WRITING PROSE

Writing Prose
TECHNIQUES AND PURPOSES

Fifth Edition

EDITED BY THOMAS S. KANE
AND LEONARD J. PETERS

New York Oxford
OXFORD UNIVERSITY PRESS
1980

Library of Congress Cataloging in Publication Data
Kane, Thomas S   ed.
    Writing prose.
1. College readers. 2. English language—Rhetoric.
I. Peters, Leonard J., joint author. II. Title.
PE1417.K3 1980   808'.0427   79-16101   ISBN 0-19-502671-3

9 8 7 6

Printed in the United States of America

Preface to the Fifth Edition

In this edition of *Writing Prose,* as in those that have preceded it, we continue to think that one method of learning to write is to study good prose and to ask questions about the strategies and choices that make it good. Accordingly, the plan of the book remains the same: selections illustrating particular modes and techniques of composition are followed first by questions that focus on precise matters of purpose, organization, sentence style, and diction, and second by exercises which encourage students to apply what they have learned to their own writing. The initial section— Exposition—is composed of short, self-contained pieces, the emphasis being to acquaint students with basic ways of developing paragraphs. In other sections of the text, shorter pieces are augmented by complete essays.

We have added two features which we hope will enhance the usefulness of the book. First a brief headnote now introduces each selection, identifying the author, summarizing the context of the passage or essay, and indicating what technique of writing it principally exemplifies. Secondly, after each "Suggestion for Writing" we now include an option called "Improving Your Style," which contains several precise assignments, derived from the model, about diction and sentence structure; at their instructor's discretion students may be asked to incorporate these into their compositions.

We have tried to keep the book flexible. In a subtle and undemanding way the selections progress in complexity within each section. Yet each piece and its questions are self-contained, so that teachers may begin where they please and use as much or as little of any section as they wish. Similarly, we have grouped questions so that here too teachers and students may concentrate upon what meets their needs at the moment and ignore what does not. In a text that asks so many questions, some will prove repetitious, but we assume that since no one will study every selection the value of, say, parallelism or metaphor may properly be pointed to more than once.

We encourage teachers to select from and add to our questions and assignments according to their own insights and beliefs about writing and the requirements and abilities of their classes. Our questions certainly do not exhaust what may be learned from any selection; they merely focus upon some matters worth observing, directing attention to where we feel it belongs in a composition class—upon the written word. To look closely at what good writers do is not the only way to learn to write. But it is one way.

We would like to thank all those who sent us suggestions for this revision: Betty Beckley Styers (University of Maryland); Carl Anderson (Duke University); John B. Gleason (University of San Francisco); William D. Mowatt (West Valley Community College); William Roberts (University of Lowell).

We also thank John W. Wright of the Oxford University Press for his encouragement and perspicacious criticism. He incurs no blame, but he deserves credit.

Gerrish Island   T.S.K.
Kittery Point, Maine   L.J.P.
March 1979

Preface to the First Edition

This book offers the student examples of good writing. It assumes that the close study of good models is an indispensable aid to both teaching and learning, that one learns to write by imitation—an imitation of the basic patterns, forms, and structures that lie behind the infinite variety of all English prose. We believe that the principles of organization, sentence structure, and diction can be studied best not in the dead rules of rhetoric, but in the living example. In short, our assumption is this: the student of composition should study good prose to learn to write good prose.

There is nothing new or revolutionary in learning to write by close analysis and imitation. In one form or another this method has been used for many years in European schools. It is the method of books like J. C. Dent's *Thought in English Prose*, long familiar to American teachers of composition. Indeed, it is the method of everyone who learns to write, even if some writers have imitated more haphazardly and less consciously than others. Styles, of course, change from period to period; no two writers, however similar, write in exactly the same way; and in every age appear writers who change the shape and sound of English prose. Imitation does not mean a sterile conformity. But it does mean that any writer, if he is to be successful, must learn to use and to adapt to his own purposes the tools of others. It means that each writer must study the work of others if he is to learn to use the vast resources of the English language.

To acquaint the student with the diversity of the subjects, purposes, and techniques of good prose is the intention of this book. In selecting our models, therefore, we have made our standard not superficial journalistic appeal or timeliness or an introduction to great ideas, but high quality. We have tried to insure that the selections illustrate the most common techniques of expressing ideas and display a variety of tone, purpose, and point of view. In our arrangement we have emphasized the typical patterns of organization and paragraphing, for these are the most troublesome to the average student; and we have paid considerable attention to diction, including neglected matters like sound and rhythm, as well as to sentence structure.

The first section of the book reprints short, but self-contained, excerpts from books and essays rather than whole pieces, a procedure that we think has two advantages. First, it keeps the model closer to the length of the average student theme. Second, it allows the student to focus upon a limited number of writing problems and to study these closely without being distracted or overwhelmed by too much to consider, as he sometimes is with a long essay. The short selections are arranged in the traditional, if oversimple, categories of exposition, argument, description, and narration, though most of these pieces are expository in their chief intention. Under exposition we offer two or three examples of each of the more common patterns of development. Along the way we have tried to make clear that exposition often includes description and narration, and that narrative is often a kind of description.

For a change of pace the student and teacher may turn at any time to the study of complete essays in the second part of the book. Whole essays permit the study of more complex kinds of organization than appear in the short selections in addition to illustrating the techniques of paragraph development in a more mixed form than sometimes appears in the shorter selections. Furthermore, in the complete essays we have paid more attention to matters of reader and purpose than we have in the first part of the book. The instructor, however, need not follow the general arrangement of the book at all. If he wishes to skip about, to study the writing of characters or description as a change from exposition, he can easily do so; and he may wish to assign the material in "Beginnings and Closings" early in the course of study.

In both parts of the book we have followed each selection with analytical questions, among which the instructor can pick and choose if he wishes. Since certain technical terms are unavoidable in the questions, these have been marked with an asterisk and will be found defined and discussed briefly in a glossary at the end of the book. Following each group of questions is a list of "points to learn" about the principles of writing illustrated in the selection. These questions and the "points to learn" are intended to guide the student's reading and, if possible, to help him discover the principles of good writing for himself.

From experience we have found that the best way to use the selections is to assign them first of all for study outside the classroom. The student is encouraged to read each short piece two or three times—at least once aloud—before attempting to answer the questions. Answers are not intended to be written out by the student, although he may wish to take notes on one or two, but rather to be carried to class in his head. In class the instructor, if he wishes, may lead a discussion of those questions and answers that seem most appropriate to his teaching at the moment. Following the class discussion the instructor may want to assign a theme in which the student applies immediately the principles he has learned. Suggestions for theme topics will be found at the end of each unit of study, but the instructor may wish to supplement these or substitute better topics of his own.

If it seems that this method of study pays more attention to form than to content or meaning, we can only say that to us close attention to a writer's means of expressing what he says is the best way of reading—really reading—what the writer has to say. How a writer shapes and expresses his thought greatly affects that thought in its final form. It is just this attention to how the writer works that is most important to the student of composition. It is true that after such analysis the sudent will have no great store of knowledge about current issues and great ideas, but then he will be well on his way to acquiring one of the most valuable intellectual skills he can possess—how to say what he does know with clarity and precision. Before a student tries to wrestle with Great Ideas, he should at least have mastered some of the holds. A close analysis of techniques and purposes gives the study of prose a solid foundation and keeps the student's attention where we believe it belongs—upon the problems of writing.

Waterbury, Connecticut   THOMAS S. KANE
November 1958   LEONARD J. PETERS

A Note to the Student

Unfortunately there is no quick and easy way of learning to write. Good writing is hard work, but when you bring it off—when you really succeed in saying what you set out to say—it is among the most rewarding of all activities. One way to acquire skill in composition is to look closely at what good writers do and to ask yourself questions about it. In this text we do just that—offer you examples of well-written prose and ask questions which we hope will lead you to discover some of its techniques and strategies.

We have tried to make the questions specific and clear and self-contained. As much as possible we have avoided technicalities of grammar and rhetoric. Occasionally, of course, it is necessary to use a word from those disciplines—"appositive" or "metaphor," for example. The first time such a term appears in any set of questions it is marked by an asterisk to indicate that it is briefly defined in the Glossary beginning on page 637. Generally, however, the questions will require only that you study the selection and think about it. What you learn you should apply to your own compositions, following the directions which are given after each selection for a writing assignment. That, finally, is the whole point: not simply to understand what another writer has done, but to do it yourself.

Contents

EXPOSITION, 3

DEFINITION, 93

* An asterisk means the selection appears in its entirety.

PERSUASION, 137

DESCRIPTION, 287

DESCRIPTION OF CHARACTER, 341

NARRATION, 387

BEGINNINGS AND CLOSINGS, 417

PERSONAL WRITING, 455

WRITING ABOUT LITERATURE, 511

STYLE: A CLOSER LOOK, 589

GLOSSARY, 637

WRITING PROSE

What does the mind enjoy in books? Either the style or nothing. But, someone says, what about the thought? The thought, that is the style, too.

CHARLES MAURRAS

If the cardinal virtue of poetry is love, the cardinal virtue of prose is justice; and, whereas love makes you act and speak on the spur of the moment,
justice needs inquiry, patience, and a control even of the noblest passions . . . By justice here I do not mean justice only to particular people or
ideas, but a habit of justice in all the processes of thought, a style tranquil-
lized and a form moulded by that habit.   ARTHUR CLUTTON-BROCK

Easy writing's vile hard reading.   RICHARD SHERIDAN

Exposition

Different kinds of writing achieve different purposes. On the basis of controlling purpose we traditionally divide all prose into three kinds: narration, description, and exposition. Of these, exposition is especially important to the college student since much of what he reads, and most of what he writes, is expository prose. Exposition is writing that explains. In general, it answers the questions how? and why? If we go into any university library, most of the books we find on the shelves are examples of exposition. Philosophies, histories, literary essays, theories of economics, studies of government and law, the findings of sociology, the investigations of science—all these, however different, have for their purpose to explain. Although exposition often is formal and academic, it appears also in magazines and newspapers, in any place where people look for explanations. It is the most common kind of writing, the sort with which we conduct our workaday affairs—the business letter, the doctor's case study, the lawyer's brief, the engineer's report—and the writing with which we attempt to control our world, whether our means of doing so is a complicated system of philosophy or a cook book.

Exposition, then, is a wide net. What, we may ask, is not exposition? If the guiding purpose of the writer is to tell a story, to tell merely what happened, then we say the writing is narrative rather than exposition. If the writer intends to tell us how something looks, to re-create the thing in words, we may call it description. A narrative arranges its material in time. Description most often organizes in space. We might think of narrative as a stage play or motion picture in words, and of description as a verbal photograph or painting. Exposition organizes its subject not in time or space but by logic. The subject of the expository writer may be people, things, ideas, or some combination of these, but always he is a man thinking, interpreting, informing, and persuading. Although he may appeal to our emotions, he is more likely to appeal to our reason by using evidence and logic. In other words, exposition is less like a stage play or painting and more like a lecture, discussion, or debate.

Seldom is any piece of writing pure exposition. Just as the lecturer tells a story or uses maps, charts, or slides to interest his audience and clinch his point, so the expository writer may turn for aid to narration or description. Often these kinds of writing become so fused as to be practically indistinguishable: the description of the structure of an atom is as much an explanation as it is a picture. The historical narrative is as much concerned with the why and how as with what happened. Even so, the traditional classification of prose into description, narration, and exposition is useful so long as we are aware of its limitations. The expository writer will do well to remember that his primary purpose—the purpose that guides and shapes his total organization—is to explain by logic and to show relationships.

The writing of exposition begins, therefore, in an understanding of the broad purpose to be achieved. It begins, like all composition, in the writer's head. Even before he sharpens his pencil, the expository writer must ask himself four questions: What specific point do I intend to make? Is it worth making? For whom am I writing? How can I best convey my point to my readers? Unless the writer has carefully answered each of these questions, no amount of good grammar and correct spelling will save him, and his composition is already worthless even before he begins to scribble. Deciding upon reader and purpose is easily half the task of writing. Once the writer has determined what point he intends to make, his composition is already half organized, if not completely planned. The writer has already saved himself time by eliminating several false starts, and he has already resisted the temptation to lose himself and his reader in the thickets and bypaths of his subject. With his reader in mind he has already solved many of his problems of diction and tone as well, and, however awkwardly he has expressed himself when he has done, he will know that he has fulfilled the first requirement of all writing—a definite point for definite readers.

On paper, the writing of exposition begins with paragraphs. Within each paragraph the writer shapes and develops a single unit of his thought. Every expository writer therefore must understand the nature and construction of paragraphs. To begin our definition we may say that paragraphs are like men. Each is an individual, unlike any other. Yet, as all men are alike in having a head, eyes, two arms, and two legs, every paragraph is like all the others, all possessing, so to speak, the same anatomy. Learning to write good paragraphs must begin with an understanding of the pattern common to all. We find that paragraphs of exposition contain two different kinds of statements. The first—a *general*, rather abstract statement—is called the topic sentence. Here, the writer says, "This is what I assert or believe in a general way; this is my opinion, my evaluation or conclusion about the subject of this paragraph. For instance, Frederick Lewis Allen, writing about the great depression of 1929, begins the paragraph on page 21 with this topic sentence: "The Big Bull Market was dead." Sometimes the general drift of a paragraph is so clear that the topic idea is only implied. To be sure, it is there, but the writer feels he will not lose his reader if he fails to state his topic idea in so many words. A second class of statements in every paragraph consists of *particular* facts, examples, illustrations, and supporting details that say, in effect, "This is why I believe or conclude what I do. You may not agree with what I say, but at least you understand now why I believe or conclude it. Here is my evidence."

Most often the topic sentence stands first in the paragraph, unless one or two sentences of transition go before. Less frequently, topic sentences appear last, or nearly so, when the paragraph is developed from particular to general, a pattern useful both for variation and, building as it does to a climax, for emphasis. Sometimes for the sake of clarity or emphasis the writer may restate his topic idea in a second or third sentence and again at the end of a paragraph. With or without restatement the expository writer usually moves from topic sentence to supporting details, from general to particular.

The particulars of exposition are patterns of logic and evidence, patterns that may shape individual paragraphs, a group of several paragraphs, or the composition in its entirety. To show how often words are charged with emotional force, Louis B. Salomon (page 11) brings forward precise, vivid examples which help his readers to grasp what is rather an abstract idea. Again, the expository writer may throw new light upon two things by comparing and contrasting them, showing how they are alike and yet different, as Ruth Benedict does on page 38 when she explains how the Japanese method of bringing up children differs from the American. Or the writer may employ the logical pattern of cause and effect. "The Technological Revolution" (page 69) is organized by discussing the effects of machine production upon our society. The expository writer, in short, uses the common methods of logic and thinking: he develops his material by offering examples, by comparing and contrasting, by making analogies, by restating, by giving reasons, by classifying and analyzing his subject, by revealing cause and effect, by defining, by working from premise to conclusion. The selections that follow illustrate the common types of expository development. Every student of composition should learn to use them.

BARBARA W. TUCHMAN

Patterns

Historian and author, Barbara W. Tuchman is best known for *The Guns of August*, an account of the onset and early phases of World War I. Her other books include *The Zimmermann Telegram* (dealing with the causes of that war), *The Proud Tower* (a cultural and intellectual history of the period before the first World War), and *A Distant Mirror* (a history of Europe during the troubled fourteenth century).

This paragraph is taken from an essay, one of a collection by various authors on the problems of contemporary higher education. Tuchman's thesis is that educators must stand more firmly for the values they profess to believe and not be afraid of exercising discipline to maintain those values. The paragraph suggests that young people welcome a wise and responsible authority. It is a good instance of how to develop a topic by an illustration.

It is human nature to want patterns and standards and a structure of behavior. A pattern to conform to is a kind of shelter. You see it in kindergarten and primary school, at least in those schools where the children when leaving the classroom are required to fall into line. When the teacher gives the signal, they fall in with alacrity; they know where they belong 5 and they instinctively like to *be* where they belong. They like the feeling of being in line.

From "The Missing Element: Moral Courage" in *In Search of Leaders: Current Issues in Higher Education,* edited by G. Kerry Smith (1967). Reprinted by permission of the National Education Association.

ROGER REVELLE

Our Deteriorating Environment

Roger Revelle is an educator and scientist. He has directed the Scripps Institute of Oceanography and is a professor of science and public policy at the University of California at San Diego. Professor Revelle has written extensively about pollution and population control. This selection is taken from an essay, "Pollution and Cities" (1970), one of a collection of articles by various scholars dealing with the problems faced by modern cities. In his essay Professor Revelle surveys the various environmental dangers threatening cities and suggests possible solutions. Like the preceding paragraph by Barbara Tuchman, this one also reveals how to use illustrations effectively.

In many ways, the quality of our environment has deteriorated with each new advance of the gross national product. Increases in electric power production mean the burning of more coal and fuel oil, and hence the discharge of more sulphur dioxide into the air. The growth of the paper industry has brought a vast increase in trash. The production of new auto- 5 mobiles and the discard of old ones has resulted in unsightly piles of hulks. The growth of urban automobile transportation is choking both the mobility of the city and the lungs of city dwellers.

QUESTIONS

READER AND PURPOSE

1. Even if you knew nothing about Tuchman's larger purpose you might guess that she approves of a more patterned, disciplined mode of life that many people live today. What details in her paragraph suggest this?

2. Is Revelle trying to convince us of the truth of his assertion to the same degree that Tuchman is? If not, what is his purpose?

Reprinted by permission of the publishers from *The Metropolitan Enigma* edited by James Q. Wilson, Cambridge, Mass.: Harvard University Press, © 1967 by the Chamber of Commerce of the U.S.A.; © 1968 by the President and Fellows of Harvard College.

3. Beyond their larger aims, each writer has the immediate purpose of supporting a topic by examples, one of the easiest and most effective ways of generating an expository paragraph. Sometimes a paragraph is developed from only a single example; sometimes from several. Which of these selections uses only one illustration; which more than one?

4. Illustrations should be pertinent and specific—genuine and particular instances of the assertion stated in the topic sentence. Often specificity means translating an abstract * and general idea into an image, that is, something that we can see or hear (or grasp with any of our other senses). In Tuchman's paragraph the abstraction is "patterns and standards and a structure of behavior." What is the illustration? In what sense is it an image *? Why is it especially pertinent to the writer's point?

5. What is the abstraction in Revelle's paragraph? What images exemplify it?

ORGANIZATION

6. Identify the topic sentence in each paragraph. At what point in the paragraph is it placed?

7. A good topic statement is clear and succinct. Often, too, its key term comes at the end. ("Key term" here means the word or phrase expressing what the rest of the paragraph will be chiefly concerned with.) In the light of these characteristics are the topic sentences of these two paragraphs well or poorly written?

8. A paragraph should have unity, its sentences hanging together. Do you notice anything about sentences 2-5 of Revelle's paragraph that makes them hang together? The final two sentences of Tuchman's paragraph contain four main clauses *. How are they unified?

SENTENCES

9. In prose that reads well sentences have enough similarity to sound alike, yet enough variety not to bore the reader. One way of achieving such a style is to vary a basic sentence pattern. For example, each of the five sentences in Revelle's paragraph is simple *, containing one subject-verb link. Study the final three sentences of his selection. How has Revelle made slight changes in the simple pattern of subject-verb-object so as to prevent monotony?

10. Do the final two sentences of Tuchman's paragraph show a similar variation of a basic pattern?

DICTION

11. Look up: (in Tuchman) *conform* (2), *alacrity* (5), *instinctively* (6); (in Revelle) *environment* (1), *deteriorated* (1), *hence* (3), *sulphur dioxide* (4).

12. Explain the meanings of these phrases as fully as you can: (in Tuchman)

a structure of behavior (1); (in Revelle) *the gross national product* (2), *the mobility of the city* (7-8).

13. Tone * means roughly the feeling of a distinct personality which we intuit from a writer's words. It involves his attitudes toward his subject, his readers, and himself; and we sense it in sentence structure and especially in diction. One important aspect of tone is the degree of formality or informality in the relationship between writer and reader: whether he appears to be lecturing an audience, keeping a distance between them and himself; or seems more relaxed, as if he were talking to friends. How would Tuchman's tone be affected if we substituted *variety* for *kind* and *one* for *you* in line 2?

14. Of the two paragraphs which seems more formal in its diction?

15. Why would these changes be less effective? (in Tuchman): an unitalicized *be* (6); (in Revelle): *ugly junk heaps* for *unsightly piles of hulks* (6), *decreasing* for *choking* (7), *breathing* for *lungs* (8).

16. Put into your own words what you think the phrase *human nature* (Tuchman, 1) means. What objection might a reader unsympathetic to her argument make to Tuchman's use of the phrase?

POINTS TO LEARN

1. Good illustrations are pertinent and detailed. They support a generalization with a specific case, an abstraction with a concrete * instance.

2. A memorable sentence style has variety within similarity.

3. Read out loud what you write. Listen. Write to please your ears.

SUGGESTIONS FOR WRITING

Use one of the following assertions as a topic sentence and support it by illustration in a paragraph of five or six sentences (about 120 words). You may develop only a single example or several, but in either case be sure your examples are to the point and specific.

> Young people do not want "patterns and standards and a structure of behavior"; they do not like the "feeling of being in line."

> Some of my classmates are weird.

> Some teachers have very little sense of what students really think.

> Life in a big city is exciting and full of surprises.

IMPROVING YOUR STYLE

1. Somewhere in your paragraph compose three or four consecutive simple sentences with enough variation in each to keep them from sounding monoto-

nous. As a way of testing the result, read your paragraph out loud. If the sentences seem too much alike vary their structure a little until they do not.

2. After you have finished the paragraph rewrite it twice, altering the diction where possible to make it sound (1) less formal and (2) more formal than your original version.

LOUIS B. SALOMON

The Emotive Component of Meaning

Louis B. Salomon is a professor of English. In the book *Semantics and Common Sense*, from which the following passage is taken, he is concerned with the nature of word-meaning, which is the essential province of the scholarly discipline called semantics. The problems he discusses involve not simply the conventional meanings we find in a dictionary, but even more importantly the implications and emotional values we attach to words, sometimes not very conscious of the power of these overtones of meaning to alter our ideas and feelings. The paragraphs develop by illustration, but in a more complex way than either of the two preceding selections, using both an extended example and numerous brief ones.

1   If the human mind were a strictly logical device like a calculating machine, it would deal with words simply as names of categories, and with categories as essential tools for imposing order and system on a universe which otherwise presents itself as an unsorted chaos of sense stimuli. But human reaction to words, like much other human behavior, is also moti- 5 vated by irrational impulses such as those we label *love, hate, joy, sorrow, fear, awe,* and so forth; and, whenever the users of a language evince a fairly uniform emotional response to a given word, that response becomes part of the connotation, therefore part of the standard meaning of the word in that language. While the bulk of the vocabulary doubtless consists 10 of words that carry little or no perceptible emotional charge (*lamp, book, read, subtract, through*), there are nevertheless a good many that produce reactions of various colors and shades, with voltages ranging from mild to knockout force.

2   Not that it is always easy to distinguish the emotional response to 15 a word itself from the emotional response to the class of things or concepts

the word names. A rose or a skylark's song by any other names would smell or sound as sweet, and a dungheap or a subway train's wheel-screech by any other names would be a stench in the nostril or a pain in the eardrum; but many words are undoubtedly "loaded" with the speaker's or hearer's feel- 20 ings, independent of any observable attributes in the class of objects named. When someone says "Watch your language!" he is usually not attacking your right to refer to the thing(s) you are referring to, but only urging you to abstain from an expression that *in itself*, quite apart from its denotation and linguistic connotation, is offensive to his ear or eye. There are, as Pro- 25 fessor Hayakawa puts it, words that snarl and words that purr—and, of course, there are innumerable gradations in between. An informer and an informant deliver the same confidential information; selective service and the draft impose identical duties on young male citizens; sweat and per- spiration produce the same demand for deodorant—but the different words 30 have different odors too, and the nose that is insensitive to their scent is apt to end up a punched nose; the ear that does not hear their harmonies and discords, a cauliflower ear.

3   In *Romeo and Juliet*, for example, when hot-blooded Tybalt meets Mercutio and Benvolio, the friends of the man he is seeking, he might say 35 to Mercutio, "Thou knowest [*or* art a friend of, *or* often accompaniest] Romeo"; instead, he begins, doubtless maliciously, "Mercutio, thou con- sort'st with Romeo—." Mercutio immediately bridles in anger at the choice of a word which, being then associated with bands of wandering minstrels, could only in contempt be applied to noblemen: "Consort! What, dost 40 thou make us minstrels? . . . Zounds, consort!" A few moments later Ty- balt has "made worm's meat" of Mercutio, Romeo has slain Tybalt, and the train of circumstances leading to the tragic deaths of the two young lovers has been irrevocably set in motion. Today, although the minstrel connection no longer operates to arouse such a violent sense of insult, the 45 word *consort* still has a somewhat derogatory flavor (compare the phrase "consorting with known criminals") as compared with the almost com- pletely neutral *associate*, though both terms have the same denotation and the same linguistic connotation.

4   Sometimes even slightly different forms of the same basic verbal 50 symbol will carry widely variant emotive charges, as, for example, *informer* and *informant*, already cited. If you wanted to compliment a man on his virility of appearance or behavior you would speak of him as *manly*, cer- tainly not as *mannish* (a derogatory term applied mostly to women) or *manlike* (usually a neutral term divorced from value judgment, as in "The 55

carvings included several manlike figures"). The same emotive distinctions are to be found in the usage of *womanly, womanish, womanlike;* the form *childly* never appears, but *childish* and *childlike* convey respectively denigration and mild praise.

QUESTIONS

READER AND PURPOSE

1. What is the main point argued by Salomon in this selection?

ORGANIZATION

2. Salomon supports his topic by examples. List all the illustrations you can find in each paragraph. Given the writer's purpose in the third paragraph, justify his recounting the episode from *Romeo and Juliet* in so much detail. Which of Salomon's illustrations do you think the most effective?

3. How many of these examples are explicitly announced (that is, accompanied by some such phrase as *for instance* or *a case in point*)? Are there any that are not so introduced? If there are, do they seem confusing or is the reader easily able to infer their illustrative function? Generalize an answer to the question of when one needs to announce an example and when one can let it stand on its own feet.

4. A good writer does not begin a new paragraph whimsically, but rather because his thought is turning, however slightly, into a new channel. Show that the second, third, and fourth paragraphs of this selection represent changes in thought. (Perhaps the point will be clearer if you make a short single sentence précis of each paragraph.)

5. Is there a topic sentence in paragraph 2? If not, is the paragraph flawed?

6. How has the writer linked the beginning of the second paragraph to the first? The third to the second? The fourth to the third?

7. Study the internal coherence of paragraph 3. Here the writer is telling a story and he uses temporal connectives * to indicate the flow of events. What is the key temporal term in the second sentence? In the third? Where in the sentences are these terms placed? What does *today* (44) signal to the reader? What advantage is served by making it the very first word?

SENTENCES

8. The opening sentence of paragraph 2 would have sounded a bit more conventional if it had read: "It is not always easy to distinguish the emotional response to a word itself from the emotional response to the class of things or concepts the word names." But how would the revision subtly alter the emphasis?

9. Salomon's sentences are vigorous and rapid. Among the several reasons for

this virtue, one is that he prefers to set subordinate clauses * first. Thus his opening sentence reads: "If the human mind were a strictly logical device like a calculating machine, it would deal with words . . ."; not: "The human mind would deal with words . . . if it were a strictly logical device like a calculating machine." Point to one or two similar sentences in these paragraphs.

The final sentence of paragraph 3, however, ends loosely * with a *though* clause. Why wouldn't this sentence be improved if the *though* construction were re-arranged so as to precede the main clause?

10. We have already seen in question 4 that the paragraph structure of effective exposition reflects the order of thought. The same fact is true of sentence structure within the paragraph. Paragraph 3, for example, is constructed of four sentences. Show that these sentences constitute a reasonable analysis of the subject of the paragraph.

11. In the second sentence of paragraph 2 there are four co-ordinate * constructions in which two terms are joined by *or*. Is there any method to the order in which the two terms are placed in each of these four constructions?

12. What is the purpose of the dash in line 30? Why the brackets instead of parentheses in line 36, and why are the two *or*'s inside the brackets set in italic type?

13. An ellipsis * occurs when a writer omits certain words necessary to the grammar of his sentence but not to the sense. Leaving out such words often makes a style more emphatic, more concise, and more interesting. What words must be understood in the final clause of the sentence that closes paragraph 2?

DICTION

14. Look up: *categories* (2), *chaos* (4), *evince* (7), *concepts* (16), *attributes* (21), *denotation* (24), *linguistic connotation* (25), *irrevocably* (44), *derogatory* (46), *denigration* (58).

15. Why in line 1 does Salomon write "If the human mind were . . ." instead of "If the human mind was . . ."?

16. What, exactly, *is* the difference between an informer and an informant (51-2)?

17. V*oltages* (13) is an example of metaphor *. Describe more fully the comparison Salomon has in mind here. List one or two other examples of metaphor in this selection. Do you find any similes*?

POINTS TO LEARN

1. A common method of paragraph development is to support the topic by well-chosen examples.

2. Illustrations may be brief and numerous; they may be relatively long and de-

tailed. But in either case they should be developed only far enough to clarify the topic.

3. The paragraph structure of a well-ordered composition is determined by how the writer has organized his ideas.

4. The sentence structure of a well-ordered paragraph is determined by how the writer has organized his ideas.

5. When the subordinate construction precedes the main clause, a sentence gains emphasis.

SUGGESTIONS FOR WRITING

Young people have many slang terms that carry strong charges of approval or disapproval. Write a paragraph in which you use examples to make clear the importance of such connotations.

IMPROVING YOUR STYLE

1. Use a dash for emphasis in one or two sentences.

2. Make one of your clauses elliptical, but remember that the missing words must be clear from the context.

3. Compose a metaphor to express an important idea in a forceful and emphatic way.

The London Poor

Literary critic and scholar, John Henry Raleigh is concerned in the essay from which this passage is taken with the social background of the English novel during the second half of the nineteenth century. He uses material from Henry Mayhew (1812–87), an English journalist and writer, best known for his graphic and detailed study of lower-class London, *London Labour and the London Poor* (1851–64), the work from which Professor Raleigh quotes. Raleigh's paragraphs show again the effective use of specific details to illustrate a topic idea.

1   The life of the London poor in the nineteenth century was, for the most part, miserable, and no one who has read Henry Mayhew, that great sociologist, can ever forget his grim and heartbreaking peoples and scenes. If man had set out consciously to fashion a hell for his fellow men, he could not have done better than nineteenth-century English culture did 5 with the poor who "lived" off the streets of London. Indeed Mayhew's descriptions in *London Labour and the London Poor* sometimes convey a kind of Pandemonium quality and one can almost sniff the sulphur in the air. His description of a crowd entering a "Penny Gaff"—a kind of temporary theater which put on salacious performances—suggests some of the horror. 10

> Forward they came, bringing an overpowering stench with them, laughing and yelling as they pushed their way through the waiting room. One woman carrying a sickly child with a bulging forehead, was reeling drunk, the saliva running down her mouth as she stared about with a heavy fixed eye. Two boys were pushing her from side to side, 15 while the poor infant slept, breathing heavily, as if stupified, through the din. Lads jumping on girls, and girls laughing hysterically from be-

From "Victorian Morals and the Victorian Novel," in *Time, Place, and Idea: Essays on the Novel* by John Henry Raleigh, Preface by Harry T. Moore. Copyright © 1968 by Southern Illinois University Press. Reprinted by permission of Southern Illinois University Press.

ing tickled by the youths behind them, every one shouting and jumping, presented a mad scene of frightful enjoyment.

2   But if anything, as over against this evil of stench and noise, the ²⁰
lonely pathos of individual tragedies is even more frightful: the blind streetseller who had once been a tailor and had worked in a room seven feet
square, with six other people, from five in the morning until ten at night,
the room having no chimney or window or fire, though no fire was needed
even in the winter, and in the summer it was like an oven. This is what it ²⁵
was like in the daytime, but "no mortal tongue," the man told Mayhew,
could describe what it was like at night when the two great gaslights went
on. Many times the men had to be carried out of the room fainting for air.
They told the master he was killing them, and they knew he had other
rooms, but to no avail. The gaslights burned into the man's eyes and into ³⁰
his brain until, "at last, I was seized with rheumatics in the brain, and
obliged to go into St. Thomas's Hospital. I was there eleven months, and
came out stone blind"; or the crippled streetseller of nutmeg graters, who
crawled, literally, out into the streets where he stayed from ten to six eking
out his pitiful existence, six days a week. On wet days he would lie in bed, ³⁵
often without food. "Ah," he told Mayhew, "It *is* very miserable indeed
lying in a bed all day, and in a lonely room, without perhaps a person to
come near one—helpless as I am—and hear the rain beat against your windows, all that with nothing to put to your lips." Thus, if in what follows
the life of the poor is shown to have some moments of joy, these are, it is ⁴⁰
remembered, only oases in an illimitable desert of misery.

QUESTIONS

READER AND PURPOSE

1. This passage is preliminary to Professor Raleigh's discussion of the nineteenth-century novel. What fact does he wish to establish here?

2. A practical problem every writer faces is distinguishing between information
his readers may be expected to bring with them and special facts they probably
will not know and which therefore must be explained. To define for readers
what they already know is to risk insulting them; on the other hand, to fail to
explain what they do not know may annoy them. Where in his first paragraph
does Professor Raleigh presume his reader's ignorance? Are his explanations
necessary? Are they clear, sufficient to tell the reader what he needs to know?
Are they overelaborate?

ORGANIZATION

3. The topic sentence of paragraph 1 contains two broad ideas: express them in your own words. Does the second sentence add a new idea or merely repeat that of the first?

4. How does the extended quotation from Mayhew support Professor Raleigh's topics? That passage is not enclosed in quotation marks. Why not?

5. Why does the writer begin the second paragraph with *but*? Is there a logical contradiction here? If it is not logical, how might the "contradiction" be described? In the opening sentence of paragraph 2 what words other than *but* help to forge the link to the first paragraph?

6. What is the topic of paragraph 2? How does it differ from that of the opening paragraph? Paragraph 2 also develops by examples. How many are there?

7. The semicolon in line 33 marks a major dividing point in this paragraph. Explain why. Might it be argued that this semicolon is a bit confusing and that the organization would be clearer if a new sentence were begun at this point?

SENTENCES

8. How has the writer constructed his first sentence so as to throw great stress upon *miserable*? Why does the word merit such emphasis?

9. Professor Raleigh sets off the definition in lines 9-10 with dashes. What does this mark signal to the reader about how the enclosed material is related to the rest of the sentence? What other punctuation might have been used? Would commas have worked as well?

10. To an alert reader the colon in line 21 indicates something about how the material to follow relates to what has just been said. Explain.

11. The construction in line 24 ("the room having no chimney or fire") is called a nominative absolute *. Adapted into English from a syntactical pattern frequent in Latin prose, the nominative absolute is still useful (though generally restricted nowadays to rather formal writing). It often expresses a cause or necessary condition of an effect (which is then stated in the main clause): "Peace having been concluded, the troops returned to their homes." Sometimes it shows a looser relationship of thought described as "attendant circumstances": "They marched away, the people cheering and waving their hats." What does the nominative absolute show here: cause or attendant circumstance?

DICTION

12. Look up: grim (3), *salacious* (10), *stench* (11), *pathos* (21), *avail* (30), *eking* (34).

13. Which words or phrases in paragraph 1 repeat the idea expressed by *miserable* (2)? Which iterate the idea of *hell* (4)? What is the source of the term *Pandemonium* (8)?

14. What is the author signaling by putting *lived* (6) in quotation marks? Why does he add *literally* to *crawled* in line 34?

15. *For the most part* (1-2) is a qualifier *. What purpose does it serve? What idea does the phrase *if anything* convey in line 20?

16. Sentences sometimes begin with connecting * words that alert the reader to how the ensuing idea is related to what has just been said. For instance, *however* indicates the new thought is somehow contradictory. What relationship is suggested by *indeed* (6) and by *thus* (39)?

17. Why are the following substitutes less effective in Professor Raleigh's context: *make* for *fashion* (4), *society* for *culture* (5), *smell* for *sniff* (8), *reveals* for *suggests* (10)?

18. Identify the figure of speech * found in "oases in an illimitable desert of misery" (41). Do you think it is effective?

19. The success of an illustration often depends upon its specificity. So judged, the example taken from Mayhew is successful. Examine its diction. What words are especially detailed? (A test is to consider the problem from the point of view of an artist trying to paint the scene from this description.) To how many senses does Mayhew appeal? What attitude toward the poor is implied by his diction?

POINTS TO LEARN

1. The value of an example often depends upon the detail with which it is presented.

2. When you write, think about what your reader may be presumed to know and what needs to be explained.

3. Important words may be stressed by being isolated within the sentence.

SUGGESTIONS FOR WRITING

Develop one of these topics in a short composition of one or two paragraphs, using detailed examples. If possible, include a quotation as one of your examples and try to incorporate the author and title smoothly into your text.

For the student, schoolwork is part boredom, part desperation.

For the poor, life is still miserable.

IMPROVING YOUR STYLE

1. Employ a colon to set up a specification of a general idea.

2. Expand or define an important point with a phrase set between dashes.

3. Compose a nominative absolute.

4. Use the connectives *however, indeed,* and *thus* to open sentences; be sure, of course, that the sentences are appropriately related in their logic to the preceding ideas.

The Big Bull Market

Frederick Lewis Allen (1890-1954) was an editor and author. His most popular work is *Only Yesterday* (1931), an informal social and cultural history of the United States during the 1920's. The book is still in print and easily available in a paperback edition. It culminates in the beginnings in 1929 of the Great Depression, and these paragraphs come from that section, specifically from an account of the collapse of the stock market, the event which initiated the Depression. The selection exemplifies the technique of restatement—of building a paragraph by the simple device of repeating the topic idea.

1   The Big Bull Market was dead. Billions of dollars' worth of profits and paper profits—had disappeared. The grocer, the window-cleaner, and the seamstress had lost their capital. In every town there were families which had suddenly dropped from showy affluence into debt. Investors who had dreamed of retiring to live on their fortunes now found them- 5 selves back once more at the very beginning of the long road to riches. Day by day the newspapers printed the grim reports of suicides.

2   Coolidge-Hoover Prosperity was not yet dead, but it was dying. Under the impact of the shock of panic, a multitude of ills which hitherto had passed unnoticed or had been offset by stock-market optimism began 10 to beset the body economic, as poisons seep through the human system when a vital organ has ceased to function normally. Although the liquidation of nearly three billion dollars of brokers' loans contracted credit, and the Reserve Banks lowered the rediscount rate, and the way in which the larger banks and corporations of the country had survived the emergency 15 without a single failure of large proportions offered real encouragement, nevertheless the poisons were there: overproduction of capital; overambitious expansion of business concerns; overproduction of commodities under the stimulus of installment buying and buying with stock-market profits;

the maintenance of an artificial price level for many commodities; the de-   20
pressed condition of European trade. No matter how many soothsayers of
high finance proclaimed that all was well, no matter how earnestly the
President set to work to repair the damage with soft words and White
House conferences, a major depression was inevitably under way.

3   Nor was that all. Prosperity is more than an economic condition; it   25
is a state of mind. The Big Bull Market had been more than the climax of
a business cycle; it had been the climax of a cycle in American mass thinking and mass emotion. There was hardly a man or woman in the country
whose attitude toward life had not been affected by it in some degree and
was not now affected by the sudden and brutal shattering of hope. With   30
the Big Bull Market gone and prosperity going, Americans were soon to
find themselves living in an altered world which called for new adjustments, new ideas, new habits of thought, and a new order of values. The
psychological climate was changing; the ever-shifting currents of American
life were turning into new channels.   35

4   The Post-war Decade had come to its close. An era had ended.

QUESTIONS

READER AND PURPOSE

1. For whom is the author writing? If he had been writing for high school students, where might he have changed his diction? What, if anything, might he
have added or omitted?

2. When *Only Yesterday* was first published in 1931, the depression was still
affecting the lives of all Americans. Quite plainly the writer's purpose was not to
report the news. What is he attempting to do in this selection?

ORGANIZATION

3. In these paragraphs the writer organizes his material by restatement. After
the first strong statement of his subject in the first sentence, he tells us over and
over that the big bull market was dead. But he does not merely repeat himself.
Each sentence, each paragraph shows us a different and interesting view of the
same topic. For example, the key word *dead* (1) is echoed in every other sentence in the first paragraph. Identify these echoes.

4. How does paragraph 2 carry on the restatement? Study especially the simile *
in the second sentence. Where does this simile appear later in the paragraph to
organize a group of ideas?

5. Where in paragraph 2 does the writer carefully qualify * his topic idea?
What words in the final sentence of paragraph 2 repeat his qualification?

Which repeat the main subject of economic disaster? After making a qualification, a writer needs to indicate clearly the end of his short digression. What connective * signals the writer's return to the main point of the paragraph?

6. Find the topic sentence of paragraph 3 and its key words. What terms repeat the meanings of these key words?

7. Paragraph 4 is unusual for its brevity. It does not conform to the usual pattern of topic sentence and supporting particulars. Yet precisely because of its brevity, it is all the more striking. Obviously a writer could not compose an essay of paragraphs like this one, but used rarely—most often as a closing—the abbreviated paragraph is powerful. Compare the last paragraph with the opening sentence. In this last paragraph the author returns to the rhythm and the sense of his beginning. His idea has come full circle, and by that means he has neatly signalled his closing. Study this technique carefully. It may be called completing a cycle or closing by return *.

SENTENCES

8. The first sentence of this selection is short and strong. Its emphasis in part stems from its rhythm. Of the seven syllables, how many are stressed? Following *The* are three successive stresses. What is their effect? Substitute *Colossal* for *Big*. What happens to the rhythm and emphasis?

9. The final words of the sentences of paragraph 1 are *dead, disappeared, capital, debt, riches, suicides.* How important are these words to the meaning of the paragraph?

10. In good writing form mirrors content. In restatement the sentence pattern as well as the content must be repeated, but without monotony. Analyze the repetition of ideas and constructions in paragraph 1. Study the second sentence of paragraph 3. Where else in this paragraph is the pattern of that sentence repeated?

DICTION

11. Look up: *bull market* (1), *seamstress* (3), *affluence* (4), *impact* (9), *liquidation* (12), *commodity* (18), *stimulus* (19), *proclaim* (22), *climax* (26).

12. Suppose that *go* had been used in place of *seep* (11); *experts* in place of *soothsayers* (21). What would have been lost? Think of an acceptable substitute for *soothsayers*. Why *soft* (23)? *Brutal* (30) is better than *cruel* or *unkind*. Why?

POINTS TO LEARN

1. In restatement the writer repeats key ideas in different words, taking care to avoid monotony. Restatement is a simple kind of development, but difficult to do well.

2. When restating, the writer often repeats sentence form as well as meaning.

3. A writer often ends an essay, or part of an essay, by completing a cycle or closing by return *.

4. Too many colorless verbs, like *are, is, have,* and *get,* sap the vigor of a writer's sentences. Every writer should build a vocabulary of strong, descriptive verbs.

5. Words must be chosen with careful attention to their connotations *.

SUGGESTIONS FOR WRITING

Develop a simple restatement paragraph of four or five sentences on one of these topics. Tempting though it may be to explore the causes and consequences of these ideas, restrain yourself (at least for this exercise) to reiteration. Your purpose is to convince your reader, but it is not to bore him and therefore you should vary the phrasing of the topic.

My college career has begun in earnest.

I hate mathematics (or English, Latin, history—what have you).

Today the gap between young people and the older generation is wider than ever before.

IMPROVING YOUR STYLE

1. Compose a brief simple sentence of less than ten words. Cluster stressed syllables so as to make the sentence an emphatic assertion of an important point.

2. Try to end at least three of your sentences on the key term.

MARQUIS W. CHILDS

They Hate Roosevelt

Marquis W. Childs is a journalist and writer on politics. His books include *They Hate Roosevelt* (1936), *Sweden: The Middle Way* (1936), and *The Peacemakers* (1961). In these paragraphs he discusses the hatred many wealthy Americans felt for Franklin Delano Roosevelt, president from 1932 until his death in 1945. Roosevelt was born to money and privilege and educated in the traditions of his class. But when as President he taxed the rich to help the poor, the anger of the well-to-do was intensified by the feeling that they had been betrayed by one of their own. Here Childs's technique is to restate his point in a variety of ways, a method of developing a paragraph that is less easy than you might suppose.

1 No other word than hatred will do. It is a passion, a fury, that is wholly unreasoning. Here is no mere political opposition, no mere violent disagreement over financial policies, no mere distrust of a national leader who to these men and women appears to be a demagogue. Opposition, disagreement, distrust, however strong, are quite legitimate and defensible, 5 whether or not one agrees that they are warranted. But the phenomenon to which I refer goes far beyond objection to policies or programs. It is a consuming personal hatred of President Roosevelt and, to an almost equal degree, of Mrs. Roosevelt.

2 It permeates, in greater or less degree, the whole upper stratum of 10 American society. It has become with many persons an *idée fixe*. One encounters it over and over again in clubs, even in purely social clubs, in locker and card rooms. At luncheon parties, over dinner tables, it is an incessant theme. And frequently in conversation it takes a violent and unlawful form, the expression of desires and wishes that can be explained 15 only, it would seem, in terms of abnormal psychology.

QUESTIONS

1. Is Childs addressing those who are violently opposed to Roosevelt? If not, what sort of reader is he aiming at? What presumably does he feel this reader needs to understand?
2. Would you guess that Childs himself is on the side of the haters or of President Roosevelt? Why?
3. Childs's immediate purpose is to stress a topic by repeating it over and over, a technique of paragraph development called restatement. What words in the first paragraph echo the key term "hatred"?

4. In paragraph 1 the second sentence directly repeats the topic. The third sentence, on the other hand, restates it a little differently. How?
5. How is the idea expressed in the fourth sentence of the paragraph related to the topic? Show how Childs uses repetition of words to tie this sentence to the one preceding it.
6. Where does the writer return to a more positive restatement of the topic? What connecting word signals that return?
7. Why does Childs organize his material in two paragraphs: is there a change of topic in line 10?
8. What pronoun is used to unify paragraph 2? In most of the sentences the pronoun is followed immediately by the verb so that the sentences resemble each other in having the same basic subject-verb nucleus. Which sentence is an exception?

9. Which is the shortest sentence in this selection? Can you think of any reason why this particular one is the briefest?
10. The opening sentence of paragraph 2 uses interrupted movement *, setting the phrase "in greater or less degree" between the verb ("permeates") and the direct object ("stratum"). Suppose that the phrase were moved to a non-interrupting position:

> In greater or less degree it permeates the whole upper stratum of American society.

What word or words would now have less emphasis?
11. How would the emphasis be altered if we reversed the constructions in the sentence in lines 13-14?

> It is an incessant theme at luncheons and over dinner tables.

DICTION

12. Look up: *warranted* (6), *consuming*, (8), idée fixe (11), *incessant* (13), *abnormal psychology* (16).

13. How does a knowledge of the etymology * of these words help to clarify their modern use: *demagogue* (4), *legitimate* (5), *stratum* (10)?

14. Why would each of these substitutions be less effective for Childs's purpose: *fact* for *phenomenon* (6), *is found in* for *permeates* (10), *observes* for *encounters* (11)?

15. Childs could have economized in his second sentence by using "no mere" only once to modify all three nouns: "Here is no mere political opposition, violent disagreement over financial matters, distrust of a national leader . . ." Can you justify his writing the phrase three times?

POINTS TO LEARN

1. Restatement works by saying the topic over again in different ways.

2. Restatement may take a negative form, repeating the point in terms of what it is not.

3. Interrupted movement creates pauses in a sentence and tends to emphasize the word preceding the pause.

SUGGESTIONS FOR WRITING

1. Compose a paragraph of five or six sentences (including the topic statement) developing one of the following topics by restatement.

> I do not like _____. (Select your own topic.)
>
> No other word than (choose your own adjective) will do.

2. Use restatement to support one of these topics in a paragraph of five or six sentences.

> One thing in life is all-important: sincerity. (Select another quality if this does not appeal to you.)
>
> For me writing an essay, or even a single paragraph, is a terrible chore.

IMPROVING YOUR STYLE

1. In one sentence of your paragraph restate the topic negatively, in terms of what it is not.

2. In another of the sentences stress a key term by placing an interrupting phrase or clause after it. This has to be done carefully so that the result does not sound unidiomatic.

American Men Don't Cry

Ashley Montagu is an anatomist and anthropologist and has published widely in both fields. His books include *Atlas of Human Anatomy* (1961), *Culture and the Evolution of Man* (1962), and *The Nature of Human Aggression* (1976). *The American Way of Life* (1952), from which this paragraph is taken, is concerned with the cultural patterns of our society. Specifically, the context is about the taboos we place upon men weeping or showing any other emotions of "softness." The paragraph is a fine example of restatement, of hammering a point home by repeated assertions.

American men don't cry, because it is considered unmasculine to do so. Only sissies cry. Crying is a "weakness" characteristic of the female, and no American male wants to be identified with anything in the least weak or feminine. Crying, in our culture, is identified with childishness, with weakness and dependence. No one likes a crybaby, and we disapprove of 5 crying, even in children, discouraging it in them as early as possible. In a land so devoted to the pursuit of happiness as ours, crying really is rather un-American. Adults must learn not to cry in situations in which it is permissible for a child to cry. Women being the "weaker" and "dependent" sex, it is only natural that they should cry in certain emotional situations. 10 In women, crying is excusable. But in men, crying is a mark of weakness. So goes the American credo with regard to crying.

QUESTIONS

READER AND PURPOSE

1. The remainder of Montagu's chapter makes it clear that he disapproves of the American disapproval of men crying. In his very next paragraph he asserts

that "there is good reason to believe that the American male's trained incapacity to cry is seriously damaging to him." If this passage does not represent Montagu's own beliefs, whose attitude does it summarize?

2. This paragraph comes early in Montagu's chapter. Might readers misinterpret these words, or do they contain enough clues to show that they do not express the writer's own opinion? Why does he place this paragraph early? What purpose do you suppose it has in relation to the rest of the chapter?

ORGANIZATION

3. The paragraph develops by restatement. It does not explain the historical reasons for the bias against crying; it does not offer examples or draw contrasts between American males and men of other cultures. It simply says over and over what is asserted in the opening sentence, whose key terms are "crying" and "unmasculine." How many times is *cry* (in one form or another) used? What words repeat the idea conveyed by "unmasculine"?

4. How does the final sentence function in relation to the rest of the paragraph?

SENTENCES

5. Montagu's first sentence opens with the subject-verb nucleus. Which subsequent sentences begin in the same way? Which do not? Suppose each of the eleven sentences had opened directly with the subject and verb. Would the passage have sounded better or worse?

6. Imagine that the fourth sentence (beginning in line 4) were written like this:

> In our culture crying is identified with childishness and with weakness and dependence.

How does placing the phrase first instead of in an interrupting position between subject and verb change the emphasis? Does the addition of "and" subtly alter the sense?

7. The sentence in lines 5-6 contains a participial * construction ("discouraging it in them as early as possible"). This could have been expressed as an independent clause:

> No one likes a crybaby, and we disapprove of crying, even in children, and we discourage it in them as early as possible.

What advantages does the participial phrase have? (Such constructions are very useful; learn to handle them.)

8. "Women being the 'weaker' and 'dependent' sex" is an example of a nominative absolute *. How does the idea it expresses relate logically to the point stated in the main clause that follows it?

9. Sentences 9 and 10 (line 11) are constructed in the same pattern. Is there a reason for this?

10. Look up: *unmasculine* (1), *culture* (4), *credo* (12).
11. Why does the author place quotation marks around *weakness* (2), *weaker* (9), and *dependent* (9)?
12. To what is the phrase *pursuit of happiness* (7) an allusion *?

POINTS TO LEARN
1. Restatement may involve repeating the same key word or repeating the same idea in different words.
2. Sentence openings need to be varied occasionally.
3. A contrast is reinforced if the differing ideas are expressed in clauses or sentences of the same pattern.
4. Participial phrases are economic and allow you to subordinate ideas of secondary importance.

SUGGESTIONS FOR WRITING
Compose a short paragraph of six or seven sentences (about 120 words) in which you develop one of these topics by restatement. (If none of the following appeals to you, devise your own topic.)

I hate mathematics (or English, German, chemistry, whatever).

My aunt (or uncle, cousin) never laughs.

Women are the weaker, dependent sex.

Men are really the weaker sex.

In our culture children have too much (too little) freedom.

IMPROVING YOUR STYLE
1. Conclude one of your sentences with a participial phrase.
2. Vary your sentence opening as follows:

Begin two sentences directly with the subject-verb nucleus.
Begin one with a prepositional phrase.
Begin one with the subject followed by an interrupting phrase followed by the verb.
Begin one with a participial phrase.
Begin one with a nominative absolute.

Endless Recurrence and Messianic Hope

Barbara Ward is an English economist and writer on political and economic subjects. In *The Rich Nations and the Poor Nations* (1962), the book from which this selection is taken, she discusses the disparities in national wealth and the problems confronting poorer nations attempting to achieve a higher standard of living. In the context of the following paragraph she is arguing that non-Western peoples view history differently and that their view does not promote the optimism and effort they need to escape the cycle of poverty. The paragraph itself develops by comparison, more specifically by contrast, which is comparison stressing differences.

But perhaps the sharpest break in Western tradition from the basic ideas of other civilizations lies in its vision of reality as an unfolding drama, as an immense dialogue between God and man crowned at some inconceivable end in an outcome of fulfilment and bliss. All archaic societies feel themselves bound to a "melancholy wheel" of endless recurrence. Seasons, the life cycle, planetary order, all revealed the return of things to their origins, and life swung round in the orbit fixed by destiny. Marcus Aurelius, wisest of Roman emperors, believed that at forty a man had experienced all there was to experience. No vision of reality as progressing forward to new possibilities, no sense of the future as better and fuller than the present, tempered the underlying fatalism of ancient civilization. It is only in the Jewish and Christian faith that a Messianic hope first breaks upon mankind. In Christianity, the hope is expressed in religious terms of deliverance and salvation. But over the centuries the idea became transmuted into this-worldly terms, in fact into the dominant idea of progress, of getting forward, of being able to see hope ahead, and of working for a better future, not hereafter, but here and now.

QUESTIONS

READER AND PURPOSE

1. Ward draws an essential distinction between the Western view of history and that of other societies. Put that difference into your own words.
2. Does Ward assume her readers to be knowledgeable and well educated or to be relatively ignorant? Be able to explain your answer.
3. Where is the focus of the contrast: upon the West? Upon other nations? Or equally upon both?

ORGANIZATION

4. What is the topic sentence of this paragraph?
5. The contrast is organized by discussing "endless recurrence" in the first part of the paragraph and "Messianic hope" in the second. Where is the shift from one to the other?
6. Which preceding sentence does the final sentence of the paragraph especially relate to?

SENTENCES

7. The phrase "an immense dialogue between God and man" (3) is an appositive *. To what? Where else does Ward use appositives? They allow a writer to expand ideas without having to repeat other words unnecessarily. For example, instead of using an appositive Ward might have begun a new sentence:

> It sees reality as an immense dialogue between God and man. . . .

But this would have meant repeating ideas already expressed in "Western tradition" and "vision of reality."
8. Suppose that the word "all" in line 6 were omitted: would the sentence be more difficult to understand? What purpose does the word have here?
9. In line 8 the phrase "wisest of Roman emperors" is a non-restrictive modifier, that is, not essentially related to the term it modifies ("Marcus Aurelius") as that term functions in the meaning of the sentence. Notice how the phrase is punctuated. While a non-restrictive modifier is not essential to the meaning of its headword, it should supply information relevant to the sentence. Presumably Ward's readers know who Marcus Aurelius was: why then does she stress that he was the "wisest of emperors"?
10. Imagine that the phrase "in Christianity" (13) were shifted to the end of its sentence:

> The hope is expressed in religious terms of deliverance and salvation in Christianity.

Does the revision clarify or obscure the writer's flow of thought?
11. This paragraph consists of eight sentences. Count the number of words in each. Do you notice anything significant?

12. Look up: *inconceivable* (3), *bliss* (4), *archaic* (4), *recurrence* (5), *destiny* (7), *tempered* (11), *fatalism* (11), *transmuted* (14).
13. What are the etymologies * of these words: *civilization* (2), *dialogue* (3), *Messianic* (12), *salvation* (14), *dominant* (15)?
14. Explain as fully as you can what is meant by each of these phrases: *Western tradition* (1), *vision of reality* (2), *planetary order* (6), *Messianic hope* (12), *this-worldly terms* (15).
15. Who was Marcus Aurelius (aside from being the "wisest of Roman emperors")? To what is the "melancholy wheel" (5) an allusion *?
16. What subsequent words or phrases echo the idea expressed by "endless recurrence" (5)?
17. In line 7 the expression "life swung round in its orbit" is a metaphor *. What is life being compared to? Is the comparison apt in this context?

POINTS TO LEARN
1. A contrast may be organized by devoting the first part of a paragraph to one point, the second part to the other.
2. Appositives are a useful way of increasing the information carried by a sentence without undue repetition.
3. Varying sentence length helps to keep a style from becoming monotonous.

SUGGESTIONS FOR WRITING
In a paragraph of 150-200 words develop one of these contrasts:

The essential difference between high school and college is _____.

The basic difference between my parents' attitude toward (school, life, marriage, sex, or any point of contention you think significant) and my own is _____.

IMPROVING YOUR STYLE
1. Use an appositive in one of your sentences.
2. Alternate sentence length between longer and shorter (roughly, not with perfect regularity).
3. Somewhere in your paragraph include a metaphor.

A Report on the New Feminism

A journalist and free-lance writer, Ellen Willis is also rock critic for *The New Yorker* magazine. In the essay from which this selection comes she discusses the development of and justification for women's liberation. Here she offers a striking comparison between the situations of women and of black people. She confines herself to similarities, a reminder that it is important when developing a comparison to decide what you want to emphasize: likenesses, dissimilarities, or both.

1   Like the early feminist movement, which grew out of the campaign to end slavery, the present-day women's movement has been inspired and influenced by the black liberation struggle. The situation of women and blacks is similar in many ways. Just as blacks live in a world defined by whites, women live in a world defined by males. (The generic 5 term for human being is "man"; "woman" means "wife of man.") To be female or black is to be peculiar; whiteness and maleness are the norm. Newspapers do not have "men's pages," nor would anyone think of discussing the "man problem." Racial and sexual stereotypes also resemble each other: women, like blacks, are said to be childish, incapable of ab- 10 stract reasoning, innately submissive, biologically suited for menial tasks, emotional, close to nature.

2   Most important, both women and blacks have a history of slavery—only female slavery goes back much further. From the beginnings of civilization until very recently, women in most societies were literally the 15 property of their husbands and fathers. Even now, many vestiges of that chattel status persist in law and custom. Wives are still known by their husbands' names. In many states, a wife is legally required to perform domestic services, have sexual relations on demand if her health permits, and live with her husband wherever *he* chooses or be guilty of desertion. Res- 20

taurants, bars, and other public accommodations can legally refuse to admit a woman without a male escort or exclude her altogether. And vote or no vote, politics has remained a male preserve. Women make up more than half the population, but hold less than 1 per cent of elected offices. They also get few political appointments, except for the inevitable "ad- 25 viser on consumer affairs" (women's place is in the supermarket).

3   In any case, the "emancipated" woman, like the freed slaves, has merely substituted economic dependence for legal subjection. According to Government statistics, white women workers earn even less than black men. Most women, especially mothers, must depend on men to support 30 them, and that fact alone gives men power over their lives.

QUESTIONS

READER AND PURPOSE

1. Where is the focus of Willis' comparison—on blacks, on women, or equally on both?

2. In her essay Willis is trying to convince her readers that women deserve true equality but do not yet have it. How might this comparison between women and blacks fit into her overall strategy? (Her next paragraph begins: "By now, almost everyone recognizes racism as an evil. But in spite of all the parallels, most people either defend sexism or deny its existence.")

ORGANIZATION

3. Which one sentence best serves as the topic of all three paragraphs?

4. Which serves as the topic of paragraph 1? Is the comparison in this paragraph organized by devoting one part to women and another part to blacks? If not, how is it organized?

5. Where in paragraph 1 does the writer use illustrations?

6. How is the parenthetical statement in lines 5-6 related to the preceding idea? Do the parentheses help to signal the relationship?

7. What is the topic sentence of paragraph 2? How does the focus of this paragraph change from that of the first?

8. The second paragraph develops two points. Which sentence sets up the first? The second? Such sentences might be called "sub-topic statements"; they are useful for organizing portions of a paragraph.

9. Are there any illustrations in paragraph 2?

10. How is the parenthetical remark in line 26 related to what has just been said? What is Willis implying here?

11. What is the topic of paragraph 3? How is it supported?

12. The third sentence of paragraph 1 is balanced *, that is, split into roughly equal halves by a central pause. How many other sentences in this paragraph are balanced?

13. The longest sentences of paragraph 1 are the first and the last. How many words has each? How many words has each of the five sentences between them? Notice a pattern of sentence structure here: a series of shorter sentences of similar length enclosed within two longer statements.

14. Identify the parallel * elements in the sentence in lines 18-20. Point out one or two other instances of parallelism in this selection.

15. What does the colon in line 10 signal?

16. Suppose the two sentences in lines 5-7 used coordination * instead of semicolons:

> (The generic term for human being is "man," and "woman" means "wife of man.") To be female or black is to be peculiar, and whiteness and maleness are the norm.

Would the passage be as clear? If not, why? What rule might you suggest about when independent clauses are better separated by a semicolon than joined by *and?*

17. Look up: *peculiar* (7), *norm* (7), *stereotype* (9), *menial* (11), *literally* (15), *vestiges* (16), *exclude* (22).

18. Express the meanings of these phrases in your own words: *feminist movement* (1), *generic term* (5), *abstract reasoning* (10), *innately submissive* (11), *biologically suited* (11), *chattel status* (17), *male preserve* (23).

19. What is implied by the italicization of *he* in line 20? In what sense is *inevitable* (25) used ironically *? Why does Willis place quotation marks around *emancipate* (27)?

20. What relationships in thought do these connectives * signal: *nor* (8), *and* (22), *in any case* (27)?

POINTS TO LEARN

1. A broad topic statement, sometimes called a thesis statement, may introduce several paragraphs or even an entire essay.

2. Portions of a paragraph are sometimes set up by sub-topic statements.

3. A comparison may be developed within a single sentence, the total effect being built up by a series of such sentences.

4. Parentheses usually signal a special relationship between the enclosed remark

and its context—for instance, that the remark is a definition, an illustration, an ironic comment.

5. A well-written paragraph often reveals some pattern in the structure and length of its sentences.

6. Semicolons are preferable to *and* between independent clauses when the second clause simply restates or particularizes what is expressed in the first.

SUGGESTIONS FOR WRITING

In two paragraphs (about 300 words total) develop the similarities between one of the following pairs of subjects:

Husbands (or wives) and slavemasters

Grade-school children and slaves (or composition students and slaves)

Babies and pets

Give thought to focus—whether to concentrate upon one subject at the expense of the other or to deal evenly with both. Consider, too, whether you want to organize the comparison by devoting one paragraph to subject A, the other to B; by giving part of each paragraph to A, part to B; or by building the total comparison out of a series of specific similarities, each expressed within a single sentence.

IMPROVING YOUR STYLE

1. Compose several balanced sentences in your paragraphs.

2. Use parentheses to enclose an ironic comment, but let the reader see the irony for himself.

3. Introduce a clause or sentence by *nor*.

Bringing Up Children

Ruth Benedict (1887-1948) was an American anthropologist. Her most famous work is *Patterns of Culture*. *The Chrysanthemum and the Sword*, from which this excerpt comes, is a study of Japanese culture, a subject of much interest to Americans during and immediately after World War II. Here she contrasts the modes of child-rearing in Japan and the United States.

1   Japanese babies are not brought up in the fashion that a thoughtful Westerner might suppose. American parents, training their children for a life so much less circumspect and stoical than life in Japan, nevertheless begin immediately to prove to the baby that his own little wishes are not supreme in this world. We put him immediately on a feeding schedule 5 and a sleeping schedule, and no matter how he fusses before bottle time or bed time, he has to wait. A little later his mother strikes his hand to make him take his finger out of his mouth or away from other parts of his body. His mother is frequently out of sight and when she goes out he has to stay behind. He has to be weaned before he prefers other foods, or if he is bot- 10 tle fed, he has to give up his bottle. There are certain foods that are good for him and he must eat them. He is punished when he does not do what is right. What is more natural for an American to suppose than that these disciplines are redoubled for the little Japanese baby who, when he is a finished product, will have to subordinate his own wishes and be so care- 15 ful and punctilious an observer of such a demanding code?

2   The Japanese, however, do not follow this course. The arc of life in Japan is plotted in opposite fashion to that in the United States. It is a great shallow U-curve with maximum freedom and indulgence allowed to babies and to the old. Restrictions are slowly increased after babyhood till 20

having one's own way reaches a low just before and after marriage. This low line continues many years during the prime of life, but the arc gradually ascends again until after the age of sixty men and women are almost as unhampered by shame as little children are. In the United States we stand this curve upside down. Firm disciplines are directed toward the in- 25 fant and these are gradually relaxed as the child grows in strength until a man runs his own life when he gets a self-supporting job and when he sets up a household of his own. The prime of life is with us the high point of freedom and initiative. Restrictions begin to appear as men lose their grip or their energy or become dependent. It is difficult for Americans even to 30 fantasy a life arranged according to the Japanese pattern. It seems to us to fly in the face of reality.

3   Both the American and the Japanese arrangement of the arc of life, however, have in point of fact secured in each country the individual's energetic participation in his culture during the prime of life. To se- 35 cure this end in the United States, we rely on increasing his freedom of choice during this period. The Japanese rely on maximizing the restraints upon him. The fact that a man is at this time at the peak of his physical strength and at the peak of his earning powers does not make him master of his own life. They have great confidence that restraint is good mental 40 training (shuyo) and produces results not attained by freedom. But the Japanese increase of restraints upon the man or woman during their most active producing periods by no means indicates that these restraints cover the whole of life. Childhood and old age are "free areas."

QUESTIONS

READER AND PURPOSE

1. Interest in Japan had been thrust upon Americans by Pearl Harbor and the ensuing war. Usually the Japanese were presented in the garish colors of propaganda. Does Benedict's purpose seem propagandistic? If not, how would you describe it? What attitude toward the Japanese does she assume to exist in her readers?

ORGANIZATION

2. The opening sentence is not really the topic of paragraph 1. What does it set up? Which sentence does state the topic of the first paragraph? Where in that paragraph does the writer return to the idea expressed in the opening sentence?

3. Does the first paragraph focus equally upon both terms of the comparison?
4. How does the sentence in lines 13-16 prepare for paragraph 2?
5. Why is *however* used in the opening of the new paragraph? What words in this same sentence point back to the first paragraph? What phrase in the initial sentence of paragraph 3 has a similar linking function?
6. How does the focus of the comparison change in paragraph 2? This paragraph falls into two parts. Mark the dividing point. Here is a good example of one way of developing a contrast within a single paragraph.
7. Summarize how the focus of Benedict's comparison shifts from paragraph to paragraph. Where is it primarily concerned with America? Where with Japan? Where does it deal chiefly with a difference between the two cultures? Where with something they have in common?

SENTENCES

8. Benedict's writing avoids monotony by several means. For one thing, some sentences move straight through to their conclusions (the opening sentence, for example), while others employ interrupted movement * (the first sentence of paragraph 2). Find several other instances of each kind of sentence.
9. Another way she keeps her style interesting is by varying sentence length so that relatively long and complicated statements are relieved by shorter, simpler ones. Thus in paragraph 3 the final sentence is much shorter than the one that precedes it. Where else in this selection do you find such brief sentences? How, incidentally, is the idea expressed in the last sentence of paragraph 3 related to the preceding thought?
10. But while she skillfully varies her sentence style, Benedict also exploits similarity of pattern. In the first paragraph what other clauses repeat the syntactic pattern of "he has to wait"? Why is the repetition advantageous here?
11. The second sentence contains a participial phrase * ("training their children for a life so much less circumspect and stoical than life in Japan"). Would it blur the emphasis of the paragraph to express this as a separate sentence: "American parents train their children for a life so much less circumspect and stoical than life in Japan. Nevertheless they begin immediately . . ."?
12. The participial phrase is followed by a strong word of contradiction. What contradiction in thought is signalled by *nevertheless*?

DICTION

13. Look up: *thoughtful* (1), *unhampered* (24), *initiative* (29), *restraint* (40).
14. Check the etymologies * of the following words and explain how their present meanings evolve naturally out of their original senses: *schedule* (5), *punctilious* (16), *indulgence* (19).
15. Express in your own words what is meant by a life that is *circumspect and stoical* (3).

16. Why are the following substitutions less effective in Benedict's context: *complains* for *fusses* (6), *adult* for *finished product* (15), *imagine* for *fantasy* (31)?

17. *Arc of life* (17) is a figure of speech *. What kind? Why is it effective here?

18. What relationship in thought is conveyed by the phrase *in point of fact* (34)? For example, if the sentence "We had a poor day of fishing" were followed by a sentence beginning "In point of fact," what would you expect the second sentence to say? What variations of this phrase can you think of? You should add these to your working list of connectives.

POINTS TO LEARN

1. The focus of a comparison need not remain fixed; it may be adjusted from time to time as suits the writer's needs.

2. A topic statement may set up more than a single paragraph.

3. Some variety in the length and complexity of sentences helps to sustain the reader's interest.

SUGGESTIONS FOR WRITING

You may know enough about two different ethnic groups to compose a short composition of two or three paragraphs contrasting how they rear their children. Or if not differences in child-rearing, perhaps in wedding customs, recreations, and so on. Should you have no knowledge of cultures other than your own, contrast how two friends or relatives handle their children. Do not be afraid to alter the focus of your comparison, but do it purposefully rather than haphazardly.

IMPROVING YOUR STYLE

1. In at least two places use short sentences for variety and emphasis.

2. Include a sentence with a participial phrase in an interrupting position between subject and verb.

3. Compose a metaphor *.

4. Begin one sentence with *in point of fact* (or simply *in fact*).

L. M. MYERS

The Parts of Speech

L. M. Myers is a professor of English, whose book *The Roots of Modern English* is a very readable history of the language. In this excerpt he is presenting the case for a change in the kind of grammar we use to analyze and talk about our language. His strategy is to employ an analogy, which is a special kind of comparison. Analogies compare two things, often of dissimilar natures, in order to suggest that what is true of one applies to the other.

1   It is quite easy for an American to see that our decimal system of coinage is better than the traditional (but soon to be changed) British system of pounds, shillings, and pence (not to mention half-crowns and guineas), because it is simpler in principle and very much more convenient to handle. But it is not nearly so easy for us to see that the metric system 5
of weights and measures has exactly the same advantage over our curious conglomeration of ounces and pounds, inches, feet, yards, and miles, pints, quarts, and gallons, and so forth. We may admit the advantage in theory, but we are likely to have a deep-seated feeling that our units are somehow real, and the metrical ones merely clever tricks. It is very hard indeed for 10
most of us to think of a hundred meters as simply a hundred meters, or as a tenth of a kilometer. We feel that it is really a hundred and nine-point-something yards, and wonder why the silly foreigners couldn't at least have made it come out an even hundred and ten. And of course the kilometer is too short to be a serious way of measuring long distances. How can any- 15
body be satisfied with anything that isn't quite five-eighths of a mile?
2   In a very similar way most of us have a strong feeling that the sort of grammar to which we were exposed when young is somehow real, and that any different analysis of our language is tampering with the truth. But there is no more reason to believe that all words fall naturally into eight 20

parts of speech than there is to think that silver comes naturally in either dollars or shillings, or butter in pounds or kilograms. We may have been taught that the sacred eight were permanent realities, no more open to question than the Ten Commandments or the multiplication table. Yet, since the second English grammar was written, there has never been a time 25 when "the authorities" agreed on what or how many the parts were (every number from zero to ten has been advocated), to say nothing of what words belonged in each part; and just now the disagreement is particularly acute.

QUESTIONS

READER AND PURPOSE

1. Professor Myers wishes to drive home an elusive idea: that it is nonsense to believe, as some people do, that there must be eight parts of speech and only eight. To make his point he employs an analogy, comparing the rather abstruse subject of parts of speech to something with which his readers are more familiar. Thus he draws a contrast between how Americans feel about their system of coinage (as compared with that then in use in Great Britain) and how they feel about the inch-pound system of measurements (as compared with the metric system). How do their attitudes differ in these two cases? Are their reactions consistent or illogical?
2. Explain how the analogy of coinage and of weights and measures supports Professor Myers' contention about the eight parts of speech.

ORGANIZATION

3. Does the writer begin with his main point or with his analogy?
4. In which sentence does he make it clear that he is developing his topic by analogy?
5. Which words in the first sentence of the opening paragraph are repeated in the second sentence? Where else in this paragraph do you find similar repetition of key terms? Note that these repetitions help to unify the paragraph. Unity is also aided by beginning some sentences with connectors *. Point these out.
6. How is the second paragraph tied to the first? Show how each sentence in this paragraph is linked to what precedes it.

SENTENCES

7. Suppose the word *that* were omitted in line 19: how would this affect the clarity of the sentence? To what earlier construction is the *that*-clause in line 19 parallel *?

8. Is Professor Myers asking a genuine question in lines 15-16?

9. Why is this revision inferior to the sentence in the text?

> Revision: We are likely to have a deep-seated feeling that our units are somehow real, and the metrical ones merely clever tricks, but we may admit the advantage in theory.

> Myers: "We may admit the advantage in theory, but we are likely to have a deep-seated feeling that our units are somehow real, and the metrical ones merely clever tricks." (8-10)

DICTION

10. Look up: *half-crowns* (3), *guineas* (4), *conglomeration* (7), *grammar* (18), *tampering* (19), *advocated* (27).

11. Why is *the authorities* (26) in quotation marks? Is there any irony * in Professor Myers' use of the term *sacred* in line 23? What is he mocking by his use of *silly* in the phrase *silly foreigners* (13)? And why, finally, does he preface *real* with *somehow*, both in line 9 and again in line 18?

POINTS TO LEARN

1. Analogy is a useful way of developing a subject.

2. Although analogy does not constitute logical proof (except under very special circumstances), it is an effective means of explaining a difficult or unfamiliar subject.

SUGGESTIONS FOR WRITING

Write a short essay developed by an analogy, choosing one of the subjects listed below or a comparable topic. Obviously there are differences between the things to be compared, but in developing your analogy do not waste time enumerating the differences, for that will only blur your focus and weaken your analogy. Work only with similarities.

> Learning the parts of a piece of machinery and learning grammar (of English or any other language). In either case one must learn new names, get to know how the various parts work, and so on.

> A cafeteria and college. Each offers a bewildering number of choices, and in each one may choose unwisely.

> Jugglers and good writers. Both must keep several things going at once.

> Algebra and abstract art. Both are concerned with patterns and relationships rather than with specific things, not with John who has three more apples than Mary, but with x + 3.

IMPROVING YOUR STYLE

1. Somewhere in your essay employ a rhetorical question *.

2. Be sure to provide an adequate link when you move from the first part of your analogy to the second.

3. Experiment with irony *, using one or two words in an ironic sense. Don't be heavy-handed; let the reader get the point for himself.

The Dissertation and the Mime

Nannette Vonnegut Mengel's essay appeared in an anthology by various women scholars, writers, and artists discussing the problems of work—especially professional and creative work—faced by women in our society. Mengel describes her experience in graduate school, in this excerpt the difficulties of writing her dissertation. She focuses her anxieties and frustrations by means of a compelling analogy.

1   The hardest part of graduate school was the dissertation. Yet, it was only here that the pieces of the work puzzle fell into place and that I gradually came to find myself in my work.

2   I remember many images of emotional hardship in dreams and fantasies during the three and a half years that I struggled to write my 5 thesis, to find ways to "see" Dickens' novels whole and my own relationship to them clearly. The most persistent image—the one that best describes my fears as I worked—was of Svi Kanar, a student of Marcel Marceau, performing a pantomime called "The Ball."

3   It was May 1968; the thesis I was hatching on Dickens' comic 10 technique in *Pickwick Papers*, a subject I had chosen because I thought I could live with it happily for months, was something I was not often proud of. It seemed a kind of comic luxury in a world that was everywhere in trouble. President Johnson had recently announced that he would not run for a second term and the black-student movement had just struck the 15 campus with disturbing force. My Ph.D. orals were postponed because tear gas filled the English building. Who wouldn't have doubted, daily, the value of scholarship such as mine? But I always came back to my thesis. At the age of thirty-four I had gone too far in my graduate work to turn back.

From "Coming of Age the Long Way Around" in *Working It Out*, edited by Sara Ruddick and Pamela Daniels. Copyright © 1977 by Sara Ruddick and Pamela Daniels. Reprinted by permission of Pantheon Books, a Division of Random House, Inc.

4   It was 1968, and Kanar's mime gave symbolic shape to my anxi-   20
eties about myself as an academic. As his act began, Kanar, alone on the
stage, playfully bounced an imaginary basketball, tossed it in the air, and
dribbled rhythmically at varying speeds. Suddenly the imaginary ball asserted a life of its own; it began to expand at a frightening rate so that his
pleasure, and ours as well, turned to panic—it seemed unlikely that he   25
could regain control of the ball. It was a relief to see him stop the ball by
main force from expanding, and then to watch him, with enormous exertion, force it back toward its original size until, finally, he had a basketball
again. True, he handled the ball more warily now, but it was once again
manageable. The game could go on.   30
5   The next time the ball asserted its mysterious growing-power,
Kanar was not so successful. He strained valiantly to contain it, but it became so large that his arms could barely support it. He ended the act in
the posture of Atlas, one knee on the floor, the ball weighing on his shoulders and the back of his neck. I remember that I clapped very hard for   35
Kanar's performance and that my hands were cold. There was something
familiar in it that frightened me. In retrospect, his act seems to have prefigured the life that lay ahead of me as I tried to control my thesis, to keep
it within bounds.
6   I do not remember that Kanar acted out the opposite problem—   40
shrinkage, the fear that the ball would diminish to the size of a jaw-
breaker and slip between the boards—but I retain that image of him as
clearly in my mind's eye as if he had. What if my ideas came to nothing?
What if my dissertation went the other way and vanished? These two fantasies of myself as Atlas and anti-Atlas were especially strong as my topic   45
slowly evolved. I was dismayed at the accumulation of my earlier drafts
and papers. Although it was painfully clear that I could not use most of
them, I was determined to do something with those excruciatingly hard-
won bits of work. Stubbornly, I filed them for later use, and at the same
time loaded my dissertation for a while with a pointless accumulation of   50
pages—until it reminded me of the children's book *Every Haystack Doesn't
Have a Needle*.
7   Weeding lines from draft after draft as my adviser returned them,
trying to glean whatever was salvageable, endlessly, gratefully, unquestion-
ingly, I retyped the phrases he liked. If he made the smallest positive sign   55
in the margin, I would not let that sentence go. Those phrases asserted a
claim to immortality even stronger than the mortification I felt each time
I redid them. On the one side, then, I was forever discarding, and on the

other, I was forever preserving, as I swung between the polar fears sym-
bolized in Kanar's mime: the fear that my work was trivial and liable to   6o
evaporate, and the fear that it was so enormous it would immobilize me.

QUESTIONS

READER AND PURPOSE

1. What advantages are there in explaining anxiety in terms of a pantomimist
struggling with an imaginary ball?
2. Do you think that Mengel is writing for people much like herself, or for
readers whose backgrounds and experience are very different? What kind of
knowledge does she expect her readers to have?

ORGANIZATION

3. How do paragraphs 1 and 2 relate to the rest of this selection? How does
paragraph 3? How do 4 and 5? 6 and 7? Make a rough outline of the passage,
giving a synoptic title to each major section and indicating which paragraphs
it includes.
4. What is the topic sentence of the third paragraph? How is it supported?
Do the final two sentences of this paragraph change the topic slightly?
5. The first sentence of paragraph 4 does not state the topic of this paragraph.
What does it do? Which is the topic sentence of paragraph 4? How is the
paragraph organized?
6. What is the topic sentence of the fifth paragraph? Where does the paragraph change direction?

SENTENCES

7. Most of Mengel's sentences are relatively long, containing at least two
clauses. Where does she use short simple * sentences effectively?
8. The rhetorical question * in lines 17-18 is a device of emphasis. What is
the writer asserting here? Are the two rhetorical questions in 43-44 also a form
of emphatic statement?
9. The phrase "to find ways to 'see' Dickens' novels" (6) is an appositive *.
To what? There is also an appositive in the very next line; identify it.
10. Notice that Mengel puts dashes around the appositive in lines 7-8. Would
commas have worked? Are dashes preferable here? Would the construction in
line 25 be clearer if the dashes were replaced by a comma plus *and*?
11. Suppose the semicolon in line 24 were similarly replaced by a comma plus
and: would it be an improvement?
12. Identify the parallel * elements in the sentence in lines 21-23. Why is
parallelism an especially good way of organizing this sentence?

13. Where is the norminative absolute * in the sentence in lines 33-35?

14. In each of the following revisions the emphasis is altered for the worse. Explain why.

  (a) *Revision:* The imaginary ball suddenly asserted a life of its own. . . .
  Mengel: "Suddenly the imaginary ball asserted a life of its own. . . ." (23-24)

  (b) *Revision:* . . . it began to expand at a frightening rate so that his pleasure, and ours as well, turned to panic and it seemed unlikely that he could regain control of the ball.
  Mengel: ". . . it began to expand at a frightening rate so that his pleasure, and ours as well, turned to panic—it seemed unlikely that he could regain control of the ball." (24-26)

  (c) *Revision:* It was a relief to see him stop the ball by main force from expanding, and then to watch him force it back toward its original size with enormous exertion until he finally had a basketball again.
  Mengel: "It was a relief to see him stop the ball by main force from expanding, and then to watch him, with enormous exertion, force it back toward its original size until, finally, he had a basketball again." (26-29)

  (d) *Revision:* Kanar was not so successful the next time the ball asserted its mysterious growing-power.
  Mengel: "The next time the ball asserted its mysterious growing-power, Kanar was not so successful." (31-32)

DICTION

15. Look up: *scholarship* (18), *asserted* (23), *warily* (29), *valiantly* (32), *prefigured* (37), *evolved* (46), *drafts* (46), *excruciatingly* (48), *trivial* (60), *immobilize* (61).

16. How do the etymologies * of these words help to clarify their modern meanings: *dissertation* (1), *pantomime* (9), *retrospect* (37), *mortification* (57)?

17. Explain the meanings of these phrases as fully as you can: *dreams and fantasies* (4), *comic luxury* (13), *symbolic shape* (20), *an academic* (21), *playfully bounced* (22), *pointless accumulation* (50).

18. *Hatching* (10), *weeding* (53), and *to glean* (54) are all metaphors *. Why are they better than more commonplace terms such as *working on, removing,* and *to keep?*

19. To whom is *Atlas* (34) an allusion *? Is the comparison apt? Where does the writer pick it up again?

20. *Yet* (1), *true* (29), and *then* (58) all signal the reader that the statements they introduce stand in particular logical relationships to what precedes them. Explain the relationship in each case.

POINTS TO LEARN

1. Analogies explain the unfamiliar in terms of the familiar, the abstract in an image the reader can see or hear.
2. Metaphors * and allusions * similarly express ideas in more familiar or concrete terms.
3. A topic sentence may set up several paragraphs rather than just one.
4. An occasional short simple sentence varies a style composed of relatively long ones.

SUGGESTIONS FOR WRITING

1. A famous bit of pantomime shows an actor trapped within four invisible walls trying vainly to escape, and finally accepting the reality of his absolute imprisonment. You may have seen Marcel Marceau or another mime act out this scene, but even if you haven't you can imagine what he would do. In a short essay of three or four paragraphs (totaling 400-600 words) describe the pantomime and apply it to one of your own frustrations. (If you are familiar with some other piece of pantomime, you may substitute this for the "invisible walls.")
2. In an essay of similar length use a scene or a plot from a movie or television show to explain a personal feeling or problem. First describe the scene or plot so that the reader understands its essentials, then apply it to your situation.

IMPROVING YOUR STYLE

Somewhere in your essay include the following:

1. Several short emphatic sentences.
2. A rhetorical question.
3. A parallel sentence describing the actions of the mime or the actor.
4. The word *true* to introduce a qualification *, and the word *then* to signal a conclusion.
5. One or two verbs like *hatching* or *to glean* to describe an abstract activity in a vivid image.

The Nineteenth Century

Bertrand Russell (1872-1970) was a British philosopher, one of the most important of this century, especially noted for his work in mathematics and symbolic logic. He was the author of many books, some of a technical nature, others directed at a general audience. Among the latter, A *History of Western Philosophy* (1945) was widely read and is the source of the following paragraph. The paragraph, taken from a chapter dealing with the nineteenth century, develops the topic by discussing why it is true, that is, by giving reasons.

The intellectual life of the nineteenth century was more complex than that of any previous age. This was due to several causes. First: the area concerned was larger than ever before; America and Russia made important contributions, and Europe became more aware than formerly of Indian philosophies, both ancient and modern. Second: science, which had been 5 a chief source of novelty since the seventeenth century, made new conquests, especially in geology, biology, and organic chemistry. Third: machine production profoundly altered the social structure, and gave men a new conception of their powers in relation to the physical environment. Fourth: a profound revolt, both philosophical and political, against tradi- 10 tional systems in thought, in politics, and in economics, gave rise to attacks upon many beliefs and institutions that had hitherto been regarded as unassailable. This revolt had two very different forms, one romantic, the other rationalistic. (I am using these words in a liberal sense.) The romantic revolt passes from Byron, Schopenhauer, and Nietzsche to Mus- 15 solini and Hitler; the rationalistic revolt begins with the French philosophers of the Revolution, passes on, somewhat softened, to the philosophical radicals in England, then acquires a deeper form in Marx and issues in Soviet Russia.

QUESTIONS

1. Is Russell writing for a college freshman or for a reader with more general information than the freshman usually has? Explain what Russell assumes that his reader already knows.

2. Russell organizes this paragraph by listing reasons. After a general statement at the beginning, he gives reasons intended to convince the reader of the truth of his statement. This is one of the most common and useful methods of paragraph development, and it may be used to organize the whole or a part of an essay. How many reasons does this paragraph contain? Are they arranged in any significant order? Which does Russell regard as the most important?
3. With what words does Russell clearly separate and organize his reasons? Explain the advantages and disadvantages of this device. Compare the first part of sentence 3 with the second part. What is the pattern of development? Is the same pattern apparent in any of the other reasons?
4. What sentence organizes the last part of the paragraph?

5. Write down the subject, the verb, and the object (or complement) of the first sentence. Do the same for the third, fourth, and fifth sentences. In each case you have groups of three words (but several more for sentence 5). Do these words communicate the core of the meanings of their sentences? Do the same for this sentence from a student theme: "Barbaric ways became civilized ones." What is the difference? Improve the student sentence.
6. Examine each sentence of Russell's paragraph. Do you find many qualifications *, many *maybe's, perhaps's*, or *would seem's*? Does the absence of hedging really harm this passage? Does it have any positive value? When should the writer carefully qualify his generalizations? A good writer must avoid qualifying a statement out of existence, and he must also learn under what conditions a qualification makes his point all the more convincing.
7. Point out all the parallel * elements in the last sentence of the paragraph (14-19).

8. Look up: *intellectual* (1), *philosophical* (10), *hitherto* (12), *romantic* (13), *Byron* (15), *Schopenhauer* (15), *Nietzsche* (15), *radical* (18).
9. Remove the adjectives from these expressions: *intellectual life* (1), *social structure* (8), *new conception* (8), *traditional systems* (10), and *physical en-*

vironment (9). Remove the adjectives from this sentence: *Upward progress characterizes this modern age.* What conclusions can you draw about the purpose of modifiers?

10. Notice the verbs in the clause beginning *the rationalistic revolt* (16-19). What is their voice? Are they important in themselves to the meaning of the clause, or do they merely link together the words that are important?

POINTS TO LEARN
1. Framing words *, like *First, Second, Third,* often help to organize a paragraph.
2. The writer often uses an organizing sentence *.
3. Words in the position of subject-verb-object should carry the heart of meaning in any sentence. These important positions should not be thrown away by being filled with unimportant words.
4. Of any qualifier always ask, "Is it necessary?" Don't be one of those who are afraid to say, "It is noon"—who say instead, "It would seem as if it were perhaps in the vicinity of noon." But do not be afraid to make honest qualifications in the interest of truth and accuracy.
5. Development by reasons will quickly organize many answers during your examinations.
6. Avoid verbs in the passive voice wherever possible. Active verbs generally improve the clarity and vigor of a sentence.

SUGGESTIONS FOR WRITING
Write a single paragraph about one of these topics, advancing three or four reasons to support the topic idea. Introduce each reason with a framing word.

I have chosen _____ as my profession for several reasons.

I should never have come to school this morning.

_____ lost the World Series for several reasons.

Modern painting reflects (or does not reflect) a sharp break with tradition.

Psychology ought to be a required subject for college students.

College students are becoming increasingly restless.

IMPROVING YOUR STYLE
1. Compose a sentence in which three or four predicates are made parallel to a single subject, as in the second clause of Russell's final sentence (16-18).
2. Be sure the verbs in that sentence, as well as throughout your paragraph, are precise, clear, and in the active voice.

The Evil of My Tale

T. E. Lawrence (1888-1935), popularly known as Lawrence of Arabia, was a British officer in the Near East during World War I. He organized and led Arab tribesmen in a revolt in the desert areas now part of Israel and Jordan, then belonging to the Turks, who were allied with Germany against England. The revolt played an important part in the British victory in the Near East, which led ultimately to the establishment of the modern Arab states. After the war Lawrence published a famous account of his exploits entitled *The Seven Pillars of Wisdom* (1926). These paragraphs open that book. They develop by giving reasons, though in a more complex manner than in the previous selection by Bertrand Russell.

1 Some of the evil of my tale may have been inherent in our circumstances. For years we lived anyhow with one another in the naked desert, under the indifferent heaven. By day the hot sun fermented us; and we were dizzied by the beating wind. At night we were stained by dew, and shamed into pettiness by the innumerable silences of stars. We were a 5 self-centered army without parade or gesture, devoted to freedom, the second of man's creeds, a purpose so ravenous that it devoured all our strength, a hope so transcendent that our earlier ambitions faded in its glare.

2 As time went by our need to fight for the ideal increased to an unquestioning possession, riding with spur and rein over our doubts. Willy- 10 nilly it became a faith. We had sold ourselves into its slavery, manacled ourselves together in its chain-gang, bowed ourselves to serve its holiness with all our good and ill content. The mentality of ordinary human slaves is terrible—they have lost the world—and we had surrendered, not body alone, but soul to the overmastering greed of victory. By our own act we 15

were drained of morality, of volition, of responsibility, like dead leaves in the wind.

3   The everlasting battle stripped from us care of our own lives or of others'. We had ropes about our necks, and on our heads prices which showed that the enemy intended hideous tortures for us if we were caught. 20 Each day some of us passed; and the living knew themselves just sentient puppets on God's stage: indeed, our taskmaster was merciless, merciless, so long as our bruised feet could stagger forward on the road. The weak envied those tired enough to die; for success looked so remote, and failure a near and certain, if sharp, release from toil. We lived always in the stretch 25 or sag of nerves, either on the crest or in the trough of waves of feeling. This impotency was bitter to us, and made us live only for the seen horizon, reckless what spite we inflicted or endured, since physical sensation showed itself meanly transient. Gusts of cruelty, perversions, lusts ran lightly over the surface without troubling us; for the moral laws which had 30 seemed to hedge about these silly accidents must be yet fainter words. We had learned that there were pangs too sharp, griefs too deep, ecstasies too high for our finite selves to register. When emotion reached this pitch the mind choked; and memory went white till the circumstances were humdrum once more. 35

4   Such exaltation of thought, while it let adrift the spirit, and gave it licence in strange airs, lost it the old patient rule over the body. The body was too coarse to feel the utmost of our sorrows and of our joys. Therefore, we abandoned it as rubbish: we left it below us to march forward, a breathing simulacrum, on its own unaided level, subject to influences from which 40 in normal times our instincts would have shrunk. The men were young and sturdy; and hot flesh and blood unconsciously claimed a right in them and tormented their bellies with strange longings. Our privations and dangers fanned this virile heat, in a climate as racking as can be conceived. We had no shut places to be alone in, no thick clothes to hide our nature. Man 45 in all things lived candidly with man.

QUESTIONS

READER AND PURPOSE

1. In effect these paragraphs constitute a kind of apology. For what? What advantages do you see to beginning in this way?

2. Lawrence's prose is more difficult to read than that of Bertrand Russell in

the preceding selection. In part this is because he employs language for a somewhat different purpose. Russell is concerned chiefly with conveying information and ideas, and, since he is a master expositor, his style is transparent, allowing us immediate access to his thought. Lawrence's style, on the other hand, is denser, more opaque. He uses words not only to convey ideas but also to suggest a wide range of feeling, in short to re-create the experience of being in the desert, close by death. Point to words and phrases that are especially loaded with feeling. Would Russell's textbook on the history of philosophy have been so successful had it been written in Lawrence's style? Would *Seven Pillars of Wisdom* have been so impressive composed in the style of Russell?

ORGANIZATION

3. Make an analysis of this selection, outlining the relationships between the various causes and effects that Lawrence describes.
4. Why does Lawrence begin new paragraphs at lines 9, 18, and 36? How is paragraph 4 linked to the preceding one?
5. Study the internal coherence of paragraph 2, underlining in each sentence the word(s) linking it to what has gone before.

SENTENCES

6. In the sentence in lines 5-8 ("We were . . . in its glare") the word *second* (6) is an appositive *. To what? Is *purpose* (7) also an appositive? If so, to what? If not, what is it? What about *hope* (8)? The value of such words is that they enable a writer to predicate new ideas without the tiresome repetition of a subject already stated. For instance, one could break Lawrence's sentence into a series of briefer, self-contained propositions: "We were a self-centred army without parade or gesture. We were devoted to freedom. Freedom is the second of man's creeds. Our devotion to it constituted a purpose so ravenous that it devoured all our strength. It became a hope so transcendent that our earlier ambitions faded in its glare." This is plainly a very bad version of what Lawrence wrote. Why? Find one or two other sentences in these paragraphs that reveal such effective use of appositives.
7. In the sentence in lines 11-13 ("We had sold . . . ill content") what words parallel * sold?
8. The interrupting * construction in line 14 is set off by dashes. Why would it be confusing here to substitute commas? What other mark of punctuation might Lawrence have used? Why are dashes—given Lawrence's purpose—probably better than that other mark?
9. In the series in line 29 Lawrence does not write *and* between the two final items, which would have been conventional ("Gusts of cruelty, perversions, and lusts . . ."). He seems to prefer to handle series in this way; you should

easily be able to find several other examples. How does this treatment of a series subtly affect the tone * of Lawrence's prose?

10. Explain why the following revisions are not as good as Lawrence's sentences:

(a) *Revision:* . . . and we had surrendered both body and soul to the overmastering greed of victory.
Lawrence: ". . . and we had surrendered, not body alone, but soul to the overmastering greed of victory." (14-15)

(b) *Revision:* While it let adrift the spirit, and gave it licence in strange airs, such exaltation of thought lost it the old patient rule over the body.
Lawrence: "Such exaltation of thought, while it let adrift the spirit, and gave it licence in strange airs, lost it the old patient rule over the body." (36-37)

DICTION

11. Look up: *pettiness* (5), *volition* (16), *sentient* (21), *ecstasies* (32), *exaltation* (36), *privations* (43), *candidly* (46).

12. Be able briefly to discuss the etymologies of these words: *willy-nilly* (10), *silly* (31), *simulacrum* (40).

13. Lawrence employs figurative * language more than is common in exposition; *like dead leaves in the wind* (16), for example, is a simile*, while *sentient puppets on God's stage* (21) is a metaphor *. Think about both these figures for a few minutes and write down all the implications you can see in them. Do the same for two or three other similes or metaphors in this selection. What advantages does figurative language offer the expository writer? Has it any dangers?

14. In line 22 Lawrence repeats *merciless* for emphasis. Could he have gotten the same effect by using an intensive (say, ". . . our taskmaster was exceedingly merciless, so long as our bruised feet . . ."), or by employing a synonym (". . . our taskmaster was merciless, without pity, so long as . . .")?

15. Why are these alternates less effective for Lawrence's purpose: *somehow* for *anyhow* (2), *empty* for *indifferent* (3), *cooked* for *fermented* (3), *ate* for *devoured* (7), *nervous agitation* for *stretch or sag of nerves* (25), *spells* for *gusts* (29), *blank for white* (34), *abdomens for bellies* (43), *manly for virile* (44)?

POINTS TO LEARN

1. Development by reasons and effects can become extremely subtle as the writer reveals the complex interplay of consequences and causes.

2. Appositives are an efficient, even elegant, way of introducing new ideas into a sentence.

3. Metaphors and similes are richly suggestive. For that reason they can enormously expand the writer's meaning in relatively few words. But for that reason, too, they must be carefully controlled.

SUGGESTIONS FOR WRITING

Lawrence is not an easy writer to model oneself upon. He possessed a sensitivity to experience and a sense of style most of us do not have. Still, try to analyze some deeply felt experience—a serious illness or accident (if you have been so unfortunate), a brush with danger, service in the army or navy. Compose your short essay (about 500 words) in three or four paragraphs and concentrate upon why you felt or reacted as you did, that is, upon giving reasons.

IMPROVING YOUR STYLE

Somewhere in your paragraphs attempt the following:
1. An appositive.
2. A series of parallel verbs.
3. An interrupter set off by dashes.
4. At least one simile and one metaphor.

The Fall of Rome

Colin McEvedy is the editor of a three-volume historical atlas published by Penguin Books. These paragraphs come from his Introduction to the second volume, *The Penguin Atlas of Medieval History*. In them McEvedy offers his answer to the perennial question of why the Roman Empire came apart. The problem demands, of course, that he discuss reasons.

1   The final end of the classical world is a subject which for most people has a tragic aspect and this reaction is worth some analysis. Both the sheer size of the Empire, never equalled in the West before or since, and the many characteristics, absent in the Dark Ages, which our civilization shares with the Roman in the fields of culture, law, and administra- 5 tion, contribute to this feeling. But were the victories of the Germans really a disaster for mankind? Such a view is best examined by considering what would have happened if the Empire had survived—by considering China, for example, where, although individual Empires existed only for a span, it was fundamentally the same Empire that was recreated each 10 time. The result was a tendency to stagnation or at least the mere reshuf- fling of elements that had been created in the early days of Chinese his- tory. The concept of a few eternal verities may be attractive, but there is a lot to be said for searching for new truths even at the expense of the old. Rome had given all it had to give, and, though considerable flexibility was 15 still exhibited in some ways, late Roman society lacked vitality. At the end, the talents were not multiplying, they were simply buried.

2   This brings us to a problem that can be considered in more con- crete terms; why did the Western Empire fall when it did? The immediate answer is, of course, the advance of the Huns, which frightened the Ger- 20 mans into doing what they had long had the capacity to do, for both in

numbers and in arms they were by then superior to the legionaries who manned the frontiers. The decline in the Empire's total population may have been absolute or merely comparative to barbarian increase. It may have been due to the fact that a sizeable proportion of the masses were 25 slaves (slaves had a notoriously low reproduction rate), or to a high death rate in the urban proletariat, which must have been decimated by endemic and epidemic diseases. But whatever the extent or the reason, the manpower situation of the Empire certainly deteriorated *vis-à-vis* the German, and this deterioration was exaggerated by the specialization of Roman so- 30 ciety. While every adult male German was a seasonal soldier, each Roman legionary represented the defence effort of some tens or even hundreds of civilians. Though professional soldiery has advantages of discipline and experience and can usually be relied on to defeat several times their number of amateurs, their capacity for doing so is heavily dependent on their being 35 well equipped, and it so happened that, at the moment when sheer numbers were beginning to tell against them, the legionaries found that their methods and equipment were hopelessly obsolete. The German soldier of the end of the fourth century had a better sword made of better steel, and the Goths had learnt the latest techniques of cavalry warfare from the no- 40 mads of the Russian steppe. The Romans were left dependent on discipline and generalship, and when these failed, as fail they must in the long run, on the hiring of Germans to fight Germans. This last could only be a stop-gap, for an indispensable soldier will set up on his own if even his most irresponsible demands are not met. In the end, the Western Empire 45 was destroyed by the arms of the professional German soldiery that imperial necessity had created.

3   But if all this is true, why did not the East fall as well as the West? The answer here goes back to Julius Caesar, who, by conquering Gaul out of personal ambition, carried the Roman eagles into continental Europe. 50 The Greeks and Carthaginians had colonized and economically unified the Mediterranean littoral, providing the basis for its political unification as achieved by Rome. Julius Caesar marched beyond the confines of this natural unit and introduced Mediterranean culture into France and England. There it flourished in an etiolated manner while the political climate 55 was favourable. But when the Roman frontiers ceased to expand and defence costs began to rise, the slender trade of the north-west dried up in the hotter taxation, and the people left the cities, the foci of the tax man's attention. The West soon proved completely unable to pay its way. Once the division of the Empire became a reality and the West was deprived 60

of the support of the far wealthier, far more urbanized East, it collapsed almost spontaneously. The East was just rich enough to buy off invaders and hire guards. Thus it survived ingloriously for a century and by Justinian's time had rebuilt a native army on new lines.

QUESTIONS

READER AND PURPOSE

1. This selection is generally informative in purpose. The first paragraph, however, may be described as argumentative. Why?
2. Does McEvedy assume his reader to be an advanced student of Roman history, to be moderately informed, or to be completely ignorant of the ancient world?

ORGANIZATION

3. In three sentences (one devoted to each paragraph) totaling no more than one hundred words, summarize the main points of this selection.
4. What is the topic statement of paragraph 1? What phrase in the sentence suggests how the writer will develop the paragraph?
5. The rhetorical question * in lines 6-7 marks a turn of thought. Explain. Where else does the writer employ rhetorical questions to organize his material?
6. Which words at the beginning of paragraph 2 link it to paragraph 1? Which words provide a similar linkage at the beginning of paragraph 3?
7. How many reasons does McEvedy advance in the second paragraph to support his topic? List them. In paragraph 3 does he develop several reasons or only one?

SENTENCES

8. Explain how these revisions alter the emphasis of McEvedy's sentences and decide whether the change is for the better or the worse:

> (a) *Revision:* This feeling is contributed to both by the sheer size of the Empire, never equalled in the West before or since, and the many characteristics, absent in the Dark Ages, which our civilization shares with the Romans in the fields of culture, law, and administration.
>
> *McEvedy:* "Both the sheer size of the Empire, never equalled in the West before or since, and the many characteristics, absent in the Dark Ages, which our civilization shares with the Roman in the fields of culture, law, and administration, contribute to this feeling." (2-6)

(b) *Revision:* Rome had given all it had to give, and late Roman society lacked vitality, though considerable flexibility was still exhibited in some ways.

McEvedy: "Rome had given all it had to give, and, though considerable flexibility was still exhibited in some ways, late Roman society lacked vitality." (15-16)

(c) *Revision:* The West collapsed almost spontaneously once the division of the Empire became a reality and the West was deprived of the support of the far wealthier, far more urbanized East.

McEvedy: "Once the division of the Empire became a reality and the West was deprived of the support of the far wealthier, far more urbanized East, it collapsed almost spontaneously." (59-62)

9. What general conclusion may be drawn from question 8 about the importance of the closing position in a sentence?

10. The complex sentence * in lines 41-43 might be broken down into four shorter statements: "The Romans were left dependent on discipline and generalship. These failed. In the long run these must always fail. The Romans then had to hire Germans to fight Germans." Why would such a simplification be inferior to McEvedy's longer construction, with its much greater use of subordination *?

11. The compound sentence * in lines 16-17 is constructed so as to throw great weight on what two words?

12. Is the parenthetical remark in lines 25-26 integrated into the grammar of the sentence containing it, or is it simply a new and independent statement that has been intruded into the middle of the longer sentence? Could it be punctuated by dashes? By commas? What rule may be suggested about when such interrupting constructions have to be set off by dashes or parentheses and when they may be handled by commas?

13. What is the logical relationship between the idea expressed in the parenthetical statement and that conveyed by the larger sentence? What logical relationship is implicit between the participial construction * in lines 52-53 ("providing the basis for its political unification as achieved by Rome") and the main clause about the Greeks and Carthaginians?

14. In line 58 *foci* is an appositive *: to what?

DICTION

15. Look up: *tragic* (2), *stagnation* (11), *legionaries* (22), *vis-à-vis* (29), *deterioration* (30), *obsolete* (38), *steppe* (41), *littoral* (52).

16. Explain the meanings of these phrases: *classical world* (1), *eternal verities* (13), *urban proletariat* (27), *seasonal soldier* (31), *irresponsible demands* (45), *imperial necessity* (46), *Roman eagles* (50), *etiolated manner* (55).

17. How does a knowledge of the etymologies * of the following words help one to understand their meanings: *civilization* (4), *barbarian* (24), *decimated* (27), *sheer* (36), *nomads* (40)?

18. What precisely is the difference between a population decline that is *absolute* and one that is *merely comparative to barbarian increase* (24)? Between *endemic and epidemic diseases* (27-28)?

POINTS TO LEARN

1. Although they can be overused, rhetorical questions are an effective way of organizing paragraphs.

2. Dealing with complex intellectual problems requires a complex sentence style, in which several ideas are worked together, often with one or more subordinated to the main point.

3. When you look up a word, check its etymology; the information may help to explain how the word is used.

SUGGESTIONS FOR WRITING

You cannot tackle so grand a theme as the decline of Rome. However, try to explain in one or two paragraphs why a local business failed, or why one politician lost an election, or why a sports team was defeated.

IMPROVING YOUR STYLE

1. Someplace in your paragraph(s) construct a compound sentence like the one that closes McEvedy's first paragraph in which you emphasize an idea by negative-positive restatement *.

2. Compose an independent parenthetical sentence set between parentheses or dashes which explains something concerning the sentence within which it is enclosed without being grammatically a part of that sentence.

3. Include an appositive in one of your sentences.

GEORGE F. KENNAN

The Student-Activist of the 1960's

George F. Kennan is a diplomat and historian. He served as the U.S. ambassador to Russia in 1952-53 and has written numerous articles and books on foreign affairs. In the work from which the following selection is taken he discusses the radical student movement of the 1960's and the dangers it posed to democracy as democracy has traditionally been understood in this country. In these paragraphs he considers specifically why the radical activist is as he is, thus developing his topic by reasons.

1   Today's radical student . . . is, as he might be expected to be in an overwhelmingly urban society, a distinctly urban creature. He is anxious, angry, humorless, suspicious of his own society, apprehensive with relation to his own future. Overexcited and unreflective, lacking confidence in anyone else, impatient and accustomed to look for immediate results, he 5 fairly thirsts for action. Romantic and quixotic, he is on the prowl for causes. His nostrils fairly quiver for the scent of some injustice he can sally forth to remedy. Devoid of any feeling for the delineation of function and responsibility, he finds all the ills of his country, real or fancied, pressing on his conscience. He is not lacking in courage: he is prepared, in fact, 10 to charge any number of windmills. But in doing so he is often aggressive and unintentionally destructive toward what he needs to live by, destructive sometimes toward himself.

2   What makes him this way? Certain of the causes are external, temporary and relatively superficial: I have already mentioned the devas- 15 tatingly unsettling effect of Vietnam and the draft. But underlying the very intensity with which he reacts to these things, there are obviously far deeper, and largely subconscious, sources of discomfort.

From *Democracy and the Student Left*. Copyright © 1968 by George F. Kennan. Reprinted by permission of Little, Brown and Company, and Hutchinson Publishing Group Limited.

3   He is the product of his national culture and his time. He reflects faithfully, but in expanded, oversized dimensions, like shadows on the wall, the bewilderments and weakness of parents, teachers, employers, molders of opinion, leaders of government. He comes, often, from a home that is affluent yet insecure. He senses in his parents, and feels in himself, the malaise of material satiety without the balancing influence of any inner security. Imagination, fears, hopes, desires: all these are overstimulated, and prematurely stimulated, by exposure to the products of the commercialized mass media. Yet there are no adequate countervailing sources of strength, confidence and hope. There is no strong and coherent religious faith, no firm foundation of instruction in the nature of individual man, no appreciation for the element of tragedy that unavoidably constitutes a central component of man's predicament, and no understanding for the resulting limitations on the possibilities for social and political achievement. The student is the victim of the sickly secularism of this society, of the appalling shallowness of the religious, philosophic and political concepts that pervade it. And in addition to all this, his estrangement from nature, his intimacy with the machine, his familiarity with the world of gadgetry, and his total lack of understanding for the slow powerful processes of organic growth, all these imbue him with an impatience and an expectation of an immediate connection between stimulus and effect that do not fit even with the realities of his own development as a person, and even less with those of the development of a society.

4   As a result of this complex of formative influences, the student suffers at college age from the effects of an extreme disbalance in emotional and intellectual growth. In certain ways he is precocious and overmature. In other ways he is much more childlike than were students of an earlier and simpler age. Between these extremes of over- and underdevelopment a tension is created which causes him acute unease, while the origins of it largely escape his consciousness. It is from this that there flows the frantic, anxious, troubled nature of his behavior. It renders him ill-prepared to meet the demands on his patience that the slow process of educational growth inevitably imposes. For this reason, while his unhappiness could certainly be greatly alleviated by the removal of Vietnam and the draft as aggravating factors, this would still not really solve the problem, as he would himself search for others to take their place. His misery has its roots in the society out of which he emerged, and it can be entirely cured only in the sanification of that society itself.

QUESTIONS

READER AND PURPOSE

1. What words in the opening paragraph reveal that Kennan looks upon the radical student unsympathetically? Does he qualify his general disapproval?
2. Is Kennan writing for an audience of college radicals? If not, what sort of reader does he have in mind?
3. Do you think his purpose is to warn us against these students, to mock and ridicule them, to explain why they are as they are, or to use them as a springboard to criticize American society?
4. Which of these best describes Kennan's tone *: (a) angry and bitter, (b) hysterical, (c) amused and tolerant, (d) serious and thoughtful?

ORGANIZATION

5. Make a simple outline of this selection by giving a brief title to each paragraph that describes what it contributes to the overall strategy. For instance, the first paragraph might be called "The Nature of the Radical Student."
6. In paragraph 2 the first sentence asks the question of causation in a general way. Which sentence focuses the question more sharply, thus setting up the remaining two paragraphs? How do the other sentences of paragraph 2 relate to the general problem?
7. What is the topic sentence of paragraph 3? That topic is developed by specification, that is, by enumerating a general idea or fact in a series of particulars. In this case the general point is "national culture and time." How is it specified in the following sentences? Where does the paragraph change direction? What word prepares us for the change?
8. How are the first four sentences of paragraph 3 held together? Are any sentences elsewhere in this paragraph unified in the same way?
9. In paragraph 4 is Kennan concerned more with cause or with effect in discussing the radical student? What words link this paragraph to the third? Which specific term in the opening sentence sets up the next two statements? How is the fourth sentence connected to what precedes it? Point out the link words or phrases in the remaining sentences of paragraph 4.

SENTENCES

10. The second and third sentences of this selection are a fine example of how to use a series of adjectives to modify a single noun or pronoun, thus increasing what you assert about the subject without actually having to repeat the word. In the first case the adjectives are predicatives, attached to "He" by the verb "is." Where are the adjectives in the second of these two sentences? Three of

them are participles—which three? Where else in this paragraph do you find adjectives used as they are in the third sentence?

11. The colon in line 10 could not be replaced by a semicolon or a comma plus conjunction without subtly altering the sense. What relationship between the two independent clauses does the colon signal? Does the colon in line 25 have the same function? If not, what does it signify?

12. Point out the parallel * elements in the sentence in lines 28-33. Find at least one other sentence which uses parallelism.

13. How does the writer use sentence structure in lines 44-46 to reinforce the contrast he is making?

DICTION

14. Look up: *radical* (1), *unreflective* (4), *delineation* (8), *fancied* (9), *superficial* (15), *devastatingly* (15), *subconscious* (18), *bewilderments* (21), *countervailing* (27), *coherent* (28), *tragedy* (30), *pervade* (35), *imbue* (38), *precocious* (44), *frantic* (49), *imposes* (51), *alleviated* (52), *sanification* (56).

15. What do these phrases mean: *urban society* (2), *national culture* (19), *malaise of material satiety* (24), *commercialized mass media* (26), *sickly secularism* (33), *appalling shallowness* (34), *world of gadgetry* (36), *organic growth* (38)?

16. *Romantic* (6) is a word with an enormous range of meaning. What exactly do you think Kennan means by it? His intention is clarified by the adjective with which it is coupled: *quixotic*. Explain the allusion *. Where does the writer repeat it?

17. Study the diction in this sentence:

> His nostrils fairly quiver for the scent of some injustice he can sally forth to remedy. (7-8)

Are the words prejudicial? Do you think this is a legitimate use of language?

18. Identify the simile * in line 20. Is it effective? Why or why not?

19. Why is the following revision less memorable than what Kennan wrote?

> *Revision:* He is the victim of the unhealthy secularism of our time . . .
> *Kennan:* "The student is the victim of the sickly secularism of this society . . ." (33)

20. What relationship in thought do these connectives * signal: *in fact* (10), *yet* (27), *and* (35)?

POINTS TO LEARN

1. Topics may be developed by specification—restating a generalization in a set of particulars.

2. A group of sentences may be unified by opening them in the same way.

3. Initial adjectives (including participles) convey additional information about the subject efficiently, that is, without requiring the constant repetition of the subject.

4. A contrast is reinforced if the sentences or clauses expressing it are constructed along the same lines.

5. Subtle repetitions of sound help readers remember.

SUGGESTIONS FOR WRITING

Compose a short theme (3 or 4 paragraphs, 400-500 words) on one of these topics, answering the question: what makes him or her this way?

> The politically apathetic person, the swinger, the macho male, the dropout, the cult follower, the teen-age rebel.

IMPROVING YOUR STYLE

In your essay attempt the following:

1. A sentence beginning with a series of four or five adjectives.

2. A colon used to signal a strong reassertion.

3. A simile.

4. A repetition of sound to stress a point.

5. Similar syntactic patterns to reinforce a contrast.

CARL BECKER

The Technological Revolution

Carl Becker (1873-1945) was an American historian whose books include *Beginnings of the American People* (1915), *Progress and Power* (1936), and *The Declaration of Independence* (1942). These paragraphs are from *Modern Democracy* (1941) and discuss how the enormous increase in machine production has affected contemporary society. The paragraphs develop by treating the topic as a cause and tracing the consequences or effects that follow from it. Becker's prose is a model of the lucid exposition of subtle and complicated ideas.

1   . . . we are now living in the second great epoch of discovery and invention. Since the seventeenth century, the discovery of steam power, gas, electricity, and radiation have made possible those innumerable tools and appliances, those complicated and powerful machines, and those delicate instruments of precision which elicit our wonder and our admiration. The 5 result has been that the new technology, by giving men unprecedented control over material things, has transformed the relatively simple agricultural communities of the eighteenth century into societies far more complex and impersonal than anything the prophets of liberal-democracy could have imagined—mechanized Leviathans which Thomas Jefferson at least would 10 have regarded as unreal and fantastic and altogether unsuited to the principles of liberty and equality as he understood them.

2   I need not say that the influence of the technological revolution has not been confined to any particular aspect of social life. On the contrary, it has exerted and still exerts a decisive influence in modifying all the habitual 15 patterns of thought and conduct. But I am here concerned with the influence of the technological revolution in accelerating and intensifying that concentration of wealth and power in the hands of a few which the prin-

ciples of individual freedom in the economic realm would in any case have
tended to bring about.   20
3   The first and most obvious result of the technological revolution
has been to increase the amount of wealth in the form of material things
which can be produced in a given time by a given population. For example,
in 1913 there was produced in Great Britain seven billion yards of cotton
cloth for export alone. In 1750 the total population of Great Britain, 25
working with the mechanical appliances then available, could have produced only a small fraction of that amount. A second result of the technological revolution is that, as machines are perfected and become more
automatic, man power plays a relatively less important part in the production of a given amount of wealth in a given time. Fifty years ago, when 30
all type was set by hand, the labor of several men was required to print,
fold, and arrange in piles the signatures of a book. Today machines can
do it all, and far more rapidly; little man power is required, except that a
mechanic, who may pass the time sitting in a chair, must be present in
case anything goes wrong with the machine. And finally, a third result of 35
the technological revolution is that, under the system of private property
in the means of production and the price system as a method of dis-
tributing wealth, the greater part of the wealth produced, since it is
produced by the machines, goes to those who own or control the machines,
while those who work the machines receive that part only which can be 40
exacted by selling their services in a market where wages are impersonally
adjusted to the necessities of the machine process.

QUESTIONS

READER AND PURPOSE
1. Is Becker's tone * formal or informal? What is his point of view *? Suggest
several subjects that demand an impersonal, formal point of view. Suggest others
that must be treated informally and personally. Try to think of two or three subjects that may be handled either way. Describe Becker's reader and purpose.

ORGANIZATION
2. What does paragraph 1 contribute to our understanding of the subject? Does
it anticipate the remainder of the selection? Paragraph 2 divides into two parts.
Where? Why may the first part be called a qualification *? What does the
second part of paragraph 2 add to the development of the topic? Explain why
the last is obviously the most important of the three paragraphs.

3. Identify the parts of paragraph 3 and explain what device welds them together.

4. In this selection Becker develops his subject by listing the effects of a cause—here the technological revolution. Paragraph 3 is a very good example of development by effects. Show that the effects are arranged in a purposeful order, not simply put down haphazardly as they might have occurred to the writer. Along with his development by effects the writer has also used illustrations. Identify each one. Would the paragraph have been as clear and as effective without them? Observe that in addition to effects and illustration the third paragraph also involves comparison. Explain why comparisons are a necessary part of the writer's subject in this selection.

SENTENCES

5. A less experienced writer might have used a complete adjective clause in line 8, writing "societies *which are* far more complex and impersonal." Are the words omitted really necessary? What has the writer gained by omitting them? With what preceding word is *Leviathans* (10) in apposition *?

6. In his illustrations Becker's sentences become somewhat simpler. What is the reason for this easier style? The two sentences comprising the first illustration in paragraph 3 begin in much the same way. Why? Is this similarity of beginning also true of the sentences which develop the second illustration?

7. Becker's sentences are generally quite complicated, a style suited to the exposition of subtly related and highly abstract ideas. A good example is the final sentence (35-42). How many ideas does it contain? Rewrite this sentence in five or six shorter ones, keeping as much of the writer's phrasing as you can. Is the revision more, or less, clear than the original? Can you remove any words from the final sentence without damaging its meaning?

8. Label examples of interrupted movement *. In what way are these constructions useful to the writer of a rather formal, complex subject?

DICTION

9. Look up: *radiation* (3), *elicit* (5), *technology* (6), *unprecedented* (6), *exert* (15), *modifying* (15), *habitual* (15), *material* (22), *signatures* (32), *exacted* (41).

10. Becker uses *machine* and *instrument* (4-5) with a nice discrimination. How does *appliance* differ from both *machine* and *instrument*? Substitute *changed* for *transformed* (7) and *on the other hand* for *on the contrary* (14). Do these substitutions change the sense of either passage?

POINTS TO LEARN

1. In developing effects it is not enough simply to list them at random. They must be arranged according to a plan and held together in a unified whole.

2. Most exposition relies upon a number of developing techniques. Learn to use not effects alone, but effects assisted by other methods like illustration and comparison.

3. The writer must prune all words not absolutely necessary. To achieve this economy he may (1) use appositives * frequently; (2) abbreviate adjective clauses by omitting the relative pronoun, the auxiliary verb or the linking verb: "societies far more complex and impersonal" in place of "societies *which are* far more complex and impersonal."

SUGGESTIONS FOR WRITING

In several paragraphs explain three or four additional effects of the technological revolution: for example, the effect of the mass production of automobiles on the American city; how the forty-hour week has changed American recreation; the influence of television upon home life and habits. Choose one of these or a similar topic. Support your effects with brief but detailed illustrations. Make the reader see.

IMPROVING YOUR STYLE

1. Somewhere in your paragraphs construct two sentences that use interrupted movement.

2. Attempt a long, complex sentence *, something like Becker's in lines 35-42, bringing together five or six ideas in a subtle relationship of cause and effect.

Los Angeles Notebook

Joan Didion is an essayist and novelist. The paragraphs below come from the essay "Los Angeles Notebook," one of a collection published in the book *Slouching Towards Bethlehem* (1961). Like Becker in the preceding selection, Didion develops her topic primarily by effects. Her prose, however, is more personal and less formal than Becker's, a fact which suits her subject matter and which is also typical of the trend of modern exposition toward informality and the personal vision.

1   There is something uneasy in the Los Angeles air this afternoon, some unnatural stillness, some tension. What it means is that tonight a Santa Ana will begin to blow, a hot wind from the northeast whining down through the Cajon and San Gorgonio Passes, blowing up sandstorms out along Route 66, drying the hills and the nerves to the flash point. For a 5 few days now we will see smoke back in the canyons, and hear sirens in the night. I have neither heard nor read that a Santa Ana is due, but I know it, and almost everyone I have seen today knows it too. We know it because we feel it. The baby frets. The maid sulks. I rekindle a waning argument with the telephone company, then cut my losses and lie down, given over 10 to whatever it is in the air. To live with the Santa Ana is to accept, consciously or unconsciously, a deeply mechanistic view of human behavior.

2   I recall being told, when I first moved to Los Angeles and was living on an isolated beach, that the Indians would throw themselves into the sea when the bad wind blew. I could see why. The Pacific turned omi- 15 nously glossy during a Santa Ana period, and one woke in the night troubled not only by the peacocks screaming in the olive trees but by the eerie absence of surf. The heat was surreal. The sky had a yellow cast, the kind of light sometimes called "earthquake weather." My only neighbor would

not come out of her house for days, and there were no lights at night, and 20
her husband roamed the place with a machete. One day he would tell me
that he had heard a trespasser, the next a rattlesnake.

3   "On nights like that," Raymond Chandler once wrote about the
Santa Ana, "every booze party ends in a fight. Meek little wives feel the
edge of the carving knife and study their husbands' necks. Anything can 25
happen." That was the kind of wind it was. I did not know then that there
was any basis for the effect it had on all of us, but it turns out to be another of those cases in which science bears out folk wisdom. The Santa
Ana, which is named for one of the canyons it rushes through, is a *foehn*
wind, like the *foehn* of Austria and Switzerland and the *hamsin* of Israel. 30
There are a number of persistent malevolent winds, perhaps the best known
of which are the mistral of France and the Mediterranean sirocco, but a
foehn wind has distinct characteristics: it occurs on the leeward slope of a
mountain range and, although the air begins as a cold mass, it is warmed
as it comes down the mountain and appears finally as a hot dry wind. 35
Whenever and wherever a *foehn* blows, doctors hear about headaches and
nausea and allergies, about "nervousness," about "depression." In Los
Angeles some teachers do not attempt to conduct formal classes during a
Santa Ana, because the children become unmanageable. In Switzerland the
suicide rate goes up during the *foehn*, and in the courts of some Swiss can- 40
tons the wind is considered a mitigating circumstance for crime. Surgeons
are said to watch the wind, because blood does not clot normally during a
foehn. A few years ago an Israeli physicist discovered that not only during
such winds, but for the ten or twelve hours which precede them, the air
carries an unusually high ratio of positive to negative ions. No one seems 45
to know exactly why that should be; some talk about friction and others
suggest solar disturbances. In any case the positive ions are there, and what
an excess of positive ions does, in the simplest terms, is make people unhappy. One cannot get much more mechanistic than that.

4   Easterners commonly complain that there is no "weather" at all 50
in Southern California, that the days and the seasons slip by relentlessly,
numbingly bland. That is quite misleading. In fact the climate is characterized by infrequent but violent extremes: two periods of torrential sub-
tropical rains which continue for weeks and wash out the hills and send
subdivisions sliding toward the sea; about twenty scattered days a year of 55
the Santa Ana, which, with its incendiary dryness, invariably means fire. At
the first prediction of a Santa Ana, the Forest Service flies men and equipment from northern California into the southern forests, and the Los An-

geles Fire Department cancels its ordinary non-firefighting routines. The Santa Ana caused Malibu to burn the way it did in 1956, and Bel Air in 60 1961, and Santa Barbara in 1964. In the winter of 1966-67 eleven men were killed fighting a Santa Ana fire that spread through the San Gabriel Mountains.

5   Just to watch the front-page news out of Los Angeles during a Santa Ana is to get very close to what it is about the place. The longest 65 single Santa Ana period in recent years was in 1957, and it lasted not the usual three or four days but fourteen days, from November 21 until December 4. On the first day 25,000 acres of the San Gabriel Mountains were burning, with gusts reaching 100 miles an hour. In town, the wind reached Force 12, or hurricane force, on the Beaufort Scale; oil derricks were top- 70 pled and people ordered off the downtown streets to avoid injury from flying objects. On November 22 the fire in the San Gabriels was out of control. On November 24 six people were killed in automobile accidents, and by the end of the week the Los Angeles *Times* was keeping a box score of traffic deaths. On November 26 a prominent Pasadena attorney, depressed 75 about money, shot and killed his wife, their two sons, and himself. On November 27 a South Gate divorcée, twenty-two, was murdered and thrown from a moving car. On November 30 the San Gabriel fire was still out of control, and the wind in town was blowing eighty miles an hour. On the first day of December four people died violently, and on the third the wind 80 began to break.

6   It is hard for people who have not lived in Los Angeles to realize how radically the Santa Ana figures in the local imagination. The city burning is Los Angeles's deepest image of itself: Nathanael West perceived that, in *The Day of the Locust*; and at the time of the 1965 Watts 85 riots what struck the imagination most indelibly were the fires. For days one could drive the Harbor Freeway and see the city on fire, just as we had always known it would be in the end. Los Angeles weather is the weather of catastrophe, of apocalypse, and, just as the reliably long and bitter winters of New England determine the way life is lived there, so the violence 90 and the unpredictability of the Santa Ana affect the entire quality of life in Los Angeles, accentuate its impermanence, its unreliability. The wind shows us how close to the edge we are.

QUESTIONS

READER AND PURPOSE

1. Didion's aim is not simply to communicate information, though she does tell us a great deal about what the Santa Ana is and about how it affects life in Los Angeles. More than reporting facts, however, she re-creates and comments upon experience. Accordingly her point of view * is personal, and in the first paragraph she uses verbs in a way calculated to suggest immediacy. How does she do this?

2. Ultimately her purpose includes even more than re-creating what it is to endure a Santa Ana. While Didion begins these paragraphs by putting us into the experience, she moves in the direction of philosophical speculation. Her final sentence is an example of such speculation. What does she mean by "close to the edge"? "Close to the edge" of what? Where earlier in the selection is this philosophical note sounded?

ORGANIZATION

3. Make a brief outline of this selection, giving an explanatory title to each paragraph. Is each new paragraph justified by a shift in topic?

4. Paragraph 3 is a bit longer and more complicated than the others. In terms of its development of thought divide it into its several parts and briefly describe the major idea in each part.

5. What single word toward the middle of paragraph 4 sets up the effects which Didion discusses?

6. Paragraph 5 describes a number of consequences of a particularly severe Santa Ana. How does the writer impose order upon these effects and thereby unify her paragraph?

SENTENCES

7. Why are the short, terse sentences in lines 8-9 particularly appropriate? There are individual short sentences elsewhere in this selection—in lines 15, 18, 25-26, and 92-93, for example. Consider what advantage each of these possesses.

8. In the sentence in lines 9-11 what verbs parallel * rekindle? Is given one of them? In the sentence in lines 18-19, to what is the phrase kind of light in apposition *?

9. Explain why each of the following revisions is inferior to Didion's sentence:

(a) Revision: There is something uneasy, some unnatural stillness, some tension in the Los Angeles air this afternoon.
Didion: "There is something uneasy in the Los Angeles air this afternoon, some unnatural stillness, some tension." (1-2)

(b) *Revision:* I recall being told that the Indians would throw themselves into the sea when the bad wind blew when I first moved to Los Angeles and was living on an isolated beach.

Didion: "I recall being told, when I first moved to Los Angeles and was living on an isolated beach, that the Indians would throw themselves into the sea when the bad wind blew. (13-15)

(c) *Revision:* Easterners commonly complain that there is no "weather" at all in Southern California, that the days and the seasons slip by relentlessly, numbingly bland, but that is quite misleading.

Didion: "Easterners commonly complain that there is no 'weather' at all in Southern California, that the days and the seasons slip by relentlessly, numbingly bland. That is quite misleading." (50-52)

10. The sentence in lines 19-21 is an example of what is sometimes called the "freight-train" style *. Why is that an appropriate name?

11. What is signaled by the colon in line 53?

12. Explain how the idea expressed in the participial * construction in lines 75-76 ("depressed about money") is related to the main thought of the sentence.

13. Slowly read aloud the sentence in lines 50-52. It is made interesting by—among other things—the repetition of sound. Point out several of these echoes, and find one or two other sentences in the selection which show a similar repetition of sound.

DICTION

14. Look up: *surreal* (18), *cast* (18), *malevolent* (31), *leeward* (33), *ions* (45), *gusts* (69), *Beaufort Scale* (70), *radically* (83), *indelibly* (86), *apocalypse* (89), *accentuate* (92).

15. Explain the meanings of these phrases: *mechanistic view of human behavior* (12), *ominously glossy* (15-16), *eerie absence* (17-18), *folk wisdom* (28), *numbingly bland* (52), *incendiary dryness* (56).

16. Why is *weather* (50) in quotation marks?

17. What relationship in thought does *in fact* (52) signal?

18. In the sentence beginning *I rekindle* (9) what metaphors * can you find?

19. Each of these is a poor substitute for Didion's word. Why? *Whistling* for *whining* (3), *singing* for *screaming* (17), *falling into* for *sliding toward* (55).

POINTS TO LEARN

1. Exposition may involve more than "facts"; often it expresses a mind sensitively responding to facts.

2. Chronological sequence is one way of unifying a paragraph.

3. Learn to listen to your sentences; good prose pleases the ear.

SUGGESTIONS FOR WRITING

If you live in New England, or any other area with "long and bitter winters," discuss how the cold weather affects the quality of life. Alternatively, if you do not know winter as New Englanders do, explain the effects of some other aspect of climate—the summer heat of the deep South, for example, or the dry, dusty winds of the plains states, or a severe northeaster along the Atlantic coast.

IMPROVING YOUR STYLE

Somewhere in your composition include the following:

1. A series of three or four short emphatic sentences like Didion's in lines 8-9.
2. A sentence in which several verbs are paralleled to a single subject.
3. A freight-train * sentence.
4. An emphatic restatement introduced by *in fact.*
5. A metaphor *.

The Imperial Legion

The historian Edward Gibbon (1737-94) wrote *The Decline and Fall of the Roman Empire* (1776-88), one of the greatest works of history in English. In this selection he discusses the organization of the legion, a unit of the Roman army roughly equivalent in terms of relative strength and strategic function to a division in a modern army. Gibbon's method is to analyze his topic, that is, to break it into its parts and present each in turn. With something like a military unit, analysis is a natural way to proceed, since one need only follow principles of organization inherent in the subject. Gibbon's paragraphs are a lucid example of analysis in exposition, of explaining a complicated topic by saying, in effect: here are its parts and this is how they relate.

1 . . . The constitution of the Imperial legion may be described in a few words. The heavy armed infantry, which composed its principal strength, was divided into ten cohorts, and fifty-five companies, under the orders of a correspondent number of tribunes and centurions. The first cohort, which always claimed the post of honour and the custody of the eagle, 5 was formed of eleven hundred and five soldiers, the most approved for valour and fidelity. The remaining nine cohorts consisted each of five hundred and fifty-five; and the whole body of legionary infantry amounted to six thousand one hundred men. Their arms were uniform, and admirably adapted to the nature of their service: an open helmet, with a lofty crest; 10 a breast-plate, or coat of mail; greaves on their legs, and an ample buckler on their left arm. The buckler was of an oblong and concave figure, four feet in length, and two and a half in breadth, framed of a light wood, covered with a bull's hide, and strongly guarded with plates of brass. Besides a lighter spear, the legionary soldier grasped in his right hand the formidable 15 *pilum*, a ponderous javelin, whose utmost length was about six feet, and which was terminated by a massy triangular point of steel of eighteen inches. This instrument was indeed much inferior to our modern fire-arms;

From *The Decline and Fall of the Roman Empire*, 1788.

since it was exhausted by a single discharge, at the distance of only ten or twelve paces. Yet when it was launched by a firm and skilfull hand, there 2c was not any cavalry that durst venture within its reach, nor any shield or corslet that could sustain the impetuosity of its weight. As soon as the Roman had darted his *pilum*, he drew his sword, and rushed forwards to close with the enemy. His sword was a short well-tempered Spanish blade, that carried a double edge, and was alike suited to the purpose of striking 25 or of pushing; but the soldier was always instructed to prefer the latter use of his weapon, as his own body remained less exposed, whilst he in- flicted a more dangerous wound on his adversary. The legion was usually drawn up eight deep; and the regular distance of three feet was left be- tween the files as well as ranks. A body of troops, habituated to preserve 30 this open order, in a long front and a rapid charge, found themselves pre- pared to execute every disposition which the circumstances of war, or the skill of their leader, might suggest. The soldier possessed a free space for his arms and motions, and sufficient intervals were allowed, through which seasonable reinforcements might be introduced to the relief of the ex- 35 hausted combatants. The tactics of the Greeks and Macedonians were formed on very different principles. The strength of the phalanx depended on sixteen ranks of long pikes, wedged together in the closest array. But it was soon discovered by reflection as well as by the event, that the strength of the phalanx was unable to contend with the activity of the legion.   40

2   The cavalry, without which the force of the legion would have re- mained imperfect, was divided into ten troops or squadrons; the first, as the companion of the first cohort, consisted of an hundred and thirty-two men; whilst each of the other nine amounted only to sixty-six. The entire estab- lishment formed a regiment, if we may use the modern expression, of seven 45 hundred and twenty-six horse, naturally connected with its respective le- gion, but occasionally separated to act in the line, and to compose a part of the wings of the army. The cavalry of the emperors was no longer com- posed, like that of the ancient republic, of the noblest youths of Rome and Italy, who by performing their military service on horseback, prepared 50 themselves for the offices of senator and consul; and solicited, by deeds of valour, the future suffrages of their countrymen. Since the alteration of manners and government, the most wealthy of the equestrian order were engaged in the administration of justice, and of the revenue; and whenever they embraced the profession of arms, they were immediately intrusted 55 with a troop of horse, or a cohort of foot. Trajan and Hadrian formed their cavalry from the same provinces, and the same class of their subjects, which

recruited the ranks of the legion. The horses were bred, for the most part, in Spain or Cappadocia. The Roman troopers despised the complete armour with which the cavalry of the East was encumbered. *Their* more 60 useful arms consisted in a helmet, an oblong shield, light boots, and a coat of mail. A javelin, and a long broad sword, were their principal weapons of offense. The use of lances and of iron maces they seemed to have borrowed from the barbarians.

3   The safety and honour of the empire were principally intrusted to 65 the legions, but the policy of Rome condescended to adopt every useful instrument of war. Considerable levies were regularly made among the provincials, who had not yet deserved the honourable distinction of Romans. Many dependent princes and communities, dispersed round the frontiers, were permitted, for a while, to hold their freedom and security by 70 the tenure of military service. Even select troops of hostile barbarians were frequently compelled or persuaded to consume their dangerous valour in remote climates, and for the benefit of the state. All these were included under the general name of auxiliaries; and howsoever they might vary according to the difference of times and circumstances, their numbers were 75 seldom much inferior to those of the legions themselves. Among the auxiliaries, the bravest and most faithful bands were placed under the command of praefects and centurions, and severely trained in the arts of Roman discipline; but the far greater part retained those arms, to which the nature of their country, or their early habits of life, more peculiarly 80 adapted them. By this institution each legion, to whom a certain proportion of auxiliaries was alloted, contained within itself every species of lighter troops, and of missile weapons; and was capable of encountering every nation, with the advantages of its respective arms and discipline. Nor was the legion destitute of what, in modern language, would be styled 85 a train of artillery. It consisted in ten military engines of the largest, and fifty-five of a smaller size; but all of which, either in an oblique or horizontal manner, discharged stone and darts with irresistible violence.

4   The camp of a Roman legion presented the appearance of a fortified city. As soon as the space was marked out, the pioneers carefully 90 levelled the ground, and removed every impediment that might interrupt its perfect regularity. Its form was an exact quadrangle; and we may calculate, that a square of about seven hundred yards was sufficient for the encampment of twenty thousand Romans; though a similar number of our own troops would expose to the enemy a front of more than treble that 95 extent. In the midst of the camp, the praetorium, or general's quarters,

rose above the others; the cavalry, the infantry, and the auxiliaries, occupied their respective stations; the streets were broad, and perfectly straight, and a vacant space of two hundred feet was left on all sides, between the tents and the rampart. The rampart itself was usually twelve feet high, armed with a line of strong and intricate palisades, and defended by a ditch of twelve feet in depth as well as in breadth. This important labour was performed by the hands of the legionaries themselves; to whom the use of the spade and the pick-axe was no less familiar than that of the sword or *pilum*. Active valour may often be the present of nature; but such patient diligence can be the fruit only of habit and discipline.

QUESTIONS

READER AND PURPOSE

1. Gibbon's purpose is to make clear how a Roman legion was organized and equipped. Does he succeed?

2. Does he appear to be writing for mature, educated readers or for school-children?

ORGANIZATION

3. Gibbon develops his topic by analysis. First he divides it into primary parts. Do these correspond to the paragraph structure—that is, does each paragraph represent a major division of the subject?

4. One might entitle the first paragraph "The Infantry." Give similar titles to the remaining three paragraphs.

5. Make an outline showing how Gibbon analyzes the infantry. There are seventeen sentences in this first paragraph. Show that they correspond, roughly if not perfectly, to the way in which the writer has divided his material.

6. In lines 10-12 Gibbon lists the legionary's armor as "an open helmet, with a lofty crest; a breast-plate, or coat of mail; greaves on their legs, and an ample buckler on their left arm." Why this particular order? Later in the paragraph he describes their weapons in the sequence "lighter spear . . . *pilum* . . . sword." Again, why this order?

7. Why does Gibbon italicize *Their* (60)? Is this device clumsy? Can it be defended?

8. Gibbon occasionally develops his subject by comparison and contrast. Mark two or three examples in your book.

SENTENCES

9. Would you describe Gibbon's sentences as very long, moderately long, or quite short? Can you find examples of short, simple sentences?

10. In the sentence beginning "The buckler" (12), what words are parallel *
to "framed" (13)? Find other examples of parallelism in Gibbon's writing. The
last sentence contains both parallelism and balance *, two clauses of about the
same length standing on either side of the semicolon. "Active valour" (105)
balances what words in the second clause? What other words and phrases in
this sentence exactly balance one another? In normal speech is this construction
common or rare? Is it more appropriate to a formal tone and subject or to informal writing?

11. Why in the list quoted in question 6 does Gibbon use semicolons between
the separate items instead of commas, which are more usual?

DICTION

12. Look up: *constitution* (1), *files* (30), *ranks* (30), *disposition* (32), *tactics*
(36), *phalanx* (37), *pikes* (38), *equestrian order* (53), *maces* (63), *levies*
67), *peculiarly* (80), *pioneers* (90), *rampart* (100).

13. Substitute simpler, less formal words for these: *constitution* (1), *discharge*
(19), *launched* (20), *durst* (21), *impetuosity* (22), *adversary* (28), *habituated*
(30), *solicited* (51), *suffrages* (52). Do you think any of these substitutions
improve the vigor of the writing?

14. What does Gibbon mean by "dangerous valour" (72)? Why is it an accurate and forceful phrase?

15. Find the etymologies * of *ponderous* (16), *equestrian* (53), *barbarians*
(64).

16. Describe Gibbon's tone *. Does he regard the Roman legion as a paltry
affair in comparison with modern army units? Or does he greatly admire the
legion? Underline words and phrases that support your answer.

POINTS TO LEARN

1. Broadly speaking, we say that Gibbon's purpose is description. Yet he has ordered his description by carefully dividing and subdividing the thing described
into its parts. In developing these parts, Gibbon uses illustration and comparison. A single paragraph or essay is seldom developed by one technique. Yet one
or two techniques usually stand out above the others and govern their use.

2. Two seemingly different subjects may appear in a single paragraph if their
relationship is made clear in the topic sentence.

3. Parallelism varies the rhythm of the prose and permits an economy especially
desirable when the subject is composed of many details. Parallelism appears in
almost all kinds of writing, both formal and informal, being particularly useful
in description. But the combination of parallelism and balance most often belongs to a formal style.

4. A knowledge of etymologies helps us to remember the meaning of a word and to use it accurately.

5. The careful reader will catch the tone * of whatever he reads. Through his sentence structure and diction, almost every writer will suggest how he feels toward his subject and his reader.

SUGGESTIONS FOR WRITING

Taking Gibbon's organization as a model, describe one of the following: a unit of the armed services, a sports team, an institution, a business, a club.

IMPROVING YOUR STYLE

1. In your composition write two parallel sentences. In one make three or four verbs parallel to a single subject; in the other make three or four subjects parallel to one verb.

2. Include as well a balanced sentence.

From The White Race and Its Heroes

Eldridge Cleaver is a black writer and activist. In the following selection—more specifically in its final five paragraphs—Cleaver uses analysis to develop his topic: the rebellion of white youth. Here the problem of analysis is more difficult than in the previous selection by Edward Gibbon. Gibbon had only to observe and follow a structure clearly inherent in the subject; the subject, in effect, presented its own analysis. Cleaver, on the other hand, deals with a more abstract and less obviously structured topic, and the analysis depends more upon the sensitivity and judgment of the writer. In exposition analysis often requires this kind of creative ability to discern patterns that lie below the surface rather than upon it.

1   At the close of World War Two, national liberation movements in the colonized world picked up new momentum and audacity, seeking to cash in on the democratic promises made by the Allies during the war. The Atlantic Charter, signed by President Roosevelt and Prime Minister Churchill in 1941, affirming "the right of all people to choose the form of 5 government under which they may live," established the principle, although it took years of postwar struggle to give this piece of rhetoric even the appearance of reality. And just as world revolution has prompted the oppressed to re-evaluate their self-image in terms of the changing conditions, to slough off the servile attitudes inculcated by long years of subordination, 10 the same dynamics of change have prompted the white people of the world to re-evaluate their self-image as well, to disabuse themselves of the Master Race psychology developed over centuries of imperial hegemony.

2   It is among the white youth of the world that the greatest change is taking place. It is they who are experiencing the great psychic pain of 15 waking into consciousness to find their inherited heroes turned by events into villains. Communication and understanding between the older and

younger generations of whites has entered a crisis. The elders, who, in the
tradition of privileged classes or races, genuinely do not understand the
youth, trapped by old ways of thinking and blind to the future, have only   20
just begun to be vexed—because the youth have only just begun to rebel.
So thoroughgoing is the revolution in the psyches of white youth that the
traditional tolerance which every older generation has found it necessary
to display is quickly exhausted, leaving a gulf of fear, hostility, mutual mis-
understanding, and contempt.   25

3   The rebellion of the oppressed peoples of the world, along with
the Negro revolution in America, have opened the way to a new evaluation of history, a re-examination of the role played by the white race since
the beginning of European expansion. The positive achievements are also
there in the record, and future generations will applaud them. But there   30
can be no applause now, not while the master still holds the whip in his
hand! Not even the master's own children can find it possible to applaud
him—he cannot even applaud himself! The negative rings too loudly. Slave-
catchers, slaveowners, murderers, butchers, invaders, oppressors—the white
heroes have acquired new names. The great white statesmen whom school   35
children are taught to revere are revealed as the architects of systems of
human exploitation and slavery. Religious leaders are exposed as condoners
and justifiers of all these evil deeds. Schoolteachers and college professors
are seen as a clique of brainwashers and whitewashers.

4   The white youth of today are coming to see, intuitively, that to   40
escape the onus of the history their fathers made they must face and admit
the moral truth concerning the works of their fathers. That such venerated
figures as George Washington and Thomas Jefferson owned hundreds of
black slaves, that all of the Presidents up to Lincoln presided over a slave
state, and that every President since Lincoln connived politically and cyni-   45
cally with the issues affecting the human rights and general welfare of the
broad masses of the American people—these facts weigh heavily upon the
hearts of these young people.

5   The elders do not like to give these youngsters credit for being able
to understand what is going on and what has gone on. When speaking of   50
juvenile delinquency, or the rebellious attitude of today's youth, the elders
employ a glib rhetoric. They speak of the "alienation of youth," the desire
of the young to be independent, the problems of "the father image" and
"the mother image" and their effect upon growing children who lack sound
models upon which to pattern themselves. But they consider it bad form   55

to connect the problems of the youth with the central event of our era—
the national liberation movements abroad and the Negro revolution at
home. The foundations of authority have been blasted to bits in America
because the whole society has been indicted, tried, and convicted of injustice. To the youth, the elders are Ugly Americans; to the elders, the youth 60
have gone mad.

6   The rebellion of the white youth has gone through four broadly
discernible stages. First there was an initial recoiling away, a rejection of
the conformity which America expected, and had always received, sooner
or later, from its youth. The disaffected youth were refusing to participate 65
in the system, having discovered that America, far from helping the under-
dog, was up to its ears in the mud trying to hold the dog down. Because
of the publicity and self-advertisements of the more vocal rebels, this
period has come to be known as the beatnik era, although not all of the
youth affected by these changes thought of themselves as beatniks. The 70
howl of the beatniks and their scathing, outraged denunciation of the system—characterized by Ginsberg as Moloch, a bloodthirsty Semitic deity to
which the ancient tribes sacrificed their first-born children—was a serious,
irrevocable declaration of war. It is revealing that the elders looked upon
the beatniks as mere obscene misfits who were too lazy to take baths and 75
too stingy to buy a haircut. The elders had eyes but couldn't see, ears but
couldn't hear—not even when the message came through as clearly as in
this remarkable passage from Jack Kerouac's *On the Road:*

> At lilac evening I walked with every muscle aching among the lights of
> 27th and Welton in the Denver colored section, wishing I were a 80
> Negro, feeling that the best the white world had offered was not
> enough ecstasy for me, not enough life, joy, kicks, darkness, music, not
> enough night. I wished I were a Denver Mexican, or even a poor over-
> worked Jap, anything but what I so drearily was, a "white man" disillu-
> sioned. All my life I'd had white ambitions. . . . I passed the dark 85
> porches of Mexican and Negro homes; soft voices were there, occa-
> sionally the dusky knee of some mysterious sensuous gal; the dark faces
> of the men behind rose arbors. Little children sat like sages in ancient
> rocking chairs.

7   The second stage arrived when these young people, having decided 90
emphatically that the world, and particularly the U.S.A., was unacceptable
to them in its present form, began an active search for roles they could play

in changing the society. If many of these young people were content to lay up in their cool beat pads, smoking pot and listening to jazz in a perpetual orgy of esoteric bliss, there were others, less crushed by the system, who rec- 95 ognized the need for positive action. Moloch could not ask for anything more than to have its disaffected victims withdraw into safe, passive, apolitical little nonparticipatory islands, in an economy less and less able to provide jobs for the growing pool of unemployed. If all the unemployed had followed the lead of the beatniks, Moloch would gladly have legalized 100 the use of euphoric drugs and marijuana, passed out free jazz albums and sleeping bags, to all those willing to sign affidavits promising to remain "beat." The non-beat disenchanted white youth were attracted magnetically to the Negro revolution, which had begun to take on a mass, insurrectionary tone. But they had difficulty understanding their relationship to the 105 Negro, and what role "whites" could play in a "Negro revolution." For the time being they watched the Negro activists from afar.

8   The third stage, which is rapidly drawing to a close, emerged when white youth started joining Negro demonstrations in large numbers. The presence of whites among the demonstrators emboldened the Negro lead- 110 ers and allowed them to use tactics they never would have been able to employ with all-black troops. The racist conscience of America is such that murder does not register as murder, really, unless the victim is white. And it was only when the newspapers and magazines started carrying pictures and stories of white demonstrators being beaten and maimed by mobs and 115 police that the public began to protest. Negroes have become so used to this double standard that they, too, react differently to the death of a white. When white freedom riders were brutalized along with blacks, a sigh of relief went up from the black masses, because the blacks knew that white blood is the coin of freedom in a land where for four hundred years 120 black blood has been shed unremarked and with impunity. America has never truly been outraged by the murder of a black man, woman, or child. White politicians may, if Negroes are aroused by a particular murder, say with their lips what they know with their minds they should feel with their hearts—but don't.   125

9   It is a measure of what the Negro feels that when the two white and one black civil rights workers were murdered in Mississippi in 1964, the event was welcomed by Negroes on the level of understanding beyond and deeper than the grief they felt for the victims and their families. This welcoming of violence and death to whites can almost be heard—indeed it 130

can be heard—in the inevitable words, oft repeated by Negroes, that those whites, and blacks, do not die in vain. So it was with Mrs. Viola Liuzzo.[1] And much of the anger which Negroes felt toward Martin Luther King during the Battle of Selma stemmed from the fact that he denied history a great moment, never to be recaptured, when he turned tail on the Ed- 135 mund Pettus Bridge and refused to all those whites behind him what they had traveled thousands of miles to receive. If the police had turned them back by force, all those nuns, priests, rabbis, preachers, and distinguished ladies and gentlemen old and young—as they had done the Negroes a week earlier—the violence and brutality of the system would have been 140 ruthlessly exposed. Or if, seeing King determined to lead them on to Montgomery, the troopers had stepped aside to avoid precisely the confrontation that Washington would not have tolerated, it would have signaled the capitulation of the militant white South. As it turned out, the March on Montgomery was a show of somewhat dim luster, stage-managed by the 145 Establishment. But by this time the young whites were already active participants in the Negro revolution. In fact they had begun to transform it into something broader, with the potential of encompassing the whole of America in a radical reordering of society.

10   The fourth stage, now in its infancy, sees these white youth taking 150 the initiative, using techniques learned in the Negro struggle to attack problems in the general society. The classic example of this new energy in action was the student battle on the UC campus at Berkeley, California— the Free Speech Movement. Leading the revolt were veterans of the civil rights movement, some of whom spent time on the firing line in the wilder- 155 ness of Mississippi/Alabama. Flowing from the same momentum were student demonstrations against U.S. interference in the internal affairs of Vietnam, Cuba, the Dominican Republic, and the Congo and U.S. aid to apartheid in South Africa. The students even aroused the intellectual community to actions and positions unthinkable a few years ago: witness the 160 teach-ins. But their revolt is deeper than single-issue protest. The characteristics of the white rebels which most alarm their elders—the long hair, the new dances, their love for Negro music, their use of marijuana, their mystical attitude toward sex—are all tools of their rebellion. They have turned these tools against the totalitarian fabric of American society—and 165 they mean to change it.

[1] A worker for the Southern Christian Leadership Conference who was shot and killed on March 26, 1965, on a highway near Lowndesboro, Alabama. [Editors' note]

QUESTIONS

READER AND PURPOSE

1. This analysis of what Cleaver calls the rebellion of white youth is part of a longer discussion of changing white attitudes. In itself the analysis is expository. Cleaver's larger purpose, however, is not merely to explain a historical phenomenon. Can you suggest what that larger purpose is?

2. Does Cleaver assume his readers generally to be sympathetic or unfriendly?

ORGANIZATION

3. The actual analysis of the phases of the rebellion begins in paragraph 6. What do the first five paragraphs contribute to the discussion? Make a brief outline of these paragraphs.

4. The opening sentence of paragraph 2 does not state the topic. Which one does? What does the first sentence set up?

5. Why does the writer begin a new paragraph at line 26? Where is the topic statement here? In this paragraph how does Cleaver meet the objection that he is unfairly neglecting the achievements of European culture?

6. Which sentence states the general topic of paragraphs 6-10? Explain how in these paragraphs Cleaver keeps his organizational scheme before the reader.

7. Cleaver uses examples to clarify what he means by the first stage of the youth rebellion. How does he develop the topic in paragraph 7? In paragraphs 9 and 10?

8. The eighth paragraph develops a little differently. Study how the thought expands through the eight sentences that make up this paragraph. How, for example, is the second sentence related to the first? Sentences 3 and 4 compose a new logical unit, as do sentences 5 and 6. How do each of these units connect with the idea expressed in the second sentence? Does sentence 7 introduce a brand-new thought or restate one expressed earlier? The closing sentence, finally, appears to contradict the seventh. Does it?

9. Each of the stages of the rebellion is treated in a single paragraph except for the third, which is given two. Why does Cleaver divide his material here into two paragraphs?

SENTENCES

10. The last two sentences of paragraph 3 are constructed along the same lines. Does this similarity of form reflect a similarity of idea? Point out one or two other places where Cleaver employs the same syntactic pattern for successive sentences.

11. The sentence beginning paragraph 2 is an example of what is called an-

ticipatory construction: a pronoun (here *it*) acts as the formal subject but merely anticipates the conceptual subject, which follows a linking verb (here *is*). Anticipatory constructions require extra words. This statement, for instance, could be shortened to "The greatest change is taking place among the white youth of the world." What advantage, however, does the anticipatory pattern have that justifies its use here?

12. How is sentence structure used to sharpen the contrast at the end of paragraph 5?

13. The logic of the sentence in lines 18-21 is complicated. The main point is that the older generation is just beginning to be annoyed by young people. But the sentence contains several other ideas: that older people do not understand the young, that they are caught up in the past, that they cannot see the future, that they belong to a tradition of privilege, and that the young have only just begun their rebellion. How are these ideas related to the main thought? All in all this is a fine example of the complex sentence *, in which a number of ideas are ordered around one major concept. Notice that Cleaver skillfully uses interrupted movement * to gather most of the subordinate constructions within the main clause.

14. What logical connection is implied between the participial construction * beginning in line 66 ("having discovered . . .") and the main clause?

15. What relationship in idea is implied by the colon in line 160? By the dashes in lines 162 and 164? Does the dash in the final sentence show the same thing?

DICTION

16. Look up: *inculcated* (10), *psyches* (22), *revere* (36), *exploitation* (37), *condoners* (37), *intuitively* (40), *impunity* (121), *Establishment* (146), *transform* (147), *encompassing* (148), *apatheid* (159).

17. Explain as fully as you can all that is conveyed by these phrases: *slough off the servile attitudes* (10), *dynamics of change* (11), *Master Race psychology* (12), *imperial hegemony* (13), *onus of history* (41).

8. What unfavorable connotation * is carried by each of the following expressions? *Piece of rhetoric* (7), *clique of brainwashers* (39), *connived politically and cynically* (45-46), *stage-managed* (145), *totalitarian fabric* (165).

19. Is there any irony * in the phrase *distinguished ladies and gentlemen* as used in lines 138-39?

20. What words might a political conservative employ to phrase the idea Cleaver expresses in line 149 as a *reordering of society*?

21. In lines 76-77 there is an allusion * to the Bible. Try to track it down.

22. *Lilac evening* (in the first line of the passage quoted from Jack Kerouac) is a fine piece of diction. Why is *lilac* a very effective epithet here—much better than *twilit*, say, or *dusky* or *darkening*?

POINTS TO LEARN

1. Topic statements may set up groups of paragraphs as well as a single paragraph.

2. One test of good expository writing is that it possesses conceptual toughness, enabling it to stand up to logical analysis.

3. Ideas of parallel logical value may be expressed effectively in sentences of similar syntactic pattern.

4. Words do more than convey facts and ideas; they also play upon and direct our emotions.

SUGGESTIONS FOR WRITING

1. If you think the older generation does not understand the younger (or that the young do not comprehend the old) write an essay of three or four paragraphs analyzing the reasons for the failure.

2. Many people feel that the young are no longer as rebellious as they were ten or fifteen years ago. If you agree, analyze why this is so.

3. Perhaps your attitude toward something or someone has passed through several stages (school or church or athletics or your parents). Analyze such a process in several paragraphs.

IMPROVING YOUR STYLE

In your essay attempt the following:

1. A long complex sentence using interrupted movement (like Cleaver's in lines 18-21). Select one idea as paramount and subordinate the others to it.

2. A participial phrase, placed either before or after the subject and expressing a cause of the effect stated in the main predicate of the sentence.

3. An allusion—if not to the Bible to a literary or historical personage or event.

4. Two or three examples of loaded diction—either favorable or unfavorable.

Definition

Although by placing it in a separate section we seem to be treating definition as something different from exposition, definition is in fact a form of expository writing. Indeed, it is a very important form, for to define something is certainly to explain it, and very often in order to explain one must first define. But because definition presents certain problems of its own, we have felt it convenient to treat it separately.

The Meaning of Definition

A definition is the effort to distinguish an entity from all other things for the purpose of being able to recognize it or in some way to understand it. To define "apple," for instance, is to find some means of isolating "apple" from all other things, especially from those things that superficially resemble it, like quinces or pomegranates. We must show that "apple" refers to a combination of features possessed by no other thing. But to find this combination of distinguishing features is not always easy; moreover, there are many ways to define and many complicated questions of psychology, philosophy, and logic concealed in the intellectual operation we call definition. One of the most significant concerns the thing-to-be-defined. In one sense, the term *apple* is merely a symbol—a combination of sounds made by the vocal apparatus or a certain combination of letters that stand for these sounds. In another sense *apple* signifies the physical object, the thing one can hold in one's hand and eat. We may reasonably ask, therefore, is definition concerned primarily with *apple* as word or with "apple" as thing? Although not all logicians would agree upon a single answer, most seem to admit that definition may deal either with words or with things. Some definitions focus our attention chiefly upon the thing, no matter whether we call it *apple, pomme,* or *Apfel.* This kind of definition attempts to give, as best it can, accurate, factual information about what an apple *is,* in some particular frame of reference. It is often concerned with the analysis of the thing, with its constituent

93

parts, their nature, function, and purpose. It describes the thing in relation to other things. In contrast, other definitions stress the word or the word-thing relationship. Either they call our attention to how a word has been used in the past, or else they explain—by whatever the process—what words mean. Philosophers and logicians have called the former *real definition*, and the latter *nominal definition*. These terms designate the two most general purposes of definition, both of which are important intellectual goals, and it would be a mistake, no doubt, to regard one as, in itself, superior to the other. We must acknowledge, however, an understandable human tendency to regard real definition as the only kind that matters and to dismiss nominal definition as only juggling with words, as being "merely verbal." Yet real definition is probably the much rarer of the two. It is, most usually, the contribution of an original and creative thinker or of a pioneer in some form of research. More commonly, our definition of *atom* or *quantum* is likely to be an explanation of how original thinkers and research workers have used the term, a nominal rather than a real definition. But this fact need not humble us or dismay us, for surely one of man's greatest achievements is his ability to use words accurately and wisely both for learning and for communicating. Furthermore, concern with words always implies a concern for things. With words we are able to think clearly about things, to devise new concepts, and to gain increasing mastery over our world. Defining words is therefore among the most important of our intellectual activities.

Methods of Definition

How does one go about defining a word or thing? Since there is no one "correct" method, we must say that it all depends upon one's reader and purpose. Or put in a different way, the general principle is this: the writer may use any method or combination of methods known or devisable so long as he efficiently brings his reader to understand what something is or what a word means. The following is a list of some of the most common methods of definition, a list that does not claim to be either exhaustive or exclusive.

1. *Analysis.* The type of definition that is perhaps most familiar to the average reader consists of placing a word in a large class called the *genus* and then differentiating the word from other members of that class. This method, as old as Aristotle, results in the dictionary kind of definition, though it is by no means confined to dictionaries. A typical entry in *Webster's New Collegiate Dictionary*, for example, reads in part: "*spin-*

naker . . . Naut. A large triangular sail set upon a long light pole (*spin-naker boom*), used when running before the wind." This same kind of analysis appears in the first sentence of an essay defining *semantics* by Hugh R. Walpole: "Semantics, or semasiology, is the study of the meaning of words." But analysis does not always consist of this kind of classification into genus and differentia. Another form of analysis lists the most important characteristics of the thing-to-be-defined, as we see in Aldous Huxley's definition of *ectomorph*, one of three major body types:

> The extreme ectomorph is neither comfortably round nor compactly hard. His is a linear physique with slender bones, stringy, unemphatic muscles, a short and thin-walled gut. The ectomorph is a light-weight, has little muscular strength, needs to eat at frequent intervals, is often quick and highly sensitive. The ratio of skin surface to body mass is higher than in endomorphs or mesomorphs, and he is thus more vulnerable to outside influences, because more extensively in contact with them. His body is built, not around the endomorph's massively efficient intestine, not around the mesomorph's big bones and muscles, but around a relatively predominant and unprotected nervous system.

Both definition by genus and differentia, and definition by division into parts are common and extremely useful, but it would be a mistake to assume that all definitions must proceed by analysis.

2. *Synthesis.* Just as important is definition by synthesis. This form of definition relates the thing-to-be-defined to something already familiar to the reader or listener. It often reveals the thing-to-be-defined as part of some larger whole. Thus, it might also be called "relational definition." Consider the following definition of thirst:

> . . . the entire theory of the mechanism of thirst has been formulated on this basis: "When there is a diminution of the water content of the blood and tissues generally, the secretions of the body, including saliva, are diminished in volume. Because less saliva is secreted, the mouth and throat become dry. It is this sensation of dryness that has been called "thirst." (Anton J. Carlson and Victor Johnson, *The Machinery of the Body*)

It is possible to define *thirst* by analyzing it, by saying that it consists of unpleasant tension, burning, and tickling, instead of relating the sensation to the chemistry of the body. But some things cannot be analyzed in this way and must be defined by synthesis or by some other method. *Blue* is such a thing. To define *blue*, other than by pointing to some blue object, we shall have to say that *blue* is the color produced by light of a wavelength .000047 cm. Or we might define blue as the color of the sky on a cloudless day. Either is an example of definition by synthesis.

3. *Negative Definition.* Closely related to synthetic definition, indeed what may be a special form of it, is negative definition, which helps to define a thing by making clear what it is not. "Electricity," says Bertrand Russell, "is not a thing like St. Paul's Cathedral; it is a way in which things behave. When we have told how things behave when they are electrified, and under what circumstances they are electrified, we have told all there is to tell." Or again, when defining the modern cowboy, Donald Hough observes that "Cowboys do not know how to fire a six-shooter. Most of them have never seen one. They used to wear revolvers for much the same reason as those that prompted early-day farmers to carry a scythe over one shoulder and a blunderbuss over the other when they went to work in their fields. Their herds are now protected by the cops . . ." By itself, negative definition is of little value, but as an accessory method of development and definition it is a striking device. In connection with negative definition, we might add that definitions sometimes carefully distinguish the thing-to-be-defined from something resembling it and often confused with it. Thus, a definition of *stalactite* might very well distinguish that formation from *stalagmite*. As with negative definition, to make this kind of distinction is to define the thing by means of relationships, by synthesis.

4. *Exemplification.* Often appearing as an aid to definition by analysis or by synthesis is definition by example, for one of the best ways to define something is to give one or more examples of it. At times, however, the method of example by itself is sufficient. Lincoln Barnett, for instance, after discussing *relativity of place*, defines *relativity of motion* in this way: "Anyone who has ever ridden on a railroad train knows how rapidly another train flashes by when it is traveling in the opposite direction, and conversely how it may look almost motionless when it is moving in the same direction." The example is developed at greater length than is indicated here and is made to serve, quite properly, as the writer's definition. Sometimes, then, one example can define all by itself, but other methods of definition can seldom do without examples.

5. *Synonyms.* Almost as familiar as definition by example is definition by synonyms. Dictionaries often define words by listing synonyms of the word-to-be-defined. This method has the advantage of being brief, but

unless it is accompanied by some other method of definition, it runs the risk of misleading the reader, for no two words mean exactly the same thing, and, quite often, approximations are not good enough. For this reason, many small abridged dictionaries have a limited value. Still, this method is useful, if our purpose is simply to clarify the meaning of a word or term in passing, as in this sentence by Alfred North Whitehead: "It would therefore appear as if the idea of congruence, or metrical equality, of two portions of space (as empirically suggested by the motion of rigid bodies) must be considered as a fundamental idea incapable of definition in terms of those geometrical concepts which have already been enumerated."

Types of Definition

1. *Consensual Definition*. Whatever the method of definition, the purpose remains the same—to make clear what the word means. Usually the writer will mean by it what most others in his culture mean. Thus in defining *apple* he is trying to state the common public definition of the term, what it means by the consensus of its users. We may, in fact, call such a statement a consensual definition.

2. *Stipulative Definition*. On the other hand, a writer may occasionally want to assign to a word a meaning more precise or in some other way slightly different from that which it commonly has. H. W. Fowler, for example, stipulates a definition of *genteelism* in this way: "By *genteelism* is here to be understood the substituting, for the ordinary natural word that first suggests itself to the mind, of a synonym that is thought to be less soiled by the lips of the common herd, less familiar, less plebian, less vulgar, less improper, less apt to come unhandsomely between the wind & our nobility." What is the advantage of creating one's own definition? The answer is that one does so, first, for clarity, and second, for convenience. Words, often, have so many different meanings that they are potential sources of ambiguity. Whenever abstractions like *beauty, liberty, justice, Romanticism* are key words in an essay, it is wise to announce that, for this particular discourse, we intend to use the word in one sense only. *Genteelism*, for example, may refer to many kinds of affected behavior, but Fowler wishes, for his purpose, to restrict the term to affectation in one's choice of words. The result is concentration and clarity. In addition, making a stipulative definition is more convenient than each time dragging along a cumbersome phrase like "genteelism in one's choice of words." Stipulative definitions are closely related to the consensual meaning, being

essentially a precise denotation selected out of the several contained within the general definition. Of course, stipulative definitions do not have to be related to consensual definitions. A writer is free to stipulate any meaning he chooses for his words, as did Humpty Dumpty when he told Alice that when "I use a word . . . it means just what I choose it to mean—neither more nor less." Still, when stipulative meanings grow too idiosyncratic the writer ceases to communicate and thus ceases to be a writer. There must always be some good reason for making a stipulative definition, some kind of ambiguity in the writing situation that cannot otherwise be avoided, since a stipulative definition always places an extra burden of attention upon the reader. But a wise use of stipulation is one of the writer's sharpest tools in exposition and argument.

3. *Normative Definition.* Finally, a writer may make what is called a normative definition, which may or may not be more precise than the consensual one, but which is, in the writer's opinion, better. A political theorist, for example, might feel that most of us misuse the word *democracy*. We employ it, he complains, to mean X when it should mean Y. If he defines it to mean Y and says that it should never be used by anyone except to mean Y, he has framed a normative definition. This might seem to be a special kind of stipulative definition, but actually it is different. In a stipulative definition the writer says: "In this work I shall use *democracy* to mean Y"; he says nothing about how he may define it in other contexts, and he says nothing about how other people should use it. In a normative definition the writer says not only that "I shall define *democracy* here to mean Y"; he asserts, or implies, that he will always use it with that meaning and that so should everyone else, for it—and it alone—is the proper meaning. Both types, however, have in common the fact that they cannot depart too far from commonly accepted meanings.

In exposition and argument, as we have demonstrated, the writer is constantly defining. Sometimes his definition is a single word. Sometimes it is only a sentence or two. But almost as often it is a paragraph, a section, or even a chapter; and, at times, to make his definition clear the writer needs the space of an entire book, for a definition is not complete until a writer can be sure that his reader knows what his term means. Writing good definition thus depends upon a thorough knowledge of one's subject, a rudimentary acquaintance with logic, common sense, and good manners. The following selections illustrate these characteristics as they appear in the work of skillful writers.

C. C. WYLIE

Maps

In the following selection C. C. Wylie develops a simple analytical definition. First he classifies the definiendum (the word or thing being defined), and then he differentiates it from others in its class. Notice particularly how he uses paragraphing to organize his definition. Had all this been composed in a single paragraph—which could have been done—the phases of the definition would have been less clear.

1   A map is a conventional picture of an area of land, sea, or sky. Perhaps the maps most widely used are the road maps given away by the oil companies. They show the cultural features such as states, towns, parks, and roads, especially paved roads. They show also natural features, such as rivers and lakes, and sometimes mountains. As simple maps, most auto- 5 mobile drivers have on various occasions used sketches drawn by service station men, or by friends, to show the best automobile route from one town to another.

2   The distinction usually made between "maps" and "charts" is that a chart is a representation of an area consisting chiefly of water; a 10 map represents an area that is predominantly land. It is easy to see how this distinction arose in the days when there was no navigation over land, but a truer distinction is that charts are specially designed for use in navigation, whether at sea or in the air.

3   Maps have been used since the earliest civilizations, and explorers 15 find that they are used in rather simple civilizations at the present time by people who are accustomed to traveling. For example, Arctic explorers have obtained considerable help from maps of the coast lines showing settlements, drawn by Eskimo people. Occasionally maps show not only the roads, but pictures of other features. One of the earliest such maps 20

From *Astronomy, Maps and Weather*. Copyright 1942 by Harper & Row, Publishers, Inc. Reprinted by permission of the publisher.

dates from about 1400 B.C. It shows not only roads, but also lakes with fish, and a canal with crocodiles and a bridge over the canal. This is somewhat similar to the modern maps of a state which show for each large town some feature of interest or the chief products of that town.

QUESTIONS

READER AND PURPOSE

1. Is Wylie's purpose to define *map* or map—that is, the word or the thing? How do you know?
2. What inferences can you draw about the kind of readers he is aiming at? Does he assume they are interested in the subject? Knowledgeable?

ORGANIZATION

3. This selection is a good example of definition by analysis. What words in the first sentence name the genus, or class, to which map belongs? Is the remainder of the paragraph (that is, after the first sentence) *essential* to the definition of map? If not, how does it contribute to our understanding?
4. Show that paragraph 1 is unified by the repetition of key words.
5. What important aspect of an analytical definition does the second paragraph fulfill? In drawing the distinction between map and chart what strategy does Wylie follow?
6. The third paragraph has two topics. Which sentence sets up the first? How is it supported? Which sentence introduces the second topic? What method of support is used here?
7. Are either of the topics of paragraph 3 absolutely necessary to the definition? If they aren't, what value do they have?

SENTENCES

8. Wylie's sentences are straightforward, without interrupting constructions * or numerous subordinated clauses * and phrases. Is this a good style for his purpose?
9. The opening sentence is simple *, having one subject-verb nucleus ("a map is"). Point out one or two other simple sentences. Are most of the sentences in this selection grammatically simple?
10. What technique of sentence structure does the writer use to pack more information into the first sentence?
11. The sentence in lines 17-19 makes use of participial phrases * to convey ideas of secondary importance ("showing settlements, drawn by Eskimo people"). Where is another example of such a phrase? Incidentally, is that comma after "settlement" really necessary?

DICTION
12. Look up: *conventional* (1), *cultural* (3), *distinction* (9), *navigation* (12).
13. In line 22 does *this* refer to any specific word in the preceding sentence? If not, to what does it refer? Can you think of a way of opening the sentence with *this* without risk of puzzling the reader?

POINTS TO LEARN
1. The analytical definition first classifies, then differentiates.
2. A paragraph may have two topics, each introduced by its own sentence.
3. An uncomplicated, straightforward sentence style conveys information easily and clearly.
4. When using *this* as the subject of a sentence, be certain that the reader understands what it refers to. If there is any doubt, make *this* an adjective modifying a noun that clearly sums up the preceding idea.

SUGGESTIONS FOR WRITING
In two paragraphs (about 300 words total) compose an analytical definition of one of the following topics. The essential problem is to classify the definiendum and then to distinguish it from other members of the class. However, include whatever additional, non-essential information you think will help your reader's understanding.

book, desk, recipe, office, college, statue, boat, turnpike

IMPROVING YOUR STYLE
In your paragraphs strive for a straightforward, uncomplicated sentence style. Include:
1. At least two grammatically simple sentences.
2. Two or three sentences using participial phrases.

Plot

E. M. Forster (1879-1970) was an English novelist, short story writer, and essayist. His best known novels include A *Passage to India, Howard's End,* and A *Room with a View.* This selection comes from *Aspects of the Novel,* the printed version of a series of lectures Forster delivered at Cambridge University in 1927. Like C. C. Wylie in the preceding selection Forster defines by genus and species. He spends, however, considerably more time on differentiation.

1   Let us define a plot. We have defined a story as a narrative of events arranged in their time-sequence. A plot is also a narrative of events, the emphasis falling on causality. "The king died and then the queen died," is a story. "The king died, and then the queen died of grief," is a plot. The time-sequence is preserved, but the sense of causality over- 5
shadows it. Or again: "The queen died, no one knew why, until it was discovered that it was through grief at the death of the king." This is a plot with a mystery in it, a form capable of high development. It suspends the time-sequence, it moves as far away from the story as its limitations will allow. Consider the death of the queen. If it is in a story we say "and 10
then?" If it is in a plot we ask "why?" That is the fundamental difference between these two aspects of the novel. A plot cannot be told to a gaping audience of cave men or to a tyrannical sultan or to their modern descendant the movie-public. They can only be kept awake by "and then—and then." They can only supply curiosity. But a plot demands intelligence and 15
memory also.

2   Curiosity is one of the lowest of the human faculties. You will have noticed in daily life that when people are inquisitive they nearly always have bad memories and are usually stupid at bottom. The man who begins by asking you how many brothers and sisters you have, is 20

never a sympathetic character, and if you meet him in a year's time he will probably ask you how many brothers and sisters you have, his mouth again sagging open, his eyes still bulging from his head. It is difficult to be friends with such a man, and for two inquisitive people to be friends must be impossible. Curiosity by itself takes us a very little way, nor does it take 25 us far into the novel—only as far as the story. If we would grasp the plot we must add intelligence and memory.

3   Intelligence first. The intelligent novel-reader, unlike the inquisitive one who just runs his eye over a new fact, mentally picks it up. He sees it from two points of view; isolated, and related to the other facts 30 that he has read on previous pages. Probably he does not understand it, but he does not expect to do so yet awhile. The facts in a highly organized novel (like *The Egoist*) are often of the nature of cross-correspondences and the ideal spectator cannot expect to view them properly until he is sitting up on a hill at the end. This element of surprise or mystery—the 35 detective element as it is sometimes rather emptily called—is of great importance in a plot. It occurs through a suspension of the time-sequence; a mystery is a pocket in time, and it occurs crudely, as in "Why did the queen die?" and more subtly in half-explained gestures and words, the true meaning of which only dawns pages ahead. Mystery is essential to a plot, 40 and cannot be appreciated without intelligence. To the curious it is just another "and then—" To appreciate a mystery, part of the mind must be left behind, brooding, while the other part goes marching on.

4   That brings us to our second qualification: memory.

5   Memory and intelligence are closely connected, for unless we re- 45 member we cannot understand. If by the time the queen dies we have forgotten the existence of the king we shall never make out what killed her. The plot-maker expects us to remember, we expect him to leave no loose ends. Every action or word ought to count; it ought to be economical and spare; even when complicated it should be organic and free from dead 50 matter. It may be difficult or easy, it may and should contain mysteries, but it ought not to mislead. And over it, as it unfolds, will hover the memory of the reader (that dull glow of the mind of which intelligence is the bright advancing edge) and will constantly rearrange and reconsider, seeing new clues, new chains of cause and effect, and the final sense (if the plot has 55 been a fine one) will not be of clues or chains, but of something aesthetically compact, something which might have been shown by the novelist straight away, only if he had shown it straight away it would never have become beautiful. We come up against beauty here—for the first time in

our enquiry: beauty at which a novelist should never aim, though he fails   60
if he does not achieve it. I will conduct beauty to her proper place later
on. Meanwhile please accept her as part of a completed plot. She looks a
little surprised at being there, but beauty ought to look a little surprised:
it is the emotion that best suits her face, as Botticelli knew when he painted
her risen from the waves, between the winds and the flowers. The beauty   65
who does not look surprised, who accepts her position as her due—she
reminds us too much of a prima donna.

QUESTIONS

READER AND PURPOSE

1. Does Forster assume that his readers know a great many novels and short
stories or that they have read very little fiction? Is his purpose anything more
than to make them understand clearly what *plot* means?

ORGANIZATION

2. What is the genus of *plot?* Name several other things that belong to the
same family. What characteristic of *plot* differentiates it from them? Does
Forster differentiate *plot* explicitly or implicitly?

3. How do the last two sentences of the first paragraph organize the rest of the
selection?

4. In Forster's sense, *plot* signifies a quality abstracted from narrative literature.
Curiosity, intelligence, and memory, however, belong to the reader of the story
rather than to any quality of the story itself. Can they be, then, part of a definition of *plot?* To put this another way, are these mental qualities essential
to Forster's definition, or are they accidental attributes of *plot?* Can you add
to Forster's third sentence so that curiosity, intelligence, and memory become
part of his formal definition: "A plot is . . . a narrative of events, the emphasis falling upon causality, which . . ."?

5. Why in line 44 does the writer set off his short sentence as a new paragraph?

6. Call to mind well-known narratives that merely tell stories and narratives
that have plots. Should the writer have named particular novels in the first
paragraph?

SENTENCES

7. In his introductory note Forster says of the lectures he delivered at Cambridge that "they were informal, indeed talkative in their tone *, and it seemed
safer when presenting them in book form not to mitigate the talk, in case

nothing should be left at all. Words such as 'I,' 'you,' 'one,' 'we,' 'curiously enough,' 'so to speak,' and 'of course,' will consequently occur on every page." The fact that he was talking has also influenced Forster's sentence structure. How?

8. Why does the writer begin by saying, "Let us define a plot"? Is that beginning more effective for his purpose than this opening: "If a story is a narrative of events arranged in their time-sequence, a plot is also a narrative of events, the emphasis falling on causality"? Forster's sentences are relatively short and their effect is one of simplicity. Yet they are not monotonous or flat. How does he vary his sentence structure?

DICTION

9. Look up: *faculties* (16), *cross-correspondences* (33), *organic* (50), *Botticelli* (64), *prima donna* (67).

10. Why does the writer refer to a "tyrannical sultan" (13)? Explain what he means by "the detective element as it is sometimes rather emptily called" (36). Demonstrate how Forster uses the connotations * of words to express his preference for plot over story.

11. Describe the writer's tone and point of view *. What is the advantage of his point of view?

POINTS TO LEARN

1. Good definitions give several concrete examples of the thing defined.
2. A writer may define something by contrasting it with something similar, something with which it may be confused.
3. A writer may define by telling what a thing is not.
4. In defining, a writer may list the essential qualities or characteristics of a thing.
5. Writing intended to be read aloud must use short, emphatic sentences of transition and relatively simple constructions.

SUGGESTIONS FOR WRITING

Prepare a definition to be read aloud to your class. Make your purpose to inform without being dull or losing the attention of your audience. Pay careful attention to your sentence structure. Write down a number of things that one might define for an audience of college students. Choose one of these or define one of the following: theater in the round, surrealism, a stock car, culture (as used by the sociologist or anthropologist), the stock market, outer space.

IMPROVING YOUR STYLE

Your style should be that of someone talking, talking to a friendly and sophisticated audience. Avoid slang and street argot but work for a relaxed informal tone. Remember that a personality is inevitably revealed in your language and that your audience will respond to that personality. Seek therefore to be pleasing. Strive for modesty without appearing hesitant or wishy-washy, for confidence without seeming overbearing, for originality in idea and diction without sounding idiosyncratic. Use "I" and "me," and by an occasional judicious "we" or "us" suggest an identification between yourself and your listeners.

Some Notes on Parody

Dwight Macdonald is a journalist and critic, whose books include: *Against the Grain: Essays on the Effects of Mass Culture* (1962), *Dwight Macdonald on Movies* (1969), and *Discriminations: Essays and Afterthoughts* (1974). These paragraphs are taken from the appendix to an anthology of parody edited by Macdonald. Parody is literature that mocks the style, sentiments, or ideas of other literature, a type of satire of which other species are travesty and burlesque. Macdonald attempts, successfully, to define all three of these varieties of literary satire. Such field definitions are not uncommon, for often entities, or words, derive much of their meanings from a close relationship to similar entities or terms. In such cases definition must involve not a single concept but a field—or linked series—of concepts, each being understood, in part, with reference to the others. So it is with parody, travesty, and burlesque.

1   The first question is: What *is* parody? The dictionaries are not helpful. Dr. Johnson defines parody as "a kind of writing in which the words of an author or his thoughts are taken and by a slight change adapted to some new purpose," which is imprecise and incomplete. The Oxford dictionary comes closer: "a composition . . . in which characteris- 5 tic turns of an author . . . are imitated in such a way as to make them appear ridiculous, especially by applying them to ludicrously inappropriate subjects." This at least brings in humor. But it does not distinguish parody from its poor relations, *travesty* ("a grotesque or debased imitation or likeness") and *burlesque* ("aims at exciting laughter by caricature of the man- 10 ner or spirit of serious works, or by ludicrous treatment of their subjects"). Such definitions tend to run together, which is just what a definition shouldn't do, since *definire* means "to set limits." I therefore propose the following hierarchy:

2   TRAVESTY (literally "changing clothes," as in "transvestite") is   15
the most primitive form. It raises laughs, from the belly rather than the
head, by putting high, classic characters into prosaic situations, with a corresponding stepping-down of the language. Achilles becomes a football
hero, Penelope a suburban housewife, Helen a beauty queen. Scarron did
it in the seventeenth century with his enormously popular *Virgile Travesti,*   20
John Erskine in the twentieth with his *The Private Life of Helen of Troy.*
Boileau was severe on Scarron:

> Au mépris du bon sens, le burlesque effronté
> Trompa les yeux d'abord, plut par sa nouveauté. . . .
> Cette contagion infecta les provinces,   25
> Du clerc et du bourgeois passa jusques aux princes.

It hardly bears thinking what his reaction would have been to Erskine's
book. Or to the contemporary imitation of Scarron by the English poetaster, Charles Cotton, which begins:

> I sing the man (read it who list)   30
> A Trojan true as ever pist,
> Who from Troy-Town by wind and weather
> To Italy (and God knows whither)
> Was pack'd and rack'd and lost and tost
> And bounced from pillar unto post.   35

3   BURLESQUE (from Italian *burla,* "ridicule") is a more advanced
form since it at least imitates the style of the original. It differs from parody
in that the writer is concerned with the original not in itself but merely as
a device for topical humor. Hawthorne's charming *The Celestial Railway,*
for example, is not a parody of Bunyan but a satire on materialistic progress   40
that is hung on the peg of *Pilgrim's Progress.* The instinct for filling a familiar form with a new content is old as history. The *Iliad* was burlesqued
a few generations after it was composed. Sacred themes were popular in the
Middle Ages, such as the Drunkards' Mass (*Missa de Potatoribus*), which
began: 45

> V*a.* Introibo ad altare Bachi
> R. Ad eum qui letificat cor homins.
>   Confiteor reo Bacho omnepotanti, et reo vino coloris rubei, et
> omnibus ciphis eius, et vobis potatoribus, me nimis gulose potasse per
> nimian nauseam rei Bachi dei mei potatione, sternutatione, ocitatione   50
> maxima, mea crupa, mea maxima crupa. . . . Potemus.

Twenty-five years ago, when the eleven-year-old Gloria Vanderbilt was the subject of a famous custody suit between her mother and her aunt, the court's decision awarding her to the aunt except for week ends was summarized by an anonymous newspaper wit: 55

> Rockabye baby
> Up on a writ,
> Monday to Friday, mother's unfit.
> As the week ends, she rises in virtue;
> Saturday, Sunday,   60
> Mother won't hurt you.

And last year, the London *Economist* printed a political carol:

> On the tenth day of Cwthmas,[1] the Commonwealth
>   brought to me
> Ten Sovereign Nations   65
> Nine Governors General
> Eight Federations
> Seven Disputed Areas
> Six Trust Territories
> Five Old Realms   70
> Four Present or Prospective Republics
> Three High Commission Territories
> Two Ghana-Guinea Fowl
>
> One Sterling Area
> One Dollar Dominion   75
> One Sun That Never Sets
> One Maltese Cross
> One Marylebone Cricket Club
> One Trans-Arctic Expedition
>
> And a Mother Country up a Gum Tree.   80

4   Finally and at last, PARODY, from the Greek *parodia* ("a beside- or against-song"), concentrates on the style and thought of the original.[2]

---

[1] Contraction of "Commonwealthmas." [Mr. Macdonald's note]

[2] Parody belongs to the family of para-words: parasite, parapsychology, paratyphoid, paranoia (against mind), paradox (against received opinion), paraphrase, paranymph (bridesmaid). It is not related to Paraguay, although that country is beside and against Uruguay. [Mr. Macdonald's note]

If burlesque is pouring new wine into old bottles, parody is making a new wine that tastes like the old but has a slightly lethal effect. At its best, it is a form of literary criticism. The beginning of Max Beerbohm's parody of 85 a Shaw preface may give the general idea:

A STRAIGHT TALK

When a public man lays his hand on his heart and declares that his conduct needs no apology, the audience hastens to put up its umbrellas against the particularly severe downpour of apologies in 90 store for it. I won't give the customary warning. My conduct shrieks aloud for apology, and you are in for a thorough drenching.

Flatly, I stole this play. The one valid excuse for the theft would be mental starvation. That excuse I shan't plead. I could have made a dozen better plays than this out of my own head. You don't 95 suppose Shakespeare was so vacant in the upper storey that there was nothing for it but to rummage through cinquecento romances, Towneley mysteries, and such-like insanitary rubbishheaps in order that he might fish out enough scraps for his artistic fangs to fasten on. Depend on it, there were plenty of decent original notions seething behind yon mar- 100 ble brow. Why didn't our William use *them?* He was too lazy. And so am I.

Shaw's polemical style is unerringly reproduced—the short, punchy sentences; the familiarity ("yon marble brow . . . our William"), the Anglo-Saxon vigor, the calculated irreverences ("and suchlike insanitary rubbish- 105 heaps"). But Beerbohm goes deeper, into the peculiar combination in Shaw of arrogance and self-depreciation, of aggressiveness and mateyness, so that the audience is at once bullied and flattered; shocking ideas are asserted but as if they were a matter of course between sensible people. Beerbohm's exposé of this strategy is true parody. 110

QUESTIONS

READER AND PURPOSE

1. Sometimes a writer, in order to define one word, has perforce to define two. Macdonald deals with an even more extensive field of meaning involving three terms. Think of a phrase (as brief as possible) that would label the general type of writing of which travesty, burlesque, and parody are the species.

2. Is Macdonald making a nominal or a real definition? Much effort is given in scholarship to establishing the limits of closely related terms. You can easily

appreciate, for example, the confusion that would result in literary criticism from the careless interchange of the words with which Macdonald is concerned. Do you think he clearly differentiates travesty, burlesque, and parody? Explain. Look up these words in a good unabridged dictionary. Are Macdonald's definitions an improvement?

ORGANIZATION

3. The rhetorical question * that opens this selection is the topic sentence for all four paragraphs which follow. What other sentence in this paragraph helps to organize the rest of the selection? What is the topic sentence of paragraph 1?

4. Notice that at the beginnings of paragraphs 2 and 3 there are no explicit transitional words or phrases linking them with the preceding material. Why are such links unnecessary in these cases? What signpost * is set at the beginning of paragraph 4?

5. In paragraphs 2 and 3 Macdonald supports his topic by several illustrations. He does not literally announce these examples, writing, say, in line 18: "Achilles, for instance, becomes a football hero. . . ." Is the absence of such labels (*for example, thus, say* would be others) a virtue or a disadvantage here? Why? In the third paragraph what sentence sets up the last three illustrations? What principle governs the order in which they are presented?

SENTENCES

6. Point out two or three examples of effective short sentences in Macdonald's prose.

7. The sentence in line 28 beginning "Or to the contemporary imitation . . ." is a fragment *. Why? What words would have to be added to make it a complete sentence? What advantage is there to keeping it a fragment?

DICTION

8. Look up: *Dr. Johnson* (2), *ludicrously* (7), *caricature* (10), *wit* (55), *writ* (57), *lethal* (84), *parapsychology* (footnote on page 109), *polemical* (103).

9. Precisely what do these phrases mean: *prosaic situations* (17), *topical humor* (39), *cinquecento romances* (97), *calculated irreverences* (105), *self-deprecation* (107)?

10. Why are the following substitutions inferior to Macdonald's words: *set of definitions* for *hierarchy* (14), *poet* for *poetaster* (28), *pithy* for *punchy* (103), *camaraderie* for *mateyness* (107)?

11. In line 41 Macdonald writes that Hawthorne's story was "hung on the peg of *Pilgrim's Progress.*" The metaphor * *hung on the peg of* is better than a phrase like *based on* because it is a fresher image *; it conveys the relationship between Hawthorne's story and Bunyan's allegory in sharper visual terms.

Where else in this selection does the writer employ an image to communicate an abstract idea visually?

12. Study the metaphors in the sentence in lines 95-99. What is Beerbohm making fun of here?

13. Are both *finally* and *at last* necessary in line 81? If they are not, can you think of any justification for using both?

POINTS TO LEARN

1. Often a set of closely related terms conveys a field of meaning. It is especially important that such terms be clearly differentiated, with as little overlapping as possible.

2. Fresh, sharp images often help a reader understand abstract conceptual relationships.

SUGGESTIONS FOR WRITING

Listed below are several three-term sets, each of which involves a field of related meanings. Select any one and in an essay of about four or five paragraphs define each term in the set. You may use examples; in fact you will probably find that you must use examples if you are successfully to distinguish each term in the set from the others.

> sport-game-hobby, opera-musical comedy-revue, panic-fear-dread, short story-novel-novella, magazine-journal-pamphlet, teacher-tutor-instructor, satire-irony-sarcasm, supper-dinner-meal, friend-acquaintance-pal, humor-wit-slapstick, sympathy-pity-compassion, happiness-joy-satisfaction, work-labor-toil, job-profession-career, love-lust-passion, chuckle-titter-snicker

IMPROVING YOUR STYLE

Somewhere in your composition attempt the following:

1. Three or four short emphatic sentences set against longer ones.

2. (With your instructor's approval) an effective fragment.

3. Several metaphors which convey an abstract idea or relationship in a sharp visual image.

Nebech . . . Schlemiel . . . Shlimazl

Leo Rosten has many talents. He has taught at major American universities; he writes short stories, movies, and books on a variety of non-fictional subjects. Probably he is best known for his humorous stories about H*Y*M*A*N K*A*P*L*A*N (as his hero likes to sign himself), a shrewd and likeable Jewish immigrant to the United States. This selection comes from *The Joys of Yiddish* (1968), described by Rosten as a "relaxed lexicon of Yiddish, Hebrew and Yinglish words often encountered in English. . . ." *The Joys of Yiddish* is both a mine of information and a vast entertainment. In this passage— actually a combination of three related entries in the book, each printed in its entirety—Rosten is defining words used to designate different kinds of fools. Like the preceding selection by Dwight Macdonald, this is a field, or group, definition, each term being defined, in part, with reference to the others. Like Macdonald, too, Rosten uses examples liberally to flesh out his definitions. He includes, however, more information of a strictly lexicographical nature, as his subject requires.

Nebech
Nebbech
Nebish
Nebbish

Pronounced NEB-*ekh* or NEB-*ikh*, with the *ch* as sounded by Scots or Germans, not the *ch* of "choo-choo." From Czech: *neboky*.

In recent years, no doubt to help the laryngeally unagile, the pronunciation NEB-*bish* (note the *sh*) has gained currency. The word is even spelled *nebbish*, notably in a collection of cartoons on cocktail 5 napkins, matchbooks, ashtrays and, for all I know, Cape Cod lighters. My feeling is that *nebbish* should be used only by people unable to clear their throats.

113

As an interjection, *nebech* means:

1. Alas, too bad, unfortunately, "the poor thing." "He went to the doctor, *nebech*." "She, *nebech*, didn't have a dime."

    In this usage, *nebech* expresses:

(a) Sympathy. "He lost his job, *nebech*."

(b) Regret. "They asked me, *nebech*, to break the sad news."

(c) Dismay. "He looked, *nebech*, like a ghost!"

(d) "Poor thing." "His wife, *nebech*, has to put up with him."

    Never say *nebech* about something you welcome, enjoy, are happy to report, or are glad happened. Hence the irony of this: "What would make me the happiest man in the world? To be sitting on a park bench in the sun, saying to my best friend, 'Look! There, *nebech*, goes Hitler.'"

As a noun, *nebech* means:

2. An innocuous, ineffectual, weak, helpless or hapless unfortunate. A Sad Sack. A "loser." First cousin to a *shlemiel*. "He's a *nebech*." "Once a *nebech*, always a *nebech*." "Whom did she marry? A real *nebech*!"

3. A nonentity; "a nothing of a person."

To define a *nebech* simply as an unlucky man is to miss the many nuances, from pity to contempt, the word affords.

Nebech is one of the most distinctive Yiddish words; it describes a universal character type.

A *nebech* is sometimes defined as the kind of person who always picks up—what a *shlemiel* knocks over.

A *nebech* is more to be pitied than a *shlemiel*. You feel sorry for a *nebech*; you *can* dislike a *shlemiel*.

There is a well-known wiscrack: "When a *nebech* leaves the room, you feel as if someone came in."

Stories, jokes, and wisecracks about the *nebech* are, by careful count, countless.

As the apothegm has it: "A man is, *nebech*, only a man."

A *nebech* went into a store to buy a little hand fan for his wife, who liked to fan herself while rocking on the porch. He examined a hundred fans, unable to make up his mind. The *baleboss*,[1] disgusted, exclaimed, "What's so hard?"

"I can't decide between the fans that cost a nickel and the fans that cost a dime. . . . What's the difference?"

[1] The owner of the store: the boss.

"The difference is this," said the owner. "With a ten-cent fan, you make like this"—he waved a fan vigorously in front of his face; then he lifted a five-cent fan—"and with the five-cent model, you do like this." He held the fan still—and waved his head.

This mordant reprimand went for naught.   50

Said the *nebech*: "I wonder if my wife will think it's worth it."

"Better ten enemies than one *nebech*."

—PROVERB

A *nebech* pulled into a parking place on a busy street in Tel Aviv. Along came a policeman.

"Is it all right to park here?" asked the *nebech*.   55

"No," said the cop.

"*No?* But look at all those other parked cars! How come?"

"They didn't ask."

A seventh-grader was so late coming home from his suburban school that his mother was frantic.   60

"What happened to you?" she cried.

"I was made traffic guard today, Mamma, and all the kids have to wait for my signal, after I stop a car, before they cross the street."

"But you were due home two *hours* ago!"

"Mamma, you'd be surprised how long I had to wait before a car came   65 along I could stop!"

He had the makings of a *nebech*—maybe even a *shlemiel*.

Shlemiel
Schlemiel
Shlemiehl
Shlemihl

Pronounced *shleh*-MEAL, to rhyme with "reveal." (NOTE: *Shlemiel* is often spelled *schlemiel*, or even *schlemiehl*, but I sternly oppose such complications. In Hebrew and Yiddish, the single letter, *shin*, repre-   70 sents the *sh* sound. And in English, to begin a word with *sch* is to call for the *sk* sound, as in "school," "scheme," "schizophrenic." Anyway,

I think a *shlemiel* is plagued by enough burdens without our adding orthographic *tsuris*[2] to them.)

1. A foolish person; a simpleton. "He has the brains of a *shlemiel*."   75
2. A consistently unlucky or unfortunate person; a "fall guy"; a hard-luck type; a born loser; a submissive and uncomplaining victim. "That poor *shlemiel* always gets the short end of the stick." A Yiddish proverb goes: "The *shlemiel* falls on his back and breaks his nose."
3. A clumsy, butterfingered, all-thumbs gauche type. "Why does a   80 *shlemiel* like that ever try to fix anything?"
4. A social misfit, congenitally maladjusted. "Don't invite that *shlemiel* to the party."
5. A pipsqueak, a Caspar Milquetoast. "He throws as much weight as a *shlemiel*." "No one pays attention to that *shlemiel*."   85
6. A naive, trusting, gullible customer. This usage is common among furniture dealers, especially those who sell the gaudy, gimcrack stuff called "borax."
7. Anyone who makes a foolish bargain, or wagers a foolish bet. This usage is wide in Europe; it probably comes from Chamisso's tale, *Peter*   90 *Schlemihl's Wunderbare Geschichte*, a fable in which the protagonist sold his shadow and, like Faust, sold his soul to Satan.

It is important to observe that *shlemiel*, like *nebech*, carries a distinctive note of pity. In fact, a *shlemiel* is often the *nebech's* twin brother. The classic definition goes: "A *shlemiel* is always knocking things off a table;   95 the *nebech* always picks them up."

Shlemiel is said to come from the name Shlumiel, the son of a leader of the tribe of Simeon (Numbers, 2). Whereas the other generals in Zion often triumphed on the field of war, poor Shlumiel was always losing.

Another theory about the origin of *shlemiel* runs that it is a variation of   100 *shlimazl* or *shlemozzl*. (See SHLIMAZL.) I can't quite see how *shlimazl* gave birth to *shlemiel*; the words are as different as "hard luck" is from "that jerk."

The classic attempt to discriminate between the two types runs: "A *shlemiel* is a man who is always spilling hot soup—down the neck of a   105 *shlimazl*." Or, to make a triple distinction: "The *shlemiel* trips, and knocks down the *shlimazl*; and the *nebech* repairs the *shlimazl's* glasses."

I suppose that *shlemiels* often are *shlimazls*—but that need not be. A *shlemiel* can make a fortune through sheer luck; a *shlimazl* can't: He loses a fortune, through bad luck.   110

---

[2] Troubles; worries.

Nor is every *shlimazl* a *shlemiel:* e.g., a gifted, able, talented man is no *shlemiel,* but he may run into such bad luck that he is a *shlimazl:* thus, Gregor Mendel and Thomas Alva Edison, both of whom encountered strings of perverse fortune in their experiments; one might have called them *shlimazls,* but surely never *shlemiels.*   115

Can a brilliant or learned man be a *shlemiel?* Of course he can; many a savant is: the absentminded professor, the impractical genius, are paradigms of *shlemielkeit* (*shlemiel*-ness). N.B.: Neither *shlemiel, schlemiehl,* nor *schlemiel* appears in the *Oxford English Dictionary.* Nor were they in the *Webster's New International,* second edition.* Nor are they in H. L.   120 Mencken's *The American Language.*** I am as surprised as you.

"A *shlemiel* takes a bath, and forgets to wash his face."

A *shlemiel* came to his rabbi, distraught. "Rabbi, you've got to advise me. Every year my wife brings forth a baby. I have nine children already, and barely enough money to feed them—Rabbi, what can I do?"   125

The sage thought not a moment. "Do nothing."

A man came home from the steam baths—minus his shirt.

"*Shlemiel!*" cried his wife. "Where's your shirt?"

"My shirt? That's right. Where can it be? Aha! Someone at the baths must have taken my shirt by mistake, instead of his."   130

"So where is *his* shirt?"

The *shlemiel* scratched his head. "The fellow who took my shirt—he forgot to leave his."

Two *shlemiels* were drinking tea. In time, one looked up and announced portentously: "Life! What is it? Life—is like a fountain!"   135

The other pondered for a few minutes, then asked, "Why?"

The first thought and thought, then sighed, "So O.K.: life *isn't* like a fountain."

* G. & C. Merriam, 1961.
** Knopf, 1962.

Shlimazl
Schlimazel (not shemozzl, not shlemozzl)

Pronounced *shli*-MOZ-*zl*, to rhyme with "thin nozzle." From the German: *schlimm*: "bad" and the Hebrew: *mazel*: "luck." (It is not un-   140
usual for a Yiddish word to combine Hebrew with German, Hebrew
with English, Hebrew with Russian or Polish or Hungarian.)

A chronically unlucky person; someone for whom nothing seems to go
right or turn out well; a born "loser." Let me illustrate by combining
four folk sayings: "When a *shlimazl* winds a clock, it stops; when he   145
kills a chicken, it walks; when he sells umbrellas, the sun comes out;
when he manufactures shrouds, people stop dying."

A *shlimazl* wryly sighed: "From *mazel* to *shlimazl* is but a tiny step; but
from *shlimazl* to *mazel—oy*, is that far!"

A world-weary Jew once said: "They say that the poor have no *mazel*, which   150
is undeniably true, for if the poor had *mazel* would they be poor?"

"Only *shlimazls* believe in *mazel*."

—PROVERB

The twelfth-century poet Abraham ibn Ezra, whom you encountered in
high school as Browning's Rabbi ben Ezra (may his tribe increase), limpidly described the *shlimazl*'s lot when he wrote: 155

> If I sold lamps,
> The sun,
> In spite,
> Would shine at night.

Mintz came to his rabbi and said, "Whatever I do goes sour. My wife and   160
children soon won't have anything to eat. What can I *do*?"
    "Become a baker," said the rabbi.
    "A baker? Why?"
    "Because if you're a baker, even if business is bad, you and your loved
ones will have bread!"   165

LEO ROSTEN   119

Mintz pondered. "And what if the day comes when I don't have enough money to buy flour?"
"Then you won't be a baker," said the rabbi, "but a *shlimazl.*"

"Hello, Yussel! V*ie gehts?*" ("How are things?")
"Good. Everything is good!"   170
"Really? I hear you've had a terrible year. How can you say everything's *good?*"
"It is," said Yussel. "Every morning, I'm good and depressed. Every evening, I'm good and tired. In the summer, I'm good and hot, and in the winter, I'm good and cold. My roof has so many leaks that I get good   175
and wet, and my floors are so rickety that to take five steps makes me good and angry. My children are so lazy I'm good and disgusted with them, and my wife is such a *yenta** that I'm good and sick of her. In fact, everything about my life is so good, I'm good and tired of living!"

QUESTIONS

READER AND PURPOSE

1. Rosten's definitions are lexicographical. Like the editor of the dictionary you consult in your schoolwork, he tells you how a word is used. However, there are several differences between Rosten's approach and that of the more conventional lexicographer. One difference is in his point of view *. Would the usual dictionary editor write, "My feeling is . . ." (7)? Why not? Is it a fault that Rosten employs a personal point of view?
2. Another difference is in tone and purpose. How does Rosten regard his subject? His reader? What does this sentence suggest about his purpose and tone: "Stories, jokes, and wisecracks about the *nebech* are, by careful count, countless" (37-38)?

ORGANIZATION

3. A dictionary entry gives us information about the meaning of a word and also about its spelling, etymology *, grammatical function, pronunciation, and range of use. Does Rosten cover most of these matters for each of his three words? In defining *nebech* what does he do first? The material from lines 9 to 26 constitutes the formal definition. How in this section has the writer helped readers to follow his analysis?
4. What does the material in lines 27-67 contribute to the definition of *nebech*?

---

* A nag; a vulgar, coarse-mannered woman.

5. Using line references to indicate the beginnings and endings of various sections, make a rough outline of Rosten's treatment of *shlemiel*. Do the same for *shlimazl*.

6. What is the function of the rhetorical question * in line 116?

7. Explain why the sentences in lines 23-24 are examples of fragments *. Usually writers avoid fragments, but here they are a virtue. To see why turn each of these abbreviated statements into a grammatically complete sentence. Have you improved the writer's style? What fact about Rosten's purpose makes fragments desirable?

8. Contrast the following revisions with Rosten's sentences:

(a) *Revision:* To define a *nebech* simply as an unlucky man is missing the many nuances, from pity to contempt, the word affords.
Rosten: "To define a *nebech* simply as an unlucky man is to miss the many nuances, from pity to contempt, the word affords." (27-28)

(b) *Revision:* A *nebech*, for whom you feel sorry, is more to be pitied than a *shlemiel*. You can dislike a *shlemiel*.
Rosten: "A *nebech* is more to be pitied than a *shlemiel*. You feel sorry for a *nebech*; you *can* dislike a *shlemiel*." (33-34)

(c) *Revision:* This usage is wide in Europe. It probably comes from Chamisso's tale, *Peter Schlemihl's Wunderbare Geschichte*. This is a fable in which the protagonist sold his shadow. He also sold his soul to Satan. Like Faust.
Rosten: "This usage is wide in Europe; it probably comes from Chamisso's tale, *Peter Schlemihl's Wunderbare Geschichte*, a fable in which the protagonist sold his shadow and, like Faust, sold his soul to Satan." (89-92)

9. Sometimes Rosten employs a dash to set off the final construction of a sentence, even though the grammar does not require any pause. Why does he do this? (Consider the sentence in line 127 revised to read: "A man came home from the steam baths minus his shirt." What has been lost?)

10. How is *disgusted* (42) logically related to the main idea of its sentence? Participles * are often used this way; it is a trick of style worth learning.

11. Look up: *innocuous* (23), *apothegm* (39), *gauche* (80), *pipsqueak* (84), *Casper Milquetoast* (84), *gimcrack* (87), *paradigms* (117), N. B. (118), *distraught* (123), *portentously* (135).

12. As fully as you can explain the meanings of these phrases: *laryngeally un-*

agile (3), *mordant reprimand* (50), *congenitally maladjusted* (82), *classic definition* (95), *perverse fortune* (114), *chronically unlucky* (143), *limpidly described* (154).

13. How do their etymologies help to clarify the current senses of these words: *interjection* (9), *nonentity* (26), *nuances* (27), *orthographic* (74), *gullible* (86), *savant* (117), *wryly* (148)?

14. What relationship in thought does each of the following connectors * prepare us for: *anyway* (72), *in fact* (94), *nor* (111), *thus* (112)? Would the phrase *in any event* be more formal than *anyway*, or less?

15. Does Rosten intend *sternly* (69) to be taken at face value?

16. Why is *loser* (24) in quotation marks?

POINTS TO LEARN

1. A good lexicographer gives as much relevant information about a word as his space permits.

2. The more a word is illustrated in actual use, the clearer its nuances become.

3. A long clause or phrase is not always necessary to show causality; sometimes a single participle serves the purpose.

SUGGESTIONS FOR WRITING

Choose a set of two or three slang terms which describe a similar (but not identical) type of person or situation and compose a definition essay. Your purpose is to enable a reader unfamiliar with your slang to pronounce the word properly (if that presents a problem) and to apply it with a knowledge of its subtleties of meaning. Clarify these subtleties by illustrating the words in different contexts and by distinguishing them from each other.

IMPROVING YOUR STYLE

Include the following in your essay:

1. A sentence in which a final word or phrase is set off by a dash for extra emphasis.

2. A participle (past or present) used as a non-restrictive modifier and placed between the subject and verb (as in line 42 of Rosten).

3. (With your instructor's approval) one or two effective fragments.

4. Sentences introduced by *anyway, in fact, nor, thus.*

HENRY FAIRLIE

Love and Lust

Henry Fairlie is a British journalist and writer. This selection comes from one of a series of pieces he composed for *The New Republic* on the seven deadly sins (pride, anger, lust, envy, greed, gluttony, and sloth). In the essay which begins with the three paragraphs printed below Fairlie is concerned with more than defining love and lust. He attacks what he sees as our preoccupation with sex and our rejection of genuine love: "We have reduced love to sex, sex to the act, and the act to a mere quantitative measurement of it." He concludes by warning that permissive lust has become a dangerous social malaise working to the advantage of those who would manipulate us:

> The managers of our society much prefer that we are infatuated with our sexuality, than that we look long and steadily at what they contrive from day to day. . . . They have discovered that, now that religion has been displaced, sex can be made the opiate of the masses. When the entire society is at last tranquilly preoccupied in the morbid practices of onanism, they will know that there is nothing more for them to do but rule forever over the dead.

Thus Fairlie's broad purpose is that of social critic: to expose a vice in the hope that we shall be persuaded to lead better lives.

Here, however, his immediate concern is to define the vice he is attacking, and the selection is a good example of the fact that in composition defining is often not an end in itself but a required first step toward another goal.

1 Lust is not interested in its partners, but only in the gratification of its own craving: not even in the satisfaction of our whole natures, but in the appeasement merely of an appetite which we are unable to subdue. It is therefore a form of self-subjection; in fact of self-emptying. The sign

From "Lust or Luxuria" (*The New Republic*, October 8, 1977). © 1977 by The New Republic, Inc. Reprinted by permission.

it wears is: "This property is vacant." Anyone may take possession of it for 5
a while. Lustful people may think that they can choose a partner at will
for sexual gratification. But they do not really choose; they accept what is
available. Lust accepts any partner for a momentary service; anyone may
squat in its groin.

2   Love has meaning only insofar as it includes the idea of its con- 10
tinuance. Even what we rather glibly call a love affair, it if comes to an end,
may continue as a memory that is pleasing in our lives, and we can still
renew the sense of privilege and reward of having been allowed to know
someone with such intimacy and sharing. But Lust dies at the next dawn
and, when it returns in the evening, to search where it may, it is with its 15
own past erased. Love wants to enjoy in other ways the human being
whom it has enjoyed in bed. But in the morning Lust is always furtive. It
dresses as mechanically as it undressed, and heads straight for the door, to
return to its own solitude. Like all the sins, it makes us solitary. It is a self-
abdication at the very heart of one's own being, of our need and ability to 20
give and receive.

3   Love is involvement as well as continuance; but Lust will not get
involved. This is one of the forms in which we may see it today. If people
now engage in indiscriminate and short-lived relationships more than in
the past, it is not really for some exquisite sexual pleasure that is thus 25
gained, but because they refuse to become involved and to meet the demands that love makes. They are asking for little more than servicing, such
as they might get at a gas station. The fact that it may go to bed with a
lot of people is less its offense than the fact that it goes to bed with people for whom it does not care. The characteristic of the "singles" today is 30
not the sexual freedom they supposedly enjoy, but the fact that this freedom is a deception. They are free with only a fraction of their natures.
The full array of human emotions is hardly involved. The "singles bar"
does not have an obnoxious odor because its clients, before the night is
over, may hop into bed with someone whom they have just met, but be- 35
cause they do not even consider that, beyond the morning, either of them
may care for the other. As they have made deserts of themselves, so they
make deserts of their beds. This is the sin of Lust, just as it dries up human beings, so it dries up human relationships. The word that comes to
mind, when one thinks of it, is that it is parched. Everyone in a "singles 40
bar" seems to have lost moisture, and this is peculiarly the accomplishment
of Lust, to make the flesh seem parched, to deprive it of all real dewiness,
shrivelling it to no more than a husk.

QUESTIONS

1. Actually this is a double definition, for love and lust are best understood with reference to one another. With which is Fairlie primarily concerned?

2. Is this an example of analytical definition?[1] If not, how does the writer establish the essential natures of love and of lust? Is the definition logically complete at any specific point in these paragraphs? Could a definition like this ever be "logically complete"?

3. Love and lust both involve sexual gratification. In what way, according to Fairlie, do they differ with regard to this gratification?

4. Do you think Fairlie is writing directly for "swingers," those guilty of reducing "love to sex, [and] sex to the act"? Why or why not?

5. The opening sentence of paragraph 1 makes an assertion. Does the second sentence illustrate that assertion, repeat it, compare it to something, or explain a reason for it? How is the third sentence related in thought to the second? The fourth to the third? Each of the remaining statements to the idea(s) preceding it?

6. Is the second paragraph justifiable: is there a good reason for beginning a new paragraph here?

7. Paragraph 2 contrasts love and lust with regard to what quality? Where is the emphasis in the contrast? (How many sentences are given to love, how many to lust?) Does the material from line 16 to the end of the paragraph (beginning "Love wants to enjoy") develop a second point of difference or simply repeat the first?

8. How does the second sentence of paragraph 2 relate to the idea of "continuance"—as a qualification * or as a kind of restatement?

9. What words link the third paragraph to the second?

10. Which term (or terms) in the opening sentence of paragraph 3 expresses the topic idea? How does the paragraph develop this topic—by restatement? examples? reasons? effects?

11. In the statements in lines 7-9 and 22-23 how does the writer use sentence structure to reinforce the contrast?

12. Study the semicolons in lines 4, 7, 8, and 22. According to the conven-

1. See pages 94-95.

tional rules of punctuation could any of these be replaced by a comma? Even if they could be, are the semicolons justified? What reason is there for the colons in lines 2 and 5?

13. Point out the parallel * elements in the sentence in lines 19-21.

14. Show that the sentence in lines 33-37 is organized in a pattern of "not this, that." Is the point of the sentence emphasized by keeping the progression of ideas similar in its two parts?

15. Explain why each of the following revisions is less emphatic or clear than what Fairlie wrote:

> (a) *Revision:* Anyone may squat in its groin; lust accepts any partner for a momentary service.
> *Fairlie:* "Lust accepts any partner for a momentary service; anyone may squat in its groin." (8-9)
> (b) *Revision:* But Lust dies at the next dawn and returns with its own past erased in the evening, to search where it may.
> *Fairlie:* "But Lust dies at the next dawn and, when it returns in the evening, to search where it may, it is with its own past erased." (14-16)
> (c) *Revision:* But Lust is always furtive in the morning.
> *Fairlie:* "But in the morning Lust is always furtive." (17)

DICTION

16. Look up: *craving* (2), *glibly* (11), *intimacy* (14), *furtive* (17), *self-abdication* (19), *indiscriminate* (24), *"singles"* (30), *array* (33), *husk* (43).

17. How do the etymologies * of these words help to clarify their modern sense: *appeasement* (3), *exquisite* (25), *obnoxious* (34)?

18. Explain the metaphors * implicit in *sign* (4) and in *mechanically* (18). In the latter passage what other figure of speech * does Fairlie use to vivify lust?

19. Identify the simile * in line 27-28. Is it effective?

20. What relationships in thought are signalled by *therefore* and *in fact* in line 4?

21. To what do the *it's* refer in lines 28 and 29? Do you find the pronouns confusing? What about *this* in line 23: is its antecedent clear?

22. What subsequent terms repeat the idea conveyed by *deserts* (37)?

23. Why would the following words be less effective in Fairlie's context: *appeasement of desire* for *appeasement of appetite* (3), *lonely* for *solitary* (19), *customers* for *clients* (34)?

24. *Squat* (9) and *hop* (35) are especially expressive verbs. What overtones of meaning do they have here? (There is a faint literary allusion * in Fairlie's use of *squat*. See John Milton's *Paradise Lost*, book IV, line 800.)

POINTS TO LEARN

1. Definition is often a necessary preliminary step to some other writing goal.
2. Qualities of mind and personality may perhaps be defined most easily in terms of observable behavior.
3. Strong expressive verbs are essential to strong expressive prose.

SUGGESTIONS FOR WRITING

In two or three paragraps totaling 300-400 words, define one of the following pairs of qualities:

> fear and courage, sympathy and callousness, open-mindedness and close-mindedness, initiative and lethargy, self-confidence and timidity, generosity and stinginess.

Decide where to place your emphasis and concentrate upon showing how the qualities reveal themselves in people's actions and relationships.

IMPROVING YOUR STYLE

Incorporate the following into your essay:

1. A sentence on the pattern of "not X, but Y" (like Fairlie's sentence in lines 33-37).
2. At least one metaphor and one simile.
3. Two or three verbs denoting vigorous action and implying strong feelings of approval or disapproval.
4. One sentence beginning with *therefore* and one beginning with *in fact*.

Anger

W. H. Auden (1907-73) was an English poet (he became an American citizen), one of the most important of this century. In addition to poetry he wrote plays and numerous essays. One of these—here reprinted in its entirety—is on anger. It appeared as a contribution to a collection of pieces on the seven deadly sins (pride, anger, lust, envy, greed, gluttony, and sloth), each by a different writer. Auden's essay is more personal and less moralistic than Fairlie's treatment of a similar theme (see pages 122-23). While he is not framing a definition in a narrow, logical sense, Auden is attempting to make clear what anger is. Thus his essay is an extended, if informal, definition.

1 Like all the sins except pride, anger is a perversion, caused by pride, of something in our nature which in itself is innocent, necessary to our existence and good. Thus, while everyone is proud in the same way, each of us is angry or lustful or envious in his own way.

2 Natural, or innocent, anger is the necessary reaction of a creature 5 when its survival is threatened by the attack of another creature and it cannot save itself (or its offspring) by flight. Such anger, accompanied by physiological changes, like increased secretion of adrenalin, inhibits fear so that the attacked creature is able to resist the threat to its extinction. In the case of young creatures that are not yet capable of looking after themselves, 10 anger is a necessary emotion when their needs are neglected: a hungry baby does right to scream. Natural anger is a reflex reaction, not a voluntary one; it is a response to a real situation of threat and danger, and as soon as the threat is removed, the anger subsides. No animal lets the sun go down upon its wrath. Moreover, Lorentz has shown that, in fights between the social 15 animals, when, by adopting a submissive posture, the weaker puts itself at the mercy of the stronger, this inhibits further aggression by the latter.

3   Anger, even when it is sinful, has one virtue; it overcomes sloth. Anybody, like a schoolmaster, a stage director or an orchestral conductor, whose business it is to teach others to do something, knows that, on occasions, the quickest—perhaps the only—way to get those under him to do their best is to make them angry.

4   Anger as a sin is either futile (the situation in which one finds oneself cannot or should not be changed, but must be accepted) or unnecessary (the situation could be mastered as well or better without it). Man is potentially capable of the sin of anger because he is endowed with memory —the experience of an event persists—and with the faculty of symbolization (to him, no object or event is simply itself). He becomes actually guilty of anger because he is first of all guilty of the sin of pride, of which anger is one of many possible manifestations.

5   Because every human being sees the world from a unique perspective, he can, and does, choose to regard himself as its centre. The sin of anger is one of our reactions to any threat, not to our existence, but to our fancy that our existence is more important than the existence of anybody or anything else. None of us wishes to be omnipotent, because the desires of each are limited. We are glad that other things and people exist with their own ways of behaving—life would be very dull if they didn't—so long as they do not thwart our own. Similarly, we do not want others to conform with our wishes because they must—life would be very lonely if they did— but because they choose to; we want DEVOTED slaves.

6   The British middle-class culture in which I grew up strongly discouraged overt physical expression of anger; it was far more permissive, for example, towards gluttony, lust and avarice. In consequence, I cannot now remember "losing" my temper so that I was beside myself and hardly knew what I was doing. Since childhood, at least, I have never physically assaulted anyone, thrown things or chewed the carpet. (I do, now and again, slam doors.) Nor have I often seen other people do these things. In considering anger, therefore, most of my facts are derived from introspection and may not be valid for others, or from literature, in which truth has to be subordinated to dramatic effect. No fits of temper in real life are quite as interesting as those of Lear, Coriolanus or Timon.

7   In my own case—I must leave the psychological explanation to professionals—my anger is more easily aroused by things and impersonal events than by other people. I don't, I believe, really expect others to do what I wish and am seldom angry when they don't; on the other hand I do expect God or Fate to oblige me. I do not mind losing at cards if the other players

are more skilful than I, but, if I cannot help losing because I have been dealt a poor hand, I get furious. If traffic lights fail to change obligingly to red when I wish to cross the road, I am angry; if I enter a restaurant and it is crowded, I am angry. My anger, that is to say, is most easily aroused by a 60 situation which is (a) not to my liking, (b) one I know I cannot change, and (c) one for which I can hold no human individual responsible.

Change of Nature

8   This last condition is the most decisive. I like others to be on time and hate to be kept waiting, but if someone deliberately keeps me waiting 65 because, say, he is annoyed with me or wishes to impress me with his importance, I am far less angry than I am if I know him to be unpunctual by nature. In the first case, I feel I must be partly responsible—if I had behaved otherwise in the past, he would not have kept me waiting; and I feel hopeful—perhaps I can act in the future in such a way that our relationship 70 will change and he will be punctual next time. In the second case, I know that it is in his nature to be late for others, irrespective of their relationship, so that, in order to be on time, he would have to become another person.

9   My fantastic expectation that fate will do as I wish goes so far that my immediate reaction to an unexpected event, even a pleasant surprise, is 75 anger.

10   Among the British middle class, repressed physical violence found its permitted substitute in verbal aggression, and the more physically pacific the cultural sub-group (academic and clerical circles, for instance), the more savage the tongue—one thinks of the families in Miss Compton- 80 Burnett's novels, or of Professor Housman jotting down deadly remarks for future use.

11   Compared with physical aggression, verbal aggression has one virtue; it does not require the presence of its victim. To say nasty things about someone behind his back is at least preferable to saying them to his 85 face. On the other hand, for intelligent and talented persons, it has two great moral dangers. First, verbal malice, if witty, wins the speaker social approval. (Why is it that kind remarks are very seldom as funny as unkind?) Secondly, since, in verbal malice, the ill-will of the heart is associated with the innocent play of the imagination, a malicious person can forget 90 that he feels ill-will in a way that a physically aggressive person cannot. His audience, however, is not so easily deceived. Two people may make almost the same remark; one, we feel immediately, is being only playful, the other has a compulsive wish to denigrate others.

Self-importance

95

12   Simone Weil has described how, when she was suffering from acute migraine, she felt a desire to strike others on the same spot where she felt the pain herself. Most acts of cruelty, surely, are of this kind. We wish to make others suffer because we are impotent to relieve our own sufferings (which need not, of course, be physical). Any threat to our self-importance 100 is enough to create a lifelong resentment, and most of us, probably, cherish a great deal more resentment than we are normally aware of. I like to fancy myself as a kindhearted person who hates cruelty. And why shouldn't I be kind? I was loved as a child, I have never suffered a serious injury either from another individual or from society, and I enjoy good health. Yet, now 105 and again, I meet a man or a woman who arouses in me the desire to ill-treat them. They are always perfectly harmless people, physically unattractive (I can detect no element of sexual sadism in my feelings) and helpless. It is, I realize with shame, their helplessness which excites my ill-will. Here is someone who, whatever I did to him or her, would not fight back, an 110 ideal victim, therefore, upon whom to vent all my resentments, real or imagined, against life.

13   If it were really possible for suffering to be transferred like a coin from one person to another, there might be circumstances in which it was morally permissible; and if, however mistakenly, we believed that it was 115 possible, acts of cruelty might occasionally be excusable. The proof that we do not believe such a transfer to be possible is that, when we attempt it, we are unsatisfied unless the suffering we inflict upon others is at least a little greater than the suffering that has been inflicted upon ourselves.

14   The transferability-of-suffering fallacy underlies the doctrine of re- 120 tributive punishment, and there is so little evidence that the threat of punishment—the threat of public exposure is another matter—is an effective deterrent to crime, or that its infliction—self-inflicted penance is again another matter—has a reformatory effect, that it is impossible to take any other theory of punishment seriously. By punishment, I mean, of course, 125 the deliberate infliction of physical or mental suffering beyond what the safety of others requires. There will probably always be persons who, whether they like it or not, have to be quarantined, some, perhaps, for the rest of their lives.

"Righteous Anger"

130

15   The anger felt by the authorities which makes them eager to punish is of the same discreditable kind which one can sometimes observe among parents and dog-owners, an anger at the lack of respect for his betters which the criminal has shown by daring to commit his crime. His real offence in the eyes of the authorities is not that he has done something wrong but 135 that he has done something which THEY have forbidden.

16   "Righteous anger" is a dubious term. Does it mean anything more than that there are occasions when the sin of anger is a lesser evil than cowardice or sloth? I know that a certain state of affairs or the behaviour of a certain person is morally evil and I know what should be done to put an 140 end to it; but, without getting angry, I cannot summon up the energy and the courage to take action.

17   Righteous anger can effectively resist and destroy evil, but the more one relies upon it as a source of energy, the less energy and attention one can give to the good which is to replace the evil once it has been removed. 145 That is why, though there may have been some just wars, there has been no just peace. Nor is it only the vanquished who suffer; I have known more than one passionate anti-Nazi who went to pieces once Hitler had been destroyed. Without Hitler to hate, their lives had no *raison d'être*.

18   "One should hate the sin and love the sinner." Is this possible? 150 The evil actions which I might be said to hate are those which I cannot imagine myself committing. When I read of the deeds of a Hoess or an Eichmann, from whom I have not personally suffered, though I certainly do not love them, their minds are too unintelligible to hate. On the other hand, when I do something of which I am ashamed, I hate myself, not 155 what I have done; if I had hated it, I should not have done it.

19   I wish the clergy today—I am thinking of the Anglican Church because She is the one I know best—would not avoid, as they seem to, explaining to us what the Church means by Hell and the Wrath of God. The public is left with the impression, either that She no longer believes in 160 them or that She holds a doctrine which is a moral monstrosity no decent person could believe.

20   Theological definitions are necessarily analogical, but it is singularly unfortunate that the analogies for Hell which the Church has used in the past should have been drawn from Criminal Law. Criminal laws are 165 imposed laws—they come into being because some people are not what they should be, and the purpose of the law is to compel them by force and fear to behave. A law can always be broken and it is ineffective unless the authorities have the power to detect and punish, and the resolution to act at once.   170

21   To think of God's laws as imposed leads to absurdities. Thus, the popular conception of what the Church means by Hell could not unfairly be described as follows. God is an omniscient policeman who is not only aware of every sin we have committed but also of every sin we are going to commit. But for seventy years or so He does nothing, but lets every human 175 being commit any sin he chooses. Then, suddenly, He makes an arrest and, in the majority of cases, the sinner is sentenced to eternal torture.

Souls in Hell

22   Such a picture is not without its appeal; none of us likes to see his enemies, righteous or unrighteous, flourishing on earth like a green bay tree. 180 But it cannot be called Christian. Some tender-minded souls have accepted the analogy but tried to give eternity a time limit: in the end, they say, the Devil and damned will be converted. But this is really no better. God created the world; He was not brought in later to make it a good one. If His love could ever be coercive and affect the human will without its co- 185 operation, then a failure to exercise it from the first moment would make Him directly responsible for all the evil and suffering in the world.

23   If God created the world, then the laws of the spiritual life are as much laws of our nature as the laws of physics and physiology, which we can defy but not break. If I jump out of the window or drink too much I 190 cannot be said to break the law of gravity or a biochemical law, nor can I speak of my broken leg or my hangover as a punishment inflicted by an angry Nature. As Wittgenstein said: "Ethics does not treat of the world. Ethics must be a condition of the world like logic." To speak of the Wrath of God cannot mean that God is Himself angry. It is the unpleasant ex- 195 perience of a creature, created to love and be happy, when he defies the laws of his spiritual nature. To believe in Hell as a possibility is to believe that God cannot or will not ever compel us to love and be happy. The analogy which occurs to me is with neurosis. (This, of course, is misleading too because, in these days, many people imagine that, if they can call their 200 behaviour neurotic, they have no moral responsibility for it.) A neurotic, an alcoholic, let us say, is not happy; on the contrary, he suffers terribly, yet no one can relieve his suffering without his consent and this he so often withholds. He insists on suffering because his ego cannot bear the pain of facing reality and the diminution of self-importance which a cure would involve. 205

24   If there are any souls in Hell, it is not because they have been sent there, but because Hell is where they insist upon being.

QUESTIONS

READER AND PURPOSE

1. The essays in the collection in which this piece first appeared varied in tone * from playful to serious. Which of those two words better describes Auden's tone? Does his purpose seem to be primarily to amuse his readers, to inform them, or to persuade them of something?

2. In a strict and formal sense Auden does not define anger. In fact, he uses the word in full confidence that his readers know what it means. In a broader sense, however, his essay may be said to define anger to the degree that it expands and explores what is involved in this state of mind. For one thing Auden distinguishes natural from sinful anger. What is the difference? What other aspects of anger does he throw light upon?

ORGANIZATION

3. What does paragraph 2 contribute to Auden's discussion of anger? Paragraph 3? Paragraphs 7 and 8? Indicate the topic sentence of paragraph 8. How is it supported?

4. Make a conceptual analysis of paragraph 11. This requires that you (a) state the topic idea and (b) show how the idea conveyd by each of the following sentences in the paragraph relates to the topic. Do the same thing for paragraph 12.

5. In paragraphs 19-24 Auden argues against the popular conception of hell. His argument is built upon a distinction between imposed law (which he defines in paragraph 20) and natural law (paragraph 23). Explain this distinction. Why does it lead to the conclusion that the usual conception of hell is absurd?

6. Is the closing of this essay effective? Why or why not?

7. Auden's organization is less schematic than that of many of the selections contained in this text. Rather than follow a plan rigorously laid out beforehand, Auden seems to spin his essay by a kind of association, one aspect of the subject suggesting another. Consider, for example, paragraphs 4, 5, and 6. Is there a necessary logical progression to the thought? Are the paragraphs carefully tied together by linking words and phrases? Would you conclude from your answers to these questions that Auden's essay is poorly organized, that it lacks coherence and shape?

Contrast the structure of "Anger" with Edward Gibbon's analysis of a Roman legion (page 79). Gibbon's method of organizing is schematic while Auden's is meditative. The first presents the subject thoroughly mastered—laid out in shaped and ordered blocks. A student reviewing for an examination would be grateful for Gibbon's clear analysis. Auden's essay, on the other hand, suggests less the finished product of thought than the actual process of thinking. Before he began his final draft one suspects that Gibbon knew exactly what he wanted to say; Auden—or so his essay suggests—creates his thought in the very process of writing. The two passages, in short, represent two kinds of prose, equally valuable but profoundly different. The one is a vehicle for ideas clearly formulated before the writer puts pen to paper; the other is a voyage of exploration and discovery.

SENTENCES

8. This difference is reflected in more than organization. For example, Auden's sentences contain more interrupted movement * than Gibbon's. Interrupted movement usually is closer to the actual process of thinking than is straightforward sentence structure. When we think, our ideas do not present themselves one by one like a file of obedient soldiers. They mix and interfere and clash. We begin one thought, but, before we finish, another intrudes, with which we play before returning, after a moment, to the first. Obviously a writer can ill afford literally to write as he thinks; he would keep the attention of very few readers. He must set his ideas down on paper in more orderly fashion than that in which he conceived them. But if he is the kind of writer willing even in his last draft to continue probing his subject, the chances are that interrupted movement—a sign of the mind at work—will be relatively frequent in his style. And so it is in Auden's sentences. Read closely, for instance, the final sentence of paragraph 12. Identify the interrupters it contains. Find six or seven other sentences in this selection notable for interrupted movement. If you can, discuss any particular advantages to the interruptions in these sentences, advantages in respect to emphasis, sentence rhythm, or subtlety of thought. On the other hand, Auden also employs the short, straightforward sentence effectively. Point out several.

9. Notice how the dash is used in this essay and list the functions it appears to have.

10. The first sentence of paragraph 3 is emphatic. Why is the term *announcement* a fair label for this kind of emphatic sentence structure? Can you find another of Auden's sentences that uses this technique?

11. Why in each of the following pairs of sentences is the revision inferior to what Auden wrote?

> (a) *Revision:* I am angry if traffic lights fail to change obligingly to red when I wish to cross the road or if I enter a restaurant and it is crowded.

Auden: "If traffic lights fail to change obligingly to red when I wish to cross the road, I am angry; if I enter a restaurant and it is crowded, I am angry." (58-60)

(b) Revision: Then He suddenly makes an arrest and the sinner is sentenced to eternal torture in the majority of cases.

Auden: "Then, suddenly, He makes an arrest and, in the majority of cases, the sinner is sentenced to eternal torture." (176-77)

12. Is the question in line 150 genuine or rhetorical *? Point to several other questions in this essay and be able to explain the purpose of each. Why is the question in lines 88-89 in parentheses?

13. Why is the first sentence of paragraph 8 a good example of a topic statement?

DICTION

14. Look up: adrenalin (8), inhibits (17), overt (42), introspection (48), malice (87), denigrate (94), migraine (97), vent (111), coercive (185), physiology (189), neurosis (199).

15. Explain in your own words what each of these expressions means: faculty of symbolization (27), chewed the carpet (46), verbal aggression (78), academic and clerical circles (79), the doctrine of retributory punishment (120), dubious term (137), raison d'être (149), theological definitions are necessarily analogical (163).

16. In paragraph 4 the words futile, unnecessary, and memory are all rather abstract. How does Auden clarify these terms? Actually what he does is an example of one of the kinds of definition referred to in the introduction to this section. Can you identify it?

17. Explain what relationship in thought the following connectors * prepare us for: thus (3), similarly (38), that is to say (60), say (66), nor (147), on the other hand (154). Does surely act as a kind of pointer in line 98?

POINTS TO LEARN

1. There is more than one way to organize an essay.

2. A writer may explore his subject in the very process of writing about it. If his exploration is directed and not merely haphazard, the essay that evolves will be organized; but it will be organized in a looser, more associative pattern than the essay composed according to a carefully wrought, pre-conceived plan or outline.

3. Extensive interrupted movement may make the syntax of a sentence more difficult to follow, but at the same time it creates the illusion of the thinking mind.

SUGGESTIONS FOR WRITING

There are six deadly sins besides anger. Select one of them—or, if you prefer, some other sin less deadly—and attempt an essay like Auden's. Do not begin by making an outline; instead simply sit for a while and think about your subject. Then compose a first draft. Probably it will be quite rambling. Work it over, adding and developing neglected points, pruning or even eradicating topics that on second reading seem insignificant. Go through this process several times until you feel you have clearly told your reader what you think and feel about envy or avarice or what have you. Support generalizations with specifics and do not be afraid to draw upon your own experience.

IMPROVING YOUR STYLE

In your essay include:

1. A rhetorical question.
2. A topic sentence of no more than six words.
3. Dashes to set off an explanation or qualification *.
4. The word *say* to identify an example.
5. The connectives *thus, similarly,* and *on the other hand* to introduce sentences.

Persuasion

Thus far we have been concerned with problems of explaining and defining. Often, however, a writer desires to change his readers' beliefs or opinions, to persuade them to share his own values or conclusions. Of course, a clear-cut line is not easily drawn between exposition and persuasion. One, in fact, may imply the other. If you wish to convince someone that you are right about a controversial issue, you probably will have to define terms and explain facts and ideas. Contrarily, exposition—especially if it is effectively organized and expressed—is likely to have persuasive force, even though its composer had no persuasive intention. But however difficult it is to lay down in practice, there is a difference between writing to explain and writing to persuade.

Three modes of persuasion are common: argument, satire, and eloquence. Argument persuades by appealing to reason. To reason—the restriction is important, for it distinguishes argumentation from those other types of persuasion, which aim rather at our emotions than at our intellects. With emotion argument has little to do. Its essence is reason, and reason may work in two ways: by deduction and by induction. The first argues from general premise to particular conclusion, the second from particular fact to broad conclusion.

Deductive argumentation is usually cast in the form of a logical syllogism. At its simplest a syllogism contains two premises and an inference that necessarily follows from them. For example:

1. All hatters are mad.
2. X is a hatter.
3. Therefore X is mad.

If the major premise (1) and the minor premise (2) are true, the inference, or conclusion, (3) has got to be true, for the inference is logically valid. Logical validity, however, is not the same thing as empirical truth. Since all hatters are not mad, the factual truth of the conclusion about X is open to question. Syllogistic reasoning, in short, is no sounder than the premises upon which it rests. The writer arguing logically must begin from premises not easily denied by his opponents.

In working from these premises he must proceed carefully. It is not hard to make mistakes—called fallacies—in getting from premise to conclusion. Many arguments involve a chain of interlocked syllogisms, each more complicated than that about X the hatter. In most arguments the rigid form of the syllogism will be replaced by a more fluid prose, and here and there a premise or an inference may be omitted for economy. Under these conditions fallacies are especially easy to commit. There is no shortcut to learning sound logic. The student who wishes to argue well should consult a good textbook, master at least the rudiments of logic, and train himself to detect the common fallacies.

Exposing these fallacies is an effective way of attacking the arguments of others. One such flaw, quite frequent and quite easily demonstrated, is self-contradiction. It is a fundamental law of logic that if *a* is true, *a* cannot be non-true. For example, one cannot argue that the Romans were doomed to fall and then assert that they were fools because they failed to solve the problems that destroyed them. To argue the inevitability of their decline is to deny the Romans free will; to charge them with folly presupposes that they had the freedom to choose between acting wisely or not. All this seems very obvious; yet in more subtle matters a writer can easily contradict himself without realizing it. To be sure that he has not, he must examine, not only his argument itself, but all the assumptions which lie beneath it and all the implications which lie within.

About deductive argumentation, then, we may conclude: (1) that it must begin from true premises, and (2) that it must derive its conclusions from these premises according to the rules of inference. The writer who ignores either principle is himself open to attack. If his premises are untrue he may be answered factually; if his conclusions are invalid the fallacy can be revealed.

Inductive reasoning is somewhat more common in argumentation. The method of the scientist or the prosecutor, it begins with facts and builds from them to a general conclusion. In practice a writer will usually find it more convenient to indicate his conclusion first and then bring forward the evidence which supports it. This is only a matter of arrangement, however, and does not deny the essential order of particular to general. Like the syllogism, induction will be fallacious when it fails to observe certain rules, which may be called the laws of evidence.

The first, and most obvious, is that evidence must be accurate. The second, more easily forgotten, is that it must be relevant, relating meaningfully to the conclusion it is brought forward to support. To prove, for instance, that women have more accidents than men, a writer might cite figures which show that they bring more automobiles to body shops with damaged fenders. Granting the accuracy of the evidence, we may still question its relevancy. It may be that women are afraid of their husbands and hastily repair dents which men blithely ignore; it may be that most of the dents resulted from accidents with reckless males. Often relevancy is so obvious that it may be taken for granted, but sometimes, as in this example, the writer must show that his evidence connects with his conclusion.

The third rule is that evidence must be complete. One of the commonest mistakes in inductive reasoning is to ignore this rule, especially when dealing with what are called universal affirmative propositions. These are statements that assert a truth applicable to all members of a class; for example, All students love school. Such propositions can be proved only by testing each member to which they apply. Since so complete a demonstration is generally impossible, all that can be shown for most universal propositions is a strong probability. Usually probability will be all the argument requires, but honesty demands that the conclusion be stated as less than an absolute truth. In brief, a writer should never phrase his premise even one degree stronger than his evidence will support. Writers who scorn such qualifiers as *some* or *generally speaking,* expose themselves to easy counterattack. Their evidence may in itself be good, but they ride it too hard and are surprised when it collapses under the strain.

All evidence, then, must observe these rules; the evidence itself, however, may take different forms. Three are most frequent: common knowledge, specific examples, and statistical data. Evidence is often advanced in the form of common knowledge, which may be defined as what is so generally known that it can safely be asserted without the support of examples or statistical tables. No one can draw the line that separates common knowledge from particular assertion. It is common knowledge that school is sometimes dull. It is a particular assertion that crocodiles make fine household pets. Perhaps they do; still, most of us would require proof. Perhaps the best rule is this: if a writer is doubtful whether a statement is common knowledge or assertion, he had better support it with additional specific evidence.

Examples, especially when they are historical, often involve the problem of interpretation. For example, one might offer General Grant's

Wilderness Campaign to support the contention that professional soldiers are often unconcerned with the lives of their men. The example, however, hides an interpretation: that Grant sacrificed men simply because he was callous. It may well be that Grant did care about his troops and accepted heavy losses only because he felt them militarily necessary.

Another type of specific evidence often misused is the rhetorical analogy. For clarification or emphasis an analogy is often excellent; for proof it is meaningless. No matter how similar two things may be, there must be some differences between them. However slight, these differences deny any possibility of proof. This does not mean that analogies have no place in argumentation, simply that they should be restricted to supporting more legitimate evidence. To do this they must be fair and not force similarities where none exist. A famous instance of an unfair, or false, analogy is Thomas Carlyle's comparison of a state to a ship in order to demonstrate the weakness of democracy. The analogy is used to argue that a state cannot survive danger unless its leader, like the captain of a ship, has power independent of majority consent. But ships and states are very different things, and what may hold at sea does not therefore hold on land. Analogies, then, are valuable in argument if they are fair and if they are not used for proof.

The third sort of evidence is statistical. Although subject to the same laws that govern all evidence, statistics are often employed less critically. Consider a very simple case. We wish to answer the charge of the dented fenders and to prove that, on the contrary, American women are safer drivers than American men. Selecting a small community, we show that in a single year 100 women had accidents as compared to 500 men. The figures seem strong evidence. Yet this town may contain 5000 male drivers and only 500 female drivers, and if so then only 10 per cent of the men had accidents as opposed to 20 per cent of the women. Or perhaps the community is not a typical sample of the American population; or perhaps the police records included only some accidents, not all; or perhaps these figures cover a wide range of accidents, from mild bumps to head-on collisions.

Perhaps a great many things. As you see, statistics must be handled carefully. If it is too much to expect all writers to be trained in statistical method, it is not too much to ask them to subject any statistical data they use to the common-sense criteria of accuracy, relevancy, and completeness. So tested, statistics are good evidence.

Most of the faults of inductive reasoning follow from ignoring these criteria, or, even worse, from ignoring the spirit behind them. Induction begins with facts, and it stays with facts until it has established their truth. It does not select or distort facts to fit a preconceived notion. It is easy, for example, to blame juvenile delinquency on comic books by ignoring the complexity of forces that create juvenile crime. Such an argument may strike us for a moment, but only for a moment. It is neither true nor honest. And in argumentation, as in murder, truth will out.

We have stressed here the problems of reasoning well, for that is the essence of argumentation. Yet to be fully effective an argument must be not only well reasoned but well expressed. Its organization must be clear. The writer should make plain at the very beginning what he is arguing for or what he is contending against, and his paragraphs should march in perfect order from premise to inference or from evidence to conclusion. His syntax should be an easy yet a strong vehicle for the ideas it conveys, and his diction both honest and exact. In short, argumentation is reason finely phrased. Reason twisted in awkward prose is like a chisel of strong steel with a blunted edge. Beautiful writing that hides fallacy and misrepresentation is a shiny tool of cheap metal that soon cracks. To argue well the writer must begin with intelligence and with honesty, but he must hone them to the sharp edge of good prose.

There are times, however, when argument, no matter how beautifully expressed, is not as effective as those kinds of persuasion that appeal more directly to feeling. One way of making such an appeal is by satire. The satirist aims at our sense of the ridiculous and, latently at least, at our sense of shame. He mocks and exaggerates the faults and follies he would persuade us to disavow. His tone may range from light, witty humor to profound bitterness; but whether he be amused or enraged by human weakness, the satirist holds before us the disparity between what is and what ought to be, between the ideals we profess and the idiocies we practice.

To emphasize this disparity satirists often employ irony. Irony in its simplest form is using words so that their real significance is the reverse of their apparent meaning. If one were to say of a stingy man, "He's a generous person," the word "generous" would be ironic. (Heavy-handed and insulting irony of this sort is called sarcasm.) Irony, of course, must be clearly signaled so that the listener or reader will interpret it correctly. In speech this is often done by uttering the ironic word with a special emphasis or intonation ("He's a 'generous' person"), or by some non-verbal sign such as a raised eyebrow, a smile, a wink, a gesture, or a shrug. In writing, obviously, such cues are unavailable. While the writer can underline an ironic term or enclose it in quotation marks, these expedients are mechanical and not very effective. The skilful literary ironist depends upon the subtle use of context to make his intention clear, and usually, too, he counts upon the good sense of his readers to distinguish what he is really saying from what he appears to be saying.

Less subtly, the satirist may belabor his target with invective, hurling abuse at the faults he castigates. A famous example occurs in the second act of *King Lear*. When Oswald, a villainous steward to one of Lear's false daughters, encounters the Earl of Kent, he impudently asks, "What dost thou take me for?" Kent tells him in a classic instance of invective:

> A knave, a rascal, an eater of broken meats; a base, proud, shallow, beggarly, three-suited, hundred-pound, filthy worsted-stocking knave; a lily-livered, action-taking, whoreson, glass-gazing, superserviceable, finical rogue; one-trunk-inheriting slave; one that wouldst be a bawd in way of good service, and art nothing but the composition of a knave, beggar, coward, pander, and the son and heir of a mongrel bitch; one whom I will beat into clamorous whining if thou deny'st the least syllable of thy addition.

Such satire of insult, as we may call it, is less common than it was. Manners have softened in the modern world, and our sense of fair play is likely to be offended by invective. But it can still be wondrously effective, as H. L. Mencken's attack on William Jennings Bryan (on page 248) demonstrates.

Most of use enjoy clever, witty insult (if we are not the victims); the popularity of insult-comedians testifies to that. Still, it must be admitted that invective appeals to a base instinct: our enjoyment at seeing another person pilloried and made ridiculous. (Of course, we rationalize our pleasure by assuring ourselves that the fool had it coming.) The last type of persuasion sets its aim much higher. Eloquence evokes our noblest conceptions of humanity and elevates us to a plane of duty far above the petty preoccupation with self. It puts before us examples of great men and women, and urges, whether directly or by implication, that we imitate them. Thus the English poet Algernon Charles Swinburne—describing Lord Byron's death at Missolonghi, where he had gone to help the Greeks in their fight for independence from Turkey—concludes:

> His work was done at Missolonghi; all of his work for which the fates could spare him time. A little space was allowed him to show at least a heroic purpose, and attest a high design; then, with all things un-

finished before him and behind, he fell asleep after many troubles and triumphs. Few can ever have gone wearier to the grave; none with less fear. He had done enough to earn his rest. Forgetful now and set free for ever from all faults and foes, he passed through the doorway of no ignoble death out of reach of time, out of sight of love, out of hearing of hatred, beyond the blame of England and the praise of Greece. In the full strength of spirit and of body his destiny overtook him, and made an end of all his labours. He had seen and borne and achieved more than most men on record. "He was a great man, good at many things, and now he has attained this also, to be at rest."

Phrases such as "heroic purpose," "high design," "the full strength of spirit" express a level of being which few men attain but to which all worthy men should aspire. In a cynical age such expressions have a quaint, almost comic cast. But they possess a perennial truth: if we do not stretch toward stars, we fall back into mud.

General George Armstrong Custer

Ralph K. Andrist is an American journalist and writer. This selection is taken from *The Long Death: The Last Days of the Plains Indians* (1964), a history of the defeat by the United States Army of the Sioux, Cheyenne, Arapahoe, and other tribes inhabiting the central plains. Here Andrist considers the problem of George Armstrong Custer, a prominent actor in the Indian wars, killed, along with most of his command, by the Sioux and their confederates at the Little Big Horn River in June, 1876. Custer was and remains a problem in American history. It is not easy to read his character and to assess the degree of his responsibility for the disaster at the Little Big Horn. Patriots deify him as a brave and martyred soldier; detractors, less impressed by the Custer legend, stress his arrogance and disregard of orders. In a strict sense Andrist's purpose is less to persuade than to judge, that is, to consider a disputed question and arrive at a reasonable answer. But judgment is only a short step from persuasion, and it represents a spirit of mind which should infuse persuasive writing (though often it does not)—a rational, balanced examination of the evidence on both sides of an issue.

1   It is difficult to find a starting place for describing Custer. Those who have already formed opinions about the man have done so with such vehemence that it is hard to believe that the two sides are talking about the same person. To one group, he remains the brave and gallant soldier and peerless Indian fighter who died heroically and gloriously battling against 5 hopeless odds; to the other he was a big-mouthed braggart and incompetent who blundered away the lives of more than two hundred men by rushing joyfully into a deadly situation without taking the simplest precautions demanded by military prudence. On one point all agree: Custer was a man of supreme physical courage who apparently did not know what it was to 10 feel fear. Beyond that, there is agreement on very little.

2   Custer graduated at the bottom of his class at West Point, in large

part for demerits received for what his admirers like to describe as "boyish pranks and escapades," although a good part of his bad record was the result of slovenly habits. This last was highly ironic because no officer would demand more later from his men in the way of snap and polish and taut discipline than he. He received his commission just in time to get into the First Battle of Bull Run.

3   He had a dash about him and a vivaciousness, to say nothing of his courage, which could not help but attract the attention of his superiors, and he received choice assignments for such a very young officer. He had a superb confidence that fortune was always working for him; "Custer's luck," he called this continual smile of the gods, and for a number of years it appeared that he was right and that it actually existed. As it turned out, "Custer's luck" was not an inexhaustible commodity.

4   Some points in his career remain hazy. He was, for instance, jumped all the way from first lieutenant to brigadier general after having played only minor parts in engagements where he performed in no manner worthy of such recognition. Even Custer's luck could not explain such a promotion; it seems possible that political influence was also involved. In any event, at twenty-three, he was (and still is) the youngest man ever to have held the rank of brigadier general in the United States Army; two years later he was breveted major general and so became the youngest ever in that rank—with the single exception of the Marquis de Lafayette during the Revolution.

5   He was a flamboyant leader. He designed his own uniform which consisted of a wide-brimmed hat, trousers with a double stripe running down the seam, a sailor's wide-collared shirt, a red cravat, and on the sleeves of his jacket an intricate arabesque of interlacing loops of gold braid. Add to this the golden hair grown long and lying in ringlets on his shoulders and the man becomes rather overpowering in his gaudiness and glitter.

6   However, these were personal things; the important thing in a soldier is whether he can fight. General Custer could fight all right, but there was a great deal of question about his competence as a commander. During the war, he two or three times showed a disconcerting habit of forgetting his main responsibility to go whooping off after some side issue that was more exciting—as the time he entered a Virginia town and spied a Confederate locomotive and cars about to make their escape; he left his command to take care of itself and made a wild dash to capture the train. Such actions can turn disastrous, and it was perhaps only Custer's luck that saved him each time.

7   Because of his impulsiveness, he was not a good tactician. His joy was leading a cavalry charge, saber swinging, yellow hair streaming in the wind, the field behind him thundering with hundreds of men and horses answering to his command. He had not enough patience for the careful re- 55 connoitering, the consideration of alternatives, the working out of plans that make a good commanding officer.

8   Custer had been a teetotaler since the day when, a young and arrogant lieutenant home on furlough, he had been staggering under more than he could carry and had met Elizabeth Bacon. Miss Bacon, the future 60 Mrs. Custer, was not amused; young Custer took the pledge and never drank again. He appeared not to know the meaning of weariness; he could spend a day campaigning on the plains that exhausted the men with him, and then come back to his tent and spend most of the night writing a long letter to Mrs. Custer. On occasion, if no operations were scheduled for the 65 next day, he would be up early and out on an all-day hunt after getting only one or two hours of sleep. He seemed completely unable to understand that his men could not do likewise; the result was over-strict discipline—and a "bring-none-back-alive" incident.[1] Add miscellany on Custer: he carried hound dogs with him, sometimes as many as two or three dozen, 70 and let them share his tent and—within capacity—his bed.

9   The preceding, and all other facts about Custer, add up to a man of supreme courage and boundless energy who had retained the enthusiasm of a youth at the cost of never quite attaining the judgment of a man. His inability to accept the harsh restraints of discipline had shown itself on 75 occasion during the war; now it came to the surface once again when he received orders from General Hancock to move farther west and make his base at Fort Wallace.

QUESTIONS

READER AND PURPOSE

1. Where does Andrist identify the problem that he will judge? Does he come to a clear decision about it? Where?

2. Describe the tone * of this selection. Does Andrist belong to either of the two groups he mentions in the first paragraph? Explain.

---

[1] When twelve men deserted his command, Custer sent two officers after them with orders to "bring none in alive." The officers did not follow the orders, although in the ensuing scuffle one man was shot and killed and two others wounded. [Editors' note]

ORGANIZATION

3. Outline this selection, giving brief titles to its major parts and indicating the primary subdivisions within each of these parts.

4. Andrist begins the third sentence of paragraph 1 with the phrase *to one group*. How does that phrase link the sentence with what has gone before? Why did the writer place it first? Read aloud each of the following sentences in this paragraph. Do they begin in the same way?

5. What is the topic sentence of paragraph 4? Of 5? How is each topic supported? Does paragraph 2 contain a topic sentence? If so, which one is it? If not, can you easily supply one?

6. How does the opening sentence of paragraph 6 suggest a turn of thought? Identify the topic sentence of this paragraph and describe how it is supported. In paragraph 8 there are two topic ideas. What are they?

7. How is the seventh paragraph linked to the sixth? The ninth to the eighth?

SENTENCES

8. In lines 4-9 a balanced * sentence is used for contrast. Show that each half of the sentence follows essentially the same syntactic pattern. What advantages does such similarity have when, as here, it expresses a contrast? Point out one or two other balanced sentences in this selection.

9. Study the sentences in the first paragraph. Do you notice any pattern in terms of their relative length and complexity?

10. Someone once described the colon as being like a promissory note. Does the simile explain the function of the colon in line 9?

11. Identify the nominative absolutes * in lines 53-54. The nominative absolute—which, by the way, beginners might use a bit more often—is employed here to express attendant circumstances, that is, details or circumstances that would naturally accompany the fact or idea stated in the main clause—here the fact that Custer enjoyed leading a cavalry charge.

12. Study the first sentence of paragraph 8. What is the syntactic function of "a young and arrogant lieutenant home on furlough"? This type of construction is very useful; give it a name.

13. Point out three or four places where Andrist effectively uses short sentences.

DICTION

14. Look up: *vehemence* (3), *prudence* (9), *vivaciousness* (19), *arabesque* (39), *disconcerting* (45).

15. Necessarily Andrist employs many army terms. Explain the military senses of the following: *engagements* (28), *breveted* (33), *command* (48), *tactician* (52), *reconnoitering* (55), *compaigning* (63).

16. What are the etymologies * of *flamboyant* (36), *teetotaler* (58), *arrogant* (59)?

17. Comment upon the following substitutions: *promoted* for *jumped* (27), *shine* for *glitter* (41), *rushing* for *whooping* (46), *preference* for *joy* (52).

18. *In any event* (30) is a pointer *. To what conceptual relationship does it point?

19. In the opening paragraph Andrist distinguishes two antithetical views of General Custer. What words reveal the bias of each group? Where in the second paragraph does he use similar tendentious language to describe an extreme attitude toward Custer? In stating his own opinion does Andrist generally avoid loaded diction?

POINTS TO LEARN

1. The writer who attempts a judgment obligates himself to come to a decision at the end of his discussion, even if his decision is that the issue cannot be decided.

2. Nominative absolutes, while they can be misused and overused, are generally not utilized by inexperienced writers as often as they could be. They are especially useful for expressing attendant circumstances, the very looseness of their syntactic connection to the main clause being an advantage in such cases.

SUGGESTIONS FOR WRITING

Without getting deeply involved in historical research look up several divergent sources on one of the following controversial figures and write a judgment essay of about 1200 to 1500 words. You may quote from your sources, but quotations should be kept under control; the bulk of the words are to be your own.

Socrates, Martin Luther, Savonarola, Herbert Hoover, General George Patton, Senator Joseph McCarthy

IMPROVING YOUR STYLE

In your essay include these:

1. A balanced sentence expressing a contrast.
2. A nominative absolute showing attendant circumstances.
3. Several short emphatic sentences.
4. The phrase *in any event* to introduce a sentence.
5. Loaded diction which subtly parodies the bias of those who are excessively in favor of, or opposed to, the figure you are writing about. Be sure your readers understand that the loaded diction represents the unreasonable view of others, not of yourself (but make sure deftly; don't hang a sign on the words).

Of Marriage and Single Life

Francis Bacon (1561-1626) was an English statesman, philosopher, and writer. First under Elizabeth I (who reigned from 1558 until 1603), then under James I (1603-25), Bacon rose to high political office. He published important works on philosophy, history, and law, and he is the first English essayist. Bacon's essays (1591-ff., first collectively printed in 1625) are short, moralistic, and written in a terse, pointed prose. In the one printed below he considers the relative merits of marriage and the single life. While Bacon's diction and sentence style are old-fashioned, the issue he discusses is still alive (more alive in some ways than ever), and his approach to it can still provide a model for contemporary writers.

He that hath wife and children hath given hostages to fortune, for they are impediments to great enterprises, either of virtue or mischief. Certainly the best works, and of greatest merit for the public have proceeded from the unmarried or childless men, which both in affection and means have married and endowed the public. Yet it were great reason that those that have 5 children should have greatest care of future times, unto which they know they must transmit their dearest pledges. Some there are who though they lead a single life, yet their thoughts do end with themselves, and account future times impertinences.[1] Nay, there are some other that account wife and children but as bills of charges. Nay more, there are some foolish, rich, 10 covetous men that take a pride in having no children, because they may be thought so much the richer. For perhaps they have heard some talk, *Such an one is a great rich man,* and another except to it, *Yea, but he hath a great charge of children,* as if it were an abatement to his riches. But the most ordinary cause of a single life is liberty, especially in certain self-pleas- 15

From *Essays or Counsels, Civil and Moral,* edited by Richard Foster Jones (New York: Odyssey Press, 1937).
[1] Matters of no importance.

ing and humorous[2] minds, which are so sensible of every restraint, as they will go near to think their girdles and garters to be bonds and shackles. Unmarried men are best friends, best masters, best servants, but not always best subjects, for they are light to run away; and almost all fugitives are of that condition. A single life doth well with churchmen, for charity will 20 hardly water the ground where it must first fill a pool. It is indifferent for judges and magistrates, for if they be facile and corrupt, you shall have a servant five times worse than a wife. For soldiers, I find the generals commonly in their hortatives put men in mind of their wives and children; and I think the despising of marriage amongst the Turks maketh the vulgar 25 soldier more base. Certainly wife and children are a kind of discipline of humanity; and single men, though they may be many times more charitable, because their means are less exhaust,[3] yet, on the other side, they are more cruel and hardhearted (good to make severe inquisitors), because their tenderness is not so oft called upon. Grave natures, led by custom and 30 therefore constant, are commonly loving husbands, as was said of Ulysses, *vetulam suam prætulit immortalitati*.[4] Chaste women are often proud and froward, as presuming upon the merit of their chastity. It is one of the best bonds both of chastity and obedience in the wife, if she think her husband wise, which she will never do if she find him jealous. Wives are 35 young men's mistresses, companions for middle age, and old men's nurses. So as a man may have a quarrel[5] to marry when he will. But yet he was reputed one of the wise men, that made answer to the question, when a man should marry?—*A young man not yet, an elder man not at all*. It is often seen that bad husbands have very good wives; whether it be that it 40 raiseth the price of their husband's kindness when it comes, or that the wives take a pride in their patience. But this never fails if the bad husbands were of their own choosing, against their friends' consent, for then they will be sure to make good their own folly.

QUESTIONS

READER AND PURPOSE

1. What advantages does Bacon find in the single life? What disadvantages in marriage? Does he admit any vices in the former or virtues in the latter?

[2] Eccentric, odd.
[3] Exhausted, used up.
[4] "He preferred his old wife to immortality."
[5] A reason, an excuse.

2. Do you think Bacon is trying to persuade men either to marry or to remain single? Or is he examining both sides of a controversial issue?

3. What assumptions does Bacon appear to have made about his readers? Is he, for example, aiming at adults or at young people? At the educated or the ignorant? The worldly or the naïve?

4. In Bacon's "Essays" the term *essay* retains something of its early sense of a tentative attempt to discuss a topic and does not signify what it means today: a careful and polished composition. Even so, it would be a mistake to think of a Bacon essay as no more than the hasty jotting down of random thoughts. This paragraph is organized in the sense that it is a reasoned analysis of a topic. The analysis is revealed by considering how the sentences relate and group together. Thus sentences 1, 2, and 3 compose a unit. The first asserts that a disadvantage of married life is that it keeps men from great enterprises; the second repeats this point negatively by noting that the best and most valuable achievements have come from unmarried men; and the third reinforces the initial idea by noting the paradox that married men, having children, ought in theory to be more concerned with the public welfare than single men without offspring. What thread of thought similarly unites sentences 4 through 8? Sentences 9 through 12?

5. Try to analyze the remaining nine sentences of the paragraph (beginning with "Certainly a wife and children . . ." in line 26). Is there any place where you find it difficult to establish continuity of thought?

6. Study the following passage and answer (a) how the second sentence is logically related to the first, and (b) how the third is related to the second:

> Wives are young men's mistresses, companions for middle age, and old men's nurses. So as a man may have a quarrel to marry when he will. But yet he was reputed one of the wise men, that made answer to the question, when a man should marry?—*A young man not yet, an elder man not at all.*

7. *Nay* (9), *Nay more* (10), *For* (12), and *So as* (37) are all pointers *. For what turn of thought does each prepare us?

8. How does Bacon unify the three sentences in lines 20-23?

9. Point out the parallel * words in the sentences in lines 1-5.

10. The sentence in lines 30-32 contains three ideas: (a) that grave natures make good husbands, (b) that grave natures are led by custom and are therefore constant, and (c) that Ulysses was a loving husband. Which of these is

the main point of the sentence? How are the other two ideas logically related to it?

DICTION

11. Look up: *hostages* (1), *impediments* (2), *endowed* (5), *covetous* (11), *abatement* (14), *facile* (22), *vulgar* (25), *froward* (33), *reputed* (38), *folly* (44).

12. When studying writers who flourished several centuries in the past it is necessary to remember that some of their words have meanings very different from what the words possess for us. In Bacon's essay this fact is true of *mischief* (2), *impertinences* (9), *except* (13), *charge* (14), *humorous* (16), and *girdles* (17). How does the sense in which Bacon employs these words differ from their meaning today? (You may have to consult an unabridged dictionary such as *The Oxford English Dictionary* or *Webster's Third New International Dictionary*.)

13. Render these phrases into modern English idiom: *bills of charge* (10), *light to run away* (19), *generals in their hortatives* (24), *make good their own folly* (44).

14. What metaphor * is contained in Bacon's remark in line 17 that some men think their "girdles and garters to be bonds and shackles"? Explain the metaphor involved in the assertion that a wife and children are "hostages to fortune." In lines 20-21 Bacon says that it is better for clergymen to remain single because "charity will hardly water the ground where it must first fill a pool." Here too is a metaphor. What does *ground* stand for? Pool? Express in your own words why Bacon considers clergymen are better off unmarried. What advantage is there to expressing the idea metaphorically?

15. To what does *this* (42) refer?

POINTS TO LEARN

1. In most controversies there is something to be said on either side. A writer's task is sometimes to consider both sides without prejudice.

2. When reading older prose do not take the meanings of words for granted; they may in fact be quite different from what you suppose.

3. A metaphor may not be as immediately clear as the direct expression of an idea, but it stimulates the willing reader, forcing him to think.

SUGGESTIONS FOR WRITING

The problem Bacon discusses is still with us. Examine it from your own point of view; is it better to marry or to remain single? If the topic of marriage versus the single life does not appeal, attempt a judgment essay on one of these subjects:

Going to college or learning a skilled trade

Owning a television set or living without one

Life in the city versus life in the country

Strict discipline at home or school compared with a liberal, permissive atmosphere

IMPROVING YOUR STYLE

In your essay include:

1. Two or three examples of parallelism.

2. A sentence in which three explanatory or illustrative ideas are subordinated to a fourth, controlling idea.

3. Several metaphors.

From Our Sexist Language

In her essay "Our Sexist Language" feminist Ethel Strainchamps attacks the bias against women latent in everyday words—the use of *man*, for instance, as a generic term for human beings, or of *him* as the third-person pronoun referring to such sexually undifferentiated words as *person, student, anyone,* and so on. These paragraphs, however, are concerned less with the specific issue of biased words than with a preliminary question. Ask yourselves how the passage fits into the writer's larger purpose of exposing sexism in language, and what kind of evidence she calls upon to support her argument.

1   Few people would care to take the negative side of the proposition that the women of the world are oppressed and scorned. Statistics are against them. What has not been made so clear, however, is that the women of America, the world's most highly advanced (that is, technological) society, may be among the most oppressed and scorned of all.   5

2   Various data suggest the conclusion. Compared to other advanced nations, we have had fewer women in high government offices and fewer women in the professions. American men are more attracted by the primal aggressive activities of hunting and fishing than are men of other nations. More of them are seduced by the atavistic appeal of all-male organiza-   10 tions—reminiscent of the male-bonding propensities of the apes—from the Knights of Columbus to the Rotary Club. Our culture heroes are not benevolent rulers or noble wise men, in spite of the schools' efforts on behalf of Washington, Jefferson, and Lincoln, but aggressive men of action: cowboys, aviators, baseball players, outlaws, military men. All *muy macho*.   15

From "Our Sexist Language" in *Women in Sexist Society: Studies in Power and Powerlessness*, edited by Vivian Gornick and Barbara K. Moran. © 1971 by Basic Books, Inc., Publishers, New York. Reprinted by permission.

QUESTIONS

READER AND PURPOSE

1. An argument may be positive in the sense that it contends something *is* the case, or negative in the sense that something is *not*. (A negative argument is sometimes called a refutation.) What is Strainchamps' contention? Is her strategy * negative or positive?

2. Is the argument deductive or inductive—that is, does the author derive her conclusion from some broad, self-evident principle, or rather support it by specific evidence?

3. Strainchamps does not quote statistics, but is her argument ultimately based upon them? Does she suggest anywhere that it is? Do you think her argument is sound even though she does not cite figures and percentages? If it is not statistical, how would you describe her evidence?

4. Describe the tone of this selection. Is it angry, amused, objective?

ORGANIZATION

5. What is the strategic purpose of the first paragraph? Of the second?

6. Suppose that in paragraph 1 Strainchamps spelled out the logical relationship between the first and second sentences, writing, for instance, in line 3: "This is because statistics are against them." Would this be more, or less, effective? What word ties these sentences together?

7. Which is the topic sentence of the second paragraph? Is it a good topic statement? Outline this paragraph, showing how each sentence relates logically to what precedes it.

SENTENCES

8. Could the enclosed remark in lines 4-5 be punctuated with commas or dashes instead of parentheses?

9. Where does Strainchamps use short sentences effectively for emphasis? Besides its brevity, for what other quality is her final sentence notable?

10. The construction beginning in line 4—"the world's most highly advanced (that is, technological) society"—is an appositive *. What preceding word or idea does it repeat? Presumably, Strainchamps' readers are Americans and know that theirs is the world's most technologically advanced society: why, then, does she stress the point? Is there any irony * in Strainchamps' parenthetical explanation that by "advanced" she means "technological"?

11. What does the colon signal in line 14?

12. The final sentence of this selection is a fragment *. Is it effective, or would it have sounded better joined to the preceding idea? Something like this, perhaps:

Our culture heroes are not benevolent rulers or noble wise men, in spite of the schools' efforts on behalf of Washington, Jefferson, and Lincoln, but aggressive men of action: cowboys, aviators, baseball players, outlaws, military men, who are all *muy macho*.

DICTION

13. Look up: *oppressed* (2), *technological* (4), *professions* (8), *reminiscent* (11), *benevolent* (13).

14. Explain the meanings of these phrases: *the negative side of the proposition* (1), *primal aggressive activities* (9), *atavistic appeal* (10), *male-bonding propensities* (11), *culture heroes* (12), muy macho (15).

15. What does the phrase *that is* (4) prepare the reader to expect?

16. Why are these substitutes less effective than the words the writer chose: *prove* for *suggest* (6), *attracted* for *seduced* (10), *higher primates* for *apes* (11)?

17. What are the implications of the Spanish phrase *muy macho* (15)?

POINTS TO LEARN

1. The strategy of an argument may be positive (that is, to prove) or negative (to disprove).

2. An inductive argument rests upon specific evidence.

3. In developing an argument begin by making clear what you are for or against.

4. Short sentences are emphatic.

SUGGESTIONS FOR WRITING

Compose a short argument (three paragraphs, 400-500 words) on one of the topics below. You may argue either side, but make your position clear at the very beginning. Work inductively and cite evidence—statistics (if you can find them), examples, general knowledge.

Men are actually more oppressed than women.

The value—both economic and social—of a college degree has declined.

The typical high-school graduate today is better educated than were those of a generation ago.

IMPROVING YOUR STYLE

In your essay use:

1. Two or three short sentences for emphasis.

2. A parenthetical remark explaining or commenting upon the preceding statement.

3. The phrase *that is* to introduce an explanation.

HARRY F. HARLOW

Of Love in Infants

Harry F. Harlow is a scientist specializing in animal behavior. The following piece, which is complete, is his report on an experiment. It is a model of how to write up an experiment—beginning with the problem to be investigated, explaining the procedure and results in detail, and clearly stating the conclusion. In a narrow sense the essay is not avowedly persuasive. Yet viewed more broadly it has great persuasive force, convincing us by the careful application of reason and gathering of evidence.

1   The use of infant monkeys in many laboratory experiments is perhaps dictated by necessity, but few scientists would deny that it is also remarkably convenient. Monkeys are far better coordinated at birth than human infants; their reactions can be evaluated with confidence at an age of ten days or earlier, yet their development follows the same general line   5 as that of humans.

2   The monkeys' well-being and even survival pose a number of problems, however—particularly if they must, in the course of experimentation, be separated from their mothers only a few hours after birth. Nonetheless, at the University of Wisconsin's Primate Laboratory we were able, using   10 techniques developed by Dr. Gertrude van Wagenen of Yale, to rear infant monkeys on the bottle with a far lower mortality than is found among monkeys nursed by their mothers. Now one of the components of our technique involved the use of a gauze diaper folded on the floor of the infant monkeys' cages, following Dr. van Wagenen's observations that monkeys   15 would maintain contact with soft, pliant surfaces during nursing. We were struck by the deep attachment our monkeys formed for these diaper pads and by the distress they showed when, once a day, the pads were removed for reasons of sanitation. This observation led us into quite a new series of

157

experiments—research into the importance of bodily contact in infant love.   20

3   Love of infants for their mothers is often regarded as a sacred or mystical force, and perhaps this is why it has received so little objective study. But if facts are lacking, theory on this subject is abundant. Psychologists, sociologists, and anthropologists usually hold that the infant's love is learned through the association of the mother's face and body with the   25 alleviation of such physical tensions as hunger and thirst. Psychoanalysts specially emphasize the importance to emotional development of attaining and sucking at the breast. Our experiments suggest something else is involved.

4   We contrived two substitute "mothers." One was a bare cylinder   30 made of welded wire and surmounted by a wooden head. In the other, the wire framework was covered by a layer of terry cloth. We put eight new-born monkeys in individual cages, each with equal access to a cloth and to a wire mother. Four received their milk from one type of mother, four from the other—the milk being obtained from nursing bottles fixed in the   35 mothers' "breasts."

5   Physiologically, the two mothers proved to be equivalent—the monkeys in both groups drank as much milk and gained weight at the same rate. But psychologically, the two mothers were not at all equivalent. Both groups of monkeys spent far more time climbing over and embracing their   40 cloth mothers than they did their plain wire ones; they even left their electric heating pads to climb on the unheated cloth mother. Those that suckled from the wire mother spent no more time than feeding required.

6   The theory that infant love is related to satisfaction of hunger or thirst was thus contradicted, and the importance of bodily contact in form-   45 ing affection underscored. This finding was supported by the next phase of our investigation. The time the monkey infants spent cuddling their surrogate mothers was a strong indication of emotional attachment, but it was perhaps not conclusive. Would they also turn to their inanimate mothers for comfort when they were subjected to emotional stress?   50

7   With this question in mind, we exposed our infant monkeys to strange objects likely to frighten them, such as a mechanical teddy bear that moved forward, beating a drum. It was found that, whether the infants had nursed on the wire mother or the cloth one, they overwhelmingly sought comfort in stress from the cloth one. The infant would cling to it,   55 rubbing its body against the toweling. With its fears thus assuaged, it would turn to look at the previously terrifying bear without the slightest

sign of alarm. It might even leave the comfort of its substitute mother to approach the object that had frightened it only a minute before.

8   It is obvious that such behavior is analogous to that of human infants, and we found that the analogy held in situations that less obviously involved stress. If a human child is taken to an unfamiliar place, for example, he will usually remain calm and happy so long as his mother is nearby, but if she leaves him, fear and panic may result. Our experiments showed a similar effect in infant monkeys. We put the monkeys in a room that was much larger than their usual cages, and in the room we placed a number of unfamiliar objects—a crumpled piece of newspaper, blocks of wood, a metal plate, and a doorknob mounted on a box. If a cloth mother was present, the monkey, at the sight of these objects, would rush wildly to her and, rubbing against the toweling, cling to her tightly. Its fear would then diminish greatly or else vanish altogether, as in the previous experiment. Soon the monkey would leave its mother to explore its new world. It now regarded the objects as playthings. Returning from time to time to the mother for reassurance, it followed an outgoing pattern of behavior.

9   If, on the other hand, the cloth mother were absent, the infant would rush across the room and throw itself head down on the floor, clutching its head and body and screaming in distress. The bare wire mother afforded no more reassurance than no mother at all—even monkeys that had known only the wire mother from birth showed no affection for her and got no comfort from her presence. Indeed, this group of monkeys showed the greatest distress of all.

10   In a final comparison of cloth and wire mothers, we adapted an experiment originally devised by Robert A. Butler in this laboratory. Butler had found that monkeys enclosed in a dimly lighted box would press a lever to open and reopen a window for hours on end, with no other reward than the chance to look out. The rate of this action depended on what the monkeys saw: a glimpse of another monkey elicited far more activity than that of an empty room.

11   When we tested our infant monkeys in such a box, we found that those raised with both cloth and wire mothers showed as great an interest in the cloth mother as in another monkey but responded no more to a wire mother than to an empty room. In this test, as in all others, the monkeys that had been fed on a wire mother behaved in the same way as those that had been fed on a cloth-covered mother surrogate.

12   Thus, all objective tests we have been able to devise indicate that

the infant monkey's relationship to its substitute mother is a full one. There are, of course, factors other than bodily contact involved. For example, the simple act of clinging, in itself, seems important: a newborn monkey has difficulty surviving in a bare wire cage unless provided with a cone to which it can cling.   100

13   Yet our experiments have clearly shown the importance of the comfort derived from bodily contact in the formation of an infant's love for its mother and revealed the role of breast-feeding to be negligible or nonexistent. They have also established an experimental approach to subtle and dramatic relationships.   105

QUESTIONS

READER AND PURPOSE

1. What question is Harlow attempting to answer? Does he?
2. Harlow's argument appeals to reason, and its method is inductive, depending upon evidence. Yet its evidence differs from that of Strainchamps (page 154), who asserts generalizations based upon statistics from everyday life. Harlow devises an experiment. What essential features distinguish the experimental method of gathering data?
3. Does Harlow appear to be writing for people who share his scientific interests and knowledge or for a more general audience: would you be more likely to find this article in a scientific journal or in *The Reader's Digest*?

ORGANIZATION

4. Which paragraphs constitute the beginning of this essay? Within that beginning what one sentence most clearly sets up the problem? Which paragraphs compose the closing?
5. The middle of the essay has three major sections. Give a title to each and indicate the paragraphs it includes.
6. In paragraph 1 how is the second sentence related in idea to the first?
7. In paragraph 6, the second sentence performs an important transitional function. Which words point backward to what has just been said? Which point forward, directing the reader to the next topic?
8. What is the topic of paragraph 8? How is the second sentence related to the topic? The third? How are the remaining sentences of the paragraph related to the third?
9. What phrase at the beginning of paragraph 9 prepares the reader for a shift in idea?

SENTENCES

10. What relationship in thought does the dash in line 20 help to signal? The colon in line 87?

11. Point out the nominative absolute * in the final sentence of paragraph 4.

12. The first two sentences of paragraph 5 open in the same way. What does the similarity serve to emphasize?

13. Identify the participial * phrase in the sentence in lines 55-56. Find three or four other effective participial phrases in this selection. What advantages do such constructions offer a writer?

DICTION

14. Look up: *coordinated* (3), *pose* (7), *components* (13), *hold* (24), *access* (33), *conclusive* (49), *analogous* (60), *reassurance* (74), *devise* (95), *negligible* (103).

15. How do the etymologies * of these words help to clarify their sense: *primate* (10), *pliant* (16), *alleviation* (26), *assuaged* (56)?

16. Explain these phrases in your own words: *mystical force* (22), *surrogate mothers* (47), *objective tests* (95), *subtle and dramatic relationships* (104).

17. What is the difference between the interests or functions of *psychologists, sociologists, anthropologists* (23-24), *psychoanalysts* (26)?

18. What relationships in thought are signaled by these connecting * words: *nonetheless* (9), *now* (13), *thus* (45, 95), *of course* (97), *yet* (101)?

19. Why does Harlow put quotation marks around *mothers* in line 30?

POINTS TO LEARN

1. Effective arguments begin by making clear what is to be proved or disproved.

2. A good essay has a well-defined beginning, middle, and end.

3. Transitional sentences direct readers from one section of an essay to the next.

4. Participial phrases are an economic and efficient way of conveying subordinate information.

SUGGESTIONS FOR WRITING

1. Compose a report of 500-600 words on an experiment done in one of your lab courses. Begin by stating what you sought to determine, devote the bulk of your essay to describing the procedure, and end by drawing the appropriate conclusion.

2. If you have not had any experience in an actual laboratory, imagine an experimental situation in everyday life—for example, trying several methods of

study to decide which works best, or using various approaches to impress someone you wish to please. Follow the general organization suggested in the first exercise.

IMPROVING YOUR STYLE

1. Include participial phrases in at least six of your sentences. Vary their position—according to the logical progression of your ideas or the demands of emphasis—so that some open the sentence, others close it, and one or two occur in interrupting positions.

2. Use each of the following connective * words or phrases at least once somewhere in your essay: *of course, for example, nonetheless, thus, yet.*

The Banishment of Dramatists

Plato (the name signifies his broad shoulders) lived from 427? to 347 B.C. He was an Athenian philosopher, a disciple of Socrates, and the teacher of Aristotle. In 387 Plato founded the Academy, which evolved into the first university of the western world. Plato's philosophy is revealed in a series of *Dialogues*, discussions in dramatic, question-and-answer form between Socrates and various of his followers and opponents—the so-called Socratic method or dialectic. It is difficult to judge in the *Dialogues* when Plato is reporting what Socrates actually said or believed and when he is spreading his own ideas by putting them in the mouth of the older philosopher. In either case the *Dialogues* develop the Platonic philosophy—a set of beliefs concerning the real, the good, and the beautiful.

This selection comes from the *Republic*, one of the longest and most important of the *Dialogues*. In the *Republic* Socrates (or Plato) is concerned with the nature of justice and with how a state ought ideally to be constituted so as to serve justice. He arrives at an intellectual autocracy: sovereignty is to be exercised by a small elite circle of philosopher-kings; laws enforced by a larger, though still select, group of warrior-policemen; work provided by the masses. It all sounds suspiciously like the totalitarian state we have seen too often in the twentieth century. It is only fair to add, however, that Plato's philosopher-kings were to be chosen (never mind by whom) for their wisdom and goodness.

In this passage from the Tenth Book of the *Republic* Socrates ("I" in the dialogue) is discussing with a young man named Glaucon ("he") how poets and dramatists would fit into his ideal state. He concludes that they would not fit in at all. The conclusion must strike modern readers as peculiar, for we are accustomed to thinking of writers as ornaments and safeguards of society, not as dangers. Even so, set aside your own beliefs for a moment and try to understand the logic that leads Socrates to banish dramatists from his Utopia.

From *The Republic* by Plato, trans. Benjamin Jowett. Reprinted by permission of Tudor Publishing Company.

1   But we have not yet brought forward the heaviest count in our accusation:—the power which poetry has of harming even the good (and there are very few who are not harmed), is surely an awful thing?

2   Yes, certainly, if the effect is what you say.

3   Hear and judge: The best of us, as I conceive, when we listen to a passage of Homer, or one of the tragedians, in which he represents some pitiful hero who is drawling out his sorrows in a long oration, or weeping, and smiting his breast—the best of us, you know, delight in giving way to sympathy, and are in raptures at the excellence of the poet who stirs our feelings most.

4   Yes, of course I know.

5   But when any sorrow of our own happens to us, then you may observe that we pride ourselves on the opposite quality—we would fain be quiet and patient; this is the manly part, and the other which delighted us in the recitation is now deemed to be the part of a woman.

6   Very true, he said.

7   Now can we be right in praising and admiring another who is doing that which any one of us would abominate and be ashamed of in his own person?

8   No, he said, that is certainly not reasonable.

9   Nay, I said, quite reasonable from one point of view.

10   What point of view?

11   If you consider, I said, that when in misfortune we feel a natural hunger and desire to relieve our sorrow by weeping and lamentation, and that this feeling which is kept under control in our own calamities is satisfied and delighted by the poets;—the better nature in each of us, not having been sufficiently trained by reason or habit, allows the sympathetic element to break loose because the sorrow is another's; and the spectator fancies that there can be no disgrace to himself in praising and pitying any one who comes telling him what a good man he is, and making a fuss about his troubles; he thinks that the pleasure is a gain, and why should he be supercilious and lose this and the poem too? Few persons ever reflect, as I should imagine, that from the evil of other men something of evil is communicated to themselves. And so the feeling of sorrow which has gathered strength at the sight of the misfortunes of others is with difficulty repressed in our own.

12   How very true!

13   And does not the same hold also of the ridiculous? There are jests which you would be ashamed to make yourself, and yet on the comic stage,

or indeed in private, when you hear them, you are greatly amused by them, 40
and are not at all disgusted at their unseemliness;—the case of pity is repeated;—there is a principle in human nature which is disposed to raise a
laugh, and this which you once restrained by reason, because you were
afraid of being thought a buffoon, is now let out again; and having stimulated the risible faculty at the theatre, you are betrayed unconsciously to 45
yourself into playing the comic poet at home.

14   Quite true, he said.

15   And the same may be said of lust and anger and all the other af-
fections, of desire and pain and pleasure, which are held to be inseparable
from every action—in all of them poetry feeds and waters the passions in- 50
stead of drying them up; she lets them rule, although they ought to be controlled, if mankind are ever to increase in happiness and virtue.

16   I can not deny it.

17   Therefore, Glaucon, I said, whenever you meet with any of the
eulogists of Homer declaring that he has been the educator of Hellas, and 55
that he is profitable for education and for the ordering of human things,
and that you should take him up again and again and get to know him and
regulate your whole life according to him, we may love and honor those
who say these things—they are excellent people, as far as their lights extend; and we are ready to acknowledge that Homer is the greatest of poets 60
and first of tragedy writers; but we must remain firm in our conviction that
hymns to the gods and praises of famous men are the only poetry which
ought to be admitted into our State. For if you go beyond this and allow
the honeyed muse to enter, either in epic or lyric verse, not law and the
reason of mankind, which by common consent have ever been deemed best, 65
but pleasure and pain will be the rulers in our State.

18   That is most true, he said.

QUESTIONS

READER AND PURPOSE

1. In paragraph 15 Socrates clearly implies what the relationship between reason and emotion ought to be in a virtuous man. Express that relationship in
your own words. This is the fundamental premise upon which Socrates grounds
his argument against poetry. Where else in these paragraphs does he state or
imply that premise?

2. Essentially, what is his complaint against poetry? Does he offer evidence to
support his charge?

3. If his initial premise be granted, is Socrates' argument sound? If you wished to attack it, would it be easier to do so by disputing his evidence or by denying his premise?

4. Does Glaucon here contribute any ideas to the argument? Does he seriously oppose Socrates? What exactly is his function? Describe Socrates' attitude toward Glaucon: is he courteous, overbearing, condescending?

ORGANIZATION

5. How do paragraphs 3 and 5 contribute to the argument? Which of these two paragraphs establishes the basic ethical premise and which offers evidence that poets violate that ethical ideal?

6. In paragraph 9 Socrates appears to contradict himself: he has just gotten Glaucon to agree that it is not reasonable to admire emotionalism in drama when men repress it in their own lives; but here he tells Glaucon that it is reasonable. Actually Socrates is correcting Glaucon, who in his answer confuses "right" and "reasonable." Socrates is suggesting that while a spectator's approval of theatrical emotionalism is not right, it is reasonable, or as we might say, "natural." How in the philosopher's view does the theater encourage emotional excess? Where does he argue that this excess is bad? Does Socrates' argument in paragraph 11 suggest that he believes that men are naturally virtuous, or rather that virtue must be acquired as the result of rational effort and discipline?

7. Paragraph 13 marks a minor turn of thought. Explain. Where in this paragraph does Socrates allude to a dangerous natural tendency of man which reason must correct, but which the theater indulges?

SENTENCES

8. In line 8 Socrates repeats "the best of us," the same phrase with which he began the sentence. Partly the repetition is emphatic, but it also has a more important function. Can you explain what it is?

9. The long and complicated sentence in lines 54-63 contains a good deal of parallelism *: point out all the parallel constructions you can find.

10. In the sentence in lines 63-66 what words are set antithetically * against "law and reason"?

DICTION

11. Look up: smiting (8), fain (13), deemed (15), calamities (25), fancies (29), risible (45), lust (48), eulogists (55).

12. What are the etymologies * of oration (7), raptures (9), supercilious (32), buffoon (44), virtue (52)?

13. Socrates, a good logician, clearly establishes the connection between his ideas. Indicate the pointers * by which he does this.

14. The word *now* in line 17 is not, strictly speaking, a logical pointer. What exactly does it do here?

POINTS TO LEARN

1. The strategy in the type of argument Socrates employs is to get your opponent to accept your premise and then to demonstrate that your position logically follows from that premise.

2. Where the subject of a sentence is followed by extensive modification, it may help the reader if you repeat the subject just before the verb.

SUGGESTIONS FOR WRITING

1. Literary figures have not accepted Socrates' banishment of poets, and there have been many counterclaims of the value of poetry, among which the essays by Sir Philip Sidney and Percy Bysshe Shelley are well known in English literature. How would you answer Socrates? You might develop your reply by expanding the role of Glaucon, putting into his mouth objections to Socrates' premise or his evidence.

2. If there is a particular amusement or social activity which you feel is harmful to social order, work out a Socratic argument on the question-and-answer pattern to prove that it should be outlawed. Possibilities—which you may accept or reject as a matter of preference—include: television, pornographic films or books, football, comic cartoons for children, grand opera, rock and roll music, Lawrence Welk, hunting, literature classes, marriage.

IMPROVING YOUR STYLE

In your composition include:

1. Several examples of parallelism.

2. Several of antithesis.

3. Connectives * which mark the flow of your logic (words like *therefore, and so, consequently, thus, now, however*).

The Third Knight's Speech

T. S. Eliot (1888-1965) was one of the most important and influential poets and critics of the twentieth century. Born an American, he lived most of his life in England and adopted British citizenship. Eliot's political and moral views were generally conservative and Christian. They are expressed in *Murder in the Cathedral* (1935), a blank-verse drama about the assassination in 1170 in the Canterbury cathedral of Archbishop Thomas à Becket.

Becket had been appointed to the archbishopric through the influence of the powerful English king, Henry II. Henry hoped that Becket, who had been his political right hand as chancellor, would, in his new post, subvert the interests of the church to those of the state. Events proved very different. When Becket vigorously upheld the authority of the church, Henry discovered that he had lost the ablest man of his kingdom to his enemies. After a series of confrontations and maneuverings Becket was hacked to death by four Norman knights, followers of King Henry. Nobody then or since has proved that the King ordered the murder or conspired in it. But as someone has said, kings do not have to issue such orders: their wishes are known.

Eliot's play, roughly modeled on a Greek tragedy, has two parts separated by a brief interlude. The first dramatizes Becket's return to Canterbury (he had sought refuge from Henry in France) and his gradual understanding and acceptance of his role as God's martyr. The martyrdom itself occurs near the beginning of part II. The thematically climactic scene of that part, however, is the Knights' efforts to justify their deed. They address the audience directly, speaking not in blank verse but in modern idiomatic prose. By having them step, as it were, from the twelfth century into the twentieth, Eliot implies the essential modernity of the Knights: in their avowal of the preeminence of the state and their rejection of God they are men of our time.

The First Knight acts as master of ceremonies, introducing the other three, each of whom argues a different justification. The initial claim (that of the Second Knight) is that they really admired Becket and did not enjoy killing him. The last (by the Fourth Knight) is that they did not really kill Becket at all: in effèct he committed suicide by refusing to listen to reason. Both arguments are silly and logically pointless. But between them Eliot places the Third Knight's speech. It is a masterpiece of logic and rhetoric, thoroughly reasoned and skillfully presented by an adroit, calculating speaker who understands his audience and plays subtly upon their beliefs and prejudices. Eliot, of course, does not accept what the Third Knight says: it rests upon assumptions which the play denies. But Eliot was an artist sufficiently mature and honest to allow the other side to state its case. It could not have been stated better than it is in the speech by the Third Knight.

1   I should like first to recur to a point that was very well put by our leader, Reginald Fitz Urse: that you are Englishmen, and therefore your sympathies are always with the under dog. It is the English spirit of fair play. Now the worthy Archbishop, whose good qualities I very much admired, has throughout been presented as the under dog. But is this really the case? I am   5
going to appeal not to your emotions but to your reason. You are hard-headed sensible people, as I can see, and not to be taken in by emotional clap-trap. I therefore ask you to consider soberly: what were the Archbishop's aims? and what are King Henry's aims? In the answer to these questions lies the key to the problem.   10
2   The King's aim has been perfectly consistent. During the reign of the late Queen Matilda and the irruption of the unhappy usurper Stephen, the kingdom was very much divided. Our King saw that the one thing needful was to restore order: to curb the excessive powers of local government, which were usually exercised for selfish and often for seditious ends, and to   15
systematise the judiciary. There was utter chaos: there were three kinds of justice and three kinds of court: that of the King, that of the Bishops, and that of the baronage. I must repeat one point that the last speaker has made. While the late Archbishop was Chancellor, he whole-heartedly supported the King's designs: this is an important point, which, if necessary, I can sub-   20
stantiate. Now the King intended that Becket, who had proved himself an extremely able administrator—no one denies that—should unite the offices of Chancellor and Archbishop. No one would have grudged him that; no one than he was better qualified to fill at once these two most important posts. Had Becket concurred with the King's wishes, we should have had an   25
almost ideal State: a union of spiritual and temporal administration, under the central government. I knew Becket well, in various official relations; and I may say that I have never known a man so well qualified for the highest

rank of the Civil Service. And what happened? The moment that Becket, at the King's instance, had been made Archbishop, he resigned the office of 30 Chancellor, he became more priestly than the priests, he ostentatiously and offensively adopted an ascetic manner of life, he openly abandoned every policy that he had heretofore supported; he affirmed immediately that there was a higher order than that which our King, and he as the King's servant, had for so many years striven to establish; and that—God knows why—the 35 two orders were incompatible.

3   You will agree with me that such interference by an Archbishop offends the instincts of a people like ours. So far, I know that I have your approval: I read it in your faces. It is only with the measures we have had to adopt, in order to set matters to rights, that you take issue. No one regrets 40 the necessity for violence more than we do. Unhappily, there are times when violence is the only way in which social justice can be secured. At another time, you would condemn an Archbishop by vote of Parliament and execute him formally as a traitor, and no one would have to bear the burden of being called murderer. And at a later time still, even such temperate measures as 45 these would become unnecessary. But, if you have now arrived at a just subordination of the pretensions of the Church to the welfare of the State, remember that it is we who took the first step. We have been instrumental in bringing about the state of affairs that you approve. We have served your interests; we merit your applause; and if there is any guilt whatever in the mat- 50 ter, you must share it with us.

QUESTIONS

READER AND PURPOSE

1. Most arguments, in the modern world at least, tend to be inductive, proceeding from particular to general. This selection, however, is different: the Third Knight argues deductively. Beginning from certain general principles, he infers from them a conclusion which, in his own mind if not in everyone's, justifies the murder of Becket. Of course, he adduces facts here and there to support some of the premises of his logic, but his method is one of deductive rather than of inductive reasoning. Read as part of Eliot's play the Third Knight's defense is less imposing; we are better able to see what is wrong with it. Considered apart from the play, however, does the argument seem to achieve its purpose? Does it convince you that Becket's assassination was necessary and just? Why or why not?

2. In one or two sentences sketch the sort of people at whom the Knight is

aiming his logic, considering such matters as their social position and income, their education, their political and religious beliefs, and their general values.

ORGANIZATION

3. In paragraph 1 the Knight very skillfully does three things: he flatters his audience, sets the tone of his argument, and establishes the lines along which he will proceed. Show where he does each of these. Why is the Knight wise to begin with flattery and to end with setting up his argument, rather than the other way round?

4. Although the bones of its logic are well hidden in the enthymemes * in which it develops, the argument in paragraphs 2 and 3 is essentially a syllogism, or rather linked syllogisms, which the paragraphing is used to separate. Paragraph 2 develops the first, the major premise of which is this: the Church must be subordinated to the State. Does the Knight offer any evidence to justify this principle? What is the minor premise of this syllogism? (Do not waste your time looking for something labeled "minor premise"; the Knight is more subtle, and you will have to read carefully and think.) What conclusion follows from these two premises?

5. Fill in the missing term in this syllogism, which is, in essence, the burden of paragraph 3:

> major premise: *Becket must be removed.*
> minor premise: _____.
> conclusion: *Therefore Becket must be killed.*

6. How is the syllogism of paragraph 3 linked to that of 2?

7. Now outline the logic of the total argument. Eliot does not intend that we accept this as justifying Becket's murder. Is its logic, then, faulty? If not, what is wrong with the argument?

SENTENCES

8. The Third Knight is as able a speaker as he is a logician. Read paragraph 1 aloud. Its sentences are short and straightforward, and therefore easy for listeners to follow. Besides lucidity, such a style has here another value. What does his sentence structure suggest about the kind of man the Knight is—or at least the kind he wishes the audience to think he is?

9. At places in paragraphs 2 and 3 the sentences grow more complicated. (E.g. those in 13-16, 16-18, 29-36.) Yet how are even these kept simple to follow?

10. Read the final three sentences (46-51) out loud. The deliberate repetitions of *we have* bind the passage into unity, but they have another purpose as well. What idea do these repetitions convey?

11. Suppose the final clause were written: "and you must share with us whatever guilt there is in this matter." Why is this less effective?

DICTION

12. Look up: *clap-trap* (8), *usurper* (12), *seditious* (15), *substantiate* (20), *concur* (25), *ostentatiously* (31), *temperate* (45), *pretension* (47).

13. As logician and as political speaker, the Knight is equally adept. These make, indeed, a peculiar combination for, however well logic may serve the philosopher, it is a weaker instrument for the needs of the politician, who must often persuade audiences immune to logic. This fact, too, the Knight realizes. He seeks to move men by appealing to their self-esteem and to their prejudices as well as to their minds, the so-called *ad populum* fallacy. Thus in paragraph 1 the Knight flatters his audience. What words in paragraph 3 are similarly flattering?

14. In paragraph 2 what words descriptive of Becket are calculated to prejudice an English audience against him? This is an example of *argumentum ad hominem*. Define this phrase.

15. As his syntax suggests, the Knight is trying to play a role designed to catch the audience's sympathy and admiration. His diction reveals the role more clearly. What does *Unhappily* (41) tell us about the kind of man the Knight wishes to seem? And why does he not simply begin in line 1: *I shall first* instead of *I should like first?*

16. Notice that at the very end of his speech the Knight tells his listeners that "if there is any guilt whatever in this matter, you must share it with us." This is known as the *tu quoque* fallacy. What is it, and why is it a fallacy?

17. Although the Third Knight is not above flattery and the other fallacies we have mentioned, he does avoid more obvious excesses. What, for example, might a more impassioned speaker have done with the "chaos" to which the Knight refers in line 16? All in all, do you think the Knight's plea is dishonest? Be prepared to defend your answer.

POINTS TO LEARN

1. Logic may be more effective in persuasion when it is hidden.

2. No logical argument, however subtle, is better than the premises upon which it rests.

3. While flattery, prejudice, and the *argumentum ad hominem* are not proper to logical reasoning, they often accompany it. It is wise, both as a writer and as a reader, to learn to recognize them.

4. The *tu quoque* argument may be a clever diversion, but it is rarely to the point.

SUGGESTIONS FOR WRITING

1. Accused of one of the "crimes" listed below, you must defend your action as logical and just. Use deductive logic to build your defense, but bear in mind the values and prejudices of the particular audience that judges you.

> Refusing to obey a policeman
> Falling asleep during class
> Knocking down a man who insulted you
> Disobeying your parents or school authorities

2. Addressing yourself to the same audience, answer the Third Knight. Keep your argument essentially logical, but do not ignore the values and prejudices of your audience.

IMPROVING YOUR STYLE

In your argument observe these conditions:

1. Keep your sentence style uncomplicated and straightforward. You are writing for people's ears, not their eyes; they cannot read back over your sentences. Therefore your syntax must not become too complex. At the same time remember that you are writing for adults; do not insult them with a "Jane-sees-Jack" primer style.

2. At one place begin three or four sentences with "I" + an appropriate verb and try to establish a bond of value or interest between yourself and your audience.

3. Use specific words or phrases that will subtly please and flatter your listeners, others that will enlist their sympathy by appealing to their beliefs or biases.

The Federalist No. 10

The book we now know as *The Federalist* was originally a series of eighty-five essays, published between October 1787 and May 1788 by James Madison (1751-1836), John Jay (1745-1829), and Alexander Hamilton (1757-1804). Writing under the name of Publius, the three men urged the adoption of the Constitution, a document that to many Americans still imbued with the liberalism of the Declaration of Independence and the Revolution seemed much too conservative. Directed primarily to the voters of New York State, the articles were widely read in the other twelve, and in 1788 they were published as *The Federalist*. They have been studied ever since, for *The Federalist* is the classic of eighteenth century American political thought and it has influenced theorists and statesmen the world over.

It is also one of the finest pieces of argumentation ever written. There are places where Publius is unfair, places where he evades or oversimplifies; *The Federalist* was originally in the nature of propaganda. Yet despite occasional lapses, it has few equals as a beautiful expression of hard thinking. But it is not easy to read. The lazy reader will be repelled by *The Federalist*. The reader willing to study and to learn, will learn much.

1   *To the People of the State of New York:*

Among the numerous advantages promised by a well-constructed Union, none deserves to be more accurately developed than its tendency to break and control the violence of faction. The friend of popular governments never finds himself so much alarmed for their character and fate, as 5 when he contemplates their propensity to this dangerous vice. He will not fail, therefore, to set a due value on any plan which, without violating the principles to which he is attached, provides a proper cure for it. The instability, injustice, and confusion introduced into the public councils, have, in truth, been the mortal diseases under which popular governments have 10 everywhere perished; as they continue to be the favorite and fruitful topics

From *The Federalist*, New York, The Modern Library, 1937, pp. 53-62.

from which the adversaries to liberty derive their most specious declamations. The valuable improvements made by the American constitutions on the popular models, both ancient and modern, cannot certainly be too much admired; but it would be an unwarrantable partiality, to contend that they have as effectually obviated the danger on this side, as was wished and expected. Complaints are everywhere heard from our most considerate and virtuous citizens, equally the friends of public and private faith, and of public and personal liberty, that our governments are too unstable, that the public good is disregarded in the conflicts of rival parties, and that measures are too often decided, not according to the rules of justice and the rights of the minor party, but by the superior force of an interested and overbearing majority. However anxiously we may wish that these complaints had no foundation, the evidence of known facts will not permit us to deny that they are in some degree true. It will be found, indeed, on a candid review of our situation, that some of the distresses under which we labor have been erroneously charged on the operation of our governments; but it will be found, at the same time, that other causes will not alone account for many of our heaviest misfortunes; and, particularly, for that prevailing and increasing distrust of public engagements, and alarm for private rights, which are echoed from one end of the continent to the other. These must be chiefly, if not wholly, effects of the unsteadiness and injustice with which a factious spirit has tainted our public administrations.

2   By a faction, I understand a number of citizens, whether amounting to a majority or minority of the whole, who are united and actuated by some common impulse of passion, or of interest, adverse to the rights of other citizens, or to the permanent and aggregate interests of the community.

3   There are two methods of curing the mischiefs of faction: the one, by removing its causes; the other, by controlling its effects.

4   There are again two methods of removing the causes of faction: the one, by destroying the liberty which is essential to its existence; the other, by giving to every citizen the same opinions, the same passions, and the same interests.

5   It could never be more truly said than of the first remedy, that it was worse than the disease. Liberty is to faction what air is to fire, and aliment without which it instantly expires. But it could not be less folly to abolish liberty, which is essential to political life, because it nourishes faction, than it would be to wish the annihilation of air, which is essential to animal life, because it imparts to fire its destructive agency.

6   The second expedient is as impracticable as the first would be un-

wise. As long as the reason of man continues fallible, and he is at liberty to exercise it, different opinions will be formed. As long as the connection subsists between his reason and his self-love, his opinions and his passions will have a reciprocal influence on each other; and the former will be objects to which the latter will attach themselves. The diversity in the faculties of men, from which the rights of property originate, is not less an insuperable obstacle to a uniformity of interests. The protection of these faculties is the first object of government. From the protection of different and unequal faculties of acquiring property, the possession of different degrees and kinds of property immediately results; and from the influence of these on the sentiments and views of the respective proprietors, ensues a division of the society into different interests and parties.

7   The latent causes of faction are thus sown in the nature of man; and we see them everywhere brought into different degrees of activity, according to the different circumstances of civil society. A zeal for different opinions concerning religion, concerning government, and many other points, as well of speculation as of practice; an attachment to different leaders ambitiously contending for pre-eminence and power; or to persons of other descriptions whose fortunes have been interesting to the human passions, have, in turn, divided mankind into parties, inflamed them with mutual animosity, and rendered them much more disposed to vex and oppress each other than to co-operate for their common good. So strong is this propensity of mankind to fall into mutual animosities, that where no substantial occasion presents itself, the most frivolous and fanciful distinctions have been sufficient to kindle their unfriendly passions and excite their most violent conflicts. But the most common and durable source of factions has been the various and unequal distribution of property. Those who hold and those who are without property have ever formed distinct interests in society. Those who are creditors, and those who are debtors, fall under a like discrimination. A landed interest, a manufacturing interest, a mercantile interest, a moneyed interest, with many lesser interests, grow up of necessity in civilized nations, and divide them into different classes, actuated by different sentiments and views. The regulation of these various and interfering interests forms the principal task of modern legislation, and involves the spirit of party and faction in the necessary and ordinary operations of the government.

8   No man is allowed to be a judge in his own cause, because his interest would certainly bias his judgment, and, not improbably, corrupt his integrity. With equal, nay with greater reason, a body of men are unfit to be

both judges and parties at the same time; yet what are many of the most   90
important acts of legislation, but so many judicial determinations, not indeed concerning the rights of single persons, but concerning the rights of
large bodies of citizens? And what are the different classes of legislators
but advocates and parties to the causes which they determine? Is a law
proposed concerning private debts? It is a question to which the creditors   95
are parties on one side and the debtors on the other. Justice ought to hold
the balance between them. Yet the parties are, and must be, themselves
the judges; and the most numerous party, or, in other words, the most
powerful faction must be expected to prevail. Shall domestic manufactures
be encouraged, and in what degree, by restrictions on foreign manufactures?   100
are questions which would be differently decided by the landed and the
manufacturing classes, and probably by neither with a sole regard to justice
and the public good. The apportionment of taxes on the various descriptions of property is an act which seems to require the most exact impar-
tiality; yet there is, perhaps, no legislative act in which greater opportunity   105
and temptation are given to a predominant party to trample on the rules of
justice. Every shilling with which they overburden the inferior number, is a
shilling saved to their own pockets.

9   It is in vain to say that enlightened statesmen will be able to adjust
these clashing interests, and render them all subservient to the public good.   110
Enlightened statesmen will not always be at the helm. Nor, in many cases,
can such an adjustment be made at all without taking into view indirect
and remote considerations, which will rarely prevail over the immediate
interest which one party may find in disregarding the rights of another or
the good of the whole.   115

10   The inference to which we are brought is, that the *causes* of faction
cannot be removed, and that relief is only to be sought in the means of
controlling its *effects*.

11   If a faction consists of less than a majority, relief is supplied by
the republican principle, which enables the majority to defeat its sinister   120
views by regular vote. It may clog the administration, it may convulse the society; but it will be unable to execute and mask its violence under the
forms of the Constitution. When a majority is included in a faction, the
form of popular government, on the other hand, enables it to sacrifice to
its ruling passion or interest both the public good and the rights of other   125
citizens. To secure the public good and private rights against the danger of
such a faction, and at the same time to preserve the spirit and the form of
popular government, is then the great object to which our inquiries are

directed. Let me add that it is the great desideratum by which this form of government can be rescued from the opprobrium under which it has so long labored, and be recommended to the esteem and adoption of mankind.   130

12   By what means is this object attainable? Evidently by one of two only. Either the existence of the same passion or interest in a majority at the same time must be prevented, or the majority, having such coexistent passion or interest, must be rendered, by their number and local situation, unable to concert and carry into effect schemes of oppression. If the impulse and the opportunity be suffered to coincide, we well know that neither moral nor religious motives can be relied on as an adequate control. They are not found to be such on the injustice and violence of individuals, and lose their efficacy in proportion to the number combined together, that is, in proportion as their efficacy becomes needful.   135   140

13   From this view of the subject it may be concluded that a pure democracy, by which I mean a society consisting of a small number of citizens, who assemble and administer the government in person, can admit of no cure for the mischiefs of faction. A common passion or interest will, in almost every case, be felt by a majority of the whole; a communication and concert result from the form of government itself; and there is nothing to check the inducements to sacrifice the weaker party or an obnoxious individual. Hence it is that such democracies have ever been spectacles of turbulence and contention; have ever been found incompatible with personal security or the rights of property; and have in general been as short in their lives as they have been violent in their deaths. Theoretic politicians, who have patronized this species of government, have erroneously supposed that by reducing mankind to a perfect equality in their political rights, they would, at the same time, be perfectly equalized and assimilated in their possessions, their opinions, and their passions.   145   150   155

14   A republic, by which I mean a government in which the scheme of representation takes place, opens a different prospect, and promises the cure for which we are seeking. Let us examine the points in which it varies from pure democracy, and we shall comprehend both the nature of the cure and the efficacy which it must derive from the Union.   160

15   The two great points of difference between a democracy and a republic are: first, the delegation of the government, in the latter, to a small number of citizens elected by the rest; secondly, the greater number of citizens, and greater sphere of country, over which the latter may be extended.   165

16   The effect of the first difference is, on the one hand, to refine and enlarge the public views, by passing them through the medium of a chosen

body of citizens, whose wisdom may best discern the true interest of their country, and whose patriotism and love of justice will be least likely to sacrifice it to temporary or partial considerations. Under such a regulation, it may well happen that the public voice, pronounced by the representatives of the people, will be more consonant to the public good than if pronounced by the people themselves, convened for the purpose. On the other hand, the effect may be inverted. Men of factious tempers, of local prejudices, or of sinister designs, may, by intrigue, by corruption, or by other means, first obtain the suffrages, and then betray the interests, of the people. The question resulting is, whether small or extensive republics are more favorable to the election of proper guardians of the public weal; and it is clearly decided in favor of the latter by two obvious considerations:

17   In the first place, it is to be remarked that, however small the republic may be, the representatives must be raised to a certain number, in order to guard against the cabals of a few; and that, however large it may be, they must be limited to a certain number, in order to guard against the confusion of a multitude. Hence, the number of representatives in the two cases not being in proportion to that of the two constituents, and being proportionally greater in the small republic, it follows that, if the proportion of fit characters be not less in the large than in the small republic, the former will present a greater option, and consequently a greater probability of a fit choice.

18   In the next place, as each representative will be chosen by a greater number of citizens in the large than in the small republic, it will be more difficult for unworthy candidates to practice with success the vicious arts by which elections are too often carried; and the suffrages of the people being more free, will be more likely to centre in men who possess the most attractive merit and the most diffusive and established characters.

19   It must be confessed that in this, as in most other cases, there is a mean, on both sides of which inconveniences will be found to lie. By enlarging too much the number of electors, you render the representative too little acquainted with all their local circumstances and lesser interests; as by reducing it too much, you render him unduly attached to these, and too little fit to comprehend and pursue great and national objects. The federal Constitution forms a happy combination in this respect; the great and aggregate interests being referred to the national, the local and particular to the State legislatures.

20   The other point of difference is, the greater number of citizens and extent of territory which may be brought within the compass of repub-

lican than of democratic government; and it is this circumstance principally which renders factious combinations less to be dreaded in the former than in the latter. The smaller the society, the fewer probably will be the distinct parties and interests composing it; the fewer the distinct parties 210 and interests, the more frequently will a majority be found of the same party; and the smaller the number of individuals composing a majority, and the smaller the compass within which they are placed, the more easily will they concert and execute their plans of oppression. Extend the sphere, and you take in a greater variety of parties and interests; you make it less prob- 215 able that a majority of the whole will have a common motive to invade the rights of other citizens; or if such a common motive exists, it will be more difficult for all who feel it to discover their own strength, and to act in unison with each other. Besides other impediments, it may be remarked that, where there is a consciousness of unjust or dishonorable purposes, communi- 220 cation is always checked by distrust in proportion to the number whose concurrence is necessary.

21   Hence, it clearly appears, that the same advantage which a republic has over a democracy, in controlling the effects of faction, is enjoyed by a large over a small republic,—is enjoyed by the Union over the States com- 225 posing it. Does the advantage consist in the substitution of representatives whose enlightened views and virtuous sentiments render them superior to local prejudices and to schemes of injustice? It will not be denied that the representation of the Union will be most likely to possess these requisite endowments. Does it consist in the greater security afforded by a greater 230 variety of parties, against the event of any one party being able to outnumber and oppress the rest? In an equal degree does the increased variety of parties comprised within the Union, increase this security. Does it, in fine, consist in the greater obstacles opposed to the concert and accomplishment of the secret wishes of an unjust and interested majority? Here, again, 235 the extent of the Union gives it the most palpable advantage.

22   The influence of factious leaders may kindle a flame within their particular States, but will be unable to spread a general conflagration through the other States. A religious sect may degenerate into a political faction in a part of the Confederacy; but the variety of sects dispersed over the entire 240 face of it must secure the national councils against any danger from that source. A rage for paper money, for an abolition of debts, for an equal division of property, or for any other improper or wicked project, will be less apt to pervade the whole body of the Union than a particular member of

it; in the same proportion as such a malady is more likely to taint a par- 245
ticular county or district, than an entire State.

23   In the extent and proper structure of the Union, therefore, we
behold a republican remedy for the diseases most incident to republican
government. And according to the degree of pleasure and pride we feel in
being republicans, ought to be our zeal in cherishing the spirit and sup- 250
porting the character of Federalists.

PUBLIUS

QUESTIONS

READER AND PURPOSE

1. In common with that of the other *Federalist* papers, the purpose of "Number 10" is to justify the Federal Constitution. On what specific grounds does
Madison urge its superiority? The skillful political publicist always has in mind
a certain type of reader. In your library learn all you can about the men for
whom James Madison was writing. Then in one or two paragraphs describe the
salient characteristics of Madison's audience, and show that Madison was extremely careful to keep these characteristics in mind.

ORGANIZATION

2. Discuss paragraph 1 as a beginning, showing that Madison makes clear what
he is going to discuss and that he stresses the importance of his subject. Before
actually beginning his argument, Madison offers us a definition. Where? Why
is it essential that he do this at the beginning? Where else in the essay does he
define key terms?

3. All arguments necessarily rest upon assumptions. Sometimes these are so
obvious that no one can deny them; sometimes, however, the assumptions may
be questionable, or even wrong. Examine as many of Madison's basic assumptions as you can. For example, does he assume that men are innately good until
corrupted by some outside force? Or does he assume that men are evil by
nature?

4. Madison uses the method of dichotomy to develop his argument; that is, he
sets up two alternatives or possibilities and handles each in turn. Which paragraph sets up the primary dichotomy that, in effect, organizes the essay into its
two major parts? Does Madison again use a dichotomy to analyze the first of
these parts? Which paragraphs constitute the first section of the essay?

5. In paragraph 5 Madison introduces an analogy *. Does this use of analogy
constitute a logical fallacy and therefore a weakening of his argument, or does
the analogy actually strengthen his argument? Explain.

6. In your own words summarize the argument that Madison advances in paragraph 6 to support his belief that it is impossible to control the causes of faction "by giving to every citizen the same opinions, the same passions, and the same interests." Is the argument basically logical or empirical? Be able to support your answer. Explain whether paragraphs 7, 8, and 9 continue and support the point developed in paragraph 6 or whether they comprise an entirely new argument.

7. In what sense might the tenth paragraph be described as a "transitional paragraph"? Is the "inference to which we are brought" in this paragraph a logically valid conclusion? Do you think that it is true?

8. Show that even though he does it implicitly, Madison organizes the second half of his argument by the same method of dichotomy that he employed more explicitly in the first part. Does he use dichotomous development any place within this section?

9. A frequent theoretical argument against democracy has been that because it cannot control factionalism it inevitably degenerates into tyranny. Madison attempts to answer this charge first by distinguishing between a democracy and a republic and second by asserting the advantages of the latter which enable it to control faction. What is the distinction and what arguments does Madison adduce in favor of a republic over a democracy? List the arguments by which he tries to prove the superiority of a large republic over a small. In both cases are the arguments empirical or logical?

10. Paragraph 17 is a beautifully lucid statement of an arithmetic argument. Using the figure 100 to represent the number of voters in a "small" republic and the figure 1000 to represent the number in a "large," demonstrate whether Madison's conclusion that a large republic "will present a greater option, and consequently a greater probability of a fit choice" is mathematically justified.

11. Which paragraphs make up the closing of this essay? Is it a good closing? Why or why not? What metaphor * helps to create a closing by return?

12. Does Madison ever make concessions to the opposition? If so, where? Do these concessions damage his argument? Why or why not? Where does he refute the opposition?

SENTENCES

13. In common with many eighteenth-century writers, the authors of *The Federalist* liked rather long sentences constructed on the principle of parallelism *. Analyze the second sentence of paragraph 7, indicating (by underlining or some other means) all the parallel elements it contains. Point to one or two other sentences that are similarly elaborate in their construction.

14. At the same time, Madison's sentences are often forceful and emphatic. Frequently, his sentences are periodic * in structure. Find and label several examples. Another device that produces emphasis is the isolation of key words

and phrases by some kind of interrupting * construction. The first sentence in paragraph 8 is an example. Try to find others. What additional techniques of emphasis can you identify?

15. Point out the parallel constructions in the sentence in lines 17-23. What verbs parallel *divided* in lines 70 and 71?

16. This sentence is a fine example of balanced * construction:

> But it could not be less folly to abolish liberty, which is essential to political life, because it nourishes faction, than it would be to wish the annihilation of air, which is essential to animal life, because it imparts to fire its destructive agency. (46-49)

Logically this sentence falls into two equal parts—at what point? Each half contains three units. Are these units arranged in identical sequences in the two parts of the sentence? So nice a balance enables Madison to throw considerable emphasis on certain pairs of words. Against what term is *liberty* balanced? *Political life? Faction?*

DICTION

17. Look up: *propensity* (6), *actuated* (35), *aliment* (45), *expedient* (50), *reciprocal* (54), *latent* (63), *animosity* (70), *clog* (121), *efficacy* (141), *consonant* (172), *mean* (197), *aggregate* (203).

18. How do the etymologies * of the following words help to explain their meanings? *Faction* (4), *candid* (25), *tainted* (33), *zeal* (65), *obnoxious* (148), *delegation* (163), *cabal* (182), *suffrages* (193), *sect* (239).

19. The modern student, no longer thoroughly grounded in the classical languages, is likely to be repelled by the heavily Latinate diction of *The Federalist*. Forgetting that this was the common currency of discourse among eighteenth-century gentlemen carefully trained in Greek and Latin, the modern reader may even suspect Madison of showing off. Of course he was not. But his diction may be defended on better grounds than its being the fashion of the times. The precise distinctions permitted by these carefully articulated Latinate words are the chief source of that crystalline subtlety we admire so much in *The Federalist*. Today, however, we are liable to miss the subtlety if we do not make an effort to understand these words in their classical sense; indeed where a word has shifted from that sense in the almost two hundred years since Madison wrote, we are likely to misunderstand it altogether. What, for example, does Madison mean by a *"popular* government" (how did Lincoln once phrase much the same thing?), by *"specious* declamations"? by "the *faculties* of men"? From Madison's argument make a list of eight or ten Latinate words that seem to be examples of perfect diction. For what kind of audience, purpose, and occasion would these words be completely inappropriate?

20. From time to time Madison seems to understate his case. For example, in

line 238 Madison speaks of a "general conflagration." He might have pictured here the horrors of civil war, the destruction and misery resulting from battles of brother against brother, of father against son. He might have depicted the burning of homes, the nightmare of plunder and rapine. Instead we have only "general conflagration." Defend Madison's strategy in this instance. Point to similar examples elsewhere in the argument.

POINTS TO LEARN

1. The writer's audience should determine what kind of argument he constructs. "The Federalist No. 10" would probably not appeal to readers of little education. But then a rabble-rousing kind of argument would not appeal to the audience for whom Madison wrote.

2. In argument, especially, the writer must define key words as soon as he introduces them.

3. Latinate diction may be just as accurate, economical, and appropriate as the simpler Saxon diction. A writer's diction should be determined by his readers, his purpose, and the occasion.

SUGGESTIONS FOR WRITING

1. Refute Madison's argument in "The Federalist No. 10."

2. Today we no longer speak of factions, but we use terms like *parties, pressure groups,* and *lobbies* to mean the same thing. Selecting very concrete examples from the modern social and political scene, convince your reader that Madison's ideas in "The Federalist No. 10" have proved sound. You may wish to quote from Madison along the way.

IMPROVING YOUR STYLE

In your essay include:

1. Two periodic sentences.

2. Two balanced sentences, one consisting of simply two roughly equal units, the other of two units which each again split in half.

3. Two sentences using extensive parallelism.

The American Dilemma

Kenneth Clark is a prominent psychologist and educator, especially noted for his studies of the black ghetto. This selection, however, deals with a more pervasive problem of American life. It appeared originally in *The New York Times*, which accounts for its journalistic mode of paragraphing. While he is not presenting a formal argument, like Eliot's Third Knight or James Madison in the preceding selections, Clark does wish to convince us of something, and he offers evidence to support his contention. The title, incidentally, echoes that of a famous book: Gunnar Myrdal's *An American Dilemma* (1944). The Swedish scholar, commissioned by the Carnegie Foundation, made a massive study of race relations in the United States which had great influence in the campaign for black rights. Myrdal concluded that the bias against blacks violated ideals which Americans professed to believe. By alluding to Myrdal's work, but substituting the definite for the indefinite article, Clark implies that the problem he sees is an even more fundamental contradiction of our ideals.

1 About seven years ago, I accepted an invitation to participate in a seminar on the ethical and moral problems of American society that was sponsored by the Aspen Institute in Colorado. Among the other invited guests were business executives, college presidents, judges, government officials, managing editors, professors and theologians.   5

2 Although there was no conflict or controversy in the discussions, one of the presentations has had a profound, almost obsessive, impact upon my own thoughts about the character and quality of American life.

3 In a rather quiet voice, a recently retired vice president of one of the largest corporations in America told the group that one of the per-   10 sistent problems faced by his office was how to keep the accounting records of the corporation in such a way that they would be accurate and would also obscure the fact that regular operating expenses were payoffs to

From *The New York Times*, February 16, 1975. Copyright © 1975 by The New York Times Company. Reprinted by permission.

municipal officials to expedite the installation of new construction in the large cities throughout the United States. Casually, this participant cited 15 this as just another example of a prevailing functional immorality with which big business had to come to terms.

4   When none of the other participants raised a question about the ethical implications of this practice, I eventually asked why this powerful corporation did not bring this matter to local and Federal law-enforcement 20 officials. My colleagues clearly considered my question naïve. They reacted to my persistent questions as if I were an unrealistic child who did not understand the economic and political rules of the great American game.

5   Now I was shocked not only by the disclosure but equally shocked at the fact that my fellow seminar participants were not shocked. They 25 thought themselves realistic in not permitting an academic discussion of ethical and moral values to be confused by "minor" specific examples of generally accepted institutionalized immorality.

6   In assessing the social, political and human strength and potential of America, one can concentrate on such large issues as America's role in 30 Southeast Asia and such other international problems as its fluctuating relations with its economic and ideological allies and adversaries; the persistent and manifold and overtly cruel forms of racism; the more subtle manifestations of inter-ethnic conflicts and the rejection of the poor, the aged and the infirm in a nation that prides itself on its affluence; and the 35 fact that a highly developed technological society that has pioneered in space exploration continues to tolerate large-scale decay of the residential portions of its inner cities, deterioration of public education and accelerated pollution and wastage of its natural and human resources.

7   What is the basic systemic problem—the fundamental problem 40 of perspective, value and character—that seems to be inherent in the chronic crises plaguing American society? Obviously the answer to this question is not to be found in deprivation and poverty of resources.

8   The paradoxical problem of American society is that it has been too successful; it is affluent and efficient even as it has legitimized and ac- 45 cepted pervasive dishonesties as the price of apparent success. When dishonesty appears to work, it is difficult to argue persuasively for honesty.

9   So far, America has been able to have its democratic ideals and pursue the cruelties of racism. Today the majority of Americans will vote yes in favor of desegregation of the public schools—but a greater majority 50 will vote against busing of students to obtain desegregated schools. Many

Americans under the banner of democratic egalitarianism will argue and insist upon their right to keep less desirable, "less equal," Americans out of their communities and schools.

10   These and related inconsistencies could be explained as examples of the nonrationality of the human species. On the basis of my Aspen experience I do not believe that this is a logical or rational problem. The crisis of inconsistencies in American life—the American dilemma—is primarily a crisis of moral ambivalence. It is an honesty-dishonesty dilemma that pervades all dimensions of our social, economic, political, educational and, indeed, our religious institutions.

11   This systemic dilemma within American society is complicated and probably made all the more virulent because it is inextricably entangled with status striving, success symbols, moral and ethical pretensions and the anxieties and fear of personal and family failures.

12   The conflicts in the American character structure and social system—conflicts intensified by the frequently fulfilled promises of upward mobility—must be resolved if the individuals are to continue to pursue the goals of status and success.

13   Reality, efficiency and morality are defined as if they were synonymous: That is real and moral which leads to success. If this is found to be too abstract an approach even for a pragmatic morality, then outright moral cynicism and hypocrisy are available as alternative approaches to personal success and effectiveness.

14   These devices for the resolution of the pervasive moral conflicts of our society can place tremendous stresses and strains upon some sensitive human beings. These individuals—probably a minority—are required continuously to measure their desire to function in terms of ethical and moral principles against their desire to avoid personal failure and ineffectiveness.

15   In a pragmatic, efficiency-dominated society, it is difficult for an ethically sensitive person to be taken seriously in the making of "tough-minded," "hard-headed" decisions. Promotions don't come easily to them. They are not likely to survive the severe "realistic" screening process that selects candidates for office.

16   American democracy, with its divergent and competing racial, ethnic and class groups cannot afford to elect to high office individuals who genuinely place ideals and ethical values above personal advantages and "realistic" moral compromises.

17   Indeed, the concern with honesty and human values becomes the

sign that an individual is not practical enough to be entrusted with the re-   90
sponsibilities of making realistic political and economic decisions.

18   The virulence of this ethical and moral sickness is indicated by the
fact that the symptoms, flagrant or subtle, are accepted by sophisticated
realists—the controllers, policy-makers and decision-makers of our society—
as normative, competitive, and necessary for efficiency, affluence and effec-   95
tiveness.

19   In short, they are interpreted as signs of health.

20   Those who insist that they are signs of a severe social disease can
be dismissed as starry-eyed moralists, sentimentalists and understandably
without influence or power. As a matter of fact, the few serious moral   100
critics of our society do not have constituents. Intellectually and temperamentally they cannot appeal to the masses. Neither can they expect support
from radicals of the right or the left because they tend to be as much concerned with methods as they are with ends; they cannot accept moral ends
through immoral means.   105

21   The moral schizophrenia pervasive in the American society appears
to be no more curable by words than is personal schizophrenia curable by
psychotherapeutic preachments. Political, religious, civil-rights panaceas
have been tried and found palliative at best and cruelly disillusioning at
worst.   110

22   The essential for hope is to be found in that critical minority of
human beings who insist upon being unrealistic, who for some still unknown set of reasons continue to argue that human beings are somehow
capable of the possibility of empathy, compassion and sensitivity even as
cruelty and hostility and insensitivity and rationalized dishonesty now   115
dominate.

23   Fortunately for the future of a civilized society there exist these
human beings who, while they are not nominated for high office and if
nominated are not elected, nonetheless remain concerned about moral and
ethical values and justice in the affairs of men.   120

24   They also seem to have the courage to risk the repeated expressions
of their concern and thereby serve as a gnawing and irritating conscience
to those who have attained success.

25   In the final analysis only these individuals provide the hope for
that ultimate type of realism that is defined by the capacity of a society to   125
survive rather than to be destroyed eventually on the altar of human
barbarity.

QUESTIONS

1. Professor Clark wishes to persuade us of two points about modern America, one negative, the other more positive. What are they?

2. How does he support his argument: by drawing conclusions from broad premises, or empirically by offering evidence to support his charges? If he does offer evidence, is it specific or in the nature of general assertions?

3. In his opening paragraph Professor Clark enumerates the participants at the conference. Is he simply name-dropping, or has the list a bearing upon his argument?

4. Does he appear to be aiming at the kind of "hard-headed realists" he failed to move at the Aspen meeting? At readers more sympathetic to his own position? At readers somewhere between these extremes? Does he suppose his readers to be knowledgeable?

5. Which paragraphs constitute the beginning of this selection? An effective beginning ought to establish the subject, at least generally, and to draw the reader into the essay. So judged, is this beginning successful?

6. Paragraph 25 closes the essay. What signal of ending does it contain?

7. Where does Professor Clark explicitly pose the question he is attempting to answer?

8. Paragraph 14 marks a major turn of thought. Explain why. Why does paragraph 22 also mark a turn of thought?

9. What is the topic sentence of paragraph 9? How is it supported?

10. Indicate which words tie paragraphs 10 and 14 to what precedes them.

11. This essay appeared originally in a newspaper (*The New York Times*) and its numerous short paragraphs are in the fashion of journalism. What virtues does this kind of paragraphing have? What disadvantages? Are there any places where two or three successive paragraphs could be combined with no loss of clarity? Would it be an improvement to combine paragraph 19, which consists of only one short sentence, with paragraph 18?

12. Explain why in the following pairs of sentences the revision is poorer than what Professor Clark wrote:

   (a) *Revision:* This participant cited this casually as just another example of a prevailing functional immorality with which big business had to come to terms.

Clark: "Casually, this participant cited this as just another example of a prevailing functional immorality with which big business had to come to terms." (15-17)

(b) *Revision:* Now I was shocked not only by the disclosure but equally by the fact that my fellow seminar participants were not. *Clark:* "Now I was shocked not only by the disclosure but equally shocked at the fact that my fellow seminar participants were not shocked." (24-25)

(c) *Revision:* One of the presentations has had a profound, almost obsessive, impact upon my own thought about the character and quality of American life, although there was no conflict or controversy in the discussion. *Clark:* "Although there was no conflict or controversy in the discussions, one of the presentations has had a profound, almost obsessive, impact upon my own thoughts about the character and quality of American life." (6-8)

13. The sixth paragraph consists of a single very long sentence, which is kept in order by parallelism *. Point out all the parallel elements you can find. How does the punctuation help us follow the complicated structure of this sentence?

14. In lines 40-41 Professor Clark encloses a parenthetical remark in dashes. How is this remark logically related to the immediately preceding phrase *systemic problem*? Would commas have worked as well here? Where else in this selection are dashes employed for a similar purpose?

15. How is the contrast between the key terms *dishonesty* and *honesty* emphasized in the sentence in lines 46-47?

DICTION

16. Look up: *obsessive* (7), *impact* (7), *expedite* (14), *manifold* (33), *overtly* (33), *paradoxical* (44), *egalitarianism* (52), *inextricably* (63), *synonomous* (70), *normative* (95), *temperamentally* (101), *panaceas* (108), *palliative* (109).

17. Explain as fully as you can what these phrases mean: *academic discussion* (26), *systemic problem* (40), *chronic crises* (42), *status striving* (64), *success symbols* (64), *upward mobility* (67), *pragmatic morality* (72), *moral cynicism* (73), *moral schizophrenia* (106).

18. How do the etymologies * of the following words help us to understand their current meanings? *Seminar* (2), *theologians* (5), *casually* (15), *naïve* (21), *dilemma* (62), *hypocrisy* (73), *ethnic* (86), *flagrant* (93), *radicals* (103), *civilized* (117), *ultimate* (125).

19. For the writer's purpose each of the following substitutions is poorer than

the word in the text. Why? *Danger* for *virulence* (92), *regarded* for *dismissed* (99), *idealistic* for *starry-eyed* (99), *analysis* for *preachments* (108).

20. How does the phrase *in a rather quiet voice* (9) and the word *casually* (15) bear upon Professor Clark's argument?

21. Professor Clark frequently uses the doublet *moral and ethical*. Why does he specify both words? What difference do you think he has in mind? In line 114 he distinguishes *empathy, compassion*, and *sensitivity*. What precisely is the difference?

22. Why does he place *less equal* (53), *tough-minded* (81), *hard-headed* (82), and *realistic* (88) in quotation marks?

23. The following words and phrases are all examples of pointers *; explain how each signals a particular relationship of thought between the approaching idea and what has just been said: *now* (24), *indeed* (89), *in short* (97), *as a matter of fact* (100).

POINTS TO LEARN

1.When you compose an argument make it clear what you are for or against.

2. A good beginning clarifies the subject and draws the reader's interest.

3. Parallelism helps to control a long, complicated sentence.

SUGGESTIONS FOR WRITING

Some of the faults of which Professor Clark accuses contemporary America are mentioned below. Select one and, after briefly defining it, argue that the charge is (or if you prefer, is not) true. Support your argument by offering evidence, either in the form of detailed example or in the form of more general assertions that seem obviously true.

status striving, concern with the symbols of success, pragmatic moral-ity, moral cynicism, moral schizophrenia

IMPROVING YOUR STYLE

Include the following in your argument:

1. A long sentence (40-50 words) with parallel structure.

2. An explanation or restatement set between dashes after the word it defines or repeats.

3. A sentence with a subordinate clause * followed by the main clause (like the one in lines 6-8 of Clark's passage).

4. Sentences introduced by these pointers: *now, indeed, in short, as a matter of fact*.

Mayhem of the Week

George F. Will is a newspaper columnist. Usually he writes about politics. Occasionally, however, he turns to other aspects of American life, as he does here in an indictment of the violence of football. In football Will is tackling a sacred cow of American culture—not an easy task, metaphorically or actually. As you read his argument, think about the evidence he offers and judge whether or not it supports his case.

1   The desecration of autumn by football has begun. By Christmas, 1.5 million players will have been injured seriously enough to miss practices or games. And coaches and fans will have said, 1.5 million times, that injuries are "part of the game." How big that part is has been demonstrated by Sports Illustrated's John Underwood in a three-part series on football 5 violence.

2   In 1905, President Theodore Roosevelt, who enjoyed war and other forms of the strenuous life, demanded civilizing rules changes for football, which had killed 18 players that year. In 1973, an Indiana high school team suffered four broken backs and four broken legs. Oklahoma 10 State's physician was called onto the field 13 times in one game. The Detroit Lions had 21 knee operations.

3   The NFL argues that only one percent of injuries result from acts against the rules. Underwood responds that, if 99 percent of injuries (like the broken neck that paralyzed Darryl Stingley of the New England Patriots 15 last month) result from play within the rules, the rules should be changed.

4   Helmets have virtually eliminated skull fractures, but blows by helmets cause about 30 percent of the worst injuries—spinal damage, ruptured spleens, bruised kidneys. Underwood believes helmets should be padded, and that rules should prohibit a player from using his helmet to 20 make the first contact in a block or tackle.

From *The Boston Globe* (September 7, 1978). Reprinted by permission of the publisher.

5   "Any injuries are the result of playing styles taught by coaches"—
techniques like the "chop block," where a player blocks down onto an
opponent's knees; "spearing," where a player plunges his helmet into an
opponent; and "rake-blocking," where a blocker rakes his facemask into an   25
opponent's chin. Although "clubbing" with forearms has been prohibited
in college football since 1949, Coach Fred Akers of Texas cringes when he
sees rival teams "with their arms taped to the elbows."

6   Ara Parseghian, former Notre Dame coach, favors banning all
below-the-waist blocks away from the line of scrimmage. John Madden,   30
coach of the Oakland Raiders, suggests something like a "grab" rule requiring defenders to use only hands and arms against a quarterback who is
vulnerable because he is in the act of passing. And there almost certainly
should be a rule against hitting backs or receivers (like Stingley) who do not
have the ball and who often are hit when in a vulnerable position and from   35
a blind side. But there are limits to what rules changes—even 30-yard penalties for unnecessary roughness—can do for a game that is fundamentally
unsafe.

7   Football is more than a "contact sport." As a coach has said: Dancing is a contact sport, football is a collision sport. Football is physics: Force   40
equals Mass times Acceleration. It is especially dangerous for youngsters,
whose neck muscles have not developed, but it is always dangerous to all
spines and knees. They are not built for the kinds of collisions inevitable in
football, collisions that are becoming worse as the weight differential between linemen and backs increases.   45

8   Quarterbacks suffer one-seventh of all serious injuries. On the last
weekend of this year's exhibition games, four NFL quarterbacks were injured. Last season, 20 quarterbacks on the 28 NFL teams were incapacitated.
On the first Saturday of last season, half the Big Eight teams lost their first-
string quarterbacks. By midseason, eight Southwest Conference first-string   50
quarterbacks were out, and Texas was using its fourth quarterback. Georgia
lost its fourth and fifth in the final game. Such injuries are not always
unintentional: "Taking out" quarterbacks is a tactic.

9   As Underwood says, the insecurity of coaches, the short careers of
players who are competing for high stakes, and the inherent violence, not   55
to say frenzy, of the game produce a "war ethic." And often there is chemical
warfare as players, and especially defensive linemen, use amphetamines in
order to achieve (in the decorous words of Fran Tarkenton, Minnesota
Vikings quarterback) "a final plateau of endurance and competitive zeal."

10   Most coaches want "gang tackling" in which most tackles are, as   60

Underwood says, "vicious exclamation points." Sportscasters burble praise of those who play with "complete abandon" in an atmosphere of rule-bending.

11   Football involves large squads of players who are increasingly specialized according to an elaborate division of labor ("special teams" and   65 linemen who play only on "third and short yardage"). This is why football is primarily a coaches' game. If the mayhem continues to increase, some coaches may find themselves defendants in lawsuits, and the web of liability may ensnare schools and officials.

12   It is only a matter of time before a national television audience sees   70 a player killed as "part of the game."

QUESTIONS

READER AND PURPOSE

1. What is Will arguing exactly: that football needs to be made safer, or that it should be banned altogether?

2. Is his argument deductive or inductive? If the latter, what sort of evidence does he advance?

3. Will frequently cites the remarks of coaches. Why are their comments particularly effective for his purpose?

4. Do you think that Will is writing primarily for football fans? If not, for what kind of reader? Be able to support your answer by details from the text.

5. Considering Will's purpose, is his title a good one? Is it fair? (Think carefully about what "fair" means in such a case.)

ORGANIZATION

6. This selection was written for newspapers. Compared to more formal essays it uses briefer paragraphs and looser organization. For instance, paragraphs 3, 4, 5, 9, 10, and 11 each consist of only two sentences; the final paragraph of only one. There are no explicit links between paragraphs 2 and 1, 4 and 3, 10 and 9, 11 and 10; and elsewhere the linkage is light. Such features are characteristic of journalistic prose and certainly not to be construed as flaws. What advantages do you find in the shorter paragraphing and looser structure? What disadvantages?

7. Paragraph 1 is the beginning of the article. Is it skillful—identifying the subject, establishing a point of view, attracting the reader's interest?

8. Is the final paragraph a good closing? Would it have been more effective, or less, if it had been joined to paragraph 11 instead of being paragraphed separately? Notice that it repeats a phrase used at the beginning: what phrase?

This technique of repeating at the close of an essay a word, phrase, or image used at the beginning is a way of signaling readers that you are coming to the end. It is called cyclic return.

9. Study the sentences in paragraph 2. By their similar openings the first two statements draw our attention to dates. Why does Will do this—what is he implying? Except for the phrase "In 1973" the final three sentences of this paragraph also open in the same way. What is the advantage of the similarity?

10. Paragraph 3 is a good example of "anticipation and refutation," a device of argument in which you think ahead to the kind of evidence or assertion that may be used against you and counter it in advance. What opposing argument does Will anticipate? How does he neutralize it?

11. What is the topic of the eighth paragraph? How is it supported?

SENTENCES

12. The first sentence of paragraph 2 contains three ideas: President Theodore Roosevelt demanded in 1905 that football be made safer, Roosevelt enjoyed war and the strenuous life, and in 1905 eighteen football players were killed. Which of these is the main clause *? Which two are expressed in subordinate clauses *? Why is the information conveyed by the subordinate constructions important to the writer's point? But if it is important, why doesn't he express it in independent clauses or in separate sentences, perhaps as in the following revision?

> President Theodore Roosevelt enjoyed war and other forms of the strenuous life. In 1905 he demanded civilizing rules changes for football. The game had killed 18 players that year.

13. What does the dash in line 18 signal? Suppose the series in that sentence had read "spinal damage, ruptured spleens, and bruised kidneys," instead of "spinal damage, ruptured spleens, bruised kidneys": would the sense have been subtly altered?

14. Identify the appositive * in the sentence in lines 29-30. Why is the information it conveys necessary? In line 44 there is another appositive: the repetition of "collision." Imagine the sentence without that repetition: would the point be as clear? What purpose does the appositive serve here?

15. In lines 64-66 which word(s) in the main clause does the parenthetical remark expand? Is there any advantage to placing it within parentheses?

DICTION

16. Look up: *strenuous* (8), *virtually* (17), *vulnerable* (33), *fundamentally* (37), *tactic* (53), *mayhem* (67), *liability* (68).

17. What precisely does each of these phrases mean: *blind side* (36), *weight differential* (44), *inherent violence* (55), *war ethic* (56)?

18. In paragraph 5 indicate the verbs that convey vigorous action.

19. In line 30 why does the writer use hyphens in *below-the-waist?*

20. Explain why each of these revisions is poorer than Will's diction: *marring* for *desecrating* (1), *late December* for *Christmas* (1), *praise* for *burble praise of* (61), *engulf* for *ensnare* (69).

21. In what sense is the phrase *decorous words* (58) ironic *? What is Will implying?

POINTS TO LEARN

1. Evidence is particularly compelling when it derives from those who sympathize with the other side.

2. Anticipate and neutralize the arguments of your opponents.

3. One way of signaling "the end" is to repeat a phrase or word made prominent in the beginning.

4. Subordinate ideas which are necessary to your main point but are of lesser significance.

5. In describing physical action use strong, vigorous verbs.

SUGGESTIONS FOR WRITING

Compose an essay of about 500 words on one of the topics listed below. Do not merely voice your opinion: give substance to your argument by citing specific evidence. You may use only three or four paragraphs, adequately linked, or you may imitate the short paragraphs and loose structure of Will's piece.

> An answer to Will's complaints against football

> An argument for (or against) the abolition or tighter control of automobile racing, hunting, ice hockey

> An argument that our culture's wide-spread involvement in sports is (or is not) healthy

IMPROVING YOUR STYLE

In your essay include:

1. An eye-catching title.

2. At least one place where you anticipate and refute a possible objection.

3. A brief closing paragraph using a cyclic return.

4. Several appositives.

5. Two or three ironic * words or phrases like Will's *burble the praises of* or *decorous words.*

The Iks

Lewis Thomas is a physician and scientist, president of the Memorial Sloan-Kettering Cancer Center in New York. In addition to scientific research he writes on a variety of subjects—personal, sensitive, meditative essays about the conditions of modern life. "The Iks" appears in a collection of such essays, *The Lives of a Cell* (1974). It is a response to a book by the anthropologist Colin Trumbull, who spent several years living with a primitive African tribe whose society had degenerated into a kind of demented individualism—a war of each against all. While Thomas does not quarrel with Trumbull's assessment of the Iks themselves, he does take issue with the philosophical conclusion the anthropologist draws from his experience with the tribe. As you read, consider the basis of Thomas's disagreement and what alternative meaning he sees in the Iks.

1   The small tribe of Iks, formerly nomadic hunters and gatherers in the mountain valleys of northern Uganda, have become celebrities, literary symbols for the ultimate fate of disheartened, heartless mankind at large. Two disastrously conclusive things happened to them: the government decided to have a national park, so they were compelled by law to give 5 up hunting in the valleys and become farmers on poor hillside soil, and then they were visited for two years by an anthropologist who detested them and wrote a book about them.

2   The message of the book is that the Iks have transformed themselves into an irreversibly disagreeable collection of unattached, brutish 10 creatures, totally selfish and loveless, in response to the dismantling of their traditional culture. Moreover, this is what the rest of us are like in our inner selves, and we will all turn into Iks when the structure of our society comes all unhinged.

3   The argument rests, of course, on certain assumptions about the   15
core of human beings, and is necessarily speculative. You have to agree in
advance that man is fundamentally a bad lot, out for himself alone, displaying such graces as affection and compassion only as learned habits. If
you take this view, the story of the Iks can be used to confirm it. These
people seem to be living together, clustered in small, dense villages, but they   20
are really solitary, unrelated individuals with no evident use for each other.
They talk, but only to make ill-tempered demands and cold refusals. They
share nothing. They never sing. They turn the children out to forage as soon
as they can walk, and desert the elders to starve whenever they can, and the
foraging children snatch food from the mouths of the helpless elders. It   25
is a mean society.

4   They breed without love or even casual regard. They defecate on
each other's doorsteps. They watch their neighbors for signs of misfortune,
and only then do they laugh. In the book they do a lot of laughing, having
so much bad luck. Several times they even laughed at the anthropologist,   30
who found this especially repellent (one senses, between the lines, that the
scholar is not himself the world's luckiest man). Worse, they took him
into the family, snatched his food, defecated on his doorstep, and hooted
dislike at him. They gave him two bad years.

5   It is a depressing book. If, as he suggests, there is only Ikness at the   35
center of each of us, our sole hope for hanging on to the name of humanity
will be in endlessly mending the structure of our society, and it is changing
so quickly and completely that we may never find the threads in time.
Meanwhile, left to ourselves alone, solitary, we will become the same
joyless, zestless, untouching lone animals.   40

6   But this may be too narrow a view. For one thing, the Iks are
extraordinary. They are absolutely astonishing, in fact. The anthropologist
has never seen people like them anywhere, nor have I. You'd think, if they
were simply examples of the common essence of mankind, they'd seem
more recognizable. Instead, they are bizarre, anomalous. I have known my   45
share of peculiar, difficult, nervous, grabby people, but I've never encountered any genuinely, consistently detestable human beings in all my life.
The Iks sound more like abnormalities, maladies.

7   I cannot accept it. I do not believe that the Iks are representative of
isolated, revealed man, unobscured by social habits. I believe their behavior   50
is something extra, something laid on. This unremitting, compulsive re-
pellence is a kind of complicated ritual. They must have learned to act this
way; they copied it, somehow.

8   I have a theory, then. The Iks have gone crazy.

9   The solitary Ik, isolated in the ruins of an exploded culture, has   55
built a new defense for himself. If you live in an unworkable society you
can make up one of your own, and this is what the Iks have done. Each Ik
has become a group, a one-man tribe on its own, a constituency.

10   Now everything falls into place. This is why they do seem, after all,
vaguely familiar to all of us. We've seen them before. This is precisely the   60
way groups of one size or another, ranging from committees to nations,
behave. It is, of course, this aspect of humanity that has lagged behind the
rest of evolution, and this is why the Ik seems so primitive. In his absolute
selfishness, his incapacity to give anything away, no matter what, he is a
successful committee. When he stands at the door of his hut, shouting   65
insults at his neighbors in a loud harangue, he is city addressing another
city.

11   Cities have all the Ik characteristics. They defecate on doorsteps,
in rivers and lakes, their own or anyone else's. They leave rubbish. They
detest all neighboring cities, give nothing away. They even build institutions   70
for deserting elders out of sight.

12   Nations are the most Iklike of all. No wonder the Iks seem familiar.
For total greed, rapacity, heartlessness, and irresponsibility there is nothing
to match a nation. Nations, by law, are solitary, self-centered, withdrawn
into themselves. There is no such thing as affection between nations, and   75
certainly no nation ever loved another. They bawl insults from their doorsteps, defecate into whole oceans, snatch all the food, survive by detestation,
take joy in the bad luck of others, celebrate the death of others, live for the
death of others.

13   That's it, and I shall stop worrying about the book. It does not   80
signify that man is a sparse, inhuman thing at his center. He's all right. It
only says what we've always known and never had enough time to worry
about, that we haven't yet learned how to stay human when assembled in
masses. The Ik, in his despair, is acting out this failure, and perhaps we
should pay closer attention. Nations have themselves become too frighten-   85
ing to think about, but we might learn some things by watching these
people.

QUESTIONS

READER AND PURPOSE

1. How does Thomas's conclusion about the Iks differ from Trumbull's?
2. What sort of evidence does he call upon: statistics, examples, his own beliefs, common knowledge?
3. Would you describe his tone * as formal and "lecturish," or as relaxed and conversational? Is his point of view * personal or impersonal? Which word (or words) best describes his attitude toward his subject—angry, amused, bitter, calm, contemptuous, pessimistic, optimistic?
4. Does Thomas suppose that his readers are familiar with Trumbull's book? What does he assume they know?

ORGANIZATION

5. This essay has two major sections. Which sentence swings us from the first to the second? What does Thomas do in part 1? In 2? Can you discern subdivisions within each of these parts?
6. How does the brief eighth paragraph function in the organization of the essay?
7. What words provide the linkage between paragraphs 2 and 1? Between 6 and 5? 11 and 10?
8. Study paragraphs 9-13 and show that there is a change of topic to justify each new paragraph.
9. What is the topic of paragraph 11? How is it supported?
10. Analyze the internal linkage of paragraph 3, explaining how each sentence is tied to what precedes it, whether by the repetition of key terms, by sentence pattern, or by connective words.
11. In line 32 how does *worse* help to link the last sentence of the paragraph to the one before it?

SENTENCES

12. Thomas is very readable, in part because he varies sentence length and structure. Study paragraph 4 in this regard and be able to discuss how it avoids the monotony of this revision:

> They breed without love or even casual regard. They defecate on each other's doorsteps. They watch their neighbors for signs of misfortune. Only then do they laugh. In the book they do a lot of laughing. They have had so much bad luck. Several times they even laughed at the anthropologist. He found this especially repellent. (One senses, between the lines, that the scholar himself is not the world's luckiest

man.) Worse, they took him into the family. They snatched his food. They defecated on his doorstep. They hooted dislike at him. They gave him a bad two years.

13. This essay contains a number of short sentences. Do they serve purposes other than variety?
14. Identify the appositives * in the sentences in lines 1-4 and 57-58. The parallelism * in the sentence in lines 76-79.
15. What does the colon signal in line 4?
16. How do these revisions alter the emphasis of the original sentences?

(a) *Revision:* He is city addressing another city when he stands at the door of his hut, shouting insults at his neighbors in a loud harangue.
Thomas: "When he stands at the door of his hut, shouting insults at his neighbors in a loud harangue, he is city addressing another city." (65-67)

(b) *Revision:* By law nations are solitary and self-centered, withdrawn into themselves.
Thomas: "Nations, by law, are solitary, self-centered, withdrawn into themselves." (74-75)

(c) *Revision:* In his despair the Ik is acting out this failure and perhaps we should pay closer attention.
Thomas: "The Ik, in his despair, is acting out this failure, and perhaps we should pay closer attention." (84-85)

DICTION

17. Look up: *dismantling* (11), *unhinged* (14), *assumptions* (15), *graces* (18), *forage* (23), *repellent* (31), *zestless* (40), *bizarre* (45), *compulsive* (51), *constituency* (58), *harangue* (66), *rapacity* (73), *detestation* (77), *sparse* (81).
18. What is meant by each of the following phrases: *nomadic hunters and gatherers* (1), *ultimate fate* (3), *brutish courage* (10), *traditional culture* (12), *an exploded culture* (55)?
19. How do the etymologies * of these words help to clarify their use: *anthropologist* (7), *speculative* (16), *compassion* (18), *scholar* (32), *essence* (44), *anomalous* (45), *maladies* (48), *primitive* (63).
20. Thomas frequently employs *you* (line 16, for example) in the generic sense of "anyone," "people in general," rather than in the specific sense of the individual(s) he is addressing. Does this usage make his tone more formal, or less? Some teachers object to the generic *you* (it does get out of hand easily). Do you think the objection is sound? What alternatives to the generic *you* can you think of? What rule might writers follow with regard to this use of the pronoun?

21. In the sentence in lines 35-38 what later word picks up the image suggested by *mending?* Would *fabric* be a better choice than *structure* in line 37?
22. Explain the relationship in thought signaled by these connectives *: *moreover* (12), *of course* (15), *instead* (45), *then* (54).
23. The parenthetical remark in lines 31-32 is an example of the figure of speech called "litotes." Look up this term.

POINTS TO LEARN
1. Personal beliefs and opinions are a legitimate kind of evidence, provided they are not outrageous and not disguised as something else.
2. The major sections of an essay should be clearly indicated, and transitions provided between them.
3. Varying sentence length and structure while retaining some similarity helps make prose readable.
4. Short sentences make good topic statements.
5. The generic *you* ought to be employed sparingly and only with an informal tone.

SUGGESTIONS FOR WRITING
In 500-600 words (4-5 paragraphs) compose an argument on one of the topics below. Support your contention by examples and by your own beliefs and opinions. Write from a personal point of view and try for a relaxed, conversational tone.

> Young people today are (are not) less aggressive and more tolerant than were previous generations.
>
> Human beings really are "Iks"; their "Ikness" simply does not show itself when things are going well.

IMPROVING YOUR STYLE
1. Begin at least two paragraphs of your essay with short simple sentences of no more than eight words.
2. In one paragraph unify a series of three or four sentences by keeping them all short and simple and beginning them with the same word.
3. Use *moreover, of course,* and *then* once each to introduce sentences.
4. Try an example of litotes.

From The Annual Message to Congress, December 1, 1862

Abraham Lincoln (1809-65), the sixteenth President (1861-65), was one of our most articulate, as well as able, statesmen. He is deservedly famous for the eloquence and compassion of his addresses at Gettysburg and at his second inauguration. Those speeches were not happy accidents. Lincoln usually spoke and wrote lucidly and precisely, qualities of mind and style evident in this passage from the Annual Message to Congress he delivered in 1862. Lincoln's words are a fine example of sober, thoughtful persuasion. His immediate purpose is not to attack slavery or to defend the policy of waging war to force the Confederate States back into the union. It is rather to make clear a fundamental truth about that union. As you read, look to understand the fact upon which Lincoln insists.

1   A nation may be said to consist of its territory, its people, and its laws. The territory is the only part which is of certain durability. "One generation passeth away, and another generation cometh, but the earth abideth forever." It is of the first importance to duly consider, and estimate, this ever-enduring part. That portion of the earth's surface which is owned 5 and inhabited by the people of the United States, is well adapted to be the home of one national family; and it is not well adapted for two, or more. Its vast extent, and its variety of climate and productions, are of advantage, in this age, for one people, whatever they might have been in former ages. Steam, telegraphs, and intelligence, have brought these, to be an advan- 10 tageous combination, for one united people.

2   In the inaugural address I briefly pointed out the total inadequacy of disunion, as a remedy for the differences between the people of the two sections. I did so in language which I cannot improve, and which, therefore, I beg to repeat: 15

3   "One section of our country believes slavery is *right*, and ought to be extended, while the other believes it is *wrong*, and ought not to be extended. This is the only substantial dispute. The fugitive slave clause of the Constitution, and the law for the suppression of the foreign slave trade, are each as well enforced, perhaps, as any law can ever be in a community where the moral sense of the people imperfectly supports the law itself. The great body of the people abide by the dry legal obligation in both cases, and a few break over in each. This, I think, cannot be perfectly cured; and it would be worse in both cases *after* the separation of the sections, than before. The foreign slave trade, now imperfectly suppressed, would be ultimately revived without restriction in one section; while fugitive slaves, now only partially surrendered, would not be surrendered at all by the other.

4   "Physically speaking, we cannot separate. We cannot remove our respective sections from each other, nor build an impassable wall between them. A husband and wife may be divorced, and go out of the presence, and beyond the reach of each other; but the different parts of our country cannot do this. They cannot but remain face to face; and intercourse, either amicable or hostile, must continue between them. Is it possible, then, to make that intercourse more advantageous, or more satisfactory, *after* separation than *before*? Can aliens make treaties, easier than friends can make laws? Can treaties be more faithfully enforced between aliens, than laws can among friends? Suppose you go to war, you cannot fight always; and when, after much loss on both sides, and no gain on either, you cease fighting, the identical old questions, as to terms of intercourse, are again upon you."

5   There is no line, straight or crooked, suitable for a national boundary, upon which to divide. Trace through, from east to west, upon the line between the free and slave country, and we shall find a little more than one-third of its length are rivers, easy to be crossed, and populated, or soon to be populated, thickly upon both sides; while nearly all its remaining length, are merely surveyor's lines, over which people may walk back and forth without any consciousness of their presence. No part of this line can be made any more difficult to pass, by writing it down on paper, or parchment, as a national boundary. The fact of separation, if it comes, gives up, on the part of the seceding section, the fugitive slave clause, along with all other constitutional obligations upon the section seceded from, while I should expect no treaty stipulation would ever be made to take its place.

6   But there is another difficulty. The great interior region, bounded

east by the Alleghanies, north by the British dominions, west by the Rocky 55
mountains, and south by the line along which the culture of corn and cotton meets, and which includes part of Virginia, part of Tennessee, all of
Kentucky, Ohio, Indiana, Michigan, Wisconsin, Illinois, Missouri, Kansas,
Iowa, Minnesota and the Territories of Dakota, Nebraska, and part of
Colorado, already has above ten millions of people, and will have fifty mil- 60
lions within fifty years, if not prevented by any political folly or mistake. It
contains more than one-third of the country owned by the United States—
certainly more than one million of square miles. Once half as populous as
Massachusetts already is, it would have more than seventy-five millions of
people. A glance at the map shows that, territorially speaking, it is the great 65
body of the republic. The other parts are but marginal borders to it, the
magnificent region sloping west from the rocky mountains to the Pacific,
being the deepest, and also the richest, in undeveloped resources. In the
production of provisions, grains, grasses, and all which proceed from them,
this great interior region is naturally one of the most important in the 70
world. Ascertain from the statistics the small proportion of the region
which has, as yet, been brought into cultivation, and also the large and
rapidly increasing amount of its products, and we shall be overwhelmed
with the magnitude of the prospect presented. An[d] yet this region has no
sea-coast, touches no ocean anywhere. As part of one nation, its people now 75
find, and may forever find, their way to Europe by New York, to South
America and Africa by New Orleans, and to Asia by San Francisco. But
separate our common country into two nations, as designed by the present
rebellion, and every man of this great interior region is thereby cut off from
some one or more of these outlets, not, perhaps, by a physical barrier, but 80
by embarrassing and onerous trade regulations.

7   And this is true, wherever a dividing, or boundary line, may be
fixed. Place it between the now free and slave country, or place it south of
Kentucky, or north of Ohio, and still the truth remains, that none south
of it, can trade to any port or place north of it, and none north of it, can 85
trade to any port or place south of it, except upon terms dictated by a government foreign to them. These outlets, east, west, and south, are indispensable to the well-being of the people inhabiting, and to inhabit, this
vast interior region. Which of the three may be the best, is no proper question. All, are better than either, and all, of right, belong to that people, and 90
to their successors forever. True to themselves, they will not ask where a
line of separation shall be, but will vow, rather, that there shall be no such
line. Nor are the marginal regions less interested in these communications

to, and through them, to the great outside world. They too, and each of them, must have access to this Egypt of the West, without paying toll at 95
the crossing of any national boundary.

8   Our national strife springs not from our permanent part; not from the land we inhabit; not from our national homestead. There is no possible severing of this, but would multiply, and not mitigate, evils among us. In all its adaptations and aptitudes, it demands union, and abhors separation. 100
In fact, it would, ere long, force reunion, however much of blood and treasure the separation might have cost.

9   Our strife pertains to ourselves—to the passing generations of men; and it can, without convulsion, be hushed forever with the passing of one generation. 105

QUESTIONS

READER AND PURPOSE

1. The President is required to deliver annually to Congress a statement about the condition of the nation and about what measures he thinks Congress should adopt. In this portion of his Second Annual Message Lincoln is leading up to his proposal that an act be passed freeing the slaves. (Though the Civil War was in its second year, slavery still had not been abolished by Federal legislation.) What Lincoln is arguing here is best expressed in the second paragraph. What is it?

ORGANIZATION

2. Lincoln begins with a brief definition of a nation. What element in that definition is especially important to the argument he will develop?
3. How does the Biblical allusion in the second and fourth lines (Ecclesiastes, 1:4) relate to his argument?
4. In paragraph 3 Lincoln offers one reason to support his claim that disunion will not solve the slavery question. Summarize that reason in your own words.
5. He suggests a second reason in paragraph 4, a reason which, in the immediate context of his speech, is more important. What is that? Why does he bring up (31-32) the case of a divorce between man and wife? How do the rhetorical questions in lines 34-38 support his argument?
6. Do the reasons brought forward in paragraphs 3 and 4 constitute an empirical argument?
7. What is the topic sentence of the fifth paragraph? Does this paragraph introduce a new argument, different from that in paragraph 4, or is it merely a continuation of the preceding idea?

8. What is the function of the opening sentence of paragraph 6? Do paragraphs 6 and 7 present a new argument? If so, summarize it.

9. The final two paragraphs close off Lincoln's argument. What pair of conclusions does he draw? How is the ninth paragraph tied to the eighth?

10. While paragraph 9 is not the end of Lincoln's speech, it does round off a portion of it. How does Lincoln signal that he has finished?

SENTENCES

11. Lincoln's oratorical style employs frequent parallelism * and balanced * construction (in which a sentence or part of a sentence is divided into two or more units of relatively equal length and importance). For example, in the statement "I did so in language which I cannot improve, and which, therefore, I beg leave to repeat," two parallel clauses modify "language": (1) "which I cannot improve" and (2) "which, therefore, I beg to repeat." These clauses are coordinated * and balanced against each other, and the key terms in each—"cannot improve" and "repeat"—by being placed in the same relative positions are played off one against the other. Analyze the following sentences, identifying the parallel constructions and indicating which words are made prominent and balanced together by the sentence structure.

(a) "One section of our country believes slavery is *right*, and ought to be extended, while the other believes it is *wrong*, and ought not to be extended." (16-18)

(b) "The great body of the people abide by the dry legal obligation in both cases, and a few break over in each." (22-23)

(c) "The foreign slave trade, now imperfectly suppressed, would be ultimately revived without restriction in one section; while fugitive slaves, now only partially surrendered, would not be surrendered at all by the other." (25-28)

(d) "Can aliens make treaties, easier than friends can make laws?" (36-37)

(e) "In all its adaptations and aptitudes, it demands union, and abhors separation." (99-100)

12. Lincoln skilfully varies this elaborate, literary style with occasional short, direct statements, such as "Physically speaking, we cannot separate" (29). Point to several similar sentences and consider whether they have any special virtue aside from variation.

13. Lincoln's power as a speaker came chiefly from the acuteness of his thought and from his ability to express that thought in exact and concise language. But partly, too, it came from a poetic sensitivity to the sounds of words, a sensitivity derived perhaps from frequent reading and listening to the prose of the King James Bible. The final sentence of this selection, for instance, is conceived in

rhythmic units which scan * like the passage from Ecclesiastes to which it alludes. Something of the effect of such prose may be suggested by realigning it and indicating the stresses (though it should be acknowledged that the result is to a degree subjective and that other readers may hear the sentence differently):

> "Our strife pertains to ourselves—
>
> to the passing generations of men;
>
> and it can, without convulsion,
>
> be hushed forever
>
> with the passing of one generation."

Such prose is moving and memorable; it endows its subject with an aura of momentousness. Something important, we feel, is being said. Point out one or two other of Lincoln's sentences in which the rhythm strikes you as particularly effective.

14. Another aspect of Lincoln's attention to sound is his propensity to alliteration *, as in "Our national strife springs not from our permanent part. . . ." Find other examples of this device. Prose writers are sometimes warned against alliteration as being a jarring distraction. Does it seem so in these paragraphs?

DICTION

15. Look up: *durability* (2), *abideth* (4), *inaugural* (12), *suppression* (19), *amicable* (34), *aliens* (36), *parchment* (49), *stipulation* (53), *ascertain* (71), *overwhelmed* (73), *onerous* (81), *abhors* (100), *convulsion* (104).

16. Explain as fully as you can what the following expressions mean: *substantial dispute* (18), *dry legal obligation* (22), *the culture of corn and cotton* (56-57), *political folly* (61).

17. To what Biblical story is Lincoln alluding in the phrase *Egypt of the West* (95)? Has his vision of the American midwest come true?

18. In line 10 Lincoln uses *intelligence* in an old-fashioned sense. Explain its meaning.

19. What does *but* mean in line 33?

POINTS TO LEARN

1. A bad argument is not made good by verbal style; but a good argument may be enhanced by style.

2. Well-written prose pleases the ear.

SUGGESTIONS FOR WRITING

1. In a paragraph of about two hundred words write a précis of Lincoln's argument.

2. Suppose that you are opposed to Lincoln. How would you answer his argument that the very geography of America makes the existence of two nations impossible?

IMPROVING YOUR STYLE

In your composition include:

1. Two balanced sentences.

2. Three sentences using parallelism.

3. A closing sentence like Lincoln's in which you try to create a relatively regular rhythm.

4. Several short, direct sentences of five or six words set against the more elaborate constructions.

Are Women Human?

Dorothy L. Sayers (1893-1957) was an English writer, best known for her detective fiction. She also wrote essays on more serious topics (*Begin Here,* 1940, and *The Mind of the Maker,* 1941) and was noted for her translation and scholarly editing of Dante's *The Divine Comedy* (1949). In this selection from *Unpopular Opinions* (1946) she is arguing against the view that as workers women are inferior to men. Her strategy is twofold: to attack (1) the claim that men put the job first, and (2) the criticism that women do not. Notice how she develops this strategy and the kind of evidence she adduces.

1   Now, it is frequently asserted that, with women, the job does not come first. What (people cry) are women doing with this liberty of theirs? What woman really prefers a job to a home and family? Very few, I admit. It is unfortunate that they should so often have to make the choice. A man does not, as a rule, have to choose. He gets both. In fact, if he wants the 5 home and family, he usually has to take the job as well, if he can get it. Nevertheless, there have been women, such as Queen Elizabeth and Florence Nightingale, who had the choice, and chose the job and made a success of it. And there have been and are many men who have sacrificed their careers for women—sometimes, like Antony or Parnell, very disastrously. 10 When it comes to a *choice,* then every man or woman has to choose as an individual human being, and, like a human being, take the consequences.

2   As human beings! I am always entertained—and also irritated—by the newsmongers who inform us, with a bright air of discovery, that they have questioned a number of female workers and been told by one and all 15 that they are "sick of the office and would love to get out of it." In the name of God, what human being is *not,* from time to time, heartily sick of the office and would *not* love to get out of it? The time of female office-workers

is daily wasted in sympathising with disgruntled male colleagues who yearn
to get out of the office. No human being likes work—not day in and day out. 20
Work is notoriously a curse—and if women *liked* everlasting work they
would not be human beings at all. *Being* human beings, they like work just
as much and just as little as anybody else. They dislike perpetual washing
and cooking just as much as perpetual typing and standing behind shop
counters. Some of them prefer typing to scrubbing—but that does not mean 25
that they are not, as human beings, entitled to damn and blast the type-
writer when they feel that way. The number of men who daily damn and
blast typewriters is incalculable; but that does not mean that they would be
happier doing a little plain sewing. Nor would the women.

3   I have admitted that there are very few women who would put their 30
job before every earthly consideration. I will go further and assert that there
are very few men who would do it either. In fact, there is perhaps only one
human being in a thousand who is passionately interested in his job for the
job's sake. The difference is that if that one person in a thousand is a man,
we say, simply, that he is passionately keen on his job; if she is a woman, we 35
say she is a freak. It is extraordinarily entertaining to watch the historians of
the past, for instance, entangling themselves in what they were pleased to
call the "problem" of Queen Elizabeth. They invented the most complicated and astonishing reasons both for her success as a sovereign and for her
tortuous matrimonial policy. She was the tool of Burleigh, she was the tool 40
of Leicester, she was the fool of Essex; she was diseased, she was deformed,
she was a man in disguise. She was a mystery, and must have some extraordinary solution. Only recently has it occurred to a few enlightened people that
the solution might be quite simple after all. She might be one of the rare
people who were born into the right job and put that job first. Whereupon 45
a whole series of riddles cleared themselves up by magic. She was in love
with Leicester—why didn't she marry him? Well, for the very same reason
that numberless kings have not married their lovers—because it would have
thrown a spanner into the wheels of the State machine. Why was she so
bloodthirsty and unfeminine as to sign the death-warrant of Mary Queen of 50
Scots? For much the same reasons that induced King George V to say that if
the House of Lords did not pass the Parliament Bill he would create enough
new peers to force it through—because she was, in the measure of her time, a
constitutional sovereign, and knew that there was a point beyond which a
sovereign could not defy Parliament. Being a rare human being with her eye 55
to the job, she did what was necessary; being an ordinary human being, she
hesitated a good deal before embarking on unsavoury measures—but as to

feminine mystery, there is no such thing about it, and nobody, had she been a man, would have thought either her statesmanship or her humanity in any way mysterious. Remarkable they were—but she was a very remarkable per- 60 son. Among her most remarkable achievements was that of showing that sovereignty was one of the jobs for which the right kind of woman was particularly well fitted.

QUESTIONS

READER AND PURPOSE

1. Sayers defends the intellectual quality of women, basing her case upon empirical evidence. What specific examples does she cite? In lines 20 ff. she relies upon a series of assertions rather than upon particular illustrations. Do these assertions constitute common knowledge or ought they to be proven?

2. Originally Sayers delivered this material as a speech, and, as her personal point of view * suggests, the occasion was rather informal. What details of her style indicate that these paragraphs were addressed to women rather than to men?

ORGANIZATION

3. The first complaint Sayers answers is that women do not stick to their jobs, preferring marriage to a career. Does she admit this?

4. What does the fifth sentence suggest about why women give up their jobs when they marry? What do the sixth and seventh imply about the right of men to criticize women for choosing a family? What does the eighth sentence suggest about why men stick to their jobs? What, finally, is the effect of all these points upon the admission Sayers made in the fourth sentence? All in all, the first sentences of paragraph 1 are a masterly job of concession, well worth studying.

5. The concession made, what word signals the return to the main line of argument? What is the writer's purpose in alluding to Queen Elizabeth and Florence Nightingale? What do the references to Antony and Parnell prove?

6. Sum up Sayers's answer to the "fact" that women do not stick to the job because they prefer a home and family.

7. In the second paragraph the writer answers a new charge: that women do not really like to work. Indicate the main lines of her reply to this criticism.

8. In paragraph 3 how does the writer use the historical explanations of the "problem" of Queen Elizabeth to attack the notion that women are inferior? How does her own solution to the "problem" affirm their equality? Might it even be said that in her final sentence Sayers goes somewhat beyond her original claim?

SENTENCES

9. In the following cases explain why the revision is inferior to what Sayers wrote:

> (a) *Revision:* Since he gets both, a man does not, as a rule have to choose.
> *Sayers:* "A man does not, as a rule, have to choose. He gets both." (4-5)
> (b) *Revision:* But, after all, most human beings are from time to time sick of the office and would love to get out of it.
> *Sayers:* "In the name of God, what human being is *not*, from time to time, heartily sick of the office and would *not* love to get out of it?" (16-18)
> (c) *Revision:* They were remarkable but she was a very remarkable person.
> *Sayers:* "Remarkable they were—but she was a very remarkable person." (60-61)

10. Read aloud the two sentences in lines 40-43 summing up the various explanations of Queen Elizabeth. How is Sayers subtly mocking these "explanations"?

11. Imagine how Sayers would have spoken the sentence in line 13: "As human beings!" What overtones of meaning do you hear? What is unusual about the form of this sentence?

12. How does the italicization of *choice* in line 11 affect the reading of that sentence? Where else does Sayers italicize words for a similar purpose?

DICTION

13. Look up: *asserted* (1), *Antony* (10), *Parnell* (10), *disgruntled* (19), *tortuous* (40), *spanner* (49), *constitutional sovereign* (54), *unsavoury* (57).

14. What are the connotations * of *newsmonger* (14)? Of *a bright air of discovery* (14)? Of *a few enlightened people* (43)?

15. Since Sayers was speaking informally she used colloquialisms * such as *thrown a spanner* (49). List four or five other examples. In argument people are usually impressed not only by what one says, but by how one says it. Do you think the tone * suggested by her diction helps Sayers's argument, or at least makes her audience more receptive?

16. Suppose *moreover* or *furthermore* were substituted in line 9 for *and:* how would this affect the tone?

17. Explain what relationship in idea the following pointers * prepare us for: *now* (1), *in fact* (5 and 32), *and* (9), *nor* (29), *whereupon* (45), *well* (47).

18. In line 13 Sayers tells us that she is "entertained—and also irritated—" by

those who question women's equality. Point out three or four words or phrases which reveal irritation; three or four which reveal amusement.

POINTS TO LEARN

1. The empirical argument looks to experience. It may cite examples or appeal to common knowledge.

2. Tone is important to argument. Not in itself evidence, tone creates an atmosphere in which evidence will be more readily accepted, or, if the tone is inappropriate, more summarily rejected.

SUGGESTIONS FOR WRITING

Develop an empirical argument to support one of the opinions listed below. You may use either specific illustrations or appeal to general knowledge, or you may do both.

Women are inferior to men.

Actually, women are superior to men.

Girls (or boys) are better students than boys (or girls).

Freshmen are the intellectual equals of sophomores.

IMPROVING YOUR STYLE

Assume that you are talking to an audience of your compeers and aim at a colloquial (but not slangy) style. In your composition include:

1. Two or three short sentences set beside longer ones for emphatic contrast (like Sayers's sentence in lines 4-5).

2. (With your instructor's approval) one or two fragments.

3. The connectives * now, in fact, nor, and, well to introduce sentences.

Confessions of a Female Chauvinist Sow

Anne Roiphe is an author and journalist whose works include *Digging Out*
(1967), *Up the Sandbox* (1970), and *Long Division* (1972). In the following
essay she works against the grain of feminism. Her argument, however, is not
a defense of the traditional view of women. Consider as you read, exactly what
Roiphe is arguing and what kind of evidence she calls upon.

1   I once married a man I thought was totally unlike my father and
I imagined a whole new world of freedom emerging. Five years later it was
clear even to me—floating face down in a wash of despair—that I had
simply chosen a replica of my handsome daddy-true. The updated version
spoke English like an angel but—good God!—underneath he was my father 5
exactly: wonderful, but not the right man for me.

2   Most people I know have at one time or another been fouled up
by their childhood experiences. Patterns tend to sink into the unconscious
only to reappear, disguised, unseen, like marionette strings, pulling us
this way or that. Whatever ails people—keeps them up at night, tossing 10
and turning—also ails movements no matter how historically huge or politically important. The women's movement cannot remake consciousness, or
reshape the future, without acknowledging and shedding all the unnecessary and ugly baggage of the past. It's easy enough now to see where men
have kept us out of clubs, baseball games, graduate schools; it's easy enough 15
to recognize the hidden directions that limit Sis to cake-baking and Junior
to bridge-building; it's now possible for even Miss America herself to identify what *they* have done to us, and, of course, *they* have and *they* did and
they are. . . . But along the way we also developed our own hidden prejudices, class assumptions and an anti-male humor and collection of expecta- 20
tions that gave us, like all oppressed groups, a secret sense of superiority

From *New York Magazine*. Copyright © 1972 by Anne Roiphe. Reprinted by permission of Brandt & Brandt, Literary Agents, Inc.

(co-existing with a poor self-image—it's not news that people can believe two contradictory things at once).

3   Listen to any group that suffers materially and socially. They have a lexicon with which they tease the enemy: ofay, goy, honky, gringo. "Poor pale devils," said Malcolm X loud enough for us to hear, although blacks had joked about that to each other for years. Behind some of the women's liberation thinking lurk the rumors, the prejudices, the defense systems of generations of oppressed women whispering in the kitchen together, presenting one face to their menfolk and another to their card clubs, their mothers and sisters. All this is natural enough but potentially dangerous in a revolutionary situation in which you hope to create a future that does not mirror the past. The hidden anti-male feelings, a result of the old system, will foul us up if they are allowed to persist.

4   During my teen years I never left the house on my Saturday night dates without my mother slipping me a few extra dollars—mad money, it was called. I'll explain what it was for the benefit of the new generation in which people just sleep with each other: the fellow was supposed to bring me home, lead me safely through the asphalt jungle, protect me from slithering snakes, rapists and the like. But my mother and I knew young men were apt to drink too much, to slosh down so many rye-and-gingers that some hero might well lead me in front of an oncoming bus, smash his daddy's car into Tiffany's window or, less gallantly, throw up on my new dress. Mad money was for getting home on your own, no matter what form of insanity your date happened to evidence. Mad money was also a wallflower's rope ladder; if the guy you came with suddenly fancied someone else, well, you didn't have to stay there and suffer, you could go home. Boys were fickle and likely to be unkind; my mother and I knew that, as surely as we knew they tried to make you do things in the dark they wouldn't respect you for afterwards, and in fact would spread the word and spoil your rep. Boys liked to be flattered; if you made them feel important they would eat out of your hand. So talk to them about their interests, don't alarm them with displays of intelligence—we all knew that, we groups of girls talking into the wee hours of the night in a kind of easy companionship we thought impossible with boys. Boys were prone to have a good time, get you pregnant, and then pretend they didn't know your name when you came knocking on their door for finances or comfort. In short, we believed boys were less moral than we were. They appeared to be hypocritical, self-seeking, exploitative, untrustworthy and very likely to be show-

ing off their precious masculinity. I never had a girl friend I thought would 60
be unkind or embarrass me in public. I never expected a girl to lie to me
about her marks or sports skill or how good she was in bed. Altogether—
without anyone's directly coming out and saying so—I gathered that men
were sexy, powerful, very interesting, but not very nice, not very moral, hu-
mane and tender, like us. Girls played fairly while men, unfortunately, re- 65
served their honor for the battlefield.

5   Why are there laws insisting on alimony and child support? Well,
everyone knows that men don't have an instinct to protect their young and,
given half a chance, with the moon in the right phase, they will run off and
disappear. Everyone assumes a mother will not let her child starve, yet it 70
is necessary to legislate that a father must not do so. We are taught to accept the idea that men are less than decent; their charms may be manifold
but their characters are riddled with faults. To this day I never blink if I
hear that a man has gone to find his fortune in South America, having left
his pregnant wife, his blind mother and taken the family car. I still gasp 75
in horror when I hear of a woman leaving her asthmatic infant for a rock
group in Taos because I can't seem to avoid the assumption that men are
naturally heels and women the ordained carriers of what little is moral in
our dubious civilization.

6   My mother never gave me mad money thinking I would ditch a 80
fellow for some other guy or that I would pass out drunk on the floor. She
knew I would be considerate of my companion because, after all, I was
more mature than the boys that gathered about. Why was I more mature?
Women just are people-oriented; they learn to be empathetic at an early
age. Most English students (students interested in humanity, not artifacts) 85
are women. Men and boys—so the myth goes—conceal their feelings and
lose interest in anybody else's. Everyone knows that even little boys can
tell the difference between one kind of a car and another—proof that their
souls are mechanical, their attention directed to the nonhuman.

7   I remember shivering in the cold vestibule of a famous men's ath- 90
letic club. Women and girls are not permitted inside the club's door. What
are they doing in there, I asked? They're naked, said my mother, they're
sweating, jumping up and down a lot, telling each other dirty jokes and
bragging about their stock market exploits. Why can't we go in? I asked.
Well, my mother told me, they're afraid we'd laugh at them.   95

8   The prejudices of childhood are hard to outgrow. I confess that
every time my business takes me past that club, I shudder. Images of large

bellies resting on massage tables and flaccid penises rising and falling with
the Dow Jones average flash through my head. There it is, chauvinism waving its cancerous tentacles from the depths of my psyche.   100

9   Minorities automatically feel superior to the oppressor because,
after all, they are not hurting anybody. In fact, they feel they are morally
better. The old canard that women need love, men need sex—believed too
long by both sexes—attributes moral and spiritual superiority to women
and makes of men beasts whose urges send them prowling into the night.   105
This false division of good and bad, placing deforming pressures on everyone, doesn't have to contaminate the future. We know that the assumptions we make about each other become a part of the cultural air we
breathe and, in fact, become social truths. Women who want equality must
be prepared to give it and to believe in it, and in order to do that it is not   110
enough to state that you are as good as any man, but also it must be stated
that he is as good as you and both will be humans together. If we want
men to share in the care of the family in a new way, we must assume them
as capable of consistent loving tenderness as we.

10   I rummage about and find in my thinking all kinds of anti-male   115
prejudices. Some are just jokes and others I will have a hard time aban-
doning. First, I share an emotional conviction with many sisters that
women given power would not create wars. Intellectually I know that's
ridiculous; great queens have waged war before; the likes of Lurleen Wallace, Pat Nixon and Mrs. General Lavelle can be depended upon in the   120
future to guiltlessly condemn to death other people's children in the name
of some ideal of their own. Little girls, of course, don't take toy guns out of
their hip pockets and say "Pow, pow" to all their neighbors and friends like
the average well-adjusted little boy. However, if we gave little girls the six-
shooters, we would soon have double the pretend body count.   125

11   Aggression is not, as I secretly think, a male-sex-linked characteristic: brutality is masculine only by virtue of opportunity. True, there are
1,000 Jack the Rippers for every Lizzie Borden, but that surely is the result
of social forms. Women as a group are indeed more masochistic than men.
The practical result of this division is that women seem nicer and kinder,   130
but when the world changes, women will have a fuller opportunity to be
just as rotten as men and there will be fewer claims of female moral
superiority.

12   Now that I am entering early middle age, I hear many women
complaining of husbands and ex-husbands who are attracted to younger fe-   135

males. This strikes the older woman as unfair, of course. But I remember a time when I thought all boys around my age and grade were creeps and bores. I wanted to go out with an older man: a senior or, miraculously, a college man. I had a certain contempt for my coevals, not realizing that the freshman in college I thought so desirable, was some older girl's creep. Some women never lose that contempt for men of their own age. That isn't fair either and may be one reason why some sensible men of middle years find solace in young women.

13   I remember coming home from school one day to find my mother's card game dissolved in hysterical laughter. The cards were floating in black rivers of running mascara. What was so funny? A woman named Helen was lying on a couch pretending to be her husband with a cold. She was issuing demands for orange juice, aspirin, suggesting a call to a specialist, complaining of neglect, of fate's cruel finger, of heat, of cold, of sharp pains on the bridge of the nose that might indicate brain involvement. What was so funny? The ladies explained to me that all men behave just like that with colds, they are reduced to temper tantrums by simple nasal congestion, men cannot stand any little physical discomfort—on and on the laughter went.

14   The point of this vignette is the nature of the laughter—us laughing at them, us feeling superior to them, us ridiculing them behind their backs. If they were doing it to us we'd call it male chauvinist pigness; if we do it to them, it is inescapably female chauvinist sowness and, whatever its roots, it leads to the same isolation. Boys are messy, boys are mean, boys are rough, boys are stupid and have sloppy handwriting. A cacophony of childhood memories rushes through my head, balanced, of course, by all the well-documented feelings of inferiority and envy. But the important thing, the hard thing, is to wipe the slate clean, to start again without the meanness of the past. That's why it's so important that the women's movement not become antimale and allow its most prejudiced spokesmen total leadership. The much-chewed-over abortion issue illustrates this. The women's-liberation position, insisting on a woman's right to determine her own body's destiny, leads in fanatical extreme to a kind of emotional immaculate conception in which the father is not judged even half-responsible—he has no rights, and no consideration is to be given to his concern for either the woman or the fetus.

15   Woman, who once was abandoned and disgraced by an unwanted pregnancy, has recently arrived at a new pride of ownership or disposal.

She has traveled in a straight line that still excludes her sexual partner from an equal share in the wanted or unwanted pregnancy. A better style of life 175 may develop from an assumption that men are as human as we. Why not ask the child's father if he would like to bring up the child? Why not share decisions, when possible, with the male? If we cut them out, assuming an old-style indifference on their part, we perpetuate the ugly divisiveness that has characterized relations between the sexes so far.   180

16   Hard as it is for many of us to believe, women are not really superior to men in intelligence or humanity—they are only equal.

QUESTIONS

READER AND PURPOSE

1. Roiphe's argument has two sides, one negative—something she is against —and the other positive—something she is for. In your own words summarize both aspects of her argument. Which single sentence of this selection best expresses her essential point?

2. How does Roiphe support her argument: logically, by deriving her conclusions from self-evident premises; or empirically, by offering evidence from experience?

3. Which of these adjectives best describes Roiphe's tone *, "angry," "amused," "frivolous"? If none seems adequate, how would you characterize the tone of this selection? Is she writing primarily for men or for women? Or equally for both?

ORGANIZATION

4. Which paragraph(s) constitute the beginning? Which the closing?

5. How does paragraph 1 contribute to the writer's argument? Paragraphs 2, 3, 4, and 5?

6. Is the sixth paragraph ironic * or are we intended to take it literally? How does it develop the argument?

7. Does the ninth paragraph mark a turn in thought?

8. How is paragraph 14 tied to 13? Show that in paragraph 14 Roiphe's concern becomes more positive—less with what is presently wrong and more with what ideally ought to be. How does she support the point she makes in this paragraph?

9. What is the function of the rhetorical question * in line 67?

10. Notice that in paragraph 10 Roiphe uses the organizing word *first*. Does she continue this scheme with *second, third*, and so on?

11. The ellipsis * in line 19 has a kind of organizational function. Explain.

SENTENCES

12. The sentence in lines 4-6 is colloquial * not only in its diction, but also in the way it is put together. What about its structure suggests speech?
13. *Keeps* in line 10 is an appositive *. To what? Why are the dashes more helpful here to a reader than commas would be?
14. Point out the parallelism * in the sentence in lines 27-31; that in the sentence in 55-57.
15. Suppose that in line 38 a semicolon had been used instead of a colon. Would it help or hinder clarity?
16. Consider the following pairs of sentences and discuss why in each case the revision is poorer than the sentence in the text:

(a) *Revision:* To this day I never blink if I hear that a man has gone to find his fortune in South America, having taken the family car and left his pregnant wife and blind mother.
Roiphe: "To this day I never blink if I hear that a man has gone to find his fortune in South America, having left his pregnant wife, his blind mother and taken the family car." (73-75)

(b) *Revision:* This false division of good and bad doesn't have to contaminate the future, placing deforming pressures on everyone.
Roiphe: "This false division of good and bad, placing deforming pressures on everyone, doesn't have to contaminate the future." (106-7)

(c) *Revision:* Hard as it is for many of us to believe, women are only equal and not really superior to men in intelligence and humanity.
Roiphe: "Hard as it is for many of us to believe, women are not really superior to men in intelligence or humanity—they are only equal." (181-82)

DICTION

17. Look up: *replica* (4), *lexicon* (25), *ofay* (25), *goy* (25), *exploitative* (59), *manifold* (72), *contaminate* (107), *Jack the Ripper* (128), *Lizzie Borden* (128), *coevals* (139), *vignette* (155), *perpetuate* (179).
18. What do these phrases mean: *wallflower's rope ladder* (46), *dubious civilization* (79), *cultural air we breathe* (108-109), *fanatical extreme* (168), *emotional immaculate conception* (168-69)?
19. How do the etymologies * of the following words help one understand their present meanings? *Prejudices* (19), *hypocritical* (58), *alimony* (67), *artifacts* (85), *chauvinism* (99), *psyche* (100), *canard* (103), *masochistic* (129), *cacophony* (160).
20. Point out several examples of colloquial diction; several of learned, literary

words. Such multi-level diction is typical of much contemporary prose. Successfully used, as it is here, it suggests a wide-ranging sensitivity, attuned both to books and to life, able to be serious without being pompous and learned without being pedantic.

21. Why is *they* italicized in the clause in lines 18-19? In that clause what is Roiphe implying by her use of the intensives *even* and *herself* in the expression "for even Miss America herself"?

22. Now and again Roiphe employs alliteration * effectively. Point out several examples.

23. Explain how these pointers * prepare us for the idea they introduce: *in short* (57), *altogether* (62), *well* (67), *in fact* (102), *true* (127). How does *either* (142) help to unify paragraph 12?

24. What is the reason for hyphenating *much-chewed-over* (166) and *women's-liberation* (166-67)?

25. Why are the following alternatives less effective for Roiphe's purpose than the word she employed? *Father* for *handsome daddy-true* (4), *crawling* for *slithering* (40), *realized* for *gathered* (63), *belief* for *myth* (86), *examine* for *rummage about and find in* (115)?

26. Do you think the metaphor * in line 3 and the simile * in line 9 are effective devices of communication?

POINTS TO LEARN

1. Sometimes the best and the easiest way to develop an empirical argument is to look to your own experience.

2. A modern style, especially one that leans toward informality, plucks words from various levels of use—formal and colloquial, learned and slang. The essential consideration is that the word be the best expression of what one wants to say.

SUGGESTIONS FOR WRITING

Examine your own preconceptions about the opposite sex, or about the older generation, or about a different ethnic, social, or occupational group than your own. Organize your essay by distinguishing specific prejudices and support your discussion with detailed illustrations drawn from your own experience.

IMPROVING YOUR STYLE

1. In your composition strive for a wide spectrum of diction, ranging from the slang and colloquial to the more literary. Do not throw words in just to fulfill the assignment. Remember that any word, slang or learned, is justified only if it conveys exactly what your context suggests it should convey.

2. Use at least one metaphor and one simile.
3. Compose a colloquial, interrupted sentence like Roiphe's in lines 4-6.
4. In other sentences include:

An appositive.

Parallel constructions.

At least one case of two independent * clauses joined paratactically (that is, without a conjunction and punctuated with a semicolon).

The Policeman and the Ghetto

James Baldwin is one of the best black writers in the United States. His work includes autobiography, novels, short stories, and essays; some of his best-known titles are Go Tell It on the Mountain (1953), The Fire Next Time (1963), and Nobody Knows My Name (1961). The last is the source of the paragraphs printed below.

1   Similarly, the only way to police a ghetto is to be oppressive. None of the Police Commissioner's men, even with the best will in the world, have any way of understanding the lives led by the people they swagger about in twos and threes controlling. Their very presence is an insult, and it would be, even if they spent their entire day feeding gumdrops to children. They 5 represent the force of the white world, and that world's real intentions are, simply, for that world's criminal profit and ease, to keep the black man corralled up here, in his place. The badge, the gun in the holster, and the swinging club make vivid what will happen should his rebellion become overt. Rare, indeed, is the Harlem citizen, from the most circumspect 10 church member to the most shiftless adolescent, who does not have a long tale to tell of police incompetence, injustice, or brutality. I myself have witnessed and endured it more than once. The businessmen and racketeers also have a story. And so do the prostitutes. (And this is not, perhaps, the place to discuss Harlem's very complex attitude toward black policemen, 15 nor the reasons, according to Harlem, that they are nearly all downtown.)

2   It is hard, on the other hand, to blame the policeman, blank, good-natured, thoughtless, and insuperably innocent, for being such a perfect representative of the people he serves. He, too, believes in good intentions and is astounded and offended when they are not taken for the deed. He 20 has never, himself, done anything for which to be hated—which of us has?

—and yet he is facing, daily and nightly, people who would gladly see him dead, and he knows it. There is no way for him not to know it: there are few things under heaven more unnerving than the silent, accumulating contempt and hatred of a people. He moves through Harlem, therefore, like 25 an occupying soldier in a bitterly hostile country; which is precisely what, and where, he is, and is the reason he walks in twos and threes. And he is not the only one who knows why he is always in company: the people who are watching him know why, too. Any street meeting, sacred or secular, which he and his colleagues uneasily cover has as its explicit or implicit 30 burden the cruelty and injustice of the white domination. And these days, of course, in terms increasingly vivid and jubilant, it speaks of the end of that domination. The white policeman standing on a Harlem street corner finds himself at the very center of the revolution now occurring in the world. He is not prepared for it—naturally, nobody is—and, what is pos- 35 sibly much more to the point, he is exposed, as few white people are, to the anguish of the black people around him. Even if he is gifted with the merest mustard grain of imagination, something must seep in. He cannot avoid observing that some of the children, in spite of their color, remind him of children he has known and loved, perhaps even of his own children. 40 He knows that he certainly does not want *his* children living this way. He can retreat from his uneasiness in only one direction: into a callousness which very shortly becomes second nature. He becomes more callous, the population becomes more hostile, the situation grows more tense, and the police force is increased. One day, to everyone's astonishment, someone 45 drops a match in the powder keg and everything blows up. Before the dust has settled or the blood congealed, editorials, speeches, and civil-rights commissions are loud in the land, demanding to know what happened. What happened is that Negroes want to be treated like men.

QUESTIONS

READER AND PURPOSE

1. What one sentence in this selection most clearly expresses the point Baldwin is arguing? Does he support that point by (a) offering detailed evidence, (b) drawing logical inferences from general premises, or (c) reasserting it in various ways?

2. What images * does Baldwin use to stand for the policeman?

3. Describe the tone * of this selection. Be able to support your description by specific words and images and sentences.

ORGANIZATION

4. What is the topic sentence of the first paragraph? Of the second?

5. Make a conceptual analysis of paragraph 1 by showing how the idea expressed in each sentence relates to what has preceded it. For instance, it could be a cause or a consequence, a simple restatement or an illustration, a contrast or a similarity, a qualification * or a particular part of a larger whole. Does the logic of this paragraph seem as tightly structured as that, say, of the third paragraph in the selection by Carl Becker (page 69) or that of Bertrand Russell's paragraph on page 51? If you think that it does not, discuss whether this fact means that Baldwin's paragraph is inferior. Attempt a similar analysis of paragraph 2.

6. *On the other hand* (17) establishes the transition between paragraphs 1 and 2. What relationship does it indicate? This phrase and *on the contrary* are sometimes confused; they signal different logical relationships. What is the difference?

7. Paragraph 2 is well unified, each sentence linking up with what has gone before. This flow is achieved by repeating key words or concepts (for example, *policeman. . . . He* in the first and second sentences), by pointer * words (*too*), and by similar sentence patterns. Analyze the paragraph and point out how each sentence is linked to the preceding one(s).

SENTENCES

8. A colloquial * style is one in which the writer creates a sense of normal conversation. Like a magician's trick, such a style is an artful illusion; it has to be, for simply to copy everyday talk (even literate everyday talk) would lead to very dull, repetitive writing. What the colloquial stylist does is to *suggest* a talking voice without literally imitating it, by using some of the devices of ordinary speech. One, for instance, is the intrusive sentence—a second, independent construction set inside a first sentence to which it is clearly related in thought but only loosely, or not at all related, in syntax. An example is the question set between dashes in lines 21-22. Point out one or two other interrupters like this. Another device is the short, direct sentence. Find several of these.

9. On the other hand, many of Baldwin's sentences are relatively literary, patterned on written rather than on spoken English. Indicate a few sentences that seem quite far from ordinary speech.

10. Suppose that the series of simple clauses in lines 43-45 were revised into a complex sentence *, such as: "As he becomes more callous and as the population becomes more hostile, the situation grows more tense, leading to an increase in the police force." The logic of these ideas is now more explicit. Yet the sentence is, for Baldwin's purpose, much less effective. Why? Normally independent clauses like these which are not joined by co-ordinating conjunc-

tions are separated by semicolons. What advantage is there in this case to the use of commas?

DICTION

11. Look up: *oppressive* (1), *shiftless* (11), *insuperably* (18), *unnerving* (24), *secular* (29).

12. What are the etymologies * of these words: *ghetto* (1), *overt* (10), *circumspect* (10), *callous* (43)? How does a knowledge of its etymology help you to understand Baldwin's use of each of these words?

13. We said earlier that Baldwin's sentences suggest a man speaking. Diction is equally important to such a colloquial style. Notice, for example, the use of *and* and *too* as conjunctive adverbs * instead of the more literary *furthermore* or *moreover*. People are sometimes warned never to start a sentence with *and*. Is that blanket rule sound?

14. Why is *swagger* an effective verb in line 3? Is *criminal* (7) a fair word? What is Baldwin implying by *blank* in line 17?

15. Suppose the sentence in line 19 had begun "He also believes" instead of "He, too, believes": what idea would have been obscured by the substitution of *also* for *too?* What is the logical force of *indeed* in line 10?

16. Are both *explicit* and *implicit* necessary in line 30 to the idea Baldwin is conveying? What irony * is contained in the phrase *loud in the land* (48)?

POINTS TO LEARN

1. An argument may be assertive, persuading less by evidence than by skilful restatement.

2. As the result of artfully selecting words and sentence patterns, an informal, colloquial style suggests everyday talk. But it does not literally imitate such talk.

SUGGESTIONS FOR WRITING

1. Can you answer Baldwin's charges against the policeman in the ghetto?

2. Arguing a specific complaint (which you may select for yourself), write a brief essay on the teacher in the classroom.

IMPROVING YOUR STYLE

In your composition include:

1. A series of simple clauses detailing a sequence of events or the steps in a process, joined without conjunctions (except for the last) like Baldwin's

sentence in lines 43-45, and punctuated with commas (semicolons if your instructor prefers).

2. A sentence which contains a second, intrusive statement set between dashes.

3. These connectives * to introduce sentences: *on the other hand, too, indeed.*

4. Verbs like *swagger* in line 3 of Baldwin's selection that convey a vivid sense of action.

RUSSELL BAKER

Hemlock at 65

Russell Baker writes a daily newspaper column which appears in *The New York Times*. Baker's pieces are usually humorous or satiric treatments of current political and social questions. Below the humor, however, there is serious intent. This selection, published in January 1971, concerns the attempt by some of the younger newly-elected representatives to the ninety-second Congress (1971-72) to upset the seniority system. According to seniority, House and Senate members with the longest terms of service are awarded the most prestigious and powerful committee assignments. In the view of young liberals the system results in an overly conservative Congress. Their effort was thus in part an attack of liberals upon conservatives. But in part, too, it was a denial by youth of the privileges of age. In dealing with the issue Baker's strategy is satiric. He persuades us less by logic and evidence than by irony and comic exaggeration. Yet the satire expresses a serious view of the problem— not a simple view, for Baker is not a knee-jerk defender of liberalism or conservatism, of youth or age. He sees the problem more subtly and reveals the faults both of seniority and of those who attack it without thinking through what they are doing.

Baker's title refers to the execution in 399 B.C. of the Athenian philosopher Socrates, who was made to drink hemlock after being convicted of impiety and of misleading the youth of the city. The charges were the response of reactionaries to the liberal open-mindedness of the aging philosopher, a fact not without irony in the context of Baker's essay.

1   It has been a bad week for old people. Another bad week. Bad weeks for old people seem to occur with increasing frequency. If it isn't "Where's Poppa?"[1] at the movie house it's another rise in the real-estate tax, the kind that must make you say "Oof!" if you are over 65 and, there-

From *The New York Times*, January 21, 1971. © 1971 by The New York Times Company. Reprinted by permission.
[1] A comic film about a young lawyer's efforts to get out of taking care of his aged and widowed mother. [Editors' note]

fore, automatically ineligible for those 17.4 per cent salary increases that 5
make it easier for the rest of us to roll with the punch.

2   This week there has been a sustained battery by insult on the very
fact of being old. Old people have been able to hear and see oldness
abused, ridiculed, denounced and scorned in a barrage of speeches, editorials, columns and broadcasts, most of them arguing the liberal political 10
position that the Congressional seniority system must be abolished because
old committee chairmen are mentally and socially inferior.

3   Some will dismiss the churlishness of the argument against the old
men on grounds that in any political struggle language is merely a blunt instrument, and should not be listened to seriously. In this case that argu- 15
ment is unpersuasive.

4   The attack on the seniority system is, in fact, merely a late-
in-the-day part of the same general assault upon the aged that has pretty
well cleaned them out of both corporate and public life.

5   The most effective weapon in the attack has been the policy of 20
forced retirement, usually at 65. It is, of course, job discrimination of the
most blatant sort, yet governments and companies, which wouldn't dream
of putting a person out of work on account of race, sex, religion or hair
style, blindly chop you off for the offense of becoming 65 years old.

6   Psychological warfare makes it easy to keep the old people sub- 25
dued. For one thing we have successfully promoted the idea that getting
old is an act in very bad taste. The smart people in America are the young
people, or so it must seem to anyone who keeps his eyes and ears open.

7   A person who lets himself become unyoung. . . .

8   Well! Shouldn't he be grateful that we don't put him out of work 30
without enough income to pay his way into the movies to see "Where's
Poppa?"

9   Provided the real-estate tax doesn't go up?

10   The reason the seniority system has failed in Congress is not because it concentrates power in the hands of the old. That isn't the vice at 35
all. The problem is that it concentrates power in the hands of old men who
have never had experience of democracy.

11   The prizes are awarded, not for great age, but for long service in
Congress. Long service in Congress almost invariably requires a one-party
district or state—a rotten borough, if you will, in which a Senator or Repre- 40
sentative never becomes acquainted with the democratic process.

12   The rotten borough tends to breed tyrants, and from this tendency

rises the real problem with the seniority system, which is not that it raises up old men, but that it exalts old tyrants.

13   Reforming the Congressional power structure needn't involve any 45
attack on age. The seniority rule, in fact, can be safely left as the guiding principle, with the exception that members would be unqualified for power positions if they were returned from districts where the democratic process is not in use.

14   This amended rule would still permit members in their 70's and 50
80's to rule over committees. And why not? Any man of advanced years who has been re-elected twenty times against opposition will surely have qualities that can only do the country great service at the top of its government.

15   The attack should be upon old tyrants, not old age. Old age gives 55
the country great strengths. Bob Dylan, to take a case, is fine, as are Senator Kennedy and Senator Dole. But even with all that youthful splendor, Socrates helps a lot. He was 70 when he took the hemlock, "at the peak of his powers," the obituary writers might say today.

16   Socrates would have been treated more cruelly in America. He 60
would have been forcibly retired to shuffleboard at Sunville at 65. There wouldn't have been all that disturbing thought at Athens.

17   The Athenian youth, instead of sitting around using their heads, would have been running great corporations, getting out those dynamic press releases, announcing new mergers, and there would have been a lot 65
more bankruptcy, as well as alienation, in Athens.

QUESTIONS

READER AND PURPOSE

1. Baker is arguing two related issues, one a specific instance of the other. What are these issues? Does his argument consist simply of assertions, or does he offer evidence from experience?

2. His tone is ironic *. How, for example, are we supposed to read the last sentence of paragraph 16? What is ironic in the final paragraph? Point out other instances of irony.

3. Is Baker writing for a relatively sophisticated audience? What does he expect them to know?

ORGANIZATION

4. Do you think the opening of this selection is effective? What about its closing?

5. Paragraph 10 marks a major turn of thought. What has the writer been concentrating upon up to this point? How does his focus change in paragraph 10?

6. Explain how the third paragraph contributes to Baker's argument; the fourth and fifth. Paragraphs 6, 7, and 8 make up a conceptual unit. What is their point?

7. What answer does Baker make to those who claim that old age should disqualify legislators from occupying positions of power?

8. The paragraphing in this selection is typical of journalism: numerous brief paragraphs. Some, in fact, consist of only a single short sentence. Would it be an improvement to combine such paragraphs (7 and 9 for example) with the preceding material?

9. How is the twelfth paragraph linked to the eleventh? The fourteenth to the thirteenth?

10. In the opening sentences of this selection Baker achieves a high degree of coherence by repeating the phrase *bad week(s)*. In fact, he ends the second sentence with these words and immediately picks them up to begin the third sentence, a pattern of repetition that in ancient rhetoric was called *anadiplosis* (accent on *plo*). Where else in these paragraphs do you find *anadiplosis*?

SENTENCES

11. Comment upon these revisions of Baker's sentences:

   (a) *Revision:* It has been another bad week for old people.
       Baker: "It has been a bad week for old people. Another bad week." (1)
   (b) *Revision:* Well, shouldn't he be grateful that we don't put him out of work without enough income to pay his way into the movies to see "Where's Poppa?" provided the real-estate tax doesn't go up?
       Baker: "Well! Shouldn't he be grateful that we don't put him out of work without enough income to pay his way into the movies to see 'Where's Poppa?'
       "Provided the real-estate tax doesn't go up?" (30-33)

12. "And why not?" (51) is a fragment *. Why? What other fragments can you find in this essay? Are they effective, or would Baker's points be more effectively expressed in grammatically complete sentences?

13. The ellipsis * in line 29 is an example of a thought deliberately left incom-

plete, a trick in Greek rhetoric called *aposiopesis* (accent on *pe*). What is the thought being implied here? What is the advantage of leaving it implicit?

14. What does Baker mean by the clause "if you will" in line 40?

15. The statement in lines 42-44 is a good example of how a well-constructed sentence thrusts ideas forward. The sentence consists of five clauses. How does the second derive from the first? The third, fourth, and fifth from the second? Why are the final two clauses parallel *?

DICTION

16. Look up: *barrage* (9), *liberal* (10), *abolished* (11), *assault* (18), *blatant* (22), *vice* (35), *tyrants* (42), *amended* (50), *mergers* (65), *alienation* (66).

17. What do these phrases mean: *corporate and public life* (19), *psychological warfare* (25), *guiding principle* (46-7)?

18. Explain the etymologies of these words: *salary* (5), *battery* (7), *churlishness* (13), *obituary* (59), *dynamic* (64), *bankruptcy* (66).

19. How do the following pointers * prepare us for the idea each introduces: *in fact* (17 and 46), *of course* (21), *yet* (22), *to take a case* (56)?

20. Comment upon how these suggested substitutions would alter the tone or the sense of Baker's text: *cut* for *chop* (24), *old* for *unyoung* (29), *cinema* for *movies* (31), *old man* for *man of advanced years* (51), *tennis at Phoenix* for *shuffleboard at Sunville* (61).

21. In lines 14-15 *blunt instrument* is a fine metaphor *. Applied to language, it has two senses. Explain.

22. Baker usually contracts a verb and a negative term. How would his tone change if he wrote these out in full—*is not* for *isn't* in line 2, for instance, or *need not* for *needn't* in line 45?

POINTS TO LEARN

1. Irony, while no substitute for logical proof or for empirical evidence, can prove effective strategy in argumentation.

2. Fragments and brief, single-sentence paragraphs, if not over-used, are valuable means of emphasis.

3. Sometimes it is better to let the reader complete a thought for himself.

SUGGESTIONS FOR WRITING

1. Compose a one- or two-paragraph argument against compulsory class attendance, dormitory regulations, or any aspect of life where you feel the young are discriminated against. Support your points by appealing to common knowledge and by offering examples, but try also to achieve a tone of irony.

2. Baker proposes in paragraphs 12-14 a way of reforming the Congressional

power structure without necessarily discriminating against old men. Examine the implications of his proposal and construct an argument against it.

IMPROVING YOUR STYLE

In your composition include:

1. An example of anadiplosis.
2. An example of aposiopesis.
3. (With your instructor's approval) one or two effective fragments.
4. These connectives * introducing sentences—*in fact, of course, yet, to take a case.*
5. A brief metaphor like *blunt instrument* (lines 14-15).

A Modest Proposal

Jonathan Swift (1667-1745) is the greatest writer of satire in English literature and one of the greatest in the world. He is best known for *Gulliver's Travels* (1726), popularly thought of as a fantasy for children, but actually a biting attack upon a variety of targets—politicians, courtiers, travel books, scientists, humanity in general. A *Tale of a Tub* (1704) is a funny and scandalous treatment of religious follies. The essay reprinted here satirizes England's policy toward Ireland. (Swift, though English, was born and educated in Dublin and served for many years as Dean of the Anglican St. Patrick's Cathedral in that city.)

During the eighteenth century Ireland suffered under an English rule that was repressive and exploitative. Religious intolerance was strong and Protestant England imposed harsh religious, political, and economic restrictions upon the native Irish, who were virtually all Catholic. Even the Anglo-Irish, Swift's class, who descended from English settlers and were themselves Protestant, suffered under unjust laws forbidding Ireland to trade with nations other than England. Swift had proposed solutions to some of these inequities, solutions that seemed to him workable and fair. No one listened. In "A Modest Proposal" (1729) he suggested a more horrendous scheme, saying to England, in effect: Since you are determined to destroy the Irish for profit, let me show you how to conduct your slaughter-house policy more systematically and efficiently. Although the "Irish Question" is now settled (or almost settled), Swift's "A Modest Proposal" remains the finest example of sustained irony ever written.

A Modest Proposal

for
Preventing the Children of Poor People in Ireland from Being a

The text and notes are taken from *The Restoration and the Eighteenth Century*, ed. Martin Price. Copyright © 1973 by Oxford University Press, Inc. Reprinted by permission of the publisher.

Burden to Their Parents or Country, and for Making Them Beneficial to the Public

1   It is a melancholy object to those who walk through this great town, or travel in the country, when they see the streets, the roads, and cabin-doors crowded with beggars of the female sex, followed by three, four, or six children, all in rags, and importuning every passenger for an alms. These mothers, instead of being able to work for their honest livelihood, are forced to employ all their time in strolling to beg sustenance for their helpless infants: who, as they grow up, either turn thieves for want of work, or leave their dear native country to fight for the Pretender* in Spain, or sell themselves to the Barbadoes.[1]

2   I think it is agreed by all parties, that this prodigious number of children in the arms, or on the backs, or at the heels of their mothers, and frequently of their fathers, is, in the present deplorable state of the kingdom, a very great additional grievance; and, therefore, whoever could find out a fair, cheap, and easy method of making these children sound and useful members of the commonwealth, would deserve so well of the public, as to have his statue set up for a preserver of the nation.[2]

3   But my intention is very far from being confined to provide only for the children of professed beggars; it is of a much greater extent, and shall take in the whole number of infants at a certain age, who are born of parents in effect as little able to support them as those who demand our charity in the streets.

4   As to my own part, having turned my thoughts for many years upon this important subject, and maturely weighed the several schemes of other projectors, I have always found them grossly mistaken in their computation. It is true, a child, just dropped from its dam,[3] may be supported by her milk for a solar year with little other nourishment; at most, not above the value of two shillings, which the mother may certainly get, or the value in scraps, by her lawful occupation of begging; and it is exactly at one

* The Old Pretender, James Edward, son of James II (last Catholic king of England, deposed in 1688) and Mary of Modena. The Pretender was a Catholic and, possessing a claim to the English throne, posed a threat to Protestant England. [Editors' note]

[1] Many Irish Catholics enlisted in French and Spanish forces, the latter employed in the effort to restore the Stuart Pretender to the English throne in 1718; emigration to the West Indies from Ireland had reached the rate of almost fifteen hundred a year (and often led to desperate servitude).

[2] The idiom of the "projector," the enthusiastic proponent of public remedies (often suspected of having an eye on his own glory).

[3] The idiom now of the cattle breeder.

year old that I propose to provide for them in such a manner, as, instead of being a charge upon their parents or the parish, or wanting food and 30 raiment for the rest of their lives, they shall, on the contrary, contribute to the feeding, and partly to the clothing, of many thousands.

5   There is likewise another great advantage in my scheme, that it will prevent those voluntary abortions, and that horrid practice of women murdering their bastard children, alas, too frequent among us, sacrificing 35 the poor innocent babes, I doubt more to avoid the expense than the shame, which would move tears and pity in the most savage and inhuman breast.

6   The number of souls in this kingdom being usually reckoned one million and a half, of these I calculate there may be about two hundred 40 thousand couple whose wives are breeders; from which number I subtract thirty thousand couple, who are able to maintain their own children (although I apprehend there cannot be so many, under the present distresses of the kingdom); but this being granted, there will remain an hundred and seventy thousand breeders. I again subtract fifty thousand for those women 45 who miscarry, or whose children die by accident or disease within the year. There only remain a hundred and twenty thousand children of poor parents annually born. The question therefore is how this number shall be reared and provided for? which, as I have already said, under the present situation of affairs, is utterly impossible by all the methods hitherto pro- 50 posed. For we can neither employ them in handicraft or agriculture; we neither build houses (I mean in the country) nor cultivate land: they can very seldom pick up a livelihood by stealing until they arrive at six years old, except where they are of towardly parts; although I confess they learn the rudiments much earlier; during which time they can, however, be prop- 55 erly looked upon only as probationers; as I have been informed by a principal gentleman in the county of Cavan,[4] who protested to me, that he never knew above one or two instances under the age of six, even in a part of the kingdom so renowned for the quickest proficiency in that art.

7   I am assured by our merchants that a boy or a girl before twelve 60 years old is no saleable commodity; and even when they come to this age they will not yield above three pounds or three pounds and half-a-crown at most, on the exchange; which cannot turn to account either to the parents or kingdom, the charge of nutriment and rags having been at least four times that value.   65

[4] One of the poorest districts of Ireland.

8   I shall now, therefore, humbly propose my own thoughts, which I hope will not be liable to the least objection.

9   I have been assured by a very knowing American[5] of my acquaintance in London, that a young healthy child, well nursed, is, at a year old, a most delicious, nourishing, and wholesome food, whether stewed, roasted, 70 baked, or boiled; and I make no doubt that it will equally serve in a fricassee or a ragout.[6]

10   I do therefore humbly offer it to public consideration, that of the hundred and twenty thousand children already computed, twenty thousand may be reserved for breed, whereof only one-fourth part to be males; which 75 is more than we allow to sheep, black cattle, or swine; and my reason is, that these children are seldom the fruits of marriage, a circumstance not much regarded by our savages, therefore one male will be sufficient to serve four females. That the remaining hundred thousand may, at a year old, be offered in sale to the persons of quality and fortune through the kingdom; 80 always advising the mother to let them suck plentifully in the last month, so as to render them plump and fat for a good table. A child will make two dishes at an entertainment for friends; and when the family dines alone, the fore or hind quarter will make a reasonable dish, and, seasoned with a little pepper or salt, will be very good boiled on the fourth day, especially 85 in winter.

11   I have reckoned, upon a medium, that a child just born will weigh twelve pounds, and in a solar year, if tolerably nursed, increaseth to twenty-eight pounds.

12   I grant this food will be somewhat dear, and therefore very proper 90 for landlords, who, as they have already devoured most of the parents, seem to have the best title to the children.

13   Infants' flesh will be in season throughout the year, but more plentifully in March, and a a little before and after: for we are told by a grave author, an eminent French physician,[7] that fish being a prolific[8] diet, 95 there are more children born in Roman Catholic countries about nine months after Lent than at any other season; therefore, reckoning a year after Lent, the markets will be more glutted than usual, because the num-

---

[5] Presumably American Indian, many of whom were believed by the English to enjoy cannibalism.
[6] A French stew, one of the foreign dishes ("olios and ragouts") Swift mocks elsewhere as affectations.
[7] François Rabelais (c. 1494-1553), Gargantua and Pantagruel V.29.
[8] Generative.

ber of popish infants is at least threee to one in this kingdom; and therefore it will have one other collateral advantage, by lessening the number of papists among us.

14   I have already computed the charge of nursing a beggar's child (in which list I reckon all cottagers, labourers, and four-fifths of the farmers) to be about two shillings per annum, rags included; and I believe no gentleman would repine to give ten shillings for the carcass of a good fat child, which, as I have said, will make four dishes of excellent nutritive meat, when he has only some particular friend, or his own family, to dine with him. Thus the squire will learn to be a good landlord, and grow popular among his tenants; the mother will have eight shillings net profit, and be fit for work till she produces another child.

15   Those who are more thrifty (as I must confess the times require) may flay the carcass; the skin of which, artificially dressed, will make admirable gloves for ladies, and summer-boots for fine gentlemen.

16   As to our city of Dublin, shambles[9] may be appointed for this purpose in the most convenient parts of it, and butchers we may be assured will not be wanting; although I rather recommend buying the children alive, and dressing them hot from the knife, as we do roasting pigs.

17   A very worthy person, a true lover of his country, and whose virtues I highly esteem, was lately pleased, in discoursing on this matter, to offer a refinement upon my scheme. He said, that many gentlemen of this kingdom, having of late destroyed their deer, he conceived that the want of venison might be well supplied by the bodies of young lads and maidens, not exceeding fourteen years of age, nor under twelve; so great a number of both sexes in every country being now ready to starve for want of work and service; and these to be disposed of by their parents, if alive, or otherwise by their nearest relations. But, with due deference to so excellent a friend, and so deserving a patriot, I cannot be altogether in his sentiments; for as to the males, my American acquaintance assured me from frequent experience, that their flesh was generally tough and lean, like that of our schoolboys, by continual exercise, and their taste disagreeable; and to fatten them would not answer the charge. Then as to the females, it would, I think, with humble submission, be a loss to the public, because they soon would become breeders themselves: and besides, it is not improbable that some scrupulous people might be apt to censure such a practice (although indeed

---

[9] Slaughterhouses.

very unjustly) as a little bordering upon cruelty; which, I confess hath al- 135
ways been with me the strongest objection against any project, how well
soever intended.

18   But in order to justify my friend, he confessed that this expedient
was put into his head by the famous Psalmanazar,[10] a native of the island
Formosa, who came from thence to London above twenty years ago; and 140
in conversation told my friend, that in his country, when any young person
happened to be put to death, the executioner sold the carcass to persons of
quality as a prime dainty; and that in his time the body of a plump girl of
fifteen, who was crucified for an attempt to poison the emperor, was sold to
his Imperial Majesty's prime minister of state,[11] and other great mandarins 145
of the court, in joints from the gibbet, at four hundred crowns. Neither indeed can I deny, that if the same use were made of several plump young
girls in this town, who, without one single groat to their fortunes, cannot
stir abroad without a chair, and appear at playhouse and assemblies[12] in
foreign fineries which they never will pay for, the kingdom would not be 150
the worse.

19   Some persons of a desponding spirit are in great concern about that
vast number of poor people who are aged, diseased, or maimed; and I have
been desired to employ my thoughts what course may be taken to ease the
nation of so grievous an encumbrance. But I am not in the least pain upon 155
that matter, because it is very well known, that they are every day dying,
and rotting, by cold and famine, and filth and vermin, as fast as can be
reasonably expected. And as to the younger labourers, they are now in almost as hopeful a condition: they cannot get work, and consequently pine
away for want of nourishment, to a degree, that if at any time they are ac- 160
cidentally hired to common labour, they have not strength to perform it;
and thus the country and themselves are happily delivered from the evils to
come.

20   I have too long digressed, and therefore shall return to my subject.
I think the advantages by the proposal which I have made are obvious and 165
many, as well as of the highest importance.

21   For first, as I have already observed, it would greatly lessen the
number of papists, with whom we are yearly overrun, being the principal

---

[10] George Psalmanazar (1679-1763), a Frenchman who pretended to be a Formosan
and wrote (in English) a fraudulent book about his "native" land.
[11] Probably a reference to Walpole.
[12] Social gatherings (Swift had sought an Irish boycott of all such foreign luxuries of
dress or diet).

breeders of the nation as well as our most dangerous enemies; and who stay at home on purpose with a design to deliver the kingdom to the Pretender, hoping to take their advantage by the absence of so many good Protestants, who have chosen rather to leave their country than stay at home and pay tithes against their conscience to an idolatrous Episcopal curate.[13]

22   Secondly, the poorer tenants will have something valuable of their own, which by law may be made liable to distress, and help to pay their landlord's rent; their corn and cattle being already seized, and money a thing unknown.

23   Thirdly, whereas the maintenance of an hundred thousand children, from two years old and upwards, cannot be computed at less than ten shillings a piece per annum, the nation's stock will be thereby increased fifty thousand pounds per annum; besides the profit of a new dish introduced to the tables of all gentlemen of fortune in the kingdom who have any refinement in taste. And the money will circulate among ourselves, the goods being entirely of our own growth and manufacture.

24   Fourthly, the constant breeders, besides the gain of eight shillings sterling per annum by the sale of their children, will be rid of the charge of maintaining them after the first year.

25   Fifthly, this food would likewise bring great custom to taverns; where the vintners will certainly be so prudent as to procure the best receipts for dressing it to perfection, and, consequently, have their houses frequented by all the fine gentlemen, who justly value themselves upon their knowledge in good eating: and a skilful cook, who understands how to oblige his guests, will contrive to make it as expensive as they please.

26   Sixthly, this would be a great inducement to marriage, which all wise nations have either encouraged by rewards, or enforced by laws and penalties. It would increase the care and tenderness of mothers towards their children, when they were sure of a settlement for life to the poor babes, provided in some sort by the public, to their annual profit instead of expense. We should soon see an honest emulation among the married women, which of them could bring the fattest child to the market. Men would become as fond of their wives during the time of their pregnancy,

---

[13] Swift is mocking the castigation of the Catholics, for he regarded it as a typical propaganda device of the Whigs and Protestants; his own experience as a clergyman in northern Ireland had given him reason to fear and distrust the energies of the dissenting Protestants, and he questions their motives (money or conscience) for leaving Ireland. The word "idolatrous" was added in 1735 after renewed agitation to remove the Sacramental Test, with the implication that Anglican forms and doctrines were intolerable to other Protestants.

as they are now of their mares in foal, their cows in calf, or sows when they are ready to farrow; nor offer to beat or kick them (as is too frequent a practice) for fear of a miscarriage.

27   Many other advantages might be enumerated. For instance, the 205 addition of some thousand carcasses in our exportation of barrelled beef; the propagation of swine's flesh, and improvement in the art of making good bacon, so much wanted among us by the great destruction of pigs, too frequent at our tables, which are no way comparable in taste or magnificence to a well-grown, fat yearling child, which, roasted whole, will make 210 a considerable figure at a Lord Mayor's feast, or any other public entertainment. But this, and many others, I omit, being studious of brevity.

28   Supposing that one thousand families in this city would be constant customers for infants' flesh, besides others who might have it at merry meetings, particularly weddings and christenings, I compute that Dublin 215 would take off annually about twenty thousand carcasses; and the rest of the kingdom (where probably they will be sold somewhat cheaper) the remaining eighty thousand.

29   I can think of no one objection that will possibly be raised against this proposal, unless it should be urged, that the number of people will be 220 thereby much lessened in the kingdom. This I freely own, and it was indeed one principal design in offering it to the world. I desire the reader will observe that I calculate my remedy for this one individual kingdom of Ireland, and for no other that ever was, is, or I think ever can be, upon earth. Therefore let no man talk to me of other expedients:[14] of taxing our ab- 225 sentees at five shillings a pound: of using neither clothes nor household-furniture except what is of our own growth and manufacture: of utterly rejecting the materials and instruments that promote foreign luxury: of curing the expensiveness of pride, vanity, idleness, and gaming in our women; of introducing a vein of parsimony, prudence, and temperance: of learning 230 to love our country, wherein we differ even from Laplanders, and the inhabitants of Topinamboo:[15] of quitting our animosities and factions, nor act any longer like the Jews, who were murdering one another at the very moment their city was taken:[16] of being a little cautious not to sell our country and consciences for nothing: of teaching landlords to have at least 235 one degree of mercy towards their tenants: lastly, of putting a spirit of hon-

---

[14] The following are, of course, Swift's own genuine proposals for Ireland.
[15] A region of Brazil known for wildness and barbarous stupidity.
[16] When Jerusalem fell to Nebuchadnezzar (II Kings 24, 25; II Chronicles 36), with the suggestion that English domination is Ireland's Babylonian captivity.

esty, industry, and skill into our shopkeepers; who, if a resolution could now be taken to buy only our native goods, would immediately unite to cheat and exact upon us in the price, the measure, and the goodness, nor could ever yet be brought to make one fair proposal of just dealing, though often 240 and earnestly invited to it.

30   Therefore I repeat, let no man talk to me of these and the like expedients, till he hath at least some glimpse of hope that there will ever be some hearty and sincere attempt to put them in practice.

31   But, as to myself, having been wearied out for many years with 245 offering vain, idle, visionary thoughts, and at length utterly despairing of success, I fortunately fell upon this proposal; which, as it is wholly new, so it hath something solid and real, of no expense and little trouble, full in our own power, and whereby we can incur no danger in disobliging England. For this kind of commodity will not bear exportation, the flesh being of too 250 tender a consistence to admit a long continuance in salt, although perhaps I could name a country which would be glad to eat up our whole nation without it.

32   After all, I am not so violently bent upon my own opinion as to reject any offer proposed by wise men which shall be found equally inno- 255 cent, cheap, easy, and effectual. But before something of that kind shall be advanced in contradiction to my scheme, and offering a better, I desire the author, or authors, will be pleased maturely to consider two points. First, as things now stand, how they will be able to find food and raiment for a hundred thousand useless mouths and backs? And, secondly, there being 260 a round million of creatures in human figure throughout this kingdom, whose whole subsistence put into a common stock would leave them in debt two millions of pounds sterling, adding those who are beggars by profession, to the bulk of farmers, cottagers, and labourers, with the wives and children who are beggars in effect; I desire those politicians who dislike my 265 overture, and may perhaps be so bold as to attempt an answer, that they will first ask the parents of these mortals, whether they would not at this day think it a great happiness to have been sold for food at a year old, in the manner I prescribe, and thereby have avoided such a perpetual scene of misfortunes as they have since gone through, by the oppression of land- 270 lords, the impossibility of paying rent without money or trade, the want of common sustenance, with neither house nor clothes to cover them from the inclemencies of weather, and the most inevitable prospect of entailing the like, or greater miseries, upon their breed for ever.

33   I profess, in the sincerity of my heart, that I have not the least per- 275

sonal interest in endeavouring to promote this necessary work, having no other motive than the public good of my country, by advancing our trade, providing for infants, relieving the poor, and giving some pleasure to the rich. I have no children by which I can propose to get a single penny; the youngest being nine years old, and my wife past child-bearing.   280

QUESTIONS

1. Swift's purpose, of course, is to attack English policy toward Ireland, but not so much any specific act as the fundamental attitude toward the Irish which determined policy in general. To do this he pretends to accept that attitude. In your own words express what Swift implies is the way in which the English regard the Irish.

2. In reading "A Modest Proposal" one must distinguish Swift from the "I," the pious projector ("do-gooder," we might call him today), who puts forward this cannibalistic scheme. On occasion Swift does speak almost directly through the "I"; but sometimes the "I" is part of the satire, expressing the moral platitudes typical of many Englishmen, who could see no contradiction between the Christianity they avowed and the harsh policy toward Ireland they preached and practiced. An example of this kind of shallow piety is the sympathy the speaker expresses for the Irish poor in the very opening sentence. Again, in paragraph 17 he speaks warmly of the virtues of his friend who suggests that Irish boys and girls might take the place of venison. Point out one or two other passages in which Swift, by giving pious sentiments to his speaker, reveals the disparity between Christian pretensions and political realities. Several times the "I" refers to himself as "humble." Is he?

3. On the surface the tone * of "A Modest Proposal" is sober and objective, carefully avoiding any direct expression of emotion. The Irish problem is approached simply as a matter of economics, calculable solely in terms of cost and profit. Now and then, however, the emotionless objectivity slips and we see a flash of anger. The very end of paragraph 18 is an example, where Swift lashes out at the vanity and idleness of society girls. Where else do you detect anger?

4. But such passages are exceptional. Generally the surface discipline holds, and emotion is kept in check. Below the surface, it is another story. Describe this deeper tone—"undertone," as it might be called. How does it differ from the tone of the irony * in the selection by Baker?

ORGANIZATION

5. Roughly, "A Modest Proposal" divides into these sections: (1) the introduction, in which the problem is identified and laid out; (2) the solution to the problem; (3) the advantages of that solution; (4) answers to possible objec-

tions; and (5) conclusion. Indicate in terms of paragraph numbers where each of these parts begins and ends.

6. The organizational scheme is not absolutely rigid. For instance, Swift touches upon the advantages of his proposal in places other than the third section. Where?

7. Paragraphs 8 and 20 do not really contribute to the proposal Swift is elaborating. What is their function?

8. Swift organizes the sixth paragraph by analyzing the problem in arithmetic terms. Explain why his use of arithmetic is a device of irony. Toward the end of this paragraph Swift gets involved in a discussion of whether or not children can support themselves by stealing. Is he wandering away from his point here, or does this apparent digression contribute to the general irony?

9. Paraphrase the point Swift makes in paragraph 12.

10. How are paragraphs 21-26 unified?

11. In paragraph 29 how does Swift answer the objection that his scheme would depopulate Ireland?

12. The final paragraph of "A Modest Proposal" is frequently praised as an excellent ending to the satire. Do you agree?

SENTENCES

13. Point out the parallel * constructions in these sentences:

(a) ". . . who, as they grow up, either turn thieves for want of work, or leave their dear native country to fight for the Pretender in Spain, or sell themselves to the Barbadoes." (7-9)

(b) "For we can neither employ them in handicraft or agriculture; we neither build houses (I mean in the country) nor cultivate land. . . ." (51-52)

14. Why are these revisions poorer than Swift's sentences?

(a) *Revision:* I grant this food will be somewhat dear, and therefore very proper for landlords who seem to have the best title to the children since they have already devoured most of the parents. *Swift:* "I grant this food will be somewhat dear, and therefore very proper for landlords, who, as they have already devoured most of the parents, seem to have the best title to the children." (90-92)

(b) *Revision:* Fifthly, this food would likewise bring great custom to taverns. Vintners will certainly be so prudent as to procure the best receipts for dressing it to perfection. Consequently they will have their houses frequented by all the fine gentlemen. Such gentlemen justly value themselves upon their knowledge in good eating. Therefore a skilful cook, who understands how to oblige his guests, will contrive to make it as expensive as they please.

Swift: "Fifthly, this food would likewise bring great custom to taverns; where the vintners will certainly be so prudent as to procure the best receipts for dressing it to perfection, and, consequently, have their houses frequented by all the fine gentlemen, who justly value themselves upon their knowledge in good eating: and a skilful cook, who understands how to oblige his guests, will contrive to make it as expensive as they please." (188-93)

15. Study the following sentence, which is a fine example of the kind of long, complex statement Swift was master of:

"But, as to myself, having been wearied out for many years with offering vain, idle, visionary thoughts, and at length utterly despairing of success, I fortunately fell upon this proposal; which, as it is wholly new, so it hath something solid and real, of no expense and little trouble, full in our own power, and whereby we can incur no danger in disobliging England." (245-49)

What is the main clause? What do "having been wearied" and "utterly despairing of success" modify? What does the long "which" clause modify? Point out all the parallel constructions. This sentence tells us three things: (1) what the speaker did, (2) the conditions under which he did it, and (3) why he considers it worthwhile. In what sequence are these elements placed in Swift's sentence? Why are they in that particular order?

DICTION

16. Look up: *raiment* (31), *fricassee* (71), *glutted* (98), *computed* (102), *repine* (105), *flay* (112), *discoursing* (119), *deference* (126), *expedient* (138), *gibbet* (146), *groat* (148), *idolatrous* (173), *emulation* (199), *absentees* (short for *absentee landlords*) (225), *parsimony* (230), *incur* (249).

17. Explain the etymologies * of these words: *melancholy* (1), *importuning* (4), *alms* (5), *vermin* (157), *digressed* (164), *curate* (173), *overture* (266).

18. What is the difference between *beggars by profession* (263) and *beggars in effect* (265)?

19. As the second footnote makes clear, the word *projector* meant for Swift something very different than it means for us. Similarly, the following words, still in use today, have different meanings than they had in Swift's time; explain the difference: *passenger* (4), *artificially* (112), *vintners* (189), *politicians* (265), *prudent* (189), *receipts* (189). Suggest in each case a modern word that would be the equivalent of what Swift meant.

20. Explain the irony in the following expressions: "so deserving a patriot" (127), "to fatten them would not answer the charge" (130-31), "some scrupu-

lous people might be apt to censure such a practice (although indeed very unjustly) as a little bordering upon cruelty" (133-35), "refinement in taste" (183), "vain, idle, visionary thoughts" (230), "although perhaps I could name a country which would be glad to eat up our whole nation without it" (251-53).

21. *Dam* (25) is normally applied to animals, not to human beings. Why does Swift use it as he does here? Point out other instances of his applying to humans words commonly restricted to animals.

22. One of the tricks Swift uses in "A Modest Proposal" is the inclusion of little details, seemingly irrelevant, but which have the effect of increasing our sense of horror. For instance, in arguing that the forequarter of a child will make a tasty leftover dish, he adds (85-86) "especially in winter." Or in line 117 he suggests that it might be better to buy the children alive and dress them "hot from the knife." Find several other such horrific details. If you agree that these do intensify our repulsion, can you explain why they do?

POINTS TO LEARN
1. Often an essayist who uses "I" is creating a persona, a mask through which he speaks, but which is not identical to him.
2. Moral outrage may be strengthened by being suppressed.

SUGGESTIONS FOR WRITING
1. Taking him at face value compose a character sketch in several paragraphs of the speaker of "A Modest Proposal."
2. Complete the following topic sentence and then support it in a paragraph or two by evidence from Swift's text: "The speaker of 'A Modest Proposal' considers the Irish to be _____."
3. In a paragraph or two answer this criticism of "A Modest Proposal": "The essay is too revolting to be effective; it exaggerates English policy in so disgusting a manner that it defeats its own purpose."

IMPROVING YOUR STYLE
In your composition include:

1. Two or three sentences using parallelism.
2. A complex * sentence with a main clause and three or four subordinate * constructions arranged so that their order reflects the actual sequence of events or the logic of ideas (the arrangement must still be within the patterns allowed by English grammar).
3. A series of three or four sentences tied together by *First, Second, Third, (Fourth)*.
4. Several examples of irony.

In Memoriam: W. J. B.

H. L. Mencken (1880-1956) was many things: reporter, editor, critic, essay-ist, scholar (his *The American Language,* 1918, remains one of the classics of language history). But he is best remembered as a satirist, a master of invective, who delighted in kicking sacred cows. Here he kicks William Jennings Bryan.

Bryan (1860-1925) was a Democratic politician and orator, a member of The House of Representatives for two terms, three times the unsuccessful Democratic candidate for President, and Secretary of State from 1912 to 1915 under Woodrow Wilson. In his final years he became a crusader for Christian fundamentalism and served as special prosecutor for the state of Tennessee in the 1925 trial of a Dayton, Tennessee, high school English teacher named John T. Scopes. Scopes was accused of teaching Darwinian evolutionary theory in violation of a state law which forbade any account of creation contradicting that of the Bible. Scopes was defended by the famous liberal lawyer Clarence Darrow and, while convicted, was later freed on a technicality. The trial at-tracted wide attention as a battleground between liberals and reactionaries; its outcome was generally regarded as a victory of at least a moral sort for Darwinism and for intellectual freedom. Bryan, exhausted by his efforts, died in Dayton five days after the trial ended. Mencken reported the events in Dayton for the Baltimore *Evening Sun* from a point of view sympathetic to Scopes and Darrow. His memorial essay to Bryan, while hardly a monument to the spirit of charity, is a classic example of satiric invective.

1   Has it been duly marked by historians that William Jennings Bryan's last secular act on this globe of sin was to catch flies? A curious de-tail, and not without its sardonic overtones. He was the most sedulous fly-catcher in American history, and in many ways the most successful. His quarry, of course, was not *Musca domestica* but *Homo neandertalensis.* 5 For forty years he tracked it with coo and bellow, up and down the rustic

backways of the Republic. Wherever the flambeaux of Chautauqua[1]
smoked and guttered, and the bilge of idealism ran in the veins, and Baptist pastors dammed the brooks with the sanctified, and men gathered who
were weary and heavy laden, and their wives who were full of Peruna[2] and   10
as fecund as the shad (*Alosa sapidissima*), there the indefatigable Jennings
set up his traps and spread his bait. He knew every country town in the
South and West, and he could crowd the most remote of them to suffoca-
tion by simply winding his horn. The city proletariat, transiently flustered
by him in 1896, quickly penetrated his buncombe and would have no more   15
of him; the cockney gallery jeered him at every Democratic national convention for twenty-five years. But out where the grass grows high, and the
horned cattle dream away the lazy afternoons, and men still fear the powers
and principalities of the air—out there between the corn-rows he held his
old puissance to the end. There was no need of beaters to drive in his game.   20
The news that he was coming was enough. For miles the flivver dust would
choke the roads. And when he rose at the end of the day to discharge his
Message there would be such breathless attention, such a rapt and en-
chanted ecstasy, such a sweet rustle of amens as the world had not known
since Johann fell to Herod's ax.   25

2   There was something peculiarly fitting in the fact that his last days
were spent in a one-horse Tennessee village, beating off the flies and gnats,
and that death found him there. The man felt at home in such simple and
Christian scenes. He liked people who sweated freely, and were not debauched by the refinements of the toilet. Making his progress up and down   30
the Main street of little Dayton, surrounded by gaping primates from the
upland valleys of the Cumberland Range, his coat laid aside, his bare arms
and hairy chest shining damply, his bald head sprinkled with dust—so
accoutred and on display, he was obviously happy. He liked getting up
early in the morning, to the tune of cocks crowing on the dunghill. He   35
liked the heavy, greasy victuals of the farmhouse kitchen. He liked country
lawyers, country pastors, all country people. He liked country sounds and
country smells.

3   I believe that this liking was sincere—perhaps the only sincere thing
in the man. His nose showed no uneasiness when a hillman in faded over-   40

[1] A kind of adult education program, named for Chautauqua, New York, where it began
in 1874 as a Methodist Episcopal camp-meeting offering lectures in the sciences and
humanities. For about fifty years numerous traveling Chautauquas brought enlightenment of a sort to all sections of the country. [Editors' note]
[2] A patent medicine famous as a tonic; Mencken is punning on the old expression "full
of prunes." [Editors' note]

alls and hickory shirt accosted him on the street, and besought him for light upon some mystery of Holy Writ. The simian gabble of the crossroads was not gabble to him, but wisdom of an occult and superior sort. In the presence of city folks he was palpably uneasy. Their clothes, I suspect, annoyed him, and he was suspicious of their too delicate manners. He knew 45 all the while that they were laughing at him—if not at his baroque theology, then at least at his alpaca pantaloons. But the yokels never laughed at him. To them he was not the huntsman but the prophet, and toward the end, as he gradually forsook mundane politics for more ghostly concerns, they began to elevate him in their hierarchy. When he died he was the peer 50 of Abraham. His old enemy, Wilson, aspiring to the same white and shining robe, came down with a thump. But Bryan made the grade. His place in Tennessee hagiography is secure. If the village barber saved any of his hair, then it is curing gall-stones down there today.

4   But what label will he bear in more urbane regions? One, I fear, 55 of a far less flattering kind. Bryan lived too long, and descended too deeply into the mud, to be taken seriously hereafter by fully literate men, even of the kind who write schoolbooks. There was a scattering of sweet words in his funeral notices, but it was no more than a response to conventional sentimentality. The best verdict the most romantic editorial writer could 60 dredge up, save in the humorless South, was to the general effect that his imbecilities were excused by his earnestness—that under his clowning, as under that of the juggler of Notre Dame, there was the zeal of a steadfast soul. But this was apology, not praise; precisely the same thing might be said of Mary Baker G. Eddy.[3] The truth is that even Bryan's sincerity will 65 probably yield to what is called, in other fields, definitive criticism. Was he sincere when he opposed imperialism in the Philippines, or when he fed it with deserving Democrats in Santo Domingo? Was he sincere when he tried to shove the Prohibitionists under the table, or when he seized their banner and began to lead them with loud whoops? Was he sincere when 70 he bellowed against war, or when he dreamed of himself as a tin-soldier in uniform, with a grave reserved at Arlington among the generals? Was he sincere when he fawned over Champ Clark, or when he betrayed Clark?[4]

[3] Founder of the Christian Science Movement. [Editors' note]
[4] At the Democratic Convention of 1912 Bryan deserted Champ Clark, Speaker of The House of Representatives and presidential favorite. Throwing his support to Woodrow Wilson, Bryan was rewarded by being appointed Secretary of State when Wilson was elected President. [Editors' note]

Was he sincere when he pleaded for tolerance in New York, or when he bawled for the faggot and the stake in Tennessee?   75

5   This talk of sincerity, I confess, fatigues me. If the fellow was sincere, then so was P. T. Barnum. The word is disgraced and degraded by such uses. He was, in fact, a charlatan, a mountebank, a zany without sense or dignity. His career brought him into contact with the first men of his time; he preferred the company of rustic ignoramuses. It was hard to be-   80 lieve, watching him at Dayton, that he had traveled, that he had been received in civilized societies, that he had been a high officer of state. He seemed only a poor clod like those around him, deluded by a childish theology, full of an almost pathological hatred of all learning, all human dignity, all beauty, all fine and noble things. He was a peasant come home   85 to the barnyard. Imagine a gentleman, and you have imagined everything that he was not. What animated him from end to end of his grotesque career was simply ambition—the ambition of a common man to get his hand upon the collar of his superiors, or, failing that, to get his thumb into their eyes. He was born with a roaring voice, and it had the trick of in-   90 flaming half-wits. His whole career was devoted to raising those half-wits against their betters, that he himself might shine.

6   His last battle will be grossly misunderstood if it is thought of as a mere exercise in fanaticism—that is, if Bryan the Fundamentalist Pope is mistaken for one of the bucolic Fundamentalists. There was much more in   95 it than that, as everyone knows who saw him on the field. What moved him, at bottom, was simply hatred of the city men who had laughed at him so long, and brought him at last to so tatterdemalion an estate. He lusted for revenge upon them. He yearned to lead the anthropoid rabble against them, to punish them for their execution upon him by attacking the very   100 vitals of their civilization. He went far beyond the bounds of any merely religious frenzy, however inordinate. When he began denouncing the notion that man is a mammal even some of the hinds at Dayton were agape. And when, brought upon Clarence Darrow's cruel hook, he writhed and tossed in a very fury of malignancy, bawling against the veriest elements of   105 sense and decency like a man frantic—when he came to that tragic climax of his striving there were snickers among the hinds as well as hosannas.

7   Upon that hook, in truth, Bryan committed suicide, as a legend as well as in the body. He staggered from the rustic court ready to die, and he staggered from it ready to be forgotten, save as a character in a third-   110 rate farce, witless and in poor taste. It was plain to everyone who knew him,

when he came to Dayton, that his great days were behind him—that, for all the fury of his hatred, he was now definitely an old man, and headed at last for silence. There was a vague, unpleasant manginess about his appearance; he somehow seemed dirty, though a close glance showed him as 115 carefully shaven as an actor, and clad in immaculate linen. All the hair was gone from the dome of his head, and it had begun to fall out, too, behind his ears, in the obscene manner of Samuel Gompers.[5] The resonance had departed from his voice; what was once a bugle blast had become reedy and quavering. Who knows that, like Demosthenes, he had a lisp? In the 120 old days, under the magic of his eloquence, no one noticed it. But when he spoke at Dayton it was always audible.

8   When I first encountered him, on the sidewalk in front of the office of the rustic lawyers who were his associates in the Scopes case, the trial was yet to begin, and so he was still expansive and amiable. I had printed 125 in the *Nation*, a week or so before, an article arguing that the Tennessee anti-evolution law, whatever its wisdom, was at least constitutional—that the yahoos of the State had a clear right to have their progeny taught whatever they chose, and kept secure from whatever knowledge violated their superstitions. The old boy professed to be delighted with the argument, 130 and gave the gaping bystanders to understand that I was a publicist of parts. Not to be outdone, I admired the preposterous country shirt that he wore—sleeveless and with the neck cut very low. We parted in the manner of two ambassadors.

9   But that was the last touch of amiability that I was destined to see 135 in Bryan. The next day the battle joined and his face became hard. By the end of the week he was simply a walking fever. Hour by hour he grew more bitter. What the Christian Scientists call malicious animal magnetism seemed to radiate from him like heat from a stove. From my place in the courtroom, standing upon a table, I looked directly down upon him, sweat- 140 ing horribly and pumping his palm-leaf fan. His eyes fascinated me; I watched them all day long. They were blazing points of hatred. They glittered like occult and sinister gems. Now and then they wandered to me, and I got my share, for my reports of the trial had come back to Dayton, and he had read them. It was like coming under fire.   145

10   Thus he fought his last fight, thirsting savagely for blood. All sense departed from him. He bit right and left, like a dog with rabies. He descended to demagogy so dreadful that his very associates at the trial table

[5] Samuel Gompers (1850-1924), a labor leader, one of the founders and first president of The American Federation of Labor. [Editors' note]

blushed. His one yearning was to keep his yokels heated up—to lead his forlorn mob of imbeciles against the foe. That foe, alas, refused to be 150 alarmed. It insisted upon seeing the whole battle as a comedy. Even Darrow, who knew better, occasionally yielded to the prevailing spirit. One day he lured poor Bryan into the folly I have mentioned: his astounding argument against the notion that man is a mammal. I am glad I heard it, for otherwise I'd never believe it. There stood the man who had been thrice a 155 candidate for the Presidency of the Republic—there he stood in the glare of the world, uttering stuff that a boy of eight would laugh at. The artful Darrow led him on: he repeated it, ranted for it, bellowed it in his cracked voice. So he was prepared for the final slaughter. He came into life a hero, a Galahad, in bright and shining armor. He was passing out a poor 160 mountebank.

QUESTIONS

READER AND PURPOSE

1. How might the title of this essay mislead a reader who knew nothing about H. L. Mencken or William Jennings Bryan? What are the conventions that usually govern an "in memoriam" for a dead public figure? Is the title really misleading, or is the essay genuinely a "memorial"?
2. Mencken's satire includes more than Bryan. What else is he attacking?
3. Do you think Mencken was writing for a highly sophisticated, literate audience, or for more general, less "hip" readers? For urbanites or for small-town Americans? How would you describe his tone *, especially his attitude toward Bryan?

ORGANIZATION

4. Does the rhetorical question * work as a way of opening the essay? What does Mencken mean by his remark that Bryan's final action on earth has "sardonic overtones"?
5. Mencken achieves considerable unity in his paragraphs by ringing variations on key ideas. What later terms in paragraph 1 echo the words "catch flies" (or are suggested by association with that phrase)? Which repeat "rustic backways"? Point out echoes of these expressions in later paragraphs.
6. Paragraph 2 consists of seven sentences. The first states the topic. How does the second support that topic? How does Mencken unify the remainder of the paragraph?
7. What words link the third paragraph to the second? Does paragraph 3 introduce a new idea or merely refine the topic of paragraph 2?

8. What change in thought occurs in paragraph 4? Identify the topic statement of this paragraph. In the second and third sentences Mencken answers the rhetorical question he poses in line 55. In what sense are his next two statements (58-64) a qualification * upon the answer? Where does Mencken disarm the qualification and reassert his own conclusion? How, finally, do the series of rhetorical questions support the conclusion?

9. How is paragraph 5 linked to 4? Paragraph 6 to 5? Paragraph 7 to 6?

SENTENCES

10. Comment upon the effectiveness of the following revisions in comparison to Mencken's sentences:

(a) *Revision:* It is a curious detail and one that is not without its sardonic overtones.
Mencken: "A curious detail, and not without its sardonic overtones." (2-3)

(b) *Revision:* He knew all the while that they were laughing at him—if not at his baroque theology, then at least at his alpaca pantaloons, but the yokels never laughed at him.
Mencken: "He knew all the while that they were laughing at him—if not at his baroque theology, then at least at his alpaca pantaloons. But the yokels never laughed at him." (45-48)

(c) *Revision:* What animated him from end to end of his grotesque career was simply the ambition of a common man. . . .
Mencken: "What animated him from end to end of his grotesque career was simply ambition—the ambition of a common man. . . ." (87-88)

(d) *Revision:* But that was the last touch of amiability that I was destined to see in Bryan, for the next day the battle joined and his face became hard and by the end of the week he was simply a walking fever, growing more bitter hour by hour.
Mencken: "But that was the last touch of amiability that I was destined to see in Bryan. The next day the battle joined and his face became hard. By the end of the week he was simply a walking fever. Hour by hour he grew more bitter." (135-38)

11. Something of the vitality of Mencken's prose derives from his skill in varying sentence structure. The final portion of paragraph 1 (from lines 17 to 25) offers an example. The first sentence ("But out where the grass grows high . . .") is long and leisurely, reflecting the bucolic life it ironically describes. Point out the parallel * constructions in this sentence. How does the

style change in the next three sentences? Does the last sentence of the paragraph continue the pattern of the preceding three, or is it more like the one with which this passage begins? Might it be said that the very pattern and movement of these five sentences suggest Bryan's effect upon a rural community? Explain.

12. Find one or two other places where Mencken varies long and short sentences with similar skill.

DICTION

13. Look up: *secular* (2), *sedulous* (3), *fecund* (11), *debauched* (29), *accoutred* (34), *palpably* (44), *alpaca* (47), *hierarchy* (50), *tatterdemalion* (98), *frenzy* (102), *inordinate* (102), *manginess* (114), *progeny* (128).

14. What are the etymologies * of *flambeaux* (7), *buncombe* (often shortened to *bunk*) (15), *occult* (43), *grotesque* (87), *bucolic* (95), *demagogy* (148)?

15. As fully as you can explain what Mencken conveys by the following phrases: *bilge of idealism* (8), *winding his horn* (14), *city proletariat* (14), *powers and principalities of the air* (18-19), *baroque theology* (46), *mundane politics* (49), *Tennessee hagiography* (53), *faggot and stake* (75), *pathological hatred* (84), *bucolic Fundamentalists* (95).

16. What irony * is concealed in these expressions: *sweet rustle of amens* (24) and *debauched by the refinements of the toilet* (29-30)?

17. Here are some of the nouns Mencken applies to Bryan: *charlatan* (78), *zany* (78), *clod* (83), *peasant* (85), *the Fundamentalist Pope* (94), *a dog with rabies* (147). What range of faults and follies is implied by those words?

18. Mencken also effectively characterizes Bryan's speech and actions: *coo and bellow* (6), *writhe* (104), and *bawling* (105) are examples. Find other words which throw a satiric light upon Bryan in speech and action, and be able to comment upon what they imply.

19. Similarly Mencken uses invective to mock Bryan's natural constituency, the *yahoos*, as he calls them in line 128. What is a yahoo? Where did the word originate? List other insulting expressions the writer applies to the country people who idolized Bryan.

20. Why are these alternates poorer than Mencken's words for his particular purpose? *Blazed and shone* for *smoked and guttered* (8), *fence* for *dunghill* (35), *poorly cooked* for *heavy, greasy* (36), *trousers* for *pantaloons* (47), *especially* for *even* (57), *shone* for *glittered* (142), *clever* for *artful* (157).

21. Who is *Galahad* (160)? Is Mencken applying the allusion ironically or seriously? What is a *mountebank* (161)? The two words sum up Mencken's estimate of Bryan. Would his closing have been better arranged like this: "He was passing out a poor mountebank who had begun life a hero, a Galahad, in shining armor"?

POINTS TO LEARN

1. Invective is the simplest, most direct form of satire. It is a pick-handle where irony is a rapier. Its effectiveness depends upon the variety and the originality of the insults of which it consists.

2. Long sentences need short ones. Variety is vital to a good sentence style.

SUGGESTIONS FOR WRITING

1. Mencken does not explain exactly why he despises William Jennings Bryan and the kind of people who support him. Still, it is possible to deduce his reasons. Write a short essay of two or three paragraphs explaining the grounds of Mencken's contempt and support your account with citations from Mencken's prose.

2. How would you answer the complaint that satire of this sort is unfair because it is exaggerated and one-sided?

3. A more ambitious project: consult a biography of William Jennings Bryan or a scholarly history of his times which discusses him in detail and then argue whether Mencken's account (even after we have discounted the exaggeration allowed a satirist) is fair.

4. Picking a target that engages your imagination, attempt a paragraph of invective satire. Keep it clean and avoid the clichés of name-calling. Invective works to the degree that the insults are witty and reveal genuine follies and faults.

IMPROVING YOUR STYLE

1. Whatever topic you choose work for a mix in sentence style—longer, more complicated sentences varied by shorter more direct ones.

2. Use several examples of irony.

3. Use four or five verbs which graphically express in terms of physical action how you feel about your subject.

4. Think of an allusion *, literary or historical, which, like Mencken's reference to Galahad, conveys a complex set of ideas and attitudes.

The Funeral Oration of Pericles

In 431 B.C. the Peloponnesian War broke out between Athens, along with her allies, and a rival league of Greek city-states led by Sparta. The war dragged on until 404 B.C., when it ended disastrously for Athens. At the close of the first year's campaigning, however, Athenian hopes were high, and the city's pride and faith are reflected in the famous oration of Pericles, a great war leader and statesman. He spoke at the funeral for the Athenians killed in that first year of the war, who were being buried at public expense, then as now a customary honor for soldiers killed fighting for the state. The occasion was recorded by Thucydides, himself a general on the Athenian side, who, after being dismissed from command, wrote an unfinished history of the war, one of the great works of ancient historiography.

Pericles's speech is a fine example of ancient oratory, an art carefully studied by ambitious Athenians in schools of rhetoric. More specifically this oration is of a type known as epideictic—speeches delivered on public ceremonial occasions, as distinguished from those given in courts of law (forensic oratory) and political assemblies (deliberative oratory). The epideictic oration depended upon eloquence more than logic. It persuaded by appealing to the ideals and aspirations of its audience.

While we no longer use the terms of Greek rhetoric to describe and classify the various modes and techniques of speaking, the value of eloquence is still real. A great political leader—a Lincoln, a Churchill, a Franklin Roosevelt—is marked by the capacity to lift our vision above the concerns of daily life, to inspire us to be better than we are. This can be done only by language, eloquent language that rings in our ears long after its moment has passed, memorable because it expresses in finely tuned words what men and women can be. Words like these:

> With malice toward none; with charity for all; with firmness in the right as God gives us to see the right, let us strive to finish the work we are in. . . .

From Thucydides, *The History of the Peloponnesian War*, edited in translation by Sir R. W. Livingstone. Reprinted by permission of Oxford University Press, Inc.

Let us therefore brace ourselves to our duties, and so bear ourselves that, if the British Empire and its Commonwealth last for a thousand years, men will still say: "This was their finest hour."

The only thing we have to fear is fear itself.

Eloquence involves more than noble sentiments. It requires a mastery of language—the ability to select the precise word and to control the structure and rhythm of sentences. Eloquence is noble feeling focused and intensified by words.

1   Most of those who have stood in this place before me have commended the institution of this closing address. It is good, they have felt, that solemn words should be spoken over our fallen soldiers. I do not share this feeling. Acts deserve acts, not words, in their honor, and to me a burial at the State's charges, such as you see before you, would have appeared suf- 5 ficient. Our sense of the deserts of a number of our fellow-citizens should not depend upon the felicity of one man's speech. Moreover, it is very hard for a speaker to be appropriate when many of his hearers will scarce believe that he is truthful. For those who have known and loved the dead may think his words scant justice to the memories they would hear honored: 10 while those who do not know will occasionally, from jealousy, suspect me of overstatement when they hear of any feat beyond their own powers. For it is only human for men not to bear praise of others beyond the point at which they still feel that they can rival their exploits. Transgress that boundary and they are jealous and distrustful. But since the wisdom of our 15 ancestors enacted this law I too must submit and try to suit as best I can the wishes and feelings of every member of this gathering.

2   My first words shall be for our ancestors; for it is both just to them and seemly that on an occasion such as this our tribute of memory should be paid them. For, dwelling always in this country, generation after gener- 20 ation in unchanging and unbroken succession, they have handed it down to us free by their exertions. So they are worthy of our praises; and still more so are our fathers. For they enlarged the ancestral patrimony by the Empire which we hold to-day and delivered it, not without labor, into the hands of our own generation; while it is we ourselves, those of us who are 25 now in middle life, who consolidated our power throughout the greater part of the Empire and secured the city's complete independence both in war and peace. Of the battles which we and our fathers fought, whether in the winning of our power abroad or in bravely withstanding the warfare

of foreigner or Greek at home, I do not wish to say more: they are too fa- 30
miliar to you all. I wish rather to set forth the spirit in which we faced
them, and the constitution and manners with which we rose to greatness,
and to pass from them to the dead; for I think it not unfitting that these
things should be called to mind in to-day's solemnity, and expedient too
that the whole gathering of citizens and strangers should listen to them.   35

3   For our government is not copied from those of our neighbors: we
are an example to them rather than they to us. Our constitution is named
a democracy, because it is in the hands not of the few but of the many.
But our laws secure equal justice for all in their private disputes, and our
public opinion welcomes and honors talent in every branch of achievement, 40
not for any sectional reason but on grounds of excellence alone. And as we
give free play to all in our public life, so we carry the same spirit into our
daily relations with one another. We have no black looks or angry words
for our neighbor if he enjoys himself in his own way, and we abstain from
the little acts of churlishness which, though they leave no mark, yet cause 45
annoyance to who so notes them. Open and friendly in our private intercourse, in our public acts we keep strictly within the control of law. We
acknowledge the restraint of reverence; we are obedient to whomsoever is
set in authority, and to the laws, more especially to those which offer protection to the oppressed and those unwritten ordinances whose transgres- 50
sion brings admitted shame.

4   Yet ours is no work-a-day city only. No other provides so many
recreations for the spirit—contests and sacrifices all the year round, and
beauty in our public buildings to cheer the heart and delight the eye day
by day. Moreover, the city is so large and powerful that all the wealth of 55
all the world flows in to her, so that our own Attic products seem no more
homelike to us than the fruits of the labors of other nations.

5   Our military training too is different from our opponents'. The
gates of our city are flung open to the world. We practice no periodical de-
portations, nor do we prevent our visitors from observing or discovering 60
what an enemy might usefully apply to his own purposes. For our trust is
not in the devices of material equipment, but in our own good spirits for
battle.

6   So too with education. They toil from early boyhood in a laborious
pursuit after courage, while we, free to live and wander as we please, march 65
out none the less to face the self-same dangers. Here is the proof of my
words. When the Spartans advance into our country, they do not come
alone but with all their allies; but when we invade our neighbors we have

little difficulty as a rule, even on foreign soil, in defeating men who are
fighting for their own homes. Moreover, no enemy has ever met us in full   70
strength, for we have our navy to attend to, and our soldiers are sent on
service to many scattered possessions; but if they chance to encounter some
portion of our forces and defeat a few of us, they boast that they have
driven back our whole army, or, if they are defeated, that the victors were
in full strength. Indeed, if we choose to face danger with an easy mind   75
rather than after a rigorous training, and to trust rather in native manliness
than in state-made courage, the advantage lies with us; for we are spared all
the weariness of practicing for future hardships, and when we find ourselves amongst them we are as brave as our plodding rivals. Here as elsewhere, then, the city sets an example which is deserving of admiration.   80

7   We are lovers of beauty without extravagance, and lovers of wisdom
without unmanliness. Wealth to us is not mere material for vainglory but
an opportunity for achievement; and poverty we think it no disgrace to acknowledge but a real degradation to make no effort to overcome. Our citizens attend both to public and private duties, and do not allow absorption   85
in their own various affairs to interfere with their knowledge of the city's.
We differ from other states in regarding the man who holds aloof from
public life not as "quiet" but as useless; we decide or debate, carefully and
in person, all matters of policy, holding, not that words and deeds go ill together, but that acts are foredoomed to failure when undertaken undis-   90
cussed. For we are noted for being at once most adventurous in action and
most reflective beforehand. Other men are bold in ignorance, while reflection will stop their onset. But the bravest are surely those who have the
clearest vision of what is before them, glory and danger alike, and yet not-
withstanding go out to meet it. In doing good, too, we are the exact op-   95
posite of the rest of mankind. We secure our friends not by accepting
favors but by doing them. And so we are naturally more firm in our attach-
ments: for we are anxious, as creditors, to cement by kind offices our relation towards our friends. If they do not respond with the same warmness it
is because they feel that their services will not be given spontaneously but   100
only as the repayment of a debt. We are alone among mankind in doing
men benefits, not on calculations of self-interest, but in the fearless confidence of freedom.

8   In a word I claim that our city as a whole is an education to
Greece, and that her members yield to none, man by man, for independ-   105
ence of spirit, many-sidedness of attainment, and complete self-reliance in
limbs and brain.

9   That this is no vainglorious phrase but actual fact the supremacy which our manners have won us itself bears testimony. No other city of the present day goes out to her ordeal greater than ever men dreamed; no other is so powerful that the invader feels no bitterness when he suffers at her hands, and her subjects no shame at the indignity of their dependence. Great indeed are the symbols and witnesses of our supremacy, at which posterity, as all mankind to-day, will be astonished. We need no Homer or other man of words to praise us, for such give pleasure for a moment, but the truth will put to shame their imaginings of our deeds. For our pioneers have forced a way into every sea and every land, establishing among all mankind, in punishment or beneficence, eternal memorials of their settlement.

10   Such then is the city for whom, lest they should lose her, the men whom we celebrate died a soldier's death: and it is but natural that all of us, who survive them, should wish to spend ourselves in her service. That, indeed, is why I have spent many words upon the city. I wished to show that we have more at stake than men who have no such inheritance, and to support my praise of the dead by making clear to you what they have done. For if I have chanted the glories of the city it was these men and their like who set hand to array her. With them, as with few among Greeks, words cannot magnify the deeds that they have done. Such an end as we have here seems indeed to show us what a good life is, from its first signs of power to its final consummation. For even where life's previous record showed faults and failures it is just to weigh the last brave hour of devotion against them all. There they wiped out evil with good and did the city more service as soldiers than they did her harm in private life. There no hearts grew faint because they loved riches more than honor; none shirked the issue in the poor man's dreams of wealth. All these they put aside to strike a blow for the city. Counting the quest to avenge her honor as the most glorious of all ventures, and leaving Hope, the uncertain goddess, to send them what she would, they faced the foe as they drew near him in the strength of their own manhood; and when the shock of battle came, they chose rather to suffer the uttermost than to win life by weakness. So their memory has escaped the reproaches of men's lips, but they bore instead on their bodies the marks of men's hands, and in a moment of time, at the climax of their lives, were rapt away from a world filled, for their dying eyes, not with terror but with glory.

11   Such were the men who lie here and such the city that inspired them. We survivors may pray to be spared their bitter hour, but must dis-

dain to meet the foe with a spirit less triumphant. Fix your eyes on the greatness of Athens as you have it before you day by day, fall in love with her, and when you feel her great, remember that this greatness was won by men with courage, with knowledge of their duty, and with a sense of honor in action, who, if they failed in any ordeal, disdained to deprive the city of their services, but sacrificed their lives as the best offerings on her behalf. So they gave their bodies to the commonwealth and received, each for his own memory, praise that will never die, and with it the grandest of all sepulchres, not that in which their mortal bones are laid, but a home in the minds of men, where their glory remains fresh to stir to speech or action as the occasion comes by. For the whole earth is the sepulchre of famous men; and their story is not graven only on stone over their native earth, but lives on far away, without visible symbol, woven into the stuff of other men's lives. For you now it remains to rival what they have done and, knowing the secret of happiness to be freedom and the secret of freedom a brave heart, not idly to stand aside from the enemy's onset. For it is not the poor and luckless, as having no hope of prosperity, who have most cause to reckon death as little loss, but those for whom fortune may yet keep reversal in store and who would feel the change most if trouble befell them. Moreover, weakly to decline the trial is more painful to a man of spirit than death coming sudden and unperceived in the hour of strength and enthusiasm.

12   Therefore I do not mourn with the parents of the dead who are here with us. I will rather comfort them. For they know that they have been born into a world of manifold chances and that he is to be accounted happy to whom the best lot falls—the best sorrow, such as is yours today, or the best death, such as fell to these, for whom life and happiness were cut to the self-same measure. I know it is not easy to give you comfort. I know how often in the joy of others you will have reminders of what was once your own, and how men feel sorrow, not for the loss of what they have never tasted, but when something that has grown dear to them has been snatched away. But you must keep a brave heart in the hope of other children, those who are still of age to bear them. For the newcomers will help you to forget the gap in your own circle, and will help the city to fill up the ranks of its workers and its soldiers. For no man is fitted to give fair and honest advice in council if he has not, like his fellows, a family at stake in the hour of the city's danger. To you who are past the age of vigor I would say: count the long years of happiness so much to set off against the brief

space that yet remains, and let your burden be lightened by the glory of the 185
dead. For the love of honor alone is not staled by age, and it is by honor,
not, as some say, by gold, that the helpless end of life is cheered.

13   I turn to those amongst you who are children or brothers of the
fallen, for whom I foresee a mighty contest with the memory of the dead.
Their praise is in all men's mouths, and hardly, even for supremest heroism, 190
you will be adjudged to have achieved, not the same but a little less than
they. For the living have the jealousy of rivals to contend with, but the dead
are honored with unchallenged admiration.

14   If I must also speak a word to those who are now in widowhood on
the powers and duties of women, I will cast all my advice into one brief 195
sentence. Great will be your glory if you do not lower the nature that is
within you—hers greatest of all whose praise or blame is least bruited on
the lips of men.

15   I have spoken such words as I had to say according as the law pre-
scribes, and the graveside offerings to the dead have been duly made. Hence- 200
forward the city will take charge of their children till manhood: such is the
crown and benefit she holds out to the dead and to their kin for the trials
they have undergone for her. For where the prize is highest, there, too, are
the best citizens to contend for it.

16   And now, when you have finished your lamentation, let each of you 205
depart.

QUESTIONS

READER AND PURPOSE

1. Certainly Pericles' primary aim is to praise the dead. But remembering the
occasion, do you detect any other purpose in his words? Might his oration be
described as persuasive as well as laudatory?

2. In paragraph 14 he addresses the widows of the dead soldiers, urging that
they do not lower "the nature that is within" them and that they bear their
grief in dignified silence, for the greatest credit belongs to those "whose praise
or blame is least bruited on the lips of men." The passage reveals the attitude
Pericles assumes toward his fellow-citizens. Describe that attitude.

ORGANIZATION

3. Pericles arrests his audience's attention by surprising them at the very beginning of his speech. How? What reason does he offer in paragraph 1 to support his surprising position?

4. How does the opening paragraph serve to establish an appropriate relationship between the speaker and his audience?

5. The organization of Pericles' speech reveals the close communion of spirit the ancient Greeks felt to exist between the state and the individual. The state, moreover, was conceived as extending through time, encompassing the past and the future as well as the present. Accordingly, with what subject does Pericles begin his oration proper?

6. Paragraphs 3 through 9 make up a section. What is Pericles doing here? Give a brief descriptive title to this part of the oration. Give one- or two-word titles to paragraphs 3, 4, 5, 6, and 7, and show how each of these paragraphs is linked to what precedes it.

7. To whom is Pericles contrasting the Athenians in paragraphs 5 and 6?

8. How might one answer the objection that in this portion of his oration Pericles appears to have forgotten the dead he was supposed to praise?

9. Why may we regard paragraphs 10 and 11 as making up the second major section of the speech?

10. The third section begins in paragraph 12. What has the speaker turned to here? Where does this section end?

11. Which paragraphs compose the conclusion? Does Pericles manage a skillful ending, neatly rounding off his oration? Or is his closing too abrupt, letting things down with a bump? Might it be said that, below its matter-of-fact surface, his final sentence implies a profound moral truth?

SENTENCES

12. Pericles is fond of the balanced sentence *, which divides into two roughly equal parts, as in: "For our government is not copied from those of our neighbors: we are an example to them rather than they to us" (36-37). Point out five or six other such sentences.

13. This type of structure permits the emphasis of similar, and the antithesis * of contrasting, ideas. Study the following sentences and decide what contrasts or similarities are made prominent by the sentence structure:

(a) "For our trust is not in the devices of material equipment, but in our own good spirits for battle." (61-63)

(b) "We are lovers of beauty without extravagance, and lovers of wisdom without unmanliness." (81-82)

(c) "Wealth to us is not mere material for vainglory but an opportunity for achievement; and poverty we think it no disgrace to acknowledge but a real degradation to make no effort to overcome." (82-84)

14. Look again at the sentence in lines 36-37 and identify the chiasmus * in the second clause.

DICTION

15. Look up *felicity* (7), *transgress* (14), *patrimony* (23), *consolidated* (26), *churlishness* (45), *vainglory* (82), *array* (127), *rapt* (143), *sepulchres* (155), *vigor* (183), *bruited* (197).

16. Pericles is careful to establish the logical flow of his thought. Identify in paragraph 1 those connectives * which signal the structure of his ideas.

17. Does Pericles play upon the emotions of his audience, using words which are likely to intensify their grief? Or does his diction have an emotionally dampening effect?

18. Which of his words are especially chosen to appeal to a high sense of duty? What does Pericles imply is the proper manner for Athenians to deal with the facts before them—the bones of their dead, fallen in battle?

POINTS TO LEARN

Eloquence appeals to our nobler sentiments, seeking to move us from narrow self-interest to the contemplation of wider, less egocentric values.

SUGGESTIONS FOR WRITING

1. Write a paragraph or two describing the Athenian conception of the ideal citizen.

2. How do you think a modern audience would respond to Pericles' speech? Develop your conclusions in one or two paragraphs.

IMPROVING YOUR STYLE

In your composition attempt:

1. Four or five balanced sentences in which you place key terms in the same positions in the two parts of the sentence so as to emphasize their similarity or difference.

2. An example of chiasmus.

WILLIAM FAULKNER

On Receiving the Nobel Prize

William Faulkner (1897-1962) was one of the best American novelists of the twentieth century. Born and educated in Mississippi, he wrote primarily about his native region. In 1949 he was awarded the Nobel Prize for literature. This selection is the speech he delivered on that occasion. Like the oration of Pericles in the preceding selection, this is also a fine example of eloquence. It is less formally constructed, less rhetorical in the technical sense of that term. But Faulkner's speech passes the test of true eloquence: a high-minded sense of human destiny expressed in moving and memorable language.

1   I feel that this award was not made to me as a man but to my work— a life's work in the agony and sweat of the human spirit, not for glory and least of all for profit, but to create out of the materials of the human spirit something which did not exist there before. So this award is only mine in trust. It will not be difficult to find a dedication for the money part of it 5 commensurate with the purpose and significance of its origin. But I would like to do the same with the acclaim, too, by using this moment as a pinnacle from which I might be listened to by the young men and women already dedicated to the same anguish and travail, among whom is already that one who will some day stand here where I am standing.   10

2   Our tragedy today is a general and a universal physical fear so long sustained by now that we can even bear it. There are no longer problems of the spirit. There is only the question: When will I be blown up? Because of this, the young man or woman writing today has forgotten the problems of the human heart in conflict with itself which alone can make good writ- 15 ing because only that is worth writing about, worth the agony and the sweat.

3   He must learn them again. He must teach himself that the basest of all things is to be afraid; and, teaching himself that, forget it forever,

leaving no room in his workshop for anything but the old verities and truths 20
of the heart, the old universal truths lacking which any story is ephemeral
and doomed—love and honor and pity and pride and compassion and sacrifice. Until he does so he labors under a curse. He writes not of love, but of
lust, of defeats in which nobody loses anything of value, of victories without hope and worst of all without pity or compassion. His griefs grieve on 25
no universal bones, leaving no scars. He writes not of the heart but of the
glands.
4   Until he relearns these things he will write as though he stood
among and watched the end of man. I decline to accept the end of man. It
is easy enough to say that man is immortal simply because he will endure; 30
that when the last ding-dong of doom has clanged and faded from the last
worthless rock hanging tideless in the last red and dying evening, that even
then there will still be one more sound: that of his puny inexhaustible voice
still talking. I refuse to accept this. I believe that man will not merely endure: he will prevail. He is immortal, not because he alone among creatures 35
has an inexhaustible voice, but because he has a soul, a spirit capable of
compassion and sacrifice and endurance. The poet's, the writer's, duty is to
write about these things. It is his privilege to help man endure by lifting his
heart, by reminding him of the courage and honor and hope and pride and
compassion and pity and sacrifice which have been the glory of his past. 40
The poet's voice need not merely be the record of man, it can be one of
the props, the pillars to help him endure and prevail.

QUESTIONS

READER AND PURPOSE

1. Faulkner clearly defines his purpose in the first paragraph. In which sentence?
2. To whom does he imagine himself to be talking? Of what does he wish to
persuade these listeners?

ORGANIZATION

3. If the first paragraph establishes the writer's intention, how does the second
fit into his strategy? What does it contribute to his thesis? Give it a brief descriptive title.
4. What words tie the beginning of the third paragraph to the second? How
are the topics of these two paragraphs related?
5. Make a conceptual analysis of paragraph 3, showing how the writer's thought
progresses from sentence to sentence. Explain why the passage beginning in

line 23 ("Until he does so he labors under a curse") marks a major turn of thought within the paragraph. How does Faulkner use sentence structure to unify paragraph 3?

6. What words connect the fourth paragraph to the third? Which sentence marks a major turn in this paragraph?

SENTENCES

7. Compare the following revisions with Faulkner's sentences and comment upon the differences in meaning, emphasis, or rhythm:

(a) *Revision:* The only question is when I'll be blown up.
 Faulkner: "There is only the question: When will I be blown up?" (13)

(b) *Revision:* He will write as though he stood among and watched the end of man until he relearns these things.
 Faulkner: "Until he relearns these things he will write as though he stood among and watched the end of man." (28-29)

(c) *Revision:* I believe that man will prevail and not merely endure.
 Faulkner: "I believe that man will not merely endure: he will prevail." (34-35)

8. Point out one or two places where Faulkner employs short sentences very effectively.

9. In the sentence in lines 18-23 to what are "love and honor and pity and pride and compassion and sacrifice" in apposition *? Suppose a comma rather than a dash had preceded these words—would the clarity of the sentence have been helped or hindered?

10. In that list Faulkner joins all the items with *ands* instead of following the more commonplace formula: "love, honor, pity, pride, compassion, and sacrifice." Where else does he handle a list or series with multiple conjunctions * (a technique called polysyndeton *)? Can you see any reason why he does it this way?

DICTION

11. Look up: *acclaim* (7), *anguish* (9), *travail* (9), *basest* (18), *prevail* (42).

12. Explain the etymologies * of *commensurate* (6), *verities* (20), *ephemeral* (21), *doom* (31), *endurance* (37).

13. Several times Faulkner couples *compassion* and *pity*. What is the difference?

14. Would it be an improvement in lines 25-26 to write something like "his griefs sadden no universal bones," avoiding the repetition of "griefs grieve"? What, incidentally, does Faulkner mean by "universal bones"?

15. In line 31 Faulkner uses the striking phrase "the last ding-dong of doom." *Ding-dong* and *doom* arouse quite different associations in one's mind. Explain.

Do you think this clash of associations makes the image awkward and ineffective? Why in this same passage does Faulkner specify the rock as being "tideless"?

16. Identify the alliteration * in the final sentence. What values does it have? Where else does Faulkner employ alliteration?

POINTS TO LEARN

1. Faulkner's speech is a notable testament to the human spirit. This faith in man is the foundation of all eloquence.

2. Like all effective persuasion, eloquence requires a clear sense of purpose and a strategy efficacious in achieving that purpose.

SUGGESTIONS FOR WRITING

Write a paragraph or two describing your reaction to Faulkner's words. Did they move you or not? Do you agree with what he says about man and about the moral responsibilities of the writer? Do you think he is unduly pessimistic, guilty of an unjustifiable optimism, or expresses a balanced view of human possibilities?

IMPROVING YOUR STYLE

Include in your composition:

1. A portion of the paragraph unified by several sentences beginning in the same way.

2. An appositive.

3. An instance of polysyndeton (see question 10).

4. A passage using alliteration.

The Search for Marvin Gardens

John McPhee is among the best of the so-called new journalists, who add a dimension of personal judgment and sensitivity to the reporter's traditional job of reporting the facts. His essays, often appearing in *The New Yorker* magazine, deal with people and places—Alaska, a canoe trip in northern Maine, the Jersey pine barrens, the basketball star—now Senator—Bill Bradley. In the following essay McPhee writes about Atlantic City, the once-fashionable resort on the coast of New Jersey whose fortunes declined in the 1950's and '60's. (Since McPhee wrote—1972—the city has been revived, financially at least, by the introduction of legalized casino gambling.)

McPhee organizes his essay in an unusual way, using the game of "Monopoly" to counterpoint his account of the city. The relationship between "Monopoly" and Atlantic City is not fortuitous; in its layout the game borrows street names from the resort. Probably, like most of us, you have played "Monopoly"; if so you may skip to the last paragraph of this headnote. But if you are unfamiliar with the game, a word about how it is played will help you to understand what McPhee is doing.

"Monopoly" is a board game for two, three, four, or more players. Each player is represented by a small token (a top hat, a satchel, a flat iron, a racing car) which he moves around a board nineteen inches square according to the number shown by the roll of a pair of dice. The edge of the board is divided into forty spaces. The four corner ones are labeled "Go" (the starting point), "Jail," "Free Parking," and "Go to Jail." Of the thirty-six remaining spaces, two force players landing upon them to pay a tax, three are designated "Chance" and three "Community Chest" (these six require a player to pick the top card from one of two piles and to do whatever it says—go to jail and lose his turn, pay a fine, or even by a lucky chance to receive an unexpected stock dividend). The other twenty-eight spaces represent pieces of property: four "Railroads," an "Electric Company," a "Waterworks," and twenty-two streets.

The streets are grouped in units of two or three, each street in the group being of the same color ("Atlantic Avenue," "Ventnor Avenue," and "Marvin Gardens," for example, are yellow; "Pacific," "North Carolina," and "Pennsylvania" Avenues are green). The streets increase in value as one moves around the board: "Mediterranean" and "Baltic" Avenues, immediately after "Go," are the cheapest, while "Park Place" and the "Boardwalk," farthest along, are the most expensive. These values correspond roughly with the economic realities of Atlantic City: Baltic Avenue really is a poor neighborhood while the Boardwalk is prime property.

At the beginning of the game the players are given equal sums of play money. The remaining cash, along with small cardboard "Deeds" to the properties, is placed in a "Bank," tended by one of the players (hopefully the most honest). As players move in turn round and round the board (which they continue to do until the game is over) they may buy from the bank the deed to any property they land upon, if they have the cash and if it is not already owned. Should it be owned the player landing upon it must pay a stipulated rent, keyed to the value of the property.

A player's immediate object is to acquire a monopoly—all four railroads, for instance, or all three avenues in the green group. When he has done so he may charge a higher rent and, on the street properties, build houses and hotels (purchased from the bank), which dramatically increase the charges unlucky visitors must pay. Property may be mortgaged for ready cash and, according to the ground rules adopted by the players, "deals" may be negotiated in the form of exchanging or selling properties, accepting deeds in lieu of rent, and so on. The ultimate object is to form a sufficient number of monopolies to force one's opponents into bankruptcy, at which point they must surrender to the bank whatever deeds and cash they retain and leave the game. The final player is the winner, owning, in effect, all the property and all the money.

"Monopoly" was invented in the 1930's during the great depression and was an immediate, and phenomenal, success: More than forty years later, while no longer a phenomenon, the game remains popular. It obviously appeals to a society based upon economic individualism and competition, giving us the chance to play a role real life denies: the "Grand Monopolist," financially omnipotent, owner of all he surveys.

On the surface "The Search for Marvin Gardens" is not persuasion. It mounts no formal argument; it is not a satire. Yet below the surface it implies, with considerable persuasive force, feelings and judgments about the values of our society.

1   Go. I roll the dice—a six and a two. Through the air I move my token, the flatiron, to Vermont Avenue, where dog packs range.

2   The dogs are moving (some are limping) through ruins, rubble,

fire damage, open garbage. Doorways are gone. Lath is visible in the
crumbling walls of the buildings. The street sparkles with shattered glass.
I have never seen, anywhere, so many broken windows. A sign—"Slow,
Children at Play"—has been bent backward by an automobile. At the
lighthouse, the dogs turn up Pacific and disappear. George Meade, Army
engineer, built the lighthouse—brick upon brick, six hundred thousand
bricks, to reach up high enough to throw a beam twenty miles over the
sea. Meade, seven years later, saved the Union at Gettysburg.

3   I buy Vermont Avenue for $100. My opponent is a tall, shadowy
figure, across from me, but I know him well, and I know his game like a
favorite tune. If he can, he will always go for the quick kill. And when it
is foolish to go for the quick kill he will be foolish. On the whole, though,
he is a master assessor of percentages. It is a mistake to underestimate
him. His eleven carries his top hat to St. Charles Place, which he buys
for $140.

4   The sidewalks of St. Charles Place have been cracked to shards by
through-growing weeds. There are no buildings. Mansions, hotels once
stood here. A few street lamps now drop cones of light on broken glass
and vacant space behind a chain-link fence that some great machine has in
places bent to the ground. Five plane trees—in full summer leaf, flecking
the light—are all that live on St. Charles Place.

5   Block upon block, gradually, we are cancelling each other out—in
the blues, the lavenders, the oranges, the greens. My opponent follows a
plan of his own devising. I use the Hornblower & Weeks opening and the
Zuricher defense. The first game draws tight, will soon finish. In 1971, a
group of people in Racine, Wisconsin, played for seven hundred and sixty-
eight hours. A game begun a month later in Danville, California, lasted
eight hundred and twenty hours. These are official records, and they stun
us. We have been playing for eight minutes. It amazes us that Monopoly
is thought of as a long game. It is possible to play to a complete, absolute,
and final conclusion in less than fifteen minutes, all within the rules as
written. My opponent and I have done so thousands of times. No wonder
we are sitting across from each other now in this best-of-seven series for the
international singles championship of the world.

6   On Illinois Avenue, three men lean out from second-story windows. A girl is coming down the street. She wears dungarees and a bright-
red shirt, has ample breasts and a Hadendoan Afro, a black halo, two feet
in diameter. Ice rattles in the glasses in the hands of the men.

7   "Hey, sister!"

8   "Come on up!"

9   She looks up, looks from one to another to the other, looks them
flat in the eye.   45

10   "What for?" she says, and she walks on.

11   I buy Illinois for $240. It solidifies my chances, for I already own
Kentucky and Indiana. My opponent pales. If he had landed first on Illinois, the game would have been over then and there, for he has houses
built on Boardwalk and Park Place, we share the railroads equally, and we 50
have cancelled each other everywhere else. We never trade.

12   In 1852, R. B. Osborne, an immigrant Englishman, civil engineer,
surveyed the route of a railroad line that would run from Camden to
Absecon Island, in New Jersey, traversing the state from the Delaware
River to the barrier beaches of the sea. He then sketched in the plan of 55
a "bathing village" that would surround the eastern terminus of the line.
His pen flew glibly, framing and naming spacious avenues parallel to the
shore—Mediterranean, Baltic, Oriental, Ventnor—and narrower transsect-
ing avenues: North Carolina, Pennsylvania, Vermont, Connecticut, States,
Virginia, Tennessee, New York, Kentucky, Indiana, Illinois. The place as 60
a whole had no name, so when he had completed the plan Osborne wrote
in large letters over the ocean, "Atlantic City." No one ever challenged
the name, or the names of Osborne's streets. Monopoly was invented in
the early nineteen-thirties by Charles B. Darrow, but Darrow was only
transliterating what Osborne had created. The railroads, crucial to any 65
player, were the making of Atlantic City. After the rails were down, houses
and hotels burgeoned from Mediterranean and Baltic to New York and
Kentucky. Properties—building lots—sold for as little as six dollars apiece
and as much as a thousand dollars. The original investors in the railroads
and the real estate called themselves the Camden & Atlantic Land Com- 70
pany. Reverently, I repeat their names: Dwight Bell, William Coffin, John
DaCosta, Daniel Deal, William Fleming, Andrew Hay, Joseph Porter,
Jonathan Pitney, Samuel Richards—founders, fathers, forerunners, archetypical masters of the quick kill.

13   My opponent and I are now in a deep situation of classical Mo- 75
nopoly. The torsion is almost perfect—Boardwalk and Park Place versus
the brilliant reds. His cash position is weak, though, and if I escape him
now he may fade. I land on Luxury Tax, contiguous to but in sanctuary
from his power. I have four houses on Indiana. He lands there. He
concedes.   80

14   Indiana Avenue was the address of the Brighton Hotel, gone now.

The Brighton was exclusive—a word that no longer has retail value in the city. If you arrived by automobile and tried to register at the Brighton, you were sent away. Brighton-class people came in private railroad cars. Brighton-class people had other private railroad cars for their horses— 85 dawn rides on the firm sand at water's edge, skirts flying. Colonel Anthony J. Drexel Biddle—the sort of name that would constrict throats in Philadelphia—lived, much of the year, in the Brighton.

15   Colonel Sanders' fried chicken is on Kentucky Avenue. So is Clifton's Club Harlem, with the Sepia Revue and the Sepia Follies, featuring 90 the Honey Bees, the Fashions, and the Lords.

16   My opponent and I, many years ago, played 2,428 games of Monopoly in a single season. He was then a recent graduate of the Harvard Law School, and he was working for a downtown firm, looking up law. Two people we knew—one from Chase Manhattan, the other from Morgan, Stanley—tried to get into the game, but after a few rounds we found 95 that they were not in the conversation and we sent them home. Monopoly should always be *mano a mano* anyway. My opponent won 1,199 games, and so did I. Thirty were ties. He was called into the Army, and we stopped just there. Now, in Game 2 of the series, I go immediately to 100 jail, and again to jail while my opponent seines property. He is dumbfoundingly lucky. He wins in twelve minutes.

17   Visiting hours are daily, eleven to two; Sunday, eleven to one; evenings, six to nine. "NO MINORS, NO FOOD. Immediate Family Only Allowed in Jail." All this above a blue steel door in a blue cement wall in 105 the windowless interior of the basement of the city hall. The desk sergeant sits opposite the door to the jail. In a cigar box in front of him are pills in every color, a banquet of fruit salad an inch and a half deep—leapers, co-pilots, footballs, truck drivers, peanuts, blue angels, yellow jackets, redbirds, rainbows. Near the desk are two soldiers, waiting to go 110 through the blue door. They are about eighteen years old. One of them is trying hard to light a cigarette. His wrists are in steel cuffs. A military policeman waits, too. He is a year or so older than the soldiers, taller, studious in appearance, gentle, fat. On a bench against a wall sits a good-looking girl in slacks. The blue door rattles, swings heavily open. A turn- 115 key stands in the doorway. "Don't you guys kill yourselves back there now," says the sergeant to the soldiers.

18   "One kid, he overdosed himself about ten and a half hours ago," says the M.P.

19   The M.P., the soldiers, the turnkey, and the girl on the bench are 120 white. The sergeant is black. "If you take off the handcuffs, take off the belts," says the sergeant to the M.P. "I don't want them hanging themselves back there." The door shuts and its tumblers move. When it opens again, five minutes later, a young white man in sandals and dungarees and a blue polo shirt emerges. His hair is in a ponytail. He has no beard. ⟍125 He grins at the good-looking girl. She rises, joins him. The sergeant hands him a manila envelope. From it he removes his belt and a small notebook. He borrows a pencil, makes an entry in the notebook. He is out of jail, free. What did he do? He offended Atlantic City in some way. He spent a night in the jail. In the nineteen-thirties, men visiting Atlantic 130 City went to jail, directly to jail, did not pass Go, for appearing in topless bathing suits on the beach. A city statute requiring all men to wear full-length bathing suits was not seriously challenged until 1937, and the first year in which a man could legally go bare-chested on the beach was 1940. 135

20   Game 3. After seventeen minutes, I am ready to begin construction on overpriced and sluggish Pacific, North Carolina, and Pennsylvania. Nothing else being open, opponent concedes.

21   The physical profile of streets perpendicular to the shore is something like a playground slide. It begins in the high skyline of Boardwalk 140 hotels, plummets into warrens of "side-avenue" motels, crosses Pacific, slopes through church missions, convalescent homes, burlesque houses, rooming houses, and liquor stores, crosses Atlantic, and runs level through the bombed-out ghetto as far—Baltic, Mediterranean—as the eye can see. North Carolina Avenue, for example, is flanked at its beach end by the 145 Chalfonte and the Haddon Hall (908 rooms, air-conditioned), where, according to one biographer, John Philip Sousa (1854-1932) first played when he was twenty-two, insisting, even then, that everyone call him by his entire name. Behind these big hotels, motels—Barbizon, Catalina— crouch. Between Pacific and Atlantic is an occasional house from 1910— 150 wooden porch, wooden mullions, old yellow paint—and two churches, a package store, a strip show, a dealer in fruits and vegetables. Then, beyond Atlantic Avenue, North Carolina moves on into the vast ghetto, the bulk of the city, and it looks like Metz in 1919, Cologne in 1944. Nothing has actually exploded. It is not bomb damage. It is deep and 155 complex decay. Roofs are off. Bricks are scattered in the street. People sit on porches, six deep, at nine on a Monday morning. When they go off to wait in unemployment lines, they wait sometimes two hours. Between Mediterranean and Baltic runs a chain-link fence, enclosing rubble. A pa-

trol car sits idling by the curb. In the back seat is a German shepherd. A   160
sign on the fence says, "Beware of Bad Dogs."

22   Mediterranean and Baltic are the principal avenues of the ghetto.
Dogs are everywhere. A pack of seven passes me. Block after block, there
are three-story brick row houses. Whole segments of them are abandoned,
a thousand broken windows. Some parts are intact, occupied. A mattress   165
lies in the street, soaking in a pool of water. Wet stuffing is coming out
of the mattress. A postman is having a rye and a beer in the Plantation
Bar at nine-fifteen in the morning. I ask him idly if he knows where Marvin Gardens is. He does not. "HOOKED AND NEED HELP? CONTACT N.A.R.C.O."
"REVIVAL NOW GOING ON, CONDUCTED BY REVEREND H. HENDERSON OF TEXAS."   170
These are signboards on Mediterranean and Baltic. The second one is upside down and leans against a boarded-up window of the Faith Temple
Church of God in Christ. There is an old peeling poster on a warehouse
wall showing a figure in an electric chair. "The Black Panther Manifesto"
is the title of the poster, and its message is, or was, that "the fascists have   175
already decided in advance to murder Chairman Bobby Seale in the electric chair." I pass an old woman who carries a bucket. She wears blue
sneakers, worn through. Her feet spill out. She wears red socks, rolled at
the knees. A white handkerchief, spread over her head, is knotted at the
corners. Does she know where Marvin Gardens is? "I sure don't know,"   180
she says, setting down the bucket. "I sure don't know. I've heard of it
somewhere, but I just can't say where." I walk on, through a block of shattered glass. The glass crunches underfoot like coarse sand. I remember
when I first came here—a long train ride from Trenton, long ago, games
of poker in the train—to play basketball against Atlantic City. We were   185
half black, they were all black. We scored forty points, they scored eighty,
or something like it. What I remember most is that they had glass backboards—glittering, pendent, expensive glass backboards, a rarity then in
high schools, even in colleges, the only ones we played on all year.

23   I turn on Pennsylvania, and start back toward the sea. The win-   190
dows of the Hotel Astoria, on Pennsylvania near Baltic, are boarded up. A
sheet of unpainted plywood is the door, and in it is a triangular peephole
that now frames an eye. The plywood door opens. A man answers my
question. Rooms there are six, seven, and ten dollars a week. I thank him
for the information and move on, emerging from the ghetto at the Catho-   195
lic Daughters of America Women's Guest House, between Atlantic and
Pacific. Between Pacific and the Boardwalk are the blinking vacancy signs
of the Aristocrat and Colton Manor motels. Pennsylvania terminates at

the Sheraton-Seaside—thirty-two dollars a day, ocean corner. I take a walk on the Boardwalk and into the Holiday Inn (twenty-three stories). A guest is registering. "You reserved for Wednesday, and this is Monday," the clerk tells him. "But that's all right. We have *plenty* of rooms." The clerk is very young, female, and has soft brown hair that hangs below her waist. Her superior kicks her.

24   He is a middle-aged man with red spiderwebs in his face. He is jacketed and tied. He takes her aside. "Don't say 'plenty,'" he says. "Say 'You are fortunate, sir. We have rooms available.'"

25   The face of the young woman turns sour. "We have all the rooms you need," she says to the customer, and, to her superior, "How's that?"

26   Game 4. My opponent's luck has become abrasive. He has Board-walk and Park Place, and has sealed the board.

27   Darrow was a plumber. He was, specifically, a radiator repairman who lived in Germantown, Pennsylvania. His first Monopoly board was a sheet of linoleum. On it he placed houses and hotels that he had carved from blocks of wood. The game he thus invented was brilliantly con-ceived, for it was an uncannily exact reflection of the business milieu at large. In its depth, range, and subtlety, in its luck-skill ratio, in its sense of infrastructure and socio-economic parameters, in its philosophical char-acteristics, it reached to the profundity of the financial community. It was as scientific as the stock market. It suggested the manner and means through which an underdeveloped world had been developed. It was chess at Wall Street level. "Advance token to the nearest Railroad and pay owner twice the rental to which he is otherwise entitled. If Railroad is unowned, you may buy it from the Bank. Get out of Jail, free. Advance token to nearest Utility. If unowned, you may buy it from Bank. If owned, throw dice and pay owner a total ten times the amount thrown. You are assessed for street repairs: $40 per house, $115 per hotel. Pay poor tax of $15. Go to Jail. Go directly to Jail. Do not pass Go. Do not collect $200."

28   The turnkey opens the blue door. The turnkey is known to the in-mates as Sidney K. Above his desk are ten closed-circuit-TV screens—as-sorted viewpoints of the jail. There are three cellblocks—men, women, ju-venile boys. Six days is the average stay. Showers twice a week. The steel doors and the equipment that operates them were made in San Antonio. The prisoners sleep on bunks of butcher block. There are no mattresses. There are three prisoners to a cell. In winter, it is cold in here. Prisoners burn newspapers to keep warm. Cell corners are black with smudge. The jail is three years old. The men's block echoes with chatter. The man in

the cell nearest Sidney K. is pacing. His shirt is covered with broad stains of blood. The block for juvenile boys is, by contrast, utterly silent—empty corridor, empty cells. There is only one prisoner. He is small and black   240 and appears to be thirteen. He says he is sixteen and that he has been alone in here for three days.

29   "Why are you here? What did you do?"

30   "I hit a jitney driver."

31   The series stands at three all. We have split the fifth and sixth   245 games. We are scrambling for property. Around the board we fairly fly. We move so fast because we do our own banking and search our own deeds. My opponent grows tense.

32   Ventnor Avenue, a street of delicatessens and doctors' offices, is leafy with plane trees and hydrangeas, the city flower. Water Works is   250 on the mainland. The water comes over in submarine pipes. Electric Company gets power from across the state, on the Delaware River, in Deepwater. States Avenue, now a wasteland like St. Charles, once had gardens running down the middle of the street, a horse-drawn trolley, private homes. States Avenue was as exclusive as the Brighton. Only an apartment   255 house, a small motel, and the All Wars Memorial Building—monadnocks spaced widely apart—stand along States Avenue now. Pawnshops, convalescent homes, and the Paradise Soul Saving Station are on Virginia Avenue. The soul-saving station is pink, orange, and yellow. In the windows flanking the door of the Virginia Money Loan Office are Nikons, Pola-   260 roids, Yashicas, Sony TVs, Underwood typewriters, Singer sewing machines, and pictures of Christ. On the far side of town, beside a single track and locked up most of the time, is the new railroad station, a small hut made of glazed firebrick, all that is left of the lines that built the city. An authentic phrenologist works on New York Avenue close to Frank's   265 Extra Dry Bar and a church where the sermon today is "Death in the Pot." The church is of pink brick, has blue and amber windows and two red doors. St. James Place, narrow and twisting, is lined with boarding houses that have wooden porches on each of three stories, suggesting a New Orleans made of salt-bleached pine. In a vacant lot on Tennessee is a   270 white Ford station wagon stripped to the chassis. The windows are smashed. A plastic Clorox bottle sits on the driver's seat. The wind has pressed newspaper against the chain-link fence around the lot. Atlantic Avenue, the city's principal thoroughfare, could be seventeen American Main Streets placed end to end—discount vitamins and Vienna Corset   275 shops, movie theatres, shoe stores, and funeral homes. The Boardwalk is

made of yellow pine and Douglas fir, soaked in pentachlorophenol. Down-beach, it reaches far beyond the city. Signs everywhere—on windows, lamp-posts, trash baskets—proclaim "Bienvenue Canadiens!" The salt air is full of Canadian French. In the Claridge Hotel, on Park Place, I ask a clerk 280 if she knows where Marvin Gardens is. She says, "Is it a floral shop?" I ask a cabdriver, parked outside. He says, "Never heard of it." Park Place is one block long, Pacific to Boardwalk. On the roof of the Claridge is the So-larium, the highest point in town—panoramic view of the ocean, the bay, the salt-water ghetto. I look down at the rooftops of the side-avenue mo- 285 tels and into swimming pools. There are hundreds of people around the rooftop pools, sunbathing, reading—many more people than are on the beach. Walls, windows, and a block of sky are all that is visible from these pools—no sand, no sea. The pools are craters, and with the people around them they are countersunk into the motels. 290

33   The seventh, and final, game is ten minutes old and I have hotels on Oriental, Vermont, and Connecticut. I have Tennessee and St. James. I have North Carolina and Pacific. I have Boardwalk, Atlantic, Ventnor, Illinois, Indiana. My fingers are forming a "V." I have mortgaged most of these properties in order to pay for others, and I have mortgaged the 295 others to pay for the hotels. I have seven dollars. I will pay off the mort-gages and build my reserves with income from the three hotels. My cash position may be low, but I feel like a rocket in an underground silo. Mean-while, if I could just go to jail for a time I could pause there, wait there, until my opponent, in his inescapable rounds, pays the rates of my ho- 300 tels. Jail, at times, is the strategic place to be. I roll boxcars from the Reading and move the flatiron to Community Chest. "Go to Jail. Go directly to Jail."

34   The prisoners, of course, have no pens and no pencils. They take paper napkins, roll them tight as crayons, char the ends with matches, 305 and write on the walls. The things they write are not entirely idiomatic; for example, "In God We Trust." All is in carbon. Time is required in the writing. "Only humanity could know of such pain." "God So Loved the World." "There is no greater pain than life itself." In the women's block now, there are six blacks, giggling, and a white asleep in red shoes. 310 She is drunk. The others are pushers, prostitutes, an auto thief, a burglar caught with pistol in purse. A sixteen-year-old accused of murder was in here last week. These words are written on the wall of a now empty cell: "Laying here I see two bunks about six inches thick, not counting the one I'm laying on, which is hard as brick. No cushion for my back. No 315

pillow for my head. Just a couple scratchy blankets which is best to use it's said. I wake up in the morning so shivery and cold, waiting and waiting till I am told the food is coming. It's on its way. It's not worth waiting for, but I eat it anyway. I know one thing when they set me free I'm gonna be good if it kills me."   320

35   How many years must a game be played to produce an Anthony J. Drexel Biddle and chestnut geldings on the beach? About half a century was the original answer, from the first railroad to Biddle at his peak. Biddle, at his peak, hit an Atlantic City streetcar conductor with his fist, laid him out with one punch. This increased Biddle's legend. He did not   325
go to jail. While John Philip Sousa led his band along the Boardwalk playing "The Stars and Stripes Forever" and Jack Dempsey ran up and down in training for his fight with Gene Tunney, the city crossed the high curve of its parabola. Al Capone held conventions here—upstairs with his sleeves rolled, apportioning among his lieutenant governors the states   330
of the Eastern seaboard. The natural history of an American resort proceeds from Indians to French Canadians via Biddles and Capones. French Canadians, whatever they may be at home, are Visigoths here. Bienvenue Visigoths!

36   My opponent plods along incredibly well. He has got his fourth   335
railroad, and patiently, unbelievably, he has picked up my potential winners until he has blocked me everywhere but Marvin Gardens. He has avoided, in the fifty-dollar zoning, my increasingly petty hotels. His cash flow swells. His railroads are costing me two hundred dollars a minute. He is building hotels on States, Virginia, and St. Charles. He has tempo-   340
rarily reversed the current. With the yellow monopolies and my blue monopolies, I could probably defeat his lavenders and his railroads. I have Atlantic and Ventnor. I need Marvin Gardens. My only hope is Marvin Gardens.

37   There is a plaque at Boardwalk and Park Place, and on it in relief   345
is the leonine profile of a man who looks like an officer in a metropolitan bank—"Charles B. Darrow, 1889-1967, inventor of the game of Monopoly." "Darrow," I address him, aloud. "Where is Marvin Gardens?" There is, of course, no answer. Bronze, impassive, Darrow looks south down the Boardwalk. "Mr. Darrow, please, where is Marvin Gardens?" Nothing.   350
Not a sign. He just looks south down the Boardwalk.

38   My opponent accepts the trophy with his natural ease, and I make, from notes, remarks that are even less graceful than his.

39   Marvin Gardens is the one color-block Monopoly property that is

not in Atlantic City. It is a suburb within a suburb, secluded. It is a   355
planned compound of seventy-two handsome houses set on curvilinear
private streets under yews and cedars, poplars and willows. The compound
was built around 1920, in Margate, New Jersey, and consists of solid buildings of stucco, brick, and wood, with slate roofs, tile roofs, multimullioned
porches, Giraldic towers, and Spanish grilles. Marvin Gardens, the ulti-   360
mate outwash of Monopoly, is a citadel and sanctuary of the middle class.
"We're heavily patrolled by police here. We don't take no chances. Me?
I'm living here nine years. I paid seventeen thousand dollars and I've been
offered thirty. Number one, I don't want to move. Number two, I don't
need the money. I have four bedrooms, two and a half baths, front den,   365
back den. No basement. The Atlantic is down there. Six feet down and
you float. A lot of people have a hard time finding this place. People that
lived in Atlantic City all their life don't know how to find it. They don't
know where the hell they're going. They just know it's south, down the
Boardwalk."   370

QUESTIONS

READER AND PURPOSE

1. McPhee uses a personal point of view * rather than striving for the appearance of objectivity. And his essay is richly implicative. Both of these characteristics are typical of the new journalism. The meaning of the essay does not lie
on top; it must be dug for like the theme of a short story or a poem. His piece
is not simply an account of "Monopoly," nor is it merely a report upon the
decline of Atlantic City, though it includes both these topics. But if neither
is his essential subject—what is?

2. The essay is not argument in any technical sense. Indeed, it is not even
persuasion, as we normally understand that term. Yet McPhee is trying to
convince us of something. What?

ORGANIZATION

3. McPhee does not develop his essay in a series of topics, each leading logically into the next. He organizes by moving back and forth between two related themes. Which paragraphs are concerned primarily with "Monopoly"
and which with Atlantic City?

4. The structure of the essay is almost musical in its use of alternating themes,
and we might adapt the terms *counterpoint* and *contrapuntal* to describe it.
The counterpointed themes are linked by details common to both, such as the
various streets and the jail. These details act as bridges, shifting us from one

theme to the other. Thus at the end of the opening paragraph the phrase "where the dog packs range" transposes us from the blue space on the "Monopoly" board to the actual street. Point out other details which swing us from game to city or from city to game.

5. In some cases there are no links, simply abrupt jumps from theme to theme—between paragraphs 26 and 27, for example. Where else do you find such discontinuities? Are they faults, or do they serve a purpose?

6. Is McPhee's first paragraph a good beginning? Why, or why not?

7. Which paragraph (or paragraphs) constitutes the closing of this essay? Is the closing effective?

8. Which is the topic sentence of paragraph 21? Of 22? How is each supported?

9. Does paragraph 4 have a topic statement? If not, is its absence a fault? Can you supply one easily? Try it.

SENTENCES

10. McPhee often uses a series of short simple * sentences—in lines 4-6, for instance. Point out three or four similar passages. Does he employ such sentences for particular topics?

11. The sentences in paragraph 12 are longer and more complicated. Is the subject different here than in lines 4-6?

12. McPhee sometimes omits *and* between paired constructions where normally the conjunction would appear: for example in line 28 "The first game draws tight, will soon finish" (instead of "and will soon finish"). Find other instances of this kind of ellipsis *. Why do you suppose he does it?

13. Identify the fragments * in paragraph 37. Where else in this selection do you find fragments? Would they be improved by being made grammatically complete?

14. Could commas be used instead of dashes in lines 6-7, 23-24, 87-88, 108, and 289? If they could be, is there any justification for the dashes?

15. How do these revisions alter the emphasis of McPhee's sentences?

> (a) *Revision:* We are gradually cancelling each other out, block upon block . . .
> *McPhee:* "Block upon block, gradually, we are cancelling each other out . . ." (25)
>
> (b) *Revision:* Motels such as the Barbizon and the Catalina crouch behind these big hotels.
> *McPhee:* "Behind these big hotels, motels—Barbizon, Catalina—crouch." (149-50)
>
> (c) *Revision:* It is a secluded suburb within a suburb.
> *McPhee:* "It is a suburb within a suburb, secluded." (355)

DICTION

16. Look up: *shards* (19), *traversing* (54), *glibly* (57), *transliterating* (65), *burgeoned* (67), *constrict* (87), *plummets* (141), *ghetto* (144), *mullions* (151), *rubble* (159), *pendent* (188), *abrasive* (210), *infrastructure* (218), *jitney* (244), *trolley* (254), *monadnocks* (256), *phrenologist* (265), *curvilinear* (356).

17. Explain as fully as you can the meanings of the following phrases: *master assessor of percentages* (16), *immigrant Englishmen* (52), *barrier beaches* (55), *archetypical masters of the quick kill* (74), *mano a mano* (98), *city statute* (132), *burlesque houses* (142), *business milieu* (216), *socio-economic parameters* (218), *chestnut geldings* (332), *leonine profile* (346), *ultimate outwash* (360-61).

18. McPhee uses the present tense when writing about both the game and Atlantic City. He could as easily have made the past his primary tense. What advantage does the present have for his purpose? Suppose that he had used the past throughout:

> Go. I rolled the dice—a six and a two. Through the air I moved my token, the flatiron, to Vermont Avenue, where dog packs ranged.
>
> The dogs were moving (some were limping) . . .

Would the change in tense affect the tone * of his essay in any way?

19. In the opening passage just quoted McPhee might have written simply: "I move my token to Vermont Avenue, where dog packs range," omitting the phrase *through the air* and any reference to the flatiron. It doesn't really matter if he picks up his token or shoves it, and the flatiron has no symbolic value. Why, then, do you suppose he adds these apparently trivial details?

20. Who were the Visigoths (333)? Is the allusion * apt?

21. Explain the metaphors * implicit in *seines* (101), *warrens* (141), and *the city crossed the high curve of its parabola* (328-29).

22. Certain images * are repeated throughout the essay so that they become motifs. The dog packs referred to in paragraph 1 and again in paragraphs 2 and 22 is an example. While the dogs do not symbolize anything, they are a laden image—that is, a visual detail that implies more than it literally states. What is suggested by the dog packs? Point out one or two other motifs and explain their significance.

23. What ambiguity * is contained in the word *game* as it is used in line 321?

24. All these devices—allusions, metaphors, laden images, ambiguity *—are ways of enriching meaning by adding overtones of feeling and thought. An even more important way of creating such overtones is the symbol *, a detail which functions both on the literal level of meaning and on a second level where it conveys a more abstract * idea—often moral, political, or philosophi-

cal. The culminating symbol of McPhee's essay is, of course, "Marvin Gardens." Actually Marvin Gardens is a double symbol, for it exists both in the game and in the city, and in each it has a literal and a symbolic value. Within the context of the game the author and his friend are playing, what does Marvin Gardens signify literally and what does it represent symbolically?

25. With reference to Atlantic City, what does Marvin Gardens literally designate? What does it symbolize? Is there a connection between its symbolic values in the game and in the city?

26. As a symbol Marvin Gardens operates, perhaps, on multiple levels, possessing economic, social, and political values, and, on the most abstract level of all, a philosophical significance. Can you sort out these various levels of meaning?

27. Finally, we return to the first question: What is "The Search for Marvin Gardens" about?

POINTS TO LEARN

1. Do not be afraid of the first person. You are the chief observer of what you see and do; your thoughts and feelings have value, even in reporting.

2. An essay may be organized contrapuntally by moving back and forth from one theme to another.

3. Short, strong sentences are good for rendering scene and action.

4. Think about the advantages and limitations of the tense you select as primary.

5. Laden images, metaphors, and symbols enrich—and complicate—meaning.

SUGGESTIONS FOR WRITING

1. In about 500 words describe a board game (but not "Monopoly") or an athletic sport such as baseball. Assume that your reader is intelligent but ignorant about the activity and that your job is to acquaint him with its basics (explaining baseball to an Englishman would be an example). This is not an easy assignment; in fact, describing a game clearly and succinctly is one of the most difficult of all writing tasks. It tests your ability to distinguish essentials from non-essentials and to organize the former without getting bogged down in the latter. You may be able to play baseball or chess, but are you able to lay out the fundamental facts of such games?

2. A more ambitious assignment: Compose an essay of about 1000 words using a game as a controlling metaphor to report upon some aspect of your experience, moving back and forth between the two themes as McPhee does with "Monopoly" and Atlantic City. There should be an inherent connection

between the topics, as, for example, a varsity football game counterpointed against a report on one of the colleges or a description of the spectators.

IMPROVING YOUR STYLE

1. In two or three places in your essay use a series (four or five) of short simple sentences to set a scene or render dramatic action.

2. If your teacher agrees, experiment with fragments in several places, and with the kind of elliptical construction McPhee uses in line 28.

3. (This applies only to the second assignment.) Work one or two motifs into your composition, and try to develop a culminating symbol comparable to Marvin Gardens in McPhee's essay.

Description

Description is the art of translating perceptions into words. All description thus involves two elements: the object—that which is seen or heard—and the observer—he who sees or hears it. According to which predominates, description is of two basic types: objective and impressionistic.

Objective description attempts to report accurately the appearance of the object as a thing in itself, independent of the observer's perception of it or feelings about it. It is a factual account, the purpose of which is to inform a reader who has not been able to see with his own eyes. The writer regards himself as a kind of camera, recording and reproducing, though in words, a true picture. In his detachment he becomes much like the scientist, rigorously excluding from his work his opinions and emotions.

Objective description often begins with a brief general picture comprehending the object in its entirety. This it then develops analytically, using paragraphs—or, in a short description, sentences—to divide the object into its parts, handling each in turn with as much detail as the purpose requires. These parts are placed in an order that reflects the arrangement in space of the object. Thus a writer depicting the interior of a house would likely organize his description by floors, and in describing the rooms on each floor he would probably move from left to right or from front to rear.

Usually objective description is written impersonally, and the writer wanders freely about the object or scene without bothering to record his own movements. When, for example, he has finished the first floor, he need not report, "I am now going upstairs"; he merely writes, "On the second floor . . ." Similarly the tone must be kept factual, and the writer should avoid words that connote a personal reaction. "A large elm," for example, states a fact; "a magnificent elm" suggests a feeling. This is not to say that such feelings are always a fault in composition—in much writing they are a virtue. But in objective description they are immaterial to the writer's purpose.

Given these restrictions, objective description often appears prosaic, even dull; and too often the appearance is real. It is not, however, inherently dull—it is only difficult to do well. Even though his impressions are excluded, the writer can create interest by the fidelity and the skill with which he translates into words the thing he sees. A dying goldfish is hardly an intriguing topic; yet consider this passage from *The Natural History of Selborne* by Gilbert White: "As soon as the creature sickens, the head sinks lower and lower, and it stands as it were on its head; till, getting weaker, and losing all poise, the tail turns over, and at last it floats on the surface of the water with its belly uppermost." This is interesting because it is accurate, precise, economical; because it reproduces exactly what White saw. To see accurately is, as any painter knows, far from easy; to reproduce accurately, whether in prose or paint, what one sees is even more difficult. But when it has been achieved, such description is one of the most satisfying kinds of writing.

Impressionistic description is very different. Focusing upon the mood or feeling the object evokes in the observer, rather than upon the object as it exists in itself, impressionism does not seek to inform but to arouse emotion. It attempts to make us feel more than to make us see. Thus the communication of feeling is the primary purpose of impressionistic description. The process begins in the writer, and it must originate in genuine feeling. But if he is to succeed, the writer must do more than feel deeply; he must in his own mind define that feeling. Impressionistic descriptions often fail because the writers have not really defined in their own minds what their responses are. Only when the writer has understood his own mood can he communicate that mood to his readers.

The actual communication may be achieved in two ways: directly and indirectly. The direct method, the simpler, is merely to describe the feeling itself. The indirect is to project the emotion back into the object and, by the careful selection and treatment of its details, so to infuse the object with feeling that it will arouse in the reader a response similar to the writer's. Both methods are illustrated in this brief description of a clipper ship from John Masefield's *A Tarpaulin Muster: A Memory*: "She bowed and curveted, the light caught the skylights on the poop; she gleamed and sparkled; she shook the sea from her as she rose. There was no man aboard of us but was filled with the beauty of that ship." The second sentence is direct impressionism; it tells us that in the men who watched her the clipper stirred feelings of beauty. The first is indirect. Masefield judiciously selects only those details that suggest grace, power, beauty. If there were facts about the ship inimical to his impression—stained and weathered sails, a shabby figurehead—these he has excluded.

Of the two methods, the indirect is more effective. If the writer's purpose is to communicate a mood, he succeeds better by re-creating the object as he sees it. A writer who tells us he is afraid does not necessarily frighten us; but if he can throw before us the fearsome thing in all its horror, he probably will. In practice, however, impressionistic description uses both methods, often employing direct statement of mood as a center about which to organize the more precise details of indirect description.

In his treatment of these details the writer frequently follows a technique that in art is called expressionism. Broadly, expressionism is the distortion of objective reality in order to communicate the inner reality of emotion. At its simplest, expressionism is the blurring of a film image to suggest dizziness or shock. Similarly the writer may blur or intensify the details he selects, and, by the clever use of figures of speech, he may compare them to things calculated to evoke the appropriate emotion. To impress us with the dreary ugliness of a house, he may exaggerate the drabness of its paint or metaphorically describe the flaking as *leprous*. In such exaggeration the writer is like the caricaturist, but like the caricaturist he is allowed to distort only within limits. Distortion becomes illegitimate when it passes belief and leads us, not toward, but away from the truth the writer seeks to express. It may be objected that impressionism has little to do with truth, if the writer is free to exaggerate some facts and to ignore others. Certainly it is true that impressionistic description draws no very accurate picture. But objective accuracy is not its concern; it tells the truth of feeling. Impressionism tells us not what the clipper ship is, but what it is to the man who sees it.

Thus the objective and the impressionistic are the broad categories of description. Neither ever exists purely. The most detached and scientific observer cannot totally repress his own feelings; and the most impressionistic writer suggests something about the objective reality of what he describes. Most actual description makes use of both. The two techniques are the ends of a continuum, between which, partaking of each, all descriptive writing falls. Yet if no fine line can be drawn between the objective and the impressionistic, they are essentially different in purpose and method. The competent writer must realize when to use the one, when the other. But he must know how to write both.

The Opium Den

W. Somerset Maugham (1874-1965) was an English novelist, short story writer, and playwright. His best known novels include *Of Human Bondage* (1915), *The Moon and Sixpence* (1919), and *Cakes and Ale* (1930); and his plays, *A Man of Honour* (1903), *East of Suez* (1922), and *The Constant Wife* (1927). In addition to stories and plays Maugham composed essays, travel books, and a notable autobiography. This selection comes from a book of sketches Maugham wrote about a trip to China, specifically from a piece describing a visit to an opium den. It is a particularly revealing example of how impressionistic description works. To emphasize the contrast between what he expected and what he found, Maugham carefully selects details and presents them in diction calculated to arouse appropriate responses.

On the stage it makes a very effective set. It is dimly lit. The room is low and squalid. In one corner a lamp burns mysteriously before a hideous image and incense fills the theatre with its exotic scent. A pig-tailed Chinaman wanders to and fro, aloof and saturnine, while on wretched pallets lie stupefied the victims of the drug. Now and then one of them breaks into frantic 5 raving. There is a highly dramatic scene where some poor creature, unable to pay for the satisfaction of his craving, with prayers and curses begs the villainous proprietor for a pipe to still his anguish. I have read also in novels descriptions which made my blood run cold. And when I was taken to an opium den by a smooth-spoken Eurasian, the narrow, winding stairway up 10 which he led me prepared me sufficiently to receive the thrill I expected. I was introduced into a neat enough room, brightly lit, divided into cubicles, the raised floor of which, covered with clean matting, formed a convenient couch. In one an elderly gentleman, with a grey head and very beautiful hands, was quietly reading a newspaper, with his long pipe by his side. In 15

From "Opium Den," in *On a Chinese Screen.* Copyright 1922 by W. Somerset Maugham. Reprinted by permission of Doubleday & Company, Inc., and A. P. Watt & Son Ltd.

another two coolies were lying, with a pipe between them, which they alternately prepared and smoked. They were young men, of a hearty appearance, and they smiled at me in a friendly way. One of them offered me a smoke. In a third, four men squatted over a chess-board, and a little further on a man was dandling a baby (the inscrutable Oriental has a passion for children) while the baby's mother, whom I took to be the landlord's wife, a plump, pleasant-faced woman, watched him with a broad smile on her lips. It was a cheerful spot, comfortable, home-like, and cosy. It reminded me somewhat of the little intimate beer-houses of Berlin, where the tired working-man could go in the evening and spend a peaceful hour. Fiction is stranger than fact.

QUESTIONS

READER AND PURPOSE

1. The parenthetical remark in lines 20-21 cleverly questions our conventional notions of the Chinese. What does their passion for children suggest about their inscrutability? At whom is Maugham poking fun here—the "inscrutable Oriental" or the average Westerner?

ORGANIZATION

2. Indicate the two parts of this paragraph. Which sentence makes the transition between them?
3. Study how the description in lines 1-9 is organized. What do we see first? What does the writer show us next? Then what? Explain why this pattern of development reflects the way in which we actually see things.
4. Show that the second section develops in much the same manner. What advantage is there to organizing both parts of this description according to the same pattern?
5. What function does the final sentence serve? Would its omission have improved the selection?

SENTENCES

6. Why is the style of the first few sentences well suited to the impression the writer is trying to convey?
7. In lines 9 ff. the sentences become longer and their rhythms smoother. Why does Maugham's purpose require such a change? Even here, however, he occasionally employs a shorter sentence for variety. Point out one or two examples.

DICTION

8. Look up: *squalid* (2), *exotic* (3), *aloof* (4), *saturnine* (4), *pallet* (4), *dramatic* (6), *craving* (7), *Eurasian* (10), *cubicle* (12), *inscrutable* (20).

9. In the first ten lines Maugham uses his diction, especially modifiers, to satirize the clichés of melodrama. The incense, for example, is *exotic*, an overworked adjective that suggests similarly trite stage properties. Point out three or four other modifiers that are deliberately trite. Is the very title of this selection ironic? Explain.

10. What words in the first eleven lines suggest the kind of melodramatic action which the writer is mocking?

11. Like the syntax, the diction also changes in the second part. It becomes less dramatic and more matter-of-fact. Maugham now uses words to re-create what he really saw. Notice, for instance, the details that characterize the "elderly gentleman" (14-15). What kind of man do they suggest he is? What details characterize the "landlord's wife"? What kind of woman is she?

12. The comparison of an opium den to a beer-house in line 24 is slightly shocking to a Western mind. What is Maugham implying here?

13. Comment upon these changes in diction, explaining why each substitute is a better or a poorer choice: *ugly* for *hideous* (2), *man* for *creature* (6), *holding* for *dandling* (20), *heavy* for *plump* (22).

POINTS TO LEARN

1. Good description usually develops in the natural order of general to particular.

2. Sentence rhythm can enter into and become a part of the descriptive process.

SUGGESTIONS FOR WRITING

The difference between naïve preconception and reality is a common experience, often humorous, sometimes bitterly disappointing. Choose one of the topics listed below and write a description in two parts; in the first develop what you anticipated, in the second what you found.

> a night club, a pool room, college (or high school), a blind date, your first cigar, a museum, a cocktail party, a fraternity (or sorority) house, any famous tourist attraction for which the publicity outruns the truth

IMPROVING YOUR STYLE

In your composition:

1. Use sentence structure to reinforce the contrast—short, staccato sentences to enhance drama contrasted with longer ones, more relaxed in movement.

2. Select your diction carefully to direct the readers' responses, and be able to defend your choice of particular words by explaining what emotion you wished to evoke.

Stagecoach Station

At the beginning of the Civil War in 1861, Mark Twain (1835-1910) gave up his profession of steamboat pilot on the Mississippi and traveled by stagecoach to the Nevada Territory. During 1861-66 he remained in the West as a prospector in Nevada and then as a journalist for several newspapers. Some six years later—newly married and living in Buffalo, New York—Twain began to record his western experiences in a book called *Roughing It* (1872). Twain's purpose was to tell the truth about frontier life, a truth, in Twain's opinion, not found in the idealizing novels of James Fenimore Cooper or in the sentimental tales of Bret Harte. Throughout *Roughing It*, as in others of his books, a part of Twain's theme is the difference between romantic imaginings and grotesque realities. In the following excerpt Twain describes the buildings where stagecoach passengers stopped for breakfast about a day's drive away from Kearney, Nebraska, enroute from St. Joseph, Missouri, to Carson City, capital of the Nevada Territory.

1   The station buildings were long, low huts, made of sun-dried, mud-colored bricks, laid up without mortar (*adobes*, the Spaniards call these bricks, and Americans shorten it to *'dobies*). The roofs, which had no slant to them worth speaking of, were thatched and then sodded or covered with a thick layer of earth, and from this sprung a pretty rank growth of weeds   5 and grass. It was the first time we had ever seen a man's front yard on top of his house. The buildings consisted of barns, stable-room for twelve or fifteen horses, and a hut for an eating-room for passengers. This latter had bunks in it for the station-keeper and a hostler or two. You could rest your elbow on its eaves, and you had to bend in order to get in at the door. In   10 place of a window there was a square hole about large enough for a man to crawl through, but this had no glass in it. There was no flooring, but the ground was packed hard. There was no stove, but the fireplace served all needful purposes. There were no shelves, no cupboards, no closets. In a

From Chapter Four of *Roughing It*, originally published by Harper & Row.

corner stood an open sack of flour, and nestling against its base were a couple 15
of black and venerable tin coffee-pots, a tin teapot, a little bag of salt, and a
side of bacon.

2   By the door of the station-keeper's den, outside, was a tin wash-
basin, on the ground. Near it was a pail of water and a piece of yellow bar-
soap, and from the eaves hung a hoary blue woolen shirt, significantly—but   20
this latter was the station-keeper's private towel, and only two persons in all
the party might venture to use it—the stage-driver and the conductor. The
latter would not, from a sense of decency; the former would not, because he
did not choose to encourage the advances of a station-keeper. We had towels—in the valise; they might as well have been in Sodom and Gomorrah.   25
We (and the conductor) used our handkerchiefs, and the driver his pantaloons and sleeves. By the door, inside, was fastened a small old-fashioned
looking-glass frame, with two little fragments of the original mirror lodged
down in one corner of it. This arrangement afforded a pleasant double-
barreled portrait of you when you looked into it, with one half of your head   30
set up a couple of inches above the other half. From the glass frame hung
the half of a comb by a string—but if I had to describe that patriarch or die,
I believe I would order some sample coffins. It had come down from Esau
and Samson, and had been accumulating hair ever since—along with certain
impurities. In one corner of the room stood three or four rifles and muskets,   35
together with horns and pouches of ammunition. The station-men wore
pantaloons of coarse, country-woven stuff, and into the seat and the inside of
the legs were sewed ample additions of buckskin, to do duty in place of leg-
gings, when the man rode horseback—so the pants were half dull blue and
half yellow, and unspeakably picturesque. The pants were stuffed into the   40
tops of high boots, the heels whereof were armed with great Spanish spurs,
whose little iron clogs and chains jingled with every step. The man wore a
huge beard and mustachios, an old slouch hat, a blue woolen shirt, no sus-
penders, no vest, no coat—in a leathern sheath in his belt, a great long
"navy" revolver (slung on right side, hammer to the front), and projecting   45
from his boot a horn-handled bowie-knife. The furniture of the hut was
neither gorgeous nor much in the way. The rocking-chairs and sofas were
not present, and never had been, but they were represented by two three-
legged stools, a pine-board bench four feet long, and two empty candle-
boxes. The table was a greasy board on stilts, and the table-cloth and nap-   50
kins had not come—and they were not looking for them, either. A battered
tin platter, a knife and fork, and a tin pint cup, were at each man's place,
and the driver had a queens-ware saucer that had seen better days. Of course,

this duke sat at the head of the table. There was one isolated piece of table furniture that bore about it a touching air of grandeur in misfortune. This 55 was the caster. It was German silver, and crippled and rusty, but it was so preposterously out of place there that it was suggestive of a tattered exiled king among barbarians, and the majesty of its native position compelled respect even in its degradation. There was only one cruet left, and that was a stopperless, fly-specked, broken-necked thing, with two inches of vinegar in 60 it, and a dozen preserved flies with their heels up and looking sorry they had invested there.

QUESTIONS

READER AND PURPOSE

1. Like many descriptions, "Stagecoach Station" contains both objective and impressionistic elements. List several examples of each. Overall, which predominates—impressionism or objectivity?

2. Explain how the descriptions of things—buildings, furniture, utensils, clothing—serve to characterize the stationmen and frontier life.

3. If this scene were to be shown as part of a television western, in what ways might the visual details differ from Twain's description? Would the eating room, for example, be so low "you had to bend in order to get in at the door"? What do these probable differences reveal about Twain's purpose? About the legend of the Old West then and now?

4. Is Twain writing primarily for Easterners or Westerners? Give several reasons for your conclusion.

ORGANIZATION

5. Show that Twain's first paragraph is organized by the pattern of general to particular.

6. Demonstrate that the second paragraph is organized spatially, that it falls into two parts, and that the beginning of the second part is signaled by verbal repetition.

7. The second paragraph might be said to lack unity. It can easily be divided into four shorter paragraphs without making any verbal changes. Where can these divisions occur? How might Twain's paragraph be defended against the charge that it is not unified?

SENTENCES

8. In each of the following cases, what is the significant difference between Twain's sentences and the revision?

(a) *Revision:* The latter contained bunks for the station-keeper and a hostler.
Twain: "This latter had bunks in it for the station-keeper and a hostler or two." (8-9)

(b) *Revision:* There was no flooring, but the ground was packed hard. The room was without a stove; however, the fireplace served all needful purposes. Nowhere were to be found shelves, cupboards, or closets.
Twain: "There was no flooring, but the ground was packed hard. There was no stove, but the fireplace served all needful purposes. There were no shelves, no cupboards, no closets." (12-14)

(c) *Revision:* We had towels in the valise but they might as well have been in Sodom and Gomorrah.
Twain: "We had towels—in the valise; they might as well have been in Sodom and Gomorrah." (24-25)

9. What variety of purposes do the dashes serve in lines 20, 22, 32, 44, and 51?

10. In the sentence beginning "Near it was a pail of water" (19) what word is given great emphasis by isolation?

DICTION

11. Look up: *hostler* (9), *venerable* (16), *hoary* (20), *pantaloons* (26), *horns* (36), *bowie-knife* (46), *queens-ware* (53), *caster* (56), *cruet* (59).

12. Citing specific words and phrases, show how Twain's diction reveals his attitude toward the stagecoach station and the men who tend it.

13. How does Twain's diction distance him from his subject and ally him with his Eastern readers?

14. Show that in the following instances the revision is less effective than what Twain wrote: *The comb was dirty* for *It had come down from Esau and Samson, and had been accumulating hair ever since—along with certain impurities* (33-35); *very picturesque* for *unspeakably picturesque* (40); *out of place* for *suggestive of a tattered exiled king among barbarians* (57-58); *landed* for *invested* (62).

15. Is *mustachios* (43) a better word here than *mustache?* Why or why not?

16. Like many nineteenth-century writers Twain is fond of biblical allusions *. The Bible was widely read and provided a common coin of exchange by which complex sets of feelings and attitudes and judgments could be easily conveyed. Who or what were Esau and Samson (33-34), Sodom and Gomorrah (25)? What is Twain implying by these allusions?

POINTS TO LEARN

1. Most good descriptions are a mixture of objective facts and the writer's feelings about those facts.

2. How the writer feels about his or her subject guides the selection of details and helps to give the description unity and purpose.

3. A bad description often seems pointless—a mere laundry list with no theme.

4. Descriptive details of the things people use or own may serve to characterize them.

5. Description characterizes the writer as well as the places or people he or she is describing. Obviously, if the description is to prove effective, the reader should be made to like the writer.

SUGGESTIONS FOR WRITING

1. Describe the buildings and equipment of a summer camp for young people, or those of a farm or small factory. If possible use details of places and things to characterize those who live or work at the camp, farm, factory. Be conscious of tone *, and work for one appropriate to what you feel and how you want the reader to respond.

2. Describe some work area not generally seen by the public—a warehouse, the kitchen of a restaurant, an upholsterer's shop, a lumber mill. Try for a distinct tone, while at the same time making yourself agreeable to the reader.

IMPROVING YOUR STYLE

1. In your description imitate Twain's anaphora * in lines 12-14, beginning three successive sentences (kept fairly short) with "There was (were)." Mark the anaphora in the margin of your paper.

2. Use diction that implies your feelings about what you are describing, your response to it. Don't be afraid to exaggerate, even to be outrageous. Exaggeration is one way in which Twain gets his comic effect, as in the description of the dirty comb.

Tourists

Nancy Mitford is an English writer of novels, biographies, and essays. This passage is from an essay called "The Tourist," part of a collection published under the title of *The Water Beetle* (1962). Mitford has acknowledged about herself that "when I take up my pen my thoughts are wicked." "Wicked" is a bit much, but certainly she is not given to pious platitudes. Her vision is satiric. She looks through appearances, through the phony surfaces most of us show the world, and reveals what people are in clever, mocking phrases. Notice in this selection how she uses her diction to ridicule both the tourists and the natives who make a living bamboozling them.

1   The most intensive study I ever made of tourists was at Torcello, where it is impossible to avoid them. Torcello is a minute island in the Venetian lagoon: here, among vineyards and wild flowers, some thirty cottages surround a great cathedral which was being built when William the Conqueror came to England. A canal and a path lead from the lagoon to 5 the village; the vineyards are intersected by canals; red and yellow sails glide slowly through the vines. Bells from the campanile ring out reproaches three times a day (*"cloches, cloches, divins reproches"*) joined by a chorus from the surrounding islands. There is an inn where I lived one summer, writing my book and observing the tourists. Torcello which used to be 10 lonely as a cloud has recently become an outing from Venice. Many more visitors than it can comfortably hold pour into it, off the regular steamers, off chartered motor-boats, and off yachts; all day they amble up the towpath, looking for what? The cathedral is decorated with early mosaics— scenes from hell, much restored, and a great sad, austere Madonna; Byzan- 15 tine art is an acquired taste and probably not one in ten of the visitors has acquired it. They wander into the church and look round aimlessly. They come out on to the village green and photograph each other in a stone arm-

From *The Water Beetle* by Nancy Mitford. Copyright © 1962 by Nancy Mitford. Reprinted by permission of A. D. Peters & Co., Ltd.

chair, said to be the throne of Attila. They relentlessly tear at the wild roses which one has seen in bud and longed to see in bloom and which, for a day 20 have scented the whole island. As soon as they are picked the roses fade and are thrown into the canal. The Americans visit the inn to eat or drink something. The English declare that they can't afford to do this. They take food which they have brought with them into the vineyard and I am sorry to say leave the devil of a mess behind them. Every Thursday Ger- 25 mans come up the tow-path, marching as to war, with a Leader. There is a standing order for fifty luncheons at the inn; while they eat the Leader lectures them through a megaphone. After luncheon they march into the cathedral and undergo another lecture. They, at least, know what they are seeing. Then they march back to their boat. They are tidy; they leave no 30 litter.

2   More interesting, however, than the behaviour of the tourists is that of the islanders. As they are obliged, whether they like it or not, to live in public during the whole summer, they very naturally try to extract some financial benefit from this state of affairs. The Italian is a born actor; be- 35 tween the first boat from Venice, at 11 a.m. and the last on which the ordinary tourist leaves at 6 p.m., the island is turned into a stage with all the natives playing a part. Young men from Burano, the next island, dress up as gondoliers and ferry tourists from the steamer to the village in sandolos. One of them brings a dreadful little brother called Eric who pesters every- 40 body to buy the dead bodies of sea-horses, painted gold. "Buona fortuna", he chants. I got very frond of Eric. Sweet-faced old women sit at the cottage doors selling postcards and trinkets and apparently making *point de Venise* lace. They have really got it, on sale or return, from relations in Burano, where it is made by young girls. Old women, with toil-worn hands, cannot 45 do such fine work. It is supposed that the tourists are more likely to buy if they think they see the lace being made, but hardly any of them seem to appreciate its marvellous quality. Babies toddle about offering four-leafed clovers and hoping for a tip. More cries of "Buona fortuna". The priest organizes holy processions to coincide with the arrival of the steamer. And so 50 the play goes on. The tourists are almost incredibly mean, they hardly leave anything on the island except empty cigarette boxes and flapping *Daily Mails*. The lace is expensive, but they might buy a few postcards or shell necklaces and give the children some pennies; they seem to have hearts of stone. 55

3   As soon as the last boat has gone, down comes the curtain. The "gondoliers" shed their white linen jackets and silly straw hats and go back

to Burano, taking Eric, highly dissatisfied with his earnings and saying if this goes on he will die of hunger. The sweet old women let the smiles fade from their faces, put away their lace-making pillows, and turn to ordinary 60 activities of village life such as drowning kittens. The father of the clover babies creeps about on his knees finding four-leafed clovers for the next day. The evening reproaches ring out, the moon comes up, the flapping *Daily Mails* blow into the lagoon. Torcello is itself again.

QUESTIONS

READER AND PURPOSE

1. Is Mitford a willing student of that strange animal—the modern tourist? (Perhaps her opening sentence, especially its final clause, will give you a clue.)

2. Whether or not she studies them willingly, Mitford is obviously critical of tourists. (Tourists seem to be disliked by everyone, even by other tourists.) Generally, however, she leaves her complaints implicit, contenting herself with simply describing what the visitors to Torcello do and allowing the facts to speak for themselves. Compose one or two sentences which summarize her criticisms of tourists. Do you think that Mitford's charges against sightseers would have been clearer and more effective if she had expressed them openly? Why or why not?

3. Does Mitford dislike the German tourists more than any of the others, or does she consider them the least objectionable?

4. Although she ridicules the typical tourist, Mitford resists the temptation to sentimentalize the natives of the island, to render them better than life so as to make the visitors seem worse. What details do we learn about the inhabitants of Torcello that keep them human and not impossibly idealized?

ORGANIZATION

5. Make an outline of this selection, indicating its major parts and at least the primary subdivisions under each of those.

6. What is the topic sentence of paragraph 1? Of paragraph 2? Of 3? How has the writer linked the beginning of the second paragraph to the first? The beginning of the third to the second?

7. What does the first part of paragraph 1 ("Torcello is . . . from the surrounding islands," lines 2-9) contribute to Mitford's discussion of tourists?

8. Paragraphs 2 and 3 are unified in part by the running metaphor * which compares the island to a stage set and its inhabitants to actors. What sentence sets up this comparison? Indicate all subsequent words or constructions that continue the metaphor.

9. While it is not actually the end of the essay from which this passage is taken, the third paragraph does bring the selection nicely to a close. Try to explain why it does.

SENTENCES

10. Mitford's sentences are effectively varied. She uses short, direct statements, longer sentences with several subordinate constructions, interrupted * movement, balanced * sentences, and parallelism *. Point out one or two examples of each of these sentence styles and be able to discuss why each is effective in its context. The writer even employs one fragment *. Where?
11. To what is *scenes* (15) in apposition *?
12. How does Mitford use sentence structure to help unify the portion of her first paragraph from line 17 to line 31?
13. Each of the following revisions is less effective, for Mitford's purpose, than the sentence she wrote. Why?

(a) *Revision:* They wander into the church and aimlessly look around. *Mitford:* "They wander into the church and look round aimlessly." (17)
(b) *Revision:* They know what they are seeing at least. *Mitford:* "They, at least, know what they are seeing." (29-30)
(c) *Revision:* The curtain comes down as soon as the last boat has gone. *Mitford:* "As soon as the last boat has gone, down comes the curtain." (56)

DICTION

14. Look up: *lagoon* (3), *campanile* (7), *mosaic* (14), *austere* (15), *Byzantine* (15), *Attila* (19), *coincide* (50), *mean* (51).
15. What words in the first paragraph indicate the tourists' lack of purpose?
16. The phrase *lonely as a cloud* (11) is an echo from a famous poem. Do you recognize it? Mitford embeds another well known quotation in her prose. See if you can spot it. What advantages do such literary allusions * offer a writer? The absence of quotation marks around these phrases is deliberate. Why do you suppose Mitford did not use quotes? (She is not trying to pass these expressions off as her own; she expects her readers to recognize them.)
17. Is there possibly a double meaning in the phrase *much restored* in line 15?
18. Why is *Leader* capitalized in line 26?
19. Comment upon these proposed changes in Mitford's diction: *listen to* for *undergo* (29), *go* for *march* (30), *wander* for *toddle* (48), *discarded* for *flapping* (52).

POINTS TO LEARN

1. In description, facts often speak louder than opinions.
2. A metaphor can effectively organize and unify a paragraph or even a group of paragraphs.
3. A varied sentence style is more apt to be interesting.

SUGGESTIONS FOR WRITING

1. Think of tourists you have known. Write an essay in which you classify them by type, describing each in detail and trying to convey a distinct impression by the details you select.
2. Instead of tourists, you might prefer to describe the kinds of spectators one sees at an athletic contest—a football game, say—perhaps contrasting their actions with those of the players or officials.

IMPROVING YOUR STYLE

1. In your composition use (and label in the margin) at least one of each of these kinds of sentences: short and straight-forward, balanced, parallel, a sentence showing interrupted movement, a sentence containing an appositive.
2. Try to embed a literary quotation somewhere in your prose. Do not explicitly identify it either by quotation marks or by acknowledging the source. It should be something sufficiently well-known that your reader will immediately recognize it.

Souvenir Shop

Paul Jacobs is an American journalist and social scientist. He writes on economic, political, and social themes for such periodicals as *Commentary*, *Commonweal*, and *The Reporter*. He has also authored or co-authored several books, among them: *The State of the Unions* (1963), *The New Radicals* (1966), and *Prelude to Riot: A View of Urban America from the Bottom* (1967). This selection is taken from an essay, "The Most Cheerful Graveyard in the World" (*The Reporter*, September 18, 1958), a not-very-sympathetic account of Forest Lawn, a large and fashionable cemetery in Los Angeles. The description of the souvenir shop, developed in these paragraphs, is an example of one of the simplest kinds of descriptive writing—the catalogue. Yet cataloguing is less easy than it looks; a good catalogue is not a laundry list. It is a focused collection of details, the creation of a writer who has looked closely, learned the names of things, and selected only what suits his purpose.

1 Color photos and post cards of the "Moses" statue can be purchased, along with thousands of other items, at Forest Lawn's souvenir shop. There, browsing visitors can choose from showcases displaying money clips, cocktail napkins, book matches, jigsaw puzzles, and charm bracelets—all decorated with Forest Lawn motifs. Prices range from a modest 5 twenty-nine cents for a key chain to $125 for a glass vase etched with a Forest Lawn scene.

2 There are brown plastic nutshells containing little photos of Forest Lawn, ladies' compacts, cigarette lighters, cufflinks, salt and pepper shakers, picture frames, demitasse spoons, bookmarks, cups and saucers, pen 10 and pencil sets, glass bells, wooden plaques, ashtrays, place mats and doilies, perfume and powder sets, jackknives, and a great variety of other goodies, all with an appropriate Forest Lawn theme. Books like *The*

Loved One, Evelyn Waugh's satire of Forest Lawn, are not on sale in the souvenir shop. (Eaton[1] occasionally expresses resentment over the treat- 15
ment given the cemetery by novelists—especially by one writer to whom he extended free run of the park only to be parodied later. But Eaton also understands that such novels have brought world-wide publicity to Forest Lawn and have not adversely affected his sales, which come not from England but from Los Angeles.) 20
3   Among the most popular items at the souvenir shop are those showing reproductions of Forest Lawn's three churches, the Church of the Recessional, the Little Church of the Flowers, and the Wee Kirk o' the Heather.

QUESTIONS

READER AND PURPOSE

1. California's Forest Lawn Memorial Park arouses different responses in different observers. To some it is one of the most beautiful and opulent cemeteries in the world, a fit resting place for movie stars and Hollywood aristocracy. To others, like the British writer Jessica Mitford in *The American Way of Death,* it is a "grotesque cloud-cuckooland where the trappings of gracious living are transformed, as in a nightmare, into the trappings of Gracious Dying." Evelyn Waugh, also English, savagely satirizes what he regarded as Forest Lawn's commercialism and vulgarity in his novel *The Loved One.* Can you judge from this passage how Jacobs feels about Forest Lawn? Does he admire the place, or is he closer to Mitford and Waugh in his response?
2. What impression does Jacobs convey in this description of the souvenir shop?

ORGANIZATION

3. Most of this description is a catalogue. What principle of selectivity has guided the writer? Is there any reason for the order of items? Could Jacobs just as well have mentioned first that the shop contains no books like *The Loved One?*
4. Consider this alternate way of organizing the material. The first half of the second paragraph, as far as the sentence beginning with "Books" in line 13, might be added to paragraph 1. Paragraph 3 might also be added to the first paragraph, as the concluding sentence. The second revised paragraph would then consist solely of what follows "Books" (lines 13-20). Is this revised organi-

[1] Director of Forest Lawn. [Editors' note]

zation better than, worse than, or equal to the one that Jacobs employs? Explain.

5. Is the third paragraph undeveloped? What purpose(s) does a single sentence serve when it is indented as a complete paragraph? Could the third paragraph easily lead into a full description of the three churches at Forest Lawn?

SENTENCES

6. Why is this revision less effective than Jacobs' sentence?

> *Revision:* Browsing visitors can choose from showcases displaying money clips, cocktail napkins, book matches, jigsaw puzzles, and charm bracelets decorated with Forest Lawn motifs.

> *Jacobs:* "There, browsing visitors can choose from showcases displaying money clips, cocktail napkins, book matches, jigsaw puzzles, and charm bracelets—all decorated with Forest Lawn motifs." (3-5)

7. Substitute *however* for *but* in the sentence beginning "But Eaton also understands" (17-20). Read the revision aloud. Does the word *Eaton* have the same emphasis as before, or has emphasis shifted to *however?* What general rule can you suggest about when to begin a sentence with *but* and when with *however?*

DICTION

8. Look up: *motifs* (5), *etched* (6), *demitasse* (10), *extended* (17), *parodied* (17), *adversely* (19).

9. Does the writer's diction betray any approval or disapproval of Forest Lawn? Be able to support your answer by citing specific words.

10. Why are these substitutes less effective than the words Jacobs chose: *items* for *goodies* (13), *fame* for *publicity* (18)?

POINTS TO LEARN

1. A catalogue is a useful way of describing anything composed of multiple objects. A catalogue supplies concrete imagery *, gives a feeling of multiplicity and complexity, is economical, defines the nature of the subject, and convinces by its cumulative weight.

2. By skillfully selecting the details he catalogues the writer controls the reader's response.

3. In a single sentence the number of items in a catalogue is usually more than three but less than fifteen or twenty. If it is necessary to deal with more than twenty items, it is best to organize them in several sentences, preferably separated by some organizing phrase or interpretive comment. Observe how Paul Jacobs separates two lists of items by the sentence beginning "Prices range" (5-7).

4. Catalogues may be the center of a short description, or they may be auxiliary to other descriptive techniques.

SUGGESTIONS FOR WRITING

Compose one or two catalogues to describe an antique or junk shop, a wood-worker's shop, a repair garage, a delicatessen, the vegetable section of a super-market, the patent medicine shelves of a drugstore, the town dump, or any place where there are objects in great profusion. By careful selectivity make your reader approve or disapprove, like or be repelled by, your subject.

IMPROVING YOUR STYLE

1. Experiment with the dash to isolate elements you wish to emphasize, as Paul Jacobs does in line 16, where he sets off a prepositional phrase and its modifiers.
2. Open one or two sentences with *but*.

Potter's Field

William Styron is an American novelist; his books include *The Confessions of Nat Turner, The Long March, Set This House Afire,* and *Lie Down in Darkness.* This selection is from the last work and describes the pauper burial ground of New York City, on Hart's Island, which is located where the East River widens into Long Island Sound. The writing is a wonderful specimen of impressionistic description, in which the writer's handling of details arouses and directs the reader's feelings. It is also description which enlarges its subject, moving outward from the immediate perceptions of things to a broader emotional and philosophical awareness of the conditions of human existence.

1   Potter's Field for New York City is on an island in the Sound, half a mile east of the Bronx and just inside the city limits. The island is named Hart's after a deer which, in the later days of the English settlement, was seen to swim out to the place from the mainland and apparently to establish residence there, among the scrub-oak and willow groves. The hart was   5
later shot, so the legend goes, by a man named Thwaite who rowed out to the island in a skiff, with a big gun and a hankering for venison. It was this person, a gentleman of preternatural modesty, who named the island Hart's, rather than Thwaite's, and it was also he who made a tidy living for years by rowing picnickers out to the place; at that time there were   10
sandy beaches there, woods, gentle groves—a perfect place, in short, to rest yourself, if you lived in the eighteenth century.

2   As the city expanded, however, it became necessary to find a newer and larger place to dispose of the friendless, nameless dead. Up until the middle of the last century, when Forty-Second Street was suburban and   15
sheep still nibbled placidly around Columbus Circle, this purpose had been served by the old Pauper's Burial Ground, which occupied what is now part of Washington Square. The dead do not remain long dead in big cities, or

perhaps they become deader; at any rate the markers were torn down, the
square filled in with new earth and sidewalks laid across. They have become   20
twice unremembered, those sleepers: once, though many bore no names,
they had at least a sunny plot of ground. Now no one can mark them, and
the nursemaids strolling along McDougal Street, aware only of the birds
and the boys and the dusty April light, cannot know even the fact of those
who rest beneath the asphalt—their bones shaken by the subways—and   25
await the resurrection.

3   The first person to be buried in the new Potter's Field on the island was an orphan named Louisa Van Slyke, who died in Charity Hospital
in 1869. Many followed her; there close to half a million souls have been
laid to rest, a lot of them nameless, all of them forgotten.   30

4   The island itself is bleak and unprepossessing. There are islands
like this, serving all sorts of cheerless but necessary municipal functions,
near every great city in the world—islands in the Thames and Danube and
the Seine, and in the yellow waters of the Tiber. This one, perhaps because
it is American, seems more than necessarily dreary. No blade of grass grows   35
here, only weeds. On the south end of the island stands a sewage disposal
plant. North of this is a city detention home, a great mass of soot-stained
brick and iron bars, where derelicts and drunks and the less-involved dope
addicts are "rehabilitated." Moss and flakes of pale green lichen creep
along the walls. In the treeless shade of the courtyards, flowering in cran-   40
nies below shuttered windows, are chickweed and ghostly dandelions. Still
farther north of this jail, separated from it by a quarter mile of dusty, weed-
choked rising ground, is Potter's Field. The glens and willow-groves are
gone, the picnickers and the slain deer; if you stand here on the hill beneath a dead, wind-twisted cedar, the island's only tree, you can get a good   45
view of the land—the sewage plant and the prison and the burial ground,
each recipient, in its fashion, of waste and decay.

5   The towers of Manhattan are faint and blue in the distance, rising
like minarets or monoliths; near by on summer days yachtsmen sail their
boats out of City Island, and the patterns their white sails make on the wa-   50
ter are as pretty as kites blown about against a blue March sky. Here in the
field weeds and brown, unsightly vegetation grow in thick clusters, tangled
together over the numbered concrete markers. There are no proper grave-
stones in the meadow. Rusted strands of barbed wire traverse the field,
serving no purpose, preventing no intrusion, for few people ever visit there.   55
It's an ugly place, full of rats and spiders, and crisscrossed, because of its
prominence above the water, by raw, shifting winds.

6   To transport bodies from the morgue they once had a tugboat; painted black, a flag at half-mast on its stern, it chugged up the East River on Thursdays. When it passed, barge captains and sailors would uncover 60 their heads, cross themselves, or murmur a prayer. Now a truck is used, and the dead no longer receive this final benediction: who would salute a truck, so green and so commonplace? The coffins are made of plain pine and these—twenty-five or thirty each week—are laid four deep in the big mass graves. There are no prayers said; city prisoners are used for the burying, 65 and they receive a day off from their sentence for each day's work in Potter's Field. The other dead must be crowded out—those who have lain there for twenty years. Now they are bones and dust and, taking up valuable space, must be removed. Not just twice dead like the relics beneath Washington Square, they become triply annihilated: the prisoners won't 70 let them rest, remove them—bones, rotted cerement, and rattling skull— and throw them in a smaller hole, where they take up one tenth the space they did twenty years before. The new coffins are laid in precisely, tagged and numbered; in this way many souls occupy, undisturbed, their own six feet of earth for two decades.   75

7   Then all is done. The grave is covered. The prisoners load up their spades and picks, climb back into the police van, and are driven away. On a promontory near the sea the old coffins are burning, for these too must be destroyed. They make a beautiful and lonely pyre; stacked high, they burn briskly, because the wood has become well decayed. Decay flowers in the 80 air too, ripe and fleshy, yet it is a clean decay, as natural as dying leaves; decay is being destroyed. On the broken splinters flames lick toward the remnant of a shroud, and a garland of baby's hair, preserved as in a locket all these years, is touched by the fire, shrivels away in a puff of dust. Small bones, overlooked by the buriers, become charred and fall among the 85 weeds. A rat peeps out from a burrow, sniffs the wind, then withdraws. The afternoon lengthens and evening comes, but the burning blue odor ascends, is caught by a breeze, and sweeps down among the graves, curls about the monument. It is almost as if this monument were forgotten. Who put it there is a mystery; it bears the meadow's only epitaph. It is small and 90 cracked and mostly covered by weeds; on it the graven eyes of Christ, weathered by many storms, still burn like the brightest fires. Below these the legend, obscured by brambles and the swirling blue odor of decay, can be read: *He calleth His own by Name.*

8   So the darkness comes on, covering the graves and the withered 95 cedar and the nameless dead. Lights wink on around the Sound. Rats stir

in the weeds, among the graves. The smoke still ascends in the night, clean and without guilt, borne like passion with the last dust of the nameless and the unremembered, upward and upward, toward the stars.

QUESTIONS

READER AND PURPOSE

1. Styron's description of New York City's potter's field involves much more than telling us what it looks like. A clue to this larger intention is suggested by his discussion in the second paragraph of the old burial ground in lower Manhattan. At first glance we might take this to be a digression from the subject of Hart's Island. Is it really? In that paragraph Styron remarks that the dead buried in the area of Washington Square have "become twice unremembered." Where else does he express this theme of the disturbed yet unremembered dead?

2. What was your reaction to Styron's description? Did it stimulate your thoughts or feelings in any particular way?

ORGANIZATION

3. Why may paragraphs 1-3 be said to make up a unit? Give this section a brief descriptive title.

4. How does the writer signal his turn of subject at the beginning of paragraph 4?

5. Do the remaining five paragraphs (4-8) compose a single unit, or do they comprise several? If you think several, indicate what these are and give a title to each.

6. Which words in the opening sentence of paragraph 4 establish the impression of Hart's Island Styron is conveying? What later details particularize and reinforce the impression?

7. How does our angle of vision change in paragraph 5? Where in that paragraph does the writer return us to the island? What word signals the return?

8. How does Styron control our perceptions in the seventh paragraph?

SENTENCES

9. Point out the parallel * constructions in the sentence in lines 86-89.

10. Comment upon how the following revisions affect the meaning or emphasis of Styron's sentences:

> (a) *Revision:* Many followed her; there close to half a million souls have been laid to rest, and a lot of them were nameless and all of them have been forgotten.

Styron: "Many followed her; there close to half a million souls have been laid to rest, a lot of them nameless, all of them forgotten." (29-30)

(b) *Revision:* It's an ugly place, full of rats and spiders and crisscrossed by raw shifting winds because of its prominence above the water.

Styron: "It's an ugly place, full of rats and spiders, and crisscrossed, because of its prominence above the water, by raw, shifting winds." (56-57)

(c) *Revision:* To transport bodies from the morgue they once had a tugboat, painted black, a flag at half-mast on its stern, it chugged up the East River on Thursdays.

Styron: "To transport bodies from the morgue they once had a tugboat; painted black, a flag at half-mast on its stern, it chugged up the East River on Thursdays." (57-60)

(d) *Revision:* Then when all is done and the grave is covered, the prisoners load up their spades and picks, climb back into the police van, and are driven away.

Styron: "Then all is done. The grave is covered. The prisoners load up their spades and picks, climb back into the police van, and are driven away." (76-77)

DICTION

11. Look up: *hankering* (7), *preternatural* (8), *placidly* (16), *lichen* (39), *minarets* (49), *monoliths* (49), *traverse* (54), *prominence* (57), *cerement* (71), *promontory* (78), *pyre* (79), *graven* (91), *weathered* (92).

12. Explain how these pointers * help the reader: *in short* (11) and *at any rate* (19).

13. Suppose the word *rattling* were omitted in line 71: how would our perception change?

14. Styron uses language like a poet, freeing the associations of words so as to deepen and enrich experience. Discuss as fully as you can the associations evoked by these expressions:

(a) "The towers of Manhattan are faint and blue in the distance, rising like minarets or monoliths. . . ." (48-49)
(b) "as pretty as kites blown about against a blue March sky" (51)
(c) "On a promontory near the sea the old coffins are burning . . . a beautiful and lonely pyre. . . ." (77-79)
(d) "a garland of baby's hair, preserved as in a locket" (83)
(e) "the graven eyes of Christ, weathered by many storms" (91-92)
(f) "So the darkness comes on. . . ." (95)

15. The closing sentence is especially rich in associations. What range of feeling and thought does it open up? The image * of the smoke is prominent in the last two paragraphs. Has it any symbolic * value?

POINTS TO LEARN
1. If the eye is to see, the mind must direct.
2. In impressionistic description the associations and overtones of language are of the utmost importance.

SUGGESTIONS FOR WRITING
Modeling your composition upon paragraphs 4 and 5 of Styron's selection, describe a space of ground containing several buildings or enclosed areas of various sorts. Try to make the reader visualize the buildings or areas in relation to one another, and try as well to convey a definite emotional response, an emotion related not directly but rather objectified in the descriptive details.

IMPROVING YOUR STYLE
In your composition
1. Pay some attention to directing your reader's eyes. But do it subtly: not "As we lift our eyes overhead"; simply "Overhead."
2. Include several examples of parallelism.
3. Use *in short* and *at any rate* to introduce sentences.

Bubbles in the Ice

Henry David Thoreau (1817-62) is best known for *Walden* (1854) and *Civil Disobedience* (1849), inspired by his opposition to the Mexican War. Thoreau is often thought of as a writer about nature, and indeed there is much observation of the natural world in *Walden*, as in such books as *Cape Cod* and *A Week on the Concord and Merrimack Rivers*. But Thoreau's primary subject is not really trees and rivers and ponds. It is the world within man—the world of mind and spirit. He is, finally, a moralist, not in the narrow brush-your-teeth-and-say-your-prayers sense, but in the larger meaning of a person for whom moral commitment is the essence of life. The following selection (from *Walden*) may not seem to be moralism. In its literal content it is not. Yet in a more subtle way "Bubbles in the Ice" illustrates one of Thoreau's most fundamental commitments: to see things whole, to see them as they are, and to be precise and honest about what he sees.

The pond had in the mean while skimmed over in the shadiest and shallowest coves, some days or even weeks before the general freezing. The first ice is especially interesting and perfect, being hard, dark, and transparent, and affords the best opportunity that ever offers for examining the bottom where it is shallow; for you can lie at your length on ice only an inch thick, 5 like a skater insect on the surface of the water, and study the bottom at your leisure, only two or three inches distant, like a picture behind a glass, and the water is necessarily always smooth then. There are many furrows in the sand where some creature has travelled about and doubled on its tracks; and, for wrecks, it is strewn with the cases of caddis worms made of minute 10 grains of white quartz. Perhaps these have creased it, for you find some of their cases in the furrows, though they are deep and broad for them to make. But the ice itself is the object of most interest, though you must improve the earliest opportunity to study it. If you examine it closely the morning after it freezes, you find that the greater part of the bubbles, which 15

From *Walden*, edited by Owen Thomas (New York: W. W. Norton & Co., 1966).

at first appeared to be within it, are against its under surface, and that more are continually rising from the bottom; while the ice is as yet comparatively solid and dark, that is, you see the water through it. These bubbles are from an eightieth to an eighth of an inch in diameter, very clear and beautiful, and you see your face reflected in them through the ice. There may be thirty or forty of them to a square inch. There are also already within the ice narrow oblong perpendicular bubbles about half an inch long, sharp cones with the apex upward; or oftener, if the ice is quite fresh, minute spherical bubbles one directly above another, like a string of beads. But these within the ice are not so numerous nor obvious as those beneath. I sometimes used to cast on stones to try the strength of the ice, and those which broke through carried in air with them, which formed very large and conspicuous white bubbles beneath. One day when I came to the same place forty-eight hours afterward, I found that those large bubbles were still perfect, though an inch more of ice had formed, as I could see distinctly by the seam in the edge of a cake. But as the last two days had been very warm, like an Indian summer, the ice was not now transparent, showing the dark green color of the water, and the bottom, but opaque and whitish or gray, and though twice as thick was hardly stronger than before, for the air bubbles had greatly expanded under this heat and run together, and lost their regularity; they were no longer one directly over another, but often like silvery coins poured from a bag, one overlapping another, or in thin flakes, as if occupying slight cleavages. The beauty of the ice was gone, and it was too late to study the bottom. Being curious to know what position my great bubbles occupied with regard to the new ice, I broke out a cake containing a middling sized one, and turned it bottom upward. The new ice had formed around and under the bubble, so that it was included between the two ices. It was wholly in the lower ice, but close against the upper, and was flattish, or perhaps slightly lenticular, with a rounded edge, a quarter of an inch deep by four inches in diameter; and I was surprised to find that directly under the bubble the ice was melted with great regularity in the form of a saucer reversed, to the height of five eighths of an inch in the middle, leaving a thin partition there between the water and the bubble, hardly an eighth of an inch thick; and in many places the small bubbles in this partition had burst out downward, and probably there was no ice at all under the largest bubbles, which were a foot in diameter. I inferred that the infinite number of minute bubbles which I had first seen against the under surface of the ice were now frozen in likewise, and that each, in its degree, had operated like a burning glass on the ice beneath to melt and rot it.

These are the little air-guns which contribute to make the ice crack and whoop.

QUESTIONS

READER AND PURPOSE

1. Is Thoreau observing the ice with an objective, scientific detachment; or is he viewing it impressionistically, projecting his values and emotions into what he sees? Does he do more than passively observe—conduct experiments, say, or take specimens?

2. What assumptions does Thoreau appear to have made concerning his reader's attitude toward nature? What effect do you believe Thoreau wishes to have upon his reader? Does he succeed?

ORGANIZATION

3. Which clause near the beginning of the paragraph serves as a topic statement?

4. Thoreau's paragraph is quite long (though this is not unusual; paragraphs tended to be longer in the literary prose of the nineteenth century). What is Thoreau primarily concerned with up to line 13? What shift in topic occurs at that point? There are at least two other places where similar minor turns of thought occur. Identify them.

5. Study the passage from lines 14 to 24 and be able to discuss how Thoreau organizes his discussion of the bubbles.

SENTENCES

6. Read the two following sentences carefully and decide what principle Thoreau has observed in arranging the sequence of their phrases and clauses:

> (a) "I sometimes used to cast on stones to try the strength of the ice, and those which broke through carried in air with them, which formed very large and conspicuous white bubbles beneath." (25-28)
>
> (b) "Being curious to know what position my great bubbles occupied with regard to the new ice, I broke out a cake containing a middle sized one, and turned it bottom upward." (39-41)

7. Why is this revision less effective than Thoreau's sentence?

> Revision: You find that the greater part of the bubbles are against the under surface of the ice (though at first they appeared to be within it),

if you examine the ice closely the morning after it freezes, and that more are continually rising from the bottom. . . .

Thoreau: "If you examine it closely the morning after it freezes, you find that the greater part of the bubbles, which at first appeared to be within it, are against its under surface, and that more are continually rising from the bottom. . . ." (14-17)

8. In the clause in lines 21-23, to what is *cones* in apposition *?

DICTION

9. Look up: *coves* (2), *quartz* (11), *Indian summer* (31), *opaque* (33), *cleavages* (38), *middling* (41), *lenticular* (44), *inferred* (51).

10. Find specimens of Thoreau's diction which suggest the exact, scientific eye. Find others which suggest a more impressionistic, emotionally colored vision.

11. In several places Thoreau uses similes * and metaphors *. Point these out and consider what purpose he probably intended them to serve and whether or not they succeed.

POINTS TO LEARN

1. Exactness of detail is vital to objective description.
2. When possible organize sentences to reflect the order of perception or of thought.

SUGGESTIONS FOR WRITING

Look closely at some commonplace natural object and describe it as exactly as you can: a stalk of grass or of grain, a mackerel, a pumpkin, an ear of corn, a gladiola.

IMPROVING YOUR STYLE

In your description include:

1. A sentence containing an appositive.
2. A long sentence (25-30 words minimum) in which the sequence of elements (that is, the words, phrases, clauses) exactly follows the order of events.
3. Two metaphors and two similes.

The Subway

Tom Wolfe (not to be confused with the novelist Thomas Wolfe of an earlier generation) is one of the new journalists. The new journalism, more an idea than a movement, loosely designates a group of younger authors who write, like journalists, about the people, the places, the events of the contemporary world, but who write with the imagination, the personal vision, and the rhetorical flair we usually associate with the creative writer. Indeed, in the new journalism the distinction between reporting and literature fades, and the term *story* includes in full measure of ambiguity both its newspaper and literary senses.

Wolfe's stories appear in magazines such as *Confidential* and *Harper's Bazaar*. The subjects of a few of those that were collected in his book *The Kandy-Kolored Tangerine-Flake Streamline Baby* (1965) will indicate his range: Las Vegas, Muhammad Ali, The Museum of Modern Art in New York City, the business of customizing cars (the subject of the title essay), and the penchant of New Yorkers for self-aggrandizement ("The Big League Complex," source of the following paragraphs about the subway). Wolfe, like any good reporter, observes closely, but far from striving for objectivity he observes from a particular angle of vision—often satiric—and he projects what he feels and thinks into his description by the details he selects to show us and the words he chooses to describe them.

1   In a way, of course, the subway is the living symbol of all that adds up to lack of status in New York. There is a sense of madness and disorientation at almost every express stop. The ceilings are low, the vistas are long, there are no landmarks, the lighting is an eerie blend of fluorescent tubing, electric light bulbs and neon advertising. The whole place is a gross assault 5
on the senses. The noise of the trains stopping or rounding curves has a high-pitched harshness that is difficult to describe. People feel no qualms

about pushing whenever it becomes crowded. Your tactile sense takes a cru-
cifying you never dreamed possible. The odors become unbearable when
the weather is warm. Between platforms, record shops broadcast 45 r.p.m.   10
records with metallic tones and lunch counters serve the kind of hot dogs
in which you bite through a tensile, rubbery surface and then hit a soft,
oleaginous center like cottonseed meal, and the customers sit there with
pastry and bread flakes caked around their mouths, belching to themselves
so that their cheeks pop out flatulently now and then.   15

2   The underground spaces seem to attract every eccentric passion. A
small and ancient man with a Bible, an American flag and a megaphone
haunts the subways of Manhattan. He opens the Bible and quotes from it
in a strong but old and monotonous voice. He uses the megaphone at express stops, where the noise is too great for his voice to be heard ordinarily,   20
and calls for redemption.

3   Also beggars. And among the beggars New York's status competition is renewed, there in the much-despised subway. On the Seventh Avenue IRT line the competition is maniacal. Some evenings the beggars
ricochet off one another between stops, calling one another ————s and   25
————s and telling each other to go find their own ———— car. A mere
blind man with a cane and a cup is mediocre business. What is demanded
is entertainment. Two boys, one of them with a bongo drum, get on and
the big boy, with the drum, starts beating on it as soon as the train starts
up, and the little boy goes into what passes for a native dance. Then, if   30
there is room, he goes into a tumbling act. He runs from one end of the
car, first in the direction the train is going, and does a complete somersault
in the air, landing on his feet. Then he runs back the other way and does a
somersault in the air, only this time against the motion of the train. He
does this several times both ways, doing some native dancing in between.   35
This act takes so long that it can be done properly only over a long stretch,
such as the run between 42nd Street and 72nd Street. After the act is over,
the boys pass along the car with Dixie cups, asking for contributions.

4   The Dixie cup is the conventional container. There is one young
Negro on the Seventh Avenue line who used to get on at 42nd Street and   40
start singing a song, "I Wish That I Were Married." He was young and
looked perfectly healthy. But he would get on and sing this song, "I Wish
That I Were Married," at the top of his lungs and then pull a Dixie cup
out from under the windbreaker he always wore and walk up and down the
car waiting for contributions. I never saw him get a cent. Lately, however,   45
life has improved for him because he has begun to understand status com-

petition. Now he gets on and sings "I Wish That I Were Married," only when he opens up his windbreaker, he not only takes out a Dixie cup but reveals a cardboard sign, on which is written: "MY MOTHER HAS MULTIPLE SCHLERROSSIS AND I AM BLIND IN ONE EYE." His best touch is sclerosis, which 50 he has added every conceivable consonant to, creating a good, intimidating German physiology-textbook solidity. So today he does much better. He seems to make a living. He is no idler, lollygagger or bum. He can look with condescension upon the states to which men fall.

5   On the East Side IRT subway line, for example, at 86th Street, the 55 train stops and everyone comes squeezing out of the cars in clots and there on a bench in the gray-green gloom, under the girders and 1905 tiles, is an old man slouched back fast asleep, wearing a cotton windbreaker with the sleeves pulled off. That is all he is wearing. His skin is the color of congealed Wheatena laced with pocket lint. His legs are crossed in a gentle- 60 manly fashion and his kindly juice-head face is slopped over on the back of the bench. Apparently, other winos, who are notorious thieves among one another, had stripped him of all his clothes except his windbreaker, which they had tried to pull off him, but only managed to rip the sleeves off, and left him there passed out on the bench and naked, but in a gentlemanly 65 posture. Everyone stares at him briefly, at his congealed Wheatena-and-lint carcass, but no one breaks stride; and who knows how long it will be before finally two policemen have to come in and hold their breath and scrape him up out of the gloom and into the bosom of the law, from which he will emerge with a set of green fatigues, at least, and an honorable seat at night 70 on the subway bench.

QUESTIONS

READER AND PURPOSE

1. In the essay from which these paragraphs are excerpted Wolfe is writing about the New Yorker's preoccupation with being "big league," with his never-ending struggle for status. As an example he points out that certain New Yorkers take a snobbish pride in never riding the subway, which they consider, not merely literally, to be beneath them. The example leads Wolfe into a description of the subway. What general impression of it does he convey?

2. Do you think that Wolfe is primarily concerned with affecting his readers in some particular way or with expressing clearly what he perceives and how he feels about it?

ORGANIZATION

3. Which sentence controls the entire selection? Which states the topic of paragraph 1?

4. In paragraph 1 how is the third sentence related to the second? Does it merely repeat the preceding idea in more specific terms, explain why that idea is true, or compare it with something else?

5. In the sentence in lines 5-6 ("The whole place is a gross assault on the senses"), what are the key words in relation to the series of particulars that follows?

6. Which is the topic statement of paragraph 2? Does it set up only this paragraph? How is it supported in the second paragraph? By what technique are the sentences in lines 18-21 unified?

7. Explain how the third paragraph is linked to the second. What short sentence sets up most of the third paragraph? Study the seven sentences from lines 28 to 38 and be able to show how each is tied to what precedes it.

8. What effects the link between paragraphs 4 and 3? Paragraph 4 has two parts: where is the dividing point? How is flow * maintained in its final four sentences?

9. At the beginning of paragraph 5 Wolfe uses the phrase "for example": what is he illustrating? Is there a topic statement in this paragraph? If not, what words at the end of the preceding paragraph serve that purpose?

SENTENCES

10. The sentence in lines 3-5 consists of four asyndetic * clauses (independent clauses butted together without conjunctions). Such constructions are usually separated by semicolons. Wolfe, however, uses what is called the comma link. Do you think commas are sufficient here? Why or why not? What would be the effect upon the movement of this sentence if the clauses were punctuated in the conventional manner with semicolons?

11. Do you think the fragment * that opens the third paragraph is effective? Would anything be gained by turning it into a complete sentence, such as: "There are also beggars"? Would anything be lost?

12. How do the following alter the emphasis of Wolfe's sentences?

> (a) *Revision:* The competition is maniacal on the Seventh Avenue IRT line.
> *Wolfe:* "On the Seventh Avenue IRT line the competition is maniacal." (23-24)
> (b) *Revision:* Then he goes into a tumbling act if there is room.
> *Wolfe:* "Then, if there is room, he goes into a tumbling act." (30-31)

(c) *Revision:* But he would get on and sing this song, "I Wish That I
Were Married," at the top of his lungs and then pull a Dixie cup
out from under the windbreaker he always wore and walk up and
down the car waiting for contributions, though I never saw him
get a cent.

Wolfe: "But he would get on and sing this song, 'I Wish That I
Were Married,' at the top of his lungs and then pull a Dixie cup
out from under the windbreaker he always wore and walk up and
down the car waiting for contributions. I never saw him get a
cent." (42-45)

DICTION

13. Look up: *symbol* (1), *disorientation* (2), *vistas* (3), *eerie* (4), *redemption*
(21), *intimidating* (51), *physiology* (52), *lollygagger* (53), *notorious* (62),
congealed (66).

14. Explain the meanings of these phrases: *gross assault* (5), *metallic tones*
(11), *eccentric passion* (16), *mediocre business* (27), *kindly juice-head face*
(61).

15. Why are these substitutions less effective than the words Wolfe uses?
Mushy for *oleaginous* (13), *patrols* for *haunts* (18), *crazy* for *maniacal* (24),
bump for *ricochet* (25), *pouring* for *squeezing* (56), *groups* for *clots* (56), *old*
for 1905 (57), *remove him from* for *scrape him up out of* (68-69)

16. In the description of the hot dog in lines 11-13, what words arouse unpleasant associations? What do you think Wolfe's purpose is in this description? Does he succeed? How does he wish us to respond to the customers eating
"pastry and bread" (13-15)?

17. How does the phrase *of course* (1) affect Wolfe's tone *? What does it
say to his reader?

POINTS TO LEARN

1. In writing description it is good practice to set up and control details with
short introductory sentences.

2. Sometimes (though not usually) a topic statement may be placed outside
the paragraph in which it is developed.

SUGGESTIONS FOR WRITING

1. Describe something which, like the subway, assaults the senses with multi-
farious sights and sounds and smells—an amusement park, a holiday crowd at a
bus station or airport, a supermarket on a busy shopping day. The impression
you communicate may be pleasant or unpleasant, but in either case decide beforehand what it is and select and arrange your details accordingly.

2. In a paragraph or two discuss what range of impressions (they are varied and complicated) Wolfe conveys about the naked drunkard he describes in paragraph 5. Support your discussion by specific examples of the writer's diction and by analyzing how individual words aroused particular responses in you.

IMPROVING YOUR STYLE

Include the following in your description:

1. A sentence consisting of 3 or 4 short clauses closely related in idea but grammatically independent. Punctuate them, as Wolfe does the sentence in lines 3-5, with commas.

2. (With your instructor's permission) two fragments (*effective* fragments).

3. The phrase *of course* to introduce a sentence.

4. (If it fits with your topic) a description of an item of junk food made to seem unappetizing, even sickening.

The Inner-city School

Theodore R. Sizer is a teacher and writer on education. He has taught in secondary schools and at Harvard University, where he served as Dean of the Faculty of Education. His books include *Secondary Schools at the Turn of the Century* (1964), *The Age of the Academy* (1964), and, as editor, *Religion and Public Education* (1967). The following selection is taken from an essay, "The Schools in the City," published in *The Metropolitan Enigma* (1968), a collection of articles by various scholars surveying the economic, political, social, and administrative difficulties of modern cities. The essay is thus problem-oriented, and the description reprinted here, which comes early in the essay, serves to focus some of the problems Sizer will discuss. Often in exposition or persuasion, description may be called for, as it is here, in a subsidiary but important role.

1   A typical inner-city school is on a slight rise in a previously "respectable" part of the city. Many of the houses nearby have a kind of late nineteenth-century grandeur left, with high windows, bay turrets, and flights of imposing stone steps. Pressing in upon them are frame "triple deckers" thirty to fifty years old, with porches out back covered with drying laundry. 5
The school's yard is very small and backs onto the houses. Trash is in abundance.

2   The door of the school is locked, not to keep the children in, as some critics would think, but to keep undesirables out. To get in, one pushes a button that rings in the classroom nearest the front door. An assigned stu- 10
dent comes out, peers at those who wish admittance, and either lets them in or informs the office.

3   The building dates from Grover Cleveland's second administration. It is solid, high ceilinged; the floors are well polished, but the sickly green walls need paint badly; the rooms are surprisingly cool on a warm June or 15

September day, but the antique steam heating system is raucous on winter mornings. The windows in each classroom are decorated pane by pane with colorful paper cutouts made by the teacher after school. Some rooms have new, tan-colored wood and steel movable table-desks; others have older, lift-top models. In each case, the desks are arranged in rows, though only   20
the older ones are screwed to the floor. The hall outside has a line painted down the middle; during class breaks, "no talking" and "keep to the right." Teachers are on duty at each point where the hall turns.

4   The teachers are proud and defensive; devoted and cynical; in many ways the most interesting, important, and neglected part of the school.   25
They are stereotyped as rigid and out-of-date, and they deeply resent this. They are local people, by and large, and locally trained, but they protest, quite rightly, that this does not necessarily mean that they are parochial and ill informed. They look on most visitors much as they look on the battalion of behavioral scientists, that has rushed forward to explain the "pa-   30
thology" of the urban school—with the contempt for (and fear of) the witch doctor who never seems to get at the root of the illness. They are at once critical of and loyal to the "central office," their own school administration, and they doubt the sincerity of a federal government that largely ignores them while it makes political hay out of a national "teachers' corps"   35
scheme to send eager but wholly inexperienced youngsters for brief tours into their schools. There are superb professionals among them, more than most critics suspect, but buried in the impersonality of the system and under a staggering load of work. Compared with but five years ago, they are an outspoken lot, drawing together as never before in the face of difficult teaching   4c
conditions, hostile children and parents, low salaries, and a floundering and impoverished city government. Many now belong to a labor union and speak more of "teacher power" than of "professionalism." As a group, the teachers display a new and in many ways refreshing truculence.

5   The children are quiet, well-disciplined: no "blackboard jungle"   45
here. The rein is tight and one can feel the pressure, but order and quiet are maintained. Few of the children are ragged, though some are clearly undernourished. Several of the teachers, at their own expense, keep packets of dry cereal and a bottle of milk to serve as breakfast for those youngsters who come hungry to school. Attendance at school is, however, poor. Many of   50
the students' families are constantly on the move, from one rented space in the city to another, from one school district, inevitably, to another. Statistically, 50 percent of the children in this school in September will not be there in June.

6   The children's studies are a mixture of the old and the new, all in 55
basic subjects such as reading, writing, arithmetic, social studies, civics. The
older authorities, "Dick and Jane," Muzzey, and the rest are there along
with the new Science Research Associates reading kits, Elementary Science
Study materials, and more. All are used, however, in almost identical ways,
the teacher teaching and the child listening, recording, reviewing in a work- 60
book, and taking tests. One is struck by the paradox that the key "teachers"
are the materials—the books—and yet they "teach" only as the human
teacher allows them. Ask classroom teachers about this paradox and why
there seems to be largely a single pedagogy, and they respond that the conditions require it—elementary school teachers are responsible for from 65
twenty to forty children without a break during the day and secondary
teachers may see between 150 and 250 different children during a day's five
or more periods. They assert either that "discovery" or "student-initiated"
methods are unproven with "their" kinds of children or, when tried, require more time for preparation and more materials and space than are 70
available. They also suggest that "discovery" and "non-directive" discipline
rest necessarily on middle-class values that are relatively meaningless for
their children, who come from other backgrounds.

7   What strikes one is the feeling of irrelevance. The distance between
much of what the children are asked to learn and what they perceive as their 75
needs is great. The formality of the school doesn't mesh with the informality
out of school. School language isn't their language. School music, school
stories, school expectations aren't theirs. This disjunction could cause rebellion (and does, in the form of "discipline problems" and dropping out),
but it more often causes lassitude. School in its irrelevant way is to be en- 80
dured. It is a necessary ritual, to the children meaning little more than that.
It is no surprise that the children's test scores fall further and further behind the national average for every year they stay in school.

8   Though in the halls and classrooms one gets a feeling of order, an
atmosphere of learning is virtually absent. The main worries of the teachers 85
and the administrators are social worries: principally, control and regular
attendance at school, less frequently troubles at home, inattentiveness and
hostility, medical and dental problems. There are many children and few
adults, considering the task, and the emphasis is on control. The front door
bell interrupts teaching. The public address system interrupts. The principal, 90
taking his visitors around, interrupts every class in turn. Interruption of
learning is the rule; it suggests to all, teachers and students alike, that *learning is not the prime purpose of school.* The principal is not the principal

teacher; he is the school's policeman and judge. The school's impossible
teaching schedule clearly suggests that teachers need not really teach. The 95
teachers claim that this is not anti-intellectualism, but that it is rather mis-
placed purpose. The school is in fact to control children, not to teach them.
The locked door, the childish window cutouts made not by children but by
teachers, the white line on glossy floors by walls ill cared for, the bitter and
misunderstood teachers—all add to a feeling not so much of desperation as 100
of confusion.

QUESTIONS

READER AND PURPOSE

1. Professor Sizer is concerned with the successes and failures of inner-city
schools in the United States. In the beginning of his essay he asks whether
schools can " 'succeed' for those whom society holds down irrespective of
merit," and argues that his readers are really responsible for the quality of our
city schools—teachers, students, parents, administrators, municipal officials, society as a whole—all of whom shape the character of the schools that "serve a
majority of our most desperately disadvantaged." In addressing himself to these
readers, what purpose does Sizer have in these paragraphs: is it to entertain us
with a faithful description of a familiar picture, or is it something more serious?

ORGANIZATION

2. The first three paragraphs describe the location of the school, its neighborhood, its locked door, and its appearance outside and in. Would the essay be
just as effective if the writer had placed these three paragraphs after the description of typical teachers and children instead of before? Why or why not?
3. The topic sentence of paragraph 4 suggests that the paragraph will consist
of three parts. What are these? Identify the sentences that develop each. What
is the principal method of development used in this paragraph?
4. In that same paragraph four successive sentences begin with *they* (26-37).
Ordinarily, it is wise to vary sentence openings. Yet this repetition is effective.
Explain why. Would the paragraph have been even more successful if the
writer had begun the remaining sentences with *they*? Why or why not?

SENTENCES

5. The first sentence of paragraph 8 might be more dramatic and more emphatic if it were revised to "The atmosphere of learning is absent." This revision, however, is not appropriate to the writer's tone * and purpose. Explain.
6. Paragraph 8, in any case, is a model of varied sentence structure and skillful

emphasis. In this paragraph find one or more examples of each of the following: parallelism *, interrupted movement *, repetition for emphasis, a short sentence, balance *, negative-positive restatement *, italics.

DICTION

7. Look up: *bay turrets* (3), *raucous* (16), *stereotyped* (26), *parochial* (28), *behavioral scientists* (30), *pathology* (30), *truculence* (44), *paradox* (61), *pedagogy* (64), *disjunction* (78), *lassitude* (80), *anti-intellectualism* (96).
8. Try to identify these allusions *: *Grover Cleveland* (13), *blackboard jungle* (45), *"Dick and Jane"* (57), *Muzzey* (57).
9. Why the quotation marks around *respectable* (1), *triple deckers* (4), *pathology* (30), and *their* (69)? Might the quotation marks be omitted from any of these words with little damage to the meaning?
10. In paragraph 7 Sizer might have written *does not* for *doesn't* (76), *is not* for *isn't* (77), and *are not* for *aren't* (78). Why does he choose contractions? On the other hand, he wrote *It is no surprise* in line 82 instead of *It's no surprise*. Why didn't he use a contraction here?
11. Describe Sizer's attitude toward the school building, both inside and out; the teachers; the behavioral scientists (30); the members of the "teachers' corps" (35); the children; their studies; and the principal. Be able to cite specific examples of diction to support your comments.

POINTS TO LEARN

1. Description, especially description of a type, may have a serious, persuasive purpose.
2. A good description is more than a string of vague, general adjectives. It is concrete details and precise images *. Particularly when it is intended to be persuasive, good description draws upon all the techniques of emphasis, both in diction and sentence structure.

SUGGESTIONS FOR WRITING

1. With the purpose of suggesting how it might be improved, describe your own primary or secondary school.
2. With the same purpose describe a typical public library, town hall, playground, or park.

IMPROVING YOUR STYLE

1. In your description include a balanced sentence in which the two clauses are joined by a semicolon, using as a guide Sizer's "Some rooms have new, tan-

colored wood and steel movable desks; others have older, lift-top models."
(18-20)

2. Use at least two short sentences of the type "Trash is in abundance" (6-7) and "The public address system interrupts" (90). (Notice that the second ends on the verb.)

3. Include one example each of interrupted movement, parallelism, and negative-positive restatement.

4. Repeat a word or an idea for emphasis.

A Paris Plongeur

George Orwell (1903-50) was born in India of middle-class English parents. His real name was Eric Blair; Orwell being a pen name. After being sent to England to be educated, he earned a scholarship to Eton. Upon leaving school, he worked for five years as a member of the British Imperial Police in Burma, but in 1927 he left his job and returned to England, utterly disillusioned with the injustice and oppression of colonial rule. Determined to become a writer, he went to Paris, hoping to support himself by giving English lessons. When his efforts to live by teaching failed, he became almost destitute. His life among the nearly starving poor of Paris and later as a tramp in England was the subject of his first book, *Down and Out in Paris and London* (1933). Today he is best remembered for his political satires *1984* (1949) and *Animal Farm* (1945). In the following excerpt from *Down and Out in Paris and London* he describes working as a dishwasher (*plongeur*) in a luxury hotel in Paris.

1   Our cafeterie was a murky cellar measuring twenty feet by seven by eight high, and so crowded with coffee-urns, breadcutters and the like that one could hardly move without banging against something. It was lighted by one dim electric bulb, and four or five gas-fires that sent out a fierce red breath. There was a thermometer there, and the temperature never 5 fell below 110 degrees Fahrenheit—it neared 130 at some times of the day. At one end were five service lifts, and at the other an ice cupboard where we stored milk and butter. When you went into the ice cupboard you dropped a hundred degrees of temperature at a single step; it used to remind me of the hymn about Greenland's icy mountains and India's coral 10 strand. Two men worked in the cafeterie besides Boris and myself. One was Mario, a huge, excitable Italian—he was like a city policeman with operatic gestures—and the other, a hairy, uncouth animal whom we called the

Magyar; I think he was a Transylvanian, or something even more remote. Except the Magyar we were all big men, and at the rush hours we collided 15 incessantly.

2 The work in the cafeterie was spasmodic. We were never idle, but the real work only came in bursts of two hours at a time—we called each burst *"un coup de feu."* The first *coup de feu* came at eight, when the guests upstairs began to wake up and demand breakfast. At eight a sudden bang- 20 ing and yelling would break out all through the basement; bells rang on all sides, blue-aproned men rushed through the passages, our service lifts came down with a simultaneous crash, and the waiters on all five floors be-gan shouting Italian oaths down the shafts. I don't remember all our duties, but they included making tea, coffee and chocolate, fetching meals from 25 the kitchen, wines from the cellar and fruit and so forth from the dining-room, slicing bread, making toast, rolling pats of butter, measuring jam, opening milk-cans, counting lumps of sugar, boiling eggs, cooking porridge, pounding ice, grinding coffee—all this for from a hundred to two hundred customers. The kitchen was thirty yards away, and the dining-room sixty 30 or seventy yards. Everything we sent up in the service lifts had to be cov-ered by a voucher, and the vouchers had to be carefully filed, and there was trouble if even a lump of sugar was lost. Besides this, we had to supply the staff with bread and coffee, and fetch the meals for the waiters upstairs. All in all, it was a complicated job. 35

3 I calculated that one had to walk and run about fifteen miles dur-ing the day, and yet the strain of the work was more mental than physical. Nothing could be easier, on the face of it, than this stupid scullion work, but it is astonishingly hard when one is in a hurry. One has to leap to and fro between a multitude of jobs—it is like sorting a pack of cards against 40 the clock. You are, for example, making toast, when bang! down comes a service lift with an order for tea, rolls and three different kinds of jam, and simultaneously bang! down comes another demanding scrambled eggs, coffee and grapefruit; you run to the kitchen for the eggs and to the dining-room for the fruit, going like lightning so as to be back before your toast 45 burns, and having to remember about the tea and coffee, besides half a dozen other orders that are still pending; and at the same time some waiter is following you and making trouble about a lost bottle of soda-water, and you are arguing with him. It needs more brains than one might think. Mario said, no doubt truly, that it took a year to make a reliable cafetier. 50

4 The time between eight and half-past ten was a sort of delirium. Sometimes we were going as though we had only five minutes to live; some-

times there were sudden lulls when the orders stopped and everything seemed quiet for a moment. Then we swept up the litter from the floor, threw down fresh sawdust, and swallowed gallipots of wine or coffee or water—anything, so long as it was wet. Very often we used to break off chunks of ice and suck them while we worked. The heat among the gas-fires was nauseating; we swallowed quarts of drink during the day, and after a few hours even our aprons were drenched with sweat. At times we were hopelessly behind with the work, and some of the customers would have gone without their breakfast, but Mario always pulled us through. He had worked fourteen years in the cafeterie, and he had the skill that never wastes a second between jobs. The Magyar was very stupid and I was inexperienced, and Boris was inclined to shirk, partly because of his lame leg, partly because he was ashamed of working in the cafeterie after being a waiter; but Mario was wonderful. The way he would stretch his great arms right across the cafeterie to fill a coffee-pot with one hand and boil an egg with the other, at the same time watching toast and shouting directions to the Magyar, and between whiles singing snatches from *Rigoletto*, was beyond all praise. The *patron* knew his value, and he was paid a thousand francs a month, instead of five hundred like the rest of us.

5   The breakfast pandemonium stopped at half-past ten. Then we scrubbed the cafeterie tables, swept the floor and polished the brasswork, and, on good mornings, went one at a time to the lavatory for a smoke. This was our slack time—only relatively slack, however, for we had only ten minutes for lunch, and we never got through it uninterrupted. The customers' luncheon hour, between twelve and two, was another period of turmoil like the breakfast hour. Most of our work was fetching meals from the kitchen, which meant constant *engueulades* from the cooks. By this time the cooks had sweated in front of their furnaces for four or five hours, and their tempers were all warmed up.

6   At two we were suddenly free men. We threw off our aprons and put on our coats, hurried out of doors, and, when we had money, dived into the nearest *bistro*. It was strange, coming up into the street from those firelit cellars. The air seemed blindingly clear and cold, like arctic summer; and how sweet the petrol did smell, after the stenches of sweat and food! Sometimes we met some of our cooks and waiters in the *bistros*, and they were friendly and stood us drinks. Indoors we were their slaves, but it is an etiquette in hotel life that between hours everyone is equal, and the *engueulades* do not count.

7   At a quarter to five we went back to the hotel. Till half-past six

there were no orders, and we used this time to polish silver, clean out the coffee-urns, and do other odd jobs. Then the grand turmoil of the day started—the dinner hour. I wish I could be Zola for a little while, just to describe that dinner hour. The essence of the situation was that a hundred or two hundred people were demanding individually different meals of five or six courses, and that fifty or sixty people had to cook and serve them and clean up the mess afterwards; anyone with experience of catering will know what that means. And at this time when the work was doubled, the whole staff was tired out, and a number of them were drunk. I could write pages about the scene without giving a true idea of it. The chargings to and fro in the narrow passages, the collisions, the yells, the struggling with crates and trays and blocks of ice, the heat, the darkness, the furious festering quarrels which there was no time to fight out—they pass description. Anyone coming into the basement for the first time would have thought himself in a den of maniacs. It was only later, when I understood the working of a hotel, that I saw order in all this chaos.

8   At half-past eight the work stopped very suddenly. We were not free till nine, but we used to throw ourselves full length on the floor, and lie there resting our legs, too lazy even to go to the ice cupboard for a drink. Sometimes the *chef du personnel* would come in with bottles of beer, for the hotel stood us an extra beer when we had had a hard day. The food we were given was no more than eatable, but the *patron* was not mean about drink; he allowed us two litres of wine a day each, knowing that if a *plongeur* is not given two litres he will steal three. We had the heeltaps of bottles as well, so that we often drank too much—a good thing, for one seemed to work faster when partially drunk.

9   Four days of the week passed like this; of the other two working days, one was better and one worse. After a week of this life I felt in need of a holiday. It was Saturday night, so the people in our *bistro* were busy getting drunk, and with a free day ahead of me I was ready to join them. We all went to bed, drunk, at two in the morning, meaning to sleep till noon. At half-past five I was suddenly awakened. A night-watchman, sent from the hotel, was standing at my bedside. He stripped the clothes back and shook me roughly.

10   "Get up!" he said. *"Tu t'es bien saoulé la gueule, eh?* Well, never mind that, the hotel's a man short. You've got to work to-day."

11   "Why should I work?" I protested. "This is my day off."

12   "Day off, nothing! The work's got to be done. Get up!"

13   I got up and went out, feeling as though my back were broken and

my skull filled with hot cinders. I did not think that I could possibly do a day's work. And yet, after only an hour in the basement, I found that I was perfectly well. It seemed that in the heat of those cellars, as in a turkish bath, one could sweat out almost any quantity of drink. *Plongeurs* know this, and count on it. The power of swallowing quarts of wine, and then sweating it 135 out before it can do much damage, is one of the compensations of their life.

QUESTIONS

READER AND PURPOSE

1. Orwell is not writing for the down-and-out in Paris and London. At what kind of reader is he aiming? What does he assume the reader to know and not to know?

2. Is Orwell's purpose best described as accurate, detailed reporting of a personal experience, as social criticism, as some combination of these, or as something else altogether? Give reasons for your answer, citing passages in the text.

ORGANIZATION

3. The first paragraph sets the stage and lists the cast of characters. The second and third paragraphs describe the narrator's job. What organizing principle is at work in paragraphs 4-8?

4. Give a title to paragraphs 9-13, indicating the essential topic of that section.

SENTENCES

5. In line 6 a semicolon in place of the dash would be more conventional. Why? What is the advantage of the dash, if any? Find another example of this usage in paragraph 3.

6. In lines 12 and 13 the dashes might be replaced with two commas or with parentheses. Yet dashes, commas, and parentheses would each create a slightly different effect. Explain.

7. What is the difference in the emphasis upon *drunk* in this sentence by Orwell and its revision?

> *Revision:* We all went to bed drunk at two in the morning, meaning to sleep till noon.

> *Orwell:* "We all went to bed, drunk, at two in the morning, meaning to sleep till noon." (122-23)

8. In paragraph 6 identify an example of emphasis by inversion *.

9. What three ways of achieving emphasis are at work in the sentence beginning "The Magyar was very stupid" in line 63?

DICTION

10. Look up: *Magyar* (14), *spasmodic* (17), *porridge* (28), *voucher* (32), *scullion* (38), *gallipots* (55), *Rigoletto* (69), *heeltaps* (115).

11. Throughout this passage Orwell uses French words and phrases. In one case he quotes what the nightwatchman said, using part English and part French (126-27). Should Orwell have avoided French altogether? Why or why not? What rule of thumb can you formulate about using foreign words in your own writing?

12. Does Orwell's diction tend to be abstract * and general or concrete * and particular? List examples of both types.

13. Does Orwell rely more heavily upon adjectives or upon nouns and verbs? Underline the adjectives in the first two paragraphs.

14. List Orwell's similes * and metaphors *.

15. Using examples, demonstrate the relationship between Orwell's diction and tone *. Describe his attitudes toward his job, the "Magyar," Mario, and toward himself.

SUGGESTIONS FOR WRITING

Loosely following Orwell's organization and employing the first-person point of view *, describe your job in a supermarket, restaurant, factory, hospital, department store, or elsewhere. Convey a distinct tone toward your work and your fellow employees. Your problem is to interest your reader by making clear exactly what you do and how you feel about it.

IMPROVING YOUR STYLE

1. In your composition write a sentence similar to that in lines 101-04. Use a long series of parallel * nouns (or gerunds and nouns) concluded by a dash and short clause, the subject of which refers to all the nouns in the series. A similar but slightly different pattern occurs in lines 24-30. Either model is suitable. Notice the occurrence of this kind of sentence in other descriptions or narrations. It is very useful to convey multiplicity and complexity.

2. Use a dash as Orwell employs it in line 6.

3. Include two or three metaphors and two or three similes.

4. In one sentence achieve emphasis by inversion.

People *and* The Church

William Gass is both teacher and novelist. His fiction includes *Omensetter's Luck* (1966), *Willie Master's Lonely Wife* (1968), and *In the Heart of the Heart of the Country* (1968), the source of the following two passages. Each is a fine example of what we have called impressionistic description. The impression involves more than a response to the immediate perception—people, a dusty street, the noise of a crowd in a gym—for the details are selected and "languaged" to imply a philosophical vision. As you read try to work below the surface of Gass's words and get at what he is saying about the way we live.

PEOPLE

1   Their hair in curlers and their heads wrapped in loud scarves, young mothers, fattish in trousers, lounge about in the speed-wash, smoking cigarettes, eating candy, drinking pop, thumbing magazines, and screaming at their children above the whir and rumble of the machines.

2   At the bank a young man freshly pressed is letting himself in with 5
a key. Along the street, delicately teetering, many grandfathers move in a dream. During the murderous heat of summer, they perch on window ledges, their feet dangling just inside the narrow shelf of shade the store has made, staring steadily into the street. Where their consciousness has gone I can't say. It's not in the eyes. Perhaps it's diffuse, all temperature and 10
skin, like an infant's, though more mild. Near the corner there are several large overalled men employed in standing. A truck turns to be weighed on the scales at the Feed and Grain. Images drift on the drugstore window. The wind has blown the smell of cattle into town. Our eyes have been driven in like the eyes of the old men. And there's no one to have mercy 15
on us.

THE CHURCH

Friday night. Girls in dark skirts and white blouses sit in ranks and scream
in concert. They carry funnels loosely stuffed with orange and black paper
which they shake wildly, and small megaphones through which, as drilled,
they direct and magnify their shouting. Their leaders, barely pubescent
girls, prance and shake and whirl their skirts above their bloomers. The 5
young men, leaping, extend their arms and race through puddles of amber
light, their bodies glistening. In a lull, though it rarely occurs, you can hear
the squeak of tennis shoes against the floor. Then the yelling begins again,
and then continues; fathers, mothers, neighbors joining in to form a single
pulsing ululation—a cry of the whole community—for in this gymnasium 10
each body becomes the bodies beside it, pressed as they are together, thigh
to thigh, and the same shudder runs through all of them, and runs toward
the same release. Only the ball moves serenely through this dazzling din.
Obedient to law it scarcely speaks but caroms quietly and lives at peace.

QUESTIONS

READER AND PURPOSE
1. What impression do you think Gass conveys about the women in the
laundromat? About the old men who "perch on window ledges"? About the
people at the basketball game? Be able to support your answers.

ORGANIZATION
2. The first two sentences of the second paragraph of "People" flow together
nicely, yet they are not linked either by a connective * like *therefore* or *however* or by the repetition of a key word. What does unify them? When you
compare the images in these two sentences, does an irony * suggest itself?
3. Is there a topic statement in this second paragraph? If not, could you supply
one? Is there, in other words, a controlling idea which determines the writer's
selection of details?
4. Has "The Church" a topic sentence? What slight change in the scene occurs in the sentence beginning in line 7 of this paragraph? Is there another
change in the following sentence?

SENTENCES
5. The opening sentence of "People" is long and complicated. Is its main clause
at the beginning, in the middle, or at the end? Point out the parallel * elements
in this sentence.

6. Suppose that first sentence were broken down into several shorter ones:

> The young mothers lounge about the speedwash. They are fattish in trousers. They wear their hair in curlers and wrap their heads in loud scarves. While they wait they smoke cigarettes, eat candy, drink pop, or thumb through magazines. Now and then they scream at their children above the whir and rumble of the machines.

Has our perception of the scene been altered? Does the scene seem less unified or more?

7. Comment upon how these revisions change the meaning or the emphasis of Gass's sentences:

   (a) *Revision:* Our eyes have been driven in like the eyes of the old men and there's no one to have mercy on us.
   Gass: "Our eyes have been driven in like the eyes of the old men. And there's no one to have mercy on us." ("People," 14-16)

   (b) *Revision:* The leaping young men extend their arms and race through puddles of amber light, their bodies glistening.
   Gass: "The young men, leaping, extend their arms and race through puddles of amber light, their bodies glistening." ("The Church," 5-7)

8. "Friday night" (line 1 of "The Church") is a fragment *. Would it be an improvement to write it out in a formally complete sentence: "It is Friday night"?

9. What is the grammatical name of the construction "their bodies glistening" ("The Church," 7)?

DICTION

10. Look up: (in "People") *consciousness* (9), *diffuse* (10); (in "The Church") *pubescent* (4), *lull* (7), *pulsing ululation* (10), *serenely* (13).

11. Why are the following alternates less effective than Gass's words? (In "People") *stout* for *fattish* (2), *wait* for *lounge* (2), *walking* for *teetering* (6), *sit* for *perch* (7); (in "The Church") *jump* for *prance* (5), *movement* for *shudder* (12), *deafening* for *dazzling* (13).

12. Which of Gass's words convey especially sharp visual images *? Which convey aural images? Does he appeal to any senses other than vision and hearing?

13. What kind of figure of speech * is "puddles of amber light" ("The Church," 6-7)? Do you like it? Why or why not?

14. The description of the basketball game ends with the image of the ball arcing toward the basket. In that passage what is Gass implying by his use of *only* (13)? In what specific ways is the ball described as being different from

the spectators? What general difference between them does Gass suggest? May the ball be said to embody an ideal? If so, how well do the crowd measure up to that ideal?

POINTS TO LEARN

1. Good description appeals to the eyes and ears, to the nose and the taste buds and the fingertips.

2. The impression which a writer wishes to convey need not be stated (it may indeed be better if it is not), but it must control his selection of descriptive details.

SUGGESTIONS FOR WRITING

1. Write an impressionistic description of shoppers in a supermarket or of loungers in the park or on a streetcorner.

2. Describe the crowd at a sports event or some sort of theatrical entertainment. Be clear in your own mind what impression you want your reader to obtain, but do not tell him directly.

IMPROVING YOUR STYLE

In your description include:

1. A sentence modeled on the opening of "People"—a number of details expressed in parallel participial * constructions which are gathered in two groups, one before and one after the main clause.

2. (With your instructor's approval) an effective fragment.

3. A sentence containing a nominative absolute * (see question 9).

4. Examples of precise visual and aural images.

5. Two or three metaphors.

Description of Character

Essentially the description of character is no different from the description of things. The same general principles and techniques govern both. Yet, character drawing has special problems of its own. There are different ways of approaching the description of character, and many kinds of characters for the writer to create, each serving different purposes. In the broad we can divide all characters into either types or individuals. Types, or flat characters as they are sometimes called, possess only a single trait. Individuals, or round characters, have a number of traits, a complexity that is closer to real life than the single dimension of the type.

All types fall into one of four classes, depending upon the kind of trait the writer depicts: there are (1) national types—the typical Irishman, Englishman, or Frenchman; (2) the occupational type—the typical cowboy, butler, police inspector, movie actress, disc jockey, barber, or business executive; (3) the social type—the typical bachelor uncle, the distant cousin, the blind date, the hostess, the week-end guest; (4) the personality type—The Tactful Man, The Tactless Man, The Nervous Man, The Steady Man, The Worry-Wart, The Happy-Go-Lucky Man. The types of all four categories have one thing in common—they have only a single characteristic. Actually, they are not real people at all, but only the single characteristic abstracted from an observation of many people. The type is a single trait personified.

In describing a type, therefore, the writer chooses only those details that bear directly upon the one characteristic of nationality, occupation, social role, or personality. The writer may know a New York taxi driver who spends all his leisure time reading Shakespeare; but in so far as the driver does, he is an individual, not a type. The writer rigorously excludes all details of physical description, clothing, interests, and personality that do not help to define the typical taxi driver.

What is the point behind the description of types? Besides appealing to our delight in the vivid description of the familiar and commonplace, the type may serve either of two purposes. The less common is to inform. A social historian, for example, may wish to describe the typical medieval peasant, showing how he looked, how he worked, what pleasure he had, if any, and how he felt about his station in life. More often the description of a type intends to instruct the reader in manners or behavior. If we describe The Braggart, we are saying in so many words, "Don't be like this." We may, of course, serve the same purpose in a different, more positive way by describing The Modest Man. Usually the negative, satiric approach is more effective and is more fun both to write and to read.

As the character acquires more than one trait, he becomes an individual. He is more than a walking occupation or trait of personality: he is a New York cab driver *and* a reader of Shakespeare. But the fact that the individual has many dimensions poses a problem. What traits shall the writer include and what traits shall he ignore? The answer depends upon the writer's impression of the individual, for almost all description of round characters is impressionistic. It is well-nigh impossible for any but a highly trained psychologist to write objectively about something so complex as the total personality of a human being. Character drawing of the individual must be both partial and interpretive. It may be more or less shrewd and accurate, but it remains an impression nevertheless. The impression may be simple or complex, and it may require qualification, but the impression guides the writer's selection of details. Our impression of an individual may range anywhere between love and admiration to hatred and loathing. We may see him as mysterious, a bundle of contradictions, or we may see beneath the variety of his traits a pattern that reveals some truth about human behavior or human values. In any case, we always begin with some reaction to the round character we are describing.

To convey this reaction, we may use many different kinds of details. Among the most useful are details of physical appearance, clothing, and personal belongings. These make the reader see, but they also suggest both the writer's impression and the character's personality. Whether it be sound psychology or not, the reader responds in one way to a tall, thin-lipped, steely-eyed man carrying a tightly furled umbrella, and in a totally different way to a robust, smiling, sloppily-dressed man carrying a fishing rod. In prose, a character's appearance, clothing, and possessions are, by convention, clues to his personality.

In addition to these, a writer may describe the "stage" or the setting within which the character moves about and lives—his room, his home, his place of work. For these, too, are extensions of the character's personality.

The shrewd observer can write pages about a man he has never seen—about his income, his social position, his tastes, his interests, even his values—if only he can study for a bit the room or the house in which he lives.

Viewing the individual in a wider perspective, we may describe his relation to society by making clear what he says and does, what he likes and dislikes, what goals he is seeking, what he values most. We may show him in action, in conflict with others, how they react to him, what they say about him. In short, our portrait may be static or dynamic or in part both.

How much vivid detail the writer will use and what he selects will depend both upon his purpose and the space at his disposal. A very short description may evoke the writer's impression with only two or three striking details, having the force or suggestiveness of an unfinished pencil sketch. If the writer has the space of a novel, he may use all kinds of details and dramatic situations to create his character over hundreds of pages. Ample space alone will not insure good characterization. It is the telling, the representative detail, the vividness that count. It is more effective to make the reader see a character's modesty in action, for example, than to say merely that he is modest.

Round characters in prose have the purpose of informing, instructing, entertaining, or doing all these at once. The historian who writes the character of a great man may have as his guiding intention to explain the impact of a personality upon the course of history. His character, without being obviously moralistic, may contain a lesson for the reader. Any character that is vivid can scarcely fail to entertain the reader. All of us are interested in people—in their motivations, their eccentricities, in the fascinating variety and complexity that make up the human comedy. For that reason any character of any individual, no matter how great or how obscure, is likely to be a pleasant task for the writer and a pleasure to the reader.

The Penurious Man *and* The Coward

Theophrastus (c. 371-c. 287 B.C.) was a Greek rhetorician and philosopher. Today he is best remembered for what he considered a minor work, his *Characters*, a series of sketches originally intended as models for students of rhetoric. The *Characters* (the word in Greek meant "distinctive marks") consists of satires of comic, foolish, or cloddish types. The sketches follow a formula: first a definition of the trait to be illustrated, then a number of situations and responses that dramatically reveal the trait in terms of behavior. For example: "After dinner, the waiter brings the check; the stingy man drops his napkin and hides beneath the table until someone else has paid."

The *Characters* was translated into Latin and widely imitated by French and English writers in the seventeenth and eighteenth centuries. Today the Theophrastian "Character" is no longer a literary genre. But one doesn't have to look far to find the same people—the bores and cheapskates, the know-it-alls and B.M.O.C.'s. Satirizing them is still a pleasant diversion, and the best way to do it is, as Theophrastus shows, to describe them in action.

1   Penuriousness is too strict attention to profit and loss.

2   The Penurious man is one who, while the month is current, will come to one's house and ask for a half-obol. When he is at table with others he will count how many cups each of them has drunk; and will pour a smaller libation to Artemis than any of the company. Whenever a person 5 has made a good bargain for him and charges him with it, he will say that it is too dear. When a servant has broken a jug or a plate he will take the value out of his rations; or, if his wife has dropped a three-farthing piece, he is capable of moving the furniture and the sofas and the wardrobes, and of rummaging in the curtains. If he has anything to sell he will dispose of it 10 at such a price that the buyer shall have no profit. He is not likely to let one eat a fig from his garden, or walk through his land, or pick up one of the

From *The Characters of Theophrastus*, ed. and trans. R. C. Jebb, London, Macmillan and Company, 1870.

olives or dates that lie on the ground; and he will inspect his boundaries day by day to see if they remain the same. He is apt, also, to enforce the right of distraining, and to exact compound interest. When he feasts the men of his 15 parish, the cutlets set before them will be small: when he markets, he will come in having bought nothing. And he will forbid his wife to lend salt, or a lamp-wick, or cummin, or verjuice, or meal for sacrifice, or garlands, or cakes; saying that these trifles come to much in the year. Then in general it may be noticed that the moneyboxes of the penurious are mouldy, and the 20 keys rusty; that they themselves wear their cloaks scarcely reaching to the thigh; that they anoint themselves from very small oil-flasks; that they have their hair cut close; that they take off their shoes in the middle of the day; and that they are urgent with the fuller to let their cloak have plenty of earth, in order that it may not soon be soiled. 25

1   Cowardice would seem to be, in fact, a shrinking of the soul through fear.

2   The Coward is one who, on a voyage, will protest that the promontories are privateers; and, if a high sea gets up, will ask if there is any one on board who has not been initiated. He will put up his head and ask the steers- 5 man if he is halfway, and what he thinks of the face of the heavens; remarking to the person sitting next him that a certain dream makes him feel uneasy; and he will take off his tunic and give it to his slave; or he will beg them to put him ashore.

3   On land also, when he is campaigning, he will call to him those who 10 are going out to the rescue, and bid them come and stand by him and look about them first; saying that it is hard to make out which is the enemy. Hearing shouts and seeing men falling, he will remark to those who stand by him that he has forgotten in his haste to bring his sword, and will run to the tent; where, having sent his slave out to reconnoitre the position of the 15 enemy, he will hide the sword under his pillow, and then spend a long time in pretending to look for it. And seeing from the tent a wounded comrade being carried in, he will run towards him and cry "Cheer up!"; he will take him into his arms and carry him; he will tend and sponge him; he will sit by him and keep the flies off his wound—in short he will do anything rather 20 than fight with the enemy. Again, when the trumpeter has sounded the signal for battle, he will cry, as he sits in the tent, "Bother! you will not allow the man to get a wink of sleep with your perpetual bugling!" Then, covered with blood from the other's wound, he will meet those who are returning from the fight, and announce to them, "I have run some risk to save one of 25

our fellows"; and he will bring in the men of his parish and of his tribe to see his patient, at the same time explaining to each of them that he carried him with his own hands to the tent.

QUESTIONS

READER AND PURPOSE

1. By what standard of behavior does Theophrastus judge his characters? Is Theophrastus writing, if unintentionally, for all men in all times?

ORGANIZATION

2. Theophrastus begins with a short definition of the folly, foible, or disagreeable trait being depicted and then writes, "The _____ man is one who . . ." After this beginning he follows with several sharp images of the type in action, stopping when he feels like it. Is there any plan or organization in the examples of penuriousness and cowardice? Which of the two characters is the better organized? How might one improve the character less well organized?

SENTENCES

3. The sentences of Theophrastus have two characteristic patterns. One of these is balance *. In the first half of his balanced sentence he describes briefly a setting or situation, and in the second half, the character's typical reaction in that setting or situation. For example, in "The Penurious Man" (3), we read: "When he is at table with others [situation], he will count how many cups each of them has drunk [reaction]." The first half of the balanced sentence is usually a dependent adverbial clause * or a participial * phrase. Find other examples of balanced sentences and identify the grammatical construction with which each begins. Why is it better to place the situation first rather than last, as in this revision: "He will count how many cups each of them has drunk, when he is at table with others"?

4. A second common pattern groups several illustrations of typical behavior in one sentence, making them parallel * in structure. The last sentence of "The Penurious Man" is a good example. Find others.

DICTION

5. Look up: (in "The Penurious Man") half-obol (3), libation (5), Artemis (5), distraining (15), cummin (18), verjuice (18), fuller (24) (see also the verb to full and fuller's earth); (in "The Coward") promontories (3), privateers (4), reconnoitre (15). In line 5 of "The Coward" initiated refers to initiation

into the Eleusinian Mysteries, one of the religious cults of ancient Greece. Anyone not so initiated was believed to bring bad luck to a ship. If he had lived
much later, the Theophrastian coward might have asked, "Is there anyone on
board who isn't a good Christian?"

POINTS TO LEARN

1. In the *Characters*, Theophrastus combines definition, description, and narration. Although a writer must learn the various techniques of development, he
must also learn that a single technique seldom appears by itself. Yet one technique usually organizes his use of the others.

2. Examples within a paragraph should be grouped according to some plan.
Often the various groups are introduced by framing words *. In "The Coward"
we find the phrases "on a voyage" (3) and "On land" (10).

3. Balance and parallelism are very common and very useful sentence patterns.
Balance allows the writer to make a sharp contrast. Theophrastus often implies
a contrast between what the situation calls for and the behavior of his character. For example, the image * of men at table suggests geniality and relaxa-
tion; but we find the penurious man scowling and counting cups. If the writer
uses balance frequently, he must take care to vary the grammatical construction
of the first half of the sentence.

Parallelism allows the writer to vary his sentence rhythm and sentence
structure. It has the advantage of variety, economy, and conviction by sheer bulk.

SUGGESTIONS FOR WRITING

Ever since the third century B.C. men have delighted in the creating of characters, and Theophrastus has had many imitators—among them Joseph Hall, John
Earle, Sir Thomas Overbury, Nicholas Breton, Jean de La Bruyère, Joseph Ad-
dison—some of whom wrote much better characters than the originator of this
literary form. Try your hand at one or two characters in the manner of Theophrastus.

Here is the beginning of a long list of possible subjects—The Braggart,
The Inside Dopester, The Tactless Man, The Snob, The Joiner, The Gossip,
The Name Dropper, The Big Man on Campus, The Busybody. Add ten or
fifteen titles to this list and then select one or two types you especially dislike.
Be sure to describe types, not individuals, though you may construct your type
from several individuals you have known. Begin with a short definition of the
trait. If possible, be brilliantly acidic here, but keep your definition short. Then
follow with "The _____ is one who . . ." Then group several well-
chosen examples of the type in action.

IMPROVING YOUR STYLE

1. In your sketch vary the situation-response pattern in some of these ways:

> Two balanced independent clauses separated by a semicolon.
> An adverbial clause followed by a main clause.
> A participial phrase followed by a main clause.
> Two short sentences in sequence.

2. Include at least one sentence using a series of parallel constructions to describe four or five typical actions or qualities of the subject.

The Medieval Gentleman

Morris Bishop is a teacher, poet, scholar. This selection is from his popular and eminently readable history, *The Middle Ages* (1970). Bishop's "gentleman" is a type, embodying qualities and behavior found in many aristocrats from the twelfth to the fifteenth centuries. No single specimen of the breed ever possessed all the characteristics of Bishop's gentleman or behaved in exactly the same way. Bishop's subject represents that range of possible attributes and behavior which define the aristocrat of the middle ages. The advantage of describing types is that it enables an historian or social scientist, a satirist or psychologist to depict a great many persons in a single figure. But it requires, of course, that the writer know such persons well enough to select the common attributes which make them members of the same group.

1   The proper medieval gentleman had many virtues. He was generally loyal to his feudal obligations and conscientious in the administration of justice. He was generous, particularly in bequeathing land and money to the church. He was sincerely religious, respectful of church authority, and faithful to his duties. He took his knightly vows seriously and seldom vio- 5 lated an oath or solemn promise, knowing that these are recorded in heaven and that the breach of an oath may be divinely punished as perjury. He could be sympathetic to lesser humans. "Courtesy to the poor is of a humble heart," said the thirteenth-century writer the Knight of La Tour-Landry, telling how a great lady bowed to a tailor. (Some reproached her; others 10 praised her meekness.)

2   However, the gentleman's faults loom larger in retrospect than do his virtues. Pride of birth and class turned readily into arrogance; bravery, into foolhardiness. Many great battles were lost by the knights' disregard of orders, their refusal to wait for the command to charge. The story of the 15 crusades is full of such splendid folly. The Templars especially were so eager

From *The Horizon Book of the Middle Ages.* © 1968 by American Heritage Publishing Company, Inc. Reprinted by permission of the publisher.

to be always in the van that they got themselves killed for nothing but honor, and not much of that.

3   Generosity, much extolled by the minstrels who profited by it, became absurd display. When Thomas à Becket visited Paris in 1157, his train was like a circus parade. It included a traveling chapel, wagons with vestments, carpets, and bedcoverings, twelve horses carrying table plate, grooms and hawkers with hounds and gerfalcons, and on the back of each lead horse a long-tailed ape. The whole was guarded by armed men with fierce dogs on leashes. Display developed conspicuous waste, rivalry in destruction as in an Indian potlatch. One knight had a plot of ground plowed and sown with small pieces of silver. Another used precious wax candles for his cooking; another, "through boastfulness," had thirty of his horses burned alive. The result of such rivalry was that many or most nobles were perpetually in debt to usurers. If worse came to worst, they were sometimes forced to murder their creditors.

4   They were a rapacious crew, often merely out of economic necessity. The noble troubadour Bertrand de Born speaks for his class, rejoicing in the approach of war with its breakdown of law and order: "We'll soon seize the usurer's gold; there won't be a packhorse on the roads; no burgher will go without fear, nor any merchant heading for France. If you want to be rich you have only to take!"

5   Whereas the king's authority often protected the merchant, the family feuds of the nobles were beyond control. Revenge was regarded rather as an act of private justice than as a crime. The remotest members of a clan were bound by the obligations of the vendetta, which had its special home in Italy. Its history in the Middle Ages is largely one of family feuds that turned into wars. These ended either by the extermination of one party or by the intervention of the emperor or the church, imposing reconciliation and indemnities.

6   Our courteous, chivalric knights could readily become demons of brutality. The *chansons de geste* are filled with rolling heads, strewn brains, gushing bowels, baby spearing, and nun raping. Some part of this joy in deeds of blood must be literary, an appeal to the perverse spirit, as in the sadistic fiction recrudescent today. But much of the brutality was unquestionable fact. I shall give none of the abundant examples, not to abet what I would condemn.

7   Another contrariety in noble behavior was in the matter of sex. The adept of courtly love, fresh from sighing at his unapproachable lady's feet,

could pause on his homeward journey to tumble a shepherdess in her 55
meadow, a fresh-faced village girl under a hedge. The Moslems in Spain and
Syria were shocked by the licentiousness of the French. The famous *jus
primae noctis* (the lord's right to spend the first night with a peasant bride)
may well be a fable. Nevertheless, the noble regarded his female serf as his
chattel, to do with as he would. Often, no doubt, what he would was what 60
she would; but if she defended her rustic honor and was then undone, neither she nor her family had any means of redress.

8   Such were some of the traits of the noble. He was a bundle of
paradoxes—a romantic lover and a libertine, a gallant knight and a bloodthirsty brute, a devout Christian and a flouter of the elements of morality. 65
But he shared his paradoxes with the rest of humanity.

QUESTIONS

READER AND PURPOSE

1. Describe Bishop's reader. Is he another historian? Someone who reads for
vicarious adventure and thrills? A student? What does Bishop assume his reader
knows and does not know?

2. If Bishop's purpose is to describe the Middle Ages for a twentieth-century
reader, would he have been wiser to depict in detail an actual individual like
the Knight of La Tour-Landry or Thomas à Becket? Why or why not?

ORGANIZATION

3. By omitting *however* (12) the writer might have begun with the second
paragraph and placed paragraph 1 near the end, between 7 and 8. But while it
is possible, this organization would be less effective than the plan Bishop followed. Why?

4. Paragraph development by "specification" lists all (or most) of the particular forms of the topic. In paragraph development by example, on the other
hand, only a few representative cases of the topic are treated. In paragraph 1
the topic is "virtues." Is it developed by specification or by examples?

5. Each sentence after the topic sentence of the first paragraph begins with *he*.
Is that repetition effective or awkward? Give reasons for your answer.

6. How are the following pairs of paragraphs linked: 1 and 2, 3 and 4, 6 and 7?

7. It might be argued that the coherence between paragraphs 2 and 3 is weak.
But notice that the relationship involving all the paragraphs from 2 through 7 has
been clearly established in paragraph 2. By what sentence?

8. Why are the following revisions inferior to Bishop's sentences?

   (a) *Revision:* Pride of birth and class turned readily into arrogance. Bravery often became foolishness.
   Bishop: "Pride of birth and class turned readily into arrogance; bravery, into foolishness." (13-14)
   (b) *Revision:* It included a traveling chapel, wagons with vestments, carpets, and bedcoverings, twelve horses carrying table plate, grooms and hawkers with hounds and gerfalcons, and on the back of each lead horse, a long-tailed ape, the whole being guarded by armed men with fierce dogs on leashes—display developing conspicuous waste, rivalry in destruction as in an Indian potlatch.
   Bishop: "It included a traveling chapel, wagons with vestments, carpets, and bedcoverings, twelve horses carrying table plate, grooms and hawkers, with hounds and gerfalcons, and on the back of each lead horse a long-tailed ape. The whole was guarded by armed men with fierce dogs on leashes. Display developed conspicuous waste, rivalry in destruction as in an Indian potlatch." (21-26)
   (c) *Revision:* The family feuds of the nobles were beyond control, whereas the king's authority often protected the merchant.
   Bishop: "Whereas the king's authority often protected the merchant, the family feuds of the nobles were beyond control." (38-39)

9. Look up: *Templars* (16), *minstrels* (19), *Thomas à Becket* (20), *gerfalcons* (23), *usurers* (30), *troubadour* (33), *burgher* (35), *vendetta* (41), *chansons de geste* (47), *adept* (54), *courtly love* (54), *paradoxes* (64), *libertine* (64).

10. How does *foolhardiness* (14) differ from *foolishness?*

11. Are there any cases in the following list where you can substitute a single simpler (or more familiar) word and still say the same thing? *Arrogance* (13), *van* (17), *gerfalcons* (23), *potlatch* (26), *rapacious* (32), *sadistic* (50), *recrudescent* (50), *licentiousness* (57).

12. If Bishop's final sentence were omitted how would the tone * be modified?

POINTS TO LEARN

1. Well-done, the description of a type conveys the general truth about a large number of individuals.

2. Some types embody a social or moral ideal. Other types, usually depicted by satirists such as Theophrastus, represent negative modes of behavior. Still oth-

ers, like Morris Bishop's "medieval gentleman," exhibit in one portrait the features of an historical, social, professional, or national group.

SUGGESTIONS FOR WRITING

Showing both faults and virtues, describe one of the following types: the cowboy hero of the grade-B movie, the male chauvinist, the feminist, the college teacher, the freshman or sophomore, the politician, the member of a rock group. Whatever type you select, it should involve contrarieties or paradoxes, as does Bishop's "medieval gentleman."

IMPROVING YOUR STYLE

In your composition:

1. Use an example of balance * and ellipsis *, modeling your sentence upon Bishop's in lines 13-14 beginning "Pride of birth."

2. Use three or four rare and unusual words; use them because they say precisely what you want to say and could not be replaced by simpler terms.

Rona *and* Me

Ingrid Benglis is an American writer, best known for *Combat in the Erogenous Zone* (1972), a provocative, sensitive, and profoundly revealing self-portrait of one liberated woman and the tensions and anxieties she must face. The first of the two vignettes reprinted from that book is of an aging actress Benglis met in a summer theater where the author worked as an apprentice when she was fifteen. The other is a small but focused picture of herself—more exactly of a self she used to be, fixed in a photograph and reassessed after fifteen years. Benglis' subjects are individuals, yet through them we see the types—middle-aged actress, adolescent girl—and the double vision suggests an important truth about character description: the type implies an individual; the individual implies a type.

Rona was about forty years old and seemed to be made of solid platinum: platinum hair, platinum skin, platinum voice. She was drunk a good deal of the time, was constantly surrounded by people, and told outrageous jokes. She had the beginning of a midriff bulge and greedy, erotic eyes, like the eyes of a Siamese cat that has spent its life foraging in the garbage cans of 5 greasy spoons, but still knows itself to be a Siamese. When Rona wasn't laughing, her silence was louder than her voice, and there was an odor of disintegration and waste about her, as if she were rusting away from the inside, as if the rust was just about to crack through the surface of her skin.

In the photograph I am thirteen years old. I am sitting on a wooden railing 10 overlooking a lake. I am wearing a bathing suit. It is a movie star pose: head thrown back, chest thrust forward, one leg extended just a little bit less than the other with my right big toe touching my left ankle. Both feet are pointed. I am being sexy.

Both selections are from *Combat in the Erogenous Zone* (Alfred A. Knopf, 1962). Reprinted by permission of the publisher.

QUESTIONS

READER AND PURPOSE

1. The two vignettes by Ingrid Benglis provide a revealing contrast between subjective and objective description. The picture of her adolescent self is almost completely objective. In only two places does Benglis subtly imply any judgment upon what she describes. Where? How do these brief comments suggest she feels about herself at thirteen?

2. In "Rona" the approach is much more subjective. The self-sketch is essentially observation ("my right toe touching my left ankle"). "Rona," on the other hand, is observation plus judgment. "Greedy, erotic eyes," for example, is a statement of a different order than, say, "light blue eyes." Greed and eroticism cannot be seen in a direct sense; they must be inferred, and thus they represent an infusion of the writer's sensitivity. This is not to say that such an infusion makes the description less true, simply that the description now involves more than observation of literal detail. Is there any other physical fact about Rona which is modified by a word like *greedy* or *erotic*, implying a judgment?

3. Rona's eyes and skin are literally aspects of her appearance. What about the "odor of distintegration" in lines 7-8)? Is this a literal detail or pure metaphor *?

4. Of the two vignettes, which gives the sharpest image *? Which gives more sense of personality?

5. Benglis is a feminist reacting against the tradition in our society of treating women primarily as sex objects. Knowing this, hazard an opinion about how each of these snapshots relates to her feminist theme. (They come from different parts of the book and have no direct connection. Even so, might the two passages be thought of as like "before" and "after" photographs? Before and after what?)

ORGANIZATION

6. How does Benglis begin the self-portrait? Does she focus down on her subject? Explain.

7. In the fourth sentence of "Me" what general phrase sets up the details? Are these details presented according to any plan?

8. Does "Rona" begin in much the same way as "Me"? Does it follow as clear a plan of presentation?

SENTENCES

9. In "Me" the first sentence is grammatically simple *. Which of the remaining five sentences are also simple?

10. The sentences in "Rona" are longer and more complicated: four sentences totaling 124 words, an average of 31 words per sentence, as against a 10.5 aver-

age in "Me" (63 words in 6 sentences). Does this contrast in length and complexity relate to the author's different purposes in the two descriptions?

11. Repeating a word or an idea as the subject of successive sentences is a good way of unifying a paragraph and maintaining its focus. Does Benglis do this in self-portrait? In "Rona"?

12. Using the same word or subject over and over, however, can be monotonous. Is that the case in either of these paragraphs? If not, explain how Benglis avoids monotony.

13. Which sentence is the climax of "Me"?

14. What function does the colon serve in the opening sentence of "Rona"? Where in the other selection does Benglis use a colon for a similar purpose?

15. Point out three examples of nominative absolutes * in "Me." In "Rona" identify the parallelism * in the second sentence and the appositive * in the last.

DICTION

16. Look up: (in "Rona") *platinum* (1), *erotic* (4), *foraging* (5), *disintegration* (8).

17. Explain the meaning of each of these phrases: (in "Rona") *outrageous jokes* (3), *midriff bulge* (4), *greasy spoons* (6); (in "Me") *movie star pose* (2).

18. How does the simile * in the third sentence add to our knowledge of Rona? Do its implications, on the whole, increase or decrease our sympathy and admiration for the aging actress?

19. Where else in this selection do you find a simile? Is it effective?

20. Study the use of platinum in the opening sentence of "Rona." Obviously it is a key metaphor, used four times. What is *platinum hair*? What overtones of meaning does the phrase have? *Platinum hair* (often used as *platinum blonde*) is a conventional image, but applying the word to the skin and to the voice is not commonplace. Here the metaphor is being worked in an increasingly abstract sense: platinum skin is less easy to imagine than platinum hair, and a platinum voice more difficult still. What is suggested by the phrase *platinum voice*? Are the connotations generally favorable or unfavorable?

POINTS TO LEARN

1. Objective description details facts, literally and unemotionally. Subjective description infuses the writer's feelings and values into what he or she is describing, using all the resources of language—loaded diction, similes, metaphors, and so on—to arouse similar feelings and judgments in the reader.

2. Description often begins with a general view, then focuses upon particulars.

3. A paragraph may be unified and focused not only by its topic but by its sentence structure.

SUGGESTIONS FOR WRITING

1. Find an old photograph of yourself and describe it as objectively as you can in a paragraph of about 150 words. Use a simple sentence style, but vary it enough to prevent monotony.

2. Have you known anyone like Rona—a brilliant surface hiding failure, loneliness, waste? Try to describe him or her in a paragraph of about 200 words. Your purpose is not to be objective but to react to the subject, to evaluate the person. However, do not express your judgments and feelings abstractly * and at length. Imply them by your diction.

IMPROVING YOUR STYLE

In your composition:

1. Compose a sentence like the fourth one of "Me": a simple clause setting up a series of details, introduced by a colon and expressed in nominative absolutes.

2. Include two sentences containing parallelism and one using an appositive.

3. (Applying only to the second of the assignments above) develop an extended simile like that of the Siamese cat, which conveys a rich complex of meanings in a graphic image.

William Joyce

Rebecca West is an English novelist, journalist, and critic. Her novels include *Harriet Hume* (1929), *The Thinking Reed* (1936), and *The Birds Fall Down* (1966). She is best known for *Black Lamb and Grey Falcon* (1942), a two-volume work about the Balkans, part travelogue and part social and political history, and for *The Meaning of Treason* (1945), from which the following passage comes. *The Meaning of Treason* is an account of the trial of William Joyce—known derisively as Lord Haw-Haw—a renegade Englishman who broadcast propaganda for Germany during World War II. After the war Joyce was tried as a traitor, convicted and hanged. West's book is much more than a report of the trial; it expands into a thoughtful examination of what constitutes treason in our time and of how the responsibilities of scientists and intellectuals have changed in the modern world.

The strong electrical light was merciless to William Joyce, whose appearance was a surprise to all of us who had not seen him before. His voice had suggested a large and flashy handsomeness. But he was a tiny little creature and, though not very ugly, was exhaustively so. His hair was mouse-coloured and grew thinly, particularly above his ears. His nose was joined to his face 5 at an odd angle, and its bridge and its point and its nostrils were all separately misshapen. Above his small dark-blue eyes, which were hard and shiny, like pebbles, his eyebrows were thick and pale and irregular. His neck was long and his shoulders were narrow and sloping. His arms were very short and very thick, so that his sleeves were like little bolsters. His 10 body looked flimsy yet coarse. There was nothing individual about him except a deep scar running across his right cheek from his ear to the corner of his mouth. But this did not create the savage and marred distinction that it might suggest, for it gave a mincing immobility to his mouth, which was extremely small. His smile was pinched and governessy. He was dressed 15 with an intent and ambitious spruceness which did not succeed in giving any impression of well-being, but rather recalled some Eastern European peasant, newly driven off the land by poverty into a factory town and wearing his first suit of Western clothes. He moved with a jerky formality which would have been thought strange in any society. When he bowed to the 20 Judge, his bow seemed sincerely respectful but entirely inappropriate to the occasion, and it was difficult to think of any occasion to which it would have been appropriate.

QUESTIONS

READER AND PURPOSE

1. West's purpose is to make her reader see William Joyce as he stands in the dock. Does she succeed?

2. Of course, she might simply have printed a photograph of him. Would that have been better? Or does she do with words things that a photograph could not do, or not do as effectively?

3. Do you think West is writing for her contemporaries—that is, for people who lived through the war—or for a younger generation, for whom the war and those connected with it are history rather than personal experience?

ORGANIZATION

4. Which sentence (or sentences) may be said to act as the topic statement?

5. West's paragraph is organized in a loosely analytical manner. Thus from lines 3 to 11 she describes Joyce's general physical appearance. Is there any order to how she does it? Which phrase in the third sentence sets up and controls the details West describes in lines 3-11?

6. In line 11 she makes a slight change in her focus. Explain. Where else does she shift to different aspects of her subject?

7. Study sentences 2, 3, and 4. How does West unify these sentences, preventing her reader from feeling any sense of discontinuity in the paragraph? Where else does she employ essentially the same sentence pattern? Beginning too many sentences in the same way can be dangerous. Does she vary the pattern enough to avoid monotony?

8. Find places where West uses pointers * to help the reader follow her flow of thought. Does she depend chiefly upon pointers or upon sentence structure to maintain flow *?

9. Suppose the first sentence had read like this: "To William Joyce, whose appearance was a surprise to all of us who had not seen him before, the electrical light was merciless." Would it sound more "literary" (that is, more like books, less like speech) than West's sentence? Generally does she prefer the loose * type of sentence (typical of speech) or the periodic * (which is more formal and literary)?

10. How does this revision change the emphasis of West's sentence?

> Revision: Except for a deep scar running across his right cheek from his ear to the corner of his mouth, there was nothing individual about him.
>
> West: "There was nothing individual about him except a deep scar running across his right cheek from his ear to the corner of his mouth." (11-13)

11. Point out the chiasmus * in the last sentence of West's paragraph.

12. Look up: bolsters (10), flimsy (11), coarse (11), inappropriate (21).

13. Much of the effectiveness of West's description comes from striking phrases which are rich in implications. Explain as fully as you can all that is implied by the following: a large and flashy handsomeness (3), savage and marred distinction (13), mincing immobility (14), pinched and governessy (15), an intent and ambitious spruceness (16), jerky formality (19).

14. What exactly does West mean by her remark that Joyce "though not very ugly, was exhaustively so" (4)?

15. What impression is conveyed by the description of his eyes as being "hard and shiny, like pebbles" (7-8)?

POINTS TO LEARN

1. In characterization, as in all description, impressions are more effectively communicated by being "rendered" in objective details than by being stated directly.

2. The loose sentence suggests informality.

SUGGESTIONS FOR WRITING

1. Write a one-paragraph character sketch of some public figure familiar to us from television. Your purpose is to convey an impression, but an impression rendered in physical details of appearance and mannerisms.

2. In a single paragraph discuss how West evaluates William Joyce, supporting your generalizations by citing from her text.

IMPROVING YOUR STYLE

In your composition include:

1. Two or three periodic sentences and two or three loose ones.
2. A simile * like the one West uses in lines 7-8, which conveys an impression in a sharp suggestive image *.

Ronald Reagan

Gore Vidal writes novels, plays, and essays. His novels include *Williwaw* (1946), *Julian* (1964), and *Myra Breckenridge* (1968); and his plays *Visit to a Small Planet* (1957) and *The Best Man* (1960). In his fiction and drama and in his essays, Vidal writes frequently, though not exclusively, about politics—how it works and the kinds of men and women it attracts. The following selection is from "Miami Beach, Florida, August 5-8, 1968," part of a collection of essays published under the title, *Reflections Upon a Sinking Ship* (1968). Miami was the site of that year's Republican National Convention, which Vidal attended as an observer and reporter. Among the several candidates for the Presidential nomination (which went finally to Richard M. Nixon) was Ronald Reagan, the one-time movie star and ex-governor of California. Reagan is a right-wing, or conservative, Republican. Vidal is far more liberal and views Reagan from an unsympathetic angle. Notice how he selects certain of the candidate's physical features and the language he uses to describe them. You may or may not feel that Vidal is being fair. But you must admire his skill.

Ronald Reagan is a well-preserved not young man. Close-to, the painted face is webbed with delicate lines while the dyed hair, eyebrows, and eyelashes contrast oddly with the sagging muscle beneath the as yet unlifted chin, soft earnest of wattle-to-be. The effect, in repose, suggests the work of a skillful embalmer. Animated, the face is quite attractive and at a distance 5 youthful; particularly engaging is the crooked smile full of large porcelain-capped teeth. The eyes are interesting: small, narrow, apparently dark, they glitter in the hot light, alert to every move, for this is enemy country—the liberal Eastern press who are so notoriously immune to that warm and folksy performance which Reagan quite deliberately projects over their heads to 10 some legendary constituency at the far end of the tube, some shining Carverville where good Lewis Stone forever lectures Andy Hardy on the virtues of thrift and the wisdom of the contract system at Metro-Goldwyn-Mayer.[1]

QUESTIONS

READER AND PURPOSE

1. Clearly this is subjective description. Express in your own words the impression of Ronald Reagan that Vidal wishes to convey.

2. Does Vidal seem to be writing for conservatives, hoping to persuade them to give up their support of Reagan's political philosophy, or for liberals—preaching to the converted?

3. Some readers—whatever their own political stance—might object to this treatment of Reagan. It is irrelevant and unfair, they might charge, to express disapproval of a man's political views by stressing his unattractive physical features. Is the objection reasonable? Why or why not?

ORGANIZATION

4. Like most description, the passage begins with a general impression, the key terms being "well-preserved" and "not young." Which following details are specifications of the first of these expressions? Which of the second?

5. The paragraph has two parts, the turn coming within the long final sentence. At what precise point? What does Vidal concentrate on in part one? In part two?

6. Study the arrangement of the second sentence. Is there any plan in how the details are presented?

SENTENCES

7. Vidal begins the second sentence with the modifier "close-to." A less experienced writer might have used a whole clause * or at least a phrase: "When it is seen close-to" or "Seen close-to." Vidal states only the key modifier, know-

---

[1] Lewis Stone was a character actor best known for the role of Judge Hardy, father of Andy Hardy (played by Mickey Rooney) in a series of MGM movies popular in the late 1930s and –40s. The films celebrate an idyll of the American small town (Carverville): an innocent world of puppy love and middle-class families, respected and secure, inhabiting large, comfortable homes set in spacious yards on elm- and maple-shaded streets. The plots developed out of the pranks and follies of the adolescent Andy and his friends, who were inevitably led back to safer paths by the forebearing wisdom of Judge and Mrs. Hardy.

The "contract system" refers to the fact that movie actors of the time worked under long-term contracts to large studios. The actors had relatively few legal rights concerning the roles they were assigned and could even be "loaned" to rival companies in deals concocted by the autocratic studio executives. [Editors' note]

ing that it clearly implies the condition of "being seen." Where else in this
selection does he begin a sentence in this manner?

8. At the end of the second sentence the phrase "soft earnest of wattle-to-be"
is an appositive *. To what preceding word? This too could have been written
as a full clause: "which is a soft earnest of wattle-to-be." Is it better as it is?

9. Why does the writer use a semicolon in line 6 instead of a comma? What
does the colon in line 7 prepare us for?

10. There is considerable variety in the length and complexity of Vidal's sentences. Count the words in each of the first four sentences. Is there a rough
pattern?

11. The opening sentence is grammatically simple *. Are any of the others? If
not simple, are they compound *, complex *, or compound-complex?

12. The fifth sentence is much the longest (82 words, more than half the total
of the paragraph). It is a fine example of the cumulative * style. Its logic is a
series of assertions about Reagan's eyes, followed by an explanation of why they
are "alert." The cumulation develops the explanation and occurs in the latter
half of the sentence, beginning with the phrase "the liberal Eastern press." To
what is that phrase in apposition? Analyze the rest of the sentence, identifying
the various clauses and phrases and indicating what they modify. Are there any
other appositives in this group of constructions? Could this sentence be stopped
at various places and still make sense? If so, where?

DICTION

13. Look up: *earnest* (4), *repose* (4), *animated* (5), *engaging* (6), *projects*
(10), *thrift* (13).

14. Explain the meanings of these phrases: *wattle-to-be* (4), *the liberal Eastern press* (9), *notoriously immune* (9), *legendary constituency* (11).

15. The expression *well-preserved* (1) is a calculated ambiguity *. Is it a compliment or an insult? Why does Vidal say *not young* (1) instead of *middle-
aged* or *old* or *elderly*?

16. On one level *painted face* (2) is probably literally accurate, for as the context of this paragraph makes clear Reagan was being televised at the time and
was made up, as all TV performers must be. Even so, does the expression have
implications that might prejudice a reader? With what other words in this
paragraph does *painted face* connect in a semantic sense? What's your opinion: is Vidal being fair in using the phrase?

17. Similarly, *small* and *narrow* might be defended as literally accurate. But
are these adjectives also loaded with unfavorable connotations *? Look up the
phrase *ad hominem*. Does it apply here?

18. What expression in the preceding sentence is *animated* (5) played against?

19. Why does Vidal write *the . . . hair, the . . . chin, the face, the eyes,*
instead of *his . . . hair, his . . . chin, his face, his eyes*?

20. How do these substitutes alter the connotations of Vidal's diction: *small for soft* (4), *uneven* for *crooked* (6), *shine* for *glitter* (8), *glittering* for *shining* (11), *intimate for folksy* (9)?

21. Even if you know nothing more about the Andy Hardy movies than was explained in the footnote, do you understand what Vidal is implying by his allusion * to them in lines 11-13? Do you think he admires the films in the sense that he agrees with the dreams and values they represent?

POINTS TO LEARN

1. Loaded diction—especially when it is prejudicial—poses questions of fairness.

2. An initial adjective or participle * is often clear by itself and does not need the support of a full clause or phrase.

3. The cumulative sentence works by tacking on ideas, expanding a point by adding modifying clauses and phrases, appositives, nominative absolutes *, and so on.

SUGGESTIONS FOR WRITING

Compose a description of about 150 words of a well-known TV personality—Walter Cronkite, for example, or Barbara Walters, Mike Wallace—or of a political figure who appears frequently on television. It should be someone whom most readers will be able immediately to visualize. Convey a distinct impression—it does not have to be unfavorable—by selecting words with appropriate connotations.

IMPROVING YOUR STYLE

In your paragraph include:

1. At least one simple sentence of no more than ten words, at least one compound sentence of twenty or thirty words, and one cumulative sentence of no less than eighty.

2. One or two sentences beginning with an adjective or participle.

Welcome to the Death Hilton

Paul Hemphill is a journalist whose methods, like those of John McPhee (page 270) and Tom Wolfe (page 318) exemplify what is loosely called the "new journalism." He has published articles in a number of magazines (*Cosmopolitan, Life, Sport, True*), and is the author of several books, among them *The Nashville Sound: Bright Lights and Country Music* and *The Good Old Boys* (1974). The latter, which is the source of the following essay, is a collection of pieces about interesting southerners (Hemphill is from Alabama), some famous, some once-famous, and some relatively obscure. But all are variants of a type known in the South as "the good old boy," a regionalism difficult to translate. Hemphill quotes a definition from Tom Wolfe's "The Last American Hero" which describes the qualities of the good old boy: "He has a good sense of humor and enjoys ironic jokes, is tolerant and easygoing enough to get along in long conversations at places like on the corner, and has a reasonable amount of physical courage . . ." On the whole, Hemphill admires the good old boy, but not uncritically. In this portrait of an enterprising funeral director named H. Raymond Ligon he shows both the type and its manifestation in one individual. And notice that he shows, he does not tell; he lets his subject speak and act for himself.

> Show me the manner in which a nation or a community cares for its dead, and I will measure with mathematical exactness the tender sympathies of its people, their respect for the laws of the land and their loyalty to high ideals.
>
> —*Gladstone*

1   "Wife found that quote somewhere, typed it up and gave it to me. Been carrying it around ever since. Believe in it. Ray Ligon's motto, don't you see." Reverently rereading it to himself, H. Raymond Ligon smiles at

From *The Good Old Boys*. Copyright © 1974 by Paul Hemphill. Reprinted by permission of Simon & Schuster, a Division of Gulf & Western Corporation, and The Sterling Lord Agency.

the card through black horn-rimmed glasses, stuffs the bulging billfold back
into his hip pocket, swings his dusty cowboy-booted feet onto the dishev-   5
eled desk and sways back deeply in a swivel chair. Everything is right on
this soft summer morning at the Woodlawn Cross Mausoleum and Funeral
Home, Inc., on the edge of downtown Nashville. Grieving families sit
quietly in several of the ten "repose rooms," waiting for services to begin.
Somber music drones through the carpeted hallways. Ligon's army of fu-   10
neral directors and embalmers and secretaries and janitors goes about its
business inside, while outside two dozen laborers preen the grassy undulating 192 acres representing the final resting place for some 100,000 souls.
But the true center of activity is behind the main building, where dozens
of hard-hatted construction workers swarm over a hulking square concrete-   15
and-steel edifice, now rising five stories out of the ground like one of the
Pyramids, soon to be the third tallest building in Nashville. Ray Ligon's
dream. A twenty-story mausoleum, cold storage for 129,500 bodies.

2   "Yes, sir," he is saying, "Ray Ligon is one of the most fortunate
people in the funeral business, and I'll tell you why." It is only nine o'clock,   20
but already he has been at work for nearly three hours, and the construction
on the mausoleum is going so well that he is in an ebullient mood, his
bright yellow shirt and gaudy boots and dyed black hair and leathery sunburned face belying his 70 years. "Hard work, and treating people right. I
remember one time this lady called and said she'd had a vision that her hus-   25
band was buried at my place with his head downhill. Said she couldn't
sleep for thinking about it. I told her to come on out, and I got two lawn
chairs and we sat there under a tree while the workers dug. When they put
a level on the coffin, the bubble was straight up. She appreciated what Ray
Ligon did for her, don't you see. Every human being is entitled to our love   30
and respect, and to a decent farewell."

3   Ligon's chief engineer on the mausoleum project opens the door to
the cluttered paneled office. He is wearing a bright yellow hardhat, and
holding a bill of lading in one hand. "Got a load we need you to sign for,
Mr. Ligon."   35

4   "What we got here?"

5   "One load of marble."

6   "Stuff from Italy?"

7   "Yes, sir."
on the bill. "Keep 'em rolling."

8   "Fine. You know what to do with it." Ligon scrawls his signature   40

9   That business done ("Sent my engineer all the way to Italy just to

find the right marble for the crypts"), Ligon sways back again and races off on another monologue about himself and his plans. While he talks, a 76-year-old retired newspaperman named Sewall B. Jackson—reedy, chain- 45 smoking, ruined voice, pencil-thin mustache, mod high-heeled shoes and tacky checkered suit—takes shorthand notes for the book he will write on Ligon's life. "If it's never been done before, I thrive," Ligon is saying. "Night funerals. Funeral home and cemetery combined. Mausoleum. Ray Ligon likes to do sensible things that've never been done before. I tell 'em 50 everything else in this world has changed, why not the funeral business. Know what I'm thinking about doing next?" Sewall Jackson's pen poises. He looks up at Ligon with an expectant conspiratorial grin. "Helicopters. Here's a loved one at the airport. Died in Chicago, wanted to be buried here. Put the remains on a helicopter, fly over here and land on top of the 55 mausoleum, bring him down on the elevator to the repose room. Save time, save money. I can get a helicopter for $18,000, as cheap as a fancy hearse. Got to keep thinking all the time, don't you see . . ."

10   For the time being, before he goes airborne, Raymond Ligon's latest scheme will suffice in solidifying his claim as the most innovative, 60 if not controversial, funeral director in America. The largest mausoleum in the country had been one of four floors at California's Forest Lawn, but when Ligon announced his audacious design for the Woodlawn Cross Mausoleum he left quite a target for any other entrepreneur who might care to shoot for the record. At a cost of $12 million, the mausoleum will 65 provide, Ligon boasts, "a burial as fine as the Taj Mahal." The name Cross Mausoleum comes from the shape of the building, its four wings converging in the center, the foundation and immediate grounds consuming only seven of the 300 acres held by Ligon. Each floor will have bright carpet, air conditioning, elevators, piped music, cushy sofas and seven tiers of 70 crypts beginning at floor level with the most expensive (the "Westminster" for couples buried side by side) and ending at the ceiling with the least expensive vault (the "Heaven Level"). There will be nighttime funerals ("working folks can't make it in the daytime"), visiting at all hours, and lounging downstairs in the Garden of Jesus: a natural underground spring 75 spilling water into a corner rock pile, a clear fiberglass roof allowing natural sunlight to feed the flowers, and a "tomb of Jesus" made of rocks brought over from Jerusalem.

11   The reaction to Ligon's plans ranged from utter disbelief to jollity.

"This is one time I'm sort of glad I can't see," said a blind Nashville singer 80
named Ronnie Milsap. Joked Johnny Carson on his television talk show:
"How would you like to be the elevator operator on duty about three in the
morning, and you're sitting on the sixth floor, and you hear somebody say,
'*Down*?'" One magazine referred to it as "the Death Hilton," and a Nashville newsman no longer surprised by anything Ligon does guessed that "as 85
soon as he finishes this one he'll go out and build a chain of the damned
things across the country." Buyers of space in the mausoleum were hard to
find at first, Southerners being more traditional about such matters as death
and religion than most, but an aggressive sales campaign ("Keeping up
with kings, queens and presidents costs less than you think," read one bro- 90
chure) soon brought into the coffers some $2 million in "Pre-need" sales—
the backbone of the burial business—so Ligon could begin construction.
When the first five floors were topped out and put into service this fall
(for the ribbon cutting, a state official landed atop the building in a helicopter), there remained some skeptics, one of them a disgruntled former 95
Ligon business associate: "I don't see any necessity for a 20-story mausoleum, except that it'll get Raymond a lot of publicity. He contends that
land in America is going to run out. I disagree. You can go three miles outside Nashville, on an old farm, and find plenty of land for plenty of
cemeteries."   100
12   To Ligon, though, the availability and price of land in America today make the argument for mausoleum burial overpowering. "We just can't
afford to keep on burying folks on these shady little hillsides," he says,
pointing out that he will bury the same number in a mausoleum covering
seven acres that he has buried on the 192 developed acres of his cemetery. 105
"I know what they say about the cemetery business, that you buy by the
acre and sell by the inch, but you can't even make any money that way
these days. Some of the land I paid $700 an acre for in the 1930s is worth
$35,000 today, and some adjoining property just brought $55,000 an acre.
We're sitting right next to the busiest intersection in Nashville now. I'm 110
just not going to develop another acre. It's mausoleums from now on.
Ground burial is going to go out." Armed with arguments, Ligon can
go on and on about the desirability—for himself and for the client family—
of mausoleum burial: it is dryer, less expensive (no need for a tombstone,
vault or elaborate coffin), offers lower maintenance costs (two people will 115
be able to take care of the mausoleum, while 28 are required for the cemetery grounds), and "if there was a strike, why me and the preacher could

get on the elevator and do the burying ourselves." Ligon does not mention
that 130,000 crypts sold at an average $2,000 would turn his $12 million
investment into $260 million, and that air space comes free.   120

13   "Let's go across the road for a minute and see the old place, Mr.
Jackson." Clapping his own personal yellow hardhat on his head, Ligon
strides through a maze of corridors until he bursts out into the bright
morning sun, quickly slipping behind the wheel of the luxury pickup truck
he prefers to drive. Gliding over the smooth paved lane leading to the main   125
entrance, he points straight ahead across busy Thompson Lane to a squat
two-story concrete building with the word MAUSOLEUM discreetly printed
on a green awning which shades the entrance. It was his first mausoleum—
and probably the first of any size in the South—and today, seven years later,
its 3,500 crypts are just about taken up. "I told 'em I wanted it soft and   130
beautiful like a living room, not harsh and cold," Ligon says as he steps into
the air conditioning and waves a hand over the bright carpeting and the
deep sofas. A woman is vacuuming, her machine drowning out the soft music, and Ligon asks her to stop when he sees that several people—most of
them old—are sitting around, apparently visiting family crypts.   135
14   "Mr. Ligon." Coming Ligon's way, his eyes red and bloated, is a
retired Army colonel who has lost his entire family during the past 18
months, the last a son killed in a skyjacking. The man says, "I just wanted
to thank you."
15   "What for, Colonel Giffe?"   140
16   "For this place you got here."
17   "Everything's all right, then."
18   "It's wonderful. Just wonderful. Well, you know what I mean. My
wife, she sat right there on that divan. She knew she was going. But she
wasn't horrified by this place. No, sir. Another thing, I can come visit with   145
her even if it's snowing."
19   Ligon nods to some of the others and makes a quick tour. "Here's
my first wife," he says, pointing to a crypt. The place is cool and quiet and
eerie, in spite of the flashy colors and deep carpet. Here and there against
the walls are small tables adorned with plastic flowers. On one of the tables   150
is a stack of index cards and a note inviting visitors to "leave word so we
can acknowledge your visit." One card has already been used. "Dear Lela,"
says a laborious scrawl. "Ethel and Norma came by to see you. We miss
you so much." Beside the note is a tiny framed picture of the dead woman.

20   The burial business has changed very little in the decade since the   155
publication of Jessica Mitford's scathing book *The American Way of
Death*, still regarded as the definitive work on the subject. (Who, for that
matter, can forget the grotesqueries in the movie made of Evelyn Waugh's
The Loved One?) Mitford gets to the point on the very second page of the
opening chapter: "Gradually, almost imperceptibly, over the years the fu-   160
neral men have constructed their own grotesque cloud-cuckooland where
the trappings of Gracious Living are transformed, as in a nightmare, into
the trappings of Gracious Dying." About 1 percent of America dies each
year, leaving the disposal of some 2 million bodies to 22,000 "funeral directors" (not "undertakers," please) who do a gross of $1.8 billion each   165
year. The competition is mean and often bitchy, the object of the hunt
usually a grieving widow suddenly forced to make her first major financial
decision within hours, and this fall the Federal Trade Commission announced an investigation into 76 District of Columbia funeral homes—
tantamount to a national study—following numerous complaints about in-   170
flated prices and the selling of unneeded services. In the burial business
today, as strongly as ever, "cremation" is a dirty word (35 percent of the
dead in England are cremated, only some 60,000 a year in the United
States). Indeed, semantics is important in the business: "grief therapy" and
"memory pictures" and "slumber room" are the ABCs of the burial sales-   175
man's language. Talk about everything but death. A hole in the ground is
a hole in the ground. *It's the last chance you will have to do something for
your loved one . . . Now here is a nice casket, fit for a man of his stature
. . . Oh, by all means, you'll want fresh flowers . . . For the memory picture, I would suggest a dark wool suit and a bowtie . . . It's going to be a*   180
nice funeral, I'm sure of that . . .
21   Sales, then, is the most important aspect of the business. "They say
Ray Ligon is a great salesman," says Ligon, "but he knows anybody can sell
a couple if they love each other." The head of Woodlawn's 15-man sales
force is Ligon's 34-year-old stepson, John Spivey, a handsome favorite at the   185
Tennessee statehouse, who recently received a six-year appointment to the
state's Youth Advisory Commission. When he dies, he says, somebody will
simply pull out a file in the business office at Woodlawn and it will all be
there: choice of casket, names of pallbearers, number of the crypt in the
mausoleum, and so forth. "I remember this young guy whose wife had   190
died," says Spivey. "Just before they closed the lid on her, he picked up his
four-year-old daughter and leaned her over and said, 'Kiss your mother

good-by.' A lot of people go hysterical at a funeral. You have all kinds. I don't see any reason why that should happen; any reason why it should be a hot, agonizing ordeal. It should be planned, together, in advance."   195

22   This "pre-need" selling is Spivey's responsibility, and he wraps his arguments around the low-key, sensible, pragmatic trappings of, say, a life insurance agent. "The funeral director doesn't have to put pressure on a couple, the family does that," he says. "A funeral is the third largest investment you make in your life, behind a car and a house. You going to let   200 your brother-in-law do it? It's all a process of education, like my juvenile job. I just tell them the straight true story and put it in an honest, believable, attractive package." At Woodlawn, one price covers all: coffin, hearse, police escort, flowers, "open-and-close" grave charges, and so forth. The price can vary greatly, depending on such choices as gravesite and cof-   205 fin, but Spivey says an average burial in the ground there runs around $2,500. In the new mausoleum, however, he says he "can do one" for $1,600. Woodlawn will also sell you the coffin, more than a dozen styles of them being on display in a sales room at the funeral home, and for the mausoleum there is a $495 Ligon-designed bier called the "cross repose,"   210 which is the cheapest way of all to go. "We don't back the hearse up to the door," says Spivey, "we just tell them the facts. Pre-need is the way you stop the high cost of dying." Ray Ligon, his stepson says with reverence, "is the greatest teacher who ever lived."

23   The funeral business is all Herschel Raymond Ligon has known   215 since his birth in 1903 to the owner of the local funeral home in Lebanon, one of those lovely little middle Tennessee towns about 30 miles east of Nashville. When he graduated from high school ("All I've got is that diploma and a Dale Carnegie course"), he became a partner in Ligon & Sons Funeral Home, doing everything from embalming to directing services.   220 "The first service I ever held, I was 24 years old," he recalls. "A logger had been killed on the job and he was so poor they were having to bury him out back of the house in the garden, don't you see. We fixed him up nice and took him over there, but there wasn't a preacher or any music. An old lady pulled me aside and said, 'I'll sing a song if you'll read some scripture.' The   225 next day my father got a preacher to teach me how to lead a service, and I was in business."

24   Ligon was too adventurous to stick around Lebanon forever, and his chance at much bigger things came during the Depression when a large holding company in Nashville went into bankruptcy. In addition to insur-   230

ance, real estate and a false-teeth factory, the group held a 40-acre cemetery in Nashville. One of the attorneys representing the creditors had been a high school classmate of Ligon's, so Ligon was hired as a trustee at $35 a week ("That's when folks felt lucky to make a dollar a day") and charged with disposing of the cemetery to pay off a $110,000 tax bill. He soon be-   235
came an expert on the cemetery business in America—visiting the major ones like Forest Lawn in Hollywood on fact-finding excursions—and when it came time to put the cemetery up on bids, Ligon decided *he* wanted it. His bid for $90,000 was the only one submitted, so he took over Memorial Park and prefixed Woodlawn to its name and began building an empire.   240
25   Accustomed to checking into the office at daylight, Ligon quickly became a national figure in the funeral industry and a financial power to be reckoned with in Nashville. Bit by bit he bought up surrounding land, some of it for as little as $700 an acre, ultimately acquiring a package of 300 acres. Stressing "pre-need" sales to a growing sales force, he was able to get his   245
hands on money and put it to his own use long before it was needed to service his clients. With the funds he began acquiring other cemeteries in the Nashville area and claiming endless "firsts" in the region: the first crematorium, the first funeral home-and-cemetery operation under one roof, the first night funeral services, the first weddings in the funeral home chapel,   250
the first previously all-white cemetery opened to blacks. That Ray Ligon knows how to come up with cash when necessary is never questioned around Nashville. "One time I needed some capital," he says, "so I announced plans for a white 25-foot 'Tower of Memories' across the road. I got 450 people to put up $10 each in exchange for their name on a bronze   255
plaque. Me and two Negroes built it in no time." Finally, seven years ago, he raised his first mausoleum.

26   Today Ligon lives an active life. At one time or another in the past he has had his hands in many pies—a bronze works, a concrete vault factory, a half-dozen cemeteries, a finance company, a downtown office building—   260
but has divested himself of most of these so he can concentrate on his dream mausoleum. His two sons are well-set now—one operates the Mount Olivet cemetery in Nashville, the other a bank in Lebanon and a tourist attraction in Gatlinburg called Christus Gardens—leaving Ligon and his second wife (a high-powered cemetery entrepreneur in her own right before   265
they married) alone in a roomy white brick ranch house, set on a wooded knoll across from the rising mausoleum, of a simplicity belying his estimated net worth of some $10 million. Except when he is on brief visits to

central Florida, overseeing a real estate development there, he starts his day
with a 6:30 A.M. meeting with construction engineers and spends the rest of   270
it swinging deals or hanging around the construction site. "He comes up
with the ideas," says the current Mrs. Ligon, "and we what you call 'imple-
ment' them." Says Ligon of his standing in the community: "You know
who criticizes me? Other funeral directors. You think there might be a little jealousy there?"   275

27   The man on the street in Nashville may hold little more than passing awe for a man audacious enough to build a skyscraper cemetery, but
there is a tight corps of others whose emotions toward Ligon run from be-
grudging respect to outright hostility. "He can easily differentiate between
the person who needs the services of a pious Bible-quoter and the one who   280
needs a drink," says Nat Caldwell, a veteran reporter for the *Nashville Ten-
nessean*. Says a young ex-banker who once wrote a 30-page report on Ligon's
financial empire: "It was so complex, if there was any hanky-panky going
on you couldn't find it." Says an embittered former associate who claims he
once lost $15,000 in a cemetery development scheme engineered by Ligon: 285
"Every time I get to thinking about the bastard, my angina starts acting up.
I wouldn't speak to him if I saw him on the street." Even his enemies, however, respect his drive. "If Raymond Ligon stayed straight," says one, "he'd
be the hottest thing in America."

28   The nearest Ligon has been to serious trouble was in the early   290
1960s when he became involved in the National Cemetery Development
Corporation, which eventually sued him and his sons for $240,000 in dam-
ages on the charge that "transactions . . . resulted in diversion of funds to
the Ligons." NCDC was organized in 1958 by a dozen or so Nashville businessmen, with plans to develop cemeteries and allied businesses all over the   295
nation. As soon as its formation was announced, Ligon offered his services
as an expert in the field and was promptly named president. More than
$1 million was raised in a public stock sale during the first four months, the
major partners kicking in as much as $30,000 each, and in the beginning all
was happiness and light. "People bought because of what they knew about   300
Woodlawn, because Ligon was obviously successful," says one of the original partners, Jim Bulleit, now a candy manufacturer in Nashville. "We
finally got around to going to Raymond Ligon to find out who he was."
Over the first three years the corporation lost some $300,000, bringing about
Ligon's "resignation" as president. Finally, in 1963, claiming that Ligon   305
and his sons were raking money off the top for themselves and doing little

else for the corporation, the NCDC filed suit. The NCDC lies dormant today, the suit still tabled somewhere in court, and the embittered partners
seem to have little heart to continue fighting. "Hell," says one, "our attorney moved off to Florida and won't even return my calls." The publicity did 310
little good for Ligon, for when he tried to give a farm to his Church of
Christ the church gave it right back on the grounds that it didn't want to
get involved. "But the man has good lawyers," says reporter Caldwell, "and
he always protects his flanks." Indeed, when the Securities Exchange Commission showed an interest in Ligon and the NCDC it was shut out of any 315
investigation because Ligon had seen to it that only Tennesseans bought
stock in the group.

29 Late in the afternoon, curious to see what sort of progress the engineers have made during the day, Ligon invites a visitor to ride with him to
the top of the mausoleum and check out the work. The dark elevator groans 320
and clangs as it rises from the wet and musty ground floor before finally
bursting into the sparkling summer sunlight. Looking like one of the construction workers himself, hardhat and all, Ligon waves a hand at the two
dozen men and asks the foreman to call the men together. Off in the distance can be seen Ligon's rambling house, sitting serenely in the cluster of 325
shade trees beyond the grassy acres of his cemetery. The spread is dotted
with tiny oases Ligon calls his "Biblical Gardens," each featuring a statue
of a character from the Bible standing amid a garden of flowers. "Boys,"
Ligon is saying, flopping his hardhat back and forth on his head, "this gentleman here is writing a story on us. *New York Times.* About the biggest 330
newspaper in the world. Wants to find out how excited you are about
having a part in this, don't you see. Y'all talk to him, now." It was an awkward moment. The young ones suppressed giggles. The foreman babbled
something he thought Ligon wanted to hear. "Let's go downstairs and relax," says Ligon, getting back onto the elevator and going down a couple of 335
floors.

30 He also has a conference room, which he hopes to entice various
civic and business groups to use for their meetings. "Want to get 'em used
to coming out to Woodlawn," he says. On the walls are pictures of Ligon
with beasts he once shot on safari, and one of a group of middle-aged 340
women he once threw a party for on a whim. "Bought every one of 'em, 15
of 'em, a $165 dress," he is saying. "Silly. But they had fun."

31 "You hunt?" he is asked.

32   "Used to, all the time. Quit now. Got to where I didn't want to kill anything anymore."   345

33   For several minutes, he rambled on about life and death and his own machinations. You see one cremation, he says, you'll never believe in it ("Reminds you of Hitler and the Jews"). He may lease out the rest of his land, he says, and go mausoleum all the way ("Government's going to get 30 percent of the price if I sell the land, anyway"). On the first floor 350 of the mausoleum, he says, "we are already burying beautifully." People make jokes, he says, about funeral directors ("Call me the white Southern planter"), but you have to laugh with them and forget it. What would he be, he is asked, if he had it to do over?

34   "Evangelist," he says. "I never got to be what you'd call religious 355 until I was about 15 or 16. Just went to church and slept up until then. Now I give 10 percent a year to the church. Believe in it now. But I got to thinking about these evangelists, and me. Got the same things in common. Trying to console people, don't you see. *Help* people. And here I got this way with people, know how to talk 'em into things." He bends over in his 360 chair to knock some mud off his cowboy boots. "Yes, sir, an evangelist is what I'd want to be. Instead of working with their bodies, work with their souls, don't you see."

QUESTIONS

READER AND PURPOSE

1. In journalism a distinction is made between fact and comment. Facts are the province of the reporter, commentary of the editorial writer or columnist. Is Hemphill acting primarily as a reporter in this essay or as a commentator?

2. Because a reporter sticks to facts and offers no overt comments upon them, does not mean, of course, that he makes no judgments or offers no angle of vision from which the facts may be interpreted. But he effects such judgments tacitly by the careful selection and arrangement of details. For example, what details in the first paragraph influence our perceptions of and response to Ligon?

3. How do you think Hemphill feels about his subject? Does he succeed in communicating his feelings to you?

4. The essay begins with an epigraph from the liberal statesman William Gladstone, a prime minister of Great Britain in the late nineteenth century. It serves Ligon as a credo, justifying his life's work. Might it cast a different light upon Ligon's career?

ORGANIZATION

5. By extra spacing Hemphill divides his essay into seven sections. What shifts of subject do these involve? Give a brief title to each.

6. Like some short story writers Hemphill moves back and forth between present and past. On the one hand, we follow Ligon through a day's activities. Which of the seven sections are primarily concerned with this? Identify within them the word or words establishing the chronological structure.

7. On the other hand, some sections are primarily (though not exclusively) concerned with what in fiction is called "exposition," the background information which we need to know in order to understand what is happening in the present. Identify these sections. How do they enhance our understanding of Ligon and the funeral business?

8. What detail brought to our attention in the opening paragraph is repeated in the closing? What value has such repetition as a means of ending an essay? In this case, does the detail also provide an implicit authorial "comment"?

9. What is the topic sentence of paragraph 11? How is it supported? What is the topic of paragraph 20? How is paragraph 9 tied to the material that precedes it?

SENTENCES

10. Hemphill is fond of the intrusive sentence, an independent construction which is simply inserted into the middle of another statement without being syntactically connected to it. Here is an example: "That business done ('Sent my engineer all the way to Italy just to find the right marble for the crypts'), Ligon sways back again and races off on another monologue about himself and his plans" (42-44). Hemphill prevents confusion by using parentheses or dashes to signal that the enclosed construction is absolute (not connected to the main statement). Find other examples of such intrusive sentences. While such constructions are not syntactically integrated with the sentences that enclose them, they are, of course, related in idea. How does the parenthetical remark in lines 42-43 bear upon the writer's point? Be able to explain the relevancy of the other examples you find.

11. Does this technique of the intrusive sentence make Hemphill's style sound formal and literary, or relaxed and conversational? Do you think it would be appropriate for, say, a term paper in a history course?

12. Incidentally, in that sentence quoted in question 10, what is the grammatical term for the opening construction ("That business done")?

13. Point out the parallel * elements in the very first sentence of the essay and also in the sentence in lines 73-78.

14. How do the following revisions change the emphasis or meaning of Hemphill's sentences?

(a) *Revision:* Ligon boasts that at a cost of $12 million, the mauso-
leum will provide "a burial as fine as the Taj Mahal."
Hemphill: "At a cost of $12 million, the mausoleum will provide,
Ligon boasts, 'a burial as fine as the Taj Mahal.' " (65-66)

(b) *Revision:* A retired army colonel is coming Ligon's way. His eyes
are red and bloated. He has lost his entire family during the past
18 months. The last one to die was his son. He was killed in a
skyjacking.
Hemphill: "Coming Ligon's way, his eyes red and bloated, is a
retired Army colonel who has lost his entire family during the
past 18 months, the last a son killed in a skyjacking." (136-38)

DICTION

15. Look up: *somber* (10), *Taj Mahal* (66), *coffers* (91), *eerie* (149), *bitchy*
(166), *tantamount* (170), *low-key* (197), *pragmatic* (197), *bier* (210), *dormant* (307), *musty* (321), *entice* (337), *machinations* (347).

16. As fully as possible explain the meanings of the following phrases: *dishev-
eled desk* (5-6), *scathing book* (156), *the definitive work* (157), *grotesque
cloud-cuckooland* (161), *the trappings of Gracious Living* (162), *wooded knoll*
(266-67).

17. What are the etymologies * of *mausoleum* (18), *crypts* (43), *brochure*
(90), *divested* (261), *entrepreneur* (265), *audacious* (277), *evangelist* (361)?

18. Why are the following less effective than Hemphill's words? *Floats* for
drones (10), *care for* for *preen* (12), *hums* for *groans and clangs* (320-21),
muttered for *babbled* (333)?

19. Explain how these pointers * prepare us for the writer's turn of thought:
though (101), *then* (182), *say* (197). Suppose that *though* were replaced by
however or *nevertheless:* how would the tone * alter?

20. In what sense is the title of this essay ironic *?

POINTS TO LEARN

1. Reporters may "stick to the facts" yet subtly impose an interpretation upon
the facts.

2. The intrusive sentence gives a colloquial * flavor to writing and is appropriate to a relaxed, conversational style.

SUGGESTIONS FOR WRITING

"Welcome to the Death Hilton" may be read as a criticism of the funeral business. Write a commentary upon Hemphill's essay from this point of view, discussing the more important failings that he tacitly suggests funeral directors
are guilty of and supporting your points by evidence from Hemphill's text.

IMPROVING YOUR STYLE

In your essay include:

1. Two examples of intrusive sentences—that is, independent statements related in idea but not in syntax to the sentence which encloses them. Punctuate the intrusive sentences with dashes or parentheses.

2. Two cases of parallelism.

3. A nominative absolute *.

4. These connective * words to link sentences to what precedes them: *though, then, say.*

HELEN BEVINGTON

The *Festivitas* of Sir Thomas More

Helen Bevington is a teacher and writer whose books include *Doctor Johnson's Waterfall* (1946), *When Found, Make a Verse Of* (1961), *Charley Smith's Girl* (1965), *A Book and a Love Affair* (1968), *The House Was Quiet and the World Was Calm* (1971), and *Beautiful Lofty People* (1973). The last is a collection of essays about literary figures and topics. The hero of the first essay is Sir Thomas More (1478-1535), an English statesman and author whose most famous work is *Utopia*, a fictional account of an ideal state. More became lord chancellor of England under Henry VIII but resigned rather than take an oath denying the pope's authority and upholding the legitimacy of Henry's divorce from Catherine of Aragon. More was subsequently tried for treason and beheaded.

1   The word for him is *festivitas*. Yet his life, had someone else lived it, would seem calamitous, unbearably tragic.

2   He lived for fifty-seven years and then was put to death. Through his refusal to support Henry VIII in his claim to be Supreme Head of the Church of England or to sign the Oath of Supremacy which went, More 5 said, against his conscience and would imperil his soul, More was found guilty of high treason and beheaded at the Tower of London, July 5, 1535. Afterward his head was exposed on London Bridge till his daughter Margaret took it down and carried it home to preserve in spices till she died. Perhaps it was buried with her. He was a peaceable and loving man, a just 10 and equable man, but for putting God before his king, Henry had him murdered.

3   Only Margaret knew of his punishing his body with whips to subdue it, the cords knotted to tame his flesh till the blood came. It was she who washed the hair shirt he wore next to his skin. In his youth More had 15 longed for the monastic life and for four years lived with the monks of

Charterhouse in London, tempted to take the final vows. He longed for that peace. Instead he returned to the world, went courting at the house of John Colt who had three daughters, and, though most attracted to the middle girl, married the eldest, Jane, lest she be hurt if rejected for her sister. Jane became the "little wife" he so faithfully loved, the mother of his children, Margaret, Elizabeth, Cecily, and a son John. Then Jane Colt died. More's second wife, Mistress Alice Middleton, was a widow and a scold, a dull-hearted woman older than he with whom he lived content, often adjuring her to be merry.

4   Merry. The word stayed ever on More's tongue and in his heart. To Dame Alice he said, "I pray you with my children be merry in God." From the Tower during the last fifteen months of his life, he wrote to Margaret, "I beseech Him make you all merry in the hope of Heaven." The day before his execution he sent her the hair shirt and a letter written with a piece of coal: "Tomorrow I long to go to God; it were a day very meet and convenient for me."

5   On the morrow as he climbed the scaffold, which was weak and ready to fall, More said, "I pray you, Master Lieutenant, see me safe up, and for my coming down let me shift for myself." By light words he took his leave. Without solemnity, with courtesy and compassion for others, with a cheerful serene face and three jests on the scaffold he went to die, speaking to the executioner, "Pluck up thy spirits, man, and be not afraid to do thine office. My neck is very short." He removed his beard from the block, "for it at least hath not offended the king."

6   The test of a man in the *Utopia*[1] is the way he dies. Those who die "merrily and full of good hope, for them no man mourneth." They are praised for their merry death and monuments are erected to them. More showed how it was done. He died as he had lived.

7   William Roper, More's son-in-law and husband to Margaret, attempted to measure his shining worth. In the sixteen years of living in More's genial house and being daily conversant with him, said Roper, "I could never perceive him as much as once in a fume."

8   He was never angry. His character was marked by kindness. As described by Erasmus (who loved that tranquillity he himself couldn't find and loved More, who had enough for both), he was of medium height, fair

---

[1] *Utopia* (the term translates as "Nowhere Land") is More's major literary work. Written in Latin and published in 1516, it describes an ideal society. It was early translated into English and other European languages and soon became popular and influential. [Editors' note]

complexion, auburn hair, thin beard, blue-gray eyes, his face alight forever breaking into a smile, merry of word and manner. Quarrels were unknown in his hospitable house. He loved gaiety and wit (but not at another's expense), and in fits of laughter ruled his household. His gift for friendship 55 was immense. He had an easiness that made him forget even the gravest injuries.

9   John Aubrey in *Brief Lives* calls More "extraordinary facetious." One night when More was riding with friends, suddenly he crossed himself and cried out, "Jesu Maria! doe not you see that prodigious Dragon in the 60 skye?" They all looked but nobody could see it. Then one did spy it, and the rest promptly saw it too. Everybody saw it. "Whereas there was no such phantome," says Aubrey. He tells of a time when Roper came to More's house with a proposal to marry one of his daughters. More led the young man into the bedchamber where, since it was morning, two of them lay 65 still asleep. Taking the sheet by the corner and whipping it off, More revealed the girls lying on their backs, their smocks up to their armpits. Thus awakened, they stirred and turned on their bellies. "Quoth Roper, 'I have seen both sides,' and so gave a patt on the buttock he made choice of, sayeing, 'Thou art mine.'" You can still hear the laughter at that wooing. 70

10   More's favorite jest, told him by his father, he would repeat to tease the females in his house: "A good Woman (as the old Philosopher observeth) is but like one Ele[2] put in a bagge amongst 500 Snakes, and if a man should have the luck to grope out that one Ele from all the snakes, yet he hath at best a wet Ele by the Taile." 75

11   In a letter to his children More wrote, "If ever I flogged you, it was but with a peacock's tail." By giving them the greatest praise in the world, which is approval, he taught them and made them love learning—the son and the three daughters, who studied with their father Greek and Latin, logic, philosophy, theology, astronomy. (They learned the Greek alphabet 80 by shooting bows and arrows at the letters.) As one would expect, he believed in the equality of the sexes. "Both are reasonable beings," he said, "suited equally for those studies by which reason is cultivated."

12   Incredulous and amazed, Erasmus viewed More's happy family life that grew to contain some twenty members: "There is not any man living 85 so affectionate to his children as he, and he loveth his old wife as if she were a girl of fifteen." In this commodious house in Chelsea, Holbein is

[2] Eel. [Editors' note]

said to have stayed three years. Erasmus, a difficult guest who spoke no
English, loathed the smell of fish and the taste of English beer, wrote *The
Praise of Folly* while laid up with lumbago and dedicated it to his beloved   90
friend: "I chose to amuse myself with a praise of folly (*moria*) because of
your name of More, which comes as close to the word for folly as you are
far from the thing itself." Erasmus said, "We had but one soul between
us." His praise of More became a litany.

13   Besides this huge family, More kept a noisy collection of birds and   95
animals inside the house and in the garden—a monkey, rabbits, a fox, a fer-
ret, a weasel. On all of life he lavished love; he found joy in everything; his
festivitas never forsook him. And since his fate was to die a martyr and be
made a saint, thank God he was a merry one.

QUESTIONS

READER AND PURPOSE

1. Would this essay be useful to a student trying to bone up on Sir Thomas
More before a test? Why or why not?

2. Does Bevington assume that her reader already knows the essential facts
about More? If she does, what is her purpose in writing about him?

3. The writer has a definite conception of the essential temperament of More.
Summarize her conception in a sentence.

ORGANIZATION

4. Bevington's essay in not organized in a tight analytical manner. This does
not mean, however, that her essay lacks organization. Rather it has a kind of
solar structure, in which one dominant theme or idea acts as a central mass
holding everything together. What is that central idea?

5. What is the topic of paragraph 4? Why may paragraphs 4, 5, and 6 be said
to constitute a unit? How do these paragraphs support the central thesis? Do
the first three paragraphs illustrate the thesis directly? If not, how do they relate to it?

6. There is a slight change of focus in paragraph 7. Describe it. Give a title to
paragraphs 7-13 suggesting the aspect of More's life the writer concentrates
upon here. Be able to show how each of these paragraphs supports the central
thesis.

7. How is paragraph 4 linked to paragraph 3? Paragraph 5 to 4?

8. How do the following revisions alter the emphasis of Bevington's sentences?

    (a) *Revision:* Henry had him murdered for putting God before his king, even though he was a peaceable and loving man, a just and equable man.
    Bevington: "He was a peaceable and loving man, a just and equable man, but for putting God before his king, Henry had him murdered." (10-12)

    (b) *Revision:* She washed the hair shirt he wore next to his skin.
    Bevington: "It was she who washed the hair shirt he wore next to his skin." (14-15)

    (c) *Revision:* He said, "Both are reasonable beings, suited equally for those studies by which reason is cultivated."
    Bevington: " 'Both are reasonable beings,' he said, 'suited equally for those studies by which reason is cultivated.' " (82-83)

    (d) *Revision:* He lavished love on all of life. . . .
    Bevington: "On all of life he lavished love. . . ." (97)

9. Study the following sentence:

> "Without solemnity, with courtesy and compassion for others, with a cheerful serene face and three jests on the scaffold he went to die, speaking to the executioner, 'Pluck up thy spirits man, and be not afraid to do thine office.' " (36-39)

Underline all the parallel * elements. Is the main clause * at the beginning, in the middle, or at the end of the sentence? What principle has the writer followed in arranging the ideas of the sentence?

10. What is the grammatical name of the construction in line 14: "the cords knotted to tame his flesh till the blood came"?

11. To what is "dull-hearted woman" (24) in apposition *?

12. Look up: *calamitous* (2), *equable* (11), *hair shirt* (15), *scold* (23), *adjuring* (24), *beseech* (29), *meet* (31), *scaffold* (33), *shift* (35), *tranquillity* (50), *wit* (54), *gravest* (56), *facetious* (58), *theology* (80), *commodious* (87), *loathed* (89), *lumbago* (90), *litany* (94), *lavished* (97).

13. Who were Erasmus (50), John Aubrey (58), Holbein (87)?

14. If you have access to a good Latin dictionary, look up *festivitas* and learn its full range of meaning.

15. Why are these alternates not as good as the words in the text: *executed* for *murdered* (12), *gags* for *jests* (37), *incredible* for *incredulous* (84), *happy* for *merry* (99)?

POINTS TO LEARN

1. Rather than proceeding in step-by-step analysis, an essay may be organized by centering everything on a core idea whose weight and importance holds the paragraphs together.

2. A character sketch may be less concerned with laying out the facts of someone's life than with revealing the essence of personality.

SUGGESTIONS FOR WRITING

Compare Bevington's account of Sir Thomas More with the entry in a good encyclopedia or in a handbook of history or of religion. Discuss differences in purpose and show how they influence organization, the inclusion or omission of details, and diction and sentence style.

IMPROVING YOUR STYLE

Include in your composition:

1. Two parallel sentences.
2. An appositive.
3. An elliptical nominative absolute * like Bevington's construction in line 14.

Narration

At its simplest, narrative writing is much like descriptive. As description develops by analyzing a physical object or scene into its parts and arranging these in space, so narration develops by analyzing a story into the events that compose it and arranging these in time. In its more highly evolved forms, such as novels and short stories, narration obviously includes more than a mere reporting of events. The novelist will elaborate a finely drawn plot and pay quite as much attention to the psychology of his characters as to what they do. However, such literary refinements are beyond the usual needs of the composition student. Here we are concerned with a simpler type of narration which restricts itself to action and does not probe deeply into the motives of the actors. Such narrative writing is often adapted to the needs of exposition. The historian must frequently relate stories, and the essayist depends upon narration to develop illustrations and anecdotes.

For whatever it is used, the essence of good narration is organizing the story into beginning, middle, and end. Most often these parts are arranged in their natural order. On occasion they may be inverted, so that the story opens with the end and then turns back to the beginning and middle. A film that starts with its main character already on the gallows and then relates for ninety minutes the circumstances which brought him to so uncomfortable a position, is an example of such flashback technique. But the brief narrative employed in exposition is best organized in the usual chronological order.

In how much detail these parts are developed will depend, of course, upon the writer's intention and the space he has available. Long or short, however, all narration is highly selective. No reporter or historian can afford to tell us everything. He must choose only those details relevant to his purpose, and reject those which are not. His criteria of selection will be based upon his reason for telling the story—the meaning he sees in it.

This meaning is what the writer tries to communicate to his reader. It is here that beginners most often fail. The inexperienced writer is likely to step forth before he knows where he is going, before he has determined in his own mind exactly what meaning the story has. It is hardly surprising that his narrative turns out like a poorly mixed cake, lumpy with unrelated details and without the flavor of meaning. Even when he has understood its significance, the beginner is likely to commit another error. This is to be afraid to permit the story to stand on its own legs. We have all suffered the would-be comedian who is so concerned with pointing out why his story is funny that he kills its humor. The meaning of a narrative, like the point of a joke, is best left to the reader, for a well-written narrative clearly implies its meaning. The writer's task, especially in brief narration, is to concentrate upon the story itself. If he knows to begin with why the story is important and if he has selected and arranged its details accordingly, he will communicate its meaning.

The Loss of the Cospatrick

Robert Carse has combined two professions: those of seaman and writer. He has published more than thirty books about the sea, including *The Age of Piracy*, *Ports of Call*, and *The Twilight of Sailing Ships*. It is the last of these which supplies the following account of a fire at sea. Carse's narrative is well-constructed and well-paced. Much of its sense of realism and economy comes from the use of nautical terminology. Since some of these terms may not be familiar to you, we shall define them here. If you are a sailor you may skip on to Carse's narrative. But if you are not you will find the following brief discussion helpful.

On a ship *forward* (pronounced "for'ard") means "toward the bow" or front of the vessel; *aft* (adjective *after*, preposition *abaft*) means "toward the stern" or rear. *Aloft* refers to anyplace in the masts, yards, or rigging, and *below* to anyplace under the main deck. The *fore-peak* is a small hold or cargo space close behind the bow; the *quarter* is the side of the vessel from midships to stern, the starboard quarter being on the right (facing forward) and the port quarter on the left. *Quarter galleries* are small balconies on the after sides, extending to the stern. The *focsle* (a shortening of *forecastle*) is the crew's compartment and on sailing ships was usually forward of the first mast, and the *poop* is a small raised deck near the stern. *Bulkheads* are the internal walls of a ship, stiffening it and dividing it, in modern vessels, into watertight compartments. *Hatches* cover the openings in the deck through which cargo is loaded and unloaded; they were of wood in the nineteenth century and are of steel today. On three-masted vessels the mast nearest the bow is the *foremast*, the next is the *mainmast*, and the third is the *mizzenmast*.

Usually *frigate* refers to a naval vessel. Here, however, the word designates a merchant ship of a design somewhat old-fashioned in the mid-nineteenth century, having a forecastle and a quarterdeck raised above the main deck.

Rigging designates all the ropes, wires, and chains used to steady the masts and to work the sails. *Standing rigging*, which is relatively immobile once it has been set up, consists of the ropes and wires that support the masts:

From *The Twilight of Sailing Ships*. Copyright © 1965 by Robert Carse. Reprinted by permission of Grosset & Dunlap, Inc.

these are the *shrouds*, running to the sides of the vessel from the masts and strengthening them to withstand forces at right angles to the ship; and the *stays*, leading fore and aft and resisting forces from ahead or astern. *Ratlines* (pronounced "ratluns") are short lengths of tarred rope secured between adjacent shrouds and serving as ladder rungs for sailors to climb up and handle the sails. *Running rigging* includes all the ropes and chains that lead from the yards (heavy round lengths of wood at right angles to the masts from which the sails are hung) and sails to the deck. They enable seamen to raise and lower sails and to adjust them to the wind. *Sheets, braces, clewlines,* and *halyards* are various kinds of running rigging.

A ship is *standing* when it is sailing easily, maintaining a steady course and speed. It is *off the wind* when the wind is on the quarter or astern, the best point of sailing for the old square-riggers (that is, ships with square sails set on yards across the masts—the most common design of deepwater vessels in the eighteenth and nineteenth centuries). The *run* is the distance made good in a particular direction.

A ship's captain is known among seamen as her *master*; the officers under him, in order of importance, are the *first-, second-,* and *third-mates*. The *bosun* (from *boatswain*) is a petty officer responsible for keeping the ship seaworthy, particularly its boats, rigging, sails, paint, and so on. The crew in nineteenth-century ships were divided into two work gangs called *watches*, a *port watch* and a *starboard watch* (these terms had nothing to do in practice with the sides of the vessel the men worked or lived on). The watches alternated working the ship in four-hour stints. The group on duty was called *the watch on deck*; the group off, *the watch below*. (In emergencies all hands were called on deck.) The four-hour time units are also known as *watches*, and each of the six making up the twenty-four-hour day has a name: the *middle watch* is from midnight until 4:00 a.m. An *able-bodied seaman* (or *able seaman*) is an experienced deck hand, able, in the old-fashioned phrase to "hand, reef, and steer" (that is, to work the sails and steer the ship). An *ordinary seaman* is a hand of less experience and ability and receives less pay. Collectively, a ship's personnel are referred to as her *company* or her *people*.

1   Fire at sea aboard a wooden vessel that carried highly inflammable sails and tarred hemp rigging had always been one of the greatest concerns of any shipmaster. With crude and slow, hand-operated pumps, and no other fire-fighting equipment except axes and buckets, a ship might easily be consumed, and many were.   5

2   The loss of the splendidly built teakwood frigate *Cospatrick* stayed in the minds of shipowners on both sides of the Atlantic for a long time

after the event. Her tragic circumstances represented an extreme case, yet showed what could take place at any time aboard another vessel.

3   *Cospatrick* had been built in India in 1856, and was still in first class condition in 1874 when she sailed for Auckland, New Zealand from London with general cargo, 429 emigrants, and a crew of forty-four men. She was under the command of Captain John Elmslie, a veteran master, who had his wife aboard with him. *Cospatrick* had made a good run to the southward and was standing around Cape Horn in fair weather on November 17 when fire was reported.

4   This was at night, in the middle watch. The wind was light, North-west, and on the quarter. "Fire!" had been cried from forward. The watch below came piling out of the focsle in their drawers and shirt tails. They were followed by the emigrants. Smoke plucked by the breeze billowed up from the fore-peak hatch. Captain Elmslie, quickly on deck, realized that the fire was in the fore-peak, and serious. The bosun kept the usual ship's stores there, which under the circumstances formed an almost explosive combination—shellack, varnish, turpentine, paint, oakum and rope.

5   The fire hose was connected at the main pump and led forward. *Cospatrick* was sailed off the wind. When pumping began and the fore part of the vessel was flooded, it seemed that she might be saved. But there was no fire-proof hatch that could be shut, no bulkheads that could contain the fire only to the fore-peak. Flame leaped high and streaked in the darkness along the sheets and running gear of the foremast. That finished the ship; she veered head-up into the wind.

6   The men handling the fire hose were driven aft by the thick, acrid masses of smoke. They were cut off from each other, and as the deck planks groaned and crackled under them with heat, the foresail caught fire. Emigrants panicked, the women screamed. Sailors could no longer hear the orders of their officers. Work was interrupted at the pump.

7   The fire gained furiously below. It sprang into the 'tween-decks, and then aloft through every hatchway, port-hole and ventilator shaft. Flame spiralled the rigging, raced swiftly along the tarred ratlines and shrouds. Then it widened out onto the yards. Sheets, braces, halyards and clewlines were next, and before they burned through and fell in charred tangles, they ignited the sails. The sails burned with wild, incandescent bursts of light; released from the gear, they dropped in great gouts of sparks upon the people crowding the main deck.

8   Discipline was gone. *Cospatrick's* people were seized by panic. Aflame fore and aft, there was no chance of saving her. It had taken a little

over an hour for the fire to make her condition hopeless. Captain Elmslie
gave the order to abandon ship.

9   The starboard quarter boat was lowered away and put in the water.
But then, frantic with fear, emigrants piled aboard her and she was cap-   50
sized. Flames licked forth at the longboat strakes when that craft was lowered from the ship, and she became useless. There were at last only two
boats that got clear of the ship. They were the port and starboard lifeboats,
one with forty-two persons, the other with thirty-nine aboard.

10   The starboard lifeboat was under the command of Henry Mac-   55
Donald, the second mate. He told both boats to lie off until the ship sank.
It was a slow and terrible process. *Cospatrick* took thirty-six hours to go.

11   Flame spread steadily aft towards the remaining people, crowded
together on the poop. The foremast fell blazing, and the main, and the
mizzen. When the mizzen dropped, a number of passengers on the poop   60
were crushed to death. The rest never stopped shrieking. They gestured to
Mr. MacDonald and the others in the boats—pleading for their lives.

12   But nothing could be done. Rescue was impossible with the boats
overcrowded by weak, half-crazed men and women who sat in their night
clothing, without food and water for a day and a night. Both boats lacked   65
masts and sails, and aboard Mr. MacDonald's boat there was only one oar.
He kept the craft at a safe distance from *Cospatrick*.

13   Her quarter galleries gave during the second day, let go with a fierce
gust of heat-compressed air, a belch of smoke and flame. The people left
aboard her jumped. Captain Elmslie was the last. He tossed his wife down   70
into the sea, then leaped after her.

14   They drowned. The lifeboat people, unable to help them, could
only sit and watch as the screaming victims begged for help. *Cospatrick*
burned almost to the waterline before she sank. When she slipped beneath
the waves, Mr. MacDonald gave the order, and slowly the boats moved away   75
on the course he had reckoned.

15   The boats stayed together until the night of November 21, when
the weather became heavy. MacDonald's survived. The other boat was never
again seen. MacDonald rigged a sea-anchor with the painter and the oar,
but lost it. Then, two days later, with pieces of wood ripped from the thwarts   80
and floorboards, a second sea-anchor was made.

16   It held, eased the strain on the boat, and kept her up to the wind,
although she was half-filled with water. During the night of November 26,
just before daylight, a ship passed within fifty yards of them. They cried out
with all their strength, but it was not enough, and they were not heard.   85

17   This was very hard for the survivors to take. Mr. MacDonald later testified at the inquiry that by November 27 "there were but five left—two able seamen, one ordinary, myself and one passenger. The passenger was out of his mind. All had drunk salt water. We were all dozing when the madman bit my foot and I woke up. We then saw a ship bearing down on us. She 90 proved to be the *British Sceptre*, from Calcutta to Dundee. We were then taken on board and treated very kindly. I got very bad on board of her. I was very nigh at death's door. We were not recovered when we got to St. Helena."

18   While aboard *British Sceptre*, both the ordinary seaman and the 95 passenger died. Mr. MacDonald and the two able-bodied sailors were the sole survivors out of the company of 473 persons which had left London in *Cospatrick*.

QUESTIONS

READER AND PURPOSE

1. In one or two sentences explain what you think Carse is attempting to do in this passage. Is he successful? Why or why not?

2. Does Carse assume that his readers are familiar with the sea and ships?

ORGANIZATIONS

3. In actuality an event such as a fire at sea does not divide neatly into acts and scenes like a play. The writer must impose an organization upon the continuous happening he describes and analyze it into parts. Paragraphs 1 and 2 compose the first part of Carse's narrative. What is their function?

4. The remaining sixteen paragraphs can be divided into three groups. At what points? Give a title to each section.

5. Events exist in time, and while the flow of time is more significant in some stories than in others, the writer of any narrative must establish temporal reference points. Does Carse? Can you make an outline fixing the dates and times of various events in his narrative?

6. Why does Carse make number 5 a separate paragraph? Numbers 6 and 7?

7. What word links paragraph 4 to 3? Paragraph 12 to 11? 14 to 13? 16 to 15? 17 to 16? These links are quick and light. Are they adequate for the writer's purpose?

SENTENCES

8. There is a change in sentence style after the third paragraph. Paragraph 1 has 51 words in two sentences, an average of 25.5 words per sentence. The

averages in paragraphs 2 and 3 are about the same: 23.5 and 27.3. In the fourth paragraph, however, the average drops to 11.5, even with the long final sentence; and in the eighth to 8.8. Why does Carse write shorter, simpler sentences in these places? What generalization might you make about the value of such a style in narrative?

9. What is the average number of words in the sentences of paragraph 6? Do these sentences sound too much the same, or are they varied enough to avoid monotony? If you think they are, explain generally how the variations are achieved.

10. Do these revisions improve Carse's sentences? Why or why not?

(a) *Revision:* Flame spiralled all through the rigging, and then it raced swiftly along the tarred ratlines and the shrouds.
Carse: "Flame spiralled the rigging, raced swiftly along the tarred ratlines and shrouds." (38-39)

(b) *Revision:* Because the ship was aflame fore and aft, there was no chance of saving her.
Carse: "Aflame fore and aft, there was no chance of saving her." (46) ·

(c) *Revision:* Flame spread steadily aft towards the remaining people, who were crowded together on the poop.
Carse: "Flame spread steadily aft towards the remaining people, crowded together on the poop." (58-59)

11. The sentence in lines 84-85 is an example of a tricolon *: one sentence composed of three independent clauses of roughly equal length and construction. Here the tricolon varies the simple style, linking three brief statements instead of expressing them separately. It also creates a pleasing rhythm by repeating the same pattern three times. On what word does the major emphasis come in each clause?

DICTION

12. Look up: *emigrants* (12), *oakum* (24), *acrid* (32), *incandescent* (42), *capsized* (50), *strakes* (51), *painter* (79), *thwarts* (80), *nigh* (93).

13. Why are these alternates less effective than Carse's words: *unfortunate* for *tragic* (8), *shouting* for *shrieking* (61), *burst* for *belch* (69)?

14. In paragraph 6 which words appeal to our sense of hearing?

15. In paragraph 7 *sprang, spiralled, raced, widened* all trace the progress of the fire. Are they good verbs for this purpose? Why or why not? What other words in this paragraph appeal to our vision?

POINTS TO LEARN

1. Narrative renders an event in words, showing what happened, when and where and how or why.

2. Vivid active verbs create a sense of movement, vital to good narrative.

3. Temporal reference points are important in narrative, enabling readers to trace the flow of events.

4. Short simple * sentences beginning with the subject and verb and without interruption express dramatic action.

5. Technical diction, while it makes demands upon the reader, is precise and economic.

SUGGESTIONS FOR WRITING

In three or four paragraphs (400-500 words) describe a dramatic event you have witnessed: a fire, an automobile accident, a fight, or a riot. Think carefully about the order of events and organize your narrative so that readers can grasp the pattern and time-flow. Try, however, to do this subtly; avoid such mechanical forumlae as "The first thing that happened was . . . The second thing was . . ."

IMPROVING YOUR STYLE

1. In your narrative use as many short strong sentences as you can to render the action. But vary this style occasionally so that it does not sound like a third-grade reader.

2. Include at least one tricolon.*

3. Experiment with verbs, choosing ones that convey a dramatic movement.

From Shooting an Elephant

George Orwell (pseudonym of Eric Blair, 1903-50) was a British novelist best known for his political satire *Animal Farm* (1945) and the grim futuristic novel *1984* (1949), depicting a totalitarian society in which people have surrendered freedom, individualism, and even privacy for the dubious security provided by a "Big-Brother" police state. In his youth Orwell served as a security officer in the British colony of Burma. The experience left him with an abiding distaste for colonialism, a feeling he makes clear in several of his essays. In the one from which the following paragraphs come he recounts the disagreeable duty of having to destroy a poor man's working elephant, which had gone on a rampage. At the moment when he shoots the animal—ironically it had by that time returned to sanity—a crowd of native villagers have gathered to watch the fun.

1   The crowd grew very still, and a deep, low, happy sigh, as of people who see the theatre curtain go up at last, breathed from innumerable throats. They were going to have their bit of fun after all. The rifle was a beautiful German thing with cross-hair sights. I did not then know that in shooting an elephant one would shoot to cut an imaginary bar running from ear-hole to   5 ear-hole. I ought, therefore, as the elephant was sideways on, to have aimed straight at his ear-hole; actually I aimed several inches in front of this, thinking the brain would be further forward.

2   When I pulled the trigger I did not hear the bang or feel the kick— one never does when a shot goes home—but I heard the devilish roar of glee   10 that went up from the crowd. In that instant, in too short a time, one would have thought, even for the bullet to get there, a mysterious, terrible change had come over the elephant. He neither stirred nor fell, but every line of

his body had altered. He looked suddenly stricken, shrunken, immensely old, as though the frightful impact of the bullet had paralysed him without 15 knocking him down. At last, after what seemed a long time—it might have been five seconds, I dare say—he sagged flabbily to his knees. His mouth slobbered. An enormous senility seemed to have settled upon him. One could have imagined him thousands of years old. I fired again into the same spot. At the second shot he did not collapse but climbed with desperate 20 slowness to his feet and stood weakly upright, with legs sagging and head drooping. I fired a third time. That was the shot that did it for him. You could see the agony of it jolt his whole body and knock the last remnant of strength from his legs. But in falling he seemed for a moment to rise, for as his hind legs collapsed beneath him he seemed to tower upward like a 25 huge rock toppling, his trunk reaching skywards like a tree. He trumpeted, for the first and only time. And then down he came, his belly towards me, with a crash that seemed to shake the ground even where I lay.

QUESTIONS

READER AND PURPOSE

1. These paragraphs are the climax of Orwell's essay, the actual death of the elephant. Which phrase best describes his tone *: objective and matter-of-fact, subjective and emotional, callous and unfeeling?
2. Is Orwell's point of view * personal or impersonal? Orwell functions in two roles—as a participant in the action and as an observer-commentator. Which role predominates in this passage?
3. Does he allow his feelings to enter into the narrative? If so, in which words?
4. What can you infer about Orwell's attitude toward the natives?

ORGANIZATION

5. Why does Orwell divide this passage into two paragraphs?
6. There are three participants in the story: the elephant, the crowd of Burmese natives, and Orwell himself. The elephant is the center of interest and would loom largest in any drawing depicting the scene. Where is Orwell in relation to the animal? Where, presumably, is the crowd in relation to Orwell?
7. Is there a topic sentence in the first paragraph? In the second? If so, point them out. If not, is the absence a fault? (Remember that the passage is part of a connected narrative.) Could you easily supply sentences expressing the general topic?
8. Paragraph 2 is organized around three nodes or centers. What are they?

9. In the second sentence of this paragraph what phrase sets up the details that follow?

10. Which words in paragraph 2 indicate the intervals of time through which the action occurs?

SENTENCES

11. The final sentence of paragraph 1 ends with a participial * phrase ("thinking the brain would be further forward"). How is the idea expressed in this phrase logically related to the main point?

12. Identify the nominative absolute * in the sentence in lines 24-26. How does it logically connect to the principal clause?

13. In lines 9-10 and again in lines 16 and 17 Orwell uses dashes. Are the clauses enclosed by these dashes grammatical parts of the sentences in which they occur, or are they simply independent statements stuck into the middle of those sentences? In each passage, how is the idea expressed in the intruding statement related to the main thought of the enclosing sentence? Could the dashes be replaced by commas without confusion? By parentheses?

14. Would it be possible to combine the four short sentences in lines 17-20 into one longer, more complicated statement? Even if it could be done, are the sentences better as they stand?

15. In contrast, the long sentence in lines 24-26 might be broken into several shorter ones; for example:

> But in falling he seemed for a moment to rise. For as his hind legs collapsed beneath him he seemed to tower upward. It was like a huge rock toppling. His trunk reached skywards like a tree.

Does this version clarify the experience or obscure it?

16. After comparing these two passages, what generalization might you make about when it is better to combine several details of an action or scene into one long sentence, and when to express them separately?

17. Each of these revisions changes the sense or emphasis or rhythm of Orwell's sentence for the worse. Explain how.

    (a) *Revision:* He neither stirred nor did he fall . . .
    Orwell: "He neither stirred nor fell . . ." (13)

    (b) *Revision:* A mysterious, terrible change had come over the elephant in that instant, in too short a time, one would have thought, even for the bullet to get there.
    Orwell: "In that instant, in too short a time, one would have thought, even for the bullet to get there, a mysterious, a terrible change had come over the elephant." (11-13)

DICTION

18. Look up: *impact* (15), *flabbily* (17), *senility* (18), *remnant* (23).

19. Explain the meaning of each of these phrases: *cross-hair sights* (4), *sideways on* (6), *goes home* (10).

20. What logical relationship is signaled by *for* (24)?

21. Why are these alternates poorer than Orwell's words: *excitement* for *glee* (10), *watered* for *slobbered* (18), *great* for *desperate* (20), *pain* for *agony* (23), *in* for *jolt* (23), *falling* for *toppling* (26)?

22. Study the sentence in lines 24-26. Are you able to visualize the event as in a slow-motion film? The description is paradoxical in that it involves movement both downward and upward. Which words convey the former? Which the latter? Identify the two similes* in this sentence. Do they help you see the action? Do they reveal anything about the writer's feelings? Is there a metaphor * anywhere in the passage?

POINTS TO LEARN

1. The focus of a narrative or description belongs upon the principal figure.

2. Details of a scene or action are often introduced by a general statement.

3. Participial phrases are an easy way of indicating cause or reason.

4. In narrative, short simple* sentences and longer complicated ones may be equally effective. It depends upon whether the ideas are relatively distinct or part of one continuous event.

SUGGESTIONS FOR WRITING

In a single paragraph of about 200 words narrate an episode in which you are an actor-observer but in which the focus is on someone else. It probably won't be anything as unusual and dramatic as shooting an elephant, but simpler incidents will do, such as telling momentous news to a friend or playing a practical joke. Think carefully about the tone you wish to create. Use a personal point of view and react to what is happening to the other person and to his or her responses.

IMPROVING YOUR STYLE

In your paragraph include:

1. A participial phrase to explain a cause or reason.

2. At least one intrusive statement enclosed by dashes within another sentence.

3. A nominative absolute.

4. One or two similes that make the action more dramatic visually and also express your feelings.

The Death of Captain Waskow

Ernie Pyle (1900-45) was one of the best known correspondents of World War II. He wrote more about men than about issues and was admired not only by civilians but by soldiers, whose hardships and dangers he shared. He was killed, in fact, in the battle for Okinawa in 1945, near the end of the war. This account of the death of an American officer during the fighting in Italy is from *Brave Men*, a collection of Pyle's reports published in 1944. As you read it ask yourselves what meaning Pyle sees in the episode, for it is to him more than an incident of war, to be reported and forgotten. Ask, too, how he selects and arranges details to make that meaning clear.

1   In this war I have known a lot of officers who were loved and re-spected by the soldiers under them. But never have I crossed the trail of any man as beloved as Captain Henry T. Waskow, of Belton, Texas.

2   Captain Waskow was a company commander in the Thirty-sixth Division. He had led his company since long before it left the States. He was very young, only in his middle twenties, but he carried in him a sincerity and a gentleness that made people want to be guided by him.

3   "After my father, he came next," a sergeant told me.

4   "He always looked after us," a soldier said. "He'd go to bat for us every time."

5   "I've never knowed him to do anything unfair," another said.

6   I was at the foot of the mule trail the night they brought Captain Waskow down. The moon was nearly full, and you could see far up the trail, and even partway across the valley below.

7   Dead men had been coming down the mountain all evening, lashed onto the backs of mules. They came lying belly-down across the wooden pack-saddles, their heads hanging down on one side, their stiffened legs

sticking out awkwardly from the other, bobbing up and down as the mules walked.

8   The Italian mule skinners were afraid to walk beside dead men, so 20 Americans had to lead the mules down that night. Even the Americans were reluctant to unlash and lift off the bodies when they got to the bottom, so an officer had to do it himself and ask others to help.

9   I don't know who that first one was. You feel small in the presence of dead men, and you don't ask silly questions. 25

10   They slid him down from the mule, and stood him on his feet for a moment. In the half-light he might have been merely a sick man standing there leaning on the others. Then they laid him on the ground in the shadow of the low stone wall beside the road. We left him there beside the road, that first one, and we all went back into the cowshed and sat on water cans 30 or lay on the straw, waiting for the next batch of mules.

11   Somebody said the dead soldier had been dead for four days, and then nobody said anything more about it. We talked soldier talk for an hour or more; the dead man lay all alone, outside in the shadow of the wall.

12   Then a soldier came into the cowshed and said there were some more 35 bodies outside. We went out into the road. Four mules stood there in the moonlight, in the road where the trail came down off the mountain. The soldiers who led them stood there waiting.

13   "This one is Captain Waskow," one of them said quietly.

14   Two men unlashed his body from the mule and lifted it off and 40 laid it in the shadow beside the stone wall. Other men took the other bodies off. Finally, there were five lying end to end in a long row. You don't cover up dead men in the combat zones. They just lie there in the shadows until somebody comes after them.

15   The unburdened mules moved off to their olive grove. The men 45 in the road seemed reluctant to leave. They stood around, and gradually I could sense them moving, one by one, close to Captain Waskow's body. Not so much to look, I think, as to say something in finality to him, and to themselves. I stood close by and I could hear.

16   One soldier came and looked down, and he said out loud, "God 50 damn it!"

17   That's all he said, and then he walked away.

18   Another one came, and he said, "God damn it to hell anyway!" He looked down for a few last moments and then turned and left.

19   Another man came. I think he was an officer. It was hard to tell 55 officers from men in the lim light, for everybody was bearded and grimy.

The man looked down into the dead captain's face and then spoke directly to him, as though he were alive, "I'm sorry, old man."

20   Then a soldier came and stood beside the officer and bent over, and he too spoke to his dead captain, not in a whisper but awfully tenderly, 60 and he said, "I sure am sorry, sir."

21   Then the first man squatted down, and he reached down and took the captain's hand, and he sat there for a full five minutes holding the dead hand in his own and looking intently into the dead face. And he never uttered a sound all the time he sat there.   65

22   Finally he put the hand down. He reached over and gently straightened the points of the captain's shirt collar, and then he sort of rearranged the tattered edges of the uniform around the wound, and then he got up and walked away down the road in the moonlight, all alone.

QUESTIONS

READER AND PURPOSE

1. Is Pyle's point of view * personal or impersonal? Is he more an observer of or a participant in the episode he narrates?

2. In the first two paragraphs Pyle explicitly states his attitude toward the Captain. Is that attitude borne out by what he shows us?

3. Pyle does not literally express any feelings about the soldiers. Yet what does he imply about them? Does he admire or dislike them? How does their attitude toward the Captain differ from that toward the other dead?

4. One test of a good narrative is that it creates the illusion of "being there," rendering scene and action so that the reader experiences the event. Another is that the meaning is inside, not outside, that is, implied in scene and action and not stuck on like a label in an Aesopian fable. Judging it by those tests, do you think Pyle's narrative is good? Explain.

5. On one level this story is a tribute to an uncommon soldier. On a less obvious level it is about the common soldiers. Pyle suggests this when he observes that the men addressing the dead Captain were saying "something in finality to him and to themselves" (48-49). What were they saying to themselves?

ORGANIZATION

6. Paragraphs 1-5 constitute the beginning of the narrative. What is established here?

7. How do paragraphs 3, 4, and 5 relate to paragraphs 1 and 2?

8. Can paragraphs 6-22 be divided into several sections? If so, at what point or points?

9. Does this narrative close well? Why or why not?

SENTENCES

10. Some of Pyle's sentences are short and simple *: "Another man came. I think he was an officer" (55). Find several more examples of this type.

11. Others are longer. Some of these use parallelism *:

> Two men unlashed his body from the mule and lifted it off and laid it in the shadow beside the stone wall. (40-41)

What are the parallel elements in this sentence? Is it still technically simple? Indicate two other cases of parallelism.

12. Others of the longer sentences employ freight-train coordination *, linking several independent clauses * by conjunctions, usually *and:*

> Then a soldier came and stood beside the officer, and he spoke to his dead captain, not in a whisper but awfully tenderly, and he said, "I sure am sorry, sir." (59-61)

Read this sentence aloud. How does it sound—dull? impressive? memorable? simple-minded? Does it remind you of anything you may have heard or read? Find one or two other sentences of this kind in Pyle's selection.

13. Occasionally Pyle uses participial * phrases. Point out one or two instances. In the sentence in lines 16-19 identify the nominative absolutes *. How do the details they contain relate to the main idea of the sentence?

14. All in all, Pyle's sentence style depends upon simple statements, either standing alone or linked by *and.* Does this style more suggest a man talking or a man writing? Does it tend to hide the presence of the narrator, or to remind us constantly of his mind at work—ordering, interpreting, judging? Do you think the style is, or is not, suited to Pyle's subject and purpose?

DICTION

15. Look up: *lashed* (15), *bobbing* (18), *skinners* (20), *small* (24), *finality* (48), *grimy* (56).

16. In paragraph 19 how does Pyle use diction to distinguish the officer?

17. Together the *moonlight* and the *road* constitute a motif, that is, a recurrent image *. Find the places where it occurs. Neither the road nor the moonlight is a symbol *; they do not stand for anything outside themselves. But they are a loaded image, carrying a weight of feelings and values to which a sensitive reader responds, even if unconsciously. What are some of the emotions and thoughts the image arouses in you?

18. Poised against the moonlight and road is another repeated image. What is it? What feelings does it suggest?

19. It might be argued that if Pyle wants us to understand the thoughts and emotions implied by such images he would do better to come right out and explain the ideas and feelings directly. The same objection might be made concerning the point raised in questions 4 and 5. What answer could you make to such a complaint?

20. How would Pyle's tone be altered by these substitutions: *a great many* for *a lot of* (1), *consequently* for *so* (20), *one* for *you* (25 and elsewhere), *simply* for *just* (43), *that is* for *that's* (52), *very* for *awfully* (60), *slightly* for *sort of* (67)?

21. On the whole is Pyle's diction commonplace or literary—that of a man talking or a man writing? How does it compare with his sentence style in this regard?

POINTS TO LEARN

1. Good narrative re-creates experience and gives it meaning.
2. The meaning of narrative is better implied than stated.
3. Sentence style and diction define the role of the narrator and make his presence more felt, or less.

SUGGESTIONS FOR WRITING

In several paragraphs totaling about 600 words render an episode involving loss and recognition—something either that happened to you or that you witnessed. Use a relatively simple sentence style and diction. Think about what meaning you want readers to get from your narrative, but don't tell them. Let scene and action speak for themselves.

IMPROVING YOUR STYLE

1. In your narrative compose several sentences in the freight-train * style.
2. Use parallel verbs in two or three sentences, and participial phrases in two or three others.
3. Develop a motif which suggests some of the feelings and values important to the story you are telling.

The Unicorn in the Garden

James Thurber (1894-1961) was one of the finest humorists and satirists of our time. Mostly he wrote loose personal essays and short stories, but he also collaborated with Elliot Nugent on a successful stage play, *The Male Animal* (1940) and was a notable cartoonist. He wrote too many books to list here; a good introduction to his work is *The Thurber Carnival*, an anthology published in 1945. The following piece is from *Fables for Our Time* (1940). A fable is, strictly speaking, a short tale in which birds or animals talk and act like human beings and which illustrates a simple moral truth, often literally stated in a closing tag or "moral." More loosely, the term *fable* applies to any short, illustrative tale even if the characters are human, as they are here. But even then the genre allows the use of fabulous elements, such as the unicorn. "The Unicorn in the Garden" is about one of Thurber's most constant themes: the struggle between men and women for dominance. It is funny, but below the humor—as so often in Thurber—the matter is serious.

1   Once upon a sunny morning a man who sat in a breakfast nook looked up from his scrambled eggs to see a white unicorn with a gold horn quietly cropping the roses in the garden. The man went up to the bedroom where his wife was still asleep and woke her. "There's a unicorn in the garden," he said. "Eating roses." She opened one unfriendly eye and looked 5 at him. "The unicorn is a mythical beast," she said, and turned her back on him. The man walked slowly downstairs and out into the garden. The unicorn was still there; he was now browsing among the tulips. "Here, unicorn," said the man, and he pulled up a lily and gave it to him. The unicorn ate it gravely. With a high heart, because there was a unicorn in his garden, 10 the man went upstairs and roused his wife again. "The unicorn," he said, "ate a lily." His wife sat up in bed and looked at him, coldly. "You are a

booby," she said, "and I am going to have you put in the booby-hatch." The
man, who had never liked the words "booby" and "booby-hatch," and who
liked them even less on a shining morning when there was a unicorn in the   15
garden, thought for a moment. "We'll see about that," he said. He walked
over to the door. "He has a golden horn in the middle of his forehead,"
he told her. Then he went back to the garden to watch the unicorn; but the
unicorn had gone away. The man sat down among the roses and went to
sleep.   20

2   As soon as the husband had gone out of the house, the wife got up
and dressed as fast as she could. She was very excited and there was a gloat
in her eye. She telephoned the police and she telephoned a psychiatrist; she
told them to hurry to her house and bring a strait-jacket. When the police
and the psychiatrist arrived they sat down in chairs and looked at her, with   25
great interest. "My husband," she said, "saw a unicorn this morning." The
police looked at the psychiatrist and the psychiatrist looked at the police.
"He told me it ate a lily," she said. The psychiatrist looked at the police and
the police looked at the psychiatrist. "He told me it had a golden horn
in the middle of its forehead," she said. At a solemn signal from the psy-   30
chiatrist, the police leaped from their chairs and seized the wife. They had
a hard time subduing her, for she put up a terrific struggle, but they finally
subdued her. Just as they got her into the strait-jacket, the husband came
back into the house.

3   "Did you tell your wife you saw a unicorn?" asked the police. "Of   35
course not," said the husband. "The unicorn is a mythical beast." "That's
all I wanted to know," said the psychiatrist. "Take her away. I'm sorry, sir,
but your wife is as crazy as a jay bird." So they took her away, cursing and
screaming, and shut her up in an institution. The husband lived happily
ever after.   40

4   *Moral: Don't count your boobies until they are hatched.*

QUESTIONS

READER AND PURPOSE

1. The essential elements of narrative are characters and action. Such things as
setting, symbols*, and imagery* may be made more, or less, important, but ultimately a story stands or falls on action and character. This important fact is
illustrated by Thurber's brief, but perhaps not-so-simple, fable. Consider first his
treatment of character. Deftly and quickly he creates the hero and the villain,
but he does not hang signs around their necks; he renders his characters dra-

matically, that is, in terms of what they say and do. We must infer what kind of people these are; the author does not tell us explicitly. The wife is plainly despicable. What does she do that makes her so? Although the husband is the hero in the sense of being the "good guy," he is no Achilles. Thurber's husbands are not cast in the mold of the Greek hero; they are mild little men—patient, gentle, long-suffering. Do you think that Thurber intends us to like this husband? Thurber's mild little men, however, often reveal another trait: they will be pushed just so far and then they turn upon their domineering wives and get even. At what point does this husband begin to turn?

2. Why do you suppose it is a unicorn that the man sees instead of, say, a pink elephant? Are we supposed to accept the unicorn of the story as real? It is clear that the wife, the police, and the psychiatrist do not. But has Thurber given us any reason to doubt that the unicorn the man sees is a real unicorn in a real garden, really browsing among the tulips and eating a lily? (Read the opening sentence carefully if you are unsure about how to answer this question.)

3. Assuming that he intends us to generalize from his couple, what is Thurber suggesting about marriage? He is poking fun at other things than lazy, vindictive wives. Do the psychiatrist and the police arouse our admiration? Are they any less literal-minded than the wife?

4. The "moral," with its pun upon *hatched*, suggests that sanity and insanity are less easy to distinguish than many people suppose. Has a rough sort of justice prevailed in this story—has the right booby been hatched?

5. There is more to the theme of "The Unicorn in the Garden," however, than is contained in its closing moral. In your own words discuss everything you think this story implies about men and women and the values by which they live.

ORGANIZATION

6. In the first paragraph the dramatic focus is upon which character? Does the focus shift in the second paragraph? If you think that it does, has Thurber provided an adequate transition?

7. A story is composed of bits of action called episodes, which are dramatically rendered in scenes. A scene is a unit of action defined by time, place, and characters; when any of these elements changes significantly a new scene begins. Thus in paragraph 1 the first scene depicts the man in the nook eating his breakfast and seeing the unicorn. When he goes upstairs to his wife's bedroom we have scene 2. This paragraph consists of five such scenes; identify the remaining three. Make a similar scenic analysis of paragraphs 2 and 3.

8. In a well-constructed story each scene must be informative; that is, it must relate something new about the characters, prepare for future action, clarify the theme in some way, or do all of these. What new bits of information are conveyed by each scene in paragraph 1?

9. In many stories the action is of the special kind called plot. Briefly, a plot

has these characteristics: (1) at least one character is working toward a specific goal; (2) this effort brings him into conflict with one or more of the other characters; (3) the conflict is ultimately resolved; (4) only episodes that bear upon either the goal or the conflict are included; and (5) all episodes are tied together in a tight chain of cause and effect. Show that the action of Thurber's story may properly be called a plot. In a well-made plot the action is brought to a logically satisfactory conclusion. Do you feel that such is the case here?

10. Plots begin with what we call a datum—an initial event, often implying a question or problem, out of which the goal and the conflict develop. What is the datum in Thurber's tale? Even more important is the climax. This is the scene in which the conflict is finally resolved; in a cowboy movie, for instance, the climax is the shoot-out between the white hat and the black. Which scene in Thurber's story constitutes the climax? For one character or another the climax of a plot usually involves a reversal—the black hat, for example, expects to win, not to be shot down in the dust. What is the reversal in "The Unicorn in the Garden"?

11. The plot generally carries an important part of the meaning of a story. Often in tragic drama, for instance, the plot demonstrates that the hero's destruction is the logically necessary consequence of a moral lapse; had Macbeth not murdered Duncan, he would not in turn have been killed by Macduff. What meaning is conveyed by Thurber's plot? There is an important difference, however, between a play like *Macbeth* and a fable. *Macbeth* presumably reflects the real world, however it may simplify that world; what happens to Macbeth is a sign of what will happen to similar men in real life. In fables and fairy tales, on the other hand, the point may be that the universe of the story does *not* reflect the world as we experience it. Do you think that such is the case in "The Unicorn in the Garden"?

12. The final element in a plot is often called the denouement. It logically follows the climax, wrapping up any loose threads and bringing the story to a close. What is the denouement of Thurber's fable?

SENTENCES

13. A narrative writer must solve the problem of fitting the bits and pieces of his action into appropriate compositional units. In a novel such units would include groups of paragraphs, chapters, and even whole books. Thurber's units, however, are paragraphs and sentences. Study the sentence plan of the first paragraph and be able to discuss whether or not Thurber has used his sentences effectively to analyze the action.

14. Comment upon these revisions of Thurber's sentences:

(a) *Revision:* His wife sat up in bed and coldly looked at him.
   Thurber: "His wife sat up in bed and looked at him, coldly." (12)

(b) *Revision:* The wife got up and dressed as fast as she could, as soon as the husband had gone out of the house.
Thurber: "As soon as the husband had gone out of the house, the wife got up and dressed as fast as she could." (21-22)

DICTION
15. Look up: *unicorn* (2), *cropping* (3), *mythical* (6).
16. In line 22 Thurber writes of the wife "that there was a gloat in her eye." *Gleam* would be more idiomatic here, but *gloat* is better. Why? And why is *shining* better in line 15 than *bright* would be?
17. What words in the first paragraph establish the wife's reaction to her husband? The husband's reaction to his wife? What words characterize the unicorn? Is it a nice unicorn? Is there any significance in the fact that the setting is a "*sunny* morning"?

POINTS TO LEARN
1. Character and action are the essence of narrative.
2. The action of a story must be organized and it must be presented as a series of scenes.
3. Plot is a common way of organizing action. A plot begins with a datum, develops a conflict, which it resolves in the climax, and concludes with a denouement.
4. Narrative action, whether or not it is plotted, must be fitted into compositional units appropriate to the length of the story; these units include clauses, sentences, sentence groups, paragraphs, paragraph groups, and chapters.

SUGGESTIONS FOR WRITING
It is far easier to analyze a fable than to write one. Indeed, because they must be stripped down to the essentials of narrative action, fables are much more difficult to write well than you may think. Listed below are several suggestions, but you should feel free to invent your own situation if none of these appeals. Before you begin to write decide in your own mind what your theme is, and as you write control your characters and action to demonstrate that theme. Do not, however, deliver the message in person. Simply tell the story and let your reader infer its point for himself.

> The alligator in the phone booth
> The horse in the bathtub
> The yellow pussy cat who thought he was boss
> The Great Dane who felt superior

IMPROVING YOUR STYLE

Before you begin to write, make:

1. A list of the characters and a synopsis of the plot.
2. A rough outline of the scenes through which the plot will develop. Indicate briefly what you want to accomplish in each scene.

Short Trip

Robert Lipsyte is a sports reporter and writer. His books include *The Mascu-line Mystique* (1966), *Assignment Sports* (1970), and *Sports World: An American Dreamland* (1975). The following piece appeared in *The New York Times* and is about the habitués of race tracks (in this case Aqueduct in New York). Unlike Thurber's fable in the preceding selection, this is not a story imagined to illustrate a moral, but rather a report about real people and events. Yet the difference is less important than it might seem. For while Lipsyte does not invent his characters, scenes, and action, he does select, arrange, and describe them. And like Thurber he does so for a purpose; he sees a meaning in what is going on. Thus whether they begin from the actual or from an imagined world, writers of narrative must look for and reveal the significance of the events they describe.

1   The fare to the Aqueduct Race Track is 75 cents on the special sub-way train from Times Square. This includes a send-off: the narrow escalator down to the platform ends beneath the words Good Luck printed on the grimy-gold arch of a huge wooden horseshoe. The subway car is as free of talk as the reading room of a library, and, in fact, all the travelers are read- 5 ing: The Morning Telegraph, The Daily News, the latest bulletin from Clocker Lawton. They are very ordinary-looking men and a few women, a bit older than most people these days.

2   It hardly seems 30 minutes before the train bursts out of the black hole and onto an elevated track that winds above the two-family houses and 10 cemetery fields of Queens. It is nearing mid-day, in the butt-end of another year, and the travelers blink briefly in the flat, hard sunlight. They are standing long before the train skids to a stop. They run down the ramp to-ward the $2 grandstand entrances, then on to daily-double windows five minutes away from closing. 15

3   Before the race of the day, at any track, anywhere, there is a sense
of happening, of a corner that might be turned, a door that might open.
There is almost a merry ring to the parimutuel machines punching out fresh
tickets to everywhere, and the players move out smartly, clapping down the
wooden seats of chairs, briskly stepping onto the pebbled concrete areas   20
that bear the remarkable signs, "No Chairs Permitted on Lawn." Seconds
after noon, the first race starts. It lasts little more than a minute, just long
enough to hold your breath, to scream, or fall to your knees against a metal
fence and pray, "Angel, Angel, Angel."

4   But on this day, Angel Cordero, the hot young jockey, finishes   25
fourth in the first race, and the praying man collapses on the fence like a
steer caught on barbed wire. Another man smiles coldly as he tears up tickets, and says: "Dropping down so fast like that, you mean to tell me he
couldn't stay in the money? Sure. Haw."

5   It is suddenly quiet again, and the day is no longer fresh and new,   30
the day is tired and old and familiar. An old, hooded man from Allied
Maintenance moves over the asphalt picking up torn tickets with a nail-
tipped stick, tapping like a blind man among the empty wastebaskets. Men
watch him to see if he is turning over the tickets looking for a winner
thrown away by mistake. He is not.   35

6   The race track settles into a predictable rhythm. In the half hour
or so between races, men study their charts, straddling green benches or
bent over stew and stale coffee in the drab cafeteria or hunkered down beneath the hot-air ceiling vent in a cavernous men's room, the warmest spot
at Aqueduct. As the minutes move toward post time, they gather beneath   40
the approximate odds board. They interpret the flickering numbers—smart
money moving, perhaps the making of a coup. At the last moment, they
bet, then rush out on the stone lawn for the race. A minute later they are
straggling back, chanting the old litany, "I woulda . . . . coulda . . . .
shoulda . . . ."   45

7   There are ebbs and flows throughout the day. People leave, others
come, the machines jangle on. There is a great deal of shuffling in the
grandstand area, and little loud talk. People move away from strangers.
When men speak of horses, they use numbers, not names, and when they
talk of jockeys, they frequently curse. It was, they whisper, an "election";   50
the jockeys decided last night who would win.

8   The day ends pale and chilly a few minutes before 4 P.M. and the
fans troop out to the subway station. There is no special train returning:
the city will get you out fast enough, but you can find your own way home.

9   Horseplayers are smart, and they all wait in the enclosed area near   55
the change booths, ready to bolt through the turnstiles onto the outdoor
platform when the train comes, and not a moment sooner. They stamp
their feet, muttering, "Woulda . . . . coulda . . . . shoulda." The losers
rail against crooked jocks, gutless horses, callous owners, the ugly track, the
greedy state that takes 10 cents of each dollar bet.   60
10   Then they bolt through the turnstiles, quick and practiced, tokens
in and spin out upon the platform. But there is no train yet, they all followed a fool, and now they curse him for five minutes in the cold until an
old shuddering train lumbers in to carry them away.

QUESTIONS

READER AND PURPOSE

1. The job of a reporter is to tell us "how it is." This requires him to do more
than simply chronicle facts; he must reveal their meaning. To be more exact,
he must give them meaning, for in themselves facts have no significance; they
acquire it only when they are observed and organized by a guiding intelligence.
What do you think is the meaning of "Short Trip"? "How is it" with Aqueduct Race Track and the people who patronize it?

2. Unlike that by James Thurber, Lipsyte's narrative is not focused upon
specific individuals. Instead of a single central character he has a number of
them who make up a composite type—"The Horseplayer." What are the characteristics of the Horseplayer? What is Lipsyte's attitude toward him? Who,
or what, constitutes the antagonist, the force opposing those who bet the
horses?

ORGANIZATION

3. This narrative has no plot in the usual sense. But the action is organized.
One might say that it is like a three-act play, with paragraphs 1-2 making up the
first act, paragraphs 3-7 the second, and 8-10 the third. Do you think this is a
reasonable analysis? Why or why not? Give each a title.

4. Each of the acts contains several scenes. Identify those in Act I. In Acts II
and III.

5. Lipsyte's organization is essentially chronological. Underline all the words
that indicate temporal progression. Paragraph 6 is an especially good example of
chronological structure. What words in the first sentence of this paragraph set
up the topic? Point out one or two other paragraphs in this selection in which
the opening sentences contain key words or phrases. Do they usually come toward the end of the sentence?

6. A good story conveys a feeling of completeness. It must have a beginning, a middle which evolves naturally from the beginning, and an ending which is the logical conclusion of all that has gone before. Does Lipsyte's story possess this sense of a completed form? He closes his narrative by the technique we call completing the circle, that is, by repeating in the ending something he mentioned in the beginning. How does Lipsyte complete his circle?

SENTENCES

7. Can you see a reason for the colon in line 2 instead of a semicolon?

8. The sentence in lines 7-8 concludes with the modifying construction "a bit older than most people these days." If you can, explain the syntax of this construction. The sentence might have read: "They are very ordinary-looking men and a few women, who are a bit older than most people these days." What is the advantage of handling it as Lipsyte has done? Does his sentence seem more, or less, formal than the one using *who are*? This kind of modifier is very useful; learn to employ it in your own sentences.

9. Identify the parallel * elements in the sentence in lines 16-17. Find one or two others of Lipsyte's sentences that effectively use parallelism.

10. Joining together the successive items in a series with *and* is called polysyndeton *, as in the clause in line 31: ". . . the day is tired and old and familiar." What advantages does polysyndeton have over the usual way of treating a series (e.g. ". . . the day is tired, old, and familiar")?

11. Locate two or three effective short sentences in these paragraphs and be prepared to discuss why you think them effective. Considering its context, why is this sentence especially well constructed: "People leave, others come, the machines jangled on" (46-47)? (This pattern is called tricolon *.)

12. The syntax of the first sentence in paragraph 10 is a bit obscure. How, for instance, would you construe the phrase *tokens in*? Yet the movement of this sentence is wonderfully appropriate to what the writer is describing. Why?

DICTION

13. Look up: *hunkered* (38), *coup* (42), *ebbs* (46), *flows* (46), *rail* (59).

14. Necessarily Lipsyte uses a number of expressions peculiar to horseracing. Try to define these as precisely as you can: *daily-double windows* (14), *parimutuel machines* (18), *a winner* (34), *post time* (40), *the approximate odds board* (41), *smart money* (41).

15. Setting is a more important element in Lipsyte's story than it was in Thurber's. For example, at the very beginning we are told that the wooden horseshoe is painted a *grimy-gold*. What is the significance of this detail? What images * in the second paragraph suggest the idea of sterility, even death? In paragraphs 3-7 what images describe the Race Track? Underline the words in the third paragraph that characterize the players before the first race.

16. Lipsyte's verbs are especially expressive. List half a dozen that strike you; explain why they are good.

17. *Litany* (44) is a metaphor *. What is being compared? Is the comparison apt—does it reveal something about horse-players? Identify the simile * in lines 26-27. Do you like it? Point out several other similes and metaphors in this selection.

18. In lines 18-19 Lipsyte speaks of the "parimutuel machines punching out fresh tickets to everywhere." What is he implying? He tells us in the final paragraph that in rushing out upon the platform too soon the crowd had "all followed a fool." Is there perhaps a double meaning in this phrase?

POINTS TO LEARN

1. A story should not simply stop. Rather it should be brought to a close, its action completed.

2. The images which describe setting often contribute significantly to the meaning of a story.

3. Tell the story well and its meaning will take care of itself.

SUGGESTIONS FOR WRITING

Imagine that you are a reporter and that you must write a narrative on one of the subjects listed below. First make up your own mind what you want to convey about the experience you describe, and then select details and organize action accordingly. Let the story imply its own theme.

> A bingo parlor on a crowded night
> A wrestling arena in a small city
> Evening visiting hours at the hospital
> A locker-room both before and after a game
> Backstage at a play or opera

IMPROVING YOUR STYLE

In your narrative include:

1. Several short, dramatic sentences.
2. A tricolon * like the one in lines 46-47 (see question 11).
3. A sentence containing an elliptical * clause similar to the construction in lines 7-8 (question 8).
4. An example of polysyndeton (question 10).
5. Several metaphors and several similes.
6. Some strong, expressive verbs.

Beginnings and Closings

Hilaire Belloc—who knew, if anyone did, how to begin and how to end an essay—once wrote that "to begin at the beginning is, next to ending at the end, the whole art of writing." If this be right, most themes have little claim to art, for it is sad but true that students pay little attention to the beginnings and the endings of their compositions. If they consider the opening and closing paragraphs at all, they treat them like luggage tags, hurriedly tied on to announce where they are going or where they have been. Beginnings and endings are more than this, and they are important. How a writer begins will determine whether his reader bothers to go on. And how he begins greatly affects what a writer will say. Starting an essay is like starting a journey: to turn left or to turn right will lead to very different destinations. Closings are equally important. It does little good to develop an idea through five pages only to lose the reader with an abrupt, inadequate final paragraph.

It is easy to assert the importance of the opening and closing paragraphs and to tell the student that he must begin well and end well. It is more difficult to explain how he goes about it. There is no simple answer; here as elsewhere learning is a slow and personal affair. Still a few generalizations will help the inexperienced writer. First about beginnings. The purpose of an opening paragraph is to introduce the body of the essay. The introduction must include several things: the identification of the subject, indicating as well the limitations within which it will be treated; often a quick view of the organization of the essay to follow; and finally an effort to motivate the reader—to engage his interest.

The number of words required to do these things will vary according to the length and complexity of the essay they introduce. In a short, simple paper the beginning may be only a sentence; in a multi-volume historical study it may comprise fifty pages. For most student themes a single paragraph is enough, and if the essay is very short its beginning may be only a sentence or two.

417

As the length of the beginning is variable, so is the manner in which it is developed. In academic papers, designed for a narrow and professional audience, the writer often announces his subject explicitly. Thus Alfred North Whitehead begins his *Religion in the Making:* "It is my purpose to consider the type of justification which is available for belief in doctrines of religion." Whitehead is concerned to be clear and precise, and is little interested in entertaining his reader; his formal, explicit beginning exactly suits his purpose. But such an opening is usually too stiff for freshman compositions, where it is better to work implicitly. The student should not begin, for instance, "The purpose of this theme is to discuss baseball"; this is much too wooden and weighty. He need only write "Baseball is the most popular of American sports," leaving to the reader the obvious inference that the theme which follows is about baseball.

Generally the limitation of the subject goes hand in hand with its announcement and need never be pursued beyond what is absolutely necessary. If the next sentence of our imaginary baseball paper were "But few people realize the intricate business organization that supports a big league team," the broad topic of baseball would be sufficiently narrowed and the reader would know what to expect. It is sometimes desirable for the writer to tell what he is not going to do, but as a rule the subjects of student themes do not require extensive boundary fixing.

How closely the plan of the paper need be indicated in the beginning paragraphs depends upon subject, length, and purpose. In long, complicated essays a preview of the organization not only aids the reader but simplifies for the writer many future problems of transition. Here, too, the writer may work either explicitly or more subtly. Usually it is best to imply the plan of the essay, avoiding such heavy-handed obviousness as "This paper will be divided into four major sections." The typical English composition, however, is too simple and too brief to warrant laying out its organization in the beginning paragraph, whether by direct statement or by implication.

Equally variable is the effort a writer must make to engage his reader's interest. A physician reporting upon a new drug in a medical journal may safely assume that the professional audience for whom he writes is already interested, and he may concentrate upon being concise and informative. A journalist treating the same subject for a lay audience must make a greater effort to capture their attention. Generally the composition student, like the journalist, needs to think consciously of interesting his reader. This is simpler to say than to do; but there are ways.

The most common is to stress the importance of the subject. "Baseball is a popular game," for example, merely states a fact without attaching to it any special significance; as an opening sentence it would hardly awaken anyone not already a fan. But "Baseball is a uniquely American game; he who would understand America must understand baseball," now gives the subject a particular importance which is more likely to attract the reader.

A more subtle way of catching the reader's interest is to puzzle him. Charles Lamb opens "A Chapter on Ears" with the cryptic remark, " I have no ear"; and his reader is intrigued. This technique may take a stronger form and become a deliberate attempt to shock. To begin our theme on baseball with "Baseball is a game that appeals to fools," will probably stimulate a reader to go on, if only to learn more about the writer's eccentricities.

There are other devices useful in gaining the reader's attention. Cleverly employed, rhetorical questions, anecdotes, allusions, quotations, will all arouse interest. One of the finest beginnings in English is the first sentence of Bacon's essay "Of Truth": "*What is truth?* said jesting Pilate; and would not stay for an answer." Short as it is, the sentence contains a rhetorical question, an allusion, and even a brief anecdote. Another method is to begin with a brief common-place remark, which, to readers accustomed to openings of momentous significance, has the charm of surprise. "I have a wealthy friend" is all Belloc writes to begin one essay. And Dickens opens "A Christmas Carol" with the remarkably effective: "Marley was dead, to begin with. There is no doubt whatever about that."

Thus to interest the reader, to identify and limit the subject, and possibly to indicate the plan of the essay, are the purposes of the beginning. In attempting to fulfill them the inexperienced writer is liable to err in either one of two extremes. The first is to do too little, to bombard his readers with ideas before they have had a chance to settle down and learn what all this is about. The second is to do too much. A beginning introduces the subject—but it does not develop it; that is the job of what is to follow. Although learning to avoid both these extremes is not easy, it can be done. To be blunt, it must be; for no essay that begins badly can be successful.

The final paragraphs are no less important. A closing has one essential function: to say "the essay is finished." In the movie theater we do not require the words "The End" to know that a well-directed film is over. We reach for our coats when the music swells and the heroine falls into the hero's arms. So in a well-written essay—the final paragraphs tell us that the writer has no more to say, and we do not need the white space at the bottom of the page to realize the fact. On occasion a writer may feel it necessary to do more in his last paragraph than merely signal the end. The subject may demand that he draw a final conclusion, and if his paper has been long and complex he may think a summary in order. When they are present, conclusions and summaries are in themselves signs of closing. But they are not always present, for not every essay requires them. Therefore the writer must learn to use other techniques of ending. Four are most common: signal words, changing the tempo of the last sentences, figurative closing, and returning to the beginning.

Most frequent is the signal word, of which there are a great many in English. Some—like *finally, in conclusion, at last*—are obvious and rather mechanical; others—like *and so, then, thus*—are more subtle. Not all these terms are exact equivalents of course, and a good writer will have ready to hand a number of them, selecting that which best fits his context.

Altering the speed of the final sentence requires a little more skill. Usually the change is a slowing down, and often a regularizing, of the rhythm. William Prescott ends the *History of the Conquest of Peru* with this long, slow, stately sentence: "With the benevolent mission of Gasca, then, the historian of the Conquest may be permitted to terminate his labors,—with feelings not unlike those of the traveller, who, having long journeyed among the dreary forests and dangerous defiles of the mountains, at length emerges on some pleasant landscape smiling in tranquillity and peace." Less often the final sentence may be quick, brief, matter-of-fact, especially if the preceding constructions have been long and complicated. Chesterton, for example, concludes "A Piece of Chalk" with this passage: "And I stood there in a trance of pleasure, realizing that this Southern England is not only a grand peninsula, and a tradition and a civilization; it is something even more admirable. It is a piece of chalk."

The third device, which we have called figurative closing, means simply the inclusion in the final paragraph of some sort of a comparison or a figure of speech—usually a simile or metaphor—which implies the idea of ending. There was a series of movie travelogues popular about twenty-five years ago which concluded invariably—or so it seemed—with our "leaving the beautiful isle of this or that and sailing into the sunset." The image of the sunset is comparable to a figure of closing. A less trite case is Prescott's traveller emerging on "some pleasant landscape smiling in tranquillity and peace." His travels are over, and so, the figure implies, is the book. The alert reader knows there is nothing more. But remember, if it is to do its job, the closing figure must seem natural to the context of the essay and not be a completely alien idea forced upon it from the outside. When they are natural, figures of closing are neat and effective ways of ending.

The final closing technique is the return to the beginning. Having set up a word or phrase in his opening, the writer swings back to it in the final paragraph, completing the circle. Chesterton, for instance, not only entitles his essay "A Piece of Chalk," but used *chalks* in his first sentence; and on this word he ends. Of all ways of closing, the return to the beginning is perhaps the best. This is not simply because it is the least obvious. Even more importantly the cyclic return best completes the form of the essay; and such completeness is, as Belloc observes, the essence of art.

Art may seem a pretentious term in the workaday world of composition courses and term papers. Writing of this sort we do not usually dignify as art. Yet—no matter how practical and prosaic its subject—it is. A lawyer's brief, a piece of literary criticism, a freshman theme are all works of art; to say that they are well or poorly written is simply to say that they are good art or bad.

Nothing is so fatal to a work of art as failure to complete its form. A lopsided vase, a novel that fails to bring its plot to the demanded conclusion, annoy us. And so with an essay. It must be complete and whole within itself. This does not mean that the first and final paragraphs are the most important. A skillful introduction or a fine closing does not salvage an otherwise foolish or badly organized theme. It does mean that an essay must begin and must end—and not start and stop. Anyone can stop writing. Only writers can finish.

Beginnings

FRANKLIN DUCHENEAUX

From The American Indian: Beyond the Stereotypes

Franklin Ducheneaux is an American teacher and writer. As the title of his essay suggests, his purpose is to show what American Indians in fact are, as opposed to what people suppose them to be. The five paragraphs reprinted here constitute the beginning of Ducheneaux's essay. As you read them, consider his opening strategy, how he accomplishes the tasks a beginning is expected to do.

1   In the nineteenth century, the white man's image of the American Indian was either that of the noble savage or the bloodthirsty, dirty redskin. The Indian in the first image could not open his mouth without having gems of great wisdom and profound philosophy pouring out in the most poetical, oratorical style. The second Indian was not happy 5 unless he was dripping with the blood of a white man and holding aloft a scalp of flowing blond hair. Neither of these two extreme images was accurate.

2   In the twentieth century, two different images have developed in the minds of white Americans. In one—the movie/TV image—the 10 Indian is still pictured as the mighty warrior in majestic headdress, attacking the wagon train or making fervent love to a dusky young Indian maiden. In the other, he is the sullen, broken spirit who drinks cheap wine and lives on the handouts of a sometimes benign, sometimes malicious federal government. These images are also in- 15 accurate.

3   While the foregoing images still flavor white America's picture of the Indian to some extent, two new images have arisen in recent

From *Today's Education* (May 1973). Reprinted by permission of the National Education Association and the author.

years. One is that of the sophisticated, intellectual tribal leader who wears tailor-made suits and carries an attaché case. The other is that of the militant Indian; the Red Power publicity seeker, burning buildings, taking hostages, and desperately seeking identification with Crazy Horse and Sitting Bull—the Wounded Knee image of 1973. While these new images have a basis in fact, neither truly represents most American Indians.

4   This article will attempt to give the reader a more accurate picture of the Indian—the native American. Nevertheless, it will be necessarily inadequate, for Indians, like all other creatures on this earth, differ—in their physical appearance and spiritual outlook, in their ambitions and desires, in their prejudices and fears.

5   I will not discuss the Indians living in the urban areas, who were either born there or who went there from the reservations—either voluntarily or because insensitive federal Indian policies forced them to. I do not exclude them because they are not Indian. They are. I do not exclude them because they do not suffer many of the same social and cultural problems of the reservation Indian. They do, often to a more severe degree. I exclude them here because their surrounding environment is primarily non-Indian, whereas the reservation Indian lives in an Indian environment that is foreign to the adjacent non-Indian community. So the following discussion must be taken in the context of the Indian living on the reservation or near enough to be routinely affected by the problems and programs of the reservation.

QUESTIONS

READER AND PURPOSE

1. Are these paragraphs a successful opening—clarifying the subject and defining what will and will not be covered? What strategy of gaining attention does the writer use?

2. Which best describes the writer's tone *: angry, amused, objective, indignant? Support your answer by citing specific words.

3. What point of view * does Ducheneaux employ?

ORGANIZATION

4. The five paragraphs fall into two units. Where? What tasks of a beginning does the first group achieve? The second? Might Ducheneuax's strategy here be described as "negative-positive"? Explain.

5. Identify the topic sentence of paragraph 1. How do the other sentences of the paragraph relate to it in idea? Study the internal linkage of this paragraph and be able to show what words tie each sentence to the one(s) preceding it. Which of the four sentences is the shortest? Is there any advantage to its brevity?

6. Demonstrate that paragraphs 2 and 3 follow the same plan as number 1.

7. In paragraph 4 how is the second sentence related in thought to the first?

8. Paragraph 5 uses a negative-positive strategy both in its overall development and in treating specific points within the paragraph. Indicate how.

9. What words link the second paragraph to the first? The third to the second?

SENTENCES

10. Notice the two-word sentence in line 34. Would it be better to join this to the preceding statement? For example:

> I do not exclude them because they are not Indian, since they are.

11. Why are the following revisions less effective than the sentences in the text?

(a) *Revision:* He is the sullen, broken spirit in the other who drinks cheap wine and lives on the handouts of a sometimes benign, sometimes malicious government.

Ducheneaux: "In the other, he is the sullen, broken spirit who drinks cheap wine and lives on the handouts of a sometimes benign, sometimes malicious federal government." (13-15)

(b) *Revision:* Two new images have arisen in recent years, although the foregoing images still flavor white America's picture of the Indian to some extent.

Ducheneuax: "While the foregoing images still flavor white America's picture of the Indian to some extent, two new images have arisen in recent years." (17-19)

12. Which elements are parallel * in the sentences in lines 20-23 and 27-30? Identify the appositive * in the sentence in 26-27.

13. In lines 10 and 23 commas could be used instead of dashes: What is the advantage of the dashes? In line 29 no mark at all is demanded by the grammar. Why then does the writer employ a dash?

14. Would a colon or a comma be a more conventional mark than a semicolon in line 21?

DICTION

15. Look up: *stereotype* (title), *oratorical* (5), *fervent* (12), *dusky* (12), *sullen* (13), *benign* (14), *malicious* (15), *sophisticated* (19), *insensitive* (33), *exclude* (34), *adjacent* (39), *context* (40), *routinely* (41).

16. Explain the basic meanings and connotations * of these phrases: *noble savage* (2), *majestic headdress* (11), *attaché case* (20), *militant Indian* (21), *spiritual outlook* (29), *social and cultural problems* (36), *reservation Indian* (36).

17. Who were Crazy Horse and Sitting Bull (23)? What happened at Wounded Knee (22-23)?

18. How does Ducheneaux use diction ironically * in paragraphs 1, 2, and 3 to parody the popular images of the Indian that he describes?

19. Why does he specify *flowing blond hair* in line 7?

20. Of the two connectives * *nevertheless* (27) and *so* (39), which is the more formal term, which the more colloquial?

POINTS TO LEARN

1. A negative beginning may be effective—first telling the reader what is *not* the case and then focusing down on what is.

2. Opening paragraphs are important in establishing tone and point of view.

3. Successive paragraphs that develop similar topics often have similar structure.

SUGGESTIONS FOR WRITING

Imagine that you are writing an essay of 1200-1500 words on such a subject as "The College Student: Beyond the Stereotypes" (or, in place of students, teenagers, parents, teachers, football players, and so on): Compose an opening of three or four paragraphs (350-400 words) in which you first review the unrealistic, popular images and then focus upon the truth as you understand it. Make clear what you will cover and what you will not, and try to arouse your readers' interest. But remember that you are only introducing a discussion; don't try to cover the entire subject in 400 words.

IMPROVING YOUR STYLE

In your composition:

1. Parody the false images by the words you use to describe them.

2. Compose two or three short sentences (no more than seven words) for emphasis or variety, two or three containing parallelism, and one containing an appositive.

3. Use the connective *nevertheless*.

From Education as Philosophy

Brand Blanshard is an English philosopher. He has taught at universities in both Great Britain and the United States and is the author of numerous books and articles on philosophical topics. He has also published a short but valuable book about writing, *On Philosophical Style* (1954), which will reward the attention of anyone who wishes to write with lucidity and grace, whether about philosophy or any other discipline.

The paragraph reprinted here is the opening of a talk Blanshard delivered to an audience of university educators (later published as an essay). It is worth studying both for the skill with which it achieves the functions of a beginning and for its masterly control of tone. Tone is especially important for the speaker. He stands in the physical presence of those he addresses, and if he is to succeed he has to attract and hold their attention and sympathy. He must not turn them off by awkwardness, arrogance, or a tactless disregard of their feelings. Thus for the speaker tone is all-important, and he has to pay close attention to establishing exactly the right attitudes toward his subject, himself, and his audience. But the speaker's concern with tone is only more immediate than the writer's; it is not essentially different. No more than a speaker can a writer afford to bore or irritate his readers. Observe, then, how Blanshard creates tone in his opening.

There is an immense and justified pride in what our colleges have done. At the same time there is a growing uneasiness about their product. The young men and women who carry away our degrees are a very attractive lot —in looks, in bodily fitness, in kindliness, energy, courage, and buoyancy. But what of their intellectual equipment? That too is in some ways ad-   5
mirable; for in spite of President Lowell's remark that the university should be a repository of great learning, since the freshmen always bring a stock with them and the seniors take little away, the fact is that our graduates

From "Education as Philosophy," *Swarthmore College Bulletin*, XLII, No. 4 (July, 1945). Reprinted by permission of the author.

have every chance to be well informed, and usually are so. Yet the uneasiness persists. When it becomes articulate, it takes the form of wishes that these attractive young products of ours had more intellectual depth and force, more at-homeness in the world of ideas, more of the firm, clear, quiet thoughtfulness that is so potent and so needed a guard against besetting humbug and quackery. The complaint commonly resolves itself into a bill of three particulars. First, granting that our graduates know a good deal, their knowledge lies about in fragments and never gets welded together into the stuff of a tempered and mobile mind. Secondly, our university graduates have been so busy boring holes for themselves, acquiring special knowledge and skills, that in later life they have astonishingly little in common in the way of ideas, standards, or principles. Thirdly, it is alleged that the past two decades have revealed a singular want of clarity about the great ends of living, attachment to which gives significance and direction to a life. Here are three grave charges against American education, and I want to discuss them briefly. My argument will be simple, perhaps too simple. What I shall contend is that there is a great deal of truth in each of them, and that the remedy for each is the same. It is larger infusion of the philosophic habit of mind.

QUESTIONS

READER AND PURPOSE

1. Is Blanshard's point of view * personal or impersonal? Describe the kind of reader for whom you think this essay is intended.

ORGANIZATION

2. Supposing that there were no title, how far would a reader have to go in this opening paragraph before he learned the subject of the essay? How far before he knew what particular aspects of that subject Blanshard would handle? If he were alert, our reader could predict from this paragraph the major sections in the remainder of the essay. How could he? What are these sections? How is the *order* of these sections made clear? Blanshard does not literally say that "first I shall discuss this, next that." How do you know, then, what the organization will be?

3. Blanshard moves from the general to the particular, a common way of opening, sometimes described as "focusing down." At what point in the paragraph does Blanshard adjust his focus from the general to the particular?

4. On either side of this point the paragraph falls into two roughly equal halves.

Suppose the first had been omitted, and the paragraph had begun: "There are three principal complaints against our colleges. First," continuing with what are now lines 15-27. This would have made a much briefer opening, yet one which told us all we really need to know about the subject and plan of the essay to follow. But this shorter version would not have been as good a beginning. What would it have sacrificed?

5. The idea developed in lines 6-8 ("in spite of . . . little away") is not important to the establishment of the subject or plan of Blanshard's paper. What is the purpose of the allusion to President Lowell's remark?

6. One of the most difficult tasks of the writer is to avoid oversimplification. It is easy to say that something is white or that it is black. Many things, however, are a little of both, and to indicate this complexity without confusing the reader is one hallmark of skilled writing. Blanshard is worth studying in this respect, for while he both praises and criticizes the American university, he does not confuse the reader about which is his chief purpose. He succeeds because he keeps returning to his main point in short, emphatic sentences. How many times in the first eleven lines does he restate the idea that people are growing uneasy about the American college graduate?

7. In the light of the preceding question, show why the following two beginnings are less effective than lines 1-9 of the text:

> (a) There is an immense and justified pride in what our colleges have done, and at the same time there is a growing uneasiness about their product. Still the young men and women who carry away our degrees are very attractive, physically fit, kind, energetic, courageous, and buoyant; however their intellectual equipment is limited.
>
> (b) Our colleges have failed.

How does "focusing down" make it easier for a writer to avoid oversimplification?

SENTENCES

8. Study the sentence in lines 17-20. Show that it analyzes a concept in terms of cause and effect, and indicate which part of the sentence defines the cause and which the effect.

9. Why is this rendering of the final three sentences less successful than what Blanshard wrote?

> My argument will be simple, perhaps too simple, for I shall contend that there is a great deal of truth in each of them, and that the remedy for each is the same, being a larger infusion of the philosophic habit of mind.

DICTION

10. Look up: *buoyancy* (4), *repository* (7), *articulate* (10), *alleged* (20), *singular* (21), *contend* (25).

11. Explain in your own words what Blanshard means by these phrases: *besetting humbug and quackery* (14), *a tempered and mobile mind* (17), *the philosophic habit of mind* (26).

12. Look up *infusion* (26). What does this word suggest about the writer's attitude toward college education? What does it suggest about his tone *? Is he amused by the deficiencies of our graduates? Shocked and angered by the failure of higher education? Or is Blanshard's tone neither of these extremes?

POINTS TO LEARN

1. It is wise, especially in essays handling complicated, abstract * topics, to indicate something about the general plan in the very beginning.

2. "Focusing down" is a common, and advantageous, method of opening.

3. Unless the audience you are writing for is a very special one, you cannot take its interest for granted.

4. It requires constant attention to handle complex ideas honestly and clearly.

5. The proper tone is essential to effective writing, and it must be established in the beginning paragraphs.

SUGGESTIONS FOR WRITING

Write one paragraph, about as long as Blanchard's, designed to open a theme on a complex and controversial topic. Make your subject clear as quickly as possible, but begin broadly, suggesting its complexities. As you proceed, focus down, indicating the general plan and concluding with a sentence that places you in a position to step easily into the body of your essay.

IMPROVING YOUR STYLE

Before you begin your composition explain in several sentences the tone you want to achieve—that is, how you feel about your subject, how you want your readers to think of you, and how you regard them.

After you have finished, discuss in two or three sentences how you achieved the tone you aimed at, citing specific words and sentence patterns.

A Fable for Tomorrow

Rachel Carson (1907-64) was an American scientist and writer. She is best known for her popular books about oceanography, *Under the Sea Wind* (1941) and *The Sea Around Us* (1951), and for *Silent Spring* (1962), which fired one of the first shots in what has come to be called the environmental movement. The book discusses the pollution resulting from the massive and indiscriminate use of fertilizers and pesticides, a problem which most Americans were ignorant of until Carson's warning. The following paragraphs are the opening of *Silent Spring*.

1   There was once a town in the heart of America where all life seemed to live in harmony with its surroundings. The town lay in the midst of a checkerboard of prosperous farms, with fields of grain and hillsides of orchards where, in spring, white clouds of bloom drifted above the green fields. In autumn, oak and maple and birch set up a blaze of colour that 5 flamed and flickered across a backdrop of pines. Then foxes barked in the hills and deer silently crossed the fields, half hidden in the mists of the autumn mornings.

2   Along the roads, laurel, viburnum and alder, great ferns and wildflowers delighted the traveller's eye through much of the year. Even in win- 10 ter the roadsides were places of beauty, where countless birds came to feed on the berries and on the seed heads of the dried weeds rising above the snow. The countryside was, in fact, famous for the abundance and variety of its bird life, and when the flood of migrants was pouring through in spring and autumn people travelled from great distances to observe them. 15 Others came to fish the streams, which flowed clear and cold out of the hills and contained shady pools where trout lay. So it had been from the days many years ago when the first settlers raised their houses, sank their wells, and built their barns.

3   Then a strange blight crept over the area and everything began to 20
change. Some evil spell had settled on the community: mysterious maladies
swept the flocks of chickens; the cattle and sheep sickened and died. Everywhere was a shadow of death. The farmers spoke of much illness among
their families. In the town the doctors had become more and more puzzled by new kinds of sickness appearing among their patients. There had 25
been several sudden and unexplained deaths, not only among adults but
even among children, who would be stricken suddenly while at play and die
within a few hours.

4   There was a strange stillness. The birds, for example—where had
they gone? Many people spoke of them, puzzled and disturbed. The feeding 30
stations in the backyards were deserted. The few birds seen anywhere were
moribund; they trembled violently and could not fly. It was a spring without voices. On the mornings that had once throbbed with the dawn chorus
of robins, catbirds, doves, jays, wrens, and scores of other bird voices there
was now no sound; only silence lay over the fields and woods and marsh.   35

5   On the farms the hens brooded, but no chicks hatched. The farmers complained that they were unable to raise any pigs—the litters were
small and the young survived only a few days. The apple trees were coming
into bloom but no bees droned among the blossoms, so there was no pollination and there would be no fruit.   40

6   The roadsides, once so attractive, were now lined with browned
and withered vegetation as though swept by fire. These, too, were silent,
deserted by all living things. Even the streams were now lifeless. Anglers no
longer visited them, for all the fish had died.

7   In the gutters under the eaves and between the shingles of the 45
roofs, a white granular powder still showed a few patches; some weeks before it had fallen like snow upon the roofs and the lawns, the fields and
streams.

8   No witchcraft, no enemy action had silenced the rebirth of new life
in this stricken world. The people had done it themselves.   50

9   This town does not actually exist, but it might easily have a thousand counterparts in America or elsewhere in the world. I know of no community that has experienced all the misfortunes I describe. Yet every one of
these disasters has actually happened somewhere, and many real communities have already suffered a substantial number of them. A grim spectre 55
has crept upon us almost unnoticed, and this imagined tragedy may easily
become a stark reality we all shall know.

10   What has already silenced the voices of spring in countless towns in America? This book is an attempt to explain.

QUESTIONS

READER AND PURPOSE

1. Would you judge from this opening that Carson's purpose was simply to inform her readers of the problem, or to do more than inform? Do you think her beginning is adequate to her purpose? Why or why not?

2. Unlike the other beginnings we have studied, this one does not actually identify the subject. Is that a fault, or is it a deliberate and useful strategy?

3. Carson's book was criticized by spokesmen for the chemical industry as "alarmist." Could it be fairly argued that these opening paragraphs are misleading and trick the reader into taking an imaginary disaster for a real one?

ORGANIZATION

4. Paragraphs 1-8 fall into two parts: at what point? What word marks the shift of focus?

5. Analyze the unity of paragraph 1, showing how each sentence after the first is linked to the preceding statement.

6. What is the topic sentence of the fourth paragraph? Indicate the key term in that sentence and the words which echo it later in the paragraph.

7. Paragraphs 4, 5, and 6 all begin in much the same manner. What is the virtue of such similarity?

8. What is the purpose of the extra spacing between paragraphs 8 and 9?

SENTENCES

9. Point out the parallel * constructions in the sentence in lines 17-19.

10. What does the colon in line 21 signal to us about how the following construction will be related to what has just been said? Why does the writer use a semicolon in line 22 instead of a comma?

11. Explain how these revisions change the emphasis or meaning of Carson's sentences and whether you think them an improvement:

    (a) *Revision:* In the heart of America a town once existed where all life seemed to live in harmony with its surroundings.
    Carson: "There was once a town in the heart of America where all life seemed to live in harmony with its surroundings." (1-2)

    (b) *Revision:* On the farms no chicks hatched, but the hens brooded.
    Carson: "On the farms the hens brooded, but no chicks hatched."
    (36)

(c) *Revision:* This book is an attempt to explain what has already silenced the voices of spring in countless towns in America.
Carson: "What has already silenced the voices of spring in countless towns in America? This book is an attempt to explain."
(58-59)

DICTION

12. Look up: *harmony* (2), *migrants* (14), *blight* (20), *maladies* (21), *moribund* (32), *litters* (37), *pollination* (39), *granular* (46), *spectre* (55), *stark* (57).
13. Why does Carson call her account a *fable?*
14. Which subsequent words in the third paragraph pick up the idea of *blight* (20)? Which echo the idea of *now* (41) in paragraph 6?
15. Study the diction of the first two paragraphs and indicate the words which reinforce the concept of a pure, undefiled nature.

POINTS TO LEARN

1. Occasionally it is good strategy not to identify the subject, but to create a mystery and thereby to arouse the reader's curiosity.
2. A focused and coherent paragraph will often echo in subsequent sentences the key idea expressed in its topic statement.

SUGGESTIONS FOR WRITING

1. Attempt a beginning of several paragraphs modeled on Carson's dealing with some such topic as "A Fable for Teachers" or "A Fable for Students" or "A Fable for Parents."
2. In a paragraph or two discuss more fully the point raised in question 3—whether Carson has deliberately attempted here to mislead her readers.

IMPROVING YOUR STYLE

1. In your composition include two or three sentences using parallel constructions.
2. Use a colon following a general assertion to introduce a series of specific instances.
3. In one passage repeat a key idea in different words as Carson repeats the concept of blight in her third paragraph.

From American Ways of Life

George R. Stewart is an historian and writer. This selection is the beginning of *American Ways of Life* (1954). The book evolved from Stewart's experiences as a Fulbright lecturer in Greece, where he taught at the University of Athens during 1952-53. The need to satisfy the curiosity of European students about our manner of living led him to reflect upon our society; and as is so often the case when one attempts to explain something to others, Stewart found himself coming to fresh and deeper insights of American culture. The ultimate result was *American Ways of Life*. Despite its genesis, the book is addressed not merely to foreigners but to Americans as well. These opening paragraphs are especially interesting and instructive for their use of an unusual, provocative analogy.

1   As a beginning, let us momentarily make use of a device of science fiction, and imagine a "historical" event that never occurred. . . . During one of the vigorous and expansive periods of the Chinese Empire, one of their navigators (who might have been named Ko Lum Bo) conceived the idea of sailing eastward from China and thus arriving at Ireland, which was   5 known to be the farthest outpost of Europe. The Chinese wished to reach Ireland, it may be believed, because they had heard tales that those barbarous islanders made a certain drink called Wis Ki.

2   Ko Lum Bo made his voyage, and discovered a country that he supposed to be part of Ireland, although he was disappointed in not finding   10 any Wis Ki being manufactured by the natives.

3   During the course of the next two centuries the Chinese colonized this country, eventually discovering it to be not Ireland, but a wholly new continent. Nevertheless they continued to call the natives Irish, or sometimes Red Irish.   15

4   The Chinese colonists introduced their own well-established ways of life. They continued to speak Chinese, and to practice their own religion. Being accustomed to eat rice, they still ate it, as far as possible. Vast areas of the country were terraced and irrigated as rice paddies. The colonists continued to use their comfortable flowing garments, and pagodas dotted the   20
landscape. In short, the civilization was Asiatic and not European.

5   Yet it could not be wholly Asiatic. The Chinese adopted from the natives the valuable food plant known as Irish corn. They also made other adjustments to the land itself. For instance, landing on the shores of San Francisco Bay with their domestic animals, especially their pigs, they found   25
that the country, as they advanced inland, was largely open grassland and desert. Since such land was much better suited to sheep than to pigs, the colonists came to depend more upon sheep, and gradually lost some of their taste for pork. When they finally came to the forested eastern part of the country, they entered a region much more hospitable to pigs than to sheep.   30
But by this time they were so well accustomed to raising sheep that they continued to do so.

6   Thus, in the end, a student of their civilization would conclude that it showed the influence of two factors. Much of it resulted from what the colonists had brought with them, and the rest sprang chiefly from the influence of the land itself. . . . At this point let us drop science fiction. . . .   35

7   Like an individual's character, a nation's way of life may be conceived as the result of environment and heredity. The environment of a nation consists of the land that it inhabits, the seas that border that land, and the air that sweeps across it. The heredity of a nation, at any given moment in its history, consists of the sum total of the blood strains and   40
acquired habits of its people.

8   An individual's environment and a nation's may be considered essentially the same in their nature, continually changing with time. Whereas, however, an individual's heredity is to be conceived as being immutably   45
fixed from the beginning, the heredity of a nation changes with every new immigrant and emigrant.

9   This present book is twofold in its purpose. It attempts to present certain aspects of life in a particular nation, with special reference to the features that may be considered distinctive; and at the same time, to show   50
how these distinctive ways of life have arisen historically, as the result of heredity and environment.

QUESTIONS

READER AND PURPOSE

1. Suppose Stewart had dispensed with the first eight paragraphs and simply begun: "This present book is twofold in its purpose. It attempts . . ." Would you have been as impelled to read on?

2. Some openings attract us by the skill with which they lay out the subject rather than by overt attention-getting devices. Stewart's analogy, on the other hand, is calculated to startle us and thereby to pull us into the book. Do you think he succeeds?

3. There is more to Stewart's analogy, however, than its capacity to hold our attention. What facts does it help us to realize about the European settlement of the New World? A writer discussing the history and structure of his own society may find it advantageous forcibly to detach himself, and his readers, from a subject they know, in a sense, too well. Discuss whether Stewart's opening analogy wrenches us from the familiar, opening up a fresh perspective.

4. Where does the writer make formal announcement of his subject? What advantages do you see in this sort of delayed announcement? Are there any dangers?

ORGANIZATION

5. Why does Stewart begin new paragraphs at lines 9, 12, and 16?

6. Notice that between paragraphs 6 and 7 the spacing is extra wide. What does this typographical signal mean?

7. What is the topic sentence of paragraph 4? Of paragraph 5? In each case, how are these topics developed? What words link the fifth paragraph to the fourth? The sixth to the fifth?

SENTENCES

8. The sentence in line 18 begins with a participial * phrase. What is the logical relationship between the idea expressed in the phrase and that expressed in the main clause? Is there any reason for placing the phrase before, instead of after, the main clause? In the sentence in lines 12-14, on the other hand, the participial construction is put after the main idea. Is this the best place for it? Concise participial modifiers like these are efficient ways of working necessary, but subordinate, ideas into the sentence; practice using them.

9. Point out two or three effective short sentences in this selection. Why does Stewart use an ellipsis * after *never occurred* in line 2 and twice again in line 36?

10. Study the sentences in paragraphs 4 and 5 and be able to point out all instances of parallelism * and all subordinate clauses *. Read the paragraphs aloud. Do the sentences sound monotonous? Why or why not?

DICTION

11. Look up: *momentarily* (1), *expansive* (3), *colonized* (12), *terraced* (19), *pagodas* (20), *immutably* (45), *aspects* (49), *distinctive* (51).
12. Describe the difference between an *immigrant* and an *emigrant* (47). Why do each change the national heredity?
13. What is the reason for the quotation marks around *historical* in line 2?
14. Stewart frequently uses pointers *. What conceptual relationships are signalled by *in short* (21), *thus* (33), and *whereas* (44)? *Nevertheless* (14), *yet* (22), *but* (31), and *however* (45) are all pointers that show the basic relationship of contradiction. There are, however, subtle differences between them. Try to formulate some of these slight distinctions of meaning.

POINTS TO LEARN

1. A writer often cannot take his readers' interest for granted; he must work consciously to capture it.
2. Any attention-getting device such as an anecdote, an allusion *, a quotation, or an analogy must be not only interesting in itself but also legitimately related to the subject. It should throw light upon or lead naturally into what the essay is all about.
3. Participals are useful subordinating constructions, too little used by most beginning writers.

SUGGESTIONS FOR WRITING

Compose a beginning (in one paragraph or several) for a projected essay on a subject of your own choosing. Delay the announcement of the subject until the final sentences and make an overt effort to engage your reader's interest. You may try to develop an analogy like Stewart's, relate an anecdote, or work with quotations or allusions. In any case, select something that is both interesting and apposite.

IMPROVING YOUR STYLE

In your beginning paragraph(s) include:

1. Three sentences containing participial phrases, positioned (according to emphasis or progression of idea) as follows: one opening its sentence, one interrupting the subject and verb, one closing the sentence.
2. Two or three effective short sentences.
3. At least three of the following connectives *: *in short, yet, thus, whereas, nevertheless, however, but.*

From Of the Dawn of Freedom

William Edward Burghardt DuBois (1868-1963) was a Negro scholar and educator, an early advocate of black consciousness and pride. In the essays collected under the title of *The Souls of Black Folk* (1903), his best known book, he combined intellectual rigor and emotional sensitivity in writing about the situation of black people in America. The essay "Of the Dawn of Freedom" is largely an account of the Freedmen's Bureau, an agency established by Congress in 1865 to cope with the problems created by the sudden liberation of four million black men, women, and children in the aftermath of the Civil War. The Bureau offered welfare, land, jobs, and schooling to the former slaves. Partly successful and partly a source of corruption and misrule, the Freedmen's Bureau was abolished in 1874. In the following selection the first two paragraphs are the opening of DuBois' essay; the second two its conclusion. Together they illustrate how to begin and close an essay effectively.

1   The problem of the twentieth century is the problem of the color line—the relation of the darker to the lighter races of men in Asia and Africa, in America and the islands of the sea. It was a phase of this problem that caused the Civil War; and however much they who marched South and North in 1861 may have fixed on the technical points of union and local 5 autonomy as a shibboleth, all nevertheless knew, as we know, that the question of Negro slavery was the real cause of the conflict. Curious it was, too, how this deeper question ever forced itself to the surface despite effort and disclaimer. No sooner had Northern armies touched Southern soil than this old question, newly guised, sprang from the earth—What shall be done with 10 Negroes? Peremptory military commands this way and that, could not answer the query; the Emancipation Proclamation seemed but to broaden and intensify the difficulties; and the War Amendments made the Negro problems of to-day.

From *The Souls of Black Folk*, 1903.

2   It is the aim of this essay to study the period of history from 1861 to   15
1872 so far as it relates to the American Negro. In effect, this tale of the
dawn of Freedom is an account of that government of men called the Freedmen's Bureau—one of the most singular and interesting of the attempts
made by a great nation to grapple with vast problems of race and social
condition.   20

3   The passing of a great human institution before its work is done,
like the untimely passing of a single soul, but leaves a legacy of striving for
other men. The legacy of the Freedmen's Bureau is the heavy heritage of
this generation. Today, when new and vaster problems are destined to strain
every fibre of the national mind and soul, would it not be well to count this   25
legacy honestly and carefully? For this much all men know: despite com-
promise, war, and struggle, the Negro is not free. In the backwoods of the
Gulf States, for miles and miles, he may not leave the plantation of his birth;
in well-nigh the whole rural South the black farmers are peons, bound by
law and custom to an economic slavery, from which the only escape is death   30
or the penitentiary. In the most cultured sections and cities of the South the
Negroes are a segregated servile caste, with restricted rights and privileges.
Before the courts, both in law and custom, they stand on a different and
peculiar basis. Taxation without representation is the rule of their political
life. And the result of all this is, and in nature must have been, lawlessness   35
and crime. That is the large legacy of the Freedmen's Bureau, the work it
did not do because it could not.

4   I have seen a land right merry with the sun, where children sing, and
rolling hills lie like passioned women wanton with harvest. And there in
the King's Highways sat and sits a figure veiled and bowed, by which the   40
traveller's footsteps hasten as they go. On the tainted air broods fear. Three
centuries' thought has been the raising and unveiling of that bowed human
heart, and now behold a century new for the duty and the deed. The problem of the Twentieth Century is the problem of the color-line.

QUESTIONS

READER AND PURPOSE

1. The first two paragraphs set the topic. What is the subject generally?
Specifically? Does DuBois announce his subject explicitly?

2. After summarizing the work of the Freedmen's Bureau DuBois acknowledges that it was a noble effort that failed, in part because of its own inadequacies. He ends the essay with paragraphs 3 and 4 of this selection. Here he returns to the larger problem with which he began. What is that problem and what does he conclude about it?

3. In ancient rhetoric a speech was often closed with a peroration, an emotional passage which attempted to arouse the appropriate feelings in the audience. The peroration was in itself an indication that the speaker was coming to the end. Which paragraph constitutes a kind of peroration to DuBois' essay? What feelings does he try to evoke? Do you think he succeeds?

4. DuBois also signals closing by the device we called, in the introduction to this section, the "cyclic return." What does he repeat?

ORGANIZATION

5. What shift of topic justifies the new paragraph at line 15? The one at line 38?

6. Paragraph 1 is unified in large part by repeating the idea expressed by the word *problem* (1). What subsequent terms re-express this idea?

7. Study the linkage of the sentences in paragraph 3. How is the second tied to the first? The third to the second? Indicate the links for all the other sentences in this paragraph.

SENTENCES

8. In the opening sentence the word *relation* is an appositive *. To what? Appositives are an easy and efficient way of expanding ideas. There is also one in line 18: identify it.

9. Is the question in lines 24-26 genuine or rhetorical *? If you think it is the latter, what purpose does it serve?

10. What does the colon in line 26 signal?

11. Why are these revisions less effective than DuBois' sentences?

> (a) Revision: It was curious too how this deeper question ever forced itself to the surface despite effort and disclaimer.
> DuBois: "Curious it was, too, how this deeper question ever forced itself to the surface despite effort and disclaimer." (7-9)
>
> (b) Revision: For all men know that the Negro is not free despite compromise, war, and struggle.
> DuBois: "For this much all men know: despite compromise, war, and struggle, the Negro is not free." (26-27)

DICTION

12. Look up: *phase* (3), *shibboleth* (6), *guised* (10), *peremptory* (11), *singular* (18), *destined* (24), *well-nigh* (29), *peons* (29), *wanton* (39), *tainted* (41).

13. Explain the meanings of these phrases: *local autonomy* (5), *Emancipation Proclamation* (12), *untimely passing* (22), *law and custom* (30), *segregated servile caste* (32).

14. What relationships in thought do these connectives signal: *nevertheless* (6), *in effect* (16), *for* (26)?

15. To what historical event does *taxation without representation* (36) allude *? How does the allusion contribute to DuBois' argument?

16. The imagery * of the final paragraph falls into two contrasting patterns. What are these patterns? What idea or feeling does the contrast reinforce?

POINTS TO LEARN

1. Repeating at the end of an essay a key word or expression used at its beginning is a good way of signaling "the end."

2. A paragraph may be unified by repeating a key idea in every sentence.

3. Appositives expand ideas without requiring connective * words like *which is* or *this was* and so on.

SUGGESTIONS FOR WRITING

For an essay of about 600 words compose a brief beginning and a brief closing paragraph (50-75 words each). Attempt a cyclic return, ending the final paragraph with the same words that opened the first. In choosing your topic select something that you could really write about, for your instructor might ask you to complete the essay after he or she has read your beginning and closing.

IMPROVING YOUR STYLE

Somewhere in your paragraphs:

1. Use appositives in two places.
2. Include a rhetorical question.
3. Introduce sentences with these connectives: *in effect, for, nevertheless*.
4. Use a colon as DuBois uses it in line 26: to announce an emphatic idea.

Closings

W. K. FLEMING

General Lee

W. K. Fleming was a British scholar and writer. The following paragraphs close a long essay he composed on Robert E. Lee for an English periodical. The selection illustrates several of the things that a skillful closing must do—summarizing, drawing a conclusion, signaling neatly and clearly that the writer is coming to an end. Particularly instructive is the carefully controlled rhythm of Fleming's final sentence.

1   There is neither need nor space to tell again the charming anecdotes of these final years. His care for his students, his love of children, his solicitude for his old veterans, and indeed for those, if need be, who had fought against him—the stories of such traits are, or should be, familiar enough. In Lexington, and its wooded ways, there was no figure so well known and 5 loved as that of the stately and white-haired hero of many a hard-fought field, great in defeat as in victory, as he rode by on his war-horse "Traveller," exchanging with him, as he was wont to say, "many a sweet confidence."

2   What, we wonder, was the nature of those confidences? The question suggests another, asked in the early days of the war by Mrs. Chestnut 10 in her *Diary from Dixie*: "Can any one say they know General Lee?" It is certainly difficult to write Lee's life; not one of several attempts has proved satisfactory. Some great sayings of his stand out, that on the hill above Fredericksburg, for instance, as he watched the advance of Burnside's vast army: "It is well that war is so terrible, or we should grow too fond of it"; 15 or, in a very different hour, "Human virtue should equal human calamity"— surely one of the finest maxims ever heard from mortal lips! But still we want something that we shall never have. Despite his gracious geniality, and

"General Lee," from *Life and Letters* (London), Volume III, November, 1929.

442

the affection he evoked from all and sundry, from animals and children, from family and friends, there is a strange veil between Lee and even the 20 most ardent of his admirers. It might have arisen from habitual self-control, from an old-world dignity and reticence of manners. But we feel it is more than that. Some element of reserve that he could never break through screens Lee from his fellow men. He knew it. "I only am alone," he once wrote. And it has been asked: "Did he, with all his unstinted gifts of his 25 fortune, his energies, his genius, to his friends and to his cause, ever really give himself?" The solemn silence that was felt almost as a living force by the dying soldier's bedside during his last days on earth, comes almost as a significant answer. But, however that answer be interpreted, we can affirm, with reverent certitude, that Lee did give himself thrice, completely and 30 whole-heartedly. For he gave himself to his army, and to his country, and to his God.

Sir Philip Sidney

Dylan Thomas (1914-53), born in Wales, was a noted British poet; his best known volume of poems is *Deaths and Entrances* (1946). In addition to poetry Thomas wrote essays, autobiography, and drama. His prose, like his poetry, is rich and complex, in sound as well as meaning. This passage ends an essay on Sir Philip Sidney. Sidney (1554-86) was an Elizabethan version of the Renaissance man—poet, soldier, courtier. As a poet Sidney was both gifted and influential, particularly in establishing the sonnet form in English. He was killed fighting for the Dutch Protestants (Elizabeth was their silent ally) in their war to secure independence from Catholic Spain. Sidney's calmness and graciousness in accepting death following a severe wound at the siege of the Dutch town of Zutphen was widely esteemed as a model of the Christian and chivalric ideals. Thomas clearly admires him. As you read the following paragraphs compare them with Fleming's closing. Both selections end essays about famous men; both are by writers who deeply admire their subjects. But notice how different are the strategies by which Fleming and Thomas convey their admiration.

1   In the storming of Zutphen in the Netherlands, September 22, 1586, Sir Philip Sidney was struck by a musket-ball in the thigh. On his agonized way back to the camp, "being thirsty with excess of bleeding, he called for drink, which was presently brought him; but, as he was putting the bottle to his mouth, he saw a poor soldier carried along, who had eaten his last at 5 the same feast, ghastly casting up his eyes at the bottle, which Sir Philip, perceiving, took it from his head before he drank, and delivered it to the poor man with these words, 'Thy necessity is yet greater than mine.'"

2   The operations upon his wound were long and painful. "When they began to dress his wound, he, both by way of charge and advice, told 10

them that while his strength was still entire, his body free from fever, and his mind able to endure, they might freely use their art, cut, and search to the bottom."

3   They used their art, and he was taken away to Arnheim. There he suffered. He became a mere skeleton. The shoulder bones broke through the skin.

4   "He one morning lifting up the clothes for change and ease of his body, smelt some extraordinary noisome savour about him, differing from oils and salves, as he conceived. . . ." Mortification had set in.

5   He sent for ministers of many nationalities, and they prayed with him.

6   He asked for music.

7   He dictated his will.

8   He wrote a long letter in Latin.

9   He bade goodbye to his brother.

10   Very near death, he said, "I would not change my joy for the empire of the world."

QUESTIONS

READER AND PURPOSE

1. We shall consider the selections by W. K. Fleming and Dylan Thomas together. They are alike in several ways. Each describes the end of a great man. In each case, too, the writer is doing more than simply concluding his essay. What other purpose has Fleming? Thomas?

ORGANIZATION

2. If the selections are similar in purpose, they differ in the means they employ. Fleming, for example, clearly signals the fact of closing in his first sentence. In which words? Do you find equally clear signal terms in the selection by Thomas?

3. Although Fleming does not "tell again" the story of Lee's final years, he does summarize it. In which sentences?

4. A conclusion in the logical sense of a final inference is not an inevitable element in a closing. A writer's purpose may or may not require that he draw such a conclusion. Fleming does feel it a requirement. Where does he set up the question he must answer? Where does he answer it? Does he admit any qualification * upon his answer? Thomas, on the other hand, does not draw a conclusion about Sir Philip Sidney. But does he imply one? If so, what is it?

SENTENCES

5. Suppose that Fleming's final sentence were re-written like this:

> However we answer that question we can reverently affirm that Lee did give himself three times completely and whole-heartedly. He gave himself to his army, country and God.

What has been done to Fleming's sentences to make them read more rapidly? Why is the revision less effective as a closing? Is the movement of Thomas's last sentence also held back? Compare the effectiveness of the final sentences of these two selections.

6. Rewrite the following passage, adding such words and punctuation as are necessary to slow it down and make it more like Fleming's closing:

> In dignity, honor and skill America has produced no soldier greater than Robert E. Lee. He accepted defeat with fortitude and victory with humility.

7. It would be easy to combine the four statements that make up Thomas's third paragraph into one compound-complex sentence:

> They used their art, and he was taken away to Arnheim, where he suffered, becoming a mere skeleton so that the shoulder bones broke through the skin.

Would this be more suited to Thomas's purpose, or less? Notice that his sentences are short, simple, and straightforward, having little interrupted movement *. What do these facts suggest about his tone *?

DICTION

8. Look up: (in Fleming) *solicitude* (2), *maxims* (17), *sundry* (19), *reticence* (22), *unstinted* (25), *certitude* (30); (in Thomas) *ghastly* (6), *noisome* (18), *mortification* (19).

9. Thomas's diction is rather different from Fleming's. Fleming writes eloquently, trying to move us by appealing to our nobler emotions with such words as *solemn* and *reverent*. Underline in his selection other words that seem eloquent. Thomas, however, avoids direct emotionalism. He is more factual, confining himself to reporting what happened, as, for example, in the final six sentences. He is relying upon an older account of Sidney's death, which he quotes freely, and this too is essentially reportorial. Would you conclude, then, that Thomas's account of Sidney's death lacks the emotional force of Fleming's description of the last days of General Lee?

10. What does this expression mean: *"who had eaten his last at the same feast"* (Thomas, 5-6)? Explain in what sense it is ironic.

11. What, exactly, do you think Sidney meant by his last words? Is this a good note on which to end? Why or why not?

12. We said that these closings were similar in subject and purpose but different in technique. Fleming sets up a problem and attempts to resolve it, appealing at the same time to our emotions. Thomas is more restrained, reporting without directly interjecting his feelings. Of the two, which did you like the better? Why?

POINTS TO LEARN

1. The final paragraph(s) must make the reader understand that "this is the end."

2. Signal words such as *finally, and so, thus* are one way of doing this.

3. Another is to slow down and regularize the rhythms of the final sentences.

4. Depending upon subject and purpose, a logical conclusion may or may not be necessary at the end of an essay. When it is present, such a conclusion is itself a signal of closing.

5. A summary, like a conclusion, is not an invariable element in the final section. It is useful in long and complicated essays. But most freshman themes are probably too short and their subjects too simple to require summaries.

SUGGESTIONS FOR WRITING

1. Rewrite the description of Lee's death as Dylan Thomas might have handled it.

2. Rewrite the account of Sir Philip Sidney's end on the model of the paragraphs by W. K. Fleming.

IMPROVING YOUR STYLE

In your composition:

1. Use a signal word or phrase of closing.

2. (If you are using Fleming as a model) compose a slow, relatively regular final sentence.

3. (If you are using Thomas) compose a series of three or four short simple * sentences like those in Thomas's third paragraph.

From A Woman's Role

Elizabeth Janeway is an American novelist and journalist. Her novels include *The Walsh Girls* (1943) and *Accident* (1964); and her non-fiction, *Man's World, Woman's Place* (1971) and *Between Myth and Morning: Women Awakening* (1974). The last, a collection of articles on women and feminism that appeared in various magazines, is the source of the following selection. The paragraph closes a review of two books about women in our society. It is a fine example of a somewhat unusual technique of closing: the brief final sentence which points the reader in a new direction and leaves him. Such a closing is difficult to bring off; but done well—as it is here—the technique is very effective.

I don't believe that it is impossible to write a good book about the situation of women in the present world; though I believe that anyone starting with this subject will find himself moving away both from the present and from women into a discussion of the future of humanity, as he follows the trail of his questions and his discoveries toward some tentative hypotheses. But I   5 do believe that to write such a book would be difficult in any case, and is quite impossible for anyone approaching his subject with a ready-made thesis. Naturally, the people who want to undertake such a vast project are likely to be those who are fired and fueled by a thesis. Women are thus, men on the contrary are so, the only way to fulfillment is via the nursery. And   10 yet, how flexible, how malleable, humanity is! How capable still of evolution! To lock even one sex to a pattern of behavior is wasteful and burdensome. Besides—it won't stay there.

QUESTIONS

READER AND PURPOSE

1. What conclusion does Janeway draw about books "on the situation of women"?

2. Often the final sentence of an essay is longer, slower, and more regular in movement than the writer's sentences generally. Janeway uses the opposite strategy. Her final sentence is short and quick. At the same time it is more than an effective closing variation: the sentence also reinforces her main point. How?

ORGANIZATION

3. The ideas developed in this paragraph are subtle and complex. What is the major point of the first sentence? What qualification * of that point is included in the sentence?

4. How is the idea developed in the second sentence related to those in the first? Continue through the paragraph, explaining how each sentence furthers the argument—whether by restating something, contradicting a previous idea, pointing out an effect, or giving a reason. Such a conceptual analysis will reveal the writer's pattern of thought.

5. What word or words link the second sentence to the first? Indicate all the linking words you can find in subsequent sentences.

SENTENCES

6. In the final sentence clarity requires a pause after *besides*. But for simple clarity a comma would be enough. Would the sentence be just as effective with a comma instead of a dash?

7. One sentence in this paragraph is a fragment *. Which? Is it justified?

8. Why are these revisions less effective than the originals?

> (a) *Revision:* I believe that it is possible to write a good book about the situation of women in the present world . . .
> *Janeway:* "I don't believe that it is impossible to write a good book about the situation of women in the present world . . ." (1-2)
>
> (b) *Revision:* It is wasteful and burdensome to lock even one sex to a pattern of behavior.
> *Janeway:* "To lock even one sex to a pattern of behavior is wasteful and burdensome." (12-13)

DICTION

9. Look up: *via* (10), *flexible* (11), *malleable* (11), *evolution* (11), *burdensome* (12).

10. What is the meaning of these phrases: *tentative hypothesis* (5), *ready-made thesis* (7)?

11. What relationships in thought are signaled by *and yet* (10) and *besides* (13)? Suppose that *besides* were replaced by the logically equivalent phrase *in addition* or the word *furthermore*. How would the tone * change?

12. In the metaphor * *fired and fueled by a thesis* (9) to what is Janeway implicitly comparing the "people" she mentions? Does her metaphor suggest approval or disapproval? Explain. What double meaning is conveyed by *fired?*
13. In lines 3 and 4 Janeway refers to the impersonal pronoun *anyone* with the reflexive pronoun *himself*. It is sometimes argued that in such cases strict logic requires both a masculine and a feminine form (*himself or herself*). Do you think that using both reflexives is logically necessary? Would it improve the sound of the sentence?

POINTS TO LEARN
1. The final sentence of an essay is often different in form, and the difference may be that it is brief.
2. In a well-thought-out paragraph, ideas hang together and sentences are linked by repetitions of key terms or by signal words.
3. A metaphor does more than convey an image *: it often implies approval or disapproval.

SUGGESTIONS FOR WRITING
Compose a brief (about 500-words) review of one of your textbooks. Summarize what the author does (or attempts to do) and conclude by indicating whether or not the book is successful and why it is or is not. Close your final paragraph with a short sentence of four or five words.

IMPROVING YOUR STYLE
1. In your review include a metaphor that both characterizes the book or author and also implies your own response, whether negative or positive.
2. Employ the connectives * *and yet* and *besides.*
3. (With your instructor's permission) include an effective fragment.
4. Use a dash for emphasis as Janeway uses it in her final sentence.

From Plato

An American classical scholar, Edith Hamilton (1867-1963) wrote a number of books about the culture and literature of ancient Greece, including *The Greek Way* (1930), *The Echo of Greece* (1957), and *The Ever-Present Past* (1964), a collection of essays from which these paragraphs come. They end a sympathetic account of Plato, the disciple of the philosopher Socrates. Plato develops his views in a series of *Dialogues*, philosophical discussions in the form of a dialectic, or progression of questions and answers, between Socrates and various of the older philosopher's friends. In one of his most famous *Dialogues*, the *Phaedo*, Plato describes the death of Socrates, who ran afoul of the authorities of Athens because of his searching and unconventional intellect. In 399 B.C. they convicted him of impiety and of misleading the young men of the city and condemned him to drink a cup of hemlock, a deadly poison. This Socrates does after a final talk with his friends. Hamilton closes her essay with an allusion to the *Phaedo*, which serves her as a way of suggesting the essential truth about Plato.

1   So the long talk ends. The poison is drunk. The last words Socrates speaks show better than all the arguments what he believed about immortality. As he felt the cold of the poison creeping up to his heart he said: "Remember, I owe a cock to Aesculapius." It was the Greek custom on recovering from an illness to make an offering to the Divine Healer. To him-   5
self Socrates was not dying. He was entering not into death, but into life, "life more abundantly."

2   Through the centuries Plato has received his rightful tribute of deep reverence but not often of deep understanding. Indeed, he has been misunderstood to such a degree that the word "Platonic" has come to have   10
an unreal meaning, a complete misstatement of that mighty mind. He had a great vision; he had nothing of the visionary in him. He was a very great artist; he had a supreme artist's knowledge of people, and he felt that to see

them ever as finished, completed, was to stultify them. He saw them always in the presence of what he called the Beyond, never to be reached but a 15 perpetual summons to go forward. To him the proof of Socrates' truth was his life and death. The text of the Dialogues in general might well be Christ's saying, "He that willeth to do His will shall know the doctrine whether it be of God."

3   One of the young men with whom Socrates had been building the 20 Republic[1] says to him at the end, "I do not believe such a place ever has been or ever will be." "Perhaps," Socrates answers, "a pattern of it is laid up in heaven *for him who wants to see*. But whether it exists or ever will is no matter. A man can order his life by its laws."

QUESTIONS

READER AND PURPOSE

1. In a closing it is often necessary to draw a general conclusion about one's subject. What conclusion does Hamilton come to regarding Plato?

2. A quotation may prove effective in ending an essay as well as in beginning one. Does the quotation from the *Republic* suggest anything about the significance of Plato and Socrates for modern men and women?

3. Scholars have debated the significance of Socrates' very last words about owing an offering to Aesculapius. How does Hamilton interpret them?

4. Does Hamilton assume that her readers are familiar with Plato's *Dialogues*? Does she identify Aesculapius (4)? If so, how does she do it?

ORGANIZATION

5. What shift in topic justifies the second paragraph? The third?

6. Study paragraph 2 and indicate which words link each sentence to what precedes it.

7. Consider this revision of the final sentences:

> Socrates answers, "Perhaps a pattern of it is laid up in heaven *for him who wants to see*, but whether it exists or ever will is no matter since a man can order his life by its laws.

As a closing sentence is this more effective, or less? Why?

8. Identify the appositives * in the sentences in lines 6-7 and 9-11.

9. Contrast these revisions with Hamilton's sentences and decide if they are improvements:

[1] The *Republic* is one of Plato's longest and most important dialogues. In it Socrates defines justice and outlines the kind of state that would be ideally suited to achieve and maintain justice. [Editors' note]

(a) *Revision:* So the long talk ends and Socrates drinks the poison.
Hamilton: "So the long talk ends. The poison is drunk." (1)

(b) *Revision:* Socrates' life and death was the proof of his truth to
him.
Hamilton: "To him the proof of Socrates' truth was his life and
death." (16-17)

DICTION

10. Look up: *immortality* (2), *tribute* (8), *stultify* (14), *perpetual* (16),
doctrine (18).

11. What is the difference between being a *visionary* and having *a great vision*
(12)?

12. *Indeed* (8) is a signal word. What relationship of ideas does it indicate
between the statement it introduces and the preceding one?

13. Why are these revisions less successful than Hamilton's words: the *effect
of the poison* for *the cold of the poison creeping up to his heart* (3), *complete*
for the second *deep* (9), *falsification of that great mind* for *misstatement of that
mighty mind* (11)?

POINTS TO LEARN

1. An apt quotation is effective in closing an essay.

2. A closing may require a conclusion in the sense of a final assessment of
value or meaning.

3. The end of an essay is generally better if the final passage is slowed and
regulated by separating its syntactic units (within the conventions of modern
punctuation) by stops—commas, semicolons, colons, dashes.

SUGGESTIONS FOR WRITING

Imagine that you are closing an essay about a relative, friend, or teacher whom
you know well. In two or three paragraphs sum up what you consider the
individual's essential quality. End the paragraph with a quotation (probably
something you remember the person having said, or something you yourself
make up) which by implication reinforces your conclusion. Whether it be
one sentence or several, be sure that the quotation is slowed and regulated by
appropriate stops.

IMPROVING YOUR STYLE

1. Include an appositive in one or two of your sentences.

2. Begin another sentence with *indeed*.

Personal Writing

All writing, in the broadest sense, is personal. Even a laundry list reveals something about the writer. Well aware of this fact, Napoleon, it is said, demanded to see a sample of an officer's writing before promoting him to one of the highest ranks. Exposition, argument, description, narration—all gradually, but surely, show us the writer by his choice of subject, the breadth and depth of his knowledge, the skill with which he shapes his material, and his ability to find what it means. Why, then, a collection of pieces labeled personal writing? The answer is that the personal element in essays, while always present, varies widely in its prominence.

As an essay approaches the almost pure exposition of a scientific treatise, the personality of the writer quite properly diminishes. The writer's purpose is utilitarian—the logical, efficient setting down of a body of fact. The language of such a treatise should be precise and unobtrusive, attention being diverted from the writer and his words to the subject at hand. The writer avoids the pronoun *I*, or uses it sparingly; his tone tends to be colorless. His writing is technical and usually of interest only to experts.

Very different is prose whose subject is chiefly, if not exclusively, the writer himself. Such writing is informal, familiar, and its aim, most often, to entertain more than to convey factual information. It may range from the profoundly serious to the satiric and humorous, but its distinguishing characteristic is its concern with personal feelings and personal values. Most often—though not always—the writer employs the pronoun *I*, and establishes himself simply as one individual talking to another. Informal, personal prose, then, is likely to be colloquial, more loosely organized than formal, and to have a distinctive tone. It is often a stylistic performance as well. We enjoy it. Indeed, it approaches imaginative literature in the pleasures it offers and may even be a kind of poetry.

The essays in this section have been chosen to illustrate prose in which the personal element is more prominent than usual. Within the section there is an instructive range of subject matter and strategy. In the first two selections the Duc de La Rochefoucauld and Bertrand Russell are writing, quite literally, about themselves. Here subject and writer are the same, not absolutely identical, of course, for La Rochefoucauld and Russell, as writers, step back from themselves as subjects. Perhaps because they are so close to their subjects their tactic is to appear impersonal and distanced.

The other four essays have "subjects" in the more conventional sense—boxing, a visit to a lake, the experience of time, the life of blacks in the South seventy-five years ago. Yet even here the subject is not really outside the writer. In each case the writer's consciousness so infuses what he or she is writing about that the "subject" becomes part of the self, or the self part of it.

Personal writing, then, is writing focused on the beliefs, feelings, responses of the writer, whatever the ostensible subject. It is one of the most interesting kinds of prose and one of the most revealing and surprising, both to a reader and to the writer himself. People often find when they attempt to compose a personal essay that their "selves" are more complicated than they had known. One way of discovering what you are is to try to explain to others what you believe and feel and value.

Portrait of Himself

François, Duc de La Rochefoucauld was born in Paris in 1613 and died there in 1680. He was an important member of the aristocracy—a *grand seigneur*, as the French say—but for political reasons fell out of favor and was forced to retire from court life. He is best remembered for his *Maxims*, a collection of brief, pointed observations about human beings—their virtues and vices, their follies and pretensions. The maxims are often cynical, often wise, but invariably witty and pithy. Here is a brief sampling:

> We all have enough strength to bear the misfortunes of others.
> We are easily consoled for the misfortunes of our friends, if they afford us an opportunity of displaying our affections.
> True love, like a ghost, is much talked of but seldom seen.
> Old people are fond of giving good advice to console themselves for being no longer able to give bad examples.
> Young people generally mistake rudeness and roughness for freedom from affectation.

The Self-Portrait, which is sometimes reprinted as a kind of Forward to the *Maxims*, was actually published earlier. The topic was a conventional one for writers of the period, and La Rochefoucauld's was intended to amuse his friends and not to be published. (It was printed without his authorization.) By all contemporary evidence it appears to be candid and accurate.

1   I am of medium height, supple, and well-made. My complexion is dark, and fairly uniform; I have a high and tolerably broad forehead; eyes dark, small, and deep-set, eyebrows dark and bushy, but well shaped. I find it difficult to describe my nose; for it is neither snub, aquiline, thick, nor pointed, at least to the best of my belief; all I can say is that it is big rather 5 than small, and somewhat too long. My mouth is large, the lips usually fairly

From *The Maxims of François, Duc de la Rochefoucauld*, translated by F. G. Stevens. Reprinted by permission of the publisher, Oxford University Press, Inc.

red, and neither well nor ill modeled. My teeth are white and tolerably regular. I have been told at times that I have rather too much chin; I have just been examining myself in the looking-glass to ascertain the truth, and I am not quite sure what to think of it. As for the shape of my face, it is 10 either square or oval; which of the two, I should find it very hard to say. My hair is black and curls naturally, and is moreover of such length and thickness as enables me to lay claim to a handsome head.

2   My normal expression is somewhat bitter and haughty; which makes most people think me supercilious, though I am not the least so really. I 15 have a very easy bearing, in fact rather too much so, as it leads me to gesticulate too freely when speaking. This frankly is what I think I look like and will, I believe, prove to be not far from the truth. I shall be equally faithful to fact in the rest of my portrait; for I have studied myself closely enough to know myself well, and I shall lack neither the courage to mention 20 unreservedly any good points I may possess, nor the sincerity to acknowledge my faults with frankness.

3   In the first place I will speak of my temperament. I am inclined to melancholy, to such an extent that for the last three or four years there are scarcely three or four occasions on which I have been observed to laugh. 25 But if my melancholy were the result of temperament alone, I think it would prove mild enough and easy to bear; it is due, however, to so many other causes, and so vexes my imagination and dominates my mind, that either I brood in silence, or else I give very little attention to what I am saying. I am very reserved with strangers, and not particularly open with 30 most of my acquaintances. I am aware that this is a failing, and I would do my utmost to correct it; but as my somewhat gloomy expression tends to make me seem more reserved than I really am, and as it is not within our power to rid ourselves of faults of expression which are due to the natural cast of the features, I imagine that, though I should succeed in improving 35 my inner disposition, I should still not fail to show the outward tokens of imperfection.

4   I am intellectual and am not afraid to say so; for what is the use of affectation? In my opinion too much circuity and delicacy in speaking of one's good points conceals a measure of vanity under a show of modesty, 40 and is an adroit way of securing a reputation for more merit than one claims. Personally, I am content to be thought no more handsome than I claim to be, no more amiable than I depict myself, no more intellectual or sensible than I am. I repeat then that I am intellectual; but my wit is marred by my gloomy disposition: for though I possess a fair mastery of language, a good 45

memory, and a clear head, I am so much obsessed by melancholy that I often express myself indifferently.

5   One of the things which gives me most pleasure is the conversation of cultured people. I prefer that it should be serious, and principally devoted to moral subjects. Yet I can enjoy it when it is gay; and though I am not much given to light jesting, that is not because I underrate witty trifles, or fail to derive much amusement from this kind of fooling, in which some ready and joyous wits achieve such marked success. I write good prose, and compose good verse; and if I desired the fame that these accomplishments bring, I believe that I could without much labour acquire a tolerable reputation.

6   I am fond of reading in all shapes; but particularly such as tends to educate the mind and invigorate the spirit. Above all, I derive the keenest pleasure from reading in the company of a person of intelligence; for this conduces to continual reflection on the subject of the book, and from such reflections arises the pleasantest possible conversation, and the most profitable.

7   I am a fair judge of composition both in prose and verse; but I am inclined to express my opinions too freely. Another of my failings is that my taste is sometimes too fastidious, and my criticism too severe. I do not dislike hearing an argument, and sometimes I take part in it willingly enough: but I generally maintain my opinion with too much warmth; and when my opponent's contention is erroneous, sometimes, in the ardour of my passion for truth, I become unreasonable in my turn.

8   My sympathies are with virtue and I have a generous disposition, and so keen a desire to be in all respects a man of honour that my friends can give me no greater pleasure than by frankly pointing at my faults. Those more intimate acquaintances, who have at times been kind enough to give me some hints in that direction, can bear witness that I have always accepted them with the greatest delight conceivable, and with as much humility as can be desired.

9   Not one of my passions is very ardent, and all are under control. I have scarcely even been seen to lose my temper, and I have never known hatred for anybody. At the same time I should not be incapable of revenge if I were insulted, and honour demanded that I should show my resentment for the injury received. On the contrary, I am convinced that sense of duty would take the place of hatred in me so effectively that I should prosecute my vengeance even more vigorously than others.

10   I am not troubled by ambition in the least degree. I am not ap-

prehensive, and have absolutely no fear of death. I am little susceptible to   85
pity, and would prefer not to be so at all. Yet there is nothing I would not
do to alleviate another's suffering; and I am strongly of opinion that it is
our duty to do everything possible to that end, even to the extent of ex-
hibiting great sympathy; for unhappy people are so silly that that does them
all the good in the world: but I consider that we should be content to   90
exhibit sympathy, and take the greatest care not to entertain it. For it is a
feeling that is intrinsically valueless in a sound character; it tends to en-
feeble the spirit, and should be left to the common herd who, as they are
never guided by reason, need the stimulus of feeling to prompt them to
action of any kind.   95

11   I am fond of my friends, and that in such fashion that I would not
hesitate for a moment to sacrifice my own interests to theirs. I make allow-
ances for them; and I endure with patience their ill humour; but I am not
lavish with display of my affection, nor am I rendered uneasy by their
absence.   100

12   I am by nature little given to curiosity concerning most of the
matters which excite that passion in other people. I am very secretive and
no one has less difficulty in respecting the confidence of others. I am very
particular to keep my word: I never fail to do so, whatever be the consequences of my promise, and I have made this throughout my life a rule to   105
which I admit no exception. I observe towards women the strictest polite-
ness, and I believe I have never said anything in the presence of a woman
which could cause her pain. When women have wit, I prefer their conversation to that of men: they display a charm which is never found in our sex,
and besides, they seem to me to indicate their meaning with greater lucidity,   110
and give a more pleasing turn to their observations. As for light amours, I
have in the past indulged in these to some extent; but now I do so no
longer in spite of my youth. I have given up pretty compliments, and can
only wonder that there are still so many men of honour who spend their time
in peddling them.   115

13   I heartily sympathize with strong passion; it is an indication of
noble character; and though the restlessness it brings has in it something
which is repugnant to austere philosophy, it is otherwise so much in keeping with the strictest virtue that I do not think it can be fairly condemned.
Knowing as I do what a degree of strength and refinement can characterize   120
the emotions of true love, I shall assuredly love after that fashion, if I ever
fall in love at all; but, constituted as I am, I do not believe that that knowledge will ever again quit my head to find a dwelling in my heart.

QUESTIONS

READER AND PURPOSE

1. There are a number of reasons why a man should try to draw a portrait of himself with words. List as many of these as you can. Which of them seems best to describe the purpose of La Rochefoucauld?

2. Compare and contrast La Rochefoucauld's character sketch of himself with the descriptions of character on pages 341 ff. What techniques of characterization has La Rochefoucauld failed to use? Could he have used any of these with profit? Explain.

3. Some writers, in characterizing themselves, write for the eyes of no one but themselves. Does La Rochefoucauld seem to be writing for himself or for an audience? What is the evidence for your answer? What words in paragraph 1 suggest that he is attempting to be objective in his self-appraisal? Would you say that he maintains this objectivity throughout the essay? Be able to support your answer. Nonetheless, does La Rochefoucauld unintentionally reveal any traits of personality? If so, how and where?

ORGANIZATION

4. Make an outline of this essay, indicating its main sections and the major subdivisions within them. Give a brief title to each of these headings. Explain whether or not La Rochefoucauld followed any consistent plan in sketching his self-portrait. What suggestions can you give for improving the organization?

5. Study how La Rochefoucauld develops the physical description in paragraph 1. Is he following a plan here, or simply rambling on, jotting down his various features as they occur to him? Is he wise to begin with a physical description rather than, say, placing it last?

6. Why does he treat the material in paragraph 2 separately instead of including it as part of paragraph 1? Which sentences in paragraph 2 sum up the first section of the essay and prepare us for the next?

7. La Rochefoucauld does not bother with long summarizing transitions between his paragraphs, as, for instance: "Having finished describing my temperament, I will now discuss my taste in literature." Still, his paragraphs flow together. How does he unify them?

8. Discuss the beginning and the closing of this essay, explaining whether or not you think they do the jobs that a good beginning and closing should do. Try composing a final paragraph that will make a more graceful closing.

SENTENCES

9. The final sentence of paragraph 3 is a good example of the complex style. It contains a number of clauses which carefully develop and explain and qualify

the rather complicated thought the writer is trying to express. Read the sentence several times and then in your own words explain what La Rochefoucauld is saying. Point out one or two other sentences similarly complicated.

DICTION

10. Look up: *supple* (1), *haughty* (14), *gesticulate* (17), *unreservedly* (21), *temperament* (23), *melancholy* (24), *vexes* (28), *reflection* (60), *fastidious* (65), *ardent* (77), *susceptible* (85), *alleviate* (87), *lavish* (99), *lucidity* (110).

11. Explain the meanings of the following phrases: *tolerably regular* (7-8), *outward tokens of imperfection* (36-37), *gloomy disposition* (45), *witty trifles* (51), *common herd* (93), *light amours* (111), *austere philosophy* (118).

12. Rewrite paragraph 4, substituting a Saxon vocabulary for the writer's Latinate diction wherever possible. How do these changes affect the tone * of the writing? Are the changes in each instance an improvement? What do you think of the advice that one should always prefer a simple Saxon word to one of Latin derivation?

13. Look up the etymologies * of the following: *aquiline, supercilious, adroit, intrinsically*. How does knowing the etymology of a word help the writer? What, by the way, is the etymology of *etymology?*

14. It is obvious near the end of paragraph 4 that La Rochefoucauld is repeating himself when he says that he is intellectual. Why, then, does he stress the obvious by writing "I repeat"? And why does he bother to repeat at all what he said clearly enough at the beginning of the paragraph?

15. What distinction is La Rochefoucauld making in paragraph 10 when he advises his reader to *exhibit* but not to *entertain* sympathy for unhappy people? La Rochefoucauld has often been accused of cynicism. Does this seem like cynical advice to you?

POINTS TO LEARN

1. Almost all writing, no matter how formal or informal, no matter how personal or impersonal, gains from a clear plan of organization.

2. To interest is to inform. The writer who is content with generalities in place of definite information will quickly lose his reader.

3. A writer reveals his personality not only by his choice of subject and by his beliefs openly stated, he also reveals himself by his sentence structure, his diction, and, what is closely related to both, his tone.

SUGGESTIONS FOR WRITING

Compose a self-portrait, imitating in a general way the procedure of La Rochefoucauld. Include, among other things, a section of physical description, of your likes and dislikes, of your virtues and your failings, of your talents and your weaknesses. Be as objective as you can and write with a purpose.

IMPROVING YOUR STYLE

1. Before you begin your sketch make a careful outline of what you intend to cover and in what order. If your teacher asks, turn the outline in along with the composition.

2. In your sketch include a long compound-complex sentence like the one that ends La Rochefoucauld's third paragraph.

Three Passions

Bertrand Russell (1872-1970) was a most unusual combination of mathematician, philosopher, and man of letters. One of the most important British mathematicians of this century, he wrote the very influential *Principia Mathematica* (with Alfred North Whitehead) in 1910 and *Introduction to Mathematical Philosophy* (1919). At the same time he was interested in social, ethical, and political issues, which he discussed in numerous essays. During the twenties he advocated feminism and a freer attitude toward sex, opinions which cost him his teaching position at the University of California, Los Angeles. In 1950 he was awarded the Nobel Prize for literature. In 1951, at the age of 79, he published his autobiography, from which the following selection is reprinted.

1   Three passions, simple but overwhelmingly strong, have governed my life: the longing for love, the search for knowledge, and unbearable pity for the suffering of mankind. These passions, like great winds, have blown me hither and thither, in a wayward course, over a deep ocean of anguish, reaching to the very verge of despair.   5

2   I have sought love, first, because it brings ecstasy—ecstasy so great that I would often have sacrificed all the rest of life for a few hours of this joy. I have sought it, next, because it relieves loneliness—that terrible loneliness in which one shivering consciousness looks over the rim of the world into the cold unfathomable lifeless abyss. I have sought it, finally, because in the   10 union of love I have seen, in a mystic miniature, the prefiguring vision of the heaven that saints and poets have imagined. This is what I sought, and though it might seem too good for human life, this is what—at last—I have found.

3   With equal passion I have sought knowledge. I have wished to   15

understand the hearts of men. I have wished to know why the stars shine. And I have tried to apprehend the Pythagorean power by which number holds sway above the flux. A little of this, but not much, I have achieved.

4   Love and knowledge, so far as they were possible, led upward toward the heavens. But always pity brought me back to earth. Echoes of cries of 20 pain reverberate in my heart. Children in famine, victims tortured by oppressors, helpless old people a hated burden to their sons, and the whole world of loneliness, poverty, and pain make a mockery of what human life should be. I long to alleviate the evil, but I cannot, and I too suffer.

5   This has been my life. I have found it worth living, and would gladly 25 live it again if the chance were offered me.

QUESTIONS

READER AND PURPOSE

1. What do you think motivates famous men and women to write auto-biographies? Can you suggest two purposes shaping this excerpt from Russell's autobiography? What are the rewards of reading another person's life story?

2. Writing is personal when its subject is chiefly the writer's personality, values, and deeds, for then it reveals the writer, not only in terms of what he consciously tells us but what he "says" unconsciously. What can you infer about Bertrand Russell after reading his lines and whatever lies between them?

ORGANIZATION

3. Show that the first paragraph sets up the plan of the next three.

4. Does the order in which Russell discusses his "passions" suggest anything about his priorities of value? Suppose the sequence had been "pity for mankind," "search for knowledge," and "longing for love": would Russell's tone * and emphasis be changed?

5. Study the transitions between each paragraph. Are they smooth or abrupt? What words in the opening sentence of paragraph two link to what words in paragraph one? Which words link the third paragraph to the second? The fourth to the third?

6. Why do you suppose the last paragraph is so brief?

7. Show how the organization of paragraph two parallels the organization of the whole excerpt.

SENTENCES

8. Russell's prose, while its subject is formal and serious, is both forceful and emotional. These qualities result in part from his sentence structure. His most

frequent device of emphasis is interrupted movement *. How many examples can you find?

9. Repetition is another means of emphasis. Sometimes as in line 6 Russell immediately repeats a key term for emphasis, placing the second in apposition * to the first. The ancient Greeks called this rhetorical * technique *epizeuxis*; it has been common in English and other European languages for centuries. Find another example in this selection.

10. Identify examples of anaphora * in paragraphs 2 and 3. Does anaphora tend to heighten an emotional tone or to dampen it?

11. Explain why the following revisions are less emphatic than Russell's sentence:

> *Revision (a)*: A little of this I have achieved, but not much.
> *Revision (b)*: I have achieved a little of this, but not much.
> *Russell*: "A little of this, but not much, I have achieved." (18)

DICTION

12. Look up: *abyss* (10), *prefiguring* (11), *apprehend* (17), *Pythagorean* (17), *flux* (18), *alleviate* (24).

13. As important as sentence structure in creating the emotional force of Russell's prose in his diction. At least three devices are at work: figures (metaphors * and similes *), alliteration *, and adjectives with strong emotional coloring. Find examples of each.

14. Read this entire selection out loud and listen. Then read aloud the following revision of Russell's third paragraph:

> With the same interest I've looked for knowledge, since I've wanted to understand what people are thinking and how the universe is put together, so to speak. Also I've wanted to find some comprehension of what causes the eternalization of numbers when everything else is more or less in a state of deterioration. I've done something like this, but not so much as I had hoped for.

While the revision says approximately the same thing, there is a difference, the difference, to borrow a phrase from Mark Twain, between lightning and the lightning bug. Give as many reasons as you can why Russell's prose works and the revision fails.

POINTS TO LEARN

1. All writing is self-revelation. If in personal writing authors discuss themselves consciously, they reveal almost as much unconsciously by their words and sentence structure. Even the degree of clarity or of muddle in the organization

is a clue to their intelligence, their education, their willingness to work, and their consideration for others.

2. Personal writing is likely to succeed more easily than other kinds of exposition. Our own self is a subject most of us are thoroughly acquainted with and deeply care about.

3. The fact that the prose is serious does not mean that it is toneless. Russell's writing is an instructive combination of clarity, vigor, and emotion.

4. It is helpful to read good prose out loud; it is easy on the ear. You should routinely read aloud what you write, revising whatever strikes you as harsh or dull.

SUGGESTIONS FOR WRITING

1. Loosely organizing your essay on the model of the passage by Russell, list and briefly discuss the goals that shape your life.

2. Analyze and discuss briefly the values that form your personal code of ethics.

3. Write an essay in which you discuss what in your experience inclines you toward optimism (or pessimism).

IMPROVING YOUR STYLE

1. In your essay use one or two examples of *epizeuxis*. (See question 9.)

2. If your tone permits, use anaphora once or twice. (Question 10)

3. Experiment with interrupted movement in one or two sentences.

A. J. LIEBLING

Boxing with the Naked Eye

A. J. Liebling was primarily a journalist. He was a frequent contributor to *The New Yorker*, especially on the inadequacies of newspapers. Some of these pieces were collected in *The Wayward Pressman* (1947) and *The Press* (1961). But he wrote about other things: politics (*The Earl of Louisiana*, 1961); the World War (*The Road Back to Paris*, 1944); and boxing (*The Sweet Science*, 1956). The last is the source of the following essay, an account of a heavyweight championship fight between Joe Louis and Lee Savold in 1951. Liebling's title refers to the advantage of watching a bout at ringside rather than seeing it on television. (Twenty-five or thirty years ago boxing was telecast much more frequently than it is now.) As you will see, however, the essay involves more than boxing or television or even one particular fight. Most of all it involves Liebling.

1   Watching a fight on television has always seemed to me a poor substitute for being there. For one thing, you can't tell the fighters what to do. When I watch a fight, I like to study one boxer's problem, solve it, and then communicate my solution vocally. On occasion my advice is disregarded, as when I tell a man to stay away from the other fellow's left and he   5 doesn't, but in such cases I assume that he hasn't heard my counsel, or that his opponent has, and has acted on it. Some fighters hear better and are more suggestible than others—for example, the pre-television Joe Louis. "Let him have it, Joe!" I would yell whenever I saw him fight, and sooner or later he would let the other fellow have it. Another fighter like that was the   10 late Marcel Cerdan, whom I would coach in his own language, to prevent opposition seconds from picking up our signals. "*Vas-y, Marcel!*" I used to shout, and Marcel always *y allait*. I get a feeling of participation that way that I don't in front of a television screen. I could yell, of course, but I

would know that if my suggestion was adopted, it would be by the merest 15
coincidence.

2   Besides, when you go to a fight, the boxers aren't the only ones you
want to be heard by. You are surrounded by people whose ignorance of the
ring is exceeded only by their unwillingness to face facts—the sharpness of
your boxer's punching, for instance. Such people may take it upon them- 20
selves to disparage the principal you are advising. This disparagement is less
generally addressed to the man himself (as "Gavilan, you're a bum!") than
to his opponent, whom they have wrong-headedly picked to win. ("He's a
cream puff, Miceli!" they may typically cry. "He can't hurt you. He can't
hurt nobody. Look—slaps! Ha, ha!") They thus get at your man—and, by 25
indirection, at you. To put them in their place, you address neither them
nor their man but your man. ("Get the other eye, Gavilan!" you cry.) This
throws them off balance, because they haven't noticed anything the matter
with either eye. Then, before they can think of anything to say, you thun-
der, "Look at that eye!" It doesn't much matter whether or not the man has 30
been hit in the eye; he will be. Addressing yourself to the fighter when you
want somebody else to hear you is a parliamentary device, like "Mr. Chairman . . ." Before television, a prize-fight was to a New Yorker the nearest
equivalent to the New England town meeting. It taught a man to think on
his seat. 35

3   Less malignant than rooters for the wrong man, but almost as dis-
quieting, are those who are on the right side but tactically unsound. At the
moment when you have steered your boxer to a safe lead on points but can
see the other fellow is still dangerous, one of these maniacs will encourage
recklessness. "Finish the jerk, Harry!" he will sing out. "Stop holding him 40
up! Don't lose him!" But you, knowing the enemy is a puncher, protect your
client's interests. "Move to your left, Harry!" you call. "Keep moving!
Keep moving! Don't let him set!" I sometimes finish a fight like that in a cold
sweat.

4   If you go to a fight with a friend, you can keep up unilateral con- 45
versations on two vocal levels—one at the top of your voice, directed at your
fighter, and the other a running *expertise* nominally aimed at your companion but loud enough to reach a modest fifteen feet in each direction.
"Reminds me of Panama Al Brown," you may say as a new fighter enters
the ring. "He was five feet eleven and weighed a hundred and eighteen 50
pounds. This fellow may be about forty pounds heavier and a couple of
inches shorter, but he's got the same kind of neck. I saw Brown box a fellow named Mascart in Paris in 1927. Guy stood up in the top gallery and

threw an apple and hit Brown right on the top of the head. The whole house
started yelling, 'Finish him, Mascart! He's groggy!' " Then, as the bout be-   55
gins, "Boxes like Al, too, except this fellow's a southpaw." If he wins, you
say, "I told you he reminded me of Al Brown," and if he loses, "Well, well,
I guess he's no Al Brown. They don't make fighters like Al any more." This
identifies you as a man who (a) has been in Paris, (b) has been going to
fights for a long time, and (c) therefore enjoys what the fellows who write   60
for quarterlies call a frame of reference.

5   It may be argued that this doesn't get you anywhere, but it at least
constitutes what a man I once met named Thomas S. Matthews called communication. Mr. Matthews, who was the editor of *Time*, said that the most
important thing in journalism is not reporting but communication. "What   65
are you going to communicate?" I asked him. "The most important thing,"
he said, "is the man on one end of the circuit saying 'My God, I'm alive!
You're alive!' and the fellow on the other end, receiving his message, saying
'My God, you're right! We're both alive!' " I still think it is a hell of a way
to run a news magazine, but it is a good reason for going to fights in person.   70
Television, if unchecked, may carry us back to a pre-tribal state of social development, when the family was the largest conversational unit.

6   Fights are also a great place for adding to your repertory of witty
sayings. I shall not forget my adolescent delight when I first heard a fight fan
yell, "I hope youse bot' gets knocked out!" I thought he had made it up, al-   75
though I found out later it was a cliché. It is a formula adaptable to an
endless variety of situations outside the ring. The only trouble with it is it
never works out. The place where I first heard the line was Bill Brown's, a
fight club in a big shed behind a trolley station in Far Rockaway.

7   On another night there, the time for the main bout arrived and one   80
of the principals hadn't. The other fighter sat in the ring, a bantamweight
with a face like a well-worn coin, and the fans stamped in cadence and
whistled and yelled for their money back. It was thirty years before television, but there were only a couple of hundred men on hand. The preliminary fights had been terrible. The little fighter kept looking at his hands,   85
which were resting on his knees in cracked boxing gloves, and every now
and then he would spit on the mat and rub the spittle into the canvas with
one of his scuffed ring shoes. The longer he waited, the more frequently he
spat, and I presumed he was worrying about the money he was supposed to
get; it wouldn't be more than fifty dollars with a house that size, even if the   90
other man turned up. He had come there from some remote place like West
or East New York, and he may have been thinking about the last train

home on the Long Island Railroad, too. Finally, the other bantamweight
got there, looking out of breath and flustered. He had lost his way on the
railroad—changed to the wrong train at Jamaica and had to go back there   95
and start over. The crowd booed so loud that he looked embarrassed. When
the fight began, the fellow who had been waiting walked right into the new
boy and knocked him down. He acted impatient. The tardy fellow got up
and fought back gamely, but the one who had been waiting nailed him
again, and the latecomer just about pulled up to one knee at the count of   100
seven. He had been hit pretty hard, and you could see from his face that he
was wondering whether to chuck it. Somebody in the crowd yelled out,
"Hey, Hickey! You kept us all waiting! Why don't you stay around awhile?"
So the fellow got up and caught for ten rounds and probably made the one
who had come early miss his train. It's another formula with multiple ap-   105
plications, and I think the man who said it that night in Far Rockaway did
make it up.

8   Because of the way I feel about watching fights on television, I was
highly pleased when I read, back in June, 1951, that the fifteen-round match
between Joe Louis and Lee Savold, scheduled for June thirteenth at the   110
Polo Grounds, was to be neither televised, except to eight theater audiences
in places like Pittsburgh and Albany, nor broadcast over the radio. I hadn't
seen Louis with the naked eye since we shook hands in a pub in London in
1944. He had fought often since then, and I had seen his two bouts with
Jersey Joe Walcott on television, but there hadn't been any fun in it. Those   115
had been held in public places, naturally, and I could have gone, but television gives you so plausible an adumbration of a fight, for nothing, that you
feel it would be extravagant to pay your way in. It is like the potato, which
is only a succedaneum for something decent to eat but which, once introduced into Ireland, proved so cheap that the peasants gave up their grain-   120
and-meat diet in favor of it. After that, the landlords let them keep just
enough money to buy potatoes. William Cobbett, a great Englishman, said
that he would sack any workmen of his he caught eating one of the cursed
things, because as soon as potatoes appeared anywhere they brought down
the standard of eating. I sometimes think of Cobbett on my way home from   125
the races, looking at the television aerials on all the little houses between
here and Belmont Park. As soon as I heard that the fight wouldn't be on the
air, I determined to buy a ticket.

9   On the night of the thirteenth, a Wednesday, it rained, and on the
next night it rained again, so on the evening of June fifteenth the promoters,   130

the International Boxing Club, confronted by a night game at the Polo Grounds, transferred the fight to Madison Square Garden. The postponements upset a plan I had had to go to the fight with a friend, who had another date for the third night. But alone is a good way to go to a fight or the races, because you have more time to look around you, and you always get all the conversation you can use anyway. I went to the Garden box office early Friday afternoon and bought a ten-dollar seat in the side arena—the first tiers rising in back of the boxes, midway between Eighth and Ninth Avenues on the 49th Street side of the house. There was only a scattering of ticket buyers in the lobby, and the man at the ticket window was polite—a bad omen for the gate. After buying the ticket, I got into a cab in front of the Garden, and the driver naturally asked me if I was going to see the fight. I said I was, and he said, "He's all through."

10   I knew he meant Louis, and I said, "I know, and that's why it may be a good fight. If he weren't through, he might kill this guy."

11   The driver said, "Savold is a hooker. He breaks noses."

12   I said, "He couldn't break his own nose, even," and then began to wonder how a man would go about trying to do that. "It's a shame he's so hard up he had to fight at all at his age," I said, knowing the driver would understand I meant Louis. I was surprised that the driver was against Louis, and I was appealing to his better feelings.

13   "He must have plenty socked away," said the driver. "Playing golf for a hundred dollars a hole."

14   "Maybe that helped him go broke," I said. "And anyway, what does that prove? There's many a man with a small salary who bets more than he can afford." I had seen a scratch sheet on the seat next to the hackie. I was glad I was riding only as far as Brentano's with him.

15   The driver I had on the long ride home was a better type. As soon as I told him I was going to the fight, which was at about the same time that he dropped the flag, he said, "I guess the old guy can still sock."

16   I said, "I saw him murder Max Baer sixteen years ago. He was a sweet fighter then."

17   The driver said, "Sixteen years is a long time for a fighter. I don't remember anybody lasted sixteen years in the big money. Still, Savold is almost as old as he is. When you're a bum, nobody notices how old you get."

18   We had a pleasant time on the West Side Highway, talking about how Harry Greb had gone on fighting when he was blind in one eye, only nobody knew it but his manager, and how Pete Herman had been the best

infighter in the world, because he had been practically blind in both eyes, so   170
he couldn't afford to fool around outside. "What Herman did, you couldn't
learn a boy now," the driver said. "They got no patience."

19   The fellow who drove me from my house to the Garden after dinner was also a man of good will, but rather different. He knew I was going to
the fight as soon as I told him my destination, and once we had got under   175
way, he said, "It is a pity that a man like Louis should be exploited to such a
degree that he has to fight again." It was only nine-fifteen, and he agreed
with me that I had plenty of time to get to the Garden for the main bout,
which was scheduled to begin at ten, but when we got caught in unex-
pectedly heavy traffic on Eleventh Avenue he grew impatient. "Come on,   180
Jersey!" he said, giving a station wagon in front of us the horn. "In the last
analysis, we have got to get to the Garden sometime." But it didn't help
much, because most of the other cars were heading for the Garden, too. The
traffic was so slow going toward Eighth Avenue on Fiftieth Street that I
asked him to let me out near the Garden corner, and joined the people   185
hurrying from the Independent Subway exit toward the Garden marquee. A
high percentage of them were from Harlem, and they were dressed as if for
a levee, the men in shimmering gabardines and felt hats the color of freshly
unwrapped chewing gum, the women in spring suits and fur pieces—it was a
cool night—and what seemed to me the prettiest hats of the season. They   190
seemed to me the prettiest lot of women I had seen in a long time, too, and
I reflected that if the fight had been televised, I would have missed them.
"Step out," I heard one beau say as his group swept past me, "or we won't
maybe get in. It's just like I told you—he's still one hell of a draw." As I
made my way through the now crowded lobby, I could hear the special cop   195
next to the ticket window chanting, "Six-, eight-, ten-, and fifteen-dollar
tickets only," which meant that the two-and-a-halfdollar general-admission
and the twenty-dollar ringside seats were sold out. It made me feel good, because it showed there were still some gregarious people left in the world.

20   Inside the Garden there was the same old happy drone of voices   200
as when Jimmy McLarnin was fighting and Jimmy Walker was at the ringside. There was only one small patch of bare seats, in a particularly bad part
of the ringside section. I wondered what sort of occupant I would find in
my seat; I knew from experience that there would be somebody in it. It
turned out to be a small, frail colored man in wine-red livery. He sat up   205
straight and pressed his shoulder blades against the back of the chair, so I
couldn't see the number. When I showed him my ticket, he said, "I don't

know nothing about that. You better see the usher." He was offering this token resistance, I knew, only to protect his self-esteem—to maintain the shadowy fiction that he was in the seat by error. When an usher wandered within hailing distance of us, I called him, and the little man left, to drift to some other part of the Garden, where he had no reputation as a ten-dollar-seat holder to lose, and there to squat contentedly on a step.

21   My seat was midway between the east and west ends of the ring, and about fifteen feet above it. Two not very skillful colored boys were finishing a four-rounder that the man in the next seat told me was an emergency bout, put on because there had been several knockouts in the earlier preliminaries. It gave me a chance to settle down and look around. It was ten o'clock by the time the colored boys finished and the man with the microphone announced the decision, but there was no sign of Louis or Savold. The fight wasn't on the air, so there was no need of the punctuality required by the radio business. (Later I read in the newspapers that the bout had been delayed in deference to the hundreds of people who were still in line to buy tickets and who wanted to be sure of seeing the whole fight.) Nobody made any spiel about beer, as on the home screen, although a good volume of it was being drunk all around. Miss Gladys Gooding, an organist, played the national anthem and a tenor sang it, and we all applauded. After that, the announcer introduced a number of less than illustrious prizefighters from the ring, but nobody whistled or acted restless. It was a good-natured crowd.

22   Then Louis and his seconds—what the author of *Boxiana* would have called his faction—appeared from a runway under the north stands and headed toward the ring. The first thing I noticed, from where I sat, was that the top of Louis's head was bald. He looked taller than I had remembered him, although surely he couldn't have grown after the age of thirty, and his face was puffy and impassive. It has always been so. In the days of his greatness, the press read menace in it. He walked stiff-legged, as was natural for a heavy man of thirty-seven, but when his seconds pulled off his dressing robe, his body looked all right. He had never been a lean man; his muscles had always been well buried beneath his smooth beige skin. I recalled the first time I had seen him fight—against Baer. That was at the Yankee Stadium, in September, 1935, and not only the great ball park but the roofs of all the apartment houses around were crowded with spectators, and hundreds of people were getting out of trains at the elevated I.R.T. station, which overlooks the field, and trying to loiter long enough to catch a few moments of action. Louis had come East that summer, after a single year as a professional, and had knocked out Primo Carnera in a few rounds. Carnera had been the heavyweight champion of the world in 1934, when Baer knocked him out. Baer, when he fought Louis, was the most powerful and gifted heavyweight of the day, although he had already fumbled away his title. But this mature 250 Baer, who had fought everybody, was frightened stiff by the twenty-one-year old mulatto boy. Louis outclassed him. The whole thing went only four rounds. There hadn't been anybody remotely like Louis since Dempsey in the early twenties.

23   The week of the Louis-Baer fight, a man I know wrote in a maga- 255 zine: "With half an eye, one can observe that the town is more full of stir than it has been in many moons. It is hard to find a place to park, hard to get a table in a restaurant, hard to answer all the phone calls. . . . Economic seers can explain it, if you care to listen. We prefer to remember that a sudden inflation of the town's spirit can be just as much psychological or 260 accidental as economic." I figured it was Louis.

24   Savold had now come up into the other corner, a jutty-jawed man with a fair skin but a red back, probably sunburned at his training camp. He was twenty pounds lighter than Louis, but that isn't considered a crushing handicap among heavyweights; Ezzard Charles, who beat Louis the 265 previous year, was ten pounds lighter than Savold. Savold was thirty-five, and there didn't seem to be much bounce in him. I had seen him fight twice in the winter of 1946, and I knew he wasn't much. Both bouts had been against a young Negro heavyweight named Al Hoosman, a tall, skinny fellow just out of the Army. Hoosman had started well the first time, but 270 Savold had hurt him with body punches and won the decision. The second time, Hoosman had stayed away and jabbed him silly. An old third-rater like Savold, I knew, doesn't improve with five more years on him. But an old third-rater doesn't rattle easily, either, and I was sure he'd do his best. It made me more apprehensive, in one way, than if he'd been any good. I 275 wouldn't have liked to see Louis beaten by a good young fighter, but it would be awful to see him beaten by a clown. Not that I have anything against Savold; I just think it's immoral for a fellow without talent to get too far. A lot of others in the crowd must have felt the same way, because the house was quiet when the fight started—as if the Louis rooters didn't 280 want to ask too much of Joe. There weren't any audible rooters for Savold, though, of course, there would have been if he had landed one good punch.

25   I remembered reading in a newspaper that Savold had said he would walk right out and bang Louis in the temple with a right, which would

scramble his thinking. But all he did was come forward as he had against   285
Hoosman, with his left low. A fellow like that never changes. Louis walked
out straight and stiff-legged, and jabbed his left into Savold's face. He did
it again and again, and Savold didn't seem to know what to do about it. And
Louis jabs a lot harder than a fellow like Hoosman. Louis didn't have to
chase Savold, and he had no reason to run away from him, either, so the   290
stiff legs were all right. When the two men came close together, Louis jarred
Savold with short punches, and Savold couldn't push him around, so that
was all right, too. After the first round, the crowd knew Louis would win if
his legs would hold him.

26   In the second round Louis began hitting Savold with combinations—   295
quick sequences of punches, like a right under the heart and a left hook
to the right side of the head. A sports writer I know had told me that Louis
hadn't been putting combinations together for several fights back. Combinations demand a superior kind of coordination, but a fighter who has
once had that can partly regain it by hard work. A couple of times it looked   300
as if Louis was trying for a knockout, but when Savold didn't come apart,
Louis returned to jabbing. A man somewhere behind me kept saying to a
companion, "I read Savold was a tricky fighter. He's got to do something!"
But Savold didn't, until late in the fifth round, by which time his head must
have felt like a sick music box. Then he threw a right to Louis's head and it   305
landed. I thought I could see Louis shrink, as if he feared trouble. His response ten years ago would have been to tear right back into the man. Savold
threw another right, exactly the same kind, and that hit Louis, too. No good
fighter should have been hit twice in succession with that kind of foolish
punch. But the punches weren't hard enough to slow Louis down, and that   310
was the end of that. In the third minute of the sixth round, he hit Savold
with a couple of combinations no harder than those that had gone before,
but Savold was weak now. His legs were going limp, and Louis was pursuing
him as he backed toward my side of the ring. Then Louis swung like an axman with his right (he wasn't snapping it as he used to), and his left   315
dropped over Savold's guard and against his jaw, and the fellow was rolling
over and over on the mat, rolling the way football players do when they fall
on a fumbled ball. The referee was counting and Savold was rolling, and he
got up on either nine or ten, I couldn't tell which (later, I read that it was
ten, so he was out officially), but you could see he was knocked silly, and the   320
referee had his arms around him, and it was over.

27   The newspapermen, acres of them near the ring, were banging out
the leads for the running stories they had already telegraphed, and I felt sorry

for them, because they never have time to enjoy boxing matches. Since the fight was not broadcast, there was no oily-voiced chap to drag Louis over to 325 a microphone and ask him stupid questions. He shook hands with Savold twice, once right after the knockout and again a few minutes later, when Savold was ready to leave the ring, as if he feared Savold wouldn't remember the first handshake.

28   I drifted toward the lobby with the crowd. The chic Harlem people 330 were saying to one another, "It was terrific, darling! It was terrific!" I could see that an element of continuity had been restored to their world. But there wasn't any of the wild exultation that had followed those first Louis victories in 1935. These people had celebrated so many times—except, of course, the younger ones, who were small children when Louis knocked out 335 Baer. I recognized one of the Garden promoters, usually a sour fellow, looking happy. The bout had brought in receipts of $94,684, including my ten dollars, but, what was more important to the Garden, Louis was sure to draw a lot more the next time, and at a higher scale of prices.

29   I walked downtown on Eighth Avenue to a point where the crowd 340 began to thin out, and climbed into a taxi that had been stopped by the light on a cross street. This one had a Negro driver.

30   "The old fellow looked pretty good tonight," I said. "Had those combinations going."

31   "Fight over?" the driver asked. If there had been television, or even 345 radio, he would have known about everything, and I wouldn't have had the fun of telling him.

32   "Sure," I said. "He knocked the guy out in the sixth."

33   "I was afraid he wouldn't," said the driver. "You know, it's a funny thing," he said, after we had gone on a way, "but I been twenty-five years in 350 New York now and never seen Joe Louis in the flesh."

34   "You've seen him on television, haven't you?"

35   "Yeah," he said. "But that don't count." After a while he said, "I remember when he fought Carnera. The celebration in Harlem. They poisoned his mind before that fight, his managers and Jack Blackburn did. They 355 told him Carnera was Mussolini's man and Mussolini started the Ethiopian War. He cut that man down like he was a tree."

QUESTIONS

READER AND PURPOSE

1. How does Liebling regard fight fans? Read carefully these two sentences: "Such people may take it upon themselves to disparage the principal you are advising"; and " 'Gavilan, you're a bum.' " The first is Liebling's description of what the fans say; the second is what they literally do say. The diction of the first sentence is inflated—that is, it is more serious and formal than the subject it describes—which is a time-honored device of satire. Consider again—what is Liebling's attitude toward his fellow spectators? How does he regard himself in the role of fight fan? Support your answer by evidence from the essay.

2. Compare to those quoted in question 1 this sentence from paragraph 26: "Then Louis swung like an axman with his right (he wasn't snapping it as he used to), and his left dropped over Savold's guard, and the fellow was rolling over and over on the mat, rolling the way football players do when they fall on a fumbled ball." Why does it suggest that Liebling takes fighting and fighters more seriously than he takes the fans?

You begin to realize that Liebling's tone * is complex rather than simple, not easily reduced to such a label as "serious" or "amused," "respectful" or "satiric." At times Liebling is serious, and at times he is pleasantly satiric; but these are not two separate attitudes which, like masks, he puts on and off as suits him. Rather they are two aspects of the same complex attitude. This complexity of tone is reflected in the diction, the sentence structure, and the organization of the essay.

ORGANIZATION

3. What constitutes the beginning of this essay—paragraph 1? paragraphs 1-3? paragraphs 1-7? Explain.

4. The section dealing with the Louis-Savold fight has four main parts. Identify and give a title to each.

5. The organization of this selection seems simpler and looser than it is. Before the essay is over we view the fight and its spectators from numerous angles. We see the action in the ring as a camera might record it; we see the fighters and the crowd through Liebling's eyes; we see Louis as other observers regard him; we see the fight and fighters projected against a background of other bouts and other boxers; and finally we see this match set in the general framework of prize-fighting and its fans. To appreciate this complex organization, look again at the parts you identified in question 4. What does each contribute to our understanding of the Louis-Savold fight?

6. As much as the fight, the observer is here a part of the subject, and the essay moves us back and forth between the scene and the personality that watches it. Examine, for instance, paragraph 24. Although it begins with a sentence describing the scene ("Savold had now come up into the other corner . . ."), it soon slips away from the arena. In what sentence does the paragraph return to the fight? What does the writer do in between these points? Find two or three other paragraphs that illustrate this same movement between the scene and the man watching it. Do you think that a sports editor on a metropolitan morning paper would have accepted this account from a reporter assigned to cover a boxing match? Why or why not?

7. The complexity of Liebling's subject is perhaps best revealed in the attitudes he records of other fans: the "happy promoter" in lines 335-36, for example; the newsmen "banging out leads" (322); the "oily-voiced" announcer (325), happily absent on this night; the "chic Harlem people" (330); the four cabdrivers. To each of these the fight means something different. What does it mean to the promoter? to the announcer? to each of the others?

8. Of all these reactions, Liebling gives greatest weight to the comments of the fourth cabdriver. It is on his graphic description of Louis in his prime—" 'He cut that man down like he was a tree' "—that the essay stops. Is this a good closing? Why or why not? Why does Liebling end with this sudden flashback to the young, quick Louis?

9. Thus we see that the writer's purpose here is complex indeed. To describe a particular fight, the fans interested in it, their attitudes and comments, the people who profit from the fighters—and all these as they seem to a sensitive and experienced observer—this is Liebling's purpose. Yet there is one final complication; the closing suggests that Liebling is writing about more than one fight and one fighter, about more even than fighting—what?

SENTENCES

10. Liebling's sentence structure is relatively colloquial *, reflecting the rhythms of speech. This is achieved in three ways: by keeping the clauses brief; by avoiding interrupted movement *; and by multiple co-ordination *, that is, linking several clauses with *and* or *but*. All three techniques are illustrated in this sentence: "He [Louis] had fought often since then, and I had seen his two bouts with Jersey Joe Walcott on television, but there hadn't been any fun in it." Of course most of the sentences do not reveal all these devices so plainly; try, however, to find three or four others which do. Such a style appears simple, but the appearance is deceptive. Far from mechanically reproducing the actual patterns of speech, it rather suggests colloquial simplicity by careful selection and arrangement. Listen to the conversations of your friends and compare what you hear with what Liebling writes. What improvements has he made?

DICTION

11. Look up: *disparage* (21), *malignant* (36), *client* (42), *expertise* (47), *quarterlies* (61), *repertory* (73), *cliché* (76), *adumbration* (117), *hooker* (146), *beau* (193), *jabbing* (302), *leads* (323).

12. Liebling's diction is wide-ranging, sweeping from colloquialisms and even slang at one extreme (*hackies, spiel, third-rater*) to learned, Latinate terms at the other (*malignant, unilateral, succedaneum*). Point out four or five further examples of each extreme. Why is the diction of paragraphs 25 and 26 simpler than that of paragraphs 4 and 5?

13. Study paragraph 7. Economically but surely Liebling creates the scene in Brown's fight club. He does not bother to describe carefully the face of the "other fighter"; we are not told the color of his eyes, whether his cheekbones are prominent, his nose crooked, his ears large. Yet we receive a vivid impression of his face. In what words? What details of his equipment and of his actions as he waits make this fighter a real, living figure? Could an imaginative reader almost infer from these few details the life story of the "other fighter"? Try it.

14. With equal ease and brevity Liebling characterizes the four cabdrivers. What kind of man is each? Do the cabbies also serve to unify the various sections of the essay?

POINTS TO LEARN

1. Tone is not always simple. It may be exceedingly complicated.

2. The subject of an essay, like tone, may be complex and multiple.

3. Similes * are effective in description, particularly brief description.

4. Isolated, vivid details are sometimes better than a complete catalogue.

SUGGESTIONS FOR WRITING

Probably it will be better to imitate parts rather than the whole of this selection. Whichever topic you choose, write in the first person and make your own feelings and impressions a part of the subject. Work in also typical comments and attitudes of other observers. Since you are writing in the first person, remember that your sentence structure must be less formal than in a more impersonal, academic paper.

1. Modeling your treatment upon paragraphs 1-7, select one of these topics:

(a) football (or wrestling, basketball—any sport but boxing) with "the naked eye."

(b) why you prefer movies to television, or stage plays to films (reverse either topic if you wish).

2. Paragraphs 8-35:

(a) a particular baseball game (or any sport but boxing).

(b) a performance of the circus or a play, a political rally or other public event such as a parade or civic celebration.

3. Paragraphs 2-4:

(a) the types of baseball or wrestling fans.

(b) the women who attend bridge parties, the men who play poker.

4. Paragraphs 24-26:

the climactic moments of a sports event—a tennis match, say, or mile run. (Unless you have the technical knowledge required, however, leave this assignment alone.)

IMPROVING YOUR STYLE

In your composition include:

1. A colloquial freight-train * sentence like Liebling's in lines 114-15 (see Question 10).

2. Some experimentation with diction, trying especially for a wide range from colloquial even slangy words to learned, literary ones. (Remember, however, that the words, whether colloquial or literary, should be used because they convey exactly the right meaning and tone.)

Once More to the Lake

E. B. White is a humorist and satirist, best known for his editorial comments in *The New Yorker*, collected in *The Wild Flag* (1946), and for his essays, which have been published in several collections, including *One Man's Meat* (1941) and *The Points of My Compass* (1962). But White has also written short stories (*The Second Tree From the Corner*, 1952) and children's books (*Charlotte's Web*, 1952). "Once More to the Lake" is a classic of the personal essay, and it illustrates particularly well the pattern of that kind of essay, its progression from the outer world of things and other people to the inner world of the writer's responses. That inner world is the true subject of the kind of writing we call personal.

1 One summer, along about 1904, my father rented a camp on a lake in Maine and took us all there for the month of August. We all got ringworm from some kittens and had to rub Pond's Extract on our arms and legs night and morning, and my father rolled over in a canoe with all his clothes on; but outside of that the vacation was a success and from then 5 on none of us ever thought there was any place in the world like that lake in Maine. We returned summer after summer—always on August 1st for one month. I have since become a salt-water man, but sometimes in summer there are days when the restlessness of the tides and the fearful cold of the sea water and the incessant wind which blows across the afternoon and into 10 the evening make me wish for the placidity of a lake in the woods. A few weeks ago this feeling got so strong I bought myself a couple of bass hooks and a spinner and returned to the lake where we used to go, for a week's fishing and to revisit old haunts.

2 I took along my son, who had never had any fresh water up his 15 nose and who had seen lily pads only from train windows. On the journey over to the lake I began to wonder what it would be like. I wondered how

time would have marred this unique, this holy spot—the coves and streams, the hills that the sun set behind, the camps and the paths behind the camps. I was sure that the tarred road would have found it out and I won-   20 dered in what other ways it would be desolated. It is strange how much you can remember about places like that once you allow your mind to re- turn into the grooves which lead back. You remember one thing, and that suddenly reminds you of another thing. I guess I remembered clearest of all the early mornings, when the lake was cool and motionless, remembered   25 how the bedroom smelled of the lumber it was made of and of the wet woods whose scent entered through the screen. The partitions in the camp were thin and did not extend clear to the top of the rooms, and as I was always the first up I would dress softly so as not to wake the others, and sneak out into the sweet outdoors and start out in the canoe, keeping close   30 along the shore in the long shadows of the pines. I remembered being very careful never to rub my paddle against the gunwale for fear of disturbing the stillness of the cathedral.

3   The lake had never been what you would call a wild lake. There were cottages sprinkled around the shores, and it was in farming country   35 although the shores of the lake were quite heavily wooded. Some of the cottages were owned by nearby farmers, and you would live at the shore and eat your meals at the farmhouse. That's what our family did. But al- though it wasn't wild, it was a fairly large and undisturbed lake and there were places in it which, to a child at least, seemed infinitely remote and   40 primeval.

4   I was right about the tar: it led to within half a mile of the shore. But when I got back there, with my boy, and we settled into a camp near a farmhouse and into the kind of summertime I had known, I could tell that it was going to be pretty much the same as it had been before—I knew   45 it, lying in bed the first morning, smelling the bedroom, and hearing the boy sneak quietly out and go off along the shore in a boat. I began to sus- tain the illusion that he was I, and therefore, by simple transposition, that I was my father. This sensation persisted, kept cropping up all the time we were there. It was not an entirely new feeling, but in this setting it grew   50 much stronger. I seemed to be living a dual existence. I would be in the middle of some simple act, I would be picking up a bait box or laying down a table fork, or I would be saying something, and suddenly it would be not I but my father who was saying the words or making the gesture. It gave me a creepy sensation.   55

5   We went fishing the first morning. I felt the same damp moss cov-

ering the worms in the bait can, and saw the dragonfly alight on the tip of
my rod as it hovered a few inches from the surface of the water. It was the
arrival of this fly that convinced me beyond any doubt that everything was
as it always had been, that the years were a mirage and there had been no   60
years. The small waves were the same, chucking the rowboat under the chin
as we fished at anchor, and the boat was the same boat, the same color
green and the ribs broken in the same places, and under the floor-boards
the same fresh-water leavings and débris—the dead helgramite, the wisps of
moss, the rusty discarded fish-hook, the dried blood from yesterday's catch. 65
We stared silently at the tips of our rods, at the dragonflies that came and
went. I lowered the tip of mine into the water, tentatively, pensively dis-
lodging the fly, which darted two feet away, poised, darted two feet back,
and came to rest again a little farther up the rod. There had been no years
between the ducking of this dragonfly and the other one—the one that was   70
part of memory. I looked at the boy, who was silently watching his fly, and
it was my hands that held his rod, my eyes watching. I felt dizzy and didn't
know which rod I was at the end of.

6   We caught two bass, hauling them in briskly as though they were
mackerel, pulling them over the side of the boat in a businesslike manner   75
without any landing net, and stunning them with a blow on the back of
the head. When we got back for a swim before lunch, the lake was exactly
where we had left it, the same number of inches from the dock, and there
was only the merest suggestion of a breeze. This seemed an utterly en-
chanted sea, this lake you could leave to its own devices for a few hours and 80
come back to, and find that it had not stirred, this constant and trust-
worthy body of water. In the shallows, the dark, water-soaked sticks and
twigs, smooth and old, were undulating in clusters on the bottom against
the clean ribbed sand, and the track of the mussel was plain. A school of
minnows swam by, each minnow with its small individual shadow, dou-   85
bling the attendance, so clear and sharp in the sunlight. Some of the other
campers were in swimming, along the shore, one of them with a cake of
soap, and the water felt thin and clear and unsubstantial. Over the years
there had been this person with the cake of soap, this cultist, and here he
was. There had been no years.   90

7   Up to the farmhouse to dinner through the teeming, dusty field,
the road under our sneakers was only a two-track road. The middle track
was missing, the one with the marks of the hooves and the splotches of
dried, flaky manure. There had always been three tracks to choose from in

choosing which track to walk in; now the choice was narrowed down to 95
two. For a moment I missed terribly the middle alternative. But the way
led past the tennis court, and something about the way it lay there in the
sun reassured me; the tape had loosened along the backline, the alleys were
green with plantains and other weeds, and the net (installed in June and
removed in September) sagged in the dry noon, and the whole place 100
steamed with midday heat and hunger and emptiness. There was a choice
of pie for dessert, and one was blueberry and one was apple, and the waitresses were the same country girls, there having been no passage of time,
only the illusion of it as in a dropped curtain—the waitresses were still fifteen; their hair had been washed, that was the only difference—they had 105
been to the movies and seen the pretty girls with the clean hair.
8   Summertime, oh summertime, pattern of life indelible, the fade-
proof lake, the woods unshatterable, the pasture with the sweetfern and
the juniper forever and ever, summer without end; this was the background, and the life along the shore was the design, the cottages with their 110
innocent and tranquil design, their tiny docks with the flagpole and the
American flag floating against the white clouds in the blue sky, the little
paths over the roots of the trees leading from camp to camp and the paths
leading back to the outhouses and the can of lime for sprinkling, and at
the souvenir counters at the store the miniature birch-bark canoes and the 115
post cards that showed things looking a little better than they looked. This
was the American family at play, escaping the city heat, wondering whether
the newcomers in the camp at the head of the cove were "common" or
"nice," wondering whether it was true that the people who drove up for
Sunday dinner at the farmhouse were turned away because there wasn't 120
enough chicken.
9   It seemed to me, as I kept remembering all this, that those times
and those summers had been infinitely precious and worth saving. There
had been jollity and peace and goodness. The arriving (at the beginning
of August) had been so big a business in itself, at the railway station the 125
farm wagon drawn up, the first smell of the pine-laden air, the first glimpse
of the smiling farmer, and the great importance of the trunks and your father's enormous authority in such matters, and the feel of the wagon under
you for the long ten-mile haul, and at the top of the last long hill catching
the first view of the lake after eleven months of not seeing this cherished 130
body of water. The shouts and cries of the other campers when they saw
you, and the trunks to be unpacked, to give up their rich burden. (Arriving

was less exciting nowadays, when you sneaked up in your car and parked it under a tree near the camp and took out the bags and in five minutes it was all over, no fuss, no loud wonderful fuss about trunks.)   135

10   Peace and goodness and jollity. The only thing that was wrong now, really, was the sound of the place, an unfamiliar nervous sound of the outboard motors. This was the note that jarred, the one thing that would sometimes break the illusion and set the years moving. In those other summertimes all motors were inboard; and when they were at a little dis-   140 tance, the noise they made was a sedative, an ingredient of summer sleep. They were one-cylinder and two-cylinder engines, and some were make-and-break and some were jump-spark, but they all made a sleepy sound across the lake. The one-lungers throbbed and fluttered, and the twin-cylinder ones purred and purred, and that was a quiet sound too. But now the campers   145 all had outboards. In the daytime, in the hot mornings, these motors made a petulant, irritable sound; at night, in the still evening when the afterglow lit the water, they whined about one's ears like mosquitoes. My boy loved our rented outboard, and his great desire was to achieve singlehanded mastery over it, and authority, and he soon learned the trick of choking it a   150 little (but not too much), and the adjustment of the needle valve. Watching him I would remember the things you could do with the old one-cylinder engine with the heavy flywheel, how you could have it eating out of your hand if you got really close to it spiritually. Motor boats in those days didn't have clutches, and you would make a landing by shutting off the   155 motor at the proper time and coasting in with a dead rudder. But there was a way of reversing them, if you learned the trick, by cutting the switch and putting it on again exactly on the final dying revolution of the flywheel, so that it would kick back against compression and begin reversing. Approaching a dock in a strong following breeze, it was difficult to slow up sufficiently   160 by the ordinary coasting method, and if a boy felt he had complete mastery over his motor, he was tempted to keep it running beyond its time and then reverse it a few feet from the dock. It took a cool nerve, because if you threw the switch a twentieth of a second too soon you would catch the flywheel when it still had speed enough to go up past center, and the boat would   165 leap ahead, charging bull-fashion at the dock.

11   We had a good week at the camp. The bass were biting well and the sun shone endlessly, day after day. We would be tired at night and lie down in the accumulated heat of the little bed rooms after the long hot day and the breeze would stir almost imperceptibly outside and the smell of   170 the swamp drift in through the rusty screens. Sleep would come easily and

in the morning the red squirrel would be on the roof, tapping out his gay routine. I kept remembering everything, lying in bed in the mornings—the small steamboat that had a long rounded stern like the lip of a Ubangi, and how quietly she ran on the moonlight sails, when the older boys played 175 their mandolins and the girls sang and we ate doughnuts dipped in sugar, and how sweet the music was on the water in the shining night, and what it had felt like to think about girls then. After breakfast we would go up to the store and the things were in the same place—the minnows in a bottle, the plugs and spinners disarranged and pawed over by the youngsters from 180 the boys' camp, the fig newtons and the Beeman's gum. Outside, the road was tarred and cars stood in front of the store. Inside, all was just as it had always been, except there was more Coca Cola and not so much Moxie and root beer and birch beer and sarsaparilla. We would walk out with a bottle of pop apiece and sometimes the pop would backfire up our noses and hurt. 185 We explored the streams, quietly, where the turtles slid off the sunny logs and dug their way into the soft bottom; and we lay on the town wharf and fed worms to the tame bass. Everywhere we went I had trouble making out which was I, the one walking at my side, the one walking in my pants.

12   One afternoon while we were there at the lake a thunderstorm 190 came up. It was like the revival of an old melodrama that I had seen long ago with childish awe. The second-act climax of the drama of the electrical disturbance over a lake in America had not changed in any important respect. This was the big scene, still the big scene. The whole thing was so familiar, the first feeling of oppression and heat and a general air around 195 camp of not wanting to go very far away. In midafternoon (it was all the same) a curious darkening of the sky, and a lull in everything that had made life tick; and then the way the boats suddenly swung the other way at their moorings with the coming of a breeze out of the new quarter, and the premonitory rumble. Then the kettle drum, then the snare, then the 200 bass drum and cymbals, then crackling light against the dark, and the gods grinning and licking their chops in the hills. Afterward the calm, the rain steadily rustling in the calm lake, the return of light and hope and spirits, and the campers running out in joy and relief to go swimming in the rain, their bright cries perpetuating the deathless joke about how they were get- 205 ting simply drenched, and the children screaming with delight at the new sensation of bathing in the rain, and the joke about getting drenched linking the generations in a strong indestructible chain. And the comedian who waded in carrying an umbrella.

13   When the others went swimming my son said he was going in too. 210

He pulled his dripping trunks from the line where they had hung all through the shower, and wrung them out. Languidly, and with no thought of going in, I watched him, his hard little body, skinny and bare, saw him wince slightly as he pulled up around his vitals the small, soggy, icy garment. As he buckled the swollen belt suddenly my groin felt the chill of   215 death.

QUESTIONS

READER AND PURPOSE

1. "Once More to the Lake" appeals to almost everyone. Yet the degree of appeal probably varies. Describe the reader to whom it would appeal the most; the reader to whom it might appeal the least.
2. Which of the following do you think best expresses the theme of "Once More to the Lake"?

> (a) The first years of the twentieth century were more innocent, more idyllic than those of our violent, destructive, contaminated time.
> (b) Nothing ever really changes.
> (c) Summertime is the happiest season.
> (d) Expecting to find the lake changed and the past unrecapturable, the writer suddenly realizes that the real victim of time is not the lake, but himself.

ORGANIZATION

3. What does each of the first three paragraphs contribute to the beginning of the essay?
4. Among other things, a beginning often establishes the writer's tone *. What is E. B. White's feeling about the lake? About his son?
5. The middle portion of the essay (beginning with paragraph 4) is an analysis of the summer ritual. Paragraph 4 might be entitled "Settling In"; paragraphs 5 and 6, "Fishing the First Morning"; paragraph 7, "Returning to the Farmhouse for Dinner." Give a title to the remaining paragraphs of the middle section.
6. Each paragraph in the body of the essay deals with sameness, change, or a mixture of the two. Which predominates overall—change or sameness? Which appears to be the more unsettling to the writer? Underline those passages in which E. B. White expresses his deepest feelings about sameness and change.
7. What rather unusual method of development is used in paragraph 12?
8. The final paragraph is constructed so that it leads up to and ends on the

word *death*. Is this term (or rather the idea it denotes) central to White's essay? Do you think this paragraph makes an effective conclusion to the essay? Why or why not?

SENTENCES

9. The sentence in lines 61-5 ("The small waves . . .") is a detailed expansion of what key word near its beginning? Show how White similarly spins out the sentence in lines 107-16 by expanding a key term. Such expansion is not padding. What would have been lost had White simply written "The small boat was the same" and let it go at that? Too often people complain that they "can't think" of anything to write about, when all they have to do is to turn an abstract *, general statement into a series of particulars.

10. Point to places where White relieves long, complicated sentences like those referred to in the preceding question with short, direct ones.

DICTION

11. Look up: *incessant* (10), *placidity* (11), *spinner* (13), *gunwale* (32), *primeval* (41), *helgramite* (64), *undulating* (83), *mussel* (84), *cultist* (89), *teeming* (91), *plantains* (99), *indelible* (107), *juniper* (109), *petulant* (147), *Ubangi* (174), *Moxie* (183), *sarsaparilla* (184), *melodrama* (191), *premonitory* (200).

12. (For the mechanically-minded.) What do these expressions mean: *make-and-break* (142-43), *jump-spark* (143), *one-lungers* (144), *twin-cylinder ones* (144), *needle valve* (151), *flywheel* (153)?

13. This essay is remarkable for its concrete *, specific, and sensuous diction. Make a list of the various sounds, smells, tastes, and tactile sensations in "Once More to the Lake."

14. Compare the two revisions below with the sentence E. B. White wrote and explain why his diction is far better:

> *White:* "In the shallows, the dark, water-soaked sticks and twigs, smooth and old, were undulating in clusters on the bottom against the clean ribbed sand, and the track of the mussel was plain." (82-84)
> *Revision 1:* Where the water was shallow you saw the usual trash on the bottom.
> *Revision 2:* Smooth twigs and sticks bobbed near the bank, but the sand was clean. You could see the tracks made by some creature in the sand.

15. List four or five colloquial * words or phrases in this essay. The following words, on the other hand, are relatively formal: *placidity* (11), *primeval* (41), *imperceptibility* (170), *premonitory* (200). Which kind of diction is more common in this selection—formal or informal?

16. In paragraph 9 White says, "There had been jollity and peace and good-ness" (124). How would the emphasis and rhythm have changed had he written instead "jollity, peace and goodness"?

17. Point out all the similes * and metaphors * you can find in this selection. Which two or three did you like the most?

POINTS TO LEARN

1. Almost any kind of personal experience can be turned into enduring litera-ture if one has the eye, the ear, and the sensibility.

2. "Once More to the Lake" succeeds in part because the writer knows the names of things. His diction is concrete and specific. At the same time, E. B. White can use Latinate diction when precision of thought or feeling is re-quired. Colloquial diction gives the illusion of a speaking voice and reminds us that we are listening to an individual human being, to his longings, fears, joys, biases, and insights.

SUGGESTIONS FOR WRITING

1. Write your own version of "Once More to the Lake," describing a return to a place you once enjoyed. The setting, your reactions, and your interpretation will be different. But try to make your diction as wide-ranging, as specific, and therefore as interesting as E. B. White's.

2. Learning as much as you can from this essay, describe the texture of city life. Be specific and write with a definite tone so that your reader knows how you feel toward your subject.

IMPROVING YOUR STYLE

Include in your composition:

1. A long sentence like White's in lines 61-65 in which a general image * (in his case the boat) is expanded into a series of particulars.

2. Two or three short emphatic sentences.

3. Several metaphors and several similes.

From The Present

Annie Dillard grew up in Pittsburgh, Pennsylvania, attended Hollins College, and for a number of years after 1965 lived in the Roanoke Valley of Virginia. Near her home she observed the beauty and mystery and terror of the natural world. Her meditations upon what she saw are the substance of her first book of prose, *Pilgrim at Tinker Creek*, which won the Pulitzer Prize for General Non-fiction in 1975. A selection from the beginning of Chapter Six is reprinted below.

1   Catch it if you can.

2   It is early March. I am dazed from a long day of interstate driving homeward; I pull in at a gas station in Nowhere, Virginia, north of Lexington. The young boy in charge ("Chick 'at oll?") is offering a free cup of coffee with every gas purchase. We talk in the glass-walled office while my 5 coffee cools enough to drink. He tells me, among other things, that the rival gas station down the road, whose FREE COFFEE sign is visible from the interstate, charges you fifteen cents if you want your coffee in a Styrofoam cup, as opposed, I guess, to your bare hands.

3   All the time we talk, the boy's new beagle puppy is skidding around 10 the office, sniffing impartially at my shoes and at the wire rack of folded maps. The cheerful human conversation wakes me, recalls me, not to a normal consciousness, but to a kind of energetic readiness. I step outside, followed by the puppy.

4   I am absolutely alone. There are no other customers. The road is 15 vacant, the interstate is out of sight and earshot. I have hazarded into a new corner of the world, an unknown spot, a Brigadoon.[1] Before me extends a

From *Pilgrim at Tinker Creek*. Copyright © 1974 by Annie Dillard. Reprinted by permission of Harper & Row Publishers, Inc., and Blanche C. Gregory, Inc.

[1] A legendary Scotch village of perfect charm in which all the inhabitants are perfectly happy. It mysteriously appears and vanishes. A traveler may find it once and never again, or he may choose to live in Brigadoon and vanish along with it. The legend was the basis of a Broadway musical. [Editors' note]

low hill trembling in yellow brome, and behind the hill, filling the sky, rises an enormous mountain ridge, forested, alive and awesome with brilliant blown lights. I have never seen anything so tremulous and live. Overhead, great strips and chunks of cloud dash to the northwest in a gold rush. At my back the sun is setting—how can I not have noticed before that the sun is setting? My mind has been a blank slab of black asphalt for hours, but that doesn't stop the sun's wild wheel. I set my coffee beside me on the curb; I smell loam on the wind; I pat the puppy; I watch the mountain.

5   My hand works automatically over the puppy's fur, following the line of hair under his ears, down his neck, inside his forelegs, along his hot-skinned belly.

6   Shadows lope along the mountain's rumpled flanks; they elongate like root tips, like lobes of spilling water, faster and faster. A warm purple pigment pools in each ruck and tuck of the rock; it deepens and spreads, boring crevasses, canyons. As the purple vaults and slides, it tricks out the unleafed forest and rumpled rock in gilt, in shape-shifting patches of glow. These gold lights veer and retract, shatter and glide in a series of dazzling splashes, shrinking, leaking, exploding. The ridge's bosses and hummocks sprout bulging from its side; the whole mountain looms miles closer; the light warms and reddens; the bare forest folds and pleats itself like living protoplasm before my eyes, like a running chart, a wildly scrawling oscillograph on the present moment. The air cools; the puppy's skin is hot. I am more alive than all the world.

7   This is it, I think, this is it, right now, the present, this empty gas station, here, this western wind, this tang of coffee on the tongue, and I am patting the puppy, I am watching the mountain. And the second I verbalize this awareness in my brain, I cease to see the moutain or feel the puppy. I am opaque, so much black asphalt. But at the same second, the second I know I've lost it, I also realize that the puppy is still squirming on his back under my hand. Nothing has changed for him. He draws his legs down to stretch the skin taut so he feels every fingertip's stroke along his furred and arching side, his flank, his flung-back throat.

8   I sip my coffee. I look at the mountain, which is still doing its tricks, as you look at a still-beautiful face belonging to a person who was once your lover in another country years ago: with fond nostalgia, and recognition, but no real feeling save a secret astonishment that you are now strangers. Thanks. For the memories. It is ironic that the one thing that all religions recognize as separating us from our creator—our very self-consciousness—is

also the one thing that divides us from our fellow creatures. It was a bitter birthday present from evolution, cutting us off at both ends. I get in the car and drive home.

9   Catch it if you can. The present is an invisible electron; its lightning path traced faintly on a blackened screen is fleet, and fleeing, and gone.   60

10   That I ended this experience prematurely for myself—that I drew scales over my eyes between me and the mountain and gloved my hand between me and the puppy—is not the only point. After all, it would have ended anyway. I've never seen a sunset or felt a wind that didn't. The levitating saints came down at last, and their two feet bore real weight. No, the   65 point is that not only does time fly and do we die, but that in these reckless conditions we live at all, and are vouchsafed, for the duration of certain inexplicable moments, to know it.

11   Stephen Graham startled me by describing this same gift in his antique and elegant book, *The Gentle Art of Tramping*. He wrote, "And as   70 you sit on the hillside, or lie prone under the trees of the forest, or sprawl wet-legged on the shingly beach of a mountain stream, the great door, that does not look like a door, opens." That great door opens on the present, illuminates it as with a multitude of flashing torches.

12   I had thought, because I had seen the tree with the lights in it,[2]   75 that the great door, by definition, opens on eternity. Now that I have "patted the puppy"—now that I have experienced the present purely through my senses—I discover that, although the door to the tree with the lights in it was opened *from* eternity, as it were, and shone on that tree eternal lights, it neverthelss opened on the real and present cedar. It opened on time: Where   80 else? That Christ's incarnation occurred improbably, ridiculously, at such-and-such a time, into such-and-such a place, is referred to—with great sincerity even among believers—as "the scandal of particularity." Well, the "scandal of particularity" is the only world that I, in particular, know. What use has eternity for light? We're all up to our necks in this particular scandal.   85 Why, we might as well ask, not a plane tree, instead of a bo[3]? I never saw a tree that was no tree in particular; I never met a man, not the greatest theologian, who filled infinity, or even whose hand, say, was undifferentiated,

---

[2] Earlier the author tells of walking along Tinker Creek and seeing a cedar tree blazing with flames of light—a sight that symbolizes to her the reality of the power and beauty of the eternal. [Editors' note]

[3] Sitting under a bo (or pipal) tree in the village of Bodh Gaya in India, Prince Gautama received the Enlightenment, becoming free of the cycle of re-birth and being afterwards known as the Buddha, the Enlightened One. [Editors' note]

fingerless, like a griddlecake, and not lobed and split just so with the incursions of time.   90

13   I don't want to stress this too much. Seeing the tree with the lights
in it was an experience vastly different in quality as well as in import from
patting the puppy. On that cedar tree shone, however briefly, the steady, inward flames of eternity; across the mountain by the gas station raced the
familiar flames of the falling sun. But on both occasions I thought, with ris- 95
ing exultation, this is it, this is it; praise the lord; praise the land. Experiencing the present purely is being emptied and hollow; you catch grace as a man
fills his cup under a waterfall.

14   Consciousness itself does not hinder living in the present. In fact, it
is only to a heightened awareness that the great door to the present opens 100
at all. Even a certain amount of interior verbalization is helpful to enforce
the memory of whatever it is that is taking place. The gas station beagle
puppy, after all, may have experienced those same moments more purely
that I did, but he brought fewer instruments to bear on the same material,
he had no data for comparison, and he profited only in the grossest of ways, 105
by having an assortment of itches scratched.

15   *Self*-consciousness, however, does hinder the experience of the present. It is the one instrument that unplugs all the rest. So long as I lose myself
in a tree, say, I can scent its leafy breath or estimate its board feet of lumber,
I can draw its fruits or boil tea on its branches, and the tree stays tree. But 110
the second I become aware of myself at any of these activities—looking over
my own shoulder, as it were—the tree vanishes, uprooted from the spot and
flung out of sight as if it had never grown. And time, which had flowed down
into the tree bearing new revelations like floating leaves at every moment,
ceases. It dams, stills, stagnates.   115

16   Self-consciousness is the curse of the city and all that sophistication
implies. It is the glimpse of oneself in a storefront window, the unbidden
awareness of reactions on the faces of other people—the novelist's world,
not the poet's. I've lived there. I remember what the city has to offer: human
companionship, major-league baseball, and a clatter of quickening stimulus 120
like a rush from strong drugs that leaves you drained. I remember how you
bide your time in the city, and think, if you stop to think, "next year . . .
I'll start living; next year . . . I'll start my life." Innocence is a better world.

17   Innocence sees that this is it, and finds it world enough, and time.[4]

---

[4] "World enough and time" is a phrase from the poem "To His Coy Mistress" by
Andrew Marvell (1621-78). The poem stresses the transitoriness of all things and the
need to live—and love—intensely while we can. [Editors' note]

Innocence is not the prerogative of infants and puppies, and far less of 125
mountains and fixed stars, which have no prerogatives at all. It is not lost to
us; the world is a better place than that. Like any other of the spirit's good
gifts, it is there if you want it, free for the asking, as has been stressed by
stronger words than mine. It is possible to pursue innocence as hounds
pursue hares: single-mindedly, driven by a kind of love, crashing over creeks, 130
keening and lost in fields and forests, circling, vaulting over hedges and hills
wide-eyed, giving loud tongue all unawares to the deepest, most incompre-
hensible longing, a root-flame in the heart, and that warbling chorus resound-
ing back from the mountains, hurling itself from ridge to ridge over the valley, now faint, now clear, ringing the air through which the hounds tear, 135
open-mouthed, the echoes of their own wails dimly knocking in their lungs.
18   What I call innocence is the spirit's unself-conscious state at any
moment of pure devotion to any object. It is at once a receptiveness and
total concentration. One needn't be, shouldn't be, reduced to a puppy. If
you wish to tell me that the city offers galleries, I'll pour you a drink and en- 140
joy your company while it lasts; but I'll bear with me to my grave those pure
moments at the Tate[5] (was it the Tate?) where I stood planted, open-
mouthed, born, before that one particular canvas, that river, up to my neck,
gasping, lost, receding into watercolor depth and depth to the vanishing
point, buoyant, awed, and had to be literally hauled away. These are our few 145
live seasons. Let us live them as purely as we can, in the present.

QUESTIONS

READER AND PURPOSE

1. Annie Dillard's ideal reader is like herself. Describe the author (and reader)
as fully as you can. What are you able to infer about her background, her likes
and dislikes, her values?

2. The writer suggests that her purpose is more that of a poet than that of a
novelist. What does she mean?

3. "The Present" is part narration, part description, part definition. Which of
these is central? Identify examples of each type of writing.

ORGANIZATION

4. This selection is divided into two major parts, as the writer has indicated by
the wide spacing after paragraph 8. Give a title to the first eight paragraphs, another to paragraphs 9-18.

[5] One of London's most illustrious art galleries, particularly for modern and contemporary art. [Editors' note]

5. What other devices besides spacing signals this division into two parts?

6. Paragraphs 1, 5, and 9 are much shorter than the others. Should they have been combined with following or preceding paragraphs? If not, how can you defend the brevity of each one?

7. What technique of development is most prominent in paragraphs 14, 15, 16, 17, and 18?

SENTENCES

8. What is the shortest sentence in this selection? The longest? For what purposes does the writer use short sentences? The occasional long ones? Illustrate your answer by reference to particular sentences.

9. A series of short clauses * joined without conjunctions and punctuated by semicolons appears several places in Dillard's prose. Account for the difference in meaning, tone *, and effect between this revision and the original:

> *Revision:* After I set my coffee beside me on the curb, I smell loam on the wind, while I pat the puppy and watch the mountain.
>
> *Dillard:* "I set my coffee beside me on the curb; I smell the loam on the wind; I pat the puppy; I watch the mountain." (24-25)

10. Dillard employs almost every technique of emphasis. Find examples of fragments *, very short sentences, rhetorical questions *, anaphora *, interrupted movement *, italics, inversion *, parallelism *, and asyndeton *.

11. The sentence in lines 113-15 is emphatic because its structure is periodic * and because it uses interrupted movement. Revise this sentence to make it loose * rather than periodic. Note the weakening of emphasis.

12. Analyze the sentence in lines 129-36 as an example of cumulative * structure.

DICTION

13. Look up: *hazarded* (16), *brome* (18), *blown* (20), *tremulous* (20), *lobes* (30), *ruck* (31), *bosses* (35), *hummocks* (35), *oscillograph* (38), *electron* (59), *fleet* (60), *levitating* (64), *vouchsafed* (67), *shingly* (72), *incarnation* (81), *plane tree* (86), *incursions* (89), *import* (92), *grace* (97), *prerogative* (125), *keening* (131).

14. Annie Dillard uses the present tense throughout this selection and indeed throughout *Pilgrim at Tinker Creek*. What advantages does it have for her purposes over the past tense? To help think about it, contrast the following revision using the past with what Dillard wrote in lines 35-43:

> The ridge's bosses and hummocks sprouted bulging from its sides; the whole mountain loomed miles closer; the light waned and reddened; the bare forest folded and pleated itself like a living proto-

plasm before my eyes, like a running chart, a wildly scrawling oscillo-graph on that moment. The air cooled; the puppy's skin was hot. I was more alive than all the world. This is it I thought, this is it, right now, the present, the empty gas station, the western wind, that tang of coffee on the tongue, and I was patting the puppy, I was watching the mountain.

15. As is proper in personal writing the author frequently uses the pronoun *I*. But she also uses *we*, the impersonal *you* (lines 8 and 9, for example), and the impersonal *one* (139). Study Dillard's use of these pronouns. Formulate a rule of thumb governing the use of *I*, *we*, *you*, *one*.
16. *Gold rush* (21) and *plane tree* (86) are puns. Explain how.
17. Dillard's prose is conversational, informal in its overall effect. At the same time it is very precise and highly emotive. What words give her style its collo-quial * flavor? Using examples, show that the precision of her writing results in part from concrete words, technical and scientific terms, formal words, meta-phors * and similes *. Pointing to specific words and passages show how Dillard conveys emotion by metaphors and similes, by frequent (but not obvious) alliteration *, assonance *, and consonance *.

POINTS TO LEARN
1. The best personal writing does not merely describe experience; it interprets experience and gives it a uniquely personal flavor.
2. Simple, ordinary events and observations (if one has eyes to see) often make the best subjects for personal essays. The poet William Blake writes of seeing "a World in a Grain of Sand."
3. To write as Annie Dillard does requires an extraordinary sensitivity. But that sensitivity must be made visible, and that requires an extensive knowledge of sentence structure, of emphasis, and of an amazing range of meanings and emo-tional connotations * of words.

SUGGESTIONS FOR WRITING
1. Perhaps you have had an experience that in some degree matches Annie Dillard's—while you were sailing, skiing, surfing, hiking, or just observing some-thing quite ordinary. Describe it as vividly as you can and explain what it means to you.
2. Read Sylvia Plath's poem "Black Rook in Rainy Weather" for a different treatment of the kind of experience upon which Annie Dillard meditates. Com-pare and contrast the tones, values, and personalities behind the two works.

IMPROVING YOUR STYLE

1. In your essay experiment with a combination of short and long sentences. At one extreme compose a sentence of no more than four words (it can even be a fragment of one or two words). At the other construct at least one sentence of fifty or sixty words; it can be either a parallel or a cumulative sentence, or some combination of both.

2. Include several unusual metaphors and several similes. Try your hand at a pun.

Of the Meaning of Progress

W. E. B. DuBois (1868-1963), black historian, sociologist, author, one of the founders of the National Association for the Advancement of Colored People (1909), grew up in Great Barrington, Massachusetts. He earned degrees from Fisk University in Nashville, Tennessee (1888) and Harvard University (1890). Following two years study in Germany, he completed work for a Ph.D. at Harvard in 1895. Thereafter he taught economics, history, and sociology at Atlanta University (1897-1910). In 1948 he rejected the NAACP as ineffectual in the struggle for civil rights. In 1962, disillusioned with the treatment of the black intellectual in the United States, he became a citizen of Ghana. His most famous book is *The Souls of Black Folk* (1903), a collection of essays about the life of black people in America during the second half of the nineteenth century. Some of the essays are historical (see, for example, the excerpt from "Of the Dawn of Freedom," on page 438 of this text). Others, like "Of the Meaning of Progress," are personal, serving as a lens to focus and intensify the common experience of black men and women.

1   Once upon a time I taught school in the hills of Tennessee, where the broad dark vale of the Mississippi begins to roll and crumple to greet the Alleghanies. I was a Fisk student then, and all Fisk men thought that Tennessee—beyond the Veil[1]—was theirs alone, and in vacation time they sallied forth in lusty bands to meet the county school-commissioners. 5 Young and happy, I too went, and I shall not soon forget that summer, seventeen years ago.

2   First, there was a Teachers' Institute at the county-seat; and there distinguished guests of the superintendent taught the teachers fractions and spelling and other mysteries—white teachers in the morning, Negroes 10 at night. A picnic now and then, and a supper, and the rough world was softened by laughter and song. I remember how— But I wander.

From *The Souls of Black Folk*, 1903.
[1] The "Veil" is DuBois' metaphor for racial prejudice. [Editors' note]

3   There came a day when all the teachers left the Institute and began
the hunt for schools. I learn from hearsay (for my mother was mortally
afraid of firearms) that the hunting of ducks and bears and men is won-   15
derfully interesting, but I am sure that the man who has never hunted a
country school has something to learn of the pleasures of the chase. I see
now the white, hot roads lazily rise and fall and wind before me under the
burning July sun; I feel the deep weariness of heart and limb as ten, eight,
six miles stretch relentlessly ahead; I feel my heart sink heavily as I hear   20
again and again, "Got a teacher? Yes." So I walked on and on—horses were
too expensive—until I had wandered beyond railways, beyond stage lines,
to a land of "varmints" and rattlesnakes, where the coming of a stranger
was an event, and men lived and died in the shadow of one blue hill.

4   Sprinkled over hill and dale lay cabins and farmhouses, shut out   25
from the world by the forests and the rolling hills toward the east. There I
found at last a little school. Josie told me of it; she was a thin, homely girl
of twenty, with a dark-brown face and thick, hard hair. I had crossed the
stream at Watertown, and rested under the great willows; then I had gone
to the little cabin in the lot where Josie was resting on her way to town.   30
The gaunt farmer made me welcome, and Josie, hearing my errand, told
me anxiously that they wanted a school over the hill; that but once since
the war had a teacher been there; that she herself longed to learn—and
thus she ran on, talking fast and loud, with much earnestness and energy.

5   Next morning I crossed the tall round hill, lingered to look at the   35
blue and yellow mountains stretching toward the Carolinas, then plunged
into the wood, and came out at Josie's home. It was a dull frame cottage
with four rooms, perched just below the brow of the hill, amid peach-trees.
The father was a quiet, simple soul, calmly ignorant, with no touch of vulgarity. The mother was different—strong, bustling, and energetic, with a   40
quick, restless tongue, and an ambition to live "like folks." There was a
crowd of children. Two boys had gone away. There remained two growing
girls; a shy midget of eight; John, tall, awkward, and eighteen; Jim, younger,
quicker, and better looking; and two babies of indefinite age. Then there
was Josie herself. She seemed to be the centre of the family: always busy   45
at service, or at home, or berry-picking; a little nervous and inclined to
scold, like her mother, yet faithful, too, like her father. She had about her
a certain fineness, the shadow of an unconscious moral heroism that would
willingly give all of life to make life broader, deeper, and fuller for her and
hers. I saw much of this family afterwards, and grew to love them for their   50
honest efforts to be decent and comfortable, and for their knowledge of

their own ignorance. There was with them no affectation. The mother would scold the father for being so "easy"; Josie would roundly berate the boys for carelessness; and all knew that it was a hard thing to dig a living out of a rocky side-hill.   55

6   I secured the school. I remember the day I rode horseback out to the commissioner's house with a pleasant young white fellow who wanted the white school. The road ran down the bed of a stream; the sun laughed and the water jingled, and we rode on. "Come in," said the commissioner— "come in. Have a seat. Yes, that certificate will do. Stay to dinner. What   60 do you want a month?" "Oh," thought I, "this is lucky"; but even then fell the awful shadow of the Veil, for they ate first, then I—alone.

7   The schoolhouse was a log hut, where Colonel Wheeler used to shelter his corn. It sat in a lot behind a rail fence and thorn bushes, near the sweetest of springs. There was an entrance where a door once was, and   65 within, a massive rickety fireplace; great chinks betwen the logs served as windows. Furniture was scarce. A pale blackboard crouched in the corner. My desk was made of three boards, reinforced at critical points, and my chair, borrowed from the landlady, had to be returned every night. Seats for the children—these puzzled me much. I was haunted by a New En-   70 gland vision of neat little desks and chairs, but, alas! the reality was rough plank benches without backs, and at times without legs. They had the one virtue of making naps dangerous—possibly fatal, for the floor was not to be trusted.

8   It was a hot morning late in July when the school opened. I trem-   75 bled when I heard the patter of little feet down the dusty road, and saw the growing row of dark solemn faces and bright eager eyes facing me. First came Josie and her brothers and sisters. The longing to know, to be a student in the great school at Nashville, hovered like a star above this child-woman amid her work and worry, and she studied doggedly. There were   80 the Dowells from their farm over toward Alexandria—Fanny, with her smooth black face and wondering eyes; Martha, brown and dull; the pretty girl-wife of a brother, and the younger brood.

9   There were the Burkes—two brown and yellow lads, and a tiny haughty-eyed girl. Fat Reuben's little chubby girl came, with golden face   85 and old-gold hair, faithful and solemn. 'Thenie was on hand early—a jolly, ugly, good-hearted girl, who slyly dipped snuff and looked after her little bow-legged brother. When her mother could spare her, 'Tildy came—a midnight beauty, with starry eyes and tapering limbs; and her brother, correspondingly homely. And then the big boys—the hulking Lawrences;   90

the lazy Neills, unfathered sons of mother and daughter; Hickman, with a stoop in his shoulders, and the rest.

10   There they sat, nearly thirty of them, on the rough benches, their faces shading from a pale cream to a deep brown, the little feet bare and swinging, the eyes full of expectation, with here and there a twinkle of 95 mischief, and the hands grasping Webster's blue-black spelling-book. I loved my school, and the fine faith the children had in the wisdom of their teacher was truly marvellous. We read and spelled together, wrote a little, picked flowers, sang, and listened to stories of the world beyond the hill. At times the school would dwindle away, and I would start out. I would visit 100 Mun Eddings, who lived in two very dirty rooms, and ask why little Lugene, whose flaming face seemed ever ablaze with the dark-red hair uncombed, was absent all last week, or why I missed so often the inimitable rags of Mack and Ed. Then the father, who worked Colonel Wheeler's farm on shares, would tell me how the crops needed the boys; and the thin, 105 slovenly mother, whose face was pretty when washed, assured me that Lugene must mind the baby. "But we'll start them again next week." When the Lawrences stopped, I knew that the doubts of the old folks about book-learning had conquered again, and so, toiling up the hill, and getting as far into the cabin as possible, I put Cicero "pro Archia Poeta"[2] into the 110 simplest English with local applications, and usually convinced them—for a week or so.

11   On Friday nights I often went home with some of the children— sometimes to Doc Burke's farm. He was a great, loud, thin Black, ever working, and trying to buy the seventy-five acres of hill and dale where he 115 lived; but people said that he would surely fail, and the "white folks would get it all." His wife was a magnificent Amazon, with saffron face and shining hair, uncorseted and barefooted, and the children were strong and beautiful. They lived in a one-and-a-half-room cabin in the hollow of the farm, near the spring. The front room was full of great fat white beds, 120 scrupulously neat; and there were bad chromos on the walls, and a tired centre-table. In the tiny back kitchen I was often invited to "take out and help" myself to fried chicken and wheat biscuit, "meat" and corn pone, stringbeans and berries. At first I used to be a little alarmed at the approach of bedtime in the one lone bedroom, but embarrassment was very 125 deftly avoided. First, all the children nodded and slept, and were stowed

[2] A famous oration by Cicero delivered in 62 B.C. defending the claim of the Greek poet Archias to Roman citizenship. The speech included an eloquent and famous defense of literature and learning. [Editors' note]

away in one great pile of goose feathers; next, the mother and father discreetly slipped away to the kitchen while I went to bed; then, blowing out the dim light, they retired in the dark. In the morning all were up and away before I thought of awaking. Across the road, where fat Reuben lived, they all went outdoors while the teacher retired, because they did not boast the luxury of a kitchen.

12   I liked to stay with the Dowells, for they had four rooms and plenty of good country fare. Uncle Bird had a small, rough farm, all woods and hills, miles from the big road; but he was full of tales—he preached now and then—and with his children, berries, horses, and wheat he was happy and prosperous. Often, to keep the peace, I must go where life was less lovely; for instance, 'Tildy's mother was incorrigibly dirty, Reuben's larder was limited seriously, and herds of untamed insects wandered over the Eddingses' beds. Best of all I loved to go to Josie's, and sit on the porch, eating peaches, while the mother bustled and talked: how Josie had bought the sewing-machine; how Josie worked at service in winter, but that four dollars a month was "mighty little" wages; how Josie longed to go away to school, but that it "looked like" they never could get far enough ahead to let her; how the crops failed and the well was yet unfinished; and, finally, how "mean" some of the white folks were.

13   For two summers I lived in this little world; it was dull and humdrum. The girls looked at the hill in wistful longing, and the boys fretted and haunted Alexandria. Alexandria was "town"—a straggling, lazy village of houses, churches, and shops, and an aristocracy of Toms, Dicks, and Captains. Cuddled on the hill to the north was the village of the colored folks, who lived in three- or four-room unpainted cottages, some neat and homelike, and some dirty. The dwellings were scattered rather aimlessly, but they centred about the twin temples of the hamlet, the Methodist, and the Hard-Shell Baptist churches. These, in turn, leaned gingerly on a sad-colored schoolhouse. Hither my little world wended its crooked way on Sunday to meet other worlds, and gossip, and wonder, and make the weekly sacrifice with frenzied priest at the altar of the "old-time religion." Then the soft melody and mighty cadences of Negro song fluttered and thundered.

14   I have called my tiny community a world, and so its isolation made it; and yet there was among us but a half-awakened common consciousness, sprung from common joy and grief, at burial, birth, or wedding; from a common hardship in poverty, poor land, and low wages; and, above all, from the sight of the Veil that hung between us and Opportunity. All this caused us to think some thoughts together; but these, when ripe for speech, were spoken in various languages. Those whose eyes twenty-five and more years before had seen "the glory of the coming of the Lord," saw in every present hindrance or help a dark fatalism bound to bring all things right in His own good time. The mass of those to whom slavery was a dim recol- 170 lection of childhood found the world a puzzling thing: it asked little of them, and they answered with little, and yet it ridiculed their offering. Such a paradox they could not understand, and therefore sank into listless indifference, or shiftlessness, or reckless bravado. There were, however, some— such as Josie, Jim, and Ben—to whom War, Hell, and Slavery were but 175 childhood tales, whose young appetites had been whetted to an edge by school and story and half-awakened thought. Ill could they be content, born without and beyond the World. And their weak wings beat against their barriers—barriers of caste, of youth, of life; at last, in dangerous moments, against everything that opposed even a whim. 180

15   The ten years that follow youth, the years when first the realization comes that life is leading somewhere—these were the years that passed after I left my little school. When they were past, I came by chance once more to the walls of Fisk University, to the halls of the chapel of melody. As I lingered there in the joy and pain of meeting old school-friends, there swept 185 over me a sudden longing to pass again beyond the blue hill, and to see the homes and the school of other days, and to learn how life had gone with my school-children; and I went.

16   Josie was dead, and the gray-haired mother said simply, "We've had a heap of trouble since you've been away." I had feared for Jim. With a cul- 190 tured parentage and a social caste to uphold him, he might have made a venturesome merchant or a West Point cadet. But here he was, angry with life and reckless; and when Farmer Durham charged him with stealing wheat, the old man had to ride fast to escape the stones which the furious fool hurled after him. They told Jim to run away; but he would not run, and the con- 195 stable came that afternoon. It grieved Josie, and great awkward John walked nine miles every day to see his little brother through the bars of Lebanon jail. At last the two came back together in the dark night. The mother cooked supper, and Josie emptied her purse, and the boys stole away. Josie grew thin and silent, yet worked the more. The hill became steep for the quiet old 200 father, and with the boys away there was little to do in the valley. Josie helped them to sell the old farm, and they moved nearer town. Brother Dennis, the carpenter, built a new house with six rooms; Josie toiled a year in Nashville, and brought back ninety dollars to furnish the house and change it to a home.   205

17   When the spring came, and the birds twittered, and the stream ran proud and full, little sister Lizzie, bold and thoughtless, flushed with the passion of youth, bestowed herself on the tempter, and brought home a nameless child. Josie shivered and worked on, with the vision of schooldays all fled, with a face wan and tired—worked until, on a summer's day, some   210 one married another; then Josie crept to her mother like a hurt child, and slept—and sleeps.

18   I paused to scent the breeze as I entered the valley. The Lawrences have gone—father and son forever—and the other son lazily digs in the earth to live. A new young widow rents out their cabin to fat Reuben. Reuben is a   215 Baptist preacher now, but I fear as lazy as ever, though his cabin has three rooms; and little Ella has grown into a bouncing woman, and is ploughing corn on the hot hillside. There are babies a-plenty, and one half-witted girl. Across the valley is a house I did not know before, and there I found, rocking one baby and expecting another, one of my schoolgirls, a daughter of Uncle   220 Bird Dowell. She looked somewhat worried with her new duties, but soon bristled into pride over her neat cabin and the tale of her thrifty husband, and the horse and cow, and the farm they were planning to buy.

19   My log schoolhouse was gone. In its place stood Progress; and Progress, I understand, is necessarily ugly. The crazy foundation stones still   225 marked the former site of my poor little cabin, and not far away, on six weary boulders, perched a jaunty board house, perhaps twenty by thirty feet, with three windows and a door that locked. Some of the window-glass was broken, and part of an old iron stove lay mournfully under the house. I peeped through the window half reverently, and found things that were more   230 familiar. The blackboard had grown by about two feet, and the seats were still without backs. The county owns the lot now, I hear, and every year there is a session of school. As I sat by the spring and looked on the Old and the New I felt glad, very glad, and yet—

20   After two long drinks I started on. There was the great double log-   235 house on the corner. I remembered the broken, blighted family that used to live there. The strong, hard face of the mother, with its wilderness of hair, rose before me. She had driven her husband away, and while I taught school a strange man lived there, big and jovial, and people talked. I felt sure that Ben and 'Tildy would come to naught from such a home. But this is an odd   240 world; for Ben is a busy farmer in Smith County, "doing well, too," they say, and he had cared for little 'Tildy until last spring, when a lover married her.

A hard life the lad had led, toiling for meat, and laughed at because he was homely and crooked. There was Sam Carlon, an impudent old skinflint, who had definite notions about "niggers," and hired Ben a summer and would not   245
pay him. Then the hungry boy gathered his sacks together, and in broad daylight went into Carlon's corn; and when the hard-fisted farmer set upon him, the angry boy flew at him like a beast. Doc Burke saved a murder and a lynching that day.

21   The story reminded me again of the Burkes, and an impatience   250
seized me to know who won in the battle, Doc or the seventy-five acres. For it is a hard thing to make a farm out of nothing, even in fifteen years. So I hurried on, thinking of the Burkes. They used to have a certain magnificent barbarism about them that I liked. They were never vulgar, never immoral, but rather rough and primitive, with an unconventionality that spent itself   255
in loud guffaws, slaps on the back, and naps in the corner. I hurried by the cottage of the misborn Neill boys. It was empty, and they were grown into fat, lazy farm-hands. I saw the home of the Hickmans, but Albert, with his stooping shoulders, had passed from the world. Then I came to the Burkes' gate and peered through; the inclosure looked rough and untrimmed, and   260
yet there were the same fences around the old farm save to the left, where lay twenty-five other acres. And lo! the cabin in the hollow had climbed the hill and swollen to a half-finished six-room cottage.

22   The Burkes held a hundred acres, but they were still in debt. Indeed, the gaunt father who toiled night and day would scarcely be happy out of   265
debt, being so used to it. Some day he must stop, for his massive frame is showing decline. The mother wore shoes, but the lion-like physique of other days was broken. The children had grown up. Rob, the image of his father, was loud and rough with laughter. Birdie, my school baby of six, had grown to a picture of maiden beauty, tall and tawny. "Edgar is gone," said the   270
mother, with head half bowed—"gone to work in Nashville; he and his father couldn't agree."

23   Little Doc, the boy born since the time of my school, took me horseback down the creek next morning toward Farmer Dowell's. The road and the stream were battling for mastery, and the stream had the better of it.   275
We splashed and waded, and the merry boy, perched behind me, chattered and laughed. He showed me where Simon Thompson had bought a bit of ground and a home; but his daughter Lana, a plump, brown, slow girl, was not there. She had married a man and a farm twenty miles away. We wound on down the stream till we came to a gate that I did not recognize, but the   280
boy insisted that it was "Uncle Bird's." The farm was fat with the growing

crop. In that little valley was a strange stillness as I rode up; for death and marriage had stolen youth and left age and childhood there. We sat and talked that night after the chores were done. Uncle Bird was grayer, and his eyes did not see so well, but he was still jovial. We talked of the acres 285 bought—one hundred and twenty-five—of the new guest-chamber added, of Martha's marrying. Then we talked of death: Fanny and Fred were gone; a shadow hung over the other daughter, and when it lifted she was to go to Nashville to school. At last we spoke of the neighbors, and as night fell, Uncle Bird told me how, on a night like that, 'Thenie came wandering back to her 290 home over yonder, to escape the blows of her husband. And next morning she died in the home that her little bow-legged brother, working and saving, had bought for their widowed mother.

24   My journey was done, and behind me lay hill and dale, and Life and Death. How shall man measure Progress there where the dark-faced Josie 295 lies? How many heartfuls of sorrow shall balance a bushel of wheat? How hard a thing is life to the lowly, and yet how human and real! And all this life and love and strife and failure—is it the twilight or nightfall or the flush of some faint-dawning day?

25   Thus sadly musing, I rode to Nashville in the Jim Crow car.   300

QUESTIONS

READER AND PURPOSE

1. Describe as fully as you can the kind of reader DuBois seems to be writing for.

2. A writer's purpose and strategy are intimately related. For example, in *The Federalist No. 10* (page 174) James Madison wants to persuade intelligent and educated voters to ratify the Constitution; thus his strategy is a closely reasoned argument concerning principles. What is DuBois' purpose? What is his strategy. Is his title ironic *?

ORGANIZATION

3. The extra spacing between paragraphs 14 and 15 indicates a two-part organization. Give a title to each part and show how this organization is related to the writer's purpose.

4. Often, especially in personal writing, the beginning identifies who, where, when, why, and how, thus providing a context for what follows. How much space does DuBois require for his beginning identifications? What is the date of the events in part one? In part two? How old was DuBois when he first

taught school? How old when he wrote this account of his teaching experiences? 5. Which paragraph (or paragraphs) constitutes the conclusion? How has the writer signaled his closing? Is paragraph 25 undeveloped and ineffective? Why or why not?

6. Rank the following sentences from least emphatic to most:

> *DuBois:* "There were the Burkes—two brown and yellow lads, and a tiny, haughty-eyed girl." (84-85)
> *Revision (a):* There were the Burkes, two brown and yellow lads and a tiny haughty-eyed girl.
> *Revision (b):* There were the Burkes (two brown and yellow lads and a tiny haughty-eyed girl).
> *Revision (c):* There were the Burkes: two brown and yellow lads, and a tiny haughty-eyed girl.
> *Revision (d):* There were the Burkes, two of whom were brown and yellow lads while the other was a tiny haughty-eyed girl.

7. DuBois often uses a dash to set off an appositive *, especially if the appositive construction contains a comma or some other mark of punctuation. The result is greater emphasis and greater clarity than if he had used a comma. Point out examples in paragraphs 8 and 9.

8. Does any rule require the dash in line 62? Why does DuBois employ it? Find a similar construction in the seventeenth paragraph.

9. In line 12 there is a use of the dash that is striking (if it is not too frequent). The device is called aposiopoesis, or "falling silent," and it is used to give prose a conversational flavor—as here—or sometimes to insinuate something, to hint at what is best left unsaid. Since the reader is forced to complete the sentence for himself his notice is drawn to it and hence the device is emphatic. Find another example in paragraph 19.

10. In paragraph 9 point out several examples of adjectives in the post position (that is, placed after the nouns they modify instead of before). What advantages do such adjectives have?

11. The first sentence in paragraph 10 is cumulative *. Describe how it is constructed as best you can. What virtues does it have in descriptive writing?

12. Identify the parallelism * and anaphora * in the long sentence in lines 140-46. If this sentence were broken into several shorter ones, what effect would be lost?

13. Look up: *affection* (52), *certificate* (60), *hulking* (90), *inimitable* (103), *shares* (105), *slovenly* (106), *Amazon* (117), *chromos* (121), *incorrigibly*

(138), *cadences* (159), *paradox* (173), *bravado* (174), *guffaws* (256), *Jim Crow car* (300).

14. In each of the following cases explain why DuBois' diction is better than that of the revision:

> (a) *Revision:* The usual school blackboard stood in the corner.
> *DuBois:* "A pale blackboard crouched in the corner." (67)
>
> (b) *Revision:* The front room contained clean beds, colorful pictures on the wall, and an old centre-table.
> *DuBois:* "The front room was full of great fat white beds, scrupu-lously neat; and there were bad chromos on the wall, and a tired centre-table." (120-22)
>
> (c) *Revision:* How much sorrow is required to equal a bushel of wheat? Life is hard for the poor, and yet it is very real to them. Is all this life, love, trying, and failure—night or dawn?
> *DuBois:* "How many heartfuls of sorrow shall balance a bushel of wheat? How hard a thing is life to the lowly, and yet how human and real! And all this life and love and strife and failure—is it the twilight of nightfall or the flush of some faint-dawning day?" (296-99)

15. Discuss the meaning and emotional force of *an aristocracy of Toms, Dicks, and Captains.* (150-51)

16. By pointing to diction in specific passages describe the writer's attitude toward each of the following: himself, Josie, the Burkes, the Lawrences, the Neills, the commissioner (paragraph 6), the new school (paragraph 19), and his readers.

POINTS TO LEARN

1. Personal writing can be serious and persuasive.

2. Any author—but especially the writer of a personal essay—should try to be attractive. He must respect himself (which need not mean taking himself with great solemnity), and he must respect his readers by being clear and interesting and informative and by leaving no uncertainties or unanswered questions in their minds.

3. The writer of a personal narrative should quickly identify who, where, when, why, and how.

4. Personal writing should have a definite tone.

SUGGESTIONS FOR WRITING

1. Describe an encounter with persons unfamiliar to you—perhaps new neighbors, fellow workers on a new job, people you met traveling. Give your essay a

definite theme, or focus of meaning, and make it implicitly clear how you feel about yourself and the people you describe. And respect your reader.

2. After briefly describing a place as you first experienced it, tell how it has changed after some months or years. Possible subjects: an elementary school, a summer resort, a town, a park, a place of amusement, a shop, a neighborhood.

IMPROVING YOUR STYLE

1. Following DuBois' employment of the dash, use that mark three or four different ways in your composition.

2. Experiment in your assignment with alliteration *, assonance *, consonance *, and sentence rhythm. Try to be unobtrusive. Alliteration, for example, works better if the two or three words involved are separated by several others instead of following one another in immediate succession.

Writing About Literature

Why write about Literature? Why not simply read it and enjoy it? Well, in part because a short story, play, poem, or film is a clear and ready-made subject; it has distinct boundaries and greatly simplifies the problem of invention, that is of finding something to write about. More importantly, writing about literature forces one to improve his reading and to sharpen his sensibilities. Just as we don't really look at something until we are forced to draw it, so we don't really perceive a literary work until we have to write about it.

Given a story or a poem to discuss, one may proceed in two rather different ways. On the one hand, he may work impressionistically, first describing or summarizing the work in general terms and then, in more detail, writing about how the work affected him, what emotions and ideas and associations it aroused. The danger in approaching literature in this way is that it is easy to slip away from the text altogether and to ramble on about one's "feelings" in a vague and sentimental way. To be done well, impression requires not only sensitivity and precise control of the language of feeling, but also the discipline to keep one's impressions within limits appropriate to the work. Without such discipline and sensitivity, impressionistic criticism is likely to become a kind of gush, which tells a reader little or nothing about the work and which does not even help the writer focus and define his responses.

For this reason, most writing about literature is not impressionism, but a more objective kind of analysis, critical analysis we may call it, though "critical" in this context does not have its usual sense of carping or fault-finding. Critical analysis is less concerned with the reader's feelings than with the work itself. It looks closely at each of the elements that go into the making of a story, play, or poem. It attempts to identify these elements, to understand the relationships among them, and hence to comprehend what meaning they imply, what complex reaction to man or society or the universe.

The value of such analysis lies in calling attention to what might otherwise go unnoticed. The inexperienced reader of literature is all too likely to suppose that a short story is no more than its plot, or that a poem has been understood when one is able to paraphrase it. In critical analysis, however, one does not generally rehash the plot (unless one has reason to suppose his readers are unfamiliar with it) or paraphrase the poem. Rather he works below such surfaces to reveal deeper patterns of meaning and structure, revelations which will enable other readers in turn to see more in the work. Critical analysis is organized around such topics as character relationships, conflicts, the significance of setting, how a writer uses symbols, manipulates his "point of view," or develops patterns in imagery, with the ultimate purpose of showing how such matters relate to, and reveal the meaning and overall structure of, the literary work. The analytical critic does not merely retell the story or the poem in his own words.

To convince his reader of the truth or reasonableness of his conclusions about characters, say, or setting, the literary analyst sticks closely to the "facts" of the work discussed, adding nothing that cannot objectively be shown to be present and omitting nothing of obvious prominence, a procedure that introduces at least some objectivity into literary discussion. Hence, it follows that the literary analyst will support his points by referring to these "facts," whether in his own words or by quoting from his text.

How to handle such quotations, how to divide the subject into its parts, and how to achieve the proper tone—all these and more can be learned from the close study of good models. Accordingly, this section reprints various ways of writing about literature. Helen Bevington's essay, for example, is literary impressionism at its best. Her account of Hopkins's "The Wreck of the Deutschland" is a good instance of writing that arouses our interest in a piece of literature without analyzing it. Guy Davenport, on the other hand, discusses a poem in relation to varying critical attitudes toward it, while John Ciardi shows through close and sensitive reading just how much can be seen and felt in a poem. Flannery O'Connor advises young writers about the craft of fiction, and along the way gives instructive advice about reading short stories. Pauline Kael and X. J. Kennedy bring to the discussion of films the kind of close and revealing analysis applied to plays and novels. Finally, Maynard Mack's exploration of *Hamlet* reminds us that literary criticism can be not only exciting discovery, but also—sometimes—a work of art in itself.

A Nun, a Girl, and Gerard Manley Hopkins

Helen Bevington is a teacher and writer whose books include *Doctor Johnson's Waterfall* (1946), *When Found, Make a Verse Of* (1961), *Charley Smith's Girl* (1965), *A Book and a Love Affair* (1968), *The House Was Quiet and the World Was Calm* (1971), and *Beautiful Lofty People* (1973). The last is a collection of essays about literary figures and topics. In this essay (another is reprinted on pages 380 ff.) the subject is a poem by Gerard Manley Hopkins (1844-89), an English Jesuit and poet, especially noted for his religious themes. Actually Bevington's subject is more—not simply the poem, but how the poem affected a particular reader. The essay reminds us of something we are prone to forget: that literature is much more than a book or a printed page; it is an experience.

1 In my poetry class we were reading Hopkins's "The Wreck of the Deutschland," that stupendous drama of shipwreck—the true and tragic tale of a ship called the *Deutschland* that, between midnight and morning of December 7, 1875, on her way from Bremen to America, foundered on a sand bar at the mouth of the Thames. In the dark, during a blizzard of wind 5 and snow, she struck a smother of sand and was wrecked there. Of the 213 aboard her, seventy-eight lives were lost, their bodies crushed and drowned, washed into the snow-driven sea. Sailors climbed into the rigging to save themselves, while women and children screamed in terror below. One seaman out of pity tied a rope around his waist and descended, only to be dashed 10 against the side of the ship and decapitated. There he dangled like a pendulum, the headless corpse, to and fro in the roaring storm. Among the women, five Franciscan nuns, exiled from Germany by the anti-Catholic Falk Laws, joined hands and died together. The Rhine had rejected them, the Thames killed them. "Five! the finding and sake / And cipher of suffering Christ." 15

2 It was the death of one of the five—the Nun, the chief sister—that

From *Beautiful Lofty People*. © 1974 by Helen Bevington. Reprinted by permission of Harcourt Brace Jovanovich, Inc.

Hopkins sought to understand. She rose a lioness towering in the tumult above the women wailing and the children bawling, and as the night howled and the sea romped over the deck to drown them cried out before she perished, "O Christ, Christ, come quickly." 20

3   "The majesty! What did she mean?" Hopkins asks the question in wonder and grief. At the moment of death, why did she make her majestic cry? Or, rather, he asks, what did she *not* mean? With mounting tension he considers one by one all the things she could not have meant:

4   She did not merely seek to die, calling to Death as a lover to free 25 her from the horror and anguish of this night. She did not cry out for the crown then, for the martyrdom that Christ had suffered before her. She was not begging with these words for the lovely treasure of heaven. She was not seeking for herself either safety or reward. She was not asking ease for her "sodden-with-its-sorrowing heart." She called to him not out of fear, or, 30 blinded by the "sloggering brine," out of the appeal of Christ's own Passion, to relive his own death. No. It was not any of these.

5   It was something else, something the Nun saw. Choking, gasping for breath, seeking to comprehend, Hopkins reaches at last the question: what *did* she mean? What must she have meant? Struggling to speak, he 35 seems to be drowning like her. He labors to say it, pants to make it plain, find the simple words for it.

6   Do you see? he cries. "Strike you the sight of it? look at it loom there"—and there it is. Hopkins knows. He knows! The vision of the Master has transfigured her. Christ has appeared to her, he has come, he is 40 there—Himself, *ipse*, to save the Nun, to cure her of death. He is walking on the waves toward her. He has arrived in the storm to save her and take her home,

the Master,
Ipse, the only one, Christ, King, Head: 45
He was to cure the extremity where he had cast her.

7   As I read aloud these words of the poem, in a sudden burst a girl in the class broke into uncontrolled weeping. With streaming face, she wept. For the last seven stanzas, during which Hopkins adores the wisdom and mastery of God, she wept, her wailing voice rising higher than the 50 Nun's cry, while the students on either side of her turned to embrace and wipe away her tears and comfort her.

8   The rest of the class sat stunned. The room grew electric, charged with their silence. If any had been quietly dozing or daydreaming, they were

shocked into attention, staring with blank astonishment first at the weeping 55
girl, then down at the open book in front of them. What impassioned message was this? What words were these? Only Hopkins's words? Hurled off
one's feet by *Hopkins?*
9   As a performance, it seemed a bit theatrical. But, on the whole, I
was more glad than sorry for it. A poem had spoken and been listened to. 60
Only a few of them, perhaps, would remember the sound of the poetry or
the story it told. One girl in particular will never forget. I think often of her
face.

QUESTIONS

READER AND PURPOSE

1. Not all writing about literature is close analysis of structure and meaning.
Here, for example, the first six paragraphs, while they are about the poem, are
not an interpretation—a task which would require many pages. What is the
writer's purpose here if it is not to analyze the poem closely?
2. Describe the ideal reader of this selection.

ORGANIZATION

3. Suppose that in the first paragraph Bevington had omitted all reference
to her poetry class and had begun like this: "Hopkins's 'The Wreck of the
Deutschland' is a stupendous drama of shipwreck—the true and tragic tale of
a ship called the *Deutschland*. . . ." Would the beginning be improved or
damaged?
4. What would be the effect of opening with paragraphs 7, 8 and 9 (making
slightly necessary changes) and then following with the material now in paragraphs 1-6?
5. This essay falls into three parts. Indicate them and give a title to each.
6. What means does the writer employ in the last paragraph to bring her essay
to a close? Explain how the final paragraph relates to the preceding eight paragraphs.

SENTENCES

7. In the fourth paragraph Bevington skillfully exploits repetition: "She did
not merely seek. . . . She did not cry out. . . . She was not begging. . . .
She was not seeking. . . . She was not asking. . . . She called to him not out
of fear. . . . No. It was not. . . ." How do these repetitions affect the coherence and emphasis of this passage? Beginning successive sentences or clauses
with the same word or phrase is called anaphora *. Is anaphora more appro-

priate in emotional, persuasive writing or in impersonal writing, as on a scientific subject? Explain.

8. In line 35 the writer uses two rhetorical questions * in succession. How does this affect the tone *? Where else does Bevington employ rhetorical questions? Do they all serve the same purpose as those in line 35?

9. Analyze the structure, sound, and emphasis of the following sentence: "He labors to say it, pants to make it plain, find the simple words for it." (36-37)

10. Explain what makes each of these sentences emphatic:

> (a) "No." (32)
> (b) "With streaming face, she wept." (48)
> (c) "Christ has appeared to her, he has come, he is there—Himself, *ipse*, to save the Nun, to cure her of death." 40-41)
> (d) "Hurled off one's feet by *Hopkins?*" (57-58)

DICTION

11. Look up: *rigging* (8), *decapitated* (11), *Franciscan* (13), *transfigured* (40), ipse (41), *extremity* (46).

12. It adds to the pathos if we understand clearly that the nuns are refugees from religious persecution. The Falk Laws referred to in line 13 were among the drastic measures adopted by Bismarck in the 1870's to reduce the autonomy of the Catholic Church in Germany. Written by Dr. Adalbert Falk, the Liberal minister of public worship, their aim, in part, was to bring Catholic education under strict control of the state. In Hopkins's poem the nuns' pathos is underscored in line 15: "Five! the finding and sake / And cipher of suffering Christ." What is the meaning of *cipher* in this context? To what besides the number of the nuns does five refer?

13. In each of the following two passages the sea is sharply characterized by the diction, especially by *romped* in the first and by *sloggering brine* in the second. These words, however, imply rather different attitudes toward the sea. Try to explain the differences:

> (a) "and the sea romped over the deck to drown them" (19)
> (b) "blinded by the 'sloggering brine' " (31)

POINTS TO LEARN

1. Like a short poem, a short essay can have an immense emotional impact if the writer is sensitive to words and can write sentences of great vigor.

2. Vigorous, emphatic sentences are often short.

3. Good prose employs a variety of sentence patterns.

4. Anaphora is an effective device in emotive prose.

SUGGESTIONS FOR WRITING

1. After reading Hopkins's "The Wreck of the Deutschland," write an essay in which you explain how the poet's diction and sentence structure help to give the poem its power.

2. Write an extended anecdote in which you describe how a piece of literature (poem, short story, novel, play, or even movie) "had spoken and been listened to."

IMPROVING YOUR STYLE

In your essay include:

1. An example of anaphora (see Question 7).

2. Two emphatic rhetorical questions.

3. A sentence that achieves emphasis by inversion *.

4. An effective fragment *.

5. One or two unusual verbs (like *romped* in line 19), and one or two unusual adjectives (like *sloggering* in line 31).

Yes, "Trees" Is Popular With the Rotarians. Yes, It's Vulnerable. But, Then . . .

Guy Davenport is a poet and teacher and critic. In this essay he takes a fresh and unorthodox look at a famous and popular poem, "Trees" by the American poet Joyce Kilmer (1886-1918). During the nineteen forties and fifties many academic critics convicted Kilmer's poem of being trite, sentimental, abstract, confused in its imagery, full of prosy statement, and transparent—the sort of thing, the critics felt, that passes for poetry in the popular mind but is not true poetry at all. (It is to this critical disdain that Davenport alludes in his title.) Today "Trees" appears in few anthologies prepared for college students; yet it continues to be read and admired. Here is the poem in its entirety. Read it before you read what Davenport has to say.

Trees

I think that I shall never see
A poem as lovely as a tree.
A tree whose hungry mouth is prest
Against the earth's sweet flowing breast;
A tree that looks at God all day,
And lifts her leafy arms to pray;
A tree that may in summer wear
A nest of robins in her hair;
Upon whose bosom snow has lain;
Who intimately lives with rain.
Poems are made by fools like me,
But only God can make a tree.

1   In June 1918, the Cincinnati poetess Eloise Robinson was in the wasteland of Picardy handing out chocolate and reciting poetry to the American Expeditionary Forces. Reciting poetry!

518

2   It is all but unimaginable that in that hell of terror, gangrene, mustard gas, sleeplessness, lice, and fatigue, there were moments when bone-weary soldiers, for the most part mere boys, would sit in a circle around a poetess in an ankle-length khaki skirt and Boy Scout hat to hear poems. In the middle of one poem the poetess' memory flagged. She apologized profusely, for the poem, as she explained, was immensely popular back home. Whereupon a sergeant with a particularly boyish face held up his hand, as if in school, and volunteered to recite it. And did.

3   So that in the hideously ravaged orchards and strafed woods of the valley of the Ourcq, where the fields were cratered and strewn with coils of barbed wire, fields that reeked of cordite and carrion, a voice recited "Trees." How wonderful, said Eloise Robinson, that he should know it. "Well, ma'am," said the sergeant, "I guess I wrote it. I'm Joyce Kilmer."

4   He wrote it five years before, and sent it off to the newly founded magazine "Poetry," and Harriet Monroe, the editor, paid him $6 for it. Almost immediately it became one of the most famous poems in English, the staple of schoolteachers and the one poem known by practically everybody.

5   Sgt. Alfred Joyce Kilmer was killed by German gunfire on the heights above Seringes, 30 July 1918. The French gave him the Croix de Guerre for his gallantry. He was 32.

6   "Trees" is a poem that has various reputations. It is all right for tots and Middle-Western clubwomen, but you are supposed to outgrow it. It symbolizes the sentimentality and weakmindedness that characterizes middle-class muddle. It is Rotarian. Once, at a gathering of poets at the Library of Congress the poetess Babette Deutsch[1] was using it as an example of the taradiddle Congressmen recite at prayer breakfasts and other orgies, until Prof. Gordon Wayne coughed and reminded her that the poet's son Kenton was among those present. No one, however, rose to defend Rudyard Kipling and John Greenleaf Whittier, at whom La Deutsch was also having.

7   It is, Lord knows, a vulnerable poem. For one thing, it is a poem about poetry, and is thus turned in on itself, and smacks of propaganda for the art (but is therefore useful to teachers who find justifying poetry to barbarian students uphill work). For another, the opening sentiment is all too close to Gelett Burgess' "I never saw a Purple Cow," lines that had been flipping from the tongues of wits since 1895.

8   And if the tree is pressing its hungry mouth against the earth's sweet flowing breast, how can it then lift its leafy arms to pray? This is a position

[1] Babette Deutsch is known chiefly as a poet, but she is also a novelist, translator of German and Russian literature, and a distinguished teacher. [Editors' note]

worthy of Picasso but not of the Cosmopolitan Cover Art Nouveau[2] esthetic from which the poem derives. Ask any hard-nosed classicist, and she will tell you that the poem is a monster of mixed metaphors.

9   And yet there is a silvery, spare beauty about the thing that has not dated. Its six couplets have an inexplicable integrity and a pleasant, old-fashioned music. It soothes, and seems to speak of verities. 45

10   The handbooks will tell you that William Butler Yeats and A. E. Housman influenced the poem, though one cannot suspect from it that Kilmer was one of the earliest admirers of Gerard Manley Hopkins. Poems of great energy are usually distillations of words and sentiments outside them- 50 selves. Poems are by nature a compression. Another chestnut, Henry Wadsworth Longfellow's "A Psalm of Life," was generated by the Scotch geologist Hugh Miller's "Footprints of the Creator" and "The Old Red Sandstone," books made popular in America by Longfellow's colleague at Harvard, the scientist Louis Agassiz. 55

11   It is an example of the miraculous (and of the transcendentally vague) how Longfellow, reading about fossils in Miller, latched onto the sandstone and the vestiges thereupon, to intone "Lives of great men all remind us / We can make our lives sublime / And in passing leave behind us / Footprints on the sands of time." 60

12   Poets work that way, condensing, rendering down to essence. Another poem, as popular in its day as "Trees," Edwin Markham's "The Man with the Hoe" lived in Ezra Pound's mind until it became the opening line of "The Pisan Cantos": "The enormous tragedy of the dream in the peasant's bent shoulders." 65

13   "Trees" is, if you look, very much of its time. Trees were favorite symbols for Yeats, Robert Frost, and even the young Pound. The nature of chlorophyll had just been discovered, and "Tarzan of the Apes"—set in a tree world—had just been published. Trees were everywhere in art of the period, and it was understood that they belonged to the region of ideas, to 70 George Santayana's Realm of Beauty.[3]

[2] Art Nouveau (New Art), popular in the 1890's, is a style of design based upon tree and other plant motifs arranged in flat, more or less naturalistic patterns. The style greatly influenced interior decoration and the illustration of books and magazines. Davenport suggests that "Trees" owes much to the rather prettified form of Art Nouveau and its celebration of vegetable beauty, and almost nothing—at least intentionally—to the radical and conscious distortions of nature sometimes seen in the work of Picasso. [Editors' note]

[3] George Santayana (1863-1952) taught philosophy at Harvard for some twenty-five years. His study of beauty is concerned less with trees or other objects as individual entities, but rather as ideal forms. [Editors' note]

14   But Kilmer had been reading about trees in another context that we have forgotten, one that accounts for the self-effacing closing lines ("Poems are made by fools like me, / But only God can make a tree"), lines that have elevated the poem into double duty as a religious homily.   75

15   Kilmer's young manhood was in step with the idealism of the century. One of the inventions in idealism that attracted much attention was the movement to stop child labor and to set up nursery schools in slums. One of the most diligent pioneers in this movement was the Englishwoman Margaret McMillan, who had the happy idea that a breath of fresh air and   80 an intimate acquaintance with grass and trees were worth all the pencils and desks in the whole school system. There was something about trees that she wanted her slum children to feel. She had them take naps under trees, roll on grass, dance around trees. Her word for pencils and desks was "apparatus."

16   And in her book "Labour and Childhood" (1907) you will find this   85 sentence: "Apparatus can be made by fools, but only God can make a tree."

QUESTIONS

READER AND PURPOSE

1. What should Davenport's reader ideally know? Can those who know less also enjoy his essay?

2. Which of these might be said fairly to describe Davenport's purpose?

(a) To make a line-by-line analysis of "Trees"
(b) To convict Kilmer of plagiarism
(c) To acknowledge the enduring worth of "Trees" despite its obvious faults
(d) To suggest, by example, how many good poems are made
(e) To report a hitherto unknown source of "Trees"

ORGANIZATION

3. Study each of the following alternate beginnings and explain why each is less appropriate than Davenport's:

(a) Poetry can, and does, speak powerfully to all kinds of people in all stations of life and in all periods of time. One good poem that has endured in spite of adverse criticism is Joyce Kilmer's "Trees." Kilmer wrote "Trees" in 1913 and sent it off to the newly founded magazine *Poetry*, and Harriet Monroe, the editor, paid him six dollars for it.

(b) In Margaret McMillan's book *Labour and Childhood* (1907) you will find this sentence: "Apparatus can be made by fools, but only God can make a tree." Is there something familiar about these words? There should be, because some of them appear in one of the best known couplets in American poetry, the conclusion of Joyce Kilmer's "Trees." Kilmer wrote "Trees" in 1913 and sent it off to the newly founded magazine *Poetry*.

4. Davenport does not simply stop; he closes. How does he signal that he is ending?

5. This essay was first published in *The New York Times*, and the short paragraphs reflect newspaper style. In revising it for a book the writer might prefer longer paragraphs. Which paragraphs might go together? Be able to explain why you think so.

6. How is the third paragraph linked to the second? The fourth to the third? Identify the links between paragraphs 8 and 9, 13 and 14, and 15 and 16.

7. Paragraphs 10, 11, and 12 concern the American poets Longfellow and Pound more than Kilmer. Has the writer sacrificed unity here? Why or why not?

SENTENCES

8. Note the difference in tone * and emphasis between "She was reciting poetry" and "Reciting poetry!" (line 3). What three means of emphasis are employed in Davenport's sentence? How does that sentence differ in tone from the more conventionally phrased revision? Find a similar construction in paragraph 2.

9. Identify the periodic sentence * in the third paragraph.

10. Locate several examples of interrupted movement *. Revise one or two of them to eliminate the interruption. Has the revision lost emphasis?

11. Why is the following revision less successful than the original?

> *Revision:* Tragically and wastefully Sgt. Alfred Joyce Kilmer was killed by German gunfire at age 32 on the heights above Seringes, 30 July 1918, but the French gave him, for his gallantry, the Croix de Guerre. *Davenport:* "Sgt. Alfred Joyce Kilmer was killed by German gunfire on the heights above Seringes, 30 July 1918. The French gave him the Croix de Guerre for gallantry. He was 32." (21-23)

12. Identify two sentences in paragraph 8 that vary the normal order of subject-verb-object. What is the purpose of the variation?

DICTION

13. Look up: *cordite* (14), *carrion* (14), *couplets* (45), *verities* (46), *transcendentally* (55), *homily* (75).

14. How do each of the following substitutions alter the basic meaning, the connotations *, or emotional force of Davenport's diction: *Poet* for *poetess* (7), *one is* for *you are* (25), *kind of thing* for *taradiddle* (29), *functions* for *orgies* (29), *Deutsch* for *La Deutsch* (32), *directing her criticism* for *having* (32), *he* for *she* (42), *silver, thin beauty* for *silvery spare beauty* (44), *it speaks of verities* for *it seems to speak of verities* (46), *poem* for *chestnut* (51), *sing* for *intone* (58)?

POINTS TO LEARN

1. An essay about a piece of literature may discuss the reputation of the work, its effect upon both sophisticated and unsophisticated readers, its sources, and its relation to other aspects of culture.
2. Essays, if at all complex, may have more than one purpose, but usually one aim is primary and shapes and controls the work.
3. Writing about literature is seldom detached, objective, "scientific." At its best, as in Davenport's essay, we are aware of another human being engaged with a poem or story—thinking, judging, feeling.
4. In conveying attitudes toward the work, himself, and his readers—all of which compose tone—the writer must do so through the careful attention to diction and sentence structure.

SUGGESTIONS FOR WRITING

1. What do you think of "Trees"—is it "a monster of mixed metaphors" or a poem of "silvery, spare beauty"? Compose an essay of about 600 words in response.
2. In an essay of similar length try to make your readers share your pleasure in a poem written during the last ten years or so. (The poem should be short and a copy included with your paper.)

IMPROVING YOUR STYLE

1. In your essay use several examples of interrupted movement to gain the kind of emphasis Davenport achieves with it.
2. Use *but* and *and* to begin one or two sentences each. But be careful not to overuse these, or any other, sentence openings.

Robert Frost: The Way to the Poem

John Ciardi is a poet and teacher. Some of his published volumes are *Home-ward to America* (1940), *In Fact* (1963), and *Person to Person* (1964). He has also published a notable translation of Dante's *Divine Comedy* (1954-61). In this essay on a poem by Robert Frost, Ciardi shows what the ideal reader of poetry does. Reading, in the sense in which it applies here, is far from passively sitting back and letting words flow before you. It is cerebral activity of the most intense kind, an engagement of the mind on all levels with the language of the poem. Only such a total engagement will disclose something—though never everything—of what a complex poem means.

STOPPING BY WOODS ON A SNOWY EVENING
By Robert Frost

Whose woods these are I think I know.
His house is in the village, though;
He will not see me stopping here
To watch his woods fill up with snow.

My little horse must think it queer
To stop without a farmhouse near
Between the wood and frozen lake
The darkest evening of the year.

He gives his harness bells a shake
To ask if there is some mistake.
The only other sound's the sweep
Of easy wind and downy flake.

The woods are lovely, dark, and deep,
But I have promises to keep,

And miles to go before I sleep,
And miles to go before I sleep.

1   The School System has much to say these days of the virtue of
reading widely, and not enough about the virtues of reading less but in
depth. There are any number of reading lists for poetry, but there is not
enough talk about individual poems. Poetry, finally, is one poem at a time.
To read any one poem carefully is the ideal preparation for reading an-   5
other. Only a poem can illustrate how poetry works.

2   Above, therefore, is a poem—one of the master lyrics of the English language, and almost certainly the best-known poem by an American
poet. What happens in it?—which is to say, not *what* does it mean, but *how*
does it mean? How does it go about being a human reenactment of a human   10
experience? The author—perhaps the thousandth reader would need to be
told—is Robert Frost.

3   Even the TV audience can see that this poem begins as a seemingly-
simple narration of a seemingly-simple incident but ends by suggesting
meanings far beyond anything specifically referred to in the narrative. And   15
even readers with only the most casual interest in poetry might be made to
note the additional fact that, though the poem suggests those larger meanings, it is very careful never to abandon its pretense to being simple narration. There is duplicity at work. The poet pretends to be talking about one
thing, and all the while he is talking about many others.   20

4   Many readers are forever unable to accept the poet's essential duplicity. It is almost safe to say that a poem is never about what it seems to
be about. As much could be said of the proverb. The bird in the hand, the
rolling stone, the stitch in time never (except by an artful double-decep-
tion) intend any sort of statement about birds, stones, or sewing. The inci-   25
dent of this poem, one must conclude, is at root a metaphor.

5   Duplicity aside, this poem's movement from the specific to the
general illustrates one of the basic formulas of all poetry. Such a grand
poem as Arnold's "Dover Beach" and such lesser, though unfortunately
better known, poems as Longfellow's "The Village Blacksmith" and   30
Holmes's "The Chambered Nautilus" are built on the same progression.
In these three poems, however, the generalization is markedly set apart
from the specific narration, and even seems additional to the telling rather
than intrinsic to it. It is this sense of division one has in mind in speaking
of "a tacked-on moral."   35

6   There is nothing wrong-in-itself with a tacked-on moral. Frost, in fact, makes excellent use of the device at times. In this poem, however, Frost is careful to let the whatever-the-moral-is grow out of the poem itself. When the action ends the poem ends. There is no epilogue and no explanation. Everything pretends to be about the narrated incident. And that pretense sets the basic tone of the poem's performance of itself.

7   The dramatic force of that performance is best observable, I believe, as a progression in three scenes.

8   In scene one, which coincides with stanza one, a man—a New England man—is driving his sleigh somewhere at night. It is snowing, and as the man passes a dark patch of woods he stops to watch the snow descend into the darkness. We know, moreover, that the man is familiar with these parts (he knows who owns the woods and where the owner lives), and we know that no one has seen him stop. As scene one forms itself in the theater of the mind's-eye, therefore, it serves to establish some as yet unspecified relation between the man and the woods.

9   It is necessary, however, to stop here for a long parenthesis. Even so simple an opening statement raises any number of questions. It is impossible to address all the questions that rise from the poem stanza by stanza, but two that arise from stanza one illustrate the sort of thing one might well ask of the poem detail by detail.

10   Why, for example, does the man not say what errand he is on? What is the force of leaving the errand generalized? He might just as well have told us that he was going to the general store, or returning from it with a jug of molasses he had promised to bring Aunt Harriet and two suits of long underwear he had promised to bring the hired man. Frost, moreover, can handle homely detail to great effect. He preferred to leave his motive generalized. Why?

11   And why, on the other hand, does he say so much about knowing the absent owner of the woods and where he lives? Is it simply that one set of details happened-in whereas another did not? To speak of things "happening-in" is to assault the integrity of a poem. Poetry cannot be discussed meaningfully unless one can assume that everything in the poem—every last comma and variant spelling—is in it by the poet's specific act of choice. Only bad poets allow into their poems what is haphazard or cheaply chosen.

12   The errand, I will venture a bit brashly for lack of space, is left generalized in order the more aptly to suggest *any* errand in life, therefore, life itself. The owner is there because he is one of the forces of the poem.

Let it do to say that the force he represents is the village of mankind (that 75
village at the edge of winter) from which the poet finds himself separated
(has separated himself?) in his moment by the woods (and to which, he recalls finally, he has promises to keep). The owner is he-who-lives-in-his-
village-house, thereby locked away from the poet's awareness of the time-
the-snow-tells as it engulfs and obliterates the world the village man allows 80
himself to believe he "owns." Thus, the owner is a representative of an order of reality from which the poet has divided himself for the moment,
though to a certain extent he ends by reuniting with it. Scene one, therefore, establishes not only a relation between the man and the woods, but
the fact that the man's relation begins with his separation (though momen- 85
tarily) from mankind.

13   End parenthesis one, begin parenthesis two.

14   Still considering the first scene as a kind of dramatic performance
of forces, one must note that the poet has meticulously matched the simplicity of his language to the pretended simplicity of the narrative. Clearly, 90
the man stopped because the beauty of the scene moved him, but he neither
tells us that the scene is beautiful nor that he is moved. A bad writer, always ready to overdo, might have written: "The vastness gripped me, filling
my spirit with the slow steady sinking of the snow's crystalline perfection
into the glimmerless profundities of the hushed primeval wood." Frost's 95
avoidance of such a spate illustrates two principles of good writing. The
first, he has stated himself in "The Mowing": Anything *more* than the
truth would have seemed too weak" (italics mine). Understatement is one
of the basic sources of power in English poetry. The second principle is to
let the action speak for itself. A good novelist does not tell us that a given 100
character is good or bad (at least not since the passing of the Dickens
tradition): he shows us the character in action and then, watching him,
we know. Poetry, too, has fictional obligations: even when the characters
are ideas and metaphors rather than people, they must be *characterized
in action*. A poem does not *talk about* ideas; it *enacts* them. The force of 105
the poem's performance, in fact, is precisely to act out (and thereby to
make us act out empathically that is, to *feel out*, that is, *to identify with*
the speaker and why he stopped. The man is the principal actor in this
little "drama of why" and in scene one he is the only character, though as
noted, he is somehow related to the absent owner. 110

15   End second parenthesis.

16   In scene two (stanzas two and three) a *foil* is introduced. In fiction
and drama, a foil is a character who "plays against" a more important char-

acter. By presenting a different point of view or an opposed set of motives, the foil moves the more important character to react in ways that might not 115 have found expression without such opposition. The more important character is thus more fully revealed—to the reader and to himself. The foil here is the horse.

17   The horse forces the question. Why did the man stop? Until it occurs to him that his "little horse must think it queer" he had not asked himself 120 for reasons. He had simply stopped. But the man finds himself faced with the question he imagines the horse to be asking: what *is* there to stop for out there in the cold, away from bin and stall (house and village and mankind?) and all that any self-respecting beast could value on such a night? In sensing that other view, the man is forced to examine his own 125 more deeply.

18   In stanza two the question arises only as a feeling within the man. In stanza three, however (still scene two), the horse acts. He gives his harness bells a shake. "What's wrong?" he seems to say. "What are we waiting for?" 130

19   By now, obviously, the horse—without losing its identity as horse— has also become a symbol. A symbol is something that stands for something else. Whatever that something else may be, it certainly begins as that order of life that does not understand why a man stops in the wintry middle of nowhere to watch the snow come down. (Can one fail to sense by 135 now that the dark and the snowfall symbolize a death-wish, however momentary, *i.e.*, that hunger for final rest and surrender that a man may feel, but not a beast?)

20   So by the end of scene two the performance has given dramatic force to three elements that work upon the man. There is his relation to 140 the world of the owner. There is his relation to the brute world of the horse. And there is that third presence of the unownable world, the movement of the all-engulfing snow across all the orders of life, the man's, the owner's, and the horse's—with the difference that the man knows of that second dark-within-the-dark of which the horse cannot, and the owner will not, 145 know.

21   The man ends scene two with all these forces working upon him simultaneously. He feels himself moved to a decision. And he feels a last call from the darkness: "the sweep / Of easy wind and downy flake." It would be so easy and so downy to go into the woods and let himself be covered 150 over.

22   But scene three (stanza four) produces a fourth force. This fourth

force can be given many names. It is certainly better, in fact, to give it many names than to attempt to limit it to one. It is social obligation, or personal commitment, or duty, or just the realization that a man cannot indulge a   155 mood forever. All of these and more. But, finally, he has a simple decision to make. He may go into the woods and let the darkness and the snow swallow him from the world of beast and man. Or he must move on. And unless he is going to stop here forever, it is time to remember that he has a long way to go and that he had best be getting there. (So there is something   160 to be said for the horse, too.)

23   Then and only then, his question driven more and more deeply into himself by these cross-forces, does the man venture a comment on what attracted him "The woods are lovely, dark and deep." His mood lingers over the thought of that lovely dark-and-deep (as do the very syllables in which   165 he phrases the thought), but the final decision is to put off the mood and move on. He has his man's way to go and his man's obligations to tend to before he can yield. He has miles to go before his sleep. He repeats that thought and the performance ends.

24   But why the repetition? The first time Frost says "And miles to go   170 before I sleep," there can be little doubt that the primary meaning is: "I have a long way to go before I get to bed tonight." The second time he says it, however, "miles to go" and "sleep" are suddenly transformed into symbols. What are those "something-elses" the symbols stand for? Hundreds of people have tried to ask Mr. Frost that question and he has always turned   175 it away. He has turned it away *because he cannot answer it*. He could answer some part of it. But some part is not enough.

25   For a symbol is like a rock dropped into a pool: it sends out ripples in all directions, and the ripples are in motion. Who can say where the last ripple disappears? One may have a sense that he knows the approximate   180 center point of the ripples, the point at which the stone struck the water. Yet even then he has trouble marking it surely. How does one make a mark on water? Oh very well—the center point of that second "miles to go" is probably approximately in the neighborhood of being close to meaning, perhaps, "the road of life"; and the second "before I sleep" is maybe that   185 close to meaning "before I take my final rest," the rest in darkness that seemed so temptingly dark-and-deep for the moment of the mood. But the ripples continue to move and the light to change on the water, and the longer one watches the more changes he sees. Such shifting-and-being-at-the-same-instant is of the very sparkle and life of poetry. One experiences   190 it as one experiences life, for everytime he looks at an experience he sees something new, and he sees it change as he watches it. And that sense of continuity in fluidity is one of the primary kinds of knowledge, one of man's basic ways of knowing, and one that only the arts can teach, poetry foremost among them.   195

26   Frost himself certainly did not ask what that repeated last line meant. It came to him and he received it. He "felt right" about it. And what he "felt right" about was in no sense a "meaning" that, say, an essay could apprehend, but an act of experience that could be fully presented only by the dramatic enactment of forces which is the performance of the   200 poem.

27   Now look at the poem in another way. Did Frost know what he was going to do when he began? Considering the poem simply as an act of skill, as a piece of juggling, one cannot fail to respond to the magnificent turn at the end where, with one flip, seven of the simplest words in the   205 language suddenly dazzle full of never-ending waves of thought and feeling. Or, more precisely, of felt-thought. Certainly an equivalent stunt by a juggler—could there be an equivalent—would bring the house down. Was it to cap his performance with that grand stunt that Frost wrote the poem?

28   Far from it. The obvious fact is that *Frost could not have known*   210 *he was going to write those lines until he wrote them.* Then a second fact must be registered: *he wrote them because, for the fun of it, he had got himself into trouble.*

29   Frost, like every good poet, began by playing a game with himself. The most usual way of writing a four line stanza with four feet to the line   215 is to rhyme the third line with the first, and the fourth line with the second. Even that much rhyme is so difficult in English that many poets and almost all of the anonymous ballad makers do not bother to rhyme the first and third lines at all, settling for two rhymes in four lines as good enough. For English is a rhyme-poor language. In Italian and in French, for example, so   220 many words end with the same sounds that rhyming is relatively easy—so easy that many modern French and Italian poets do not bother to rhyme at all. English, being a more agglomerate language, has far more final sounds, hence fewer of them rhyme. When an Italian poet writes a line ending with "vita" (life) he has literally hundreds of rhyme choices available. When an   225 English poet writes "life" at the end of a line he can summon "strife, wife, knife, fife, rife," and then he is in trouble. Now "life-strife" and "life-rife" and "life-wife" seem to offer a combination of possible ideas that can be related by more than just the rhyme. Inevitably, therefore, the poets have had to work and rework these combinations until the sparkle has gone out   230

of them. The reader is normally tired of such rhyme-led associations. When he encounters "life-strife" he is certainly entitled to suspect that the poet did not really want to say "strife"—that had there been in English such a word as, say, "hife," meaning "infinite peace and harmony," the poet would as gladly have used that word instead of "strife." Thus, the reader feels that the writing is haphazard, that the rhyme is making the poet say things he does not really feel, and which, therefore, the reader does not feel except as boredom. One likes to see the rhymes fall into place, but he must end with the belief that it is the poet who is deciding what is said and not the rhyme scheme that is forcing the saying.

30   So rhyme is a kind of game, and an especially difficult one in English. As in every game, the fun of the rhyme is to set one's difficulties high and then to meet them skilfully. As Frost himself once defined freedom, it consists of "moving easy in harness."

31   In "Stopping by Woods on a Snowy Evening" Frost took a long chance. He decided to rhyme not two lines in each stanza, but three. Not even Frost could have sustained that much rhyme in a long poem (as Dante, for example, with the advantage of writing in Italian, sustained triple rhyme for thousands of lines in "The Divine Comedy"). Frost would have known instantly, therefore, when he took the original chance, that he was going to write a short poem. He would have had that much foretaste of it.

32   So the first stanza emerged rhymed a-a-b-a. And with the sure sense that this was to be a short poem, Frost decided to take an additional chance and to redouble: in English three rhymes in four lines is more than enough; there is no need to rhyme the fourth line. For the fun of it, however, Frost set himself to pick up that loose rhyme and to weave it into the pattern, thereby accepting the all but impossible burden of quadruple rhyme.

33   The miracle is that it worked. Despite the enormous freight of rhyme, the poem not only came out as a neat pattern, but managed to do so with no sense of strain. Every word and every rhyme falls into place as naturally and as inevitably as if there were no rhyme restricting the poet's choices.

34   That ease-in-difficulty is certainly inseparable from the success of the poem's performance. One watches the skill-man juggle three balls, then four, then five, and every addition makes the trick more wonderful. But unless he makes the hard trick seem as easy as an easy trick, then all is lost.

35   The real point, however, is not only that Frost took on a hard

rhyme-trick and made it seem easy. It is rather as if the juggler, carried 270
away, had tossed up one more ball than he could really handle, and then
amazed himself by actually handling it. So with the real triumph of this
poem. Frost could not have known what a stunning effect his repetition of
the last line was going to produce. He could not even know he was going to
repeat the line. He simply found himself up against a difficulty he almost 275
certainly had not foreseen and he had to improvise to meet it. For in picking up the rhyme from the third line of stanza one and carrying it over into
stanza two, he had created an endless chain-link form within which each
stanza left a hook sticking out for the next stanza to hang on. So by stanza
four, feeling the poem rounding to its end, Frost had to do something about 280
that extra rhyme.

36   He might have tucked it back into a third line rhyming with the
know-though-snow of stanza one. He could thus have rounded the poem
out to the mathematical symmetry of using each rhyme four times. But
though such a device might be defensible in theory, a rhyme repeated after 285
eleven lines is so far from its original rhyme sound that its feeling as rhyme
must certainly be lost. And what good is theory if the reader is not moved
by the writing?

37   It must have been in some such quandary that the final repetition
suggested itself—a suggestion born of the very difficulties the poet had let 290
himself in for. So there is that point beyond mere ease in handling a hard
thing, the point at which the very difficulty offers the poet the opportunity
to do better than he knew he could. What, aside from having that happen
to oneself, could be more self-delighting than to participate in its happening by one's reader-identification with the poem?   295

38   And by now a further point will have suggested itself: that the
human-insight of the poem and the technicalities of its poetic artifice are inseparable. Each feeds the other. That interplay is the poem's meaning, a
matter not of *what does it mean*, for no one can ever say entirely what a good
poem means, but of *how does it mean*, a process one can come much closer 300
to discussing.

39   There is a necessary epilogue. Mr. Frost has often discussed this
poem on the platform, or more usually in the course of a long-evening-
after a talk. Time and again I have heard him say that he just wrote it off,
that it just came to him, and that he set it down as it came.   305

40   Once at Bread Loaf, however, I heard him add one very essential
piece to the discussion of how it "just came." One night, he said, he had
sat down after supper to work at a long piece of blank verse. The piece

never worked out, but Mr. Frost found himself so absorbed in it that, when next he looked up, dawn was at his window. He rose, crossed to the win- 310 dow, stood looking out for a few minutes, and *then* it was that "Stopping by Woods" suddenly "just came," so that all he had to do was cross the room and write it down.

41 Robert Frost is the sort of artist who hides his traces. I know of no Frost worksheets anywhere. If someone has raided his wastebasket in secret, 315 it is possible that such worksheets exist somewhere, but Frost would not will- ingly allow anything but the finished product to leave him. Almost cer- tainly, therefore, no one will ever know what was in that piece of unsuc- cessful blank verse he had been working at with such concentration, but I for one would stake my life that could that worksheet be uncovered, it 320 would be found to contain the germinal stuff of "Stopping by Woods"; that what was a-simmer in him all night without finding its proper form, suddenly, when he let his still-occupied mind look away, came at him from a different direction, offered itself in a different form, and that finding that form exactly right the impulse proceeded to marry itself to the new shape 325 in one of the most miraculous performances of English lyricism.

42 And that, too—whether or not one can accept so hypothetical a discussion—is part of *how* the poem means. It means that marriage to the perfect form, the poem's shapen declaration of itself, its moment's monu- ment fixed beyond all possibility of change. And thus, finally, in every truly 330 good poem, "How does it mean?" must always be answered "Trium- phantly." Whatever the poem "is about," *how* it means is always how Genesis means: the word become a form, and the form become a thing, and—when the becoming is true—the thing become a part of the knowledge and experience of the race forever. 335

QUESTIONS

READER AND PURPOSE

1. Consider the following different attitudes toward poetry:

   (a) The poet has an idea (theme, content, meaning) to begin with, and he then finds a suitable vehicle or form in which to convey it. The form is the means of presenting the really important thing— the initial idea.
   (b) Any attention to the form of a poem is frivolous, even pointless.

(c) The poet always knows exactly what his poem does and does not mean.

(d) A poem means just what it literally says.

How many of these opinions did you agree with before reading Ciardi's essay? How many do you still accept? Do you think Ciardi agrees with any of them?

2. Is the writer's purpose chiefly to explain, or to persuade? Or is it some combination of the two?

ORGANIZATION

3. The organization of this essay is unusually clear. Probably most readers would agree that its main parts are as follows: I—paragraphs 1-6; II—paragraphs 7-23; III—paragraphs 24-28; IV—paragraphs 29-39; V—paragraphs 40-42. Give a title to each of these five sections.

4. The second part contains several subdivisions. Indicate what these are by paragraph numbers and give each a descriptive title. Do the same for part IV.

5. What is the organizational function of paragraphs 7, 13, 15, and 28?

6. What techniques of closing does the author use in his final paragraph?

7. Ciardi is exceedingly skillful in making transitions between paragraphs. Be able to explain how he links each paragraph with what precedes it.

8. Analyze the structure of paragraph 14. What is its topic sentence? Show how each successive sentence relates to the preceding one. What techniques of paragraph development are used here?

9. Point out a paragraph developed by analogy.

SENTENCES

10. Explain how in each of the following pairs of sentences the revision differs from Ciardi's statement:

(a) *Revision:* The thousandth reader would need to be told that the author is Robert Frost.
Ciardi: "The author—perhaps the thousandth reader would need to be told—is Robert Frost." (11-12)

(b) *Revision:* The more important character is thus more fully revealed to the reader and to himself.
Ciardi: "The more important character is thus more fully revealed—to the reader and to himself." (116-17)

(c) *Revision:* The truth is far from it.
Ciardi: "Far from it." (210)

(d) *Revision:* . . . rhyming is so easy that many modern French and Italian poets do not bother to rhyme at all.
Ciardi: ". . . rhyming is relatively easy—so easy that many mod-

ern French and Italian poets do not bother to rhyme at all."
(221-23)

11. Rhetorical questions * appear frequently in these paragraphs. Are they over-used—a mannerism? Or can one defend them as appropriate and effective?

DICTION

12. Look up: *lyrics* (7), *intrinsic* (34), *epilogue* (39), *integrity* (67), *brashly* (72), *obliterates* (80), *meticulously* (89), *spate* (96), *understatement* (98), *quandry* (289).

13. What does Ciardi mean by "TV audience" when he writes, "Even the TV audience can see that this poem begins as a seemingly-simple narration . . ." (13-14)?

14. What is meant in line 223 by the reference to English as a "more agglomerate language" than Italian or French?

15. Explain the allusion * to Genesis in the final paragraph of Ciardi's essay.

16. In paragraphs 28-31 of her essay "Writing Short Stories" (reprinted on pages 537 ff. of this text) Flannery O'Connor describes how she wrote a short story called "Good Country People." To what extent is her account similar or dissimilar to Robert Frost's experience as Ciardi reconstructs it? (Flannery O'Connor's closing paragraph is also pertinent to this question.)

POINTS TO LEARN

1. Exposition and persuasion are often blended in the same essay.

2. Persuasion rests, of course, upon the proper use of evidence and upon sound logic, but persuasion is greatly enhanced by skillful writing.

3. One way of achieving clarity in an essay is to use organizing sentences and to provide signposts * (as in Ciardi's paragraphs 13 and 28); these guide the reader from one major section of an essay to another. In well-organized writing the reader knows where he is, and where he has been, and where he is going.

4. Although the sentences in this selection are relatively short and uncomplicated, they are astonishingly emphatic. Ciardi varies the simple sentence by using rhetorical questions, fragments *, interrupted movement *, parallelism *, and by isolating important words by means of a dash. Italics indicate vocal stress on single words and call attention to important statements.

SUGGESTIONS FOR WRITING

Modeling your essay in a general way upon paragraphs 7-40 of John Ciardi's essay, write an interpretation of a short poem by Robert Frost, such as "Tree at My Window," "Acquainted with the Night," "Nothing Gold Can Stay." Do not merely paraphrase the poem, but organize your composition by sections on the speaker, listener (if any), and situation, symbols, patterns of analogy or contrast, the meaning of the poem as a whole, the relation of form to meaning.

IMPROVING YOUR STYLE

1. In your essay experiment with emphasis, using rhetorical questions, short simple * sentences, and fragments.

2. Use dashes to punctuate appositives * and interrupters and to isolate key phrases and words as Ciardi does in lines 11-12, 45, 117, and 327-28.

Writing Short Stories

Flannery O'Connor (1925-64) was one of the finest short story writers of her time. Her books include *The Artificial Nigger* (1957), *The Violent Bear It Away* (1960), and *Everything That Rises Must Converge* (1965). The principal conflict in her stories concerns the relationship of the individual to God, but her themes are "religious" in an unusual, highly personal sense, not in a conventional one. She is much interested in the grotesqueries of behavior both of those who seek God and of those who deny Him. The following piece, however, is not a story but an essay, and its topic is more mundane: the problems of writing short stories. It is from a collection of articles about literary topics: *Mystery and Manners* (1957).

1   I have heard people say that the short story was one of the most difficult literary forms, and I've always tried to decide why people feel this way about what seems to me to be one of the most natural and fundamental ways of human expression. After all, you begin to hear and tell stories when you're a child, and there doesn't seem to be anything very complicated 5 about it. I suspect that most of you have been telling stories all your lives, and yet here you sit—come to find out how to do it.

2   Then last week, after I had written down some of these serene thoughts to use here today, my calm was shattered when I was sent seven of your manuscripts to read. 10

3   After this experience, I found myself ready to admit, if not that the short story is one of the most difficult literary forms, at least that it is more difficult for some than for others.

4   I still suspect that most people start out with some kind of ability

to tell a story but that it gets lost along the way. Of course, the ability to 15
create life with words is essentially a gift. If you have it in the first place, you
can develop it; if you don't have it, you might as well forget it.

5   But I have found that people who don't have it are frequently the
ones hell-bent on writing stories. I'm sure anyway that they are the ones
who write the books and the magazine articles on how-to-write-short-stories. 20
I have a friend who is taking a correspondence course in this subject, and
she has passed a few of the chapter headings on to me—such as "The
Story Formula for Writers," "How to Create Characters," "Let's Plot!"
This form of corruption is costing her twenty-seven dollars.

6   I feel that discussing story-writing in terms of plot, character, and 25
theme is like trying to describe the expression on a face by saying where the
eyes, nose, and mouth are. I've heard students say, "I'm very good with plot,
but I can't do a thing with character," or "I have this theme but I don't
have a plot for it," and once I heard one say, "I've got the story but I don't
have any technique." 30

7   Technique is a word they all trot out. I talked to a writers' club
once, and during the question time, one good soul said, "Will you give me
the technique for the frame-within-a-frame short story?" I had to admit I
was so ignorant I didn't even know what that was, but she assured me there
was such a thing because she had entered a contest to write one and the 35
prize was fifty dollars.

8   But setting aside the people who have no talent for it, there are
others who do have the talent but who flounder around because they don't
really know what a story is.

9   I suppose that obvious things are the hardest to define. Everybody 40
thinks he knows what a story is. But if you ask a beginning student to write
a story, you're liable to get almost anything—a reminiscence, an episode, an
opinion, an anecdote, anything under the sun but a story. A story is a complete dramatic action—and in good stories, the characters are shown through
the action and the action is controlled through the characters, and the re- 45
sult of this is meaning that derives from the whole presented experience. I
myself prefer to say that a story is a dramatic event that involves a person
because he is a person, and a particular person—that is, because he shares
in the general human condition and in some specific human situation. A
story always involves, in a dramatic way, the mystery of personality. I lent 50
some stories to a country lady who lives down the road from me, and when
she returned them, she said, "Well, them stories just gone and shown you
how some folks *would* do," and I thought to myself that that was right; when

you write stories, you have to be content to start exactly there—showing how some specific folks *will* do, *will* do in spite of everything.

10   Now this is a very humble level to have to begin on, and most people who think they want to write stories are not willing to start there. They want to write about problems, not people; or about abstract issues, not concrete situations. They have an idea, or a feeling, or an overflowing ego, or they want to Be A Writer, or they want to give their wisdom to the world in a simple-enough way for the world to be able to absorb it. In any case, they don't have a story and they wouldn't be willing to write it if they did; and in the absence of a story, they set out to find a theory or a formula or a technique.

11   Now none of this is to say that when you write a story, you are supposed to forget or give up any moral position that you hold. Your beliefs will be the light by which you see, but they will not be what you see and they will not be a substitute for seeing. For the writer of fiction, everything has its testing point in the eye, and the eye is an organ that eventually involves the whole personality, and as much of the world as can be got into it. It involves judgment. Judgment is something that begins in the act of vision, and when it does not, or when it becomes separated from vision, then a confusion exists in the mind which transfers itself to the story.

12   Fiction operates through the senses, and I think one reason that people find it so difficult to write stories is that they forget how much time and patience is required to convince through the senses. No reader who doesn't actually experience, who isn't made to feel, the story is going to believe anything the fiction writer merely tells him. The first and most obvious characteristic of fiction is that it deals with reality through what can be seen, heard, smelt, tasted, and touched.

13   Now this is something that can't be learned only in the head; it has to be learned in the habits. It has to become a way that you habitually look at things. The fiction writer has to realize that he can't create compassion with compassion, or emotion with emotion, or thought with thought. He has to provide all these things with a body; he has to create a world with weight and extension.

14   I have found that the stories of beginning writers usually bristle with emotion, but *whose* emotion is often very hard to determine. Dialogue frequently proceeds without the assistance of any characters that you can actually see, and uncontained thought leaks out of every corner of the story. The reason is usually that the student is wholly interested in his thoughts and his emotions and not in his dramatic action, and that he is

too lazy or highfalutin to descend to the concrete where fiction operates. He thinks that judgment exists in one place and sense-impression in another. But for the fiction writer, judgment begins in the details he sees and how he sees them. 95

15   Fiction writers who are not concerned with these concrete details are guilty of what Henry James called "weak specification." The eye will glide over their words while the attention goes to sleep. Ford Madox Ford taught that you couldn't have a man appear long enough to sell a newspa- 100 per in a story unless you put him there with enough detail to make the reader see him.

16   I have a friend who is taking acting classes in New York from a Russian lady who is supposed to be very good at teaching actors. My friend wrote me that the first month they didn't speak a line, they only learned to 105 see. Now learning to see is the basis for learning all the arts except music. I know a good many fiction writers who paint, not because they're any good at painting, but because it helps their writing. It forces them to look at things. Fiction writing is very seldom a matter of saying things; it is a matter of showing things. 110

17   However, to say that fiction proceeds by the use of detail does not mean the simple, mechanical piling-up of detail. Detail has to be controlled by some overall purpose, and every detail has to be put to work for you. Art is selective. What is there is essential and creates movement.

18   Now all this requires time. A good short story should not have less 115 meaning than a novel, nor should its action be less complete. Nothing essential to the main experience can be left out of a short story. All the action has to be satisfactorily accounted for in terms of motivation, and there has to be a beginning, a middle, and an end, though not necessarily in that order. I think many people decide that they want to write short stories be- 120 cause they're short, and by short, they mean short in every way. They think that a short story is an incomplete action in which a very little is shown and a great deal suggested, and they think you suggest something by leaving it out. It's very hard to disabuse a student of this notion, because he thinks that when he leaves something out, he's being subtle; and when you tell 125 him that he has to put something in before anything can be there, he thinks you're an insensitive idiot.

19   Perhaps the central question to be considered in any discussion of the short story is what do we mean by short. Being short does not mean being slight. A short story should be long in depth and should give us an ex- 130 perience of meaning. I have an aunt who thinks that nothing happens in a

story unless somebody gets married or shot at the end of it. I wrote a story about a tramp who marries an old woman's idiot daughter in order to acquire the old woman's automobile. After the marriage, he takes the daughter off on a wedding trip in the automobile and abandons her in an eating 135 place and drives on by himself. Now that is a complete story. There is nothing more relating to the mystery of that man's personality that could be shown through that particular dramatization. But I've never been able to convince my aunt that it's a complete story. She wants to know what happened to the idiot daughter after that. 140

20   Not long ago that story was adapted for a television play, and the adapter, knowing his business, had the tramp have a change of heart and go back and pick up the idiot daughter and the two of them ride away, grinning madly. My aunt believes that the story is complete at last, but I have other sentiments about it—which are not suitable for public utter- 145 ance. When you write a story, you only have to write one story, but there will always be people who will refuse to read the story you have written.

21   And this naturally brings up the awful question of what kind of a reader you are writing for when you write fiction. Perhaps we each think we have a personal solution for this problem. For my own part, I have a 150 very high opinion of the art of fiction and a very low opinion of what is called the "average" reader. I tell myself that I can't escape him, that this is the personality I am supposed to keep awake, but that at the same time, I am also supposed to provide the intelligent reader with the deeper experience that he looks for in fiction. Now actually, both of these readers are 155 just aspects of the writer's own personality, and in the last analysis, the only reader he can know anything about is himself. We all write at our own level of understanding, but it is the peculiar characteristic of fiction that its literal surface can be made to yield entertainment on an obvious physical plane to one sort of reader while the selfsame surface can be made to yield 160 meaning to the person equipped to experience it there.

22   Meaning is what keeps the short story from being short. I prefer to talk about the meaning in a story rather than the theme of a story. People talk about the theme of a story as if the theme were like the string that a sack of chicken feed is tied with. They think that if you can pick out the 165 theme, the way you pick the right thread in the chicken-feed sack, you can rip the story open and feed the chickens. But this is not the way meaning works in fiction.

23   When you can state the theme of a story, when you can separate it from the story itself, then you can be sure the story is not a very good one. 170

The meaning of a story has to be embodied in it, has to be made concrete in it. A story is a way to say something that can't be said any other way, and it takes every word in the story to say what the meaning is. You tell a story because a statement would be inadequate. When anybody asks what a story is about, the only proper thing is to tell him to read the story. The meaning of fiction is not abstract meaning but experienced meaning, and the purpose of making statements about the meaning of a story is only to help you to experience that meaning more fully. 175

24   Fiction is an art that calls for the strictest attention to the real— whether the writer is writing a naturalistic story or a fantasy. I mean that we always begin with what is or with what has an eminent possibility of truth about it. Even when one writes a fantasy, reality is the proper basis of it. A thing is fantastic because it is so real, so real that it is fantastic. Graham Greene has said that he can't write, "I stood over a bottomless pit," because that couldn't be true, or "Running down the stairs I jumped into a taxi," because that couldn't be true either. But Elizabeth Bowen can write about one of her characters that "she snatched at her hair as if she heard something in it," because that is eminently possible. 180 185

25   I would even go so far as to say that the person writing a fantasy has to be even more strictly attentive to the concrete detail than someone writing in a naturalistic vein—because the greater the story's strain on the credulity, the more convincing the properties in it have to be. 190

26   A good example of this is a story called "The Metamorphosis" by Franz Kafka. This is a story about a man who wakes up one morning to find that he has turned into a cockroach overnight, while not discarding his human nature. The rest of the story concerns his life and feelings and eventual death as an insect with human nature, and this situation is accepted by the reader because the concrete detail of the story is absolutely convincing. The fact is that this story describes the dual nature of man in such a realistic fashion that it is almost unbearable. The truth is not distorted here, but rather, a certain distortion is used to get at the truth. If we admit, as we must, that appearance is not the same thing as reality, then we must give the artist the liberty to make certain rearrangements of nature if these will lead to greater depths of vision. The artist himself always has to remember that what he is rearranging *is* nature, and that he has to know it and be able to describe it accurately in order to have the authority to rearrange it at all. 195 200 205

27   The peculiar problem of the short-story writer is how to make the action he describes reveal as much of the mystery of existence as possible. He has only a short space to do it in and he can't do it by statement. He

has to do it by showing, not by saying, and by showing the concrete—so that 210
his problem is really how to make the concrete work double time for him.

28   In good fiction, certain of the details will tend to accumulate meaning from the action of the story itself, and when this happens they become
symbolic in the way they work. I once wrote a story called "Good Country
People" in which a lady Ph.D. has her wooden leg stolen by a Bible sales- 215
man whom she has tried to seduce. Now I'll admit that, paraphrased in this
way, the situation is simply a low joke. The average reader is pleased to observe anybody's wooden leg being stolen. But without ceasing to appeal to
him and without making any statements of high intention, this story does
manage to operate at another level of experience, by letting the wooden leg 220
accumulate meaning. Early in the story, we're presented with the fact that
the Ph.D. is spiritually as well as physically crippled. She believes in nothing but her own belief in nothing, and we perceive that there is a wooden
part of her soul that corresponds to her wooden leg. Now of course this is
never stated. The fiction writer states as little as possible. The reader makes 225
this connection from things he is shown. He may not even know that he
makes the connection, but the connection is there nevertheless and it has
its effect on him. As the story goes on, the wooden leg continues to accumulate meaning. The reader learns how the girl feels about her leg, how
her mother feels about it, and how the country woman on the place feels 230
about it; and finally, by the time the Bible salesman comes along, the leg
has accumulated so much meaning that it is, as the saying goes, loaded.
And when the Bible salesman steals it, the reader realizes that he has taken
away part of the girl's personality and has revealed her deeper affliction to
her for the first time.   235

29   If you want to say that the wooden leg is a symbol, you can say
that. But it is a wooden leg first, and as a wooden leg it is absolutely necessary to the story. It has its place on the literal level of the story, but it operates in depth as well as on the surface. It increases the story in every direction, and this is essentially the way a story escapes being short.   240

30   Now a little might be said about the way in which this happens. I
wouldn't want you to think that in that story I sat down and said, "I am
now going to write a story about a Ph.D. with a wooden leg, using the
wooden leg as a symbol for another kind of affliction." I doubt myself if
many writers know what they are going to do when they start out. When I 245
started writing that story, I didn't know there was going to be a Ph.D. with
a wooden leg in it. I merely found myself one morning writing a description
of two women that I knew something about, and before I realized it, I had

equipped one of them with a daughter with a wooden leg. As the story progressed, I brought in the Bible salesman, but I had no idea what I was go-   250
ing to do with him. I didn't know he was going to steal that wooden leg until ten or twelve lines before he did it, but when I found out that this was
what was going to happen, I realized that it was inevitable. This is a story
that produces a shock for the reader, and I think one reason for this is that
it produced a shock for the writer.   255

31   Now despite the fact that this story came about in this seemingly
mindless fashion, it is a story that almost no rewriting was done on. It is a
story that was under control throughout the writing of it, and it might be
asked how this kind of control comes about, since it is not entirely conscious.

32   I think the answer to this is what Maritain calls "the habit of art."   260
It is a fact that fiction writing is something in which the whole personality
takes part—the conscious as well as the unconscious mind. Art is the habit
of the artist; and habits have to be rooted deep in the whole personality.
They have to be cultivated like any other habit, over a long period of time,
by experience; and teaching any kind of writing is largely a matter of help-   265
ing the student develop the habit of art. I think this is more than just a discipline, although it is that; I think it is a way of looking at the created
world and of using the senses so as to make them find as much meaning as
possible in things.

33   Now I am not so naïve as to suppose that most people come to   270
writers' conferences in order to hear what kind of vision is necessary to
write stories that will become a permanent part of our literature. Even if
you do wish to hear this, your greatest concerns are immediately practical.
You want to know how you can actually write a good story, and further,
how you can tell when you've done it; and so you want to know what the   275
form of a short story is, as if the form were something that existed outside
of each story and could be applied or imposed on the material. Of course,
the more you write, the more you will realize that the form is organic, that
it is something that grows out of the material, that the form of each story
is unique. A story that is any good can't be reduced, it can only be ex-   280
panded. A story is good when you continue to see more and more in it, and
when it continues to escape you. In fiction two and two is always more than
four.

34   The only way, I think, to learn to write short stories is to write
them, and then to try to discover what you have done. The time to think of   285
technique is when you've actually got the story in front of you. The teacher

can help the student by looking at his individual work and trying to help him decide if he has written a complete story, one in which the action fully illuminates the meaning.

35   Perhaps the most profitable thing I can do is to tell you about some of the general observations I made about these seven stories I read of yours. All of these observations will not fit any one of the stories exactly, but they are points nevertheless that won't hurt anyone interested in writing to think about.

36   The first thing that any professional writer is conscious of in reading anything is, naturally, the use of language. Now the use of language in these stories was such that, with one exception, it would be difficult to distinguish one story from another. While I can recall running into several clichés, I can't remember one image or one metaphor from the seven stories. I don't mean there weren't images in them; I just mean that there weren't any that were effective enough to take away with you.

37   In connection with this, I made another observation that startled me considerably. With the exception of one story, there was practically no use made of the local idiom. Now this is a Southern Writers' Conference. All the addresses on these stories were from Georgia or Tennessee, yet there was no distinctive sense of Southern life in them. A few place-names were dropped, Savannah or Atlanta or Jacksonville, but these could just as easily have been changed to Pittsburgh or Passaic without calling for any other alteration in the story. The characters spoke as if they had never heard any kind of language except what came out of a television set. This indicates that something is way out of focus.

38   There are two qualities that make fiction. One is the sense of mystery and the other is the sense of manners. You get the manners from the texture of existence that surrounds you. The great advantage of being a Southern writer is that we don't have to go anywhere to look for manners; bad or good, we've got them in abundance. We in the South live in a society that is rich in contradiction, rich in irony, rich in contrast, and particularly rich in its speech. And yet here are six stories by Southerners in which almost no use is made of the gifts of the region.

39   Of course the reason for this may be that you have seen these gifts abused so often that you have become self-conscious about using them. There is nothing worse than the writer who doesn't *use* the gifts of the region, but wallows in them. Everything becomes so Southern that it's sickening, so local that it is unintelligible, so literally reproduced that it con-

veys nothing. The general gets lost in the particular instead of being shown   325
through it.

40   However, when the life that actually surrounds us is totally ig-
nored, when our patterns of speech are absolutely overlooked, then something is out of kilter. The writer should then ask himself if he is not reaching out for a kind of life that is artificial to him.   330

41   An idiom characterizes a society, and when you ignore the idiom,
you are very likely ignoring the whole social fabric that could make a
meaningful character. You can't cut characters off from their society and
say much about them as individuals. You can't say anything meaningful
about the mystery of a personality unless you put that personality in a be-   335
lievable and significant social context. And the best way to do this is through
the character's own language. When the old lady in one of Andrew Lytle's
stories says contemptuously that she has a mule that is older than Birming-
ham, we get in that one sentence a sense of a society and its history. A great
deal of the Southern writer's work is done for him before he begins, because   340
our history lives in our talk. In one of Eudora Welty's stories a character
says, "Where I come from, we use fox for yard dogs and owls for chickens,
but we sing true." Now there is a whole book in that one sentence; and
when the people of your section can talk like that, and you ignore it, you're
just not taking advantage of what's yours. The sound of our talk is too def-   345
inite to be discarded with impunity, and if the writer tries to get rid of it,
he is liable to destroy the better part of his creative power.

42   Another thing I observed about these stories is that most of them
don't go very far inside a character, don't reveal very much of the character. I don't mean that they don't enter the character's mind, but they sim-   350
ply don't show that he has a personality. Again this goes back partly to
speech. These characters have no distinctive speech to reveal themselves
with; and sometimes they have no really distinctive features. You feel in
the end that no personality is revealed because no personality is there. In
most good stories it is the character's personality that creates the action of   355
the story. In most of these stories, I feel that the writer has thought of some
action and then scrounged up a character to perform it. You will usually be
more successful if you start the other way around. If you start with a real
personality, a real character, then something is bound to happen; and you
don't have to know what before you begin. In fact it may be better if you   360
don't know what before you begin. You ought to be able to discover something from your stories. If you don't, probably nobody else will.

QUESTIONS

READER AND PURPOSE

1. What specific group was Flannery O'Connor addressing on the occasion of her lecture? Of course she was speaking, at least potentially, to a wider audience. Describe the type of reader for whom this essay would be appropriate.

2. Of special interest here is the author's tone *. What has she assumed about the interests of those in her original audience, about their knowledge of short stories, their abilities, their mistaken notions? Does she appear to take her listeners and their ambitions seriously, or does she talk down to them? Use specific passages to illustrate your answers.

3. What does Flannery O'Connor think of her aunt's literary judgment in paragraph 19? Of correspondence courses in writing short stories in paragraph 5? Of the television version of her short story in paragraph 20? Of the "average reader" in paragraph 21?

4. How does the author conceive of her own role: as a high priestess of fiction, a hard-working professional impatient with amateurs, an honest craftsman exasperated by ignorance and humbug? Or as something else?

5. If Flannery O'Connor insists upon her own superior knowledge of fiction, how does she win the approval of her audience?

ORGANIZATION

6. Which paragraphs constitute the introduction? Where does the writer indicate her subject in a broad, general sense? Where does she narrow down the subject? What else does her introduction accomplish? Suppose she had begun like this: "My subject this evening is how, and how not, to write short stories. My purpose is to give you a number of do's and don't's, with special reference to the stories you have given me to read. But first, let us attempt to define what is meant by the term *short story*." Why would such an opening be much poorer?

7. Following the introduction, Flannery O'Connor defines a short story. Which paragraphs make up this definition? What methods of defining does she use? Show that her definition is also advice about writing short stories.

8. Identify and entitle the remaining part (or parts) of this essay.

9. Which paragraphs constitute the conclusion? Does the ending seem prepared for, or abrupt and unexpected? What means of signaling conclusion has the writer employed? Can you think of any other ways of closing this essay?

10. Paragraphs 2, 3, and 8—among others—consist of a single sentence. Would the force or clarity of the essay be improved if paragraphs 2 and 3 were combined with 4? If paragraphs 5, 6, 7, and 8 were brought together? Most of

Flannery O'Connor's paragraphs consist of three or more sentences. Is it possible to justify these one-sentence paragraphs?

11. Analyze how the writer develops her topic in paragraphs 12, 24, and 28.

SENTENCES

12. The overall effect of Flannery O'Connor's sentence style is one of simplicity. Yet she skillfully varies her sentence patterns. Find examples of parallelism *, interrupted movement *, balanced construction *, and antithesis *.

13. Explain why the following sentence is an example of chiasmus *: "A thing is fantastic because it is so real; so real that it is fantastic." Find a similar sentence in paragraph 26.

14. Study these two sentences and explain why the revision is inferior to what Flannery O'Connor wrote:

> Revision: We in the South live in a society that is rich in contradiction, replete with irony, heavily endowed with contrasts, and blessed in its speech.
>
> O'Connor: "We in the South live in a society that is rich in contradiction, rich in irony, rich in contrast, and particularly rich in its speech." (316-18)

DICTION

15. Look up: highfalutin (93), concrete (93), motivation (118), disabuse (124), awful (148), naturalistic (180), fantasy (180), eminent (181), properties (192), peculiar (207), paraphrased (216), organic (278), impunity (346).

16. Carefully differentiate the meanings of these related terms in lines 42-43: reminiscence, episode, opinion, anecdote, story.

17. Point to words and expressions that are informal, even colloquial *, suggesting the rhythms of spoken English. Find examples of more formal, literary diction.

18. Why does the writer employ capitals in "they want to Be A Writer" in line 60? What does she imply by her use of hyphens in "books and magazine articles on how-to-write-short-stories" (20)?

19. The word now appears often in this essay, especially as the first word of a paragraph. What exactly does it mean? Explain how it affects the tone of the essay. If you think it has been overused, suggest one or two monosyllabic equivalents of now.

POINTS TO LEARN

1. A formal style seldom sounds effective in a lecture or a speech; on the other hand, writing designed for an audience to listen to often works very well as an informal essay.

2. Informal writing reveals a writer's personality more clearly than does a formal, literary style. Informal essays have a distinct tone, which results from a combination of diction and sentence structure and which expresses the writer's attitude toward readers (or audience), toward subject, and toward himself. Tone, skillfully managed, helps the writer to entertain his readers as well as to inform them, and may enhance any effort he makes to persuade them of something.

3. The informal essayist uses both literary and more commonplace diction. At times he is deliberately casual or colloquial; he may tell anecdotes and report bits of conversation. At other times he employs more formal words, with precision and clarity his foremost consideration.

4. And similarly the informal essayist makes use of a wide range of sentence structure, from short, simple sentences to more complex patterns such as parallelism, balance, antithesis, and an occasional chiasmus.

SUGGESTIONS FOR WRITING

1. Analyze a short story by Flannery O'Connor, Eudora Welty, or Frank Kafka in the light of Flannery O'Connor's advice to short-story writers. Pay particular attention to such matters as the principal characters' share in the "general human condition" and their relation to "the mysteries of personality." Use short quotations from the essay if you can work them in neatly.

2. Read Flannery O'Connor's story "The Life You Save May Be Your Own," which she refers to on page 541 of this essay. Analyze the story as an "experience of meaning." Show that it is complete in the sense in which Flannery O'Connor uses that term and that it deals with "the mystery of personality." Along the way you might allude to the author's exasperation with the television script of her story.

3. Imagining that you will be reading it aloud to your classmates, compose an essay in which you show how manners and speech define characters and overall meaning in a short story by Henry James, Andrew Lytle, Graham Greene, or Flannery O'Connor.

4. Flannery O'Connor suggests that the personalities of fictional characters are shaped, at least in part, by the personalities of their creators. Study several of her short stories and discuss what they (along with this essay) reveal about Flannery O'Connor's personality.

IMPROVING YOUR STYLE

1. In your essay include examples of the balanced sentence, of parallelism, and of antithesis.

2. Include also a sentence using chiasmus (see Question 13).

3. Experiment with *now* in two or three places as a transitional word, using it as O'Connor does in lines 81, 115, 241, and 256. The exact value of *now* in such passages is difficult to define. Partly it is a weak intensive asking for the reader's attention. Partly it signals movement to another topic, too loosely related to what has just been said to warrant a more precise logical connective * such as *consequently* or *for* or *hence*. And partly it is an informal, colloquial word, important in establishing a relaxed, conversational tone.

Alchemy

Pauline Kael is one of the most literate and sensitive of contemporary film critics. Her reviews appear in *The New Yorker* magazine and have been collected in several volumes, among them, *Deeper Into Movies* (1972), from which this selection comes. It is about *The Godfather*, winner of the 1972 Academy Award as best picture of the year. Kael brings to film criticism the same analytic scrutiny literary scholars use in discussing a poem or story or play. But obviously her analysis must include attention to the qualities unique to cinema—the use of light and shadow, camera work, and so on. Her essay, like John Ciardi's on page 524, illustrates the essential role of the critic: to get involved with a work of art, to know the nature of the form, to analyze and explain how its parts articulate, and to clarify what, in their totality, they signify.

1   If ever there was a great example of how the best popular movies come out of a merger of commerce and art, *The Godfather* is it. The movie starts from a trash novel that is generally considered gripping and compulsively readable, though (maybe because movies more than satisfy my appetite for trash) I found it unreadable. You're told who and what the char- 5 acters are in a few pungent, punchy sentences, and that's all they are. You're briefed on their backgrounds and sex lives in a flashy anecdote or two, and the author moves on, from nugget to nugget. Mario Puzo has a reputation as a good writer, so his potboiler was treated as if it were special, and not in the Irving Wallace–Harold Robbins class, to which, by its itch 10 and hype and juicy *roman-à-clef* treatment, it plainly belongs. What would this school of fiction do without Porfirio Rubirosa, Judy Garland, James Aubrey, Howard Hughes, and Frank Sinatra? The novel *The Godfather*,

financed by Paramount during its writing, features a Sinatra stereotype, and sex and slaughter, and little gobbets of trouble and heartbreak. It's grip- 15 ping, maybe, in the same sense that Spiro Agnew's speeches were a few years back. Francis Ford Coppola, who directed the film, and wrote the script with Puzo, has stayed very close to the book's greased-lightning sensationalism and yet has made a movie with the spaciousness and strength that popular novels such as Dickens' used to have. With the slop and sex 20 reduced and the whoremongering guess-who material minimized ("Nino," who sings with a highball in his hand, has been weeded out), the movie bears little relationship to other adaptations of books of this kind, such as *The Carpetbaggers* and *The Adventurers*. Puzo provided what Coppola needed: a storyteller's outpouring of incidents and details to choose from, 25 the folklore behind the headlines, heat and immediacy, the richly familiar. And Puzo's shameless turn-on probably left Coppola looser than if he had been dealing with a better book; he could not have been cramped by worries about how best to convey its style. Puzo, who admits he was out to make money, wrote "below my gifts," as he puts it, and one must agree. 30 Coppola uses his gifts to reverse the process—to give the public the best a moviemaker can do with this very raw material. Coppola, a young director who has never had a big hit, may have done the movie for money, as *he* claims—in order to make the pictures he really wants to make, he says—but this picture was made at peak capacity. He has salvaged Puzo's energy and 35 lent the narrative dignity. Given the circumstances and the rush to complete the film and bring it to market, Coppola has not only done his best but pushed himself farther than he may realize. The movie is on the heroic scale of earlier pictures on broad themes, such as *On the Waterfront*, *From Here to Eternity*, and *The Nun's Story*. It offers a wide, startlingly vivid 40 view of a Mafia dynasty. The abundance is from the book; the quality of feeling is Coppola's.

2   The beginning is set late in the summer of 1945; the film's roots, however, are in the gangster films of the early thirties. The plot is still about rival gangs murdering each other, but now we see the system of patronage 45 and terror, in which killing is a way of dealing with the competition. We see how the racketeering tribes encroach on each other and why this form of illegal business inevitably erupts in violence. We see the ethnic subculture, based on a split between the men's conception of their responsibilities— all that they keep dark—and the sunny false Eden in which they try to 50 shelter the women and children. The thirties films indicated some of this, but *The Godfather* gets into it at the primary level; the willingness to be

basic and the attempt to understand the basic, to look at it without the usual preconceptions, are what give this picture its epic strength.

3   The visual scheme is based on the most obvious life-and-death con-   55
trasts; the men meet and conduct their business in deep-toned, shuttered rooms, lighted by lamps even in the daytime, and the story moves back and forth between this hidden, nocturnal world and the sunshine that they share with the women and children. The tension is in the meetings in the underworld darkness; one gets the sense that this secret life has its own po-   60
etry of fear, more real to the men (and perhaps to the excluded women also) than the sunlight world outside. The dark-and-light contrast is so operatic and so openly symbolic that it perfectly expresses the basic nature of the material. The contrast is integral to the Catholic background of the characters: innocence versus knowledge—knowledge in this sense being the   65
same as guilt. It works as a visual style, because the Goyaesque shadings of dark brown into black in the interiors suggest (no matter how irrationally) an earlier period of history, while the sunny, soft-edge garden scenes have their own calendar-pretty pastness. Nino Rota's score uses old popular songs to cue the varying moods, and at one climactic point swells in a   70
crescendo that is both Italian opera and pure-forties movie music. There are rash, foolish acts in the movie but no acts of individual bravery. The killing, connived at in the darkness, is the secret horror, and it surfaces in one bloody outburst after another. It surfaces so often that after a while it doesn't surprise us, and the recognition that the killing is an integral part   75
of business policy takes us a long way from the fantasy outlaws of old movies. These gangsters don't satisfy our adventurous fantasies of disobeying the law; they're not defiant, they're furtive and submissive. They are required to be more obedient than we are; they live by taking orders. There is no one on the screen we can identify with—unless we take a fancy to the   80
pearly teeth of one shark in a pool of sharks.

4   Even when the plot strands go slack about two-thirds of the way through, and the passage of a few years leaves us in doubt whether certain actions have been concluded or postponed, the picture doesn't become softheaded. The direction is tenaciously intelligent. Coppola holds on and   85
pulls it all together. The trash novel is there underneath, but he attempts to draw the patterns out of the particulars. It's amazing how encompassing the view seems to be—what a sense you get of a broad historical perspective, considering that the span is only from 1945 to the mid-fifties, at which time the Corleone family, already forced by competitive pressures into deal-   90
ing in narcotics, is moving its base of operations to Las Vegas.

5   The enormous cast is headed by Marlon Brando as Don Vito Corleone, the "godfather" of a powerful Sicilian-American clan, with James
Caan as his hothead son, Sonny, and Al Pacino as the thoughtful, educated
son, Michael. Is Brando marvellous? Yes, he is, but then he often is; he was
marvellous a few years ago in *Reflections in a Golden Eye,* and he's shock-
ingly effective as a working-class sadist in a current film, *The Nightcomers,*
though the film itself isn't worth seeing. The role of Don Vito—a patriarch
in his early sixties—allows him to release more of the gentleness that was so
seductive and unsettling in his braggart roles. Don Vito could be played as
a magnificent old warrior, a noble killer, a handsome bull-patriarch, but
Brando manages to debanalize him. It's typical of Brando's daring that he
doesn't capitalize on his broken-prow profile and the massive, sculptural
head that has become the head of Rodin's Balzac—he doesn't play for
statuesque nobility. The light, cracked voice comes out of a twisted mouth
and clenched teeth; he has the battered face of a devious, combative old
man, and a pugnacious thrust to his jaw. The rasp in his voice is particularly effective after Don Vito has been wounded; one almost feels that the
bullets cracked it, and wishes it hadn't been cracked before. Brando interior-
izes Don Vito's power, makes him less physically threatening and *deeper*
hidden within himself.

6   Brando's acting has mellowed in recent years; it is less immediately
exciting than it used to be, because there's not the sudden, violent discharge
of emotion. His effects are subtler, less showy, and he gives himself over to
the material. He appears to have worked his way beyond the self-parody
that was turning him into a comic, and that sometimes left the other performers dangling and laid bare the script. He has not acquired the polish of
most famous actors; just the opposite—less mannered as he grows older, he
seems to draw directly from life, and from himself. His Don is a primitive
sacred monster, and the more powerful because he suggests not the strapping sacred monsters of movies (like Anthony Quinn) but actual ones—
those old men who carry never-ending grudges and ancient hatreds inside a
frail frame, those monsters who remember minute details of old business
deals when they can no longer tie their shoelaces. No one has aged better
on camera than Brando; he gradually takes Don Vito to the close of his
life, when he moves into the sunshine world, a sleepy monster, near to innocence again. The character is all echoes and shadings, and no noise; his
strength is in that armor of quiet. Brando has lent Don Vito some of his
own mysterious, courtly reserve: the character is not explained; we simply
assent to him and believe that, yes, he could become a king of the under-

world. Brando doesn't dominate the movie, yet he gives the story the legendary presence needed to raise it above gang warfare to archetypal tribal warfare.

7   Brando isn't the whole show; James Caan is very fine, and so are Robert Duvall and many others in lesser roles. Don Vito's sons suggest different aspects of Brando—Caan's Sonny looks like the muscular young Brando, but without the redeeming intuitiveness, while as the heir, Michael, Al Pacino comes to resemble him in manner and voice. Pacino creates a quiet, ominous space around himself; his performance—which is marvellous, too, big yet without ostentation—complements Brando's. Like Brando in this film, Pacino is simple; you don't catch him acting, yet he manages to change from a small, fresh-faced, darkly handsome college boy into an underworld lord, becoming more intense, smaller, and more isolated at every step. Coppola doesn't stress the father-and-son links; they are simply there for us to notice when we will. Michael becomes like his father mostly from the inside, but we also get to see how his father's face was formed (Michael's mouth gets crooked and his cheeks jowly, like his father's, after his jaw has been smashed). Pacino has an unusual gift for conveying the divided spirit of a man whose calculations often go against his inclinations. When Michael, warned that at a certain point he must come out shooting, delays, we are left to sense his mixed feelings. As his calculations will always win out, we can see that he will never be at peace. The director levels with almost everybody in the movie. The women's complicity in their husbands' activities is kept ambiguous, but it's naggingly there—you can't quite ignore it. And Coppola doesn't make the subsidiary characters lovable; we look at Clemenza (Richard Castellano) as objectively when he is cooking spaghetti and we do when he is garrotting a former associate. Many of the actors (and the incidents) carry the resonances of earlier gangster pictures, so that we almost unconsciously place them in the prehistory of this movie. Castellano, with his resemblance to Al Capone and Edward G. Robinson (plus a vagrant streak of Oscar Levant), belongs in this atmosphere; so does Richard Conte (as Barzini), who appeared in many of the predecessors of this movie, including *House of Strangers*, though perhaps Al Lettieri (as Sollozzo) acts too much like a B-picture hood. And perhaps the director goes off key when Sonny is blasted and blood-splattered at a toll booth; the effect is too garish.

8   The people dress in character and live in character—with just the gewgaws that seem right for them. The period details are there—a satin pillow, a modernistic apartment-house lobby, a child's pasted-together greet-

ing to Grandpa—but Coppola doesn't turn the viewer into a guided tourist, 170
told what to see. Nor does he go in for a lot of closeups, which are the simplest tool for fixing a director's attitude. Diane Keaton (who plays Michael's
girl friend) is seen casually; her attractiveness isn't labored. The only character who is held in frame (for us to see exactly as the character looking at
her sees her) is Apollonia (played by Simonetta Stefanelli), whom Michael 175
falls in love with in Sicily. She is fixed by the camera as a ripe erotic image,
because that is what she means to him, and Coppola, not having wasted
his resources, can do it in a few frames. In general, he tries not to fix the
images. In *Sunday Bloody Sunday*, John Schlesinger showed a messy
knocked-over ashtray being picked up in closeup, so that there was nothing 180
to perceive in the shot but the significance of the messiness. Coppola, I
think, would have kept the camera on the room in which the woman bent
over to retrieve the ashtray, and the messiness would have been just one
element among many to be observed—perhaps the curve of her body could
have told us much more than the actual picking-up motion. *The Godfather* 185
keeps so much in front of us all the time that we're never bored (though
the picture runs just two minutes short of three hours)—we keep taking
things in. This is a heritage from Jean Renoir—this uncoercive, "open" approach to the movie frame. Like Renoir, Coppola lets the spectator roam
around in the images, lets a movie breathe, and this is extremely difficult 190
in a period film, in which every detail must be carefully planted. But the
details never look planted: you're a few minutes into the movie before
you're fully conscious that it's set in the past.

9   When one considers the different rates at which people read, it's
miraculous that films can ever solve the problem of a pace at which audi- 195
ences can "read" a film together. A hack director solves the problem of pacing by making only a few points and making those so emphatically that the
audience can hardly help getting them (this is why many of the movies
from the studio-system days are unspeakably insulting); the tendency of a
clever, careless director is to go too fast, assuming that he's made everything 200
clear when he hasn't, and leaving the audience behind. When a film has as
much novelistic detail as this one, the problem might seem to be almost
insuperable. Yet, full as it is, *The Godfather* goes by evenly, so we don't feel
rushed, or restless, either; there's classic grandeur to the narrative flow. But
Coppola's attitudes are specifically modern—more so than in many films 205
with a more jagged surface. Renoir's openness is an expression of an almost
pagan love of people and landscape; his style is an embrace. Coppola's openness is a reflection of an exploratory sense of complexity; he doesn't feel the

need to comment on what he shows us, and he doesn't want to reduce the meanings in a shot by pushing us this way or that. The assumption behind 210 this film is that complexity will engage the audience.

10   These gangsters *like* their life style, while we—seeing it from the outside—are appalled. If the movie gangster once did represent, as Robert Warshow suggested in the late forties, "what we want to be and what we are afraid we may become," if he expressed "that part of the American 215 psyche which rejects the qualities and the demands of modern life, which rejects 'Americanism' itself," that was the attitude of another era. In *The Godfather* we see organized crime as an obscene symbolic extension of free enterprise and government policy, an extension of the worst in America—its feudal ruthlessness. Organized crime is not a rejection of Americanism, it's 220 what we fear Americanism to be. It's our nightmare of the American system. When "Americanism" was a form of cheerful, bland official optimism, the gangster used to be destroyed at the end of the movies and our feelings resolved. Now the mood of the whole country has darkened, guiltily; nothing is resolved at the end of *The Godfather*, because the family business 225 goes on. Terry Malloy didn't clean up the docks at the end of *On the Waterfront*; that was a lie. *The Godfather* is popular melodrama, but it expresses a new tragic realism.

QUESTIONS

READER AND PURPOSE

1. Comment on this statement: "Pauline Kael's reader is the moviegoer who reads books." Amplify your comment into a paragraph or two about the kind of reader who would understand and enjoy this selection.

2. What purpose beyond praise of *The Godfather* does this essay achieve?

3. The author announces her subject in the very first sentence. How does she immediately begin to narrow down what she will do?

ORGANIZATION

4. Often the beginning paragraph of an essay establishes its tone *. Pointing to particular words and passages, describe Kael's attitude toward the film she is reviewing, toward herself, and toward her readers.

5. The first paragraph constitutes an introduction. Give a title to each succeeding paragraph. Could paragraphs 5, 6, and 7 change places with 2, 3, and 4? Why or why not?

6. The last paragraph is an effective closing. Show that, while it does not summarize what's been said, it is a logical, satisfying conclusion.

7. How does the last sentence of this essay echo the very first? Explain why such an echo makes an effective signal of closing.

8. The first paragraph is skillfully developed. It is organized primarily by contrast, but it also employs reasons and illustration. Explain.

9. After reading the first paragraph, one understands the title of this selection. Why?

SENTENCES

10. In a number of sentences dashes are used with great effectiveness: for example, in lines 31, 34, 98 and 99, 136, 167, and 168 and 170. Might any of these dashes have been replaced by commas without sacrificing clarity? How would using commas have affected the emphasis?

11. Find examples of rhetorical questions * and of very short sentences. Point out instances of these kinds of sentence structure: periodic *, balanced *, parallel *, interrupted movement *.

12. Study a sentence that strikes you as particularly effective and explain why it is so good.

DICTION

13. Look up: *compulsively* (3), *potboiler* (9), *hype* (11), *stereotype* (14), *gobbets* (15), *sensationalism* (18), *dynasty* (41), *epic* (54), *Goyaesque* (66), *irrationally* (67), *integral* (75), *tenaciously* (85), *mannered* (118), *courtly* (129), *ominous* (139), *ostentation* (140), *jowly* (147), *ambiguous* (154), *subsidiary* (155), *hack* (196), *melodrama* (227).

14. How do their etymologies * help one to understand the current meanings of the following? *Pungent* (6), *patronage* (45), *nocturnal* (58), *crescendo* (71), *connived* (73), *furtive* (78), *patriarch* (98), *archetypal* (132), *garrotting* (157).

15. Explain the meanings of these phrases: roman-à-clef (11), *ethnic subculture* (48), *Rodin's Balzac* (104), *feudal ruthlessness* (220).

16. The diction of "Alchemy" is a combination of the formal and the informal. What words are colloquial *, even slangy? What words seem more formal and literary?

17. Kael often uses alliteration *: "You're told who and what the characters are in a few pungent, punchy sentences, and that's all they are." Point out other instances. Is her alliteration obvious and distracting, or is it a subtle means of achieving emphasis?

18. Discuss why the diction in these phrases is especially effective: *greased-lightning sensationalism* (18-19), *whoremongering guess-who material* (21), *broken-brow profile* (103), *the strapping sacred monsters of movies* (*like Anthony Quinn*) (120-21), *blasted and blood-spattered at a toll booth* (165).

19. Identify several examples of similes * and metaphors *.

POINTS TO LEARN

1. To write well about a movie or a piece of literature one must experience it, not merely look at it.

2. Punctuation not only helps to group, separate, and thereby to clarify the elements of a sentence, but also helps to establish emphasis and tone. Kael's use of parentheses and dashes, for example, is worth studying.

3. Avoid clichés if you wish to keep your prose from seeming flat and toneless. Learn the value of allusions, colloquialisms, even an occasional slang word, and unusual words (or usual words in unusual combinations, as in "sleepy monster").

SUGGESTIONS FOR WRITING

1. Write a review of a recent film which has strongly appealed to or repelled you. Model your organization in a general way upon "Alchemy."

2. Discuss the trend in recent movies in handling a particular type of character or subject. Possibilities: policemen, criminals, housewives, women's liberation, politicians, old persons, teen-agers, horror, science or science fiction.

IMPROVING YOUR STYLE

In your essay include:

1. One each of the following: a rhetorical question, a periodic sentence, a balanced sentence, and sentences using parallelism and interrupted movement.

2. Attempts at alliteration in one or two places (see question 17).

3. Several metaphors and several similes.

Who Killed King Kong?

X. J. Kennedy is a critic, teacher, and poet. His published poems include the volumes *Nude Descending a Staircase* (1961) and *Growing into Love* (1969). Here he examines the phenomenon of *King Kong*, a perennial film classic produced in 1933. While Kennedy is not, like Pauline Kael (pp. 551 ff.), primarily a film critic, he is fully sensitive to the nature of motion pictures. His focus, however, is not simply upon the movie itself but includes its relationship to our culture, the reason for *King Kong's* enduring popularity. Kennedy's forceful prose in this essay exploits almost all the resources of diction and is noteworthy also for its skillful control of tone.

1   The ordeal and spectacular death of King Kong, the giant ape, undoubtedly have been witnessed by more Americans than have ever seen a performance of *Hamlet, Iphigenia at Aulis*, or even *Tobacco Road*. Since RKO-Radio Pictures first released *King Kong*, a quarter-century has gone by; yet year after year, from prints that grow more rain-beaten, from sound tracks 5 that grow more tinny, ticket-buyers by thousands still pursue Kong's luckless fight against the forces of technology, tabloid journalism, and the DAR. They see him chloroformed to sleep, see him whisked from his jungle isle to New York and placed on show, see him burst his chains to roam the city (lugging a frightened blonde), at last to plunge from the spire of the Empire 10 State Building, machine-gunned by model airplanes.

2   Though Kong may die, one begins to think his legend unkillable. No clearer proof of his hold upon the popular imagination may be seen than what emerged one catastrophic week in March 1955, when New York WOR-TV programmed *Kong* for seven evenings in a row (a total of sixteen 15 showings). Many a rival network vice-president must have scowled when surveys showed that *Kong*—the 1933 B-picture—had lured away fat segments

From *Dissent* (Spring 1960). Reprinted by permission of the publisher.

of the viewing populace from such powerful competitors as Ed Sullivan, Groucho Marx and Bishop Sheen.

3   But even television has failed to run *King Kong* into oblivion. Coffee-   20
in-the-lobby cinemas still show the old hunk of hokum, with the apology that in its use of composite shots and animated models the film remains technically interesting. And no other monster in movie history has won so devoted a popular audience. None of the plodding mummies, the stultified draculas, the white-coated Lugosis[1] with their shiny pinball-machine labora-   25
tories, none of the invisible stranglers, berserk robots, or menaces from Mars has ever enjoyed so many resurrections.

4   Why does the American public refuse to let King Kong rest in peace? It is true, I'll admit, that Kong outdid every monster movie before or since in sheer carnage. Producers Cooper and Schoedsack crammed into it dinosaurs,   30
headhunters, riots, aerial battles, bullets, bombs, bloodletting. Heroine Fay Wray, whose function is mainly to scream, shuts her mouth for hardly one uninterrupted minute from first reel to last. It is also true that *Kong* is larded with good healthy sadism, for those whose joy it is to see the frantic girl dangled from cliffs and harried by pterodactyls. But it seems to me that the   35
abiding appeal of the giant ape rests on other foundations.

5   Kong has, first of all, the attraction of being manlike. His simian nature gives him one huge advantage over giant ants and walking vegetables in that an audience may conceivably identify with him. Kong's appeal has the quality that established the Tarzan series as American myth—for what   40
man doesn't secretly image himself a huge hairy howler against whom no other monster has a chance? If Tarzan recalls the ape in us, then Kong may well appeal to that great-granddaddy primordial brute from whose tribe we have all deteriorated.

6   Intentionally or not, the producers of *King Kong* encourage this   45
identification by etching the character of Kong with keen sympathy. For the ape is a figure in a tradition familiar to moviegoers: the tradition of the pitiable monster. We think of Lon Chaney in the role of Quasimodo, of Karloff in the original *Frankenstein*. As we watch the Frankenstein monster's fumbling and disastrous attempts to befriend a flower-picking child, our sym-   50
pathies are enlisted with the monster in his impenetrable loneliness. And so with Kong. As he roars in his chains, while barkers sell tickets to boobs who gape at him, we perhaps feel something more deep than pathos. We begin to sense something of the problem that engaged Eugene O'Neill in *The Hairy*

---

[1] An actor in many horror movies. [Editors' note]

Ape: the dilemma of a displaced animal spirit forced to live in a jungle built   55
by machines.

7   *King Kong,* it is true, had special relevance in 1933. Landscapes of
the depression are glimpsed early in the film when an impresario, seeking
some desperate pretty girl to play the lead in a jungle movie, visits souplines
and a Woman's Home Mission. In Fay Wray—who's been caught snitching   60
an apple from a fruitstand—his search is ended. When he gives her a big feed
and a movie contract, the girl is magic-carpeted out of the world of the National Recovery Act. And when, in the film's climax, Kong smashes that very
Third Avenue landscape in which Fay had wandered hungry, audiences of
1933 may well have felt a personal satisfaction.   65

8   What is curious is that audiences of 1960 remain hooked. For in the
heart of urban man, one suspects, lurks the impulse to fling a bomb. Though
machines speed him to the scene of his daily grind, though IBM comptome-
ters ("freeing the human mind from drudgery") enable him to drudge more
efficiently once he arrives, there comes a moment when he wishes to turn   70
upon his machines and kick hell out of them. He wants to hurl his combination radio-alarmclock out the bedroom window and listen to its smash. What
subway commuter wouldn't love—just for once—to see the downtown express smack head-on into the uptown local? Such a wish is gratified in that
memorable scene in *Kong* that opens with a wide-angle shot: interior of a   75
railway car on the Third Avenue El. Straphangers are nodding, the literate
refold their newspapers. Unknown to them, Kong has torn away a section of
trestle toward which the train now speeds. The motorman spies Kong up
ahead, jams on the brakes. Passengers hurtle together like so many peas in a
pail. In a window of the car appear Kong's bloodshot eyes. Women shriek.   80
Kong picks up the railway car as if it were a rat, flips it to the street and ties
knots in it, or something. To any commuter the scene must appear one of the
most satisfactory pieces of celluloid ever exposed.

9   Yet however violent his acts, Kong remains a gentleman. Remarkable
in his sense of chivalry. Whenever a fresh boa constrictor threatens Fay,   85
Kong first sees that the lady is safely parked, then manfully thrashes her at-
tacker. (And she, the ingrate, runs away every time his back is turned.) Atop
the Empire State Building, ignoring his pursuers, Kong places Fay on a
ledge as tenderly as if she were a dozen eggs. He fondles her, then turns to
face the Army Air Force. And Kong is perhaps the most disinterested lover   90
since Cyrano: his attentions to the lady are utterly without hope of reward.
After all, between a five-foot blonde and a fifty-foot ape, love can hardly be
more than an intellectual flirtation. In his simian way King Kong is the

hopelessly yearning lover of Petrarchan convention. His forced exit from his
jungle, in chains, results directly from his single-minded pursuit of Fay. He   95
smashes a Broadway theater when the notion enters his dull brain that the
flashbulbs of photographers somehow endanger the lady. His perilous shinny-
ing up a skyscraper to pluck Fay from her boudoir is an act of the kindliest of
hearts. He's impossible to discourage even though the love of his life can't
lay eyes on him without shrieking murder.   100

10   The tragedy of King Kong then, is to be the beast who at the end of
the fable fails to turn into the handsome prince. This is the conviction that
the scriptwriters would leave with us in the film's closing line. As Kong's
corpse lies blocking traffic in the street, the entrepreneur who brought Kong
to New York turns to the assembled reporters and proclaims: "That's your   105
story, boys—it was Beauty killed the Beast!" But greater forces than those of
the screaming Lady have combined to lay Kong low, if you ask me. Kong
lives for a time as one of those persecuted near-animal souls bewildered in
the middle of an industrial order, whose simple desires are thwarted at every
turn. He climbs the Empire State Building because in all New York it's the   110
closest thing he can find to the clifftop of his jungle isle. He dies, a pitiful
dolt, and the army brass and publicity-men cackle over him. His death is the
only possible outcome to as neat a tragic dilemma as you can ask for. The
machine-guns do him in, while the manicured human hero (a nice clean
Dartmouth boy) carries away Kong's sweetheart to the altar. O, the misery   115
of it all. There's far more truth about upper-middle-class American life in
King Kong than in the last seven dozen novels of John P. Marquand.

11   A Negro friend from Atlanta tells me that in movie houses in colored
neighborhoods throughout the South, *Kong* does a constant business. They
show the thing in Atlanta at least every year, presumably to the same audi-   120
ences. Perhaps this popularity may simply be due to the fact that Kong is
one of the most watchable movies ever constructed, but I wonder whether
Negro audiences may not find some archetypical appeal in this serio-comic
tale of a huge black powerful free spirit whom all the hardworking white
policemen are out to kill.   125

12   Every day in the week on a screen somewhere in the world, King
Kong relives his agony. Again and again he expires on the Empire State
Building, as audiences of the devout assist his sacrifice. We watch him die,
and by extension kill the ape within our bones, but these little deaths of ours
occur in prosaic surroundings. We do not die on a tower, New York before   130
our feet, nor do we give our lives to smash a few flying machines. It is not for
us to bring to a momentary standstill the civilization in which we move.

King Kong does this for us. And so we kill him again and again, in much-spliced celluloid, while the ape in us expires from day to day, obscure, in desperation.   135

QUESTIONS

READER AND PURPOSE

1. Which sentence in the first four paragraphs gives the clearest clue to Kennedy's purpose? Is that purpose most adequately described as: (a) to explain the enduring appeal of *King Kong*, or (b) to write a critical appreciation of the film as great art?

2. What can you infer about the sort of readers Kennedy is writing for? Are they over or under thirty? Have they gone to college? Are they city-dwellers or do they live in small towns? Politically liberal or conservative? Does he assume that they have seen *King Kong*?

ORGANIZATION

3. Which paragraphs constitute the beginning? What does each contribute?

4. A closing may employ one or more of several techniques: summation, drawing a logical conclusion, returning to the beginning, signal words and phrases (*in conclusion, finally*, and so on), referring to some natural image * of ending, varying the rhythm and pace of the final sentence. How many of these does Kennedy employ in his last paragraph?

5. Which of the following techniques of development primarily shapes the middle of the essay: illustration, cause and effect, definition, comparison and contrast, analogy, classification and division?

SENTENCES

6. Why are Kennedy's sentences more effective than the revisions?

> (a) *Revision:* Even television has failed to run *King Kong* into oblivion, however.
> *Kennedy:* "But even television has failed to run *King Kong* into oblivion." (20)
> (b) *Revision:* None of the usual movie monsters has ever enjoyed so many resurrections.
> *Kennedy:* "None of the plodding mummies, the stultified draculas, the white-coated Lugosis with their shiny pinball-machine laboratories, none of the invisible stranglers, berserk robots, or menaces from Mars has ever enjoyed so many resurrections." (24-27)

(c) *Revision:* Any subway commuter just for once would love to see the downtown express smack head-on into the uptown local.
Kennedy: "What subway commuter wouldn't love—just for once—to see the downtown express smack head-on into the uptown local?" (72-74)

(d) *Revision:* His sense of chivalry is remarkable.
Kennedy: "Remarkable is his sense of chivalry." (84-85)

(e) *Revision:* We kill him again and again in much-spliced celluloid. The obscure ape in us expires in desperation from day to day.
Kennedy: "And so we kill him again and again, in much-spliced celluloid, while the ape in us expires from day to day, obscure, in desperation." (133-35)

DICTION

7. Look up: *tabloid* (7), *stultified* (24), *carnage* (30), *harried* (35), *pterodactyls* (35), *simian* (37), *impresario* (58), *Cyrano* (91), *entrepreneur* (104), *archetypical* (123).

8. What do these phrases signify: *National Recovery Act* (63), *Petrarchan convention* (94), *much-spliced celluloid* (133-34)?

9. The following expressions attract attention because they are unusual. Explain, if you can, exactly how each is unusual: *coffee-in-the-lobby cinemas* (20-21), *draculas* (25), *good healthy sadism* (34), *great-granddaddy primordial brute* (43), *magic-carpeted* (62), *a fresh boa-constrictor* (85), *watchable* (122).

10. What is the difference between *disinterested* (90) and *uninterested?*

11. *Huge hairy howler* (41) is an example of a rhetorical * device some teachers frown on. What is that device called? Does it work here? Why or why not? Locate other examples in this essay.

12. Kennedy draws words from several levels of usage. Find examples of slang; colloquialisms *; formal, literary words; technical terms. Would the effect have been better, or worse, if he had kept his diction more uniform—all formal, say, or all colloquial? When should a writer consistently use formal diction?

13. How much can you infer from his diction about Kennedy's interests, personality, and values?

POINTS TO LEARN

1. Among the common purposes of writing about literature are these:

(a) To describe a personal, and often emotional, response to a particular work—the kind of writing we have called impressionistic.

(b) To analyze objectively the formal elements of a work to show how their relationships produce a unity of meaning and feeling.

(c) To evaluate a literary work according to some artistic standard.

(d) To help would-be authors to write.

(e) To assign a work its proper place in the history of literature.

(f) To study how the work came to be—its sources in other literary and sub-literary pieces, its roots in the author's life and sensibility.

(g) To discuss the literary work in relation to some system of psychology, philosophy, theology, politics, sociology, or myth—as Kennedy does in "Who Killed King Kong?"

2. More than one of these purposes may be at work in any critical essay, but generally one primarily controls and shapes the piece.

3. At its best writing about literature is a work of art in itself, a combination of explanation and entertainment. In such cases the personality of the writer is an important element in the total effect. Without being obtrusive, the writer must understand what his readers need to be told and what they already know, and the writer must strive to make himself or herself pleasing. Success requires careful control of diction.

SUGGESTIONS FOR WRITING

1. Loosely using Kennedy's essay as a model, explain the popularity of a well-known film other than *King Kong*.

2. Account for the popularity of a type of film or television show generally regarded as an inferior kind of art—the cowboy movie, for example, or the cops-and-robbers melodrama, science fiction films, and so on. While you probably will want to generalize, cite examples from specific TV shows or movies.

IMPROVING YOUR STYLE

1. In your essay pay close attention to diction. Avoid clichés and seek vigorous concrete * words—especially verbs—to enliven your prose. Attempt also to widen the range of your diction, as Kennedy has, by using a judicious combination of slang, colloquialisms, technical terms, and formal words. In every case, however, take care that your diction is accurate and appropriate, working with your tone *, not against it.

2. Include a rhetorical question and sentences with interrupted movement * and inversion *.

3. Model your final sentence on Kennedy's, interrupting it and slowing it as a way of signaling closing.

The World of *Hamlet*

Maynard Mack is a foremost Renaissance scholar and taught, before his retirement, at Yale University. His essay on *Hamlet* is an example of interpretative criticism, that is, of the kind of literary analysis that seeks to get at the essential meaning which informs a poem or play or story. This meaning is often referred to as the "theme," but theme should not be thought of as a more or less clear-cut and brief statement of significance which can be inferred from the work, cut loose, and tied on like a name tag. The theme of a complex drama like *Hamlet* is, in a sense, co-extensive with the work itself and not really detachable. The task of the interpretative critic is to approach as full a statement of meaning as he can see, but always with the tacit understanding that he will not see everything and that his statement will be incomplete. *Hamlet*, because of its central ambiguities, has always resisted interpretation while at the same time demanding it. Maynard Mack's remarkable effort to get to the heart of the play is interpretative criticism at its finest.

1   My subject is the world of *Hamlet*. I do not of course mean Denmark, except as Denmark is given a body by the play; and I do not mean Elizabethan England, though this is necessarily close behind the scenes. I mean simply the imaginative environment that the play asks us to enter when we read it or go to see it.   5

2   Great plays, as we know, do present us with something that can be called a world, a microcosm—a world like our own in being made of people, actions, situations, thoughts, feelings and much more, but unlike our own in being perfectly, or almost perfectly, significant and coherent. In a play's world, each part implies the other parts, and each lives, each means, with the   10 life and meaning of the rest.

3   This is the reason, as we also know, that the worlds of great plays greatly differ. Othello in Hamlet's position, we sometimes say, would have

From *The Yale Review*, XLI (1952), 502-23. Copyright 1952 by Yale University Press, and reprinted by permission.

no problem; but what we are really saying is that Othello in Hamlet's position would not exist. The conception we have of Othello is a function of the characters who help define him, Desdemona, honest Iago, Cassio, and the rest; of his history of travel and war; of a great storm that divides his ships from Cassio's, and a handkerchief; of a quiet night in Venice broken by cries about an old black ram; of a quiet night in Cyprus broken by swordplay; of a quiet bedroom where a woman goes to bed in her wedding sheets and a man comes in with a light to put out the light; and above all, of a language, a language with many voices in it, gentle, rasping, querulous, or foul, but all counterpointing the one great voice:

> Put up your bright swords, for the dew will rust them.
>
>   O thou weed
> Who art so lovely fair and smell'st so sweet
> That the sense aches at thee. . . .
>   Yet I'll not shed her blood
> Nor scar that whiter skin of hers than snow,
> And smooth as monumental alabaster.
>
>   I pray you in your letters,
> When you shall these unlucky deeds relate,
> Speak of me as I am; nothing extenuate,
> Nor set down aught in malice; then must you speak
> Of one that loved not wisely but too well;
> Of one not easily jealous, but being wrought,
> Perplex'd in th' extreme; of one whose hand,
> Like the base Indian, threw a pearl away
> Richer than all his tribe. . . .

4   Without his particular world of voices, persons, events, the world that both expresses and contains him, Othello is unimaginable. And so, I think, are Antony, King Lear, Macbeth—and Hamlet. We come back then to Hamlet's world, of all the tragic worlds that Shakespeare made, easily the most various and brilliant, the most elusive. It is with no thought of doing justice to it that I have singled out three of its attributes for comment. I know too well, if I may echo a sentiment of Mr. E. M. W. Tillyard's, that no one is likely to accept another man's reading of *Hamlet*, that anyone who tries to throw light on one part of the play usually throws the rest into deeper shadow, and that what I have to say leaves out many problems—to mention only one, the knotty problem of the text. All I would say in defense

of the materials I have chosen is that they seem to me interesting, close to the root of the matter even if we continue to differ about what the root of the matter is, and explanatory, in a modest way, of this play's peculiar hold on everyone's imagination, its almost mythic status, one might say, as a paradigm of the life of man.   55

5   The first attribute that impresses us, I think, is mysteriousness. We often hear it said, perhaps with truth, that every great work of art has a mystery at the heart; but the mystery of *Hamlet* is something else. We feel its presence in the numberless explanations that have been brought forward for Hamlet's delay, his madness, his ghost, his treatment of Polonius, or Ophe-   60
lia, or his mother; and in the controversies that still go on about whether the play is "undoubtedly a failure" (Eliot's phrase) or one of the greatest artistic triumphs; whether, if it is a triumph, it belongs to the highest order of tragedy; whether, if it is such a tragedy, its hero is to be taken as a man of exquisite moral sensibility (Bradley's view) or an egomaniac (Madariaga's   65
view).

6   Doubtless there have been more of these controversies and explanations than the play requires; for in Hamlet, to paraphrase a remark of Falstaff's, we have a character who is not only mad in himself but a cause that madness is in the rest of us. Still, the very existence of so many theories and   70
counter-theories, many of them formulated by sober heads, gives food for thought. *Hamlet* seems to lie closer to the illogical logic of life than Shakespeare's other tragedies. And while the causes of this situation may be sought by saying that Shakespeare revised the play so often that eventually the motivations were smudged over, or that the original old play has been   75
here or there imperfectly digested, or that the problems of Hamlet lay so close to Shakespeare's heart that he could not quite distance them in the formal terms of art, we have still as critics to deal with effects, not causes. If I may quote again from Mr. Tillyard, the play's very lack of a rigorous type of causal logic seems to be a part of its point.   80

7   Moreover, the matter goes deeper than this. Hamlet's world is preëminently in the interrogative mood. It reverberates with questions, anguished, meditative, alarmed. There are questions that in this play, to an extent I think unparalleled in any other, mark the phases and even the nuances of the action, helping to establish its peculiar baffled tone. There   85
are other questions whose interrogations, innocent at first glance, are subsequently seen to have reached beyond their contexts and to point towards some pervasive inscrutability in Hamlet's world as a whole. Such is that tense series of challenges with which the tragedy begins: Bernardo's of Fran-

cisco, "Who's there?" Francisco's of Horatio and Marcellus, "Who is   90
there?" Horatio's of the ghost, "What art thou . . . ?" And then there are
the famous questions. In them the interrogations seem to point not only beyond the context but beyond the play, out of Hamlet's predicaments into
everyone's: "What a piece of work is a man! . . . And yet to me what is
this quintessence of dust?" "To be, or not to be, that is the question." "Get   95
thee to a nunnery. Why wouldst thou be a breeder of sinners?" "I am very
proud, revengeful, ambitious, with more offences at my beck than I have
thoughts to put them in, imagination to give them shape, or time to act
them in. What should such fellows as I do crawling between earth and
heaven?" "Dost thou think Alexander look'd o' this fashion i' th' earth?   100
. . . And smelt so?"

8   Further, Hamlet's world is a world of riddles. The hero's own language is often riddling, as the critics have pointed out. When he puns, his
puns have receding depths in them, like the one which constitutes his first
speech: "A little more than kin, and less than kind." His utterances in mad-   105
ness, even if wild and whirling, are simultaneously, as Polonius discovers,
pregnant: "Do you know me, my lord?" "Excellent well. You are a fish-
monger." Even the madness itself is riddling: How much is real? How much
is feigned? What does it mean? Sane or mad, Hamlet's mind plays restlessly
about his world, turning up one riddle upon another. The riddle of char-   110
acter, for example, and how it is that in a man whose virtues else are "pure
as grace," some vicious mole of nature, some "dram of eale," can "all the
noble substance oft adulter." Or the riddle of the player's art, and how a
man can so project himself into a fiction, a dream of passion, that he can
weep for Hecuba. Or the riddle of action: how we may think too little—   115
"What to ourselves in passion we propose," says the player-king, "The passion ending, doth the purpose lose"; and again, how we may think too
much: "Thus conscience does make cowards of us all, And thus the native
hue of resolution Is sicklied o'er with the pale cast of thought."

9   There are also more immediate riddles. His mother—how could she   120
"on this fair mountain leave to feed, And batten on this moor?" The ghost
—which may be a devil, for "The de'il hath power T' assume a pleasing
shape." Ophelia—what does her behavior to him mean? Surprising her in
her closet, he falls to such perusal of her face as he would draw it. Even the
king at his prayers is a riddle. Will a revenge that takes him in the purging   125
of his soul be vengeance, or hire and salary? As for himself, Hamlet realizes,
he is the greatest riddle of all—a mystery, he warns Rosencrantz and Guildenstern, from which he will not have the heart plucked out. He cannot

tell why he has of late lost all his mirth, forgone all custom of exercises. Still
less can he tell why he delays: "I do not know Why yet I live to say, 'This   130
thing's to do,' Sith I have cause and will and strength and means To do't."
10   Thus the mysteriousness of Hamlet's world is of a piece. It is not
simply a matter of missing motivations, to be expunged if only we could find
the perfect clue. It is built in. It is evidently an important part of what the
play wishes to say to us. And it is certainly an element that the play thrusts   135
upon us from the opening word. Everyone, I think, recalls the mysteriousness of that first scene. The cold middle of the night on the castle platform,
the muffled sentries, the uneasy atmosphere of apprehension, the challenges
leaping out of the dark, the questions that follow the challenges, feeling out
the darkness, searching for identities, for relations, for assurance. "Ber-   140
nardo?" "Have you had quiet guard?" "Who hath reliev'd you?" "What, is
Horatio there?" "What, has this thing appear'd again tonight?" "Looks 'a
not like the king?" "How now, Horatio! . . . Is not this something more
than fantasy? What think you on 't?" "Is it not like the king?" "Why this
same strict and most observant watch . . . ?" "Shall I strike at it with my   145
partisan?" "Do you consent we shall acquaint [young Hamlet] with it?"
11   We need not be surprised that critics and playgoers alike have been
tempted to see in this an evocation not simply of Hamlet's world but of
their own. Man in his aspect of bafflement, moving in darkness on a rampart
between two worlds, unable to reject, or quite accept, the one that, when he   150
faces it, "to-shakes" his disposition with thoughts beyond the reaches of his
soul—comforting himself with hints and guesses. We hear these hints and
guesses whispering through the darkness as the several watchers speak. "At
least, the whisper goes so," says one. "I think it be no other but e'en so,"
says another. "I have heard" that on the crowing of the cock "Th' extrava-   155
gant and erring spirit hies To his confine," says a third. "Some say" at
Christmas time "this bird of dawning" sings all night, "And then, they say,
no spirit dare stir abroad." "So have I heard," says the first, "and do in part
believe it." However we choose to take the scene, it is clear that it creates a
world where uncertainties are of the essence.   160
12   Meantime, such is Shakespeare's economy, a second attribute of
Hamlet's world has been put before us. This is the problematic nature of
reality and the relation of reality to appearance. The play begins with an appearance, an "apparition," to use Marcellus's term—the ghost. And the
ghost is somehow real, indeed the vehicle of realities. Through its revelation,   165
the glittering surface of Claudius's court is pierced, and Hamlet comes to
know, and we do, that the king is not only hateful to him but the murderer

of his father, that his mother is guilty of adultery as well as incest. Yet there is a dilemma in the revelation. For possibly the apparition *is* an apparition, a devil who has assumed his father's shape.   170

13   This dilemma, once established, recurs on every hand. From the court's point of view, there is Hamlet's madness. Polonius investigates and gets some strange advice about his daughter: "Conception is a blessing, but as your daughter may conceive, friend, look to 't." Rosencrantz and Guildenstern investigate and get the strange confidence that "Man delights not   175 me; no, nor woman neither." Ophelia is "loosed" to Hamlet (Polonius's vulgar word), while Polonius and the king hide behind the arras; and what they hear is a strange indictment of human nature, and a riddling threat: "Those that are married already, all but one, shall live."

14   On the other hand, from Hamlet's point of view, there is Ophelia.   180 Kneeling here at her prayers, she seems the image of innocence and devotion. Yet she is of the sex for whom he has already found the name Frailty, and she is also, as he seems either madly or sanely to divine, a decoy in a trick. The famous cry—"Get thee to a nunnery"—shows the anguish of his uncertainty. If Ophelia is what she seems, this dirty-minded world of   185 murder, incest, lust, adultery, is no place for her. Were she "as chaste as ice, as pure as snow," she could not escape its calumny. And if she is not what she seems, then a nunnery in its other sense of brothel is relevant to her. In the scene that follows he treats her as if she were indeed an inmate of a brothel.   190

15   Likewise, from Hamlet's point of view, there is the enigma of the king. If the ghost is *only* an appearance, then possibly the king's appearance is reality. He must try it further. By means of a second and different kind of "apparition," the play within the play, he does so. But then, immediately after, he stumbles on the king at prayer. This appearance has a relish of   195 salvation in it. If the king dies now, his soul may yet be saved. Yet actually, as we know, the king's efforts to come to terms with heaven have been unavailing; his words fly up, his thoughts remain below. If Hamlet means the conventional revenger's reasons that he gives for sparing Claudius, it was the perfect moment not to spare him—when the sinner was acknowledging his   200 guilt, yet unrepentant. The perfect moment, but it was hidden, like so much else in the play, behind an arras.

16   There are two arrases in his mother's room. Hamlet thrusts his sword through one of them. Now at last he has got to the heart of the evil, or so he thinks. But now it is the wrong man; now he himself is a murderer.   205 The other arras he stabs through with his words—like daggers, says the

queen. He makes her shrink under the contrast he points between her present husband and his father. But as the play now stands (matters are somewhat clearer in the bad Quarto), it is hard to be sure how far the queen grasps the fact that her second husband is the murderer of her first. And it is hard to say what may be signified by her inability to see the ghost, who now for the last time appears. In one sense at least, the ghost is the supreme reality, representative of the hidden ultimate power, in Bradley's terms—witnessing from beyond the grave against this hollow world. Yet the man who is capable of seeing through to this reality, the queen thinks is mad. "To whom do you speak this?" she cries to her son. "Do you see nothing there?" he asks, incredulous. And she replies: "Nothing at all; yet all that is I see." Here certainly we have the imperturbable self-confidence of the worldly world, its layers on layers of habituation, so that when the reality is before its very eyes it cannot detect its presence.

17   Like mystery, this problem of reality is central to the play and written deep into its idiom. Shakespeare's favorite terms in *Hamlet* are words of ordinary usage that pose the question of appearances in a fundamental form. "Apparition" I have already mentioned. Another term is "seems." When we say, as Ophelia says of Hamlet leaving her closet, "He seem'd to find his way without his eyes," we mean one thing. When we say, as Hamlet says to his mother in the first court-scene, "Seems, Madam! . . . I know not 'seems,' " we mean another. And when we say, as Hamlet says to Horatio before the play within the play, "And after, we will both our judgments join In censure of his seeming," we mean both at once. The ambiguities of "seem" coil and uncoil throughout this play, and over against them is set the idea of "seeing." So Hamlet challenges the king in his triumphant letter announcing his return to Denmark: "Tomorrow shall I beg leave to see your kingly eyes." Yet "seeing" itself can be ambiguous, as we recognize from Hamlet's uncertainty about the ghost; or from that statement of his mother's already quoted: "Nothing at all; yet all that is I see."

18   Another term of like importance is "assume." What we assume may be what we are not: "The de'il hath power T' assume a pleasing shape." But it may be what we are: "If it assume my noble father's person, I'll speak to it." And it may be what we are not yet, but would become; thus Hamlet advises his mother, "Assume a virtue, if you have it not." The perplexity in the word points to a real perplexity in Hamlet's and our own experience. We assume our habits—and habits are like costumes, as the word implies: "My father in his habit as he liv'd!" Yet these habits become ourselves in time: "That monster, custom, who all sense doth eat Of habits evil, is angel

yet in this, That to the use of actions fair and good He likewise gives a frock of livery That aptly is put on."

19   Two other terms I wish to instance are "put on" and "shape." The shape of something is the form under which we are accustomed to apprehend it: "Do you see yonder cloud that's almost in shape of a camel?" But a shape may also be a disguise—even, in Shakespeare's time, an actor's costume or an actor's role. This is the meaning when the king says to Laertes as they lay the plot against Hamlet's life: "Weigh what convenience both of time and means May fit us to our shape." "Put on" supplies an analogous ambiguity. Shakespeare's mind seems to worry this phrase in the play much as Hamlet's mind worries the problem of acting in a world of surfaces, or the king's mind worries the meaning of Hamlet's transformation. Hamlet has put an antic disposition on, that the king knows. But what does "put on" mean? A mask, or a frock or livery—our "habit"? The king is left guessing, and so are we.

20   What is found in the play's key terms is also found in its imagery. Miss Spurgeon has called attention to a pattern of disease images in *Hamlet*, to which I shall return. But the play has other patterns equally striking. One of these, as my earlier quotations hint, is based on clothes. In the world of surfaces to which Shakespeare exposes us in *Hamlet*, clothes are naturally a factor of importance. "The apparel oft proclaims the man," Polonius assures Laertes, cataloguing maxims in the young man's ear as he is about to leave for Paris. Oft, but not always. And so he sends his man Reynaldo to look into Laertes' life there—even, if need be, to put a false dress of accusation upon his son ("What forgeries you please"), the better by indirections to find directions out. On the same grounds, he takes Hamlet's vows to Ophelia as false apparel. They are bawds, he tells her—or if we do not like Theobald's emendation, they are bonds—in masquerade, "Not of that dye which their investments show, But mere implorators of unholy suits."

21   This breach between the outer and the inner stirs no special emotion in Polonius, because he is always either behind an arras or prying into one, but it shakes Hamlet to the core. Here so recently was his mother in her widow's weeds, the tears still flushing in her galled eyes; yet now within a month, a little month, before even her funeral shoes are old, she has married with his uncle. Her mourning was all clothes. Not so his own, he bitterly replies, when she asks him to cast his "nighted color off." "Tis not alone my inky cloak, good mother"—and not alone, he adds, the sighs, the tears, the dejected havior of the visage—"that can denote me truly."

> These indeed seem,
> For they are actions that a man might play;   285
> But I have that within which passes show;
> These but the trappings and the suits of woe.

22   What we must not overlook here is Hamlet's visible attire, giving the verbal imagery a theatrical extension. Hamlet's apparel now is his inky cloak, mark of his grief for his father, mark also of his character as a man   290 of melancholy, mark possibly too of his being one in whom appearance and reality are attuned. Later, in his madness, with his mind disordered, he will wear his costume in a corresponding disarray, the disarray that Ophelia describes so vividly to Polonius and that producers of the play rarely give sufficient heed to: "Lord Hamlet with his doublet all unbrac'd, No hat upon his   295 head; his stockings foul'd, Ungarter'd, and downgyved to his ankle." Here the only question will be, as with the madness itself, how much is studied, how much is real. Still later, by a third costume, the simple traveler's garb in which we find him new come from shipboard, Shakespeare will show us that we have a third aspect of the man.   300

23   A second pattern of imagery springs from terms of painting: the paints, the colorings, the varnishes that may either conceal, or, as in the painter's art, reveal. Art in Claudius conceals. "The harlot's cheek," he tells us in his one aside, "beautied with plastering art, Is not more ugly to the thing that helps it Than is my deed to my most painted word." Art in Ophe-   305 lia, loosed to Hamlet in the episode already noticed to which this speech of the king's is prelude, is more complex. She looks so beautiful—"the celestial, and my soul's idol, the most beautified Ophelia," Hamlet has called her in his love letter. But now, what does beautified mean? Perfected with all the innocent beauties of a lovely woman? Or "beautied" like the harlot's cheek?   310 "I have heard of your paintings too, well enough. God hath given you one face, and you make yourselves another."

24   Yet art, differently used, may serve the truth. By using an "image" (his own word) of a murder done in Vienna, Hamlet cuts through to the king's guilt; holds "as 'twere, the mirror up to nature," shows "virtue her   315 own feature, scorn her own image, and the very age and body of the time" —which is out of joint—"his form and pressure." Something similar he does again in his mother's bedroom, painting for her in words "the rank sweat of an enseamed bed," making her recoil in horror from his "counterfeit presentment of two brothers," and holding, if we may trust a stage tradition,   320

his father's picture beside his uncle's. Here again the verbal imagery is realized visually on the stage.

25   The most pervasive of Shakespeare's image patterns in this play, however, is the pattern evolved around the three words, show, act, play. "Show" seems to be Shakespeare's unifying image in *Hamlet*. Through it he pulls together and exhibits in a single focus much of the diverse material in his play. The ideas of seeming, assuming, and putting on; the images of clothing, painting, mirroring; the episode of the dumb show and the play within the play; the characters of Polonius, Laertes, Ophelia, Claudius, Gertrude, Rosencrantz and Guildenstern, Hamlet himself—all these at one time or another, and usually more than once, are drawn into the range of implications flung round the play by "show."

26   "Act," on the other hand, I take to be the play's radical metaphor. It distills the various perplexities about the character of reality into a residual perplexity about the character of an act. What, this play asks again and again, is an act? What is its relation to the inner act, the intent? "If I drown myself wittingly," says the clown in the graveyard, "it argues an act, and an act hath three branches; it is to act, to do, to perform." Or again, the play asks, how does action relate to passion, that "laps'd in time and passion" I can let "go by Th' important acting of your dread command"; and to thought, which can so sickly o'er the native hue of resolution that "enterprises of great pitch and moment With this regard their currents turn awry, And lose the name of action"; and to words, which are not acts, and so we dare not be content to unpack our hearts with them, and yet are acts of a sort, for we may speak daggers though we use none. Or still again, how does an act (a deed) relate to an act (a pretense)? For an action may be nothing but pretense. So Polonius readying Ophelia for the interview with Hamlet, with "pious action," as he phrases it, "sugar [s] o'er The devil himself." Or it may not be a pretense, yet not what it appears. So Hamlet spares the king, finding him in an act that has some "relish of salvation in 't." Or it may be a pretense that is also the first foothold of a new reality, as when we assume a virtue though we have it not. Or it may be a pretense that is actually a mirroring of reality, like the play within the play, or the tragedy of *Hamlet*.

27   To this network of implications, the third term, play, adds an additional dimension. "Play" is a more precise word, in Elizabethan parlance at least, for all the elements in *Hamlet* that pertain to the art of the theatre; and it extends their field of reference till we see that every major personage in the tragedy is a player in some sense, and every major episode a play. The court plays, Hamlet plays, the players play, Rosencrantz and Guildenstern

try to play on Hamlet, though they cannot play on his recorders—here we   360
have an extension to a musical sense. And the final duel, by a further extension, becomes itself a play, in which everyone but Claudius and Laertes
plays his role in ignorance: "The queen desires you to show some gentle
entertainment to Laertes before you fall to play." "I . . . will this brother's
wager frankly play." "Give him the cup."—"I'll play this bout first."   365
28   The full extension of this theme is best evidenced in the play within
the play itself. Here, in the bodily presence of these traveling players, bringing with them the latest playhouse gossip out of London, we have suddenly
a situation that tends to dissolve the normal barriers between the fictive and
the real. For here on the stage before us is a play of false appearances in   370
which an actor called the player-king is playing. But there is also on the
stage, Claudius, another player-king, who is a spectator of this player. And
there is on the stage, besides, a prince who is a spectator of both these
player-kings and who plays with great intensity a player's role himself. And
around these kings and that prince is a group of courtly spectators—Ger-   375
trude, Rosencrantz, Guildenstern, Polonius, and the rest—and they, as we
have come to know, are players too. And lastly there are ourselves, an audience watching all these audiences who are also players. Where, it may
suddenly occur to us to ask, does the playing end? Which *are* the guilty
creatures sitting at a play? When is an act not an "act"?   380
29   The mysteriousness of Hamlet's world, while it pervades the tragedy, finds its point of greatest dramatic concentration in the first act, and
its symbol in the first scene. The problems of appearance and reality also
pervade the play as a whole, but come to a climax in Acts II and III, and
possibly their best symbol is the play within the play. Our third attribute,   385
though again it is one that crops out everywhere, reaches its full development in Acts IV and V. It is not easy to find an appropriate name for this
attribute, but perhaps "mortality" will serve, if we remember to mean by
mortality the heartache and the thousand natural shocks that flesh is heir
to, not simply death.   390
30   The powerful sense of mortality in *Hamlet* is conveyed to us, I
think, in three ways. First, there is the play's emphasis on human weakness,
the instability of human purpose, the subjection of humanity to fortune—
all that we might call the aspect of failure in man. Hamlet opens this theme
in Act I, when he describes how from that single blemish, perhaps not even   395
the victim's fault, a man's whole character may take corruption. Claudius
dwells on it again, to an extent that goes far beyond the needs of the occasion, while engaged in seducing Laertes to step behind the arras of a

seemer's world and dispose of Hamlet by a trick. Time qualifies everything, Claudius says, including love, including purpose. As for love—it has a "plurisy" in it and dies of its own too much. As for purpose—"That we would do, We should do when we would, for this 'would' changes, And hath abatements and delays as many As there are tongues, are hands, are accidents; And then this 'should' is like a spendthrift's sigh, That hurts by easing." The player-king, in his long speeches to his queen in the play within the play, sets the matter in a still darker light. She means these protestations of undying love, he knows, but our purposes depend on our memory, and our memory fades fast. Or else, he suggests, we propose something to ourselves in a condition of strong feeling, but then the feeling goes, and with it the resolve. Or else our fortunes change, he adds, and with these our loves: "The great man down, you mark his favorite flies." The subjection of human aims to fortune is a reiterated theme in Hamlet, as subsequently in Lear. Fortune is the harlot goddess in whose secret parts men like Rosencrantz and Guildenstern live and thrive; the strumpet who threw down Troy and Hecuba and Priam; the outrageous foe whose slings and arrows a man of principle must suffer or seek release in suicide. Horatio suffers them with composure: he is one of the blessed few "Whose blood and judgment are so well co-mingled That they are not a pipe for fortune's finger To sound what stop she please." For Hamlet the task is of a greater difficulty.

31   Next, and intimately related to this matter of infirmity, is the emphasis on infection—the ulcer, the hidden abscess, "th' imposthume of much wealth and peace That inward breaks and shows no cause without Why the man dies." Miss Spurgeon, who was the first to call attention to this aspect of the play, has well remarked that so far as Shakespeare's pictorial imagination is concerned, the problem in Hamlet is not a problem of the will and reason, "of a mind too philosophical or a nature temperamentally unfitted to act quickly," nor even a problem of an individual at all. Rather, it is a condition—"a condition for which the individual himself is apparently not responsible, any more than the sick man is to blame for the infection which strikes and devours him, but which, nevertheless, in its course and development, impartially and relentlessly, annihilates him and others, innocent and guilty alike." "That," she adds, "is the tragedy of Hamlet, as it is perhaps the chief tragic mystery of life." This is a perceptive comment, for it reminds us that Hamlet's situation is mainly not of his own manufacture, as are the situations of Shakespeare's other tragic heroes. He has inherited it; he is "born to set it right."

32   We must not, however, neglect to add to this what another student
of Shakespeare's imagery has noticed—that the infection in Denmark is
presented alternatively as poison. Here, of course, responsibility is implied,   440
for the poisoner of the play is Claudius. The juice he pours into the ear of
the elder Hamlet is a combined poison and disease, a "leperous distilment"
that curds "the thin and wholesome blood." From this fatal center, un-
wholesomeness spreads out till there is something rotten in all Denmark.
Hamlet tells us that his "wit's diseased," the queen speaks of her "sick soul,"   445
the king is troubled by "the hectic" in his blood, Laertes meditates revenge
to warm "the sickness in my heart," the people of the kingdom grow "mud-
died, Thick and unwholesome in their thoughts"; and even Ophelia's madness is said to be "the poison of deep grief." In the end, all save Ophelia
die of that poison in a literal as well as figurative sense.   450

33   But the chief form in which the theme of mortality reaches us, it
seems to me, is a profound consciousness of loss. Hamlet's father expresses something of the kind when he tells Hamlet how his "[most] seem-
ing-virtuous queen," betraying a love which "was of that dignity That it
went hand in hand even with the vow I made to her in marriage," had   455
chosen to "decline Upon a wretch whose natural gifts were poor To those
of mine." "O Hamlet, what a falling off was there!" Ophelia expresses it
again, on hearing Hamlet's denunciation of love and woman in the nunnery
scene, which she takes to be the product of a disordered brain:

> O what a noble mind is here o'erthrown!   460
> The courtier's, soldier's, scholar's, eye, tongue, sword;
> Th' expectancy and rose of the fair state,
> The glass of fashion and the mould of form,
> Th' observ'd of all observers, quite, quite down!

The passage invites us to remember that we have never actually seen such a   465
Hamlet—that his mother's marriage has brought a falling off in him before
we meet him. And then there is that further falling off, if I may call it so,
when Ophelia too goes mad—"Divided from herself and her fair judgment,
Without the which we are pictures, or mere beasts."

34   Time was, the play keeps reminding us, when Denmark was a differ-   470
ent place. That was before Hamlet's mother took off "the rose From the
fair forehead of an innocent love" and set a blister there. Hamlet then was
still "Th' expectancy and rose of the fair state"; Ophelia, the "rose of May."
For Denmark was a garden then, when his father ruled. There had been
something heroic about his father—a king who met the threats to Denmark   475

in open battle, fought with Norway, smote the sledded Polacks on the ice, slew the elder Fortinbras in an honorable trial of strength. There had been something godlike about his father too: "Hyperion's curls, the front of Jove himself, An eye like Mars . . . , A station like the herald Mercury." But, the ghost reveals, a serpent was in the garden, and "the serpent that did sting   480 thy father's life Now wears his crown." The martial virtues are put by now. The threats to Denmark are attended to by policy, by agents working de- viously for and through an uncle. The moral virtues are put by too. Hype- rion's throne is occupied by "a vice of kings," "A king of shreds and patches": Hyperion's bed, by a satyr, a paddock, a bat, a gib, a bloat king   485 with reechy kisses. The garden is unweeded now, and "grows to seed; things rank and gross in nature Possess it merely." Even in himself he feels the taint, the taint of being his mother's son; and that other taint, from an earlier garden, of which he admonishes Ophelia: "Our virtue cannot so inoculate our old stock but we shall relish of it." "Why wouldst thou be a   490 breeder of sinners?" "What should such fellows as I do crawling between earth and heaven?"

35   "Hamlet is painfully aware," says Professor Tillyard, "of the baffling human predicament between the angels and the beasts, between the glory of having been made in God's image and the incrimination of being de-   495 scended from fallen Adam." To this we may add, I think, that Hamlet is more than aware of it; he exemplifies it; and it is for this reason that his problem appeals to us so powerfully as an image of our own.

36   Hamlet's problem, in its crudest form, is simply the problem of the avenger: he must carry out the injunction of the ghost and kill the king. But   500 this problem, as I ventured to suggest at the outset, is presented in terms of a certain kind of world. The ghost's injunction to act becomes so inextri- cably bound up for Hamlet with the character of the world in which the action must be taken—its mysteriousness, its baffling appearances, its deep consciousness of infection, frailty, and loss—that he cannot come to terms   505 with either without coming to terms with both.

37   When we first see him in the play, he is clearly a very young man, sensitive and idealistic, suffering the first shock of growing up. He has taken the garden at face value, we might say, supposing mankind to be only a little lower than the angels. Now in his mother's hasty and incestuous marriage,   510 he discovers evidence of something else, something bestial—though even a beast, he thinks, would have mourned longer. Then comes the revelation of the ghost, bringing a second shock. Not so much because he now knows that his serpent-uncle killed his father; his prophetic soul had almost sus-

pected this. Not entirely, even, because he knows now how far below the 515
angels humanity has fallen in his mother, and how lust—these were the
ghost's words—"though to a radiant angel link'd Will sate itself in a celestial bed, And prey on garbage." Rather, because he now sees everywhere,
but especially in his own nature, the general taint, taking from life its meaning, from woman her integrity, from the will its strength, turning reason 520
into madness. "Why wouldst thou be a breeder of sinners?" "What should
such fellows as I do crawling between earth and heaven?" Hamlet is not the
first young man to have felt the heavy and the weary weight of all this unintelligible world; and, like the others, he must come to terms with it.

38   The ghost's injunction to revenge unfolds a different facet of his 525
problem. The young man growing up is not to be allowed simply to endure
a rotten world, he must also act in it. Yet how to begin, among so many
enigmatic surfaces? Even Claudius, whom he now knows to be the core of
the ulcer, has a plausible exterior. And around Claudius, swathing the evil
out of sight, he encounters all those other exteriors, as we have seen. Some 530
of them already deeply infected beneath, like his mother. Some noble, but
marked for infection, like Laertes. Some not particularly corrupt but infinitely corruptible, like Rosencrantz and Guildenstern; some mostly weak
and foolish like Polonius and Osric. Some, like Ophelia, innocent, yet in
their innocence still serving to "skin and film the ulcerous place."   535

39   And this is not all. The act required of him, though retributive
justice, is one that necessarily involves the doer in the general guilt. Not only
because it involves a killing; but because to get at the world of seeming one
sometimes has to use its weapons. He himself, before he finishes, has become a player, has put an antic disposition on, has killed a man—the wrong 540
man—has helped drive Ophelia mad, and has sent two friends of his youth
to death, mining below their mines, and hoisting the engineer with his own
petard. He had never meant to dirty himself with these things, but from the
moment of the ghost's challenge to act, this dirtying was inevitable. It is the
condition of living at all in such a world. To quote Polonius, who knew 545
that world so well, men become "a little soil'd i' th' working." Here is another matter with which Hamlet has to come to terms.

40   Human infirmity—all that I have discussed with reference to instability, infection, loss—supplies the problem with its third phase. Hamlet
has not only to accept the mystery of man's condition between the angels 550
and the brutes, and not only to act in a perplexing and soiling world. He
has also to act within the human limits—"with shabby equipment always de-
teriorating," if I may adapt some phrases from Eliot's *East Coker*, "In the

general mess of imprecision of feeling, Undisciplined squads of emotion."
Hamlet is aware of that fine poise of body and mind, feeling and thought, 555
that suits the action to the word, the word to the action; that acquires and
begets a temperance in the very torrent, tempest, and whirlwind of passion;
but he cannot at first achieve it in himself. He vacillates between undisciplined squads of emotion and thinking too precisely on the event. He learns
to his cost how easily action can be lost in "acting," and loses it there for a 560
time himself. But these again are only the terms of every man's life. As Anatole France reminds us in a now famous apostrophe to Hamlet: "What one
of us thinks without contradiction and acts without incoherence? What
one of us is not mad? What one of us does not say with a mixture of pity,
comradeship, admiration, and horror, Goodnight, sweet Prince!" 565

41   In the last act of the play (or so it seems to me, for I know there
can be differences on this point), Hamlet accepts his world and we discover
a different man. Shakespeare does not outline for us the process of acceptance any more than he had done with Romeo or was to do with Othello.
But he leads us strongly to expect an altered Hamlet, and then, in my 570
opinion, provides him. We must recall that at this point Hamlet has been
absent from the stage during several scenes, and that such absences in
Shakespearean tragedy usually warn us to be on the watch for a new phase
in the development of the character. It is so when we leave King Lear in
Gloucester's farmhouse and find him again in Dover fields. It is so when we 575
leave Macbeth at the witches' cave and rejoin him at Dunsinane, hearing of
the armies that beset it. Furthermore, and this is an important matter in the
theatre—especially important in a play in which the symbolism of clothing
has figured largely—Hamlet now looks different. He is wearing a different
dress—probably, as Granville-Barker thinks, his "seagown scarf'd" about 580
him, but in any case no longer the disordered costume of his antic disposition. The effect is not entirely dissimilar to that in *Lear*, when the old king
wakes out of his madness to find fresh garments on him.

42   Still more important, Hamlet displays a considerable change of
mood. This is not a matter of the way we take the passage about defying 585
augury, as Mr. Tillyard among others seems to think. It is a matter of Hamlet's whole deportment, in which I feel we may legitimately see the deportment of a man who has been "illuminated" in the tragic sense. Bradley's
term for it is fatalism, but if this is what we wish to call it, we must at least
acknowledge that it is fatalism of a very distinctive kind—a kind that Shake- 590
speare has been willing to touch with the associations of the saying in St.
Matthew about the fall of a sparrow, and with Hamlet's recognition that a

divinity shapes our ends. The point is not that Hamlet has suddenly become religious; he has been religious all through the play. The point is that he has now learned, and accepted, the boundaries in which human action, human   595 judgment, are enclosed.

43   Till his return from the voyage he had been trying to act beyond these, had been encroaching on the role of providence, if I may exaggerate to make a vital point. He had been too quick to take the burden of the whole world and its condition upon his limited and finite self. Faced with a task of   600 sufficient difficulty in its own right, he had dilated it into a cosmic problem—as indeed every task is, but if we think about this too precisely we cannot act at all. The whole time is out of joint, he feels, and in his young man's egocentricity, he will set it right. Hence he misjudges Ophelia, seeing in her only a breeder of sinners. Hence he misjudges himself, seeing himself   605 a vermin crawling between earth and heaven. Hence he takes it upon himself to be his mother's conscience, though the ghost has warned that this is no fit task for him, and returns to repeat the warning: "Leave her to heaven, And to those thorns that in her bosom lodge." Even with the king, Hamlet has sought to play at God. *He* it must be who decides the issue of Claudius's   610 salvation, saving him for a more damnable occasion. Now, he has learned that there are limits to the before and after that human reason can comprehend. Rashness, even, is sometimes good. Through rashness he has saved his life from the commission for his death, "and prais'd be rashness for it." This happy circumstance and the unexpected arrival of the pirate ship make it   615 plain that the roles of life are not entirely self-assigned. "There is a divinity that shapes our ends, Roughhew them how we will." Hamlet is ready now for what may happen, seeking neither to foreknow it nor avoid it. "If it be now, 'tis not to come; if it be not to come, it will be now; if it be not now, yet it will come: the readiness is all."   620

44   The crucial evidence of Hamlet's new frame of mind, as I understand it, is the graveyard scene. Here, in its ultimate symbol, he confronts, recognizes, and accepts the condition of being man. It is not simply that he now accepts death, though Shakespeare shows him accepting it in ever more poignant forms: first, in the imagined persons of the politician, the courtier,   625 and the lawyer, who laid their little schemes "to circumvent God," as Hamlet puts it, but now lie here; then in Yorick, whom he knew and played with as a child; and then in Ophelia. This last death tears from him a final cry of passion, but the striking contrast between his behavior and Laertes's reveals how deeply he has changed.   630

45   Still, it is not the fact of death that invests this scene with its peculiar power. It is instead the haunting mystery of life itself that Hamlet's speeches point to, holding in its inscrutable folds those other mysteries that he has wrestled with so long. These he now knows for what they are, and lays them by. The mystery of evil is present here—for this is after all the 635 universal graveyard, where, as the clown says humorously, he holds up Adam's profession; where the scheming politician, the hollow courtier, the tricky lawyer, the emperor and the clown and the beautiful young maiden, all come together in an emblem of the world; where even, Hamlet murmurs, one might expect to stumble on "Cain's jawbone, that did the first mur- 640 ther." The mystery of reality is here too—for death puts the question, "What is real?" in its irreducible form, and in the end uncovers all appearances: "Is this the fine of his fines and the recovery of his recoveries, to have his fine pate full of fine dirt?" "Now get you to my lady's chamber, and tell her, let her paint an inch thick, to this favor she must come." Or if we 645 need more evidence of this mystery, there is the anger of Laertes at the lack of ceremonial trappings, and the ambiguous character of Ophelia's own death. "Is she to be buried in Christian burial when she wilfully seeks her own salvation?" asks the gravedigger. And last of all, but most pervasive of all, there is the mystery of human limitation. The grotesque nature of 650 man's little joys, his big ambitions. The fact that the man who used to bear us on his back is now a skull that smells; that the noble dust of Alexander somewhere plugs a bunghole; that "Imperious Caesar, dead and turn'd to clay, Might stop a hole to keep the wind away." Above all, the fact that a pit of clay is "meet" for such a guest as man, as the gravedigger tells us in his 655 song, and yet that, despite all frailties and limitations, "That skull had a tongue in it and could sing once."

46   After the graveyard and what it indicates has come to pass in him, we know that Hamlet is ready for the final contest of mighty opposites. He accepts the world as it is, the world as a duel, in which, whether we know it 660 or not, evil holds the poisoned rapier and the poisoned chalice waits; and in which, if we win at all, it costs not less than everything. I think we understand by the close of Shakespeare's *Hamlet* why it is that unlike the other tragic heroes he is given a soldier's rites upon the stage. For as William Butler Yeats once said, "Why should we honor those who die on the field 665 of battle? A man may show as reckless a courage in entering into the abyss of himself."

QUESTIONS

1. Describe at length the author's ideal reader, and, as fully as you can, the author's tone * and purpose.
2. Good writing is an expression of good manners. Obviously, it is good manners for the writer to be as clear, as forceful, and as graceful as he can; but courtesy toward the reader may be expressed more directly, as it is, for example, in paragraph 4. Find and mark other phrases, sentences, and passages that reflect a similar tone.

ORGANIZATION

3. What paragraphs form the introduction of the essay? Imagine "The World of *Hamlet*" without the first paragraph, beginning instead with paragraph 2: "Great plays, as we know, do present us with something that can be called a world . . ." Why would this opening be less effective?
4. What is the point of discussing *Othello* in an essay about *Hamlet?* What does paragraph 3 contribute to the introduction?
5. Make a detailed outline of this essay under six or seven major headings. Explain why "The World of *Hamlet*" is easy to outline; mark words, phrases, and sentences that help the reader to follow the plan of the essay.
6. In paragraph 20 the author anticipates his order of presentation by referring in the second sentence to Spurgeon's observations about disease imagery * in *Hamlet.* Why? Where does he discuss Spurgeon's view? It may help the writer to organize clearly by occasionally pointing forward; it is also helpful to tell the reader what has been covered already. As an example of this summarizing, see the first sentence of paragraph 40. How does paragraph 29 contribute to the organization of the writer's material?
7. In paragraph 36 the author begins an interpretation of Hamlet's problem. Would placing this material first in the essay (1) improve the organization, (2) weaken it, or (3) make little difference? Explain.
8. Identify the techniques of closing in the last section of "The World of *Hamlet.*" Which of these do you consider most important? Which are accessory?
9. The simple, clear, and forceful exposition of this essay owes much to the writer's skill in constructing paragraphs. His topic sentences, especially, repay study. Write down one below the other, the topic sentences of paragraphs 18 through 28. What qualities do they have in common?
10. The author often develops his paragraphs with several quotations from *Hamlet.* What is the advantage of doing so? Observe that Professor Mack is careful to introduce each group of quotations, telling us what they illustrate;

and to follow them, usually, with some perceptive comment, thus making doubly sure that we know what each cluster of quotations has exemplified. Study paragraph 26 as a model of development by quotation.

11. Why does the writer handle some quotations by setting them off from the text, as he does in paragraph 3 and paragraph 21, and handle others by working them into the sentences of the text? Should he have identified the act and scene of each quotation? Why or why not?

12. Paragraph 6 is developed, in part, by making important qualifications * and concessions. Indicate each one. What words introduce these qualifications? What words signal a return to the main point?

SENTENCES

13. Are the following revisions acceptable substitutes for Professor Mack's sentences?

    (a) *Revision:* But the ghost reveals that a serpent was in the garden. . . .
        Mack: "But, the ghost reveals, a serpent was in the garden. . . ." (479-80)
    (b) *Revision:* Having decided the issue of Claudius's salvation, Hamlet saves him for a more damnable occasion.
        Mack: "*He* it must be who decides the issue of Claudius's salvation, saving him for a more damnable occasion." (610-11)

14. Interrupted movement * is often characteristic of formal exposition. It allows the writer to emphasize particular words or phrases within a sentence, and it is one rather graceful form of subordination *. Study the interrupted movement of the sentences in paragraph 30, observing how it establishes subtle shadings of emphasis.

15. Why the repetitions of *hence* at the beginnings of successive sentences in paragraph 43? Are there instances of similar repetition elsewhere?

16. The third sentence of paragraph 5 ("We feel its presence . . .") is long and elaborate. Is it effective? Would the substitution of two or three shorter sentences improve the writing? How would you describe the structure of this sentence?

DICTION

17. Look up: *attributes* (45), *egomaniac* (65), *evocation* (148), *rampart* (149), *dilemma* (169), *quarto* (209), *habituation* (219), *disarray* (293), *pervasive* (323), *perplexities* (334), *annihilates* (432), *denunciation* (458), *injunction* (500), *encroaching* (598), *abyss* (666).

18. Explain the meanings of the following phrases: *imaginative environment* (4), *world of surfaces* (264-65), *the dejected havior of the visage* (283), *dumb*

show (328), *network of implications* (354), *field of reference* (357), *leperous distilment* (442), *martial virtues* (481), *retributive justice* (536-37).

19. Good diction has range and richness; for example a writer may achieve a pleasing sort of emphasis by choosing from time to time words that are both precise and unusual. *Microcosm* (7) is such a word; *fictive* (369) is another. Make a list of ten or twelve such words in this essay. At the other end of the spectrum the writer may employ, for variety, words that suggest conversational expressions of the educated speaker. Hamlet's world, we are told, is "of a piece" (132). Find similar locutions.

20. Which of the following is the most effective in its diction? Which is the least effective?

    (a) *Hamlet* is a true-to-life play.
    (b) *Hamlet* is "a paradigm of the life of man." (55)
    (c) *Hamlet* is a realistic picture of life.

21. Find several examples of figurative * language in this essay. Substituting a literal, non-figurative expression for the metaphor * or simile *, rewrite the sentences, keeping as close as possible to the sense of the original. What, if anything, has been lost? Are such figures mere decoration, or do they help a writer to communicate his meaning more precisely? Explain.

22. In the first sentence of paragraph 26 we find the phrase *radical metaphor*. The careless, inexperienced reader will assume that *radical* means *extreme* or *extravagant*. But the more careful reader will see that this meaning does not harmonize with the meaning of the second sentence of the paragraph. What does *radical* mean in this context?

POINTS TO LEARN

1. Good writing is good manners. Often a writer can be more convincing if he avoids a dogmatic tone, if he acknowledges the possibility of other views than his own.

2. Well-organized writing is easy to outline.

3. Development by quotation is an important technique in the discussion of a literary text, one that most college students ought to master. Ideally, the writer should steer a middle course between using so many quotations that his work seems like a pointless job of copying out passages and using so few quotations that the reader remains unconvinced that the writer's interpretation is grounded firmly in the text. Long quotations must be used sparingly; the use of many short quotations is usually more effective. Observe, too, the possibility of paraphrasing quotations and of combining paraphrase with the quotation of a key phrase or key word.

4. To avoid "flat" diction a writer may use, if he does not overuse, rare words,

allusions *, figures of speech—especially metaphor and simile—and words that suggest educated conversation. Within the limits, always, of appropriateness, one secret of good diction is its variety.

SUGGESTIONS FOR WRITING

1. Write an essay in which you describe the "world" of *Macbeth* or *King Lear* as it is revealed in one or more scenes. Use short quotations as one means of illustrating and supporting your interpretation.

2. Study again paragraphs 20-32. Then, modelling your writing in a general way upon the presentation of Professor Mack, write a theme about one of the major images in *Macbeth*. You might want to choose as your subject one of these: clothing, sleep, feasting, seeds and growing things, darkness, storm, blood.

3. Describe the "world" of a novel or short story you have read recently. As possibilities you might consider *Wuthering Heights, The Return of the Native, Heart of Darkness, The Turn of the Screw, The Trial, 1984, The Plague, Lord of the Flies.*

IMPROVING YOUR STYLE

1. Be sure to cite specific passages from the work you are discussing, and experiment with how you incorporate them into your text. Sometimes introduce a quotation with a colon as Mack does in line 89. Sometimes fit it to your words without any mark of introduction (lines 436 and 445 ff.). And sometimes let the quotation stand against your sentence as an implicit example, that is, without any such label as "for example" or "for instance" (lines 140 ff.).

2. In your essay compose several sentences with interrupted movement.

3. Use *hence* to introduce a sentence. You might even try to employ it repetitively as Mack does in paragraph 43.

Style: A Closer Look

The ultimate, and in many ways the most interesting, problem of writing prose is style. Yet to the student—quite understandably—his first question about style is likely to be, "Why bother about style at all?" And he is likely to add that it's hard enough to be clear, concise, and emphatic, without trying to be fancy as well. This feeling about style, which unfortunately is all too common, reflects some of the misconceptions that surround and obscure this important subject. One of the most important points to realize at the outset is this: style is not a surface decoration the writer can apply to his meaning or leave off, depending upon whether he likes things fancy or plain. Every writer, no matter how humble his task, is inescapably concerned with style—whether or not he is aware of it. His problem is to choose the best way of treating his subject as he sees it. Whatever his subject (argument, narration, exposition, description) he must choose a style that will work *for* his purpose and not *against* it. Style, for example, is behind the forcefulness of a hard-hitting argument like "The Third Knight's Speech" by T. S. Eliot (p. 168).

The writer's style, then, is inseparable from his thought and his expression of that thought. Consequently, it follows that all writing—indeed all utterances of any kind—have style. Every essay the student of composition has written thus far has style—even if the style is at times defective or deplorable. Although obviously some styles are more appropriate and more effective than others and although every writer's aim is to improve his style, style is not something only great writers achieve. Nor is the ability to manage a good prose style something one is born with; it must be learned. And while no amount of study and diligence and practice will produce great writing, it is equally true that there can be no great writing without study and diligence and practice. The study of writing, in one way or another, must consider the principles of style. Therefore the study of style is important to the beginning writer—as it is to every other kind of writer—for three reasons at least: First, by understanding some of the basic problems and principles connected with style, he can improve the vigor and effectiveness of his own writing. Second, the study of style should greatly improve his ability to *read* good prose. And, third, his increased verbal skill and his increased sensitivity to language should become a source of constant pleasure.

At this point we can pose three fundamental questions. What precisely do we mean by style? How does a writer create his style? And how can the beginning writer apply to his own writing what he learns from the study of style? These questions themselves are more important than any answers we suggest in this brief introduction, answers which are only tentative and, hopefully, provocative. To begin with, we had better essay a working definition of style.

The first point to notice is that style is a pattern of linguistic features distinguishing one piece of writing from another, or one category of writings from another. Hawthorne's *The Scarlet Letter* possesses a unique combination of linguistic characteristics different from the unique traits of Hemingway's *A Farewell to Arms*: the styles of the two novels, we say, are different. And although a writer's style often varies from work to work there is usually enough uniformity in his prose to let us observe that his over-all style differs from another writer's style. Hawthorne's style differs from Hemingway's. Similarly we may say that the style of twentieth-century American writers differs from that of eighteenth-century writers. In this sense, style does not necessarily imply excellence—only a pattern of distinctive linguistic traits. Nor is style confined to what we commonly call literature. It is just as important in exposition, argument, and description as it is in fiction. But if all utterances have style, it is obvious that in some, style is more effective than in others. Our assumption, then, is that there are various kinds of style and that they vary in their effective range. We must allow, too, for the possibility of inappropriateness or the misuse of style.

Merely to point out, however, that style is a distinguishing combination of linguistic traits and that style appears in both literary and non-literary texts is not of much help to the student of composition. A really useful answer to the question, "What is style?" requires a closer look at a writer as he prepares to write and at what happens as he begins to compose sentences. We observe, for one thing, that a writer is not an entirely free agent. Provided he is to write effectively, a significant part of what he says and how he says it is more or less determined in advance by two things. One we may call the broad context of his writing: his subject and his purpose and his reader. If his purpose, for instance, is to write an objective, factual report about the ability of a new material to withstand stress, then words conveying personal feelings and evaluations should be filtered out, so that expressions like *beautiful, charming, revolting,* and *disgusting* will appear infrequently or not at all. The second thing that determines a writer's prose concerns "rules" of language so basic that ignoring them produces a total loss of communication. Among these, for example, are the rules of English word order. No one who intends to be understood is free to write "Powers he that the is of shows do everything he can thought man that human what do sphere could valuable enlarges he." English syntax, however *does* permit Samuel Johnson to say, "Everything that enlarges the sphere of human powers, that shows man he can do what he thought he could do, is valuable."

But although a part of writing is predetermined by the writer's subject, purpose, and reader as well as by certain basic conventions of his language, much of what he produces is the result of free choices he is making constantly as he writes. These choices implicitly and explicitly convey not only the writer's message, ideas, directions, descriptions, and so on, but also often the writer's cast of mind, his temperament, his taste, his values—in short, himself as he wishes us to believe he is, at least at the instant of his writing. His free choices, broadly speaking are of two types: (1) what details of the subject to include or emphasize; and (2) what linguistic forms to select in order to achieve his purpose. Since "reality" is not a simple, constant entity that each of us grasps in exactly the same way, the writer is free to select those details from the flux of experience that seem to him most significant. And just as important, of course, is the way in which the writer forms his details into meaningful patterns, the way in which he conceives his subject. Thus, two historians witnessing the same battle will perhaps agree broadly in their descriptions of it. But no doubt each will interpret it, and perhaps evaluate it, differently.

Secondly, a writer makes choices concerning matters of diction, organization, sentence structure, punctuation, and so on. Sometimes these are binary choices: shall the writer choose the active or the passive voice? shall he repeat a noun or employ a pronoun? shall he use a colon or a dash? Other choices may involve three or four alternatives as is often the case in matters of sentence structure or word order, and still others may allow an even wider range of choices, as is sometimes true of diction. Of course, some of these choices are unconscious—so much a part of a writer's training, habit, adherence to fashion, and way of thinking that they seem not to be choices at all. Still, many, perhaps most, *are* conscious, as the untidy appearance of any rough draft will show. In this area of free choice, then, the writer creates his style. As an illustration we offer three examples. The third is a passage from James Joyce's story "Two Gallants"; the first two are versions of the same passage as less gifted writers might have handled it.

1. It was Sunday night. The streets were full of people in their Sunday clothes. The street lights were on, and all sorts of people were on the sidewalks. They were walking up and down and talking.

2. In the streets the Sunday evening crowds in their awkward Sunday clothes milled about under the street lamps, their voices swelling to a monotonous din.

3. The streets, shuttered for the repose of Sunday, swarmed with a gaily-coloured crowd. Like illumined pearls the lamps shone from the summits of their tall poles upon the living texture below, which, changing shape and hue unceasingly, sent up into the warm grey evening air an unchanging, unceasing murmur.

Each of these examples conveys approximately, though by no means entirely, the same *referential* meaning: in each the time and place are the same, and each points to, or designates, the same crowd of people talking under street lights. Yet the passages produce different effects upon the reader. Each one is different, for instance, in its *expressive* meanings, that is, in the feelings it arouses in the reader about the street lamps and the people in the streets.

The first revision of Joyce's sentences communicates little expressive meaning. Its diction and sentence structure are comparatively bland and noncommittal, as if the writer neither liked nor disliked his subject, or as if he were bored by it. He chooses merely to point to the scene rather than to react to it. In place of active verbs he uses only linking verbs. He is content with the vague diction of "all sorts of people." In short, his writing reveals little awareness of the range of effects that style can produce. In order to pass a final judgment upon the success or the failure of this passage, however, we should have to see it in a much wider linguistic context. It might indeed be merely flat writing such as the inexperienced writer is likely to produce. But in another context this simple flat writing might be just what the writer wants for his particular purpose. The first example bears some faint resemblance to the kind of effect often achieved by Hemingway, who sometimes creates expressiveness by removing all overt emotional coloring from his sentences.

The hypothetical writer of the second passage exhibits a more decided emotional response. We suspect from his diction that he dislikes the people he is describing and probably feels superior to them. He is more aware, seemingly, of words as imagery and of words as sounds, although the clustering of unstressed syllables in the phrase "swelling to a monotonous din" sounds awkward. Yet this second passage seems colorless and inexpressive when placed side by side with the two sentences by James Joyce.

Joyce feels deeply about this city and its people. Phrases like "gaily-coloured," "illumined pearls," "living texture," and "warm grey evening" both designate and evaluate. But perhaps it is Joyce's sensitivity to the sound of words, as much as anything, which surrounds his subject with an aura of approval. While this short extract is ordinary enough in the context of Joyce's entire work, it is a striking example in comparison with the first two versions. One of its sound effects is the frequent use of consonance, or internal alliteration, such as the repetition of *l* sounds in "Like *il*lumined pear*l*s the *l*amps shone . . ." or the repetition of *s* and *d* sounds in the first sentence or the repetition of *-ing* toward the end of the second sentence. Emphasis and retarded movement result from the clustering of stressed syllables in the phrase "warm grey evening air." Further emphasis stems from the repetition of sounds and rhythms at the end of the second sentence in "an unchanging, unceasing murmur." In addition to using consonance, various repetitions, and unusual rhythms, Joyce creates his stylistic effects by means of active verbs, unusual words, a simile, imagery, and interrupted movement. Thus his expressive style not only gives his description force and grace, it is an important part of his meaning. It is not mere ornament.

Skillful handling of expressive meaning, such as Joyce employs in his two sentences, usually results in winning the reader's assent—at least momentarily—to the writer's feelings and viewpoint. Style, then, is also a means of persuasion. Or put another way, effective style, as opposed to awkward or inappropriate style is in part the result of taking pains to convince the reader.

But if style is a choice that persuades, style is also, in an important sense, discovery. In creating his style the writer is trying to force language to conform to all the subtleties of his thought and feeling. In *striving* to say exactly what he wants to say, the writer *discovers* a more accurate expression of what he wants to say. As he considers which of his various stylistic choices to make, a writer often recognizes the possibility of a more precise, more emphatic, more graceful manifestation of his thought and emotion than he had imagined in merely contemplating the subject in his mind. Furthermore, it may well be that style is discovery for the reader too, giving him a sharper pair of eyes or making him aware of new and fresh and possibly startling ways of thinking about the writer's subject.

By now it should be apparent that style is not merely a fancy way of expressing content. Even content, as we have seen, involves stylistic choices. And style, far from being ornamentation, is an important component of meaning. Since style is the result of many choices, it often reveals to us a portrait of the writer, or at any rate of the person the writer wishes to seem. Even if this portrait is not identical with the "real" writer, it is nevertheless a significant part of the total impression, for it does matter what kind of writer seems to be standing behind a piece of prose. From a writer's style we can often infer much about his conception of himself, his intellectual and emotional attitude toward his subject, and the way in which he regards his reader—about all, in short, that we call tone. And while it goes without saying that factual and referential information may often be more important than any other kind of meaning—especially in expository prose—style, no matter what the purpose of a piece of writing, is more than fancy dress. Style is meaning, judgment, and often the writer's moral conception—whether in argument, description, general exposition, or narration.

To summarize our tentative definition of style we might do well to repeat the following points:

1. Style includes the writer's way of thinking about his subject and his characteristic way of presenting it for a particular reader and purpose.

2. Style results from linguistic choices; the more frequently these choices are exercised and the more wide-ranging they are, the higher the probability they will effectively express the writer's unique thought and feeling.

3. Style, therefore, is, or may be, a means of discovery, for both writer and reader.

4. Style sharpens expressive meaning as well as referential meaning. Style intensifies the tone of writing, and, all else being equal, prose with a definite tone is likely to be more persuasive than writing with little tone.

5. Style is not mere ornament; rather it conveys important subtleties of meaning and evaluation, especially as they define the nature of the writer, his basic attitudes, his presuppositions, his moral stance, and his relation to his subject and his reader.

6. These points only begin to suggest the vast implications of style. They are offered only as a tentative working definition for students of composition, not as a confident solution to the enormous problems raised by the study of style.

Turning from our attempt to define style, we come to the question, What produces style? The answer involves, of course, all possible methods and techniques of expression known to rhetoric. To study the creation of style is to study the organization of the whole composition, paragraph development, sentence structure, sentence rhythm, diction, punctuation, and whatever else contributes to the process of communication. Style, however, results most frequently from those rhetorical devices of diction and sentence structure that produce emphasis and emotion.

Diction is especially useful because of the tremendous range of choice available to the writer, a fact that will become abundantly clear in the selections that follow this introduction. An author, of course, may prefer for some special purpose to keep his diction simple and fairly limited, using a large proportion of monosyllables as Hemingway sometimes does. Or he may prefer a diction of extraordinary variety as do Shakespeare, Milton, and Joyce. A writer is always free to choose (within the limits of his subject, purpose, and reader) from monosyllables, polysyllables, rare words, technical and scientific words, highly connotative words, slang, colloquialisms, vivid imagery, abstractions, dialect words, figurative expressions, archaic words, obsolete words, allusions, onomatopoeic words, and other words with appropriate sounds. He will manage different effects depending upon his vocabulary of active verbs or his handling of participles or the frequency and kind of his adjectives and adverbs.

Sentence structure is no less important than diction, for here a writer is also capable of choosing among forms that can produce surprise, emotion, variation, and emphasis. And once again variety is usually desirable. A writer uses short sentences, rhetorical questions, long sentences, parallelism, balance, antithesis, interrupted movement, periodic sentences, inversion, various kinds of repetition, and different kinds of subordinate constructions, each with a different effect.

In the study of style it is not sufficient, of course, merely to identify techniques of diction, sentence structure, and so on. Adequately to describe a writer's style, or even some feature of it, one must do a certain amount of statistical analysis, noting, say, the frequency of balanced clauses in proportion to simple, straightforward sentences. Sometimes a writer uses balance no oftener than the majority of writers. Or sometimes a writer uses balance with such significant frequency that it becomes one identifying characteristic of his work. Or again a given device may appear so often that it becomes an irritating mannerism and so loses its effectiveness. The point is that a description of style must proceed partly by making qualitative observations and judgments and partly by quantitative analysis. The purpose of such a description should be to demonstrate how a writer uniquely combines linguistic features so as to communicate his individual thought and feeling and judgment.

In the selections that follow, the comments and questions are designed to encourage the reader to identify and describe the styles of very different writers, some of whom write upon similar subjects with very different voices and with very different interpretations owing to the differences in the personalities behind each piece of prose. Not all these passages are equally effective, nor are all the styles, in our judgment, equally appropriate to their subjects. But all, we trust, have something to teach the student of composition. As exercises, we believe imitations and parodies are useful ways of expressing one's understanding of a writer's style and the principles—positive or negative—to be learned from it. The student may wish to try his hand at describing the styles of writers like Joan Didion, James Baldwin, William Styron, Brand Blanshard, and A. J. Liebling, using selections appearing earlier in this textbook.

Even this brief and simple introduction suggests that the close description and study of style can be extremely useful to a student of composition. It reveals something of the virtually infinite number of choices available to a writer. Learning what some of these are and what kinds of meaning and emotion and effect they produce is an important step toward acquiring a style of one's own. Perhaps equally important is that recognizing the subtleties of style is a source of great pleasure. Like poetry, prose has its special rewards and delights.

Young Joan

Pierre Champion was a noted historian and authority on Joan of Arc. In 1920-21 he edited the record of her trial for witchcraft (held in 1431). There was considerable interest at the time in the French heroine, who had only recently been canonized in 1920, an interest reflected not only in Champion's publication but in a famous play presented in 1924, George Bernard Shaw's *Saint Joan* (an excerpt from the Preface to the play is the next selection). The following passage is from Champion's article on Joan written for *The Encyclopaedia Britannica* (fourteenth edition, 1937). As you read Champion's prose, and later Shaw's, contrast their styles. The differences are due in part to the personalities and values of the two men, but in part also to the fact that their interests in Joan were directed to different purposes and readers.

1   . . . Hardly anything is known of Joan's childhood; from her mother she learnt her prayers and the lives of the Saints, and she played till she was 12 or 13 with the other village children. The boys of Domrémy, who were French in their sympathies, were at frequent odds with the boys of the Burgundian village, on the other side of the Meuse. Saint Remy, 5 patron saint of the cathedral of Reims, was also that of the church at Domrémy. Joan, who was baptized by the *curé* Minet, was a pious child, and often went with her companions to bear wreaths of flowers to Notre Dame de Bermont. She had heard, without believing, the story of the fairies who haunted the spring among the bushes. She was almost certainly ignorant of 10 Merlin's prophecy that a maid should come from the Bois Chenu to do great deeds.

2   Joan helped her parents in tillage, tended the animals, and was skilled with her needle and in other feminine arts. She was pious, and often went to church when the other girls were dancing. She was in her 13th year 15 when, in her father's garden, she heard for the first time a voice from God.

From "Joan of Arc," *Encyclopaedia Britannica*, 14th edition (1937), XIII, 72-73. Reprinted by permission of the *Encyclopaedia Britannica*, Inc., Chicago, Illinois.

Thereupon she vowed to remain a virgin and to lead a godly life. During the next five years she heard the voices two or three times a week. Among them she distinguished those of Saint Catherine and Saint Margaret, who appeared to her, in the guise of queens, wearing rich and precious crowns. 20 Sometimes their coming was heralded by Saint Michael. With these visions Joan became still more serious, and more given to prayer. The troubles of Domrémy between 1419 and 1428 made her early acquainted with the horrors of war. Her voices commanded her to go to France, and to raise the siege of Orleans, which had been begun in October 1428. 25

3   We do not know the exact moment at which Joan decided to obey her voices, and to go to France. The captain of the fortified town nearest to Domrémy on the French side was Robert de Baudricourt, commandant at Vaucouleurs, four leagues away. Joan approached him for the first time in May 1428, accompanied by a relative on her mother's side, one Durand 30 Laxart ou Lassois. She was in her 16th year. At this time an army was being raised in England for the conquest of the Dauphin's territory south of the Loire. The journey was made without the knowledge of her family, for when Joan had spoken of going into France, her father had said that he would rather drown her with his own hands. She told the Dauphin's com- 35 mandant that she was sent by Our Lord, and asked him to write to the Dauphin saying that, by the will of God, she was to lead him to his crown-ing. Baudricourt attached no importance to the visit, and set her back to her parents. At home Joan talked more and more of her great mission. In July 1428, the governor of Champagne, Antoine de Vergy, undertook to 40 subdue the country around Vaucouleurs for the English. The people of Domrémy retreated with their cattle to Neufchâteau where Joan spent a fortnight with a woman called La Rousse, who kept an inn. This is the origin of the false Burgundian legend that she was a light woman, liking the company of men-at-arms and horses. Some time after, she was summoned 45 for breach of promise of marriage, before the magistrates of Toul, by a young man who had sought her hand. On the return of the family to Dom-rémy, they found the village burned to the ground, and Joan had to attend the church of Greux. Towards the end of October, she learned that Orleans was besieged by the English, who had garrisoned the towns along the Loire. 50

QUESTIONS

1. What is the purpose of most encyclopedia articles? In what way does an encyclopedia article differ from a personal essay? From an argument?

2. What kind of reader does Pierre Champion seem to be writing for? Describe the "assumed" reader of "Young Joan" as fully as you can.

3. Describe the man Pierre Champion seems to be. Granted that "Young Joan" shows us only one side of the "true" man, what personal characteristics does the writer choose to reveal in this historical sketch? Support your conclusions by pointing to specific words, phrases, and sentences.

4. How does he regard Joan of Arc? With utter detachment? With strong bias in her favor? With strong bias against her? If you think his attitude is mainly, but not entirely, objective, can you detect any subtle feeling for or against her? In answering all the questions in this section be sure to support your answers by referring to the language the writer uses.

5. In short, what is the tone * of the writing? Although style includes more than the means by which a writer creates his tone—embracing his characteristic way of planning and executing every aspect of his writing—the description of a writer's style should always include a detailed description of the writer's tone.

6. Since your answers at first will be largely intuitive, you may wish to test their validity by looking more closely into the means by which Pierre Champion creates his tone and his individual manner of presenting his subject. Are the sentences in this selection for the most part varied in length? How many words appear in the longest sentence? In the shortest? Do most of the sentences vary between the very short and the very long, or do most of them have a moderate length? You may, if you wish, count the number of sentences and the number of words in each sentence. After such a count note how many sentences fall between 6-15 words; how many fall between 16-25 words; how many between 26-35 words.

7. What is the pattern of the majority of Pierre Champion's sentences—simple *, compound *, complex *, compound-complex? Is their total effect one of simplicity or complexity?

8. To what extent does the writer vary sentence beginnings? How many begin with the subject of the sentence? How many begin with something else? What is the writer's most common variation? In what way might the handling of sentence openers affect a writer's style?

9. To what extent does the writer employ rhetorical questions *, inversions *, isolation of words and phrases, parallelism *, anaphora *, polysyndeton *, repetition, figures of speech *? What different effects result from employing these devices sparingly? From employing them frequently?

10. Is interrupted movement * frequent or infrequent? Are appositives * frequent or infrequent? Why?

11. Does the writer use dashes, parentheses, exclamation marks, and italics? Why or why not?

12. How many periodic sentences occur in this selection?

13. Sometimes even good sentences require careful, close reading because of the

inherent subtlety and complexity of the writer's thought. Generally, however, such complicated syntax is inappropriate to an encyclopedia, the readers of which want readily available information. Are Champion's sentences good or bad examples of the "encyclopedia style"? You might at this point wish to summarize how this writer's sentence structure helps to create his tone and style.

14. Is the diction of "Young Joan" largely abstract and general or concrete and particular? Are the majority of the words monosyllabic and disyllabic, or polysyllabic? Is the diction mostly Latinate or Saxon? Are the qualities of his diction referred to in this question appropriate or inappropriate to his subject, purpose, and reader? Why or why not?

15. Does the writer have a fondness for unusual or rare words? Have any words been used largely for their sound? Does Champion use slang, colloquialisms *, or contractions? Are there any archaic, obsolete, or dialect words? If any such words occur, point to examples. How does the presence or absence of any of these classes of words help to create the writer's tone?

16. Do any words or expressions characterize this writing as belonging to the twentieth century rather than to earlier centuries?

17. Are allusions * and proper nouns rare or frequent? If frequent of what sort are they? Do they come from mythology, literature, history, geography, the Bible, or from some other source? Are they appropriate? Do they make the writing more or less readable? Why or why not?

18. Would you describe the writer's language as largely emotive or referential? What are the connotations of the following phrases and clauses:

> from her mother she learnt her prayers (1-2)
> a pious child (7)
> She had heard, without believing, the story of the fairies . . . (9)
> Joan . . . was skilled with her needle and in other feminine arts. (13-14)

19. In telling his story does the writer ever apply to Joan words with unfavorable connotations *?

20. Consider this revision of the passage in lines 15-21:

> She was thirteen years old when, in her father's garden, she said she heard for the first time a voice from God. Thereupon she vowed, according to her own account, to remain a virgin and lead a godly life. During the next five years she affirmed that she heard the voices two or three times a week. Among them she claimed to distinguish those of Saint Catherine and Saint Margaret, who she said appeared to her in the guise of queens, wearing rich and precious crowns. Sometimes their coming she declared to be heralded by Saint Michael.

In what way has the style changed?

SUGGESTIONS FOR WRITING

1. Revise one paragraph of this selection to show some emotion on the writer's part and subtle disapproval of Joan of Arc.

2. In one or two paragraphs attempt a parody of this writer's style, using some such subject as Hercules or Paul Bunyan. (Before attempting this subject you might wish to read or reread Dwight Macdonald's "Parody" (p. 107).

3. Using some historical figure, the facts of whose life you have gathered, write a one- or two-paragraph imitation of Pierre Champion's style.

4. After studying Shaw's style in the next selection, rewrite paragraph 3 as Shaw might have written it. In asking for parodies and stylistic imitations we are not urging you to model your future writing as closely as possible upon Shaw or upon the style of some other writer. Nor does parody necessarily imply an adverse criticism of a writer's style. But parody and imitation are useful methods of identifying a writer's distinguishing characteristics and require an understanding of the interplay between a writer's thought and his expression of that thought. Improving one's own style results from the close study of many different writers.

The Evolutionary Appetite

George Bernard Shaw (1856-1958)—playwright, critic, Fabian socialist, wit, and brilliant platform speaker—was one of the major figures of twentieth-century British literature. His devotion to liberal reforms and his constant goading of the Establishment is seen in his plays and in the long prefaces he composed for each of them. The dramas themselves range from a serious problem play like *Mrs. Warren's Profession* (1898), concerning prostitution, to the sparkling comedy *Pygmalion* (1913), the source of the Broadway musical, *My Fair Lady* (1955). Perhaps Shaw's finest play is *Saint Joan* (1924). He sees Joan as an example of the great individual whose destiny is to move humanity forward at the cost of intense personal suffering. The following excerpt from the "Preface" to *Saint Joan* passionately defends her character and analyzes the forces impelling her to greatness and to tragedy.

1   What then is the modern view of Joan's voices and visions and messages from God? The nineteenth century said that they were delusions, but that as she was a pretty girl, and had been abominably ill-treated and finally done to death by a superstitious rabble of medieval priests hounded on by a corrupt political bishop, it must be assumed that she was the in- 5 nocent dupe of these delusions. The twentieth century finds this explanation too vapidly commonplace, and demands something more mystic. I think the twentieth century is right, because an explanation which amounts to Joan being mentally defective instead of, as she obviously was, mentally excessive, will not wash. I cannot believe, nor, if I could, could I expect all 10 my readers to believe, as Joan did, that three ocularly visible well dressed persons, named respectively Saint Catherine, Saint Margaret, and Saint Michael, came down from heaven and gave her certain instructions with which they were charged by God for her. Not that such a belief would be

Reprinted from the "Preface" to *Saint Joan* in *Nine Great Plays* by Bernard Shaw, New York, Dodd, Mead and Company, 1947. Reprinted by permission of The Society of Authors on behalf of the Bernard Shaw Estate.

more improbable or fantastic than some modern beliefs which we all 15
swallow; but there are fashions and family habits in belief, and it happens
that, my fashion being Victorian and my family habit Protestant, I find
myself unable to attach any such objective validity to the form of Joan's
visions.

2   But that there are forces at work which use individuals for purposes 20
far transcending the purpose of keeping these individuals alive and prosperous and respectable and safe and happy in the middle station in life, which
is all any good bourgeois can reasonably require, is established by the fact
that men will, in the pursuit of knowledge and of social readjustments for
which they will not be a penny the better, and are indeed often many 25
pence the worse, face poverty, infamy, exile, imprisonment, dreadful hardship, and death. Even the selfish pursuit of personal power does not nerve
men to the efforts and sacrifices which are eagerly made in pursuit of extensions of our power over nature, though these extensions may not touch
the personal life of the seeker at any point. There is no more mystery about 30
this appetite for knowledge and power than about the appetite for food:
both are known as facts and as facts only, the difference between them
being that the appetite for food is necessary to the life of the hungry man
and is therefore a personal appetite, whereas the other is an appetite for
evolution, and therefore a superpersonal need.   35
3   The diverse manners in which our imaginations dramatize the approach of the superpersonal forces is a problem for the psychologist, not
for the historian. Only, the historian must understand that visionaries are
neither impostors nor lunatics. It is one thing to say that the figure Joan
recognized as St Catherine was not really St Catherine, but the dramatiza- 40
tion by Joan's imagination of that pressure upon her of the driving force
that is behind evolution which I have just called the evolutionary appetite.
It is quite another to class her visions with the vision of two moons seen by
a drunken person, or with Brocken spectres, echoes and the like. Saint
Catherine's instructions were far too cogent for that; and the simplest 45
French peasant who believes in apparitions of celestial personages to
favored mortals is nearer to the scientific truth about Joan than the Ration-
alist and Materialist historians and essayists who feel obliged to set down
a girl who saw saints and heard them talking to her as either crazy or men-
dacious. If Joan was mad, all Christendom was mad too; for people who 50
believe devoutly in the existence of celestial personages are every whit as
mad in that sense as the people who think they see them. Luther, when he
threw his inkhorn at the devil, was no more mad than any other Augus-

tinian monk: he had a more vivid imagination, and had perhaps eaten and
slept less: that was all.   55

QUESTIONS

1. In "The Evolutionary Appetite" Shaw argues that Joan is one of those superior individuals who form the advance guard of the evolutionary process. Because they belong more to the future than to the present, they are likely to be
accused, as Joan was and still is, of neurosis or lunacy. Unlike Pierre Champion's "Young Joan," therefore, "The Evolutionary Appetite" is more argument than narration. What is Shaw's attitude toward himself? Does he, for
example, regard himself seriously? Does he ever laugh at himself? Does he allow for the possibility that his view is merely one of a number of legitimate interpretations of Joan? Does he think of himself as less than infallible? Support
your answer by specific references to Shaw's language. What kind of reader
does he assume? What does Shaw suppose are his readers' probable assumptions
about Joan of Arc?

2. Shaw's sentences are longer than those in Pierre Champion's "Young Joan."
Count the number of sentences and the number of words in each sentence.
How long is Shaw's average sentence? What is the length of his shortest sentence? His longest? What kinds of subordination * does Shaw use? What is his
most common method of subordination? Why do you think Shaw writes longer
sentences than those of Pierre Champion?

3. Classify each sentence as simple *, compound *, complex *, compound-
complex. Which of these types appears most often? Which is the second most
common?

4. Shaw's sentences are much more vigorous than those of Pierre Champion.
How many examples of the following variations for emphasis can you identify
in this selection: rhetorical questions *, interrupted movement *, emphasis by
isolation of words or phrases, fragmentary * sentences or clauses, nominative
absolutes * as interrupters, parallelism *, antithesis *, short sentences or clauses,
polysyndeton *, repetition, periodic * structure? Which of these does Shaw use
most often? Why? Is Shaw over-emphatic? Is it possible to be over-emphatic?
Would Pierre Champion's prose have been improved if he had used more frequently such techniques of emphasis as those listed above?

5. Often in Shaw's prose there is a feeling that a debate is taking place. Shaw
is fond of stating his opponent's position and then demolishing it by several
smashing blows. Point to two or three examples. How does Shaw's sentence
structure help to convey this conflict of ideas?

6. Does Shaw use more or fewer emotive words than Pierre Champion? Illustrate your answer by examples.

7. Since Shaw is arguing, he naturally uses logical connectives * in the construc-

tion of his argument. What are some of the most common of these in "The Evolutionary Appetite"?

8. Shaw's argument often involves comparisons and disjunctions. Correlative conjunctions and pairs of words framing * comparisons appear often and create an effect on dignified symmetry. Examples are:

> more . . . than
> no more . . . than
> either . . . or.

Can you find similar constructions?

9. Is Shaw's diction primarily formal and Latinate or simple and informal? Make a list of polysyllabic words of Latin origin beginning with, say, *abominably*. Make a parallel list of one- or two-syllable Saxon words like *whit*. Which is the longer list? Should Shaw have used only the kind of words appearing on the longer list? Why or why not?

10. Does Shaw ever use slang or colloquial * expressions along with formal diction? Is he wise to mix the two kinds of diction? Explain.

11. Does Shaw use adjectives and adverbs more, or less, frequently than does Pierre Champion? How do Shaw's adjectives and adverbs affect his tone? Might any be omitted?

12. Most readers would probably conclude that Pierre Champion's style is appropriate to his reader and purpose. Is Shaw's very different style appropriate to *his* reader and purpose? Why or why not?

13. Which of these styles do you prefer to read? Why? Are there any criteria by which we could judge the style of one of these writer's prose to be superior to the other?

SUGGESTIONS FOR WRITING

1. Write an argument of about the same length as "The Evolutionary Appetite" in which you imitate Shaw's style as closely as you can, without slipping into parody.

2. Rewrite "The Evolutionary Appetite," making Shaw's argument as unemotional and as dispassionate as possible. Simplify his diction wherever possible.

3. Using Shaw's style as much as possible, write an unsympathetic treatment of Joan of Arc.

4. Either in class discussion or in an essay identify several characteristics of Shaw's style not mentioned in the questions.

The Hedonistic Theory of Economics

Thorstein Veblen (1857-1929), economist and critic of American society, taught at the University of Chicago, Stanford, the University of Missouri, and the New School for Social Research. He is best known for *The Theory of the Leisure Class* (1899), in which he coined the phrase "conspicuous consumption" to describe the lavish spending of the wealthy, who, Veblen believed, acquire status in proportion to the money they can waste. In *The Theory of the Leisure Class* and in studies like *The Instinct of Workmanship* (1914) Veblen stressed the relationships between economics, social institutions, and individual psychology. In spite of his sometimes difficult style, Veblen has proved one of the most important and influential of American economists. The following excerpt is from a journal article and is typical of Veblen's formal, academic prose.

1   . . . Money and the habitual resort to its use are conceived to be simply the ways and means by which consumable goods are acquired, and therefore simply a convenient method by which to procure the pleasurable sensations of consumption; these latter being in hedonistic theory the sole and overt end of all economic endeavor. Money values have therefore no 5 other significance than that of purchasing power over consumable goods, and money is simply an expedient of computation. Investment, credit extensions, loans of all kinds and degrees, with payment of interest and the rest, are likewise taken simply as intermediate steps between the pleasurable sensations of consumption and the efforts induced by the anticipation of 10 these sensations, other bearings of the case being disregarded. The balance being kept in terms of the hedonistic consumption, no disturbance arises in this pecuniary traffic so long as the extreme terms of this extended hedonistic equation—pain-cost and pleasure-gain—are not altered, what lies between these extreme terms being merely algebraic notation employed for 15

From "The Limitations of Marginal Utility" by Thorstein Veblen, *Journal of Political Economy*, Vol. XVII, 1909. Reprinted by permission of the University of Chicago Press.

convenience of accountancy. But such is not the run of the facts in modern business. Variations of capitalization, e.g., occur without its being practicable to refer them to visibly equivalent variations either in the state of the industrial arts or in the sensations of consumption. Credit extensions tend to inflation of credit, rising prices, overstocking of markets, etc., likewise without a visible or securely traceable correlation in the state of the industrial arts or in the pleasures of consumption; that is to say, without a visible basis in those material elements to which the hedonistic theory reduces all economic phenomena. Hence the run of the facts, in so far, must be thrown out of the theoretical formulation. The hedonistically presumed final purchase of consumable goods is habitually not contemplated in the pursuit of business enterprise. Business men habitually aspire to accumulate wealth in excess of the limits of practicable consumption, and the wealth so accumulated is not intended to be converted by a final transaction of purchase into consumable goods or sensations of consumption. Such commonplace facts as these, together with the endless web of business detail of a like pecuniary character, do not in hedonistic theory raise a question as to how these conventional aims, ideals, aspirations, and standards have come into force or how they affect the scheme of life in business or outside of it; they do not raise those questions because such questions cannot be answered in the terms which the hedonistic economists are content to use, or, indeed, which their premises permit them to use. The question which arises is how to explain the facts away: how theoretically to neutralize them so that they will not have to appear in the theory, which can then be drawn in direct and unambiguous terms of rational hedonistic calculation. They are explained away as being aberrations due to oversight or lapse of memory on the part of business men, or to some failure of logic or insight. Or they are construed and interpreted into the rationalistic terms of the hedonistic calculus by resort to an ambiguous use of the hedonistic concepts. So that the whole "money economy," with all the machinery of credit and the rest, disappears in a tissue of metaphors to reappear theoretically expurgated, sterilized, and simplified into a "refined system of barter," culminating in a net aggregate maximum of pleasurable sensations of consumption.

2   But since it is in just this unhedonistic, unrationalistic pecuniary traffic that the tissue of business life consists; since it is this peculiar conventionalism of aims and standards that differentiates the life of the modern business community from any conceivable earlier or cruder phase of economic life; since it is in this tissue of pecuniary intercourse and pecuni-

ary concepts, ideals, expedients, and aspirations that the conjunctures of 55
business life arise and run their course of felicity and devastation; since it
is here that those institutional changes take place which distinguish one
phase or era of the business community's life from any other; since the
growth and change of these habitual, conventional elements make the
growth and character of any business era or business community; any 60
theory of business which sets these elements aside or explains them away
misses the main facts which it has gone out to seek. Life and its conjunctures and institutions being of this complexion, however much that state
of the case may be deprecated, a theoretical account of the phenomena of
this life must be drawn in these terms in which the phenomena occur. It 65
is not simply that the hedonistic interpretation of modern economic phenomena is inadequate or misleading; if the phenomena are subjected to the
hedonistic interpretation in the theoretical analysis they disappear from the
theory; and if they would bear the interpretation in fact they would disappear in fact. If, in fact, all the conventional relations and principles of pecu- 70
niary intercourse were subject to such a perpetual rationalized, calculating
revision, so that each article of usage, appreciation, or procedure must approve itself *de novo* on hedonistic grounds of sensuous expediency to all
concerned at every move, it is not conceivable that the institutional fabric
would last over night.   75

QUESTIONS

1. Which of the following descriptions of the writer seem to you most accurate?

(a) Thorstein Veblen, a learned professor, is speaking to other experts
in a necessarily technical language that laymen—even educated laymen—can
scarcely comprehend.

(b) Thorstein Veblen is expressing a fairly simple idea in painfully
difficult and ponderous language. Perhaps he wishes to make his subject seem
more abstruse than it is; perhaps he takes a malicious delight in overwhelming
his reader with the sound of his learned words. Or perhaps he enjoys playing
the role of high priest as he presides over the mysteries of economics.

(c) Thorstein Veblen has a worthwhile purpose—to criticize the hedonistic theory of economics—but he never learned to write the clear, economical prose that displays consideration for the reader.

2. In what way does Veblen vary his sentence patterns? How many sentences
are simple *? How many are compound *? Complex *? Compound-complex?

3. Study the ways in which Veblen achieves emphasis through sentence struc-

ture. Find examples of (1) short sentences, (2) balanced constructions *, (3) periodic sentences *, (4) interrupted movement *, (5) parallelism *.

4. Does Veblen vary his sentence openers frequently or infrequently? What is his usual way of beginning a sentence? What is his most common variation?

5. One of the most obvious features of Veblen's prose is its wordiness or redundancy. Often he fails to place key ideas in the positions of subject, verb, object, preferring instead to tuck them away in some subordinate position. Thus, the clause in line 29 has for its subject *wealth* and for its verb *is not intended*. *Wealth is not intended* scarcely conveys the kernel of his meaning. Note that the 57 words of the two sentences in lines 25-31 can be expressed more clearly and vigorously in only 14 words: "Business men often accumulate more wealth than they need to satisfy their material desires." Find other instances of this kind of wordiness and try to express Veblen's idea more succinctly.

6. Veblen's sentences average about 45 words, being only a bit longer than Shaw's average of 41. How do they differ from Shaw's? Are they more or less effective? Why?

7. Study the following revisions of the first two sentences (1-7):

> According to the hedonistic theory, men work for money in order to obtain pleasure. Money has no meaning beyond allowing us to compute how much we can buy and enjoy.

Does this rewriting express the same ideas as Veblen's first two sentences? If not, why not? If so, what is the difference between the original and the revision?

8. Following in general the style and tone of the revision in question 7, rewrite the rest of the first paragraph.

9. Is Veblen's diction primarily formal or informal? What is the proportion of monosyllabic and disyllabic words to polysyllabic words?

10. Veblen uses few colloquial * expressions, contractions, dashes, italics, and parentheses. How would more frequent use of these have affected his tone *?

11. Does he use any figures of speech? Is there any place in this selection in which the writer reveals an emotional response to his subject? If so, where?

12. Does Veblen seem sensitive to the sounds of words? Does he use any rare, unusual, or surprising words?

13. Many of Veblen's words end in *-tion*, *-able*, and *-ance*. Sometimes such endings appear in the same phrase, as in "Variations of capitalization" (17) or in "sensations of consumption" (19). How does such diction affect you?

14. Does the passive voice appear frequently or infrequently in Veblen's prose? Does he employ a large vocabulary of verbs expressing action? What is the effect of a high proportion of passive verbs in expository prose?

15. If you admire this prose, what do you think are its virtues? If you deplore this kind of writing, do you think its failure results chiefly from defective sentence structure or from poor diction?

SUGGESTIONS FOR WRITING

1. Write an essay in which you contrast the prose of Shaw and Veblen. Use numerous examples.

2. Write an essay entitled "How to Write like Thorstein Veblen."

3. Choosing a trivial subject, such as "The Shortcomings of the Food in the College Dining Hall," write a parody of Veblen's style.

Courtesy to Readers—Clarity

F. L. Lucas (1894-1967)—British essayist and critic—was a Fellow of King's College, Cambridge, and a university Reader in English. His critical works reflect his interest in the personalities of writers and their moral values. Typical of his best criticism is *The Search for Good Sense; Four Eighteenth-Century Characters: Johnson, Chesterfield, Boswell, Goldsmith* (1958), a model of lively, urbane prose. Lucas was thoroughly grounded in the classics and widely acquainted with European literature. His familiarity with the finest prose in several languages accounts for the success of his book *Style* (1955), from which the following selection comes.

> One should not aim at being possible to understand, but at being impossible to misunderstand.   QUINTILIAN
>
> Obscurité . . . vicieuse affectation.   MONTAIGNE

1   Character, I have suggested, is the first thing to think about in style. The next step is to consider what characteristics can win a hearer's or a reader's sympathy. For example, it is bad manners to give them needless trouble. Therefore clarity. It is bad manners to waste their time. Therefore brevity.   5

2   There clings in my memory a story once told me by Professor Sisson. A Frenchman said to him: "In France it is the writer that takes the trouble; in Germany, the reader; in England it is betwixt and between." The generalization is over-simple; perhaps even libellous; but not without truth. It gives, I think, another reason why the level of French prose has   10 remained so high. And this may in its turn be partly because French culture has been based more than ours on conversation and the salon. In most conversation, if he is muddled, wordy, or tedious, a man is soon made,

unless he is a hippopotamus, to feel it. Further, the salon has been particularly influenced by women; who, as a rule, are less tolerant of tedium and 15
clumsiness than men.

3   First, then, clarity. The social purpose of language is communication—to inform, misinform, or otherwise influence our fellows. True, we also use words in solitude to think our own thoughts, and to express our feelings to ourselves. But writing is concerned rather with communication 20 than with self-communing; though some writers, especially poets, may talk to themselves in public. Yet, as I have said, even these, though in a sense overheard rather than heard, have generally tried to reach an audience. No doubt in some modern literature there has appeared a tendency to replace communication by a private maundering to oneself which shall inspire 25 one's audience to maunder privately to *themselves*—rather as if the author handed round a box of drugged cigarettes of his concoction to stimulate each guest to his own solitary dreams. But I have yet to be convinced that such activities are very valuable; or that one's own dreams and meditations are much heightened by the stimulus of some other voice soliloquizing in 30 Chinese. The irrational, now in politics, now in poetics, has been the sinister opium of our tormented and demented century.

4   For most prose, at all events, there is a good deal in Defoe's view of what style should be: "I would answer, that in which a man speaking to five hundred people, of all common and various capacities, idiots or lunatics 35 excepted, should be understood by them all." This is, indeed, very like the verdict of Anatole France on the three most important qualities of French style: "d'abord la clarté, puis encore la clarté, et enfin la clarté." Poetry, and poetic prose, may sometimes gain by a looming mystery like that of a mountain-cloud or thunderstorm; but ordinary prose, I think, is happiest 40 when it is clear as the air of a spring day in Attica.

5   True, obscurity cannot always be avoided. It is impossible to make easy the ideas of an Einstein, or the psychology of a Proust. But even abstruse subjects are often made needlessly difficult; for instance, by the type of philosopher who, sometimes from a sound instinct of self-preservation, 45 consistently refuses to illustrate his meaning by *examples*; or by the type of scientific writer who goes decked out with technical jargon as an Indian brave with feathers. Most obscurity is an unmixed, and unnecessary, evil.

6   It may be caused by incoherence; by inconsiderateness; by overcrowding of ideas; by pomp and circumstance; by sheer charlatanism; and 50 doubtless by other things I have not thought of.

· · ·

7   And how is clarity to be acquired? Mainly by taking trouble; and by writing to serve people rather than to impress them. Most obscurity, I suspect, comes not so much from incompetence as from ambition—the ambition to be admired for depth of sense, or pomp of sound, or wealth of ornament. It is for the writer to think and rethink his ideas till they are clear; to put them in a clear order; to prefer (other things equal, and subject to the law of variety) short words, sentences, and paragraphs to long; not to try to say too many things at once; to eschew irrelevances; and, above all, to put himself with imaginative sympathy in his reader's place. Everyone knows of Molière reading his plays to his cook; eight centuries before him, in distant China, Po Chu-i had done the like; and Swift's Dublin publisher, Faulkner, would similarly read Swift's proofs aloud to him and two of his men-servants—"which, if they did not comprehend, he would alter and amend, until they understood it perfectly well." In short, it is usually the pretentious and the egotistic who are obscure, especially in prose; those who write with wider sympathy, to serve some purpose beyond themselves, must usually be muddy-minded creatures if they cannot, or will not, be clear.

QUESTIONS

1. Contrast F. L. Lucas's sentences with those of Thorstein Veblen, especially with reference to length, the number of ideas expressed per sentence, and variety of sentence structure. How would you describe Lucas's most common type of sentence in this selection? What means does he employ to achieve emphasis in his sentences?

2. Identify the number and kind of sentence openers in this selection. Are they more or less varied than those in Thorstein Veblen's prose?

3. Most of Lucas's words are simple, and polysyllabic words do not occur as often as words of one and two syllables. Yet he sometimes uses rare or unusual words that help to give his prose interest, variety, and emphasis—*maundering*, for example (25). How many others can you identify?

4. Frequent allusions * and quotations are characteristic of Lucas's style. Point out several. Do these contribute to, or detract from, the clarity of his writing? Explain.

5. Several times Lucas uses metaphors * and similes *. Identify each one and explain its purpose. Rewrite each sentence containing one of these figures in order to express the same idea in nonfigurative language. Describe the difference in effect in each instance.

6. Does Lucas win his reader's sympathy in this selection? If so, how? If not, why not?

7. Describe as fully as you can the personality behind this prose. What are Lucas's assumptions about writing, about literature, about what we vaguely call a philosophy of life? What does he like and dislike? How does he regard his reader? What kind of reader might be hostile to this writer?

SUGGESTIONS FOR WRITING

1. Imitating this style generally, but not slavishly, write an essay on the virtue of either economy or simplicity in prose.

2. Rewrite one or two of Lucas's paragraphs in the style of Veblen.

3. Choosing your best theme, compare and contrast your own prose with that of F. L. Lucas. Try also to improve the clarity and grace of one of your less successful themes by applying Lucas's advice.

Hester Prynne

Mark Van Doren—literary critic and for many years Professor of Literature at Columbia University—is also a distinguished poet and novelist. In 1939 his *Collected Poems* won the Pulitzer Prize. Van Doren's literary criticism includes books on Henry David Thoreau, Edward Arlington Robinson, John Dryden, and Shakespeare. *Nathaniel Hawthorne* (1949) helped to re-evaluate Hawthorne as an American novelist of the first rank.

In *The Scarlet Letter*, Hawthorne's finest novel, the heroine is Hester Prynne. Hester, whose elderly husband has long been missing and presumed dead, has a child by her unmarried minister, the Reverend Arthur Dimmesdale. When she refuses to reveal the identity of her child's father, the Puritan magistrates condemn her to stand for hours on the prison scaffold and to wear a scarlet A (for adultress) upon her dress for the remainder of her life. Hester's husband re-appears in the Puritan village but calls himself Roger Chillingworth to keep his identity secret in order to find and avenge himself upon the man who has wronged him. He quickly learns that the Reverend Dimmesdale was Hester's lover. For several years he spitefully torments the minister. Hester and Dimmesdale consider escaping from the Puritan settlement, but Dimmesdale's profound guilt forces him to confess his sin publicly, and thereafter he dies.

This excerpt from *Nathaniel Hawthorne* examines the character of Hester Prynne.

1   . . . *The Scarlet Letter*, brief though it is and barren of incident though it seems, is packed with pictures and events; real at the center, it is rich at every portion of its surface. But any synopsis serves to show that the situation of the principals is indeed concrete. Never before has Hawthorne dealt with stuff so solid; and never again will he be so able or content to let his people determine his plot. His plot in this case is his people.   5

From *Nathaniel Hawthorne* by Mark Van Doren. Copyright © 1949 by William Sloane Associates, Inc. Reprinted by permission of William Morrow & Co., Inc.

615

2   Above all it is Hester Prynne, whose passion and beauty dominate every other person, and color each event. Hawthorne has conceived her as he has conceived his scene, in the full strength of his feeling for ancient New England. He is the Homer of that New England, as Hester is its most 10 heroic creature. Tall, with dark and abundant hair and deep black eyes, a rich complexion that makes modern women (says Hawthorne) pale and thin by comparison, and a dignity that throws into low relief the "delicate, evanescent, and indescribable grace" by which gentility in girls has since come to be known, from the very first—and we believe it—she is said to 15 cast a spell over those who behold her; and this is not merely because of the scarlet letter, "so fantastically embroidered and illuminated," upon the bosom of her always magnificent dress. It is because of herself, into whom Hawthorne has known how to put a unique importance. Nor is this a remote, a merely stately importance. We are close to her all of the time, and 20 completely convinced of her flesh and blood, of her heart and mind. She is a passionate woman whom Hawthorne does not need to call passionate, for he has the evidence: her state of excitement, bordering on frenzy, in the prison after her first exposure to the crowd—her "moral agony," reflected in the convulsions that have seized the child; her pride, her daring, in after 25 days when she makes more show than she needs to make of the letter on her bosom, the symbol she insists upon adorning with such "wild and picturesque peculiarity"; her alternations of despair and defiance; her continuing love, so unconfessed that we can only assume it to be there, for the man whose weakness seems so little to deserve it; her power of speech, so eco- 30 nomical and so tender, when at last she is with this man; her sudden revelation that through years of loneliness she has not consented to let her soul be killed.

3   "I pity thee," says Chillingworth near the close, "for the good that has been wasted in thy nature." These are terrible words, for they express 35 a fear we have had, the fear that this magnificent woman has lived for nothing; for a few days of love, and then for dreary years of less indeed than nothing. Hawthorne has known how to fasten this fear upon us—it could exist in us only if we loved her too—but he also has known how to make Chillingworth's words untrue. The life of Hester increases, not diminishes, 40 in the bleak world whose best citizen she is. Nor is this done by Hawthorne at the expense of that world. He deplores the "dismal severity" of its moral code, and for all we know he is presenting Hester as the blackest sacrifice it ever offered on its altar. But he is not doctrinaire against the code. His Puritan world is in its own way beautiful. It fully exists, as Hester fully 45

exists. If their existences conflict, then that is the tragedy to be understood. Hester, whose solitary thought takes her far beyond the confines of the code, is nevertheless respectful of the strength in it that could kill her were she not even stronger. She is not the subject of a sermon; she is the heroine of a tragedy, and she understands the tragedy. She understands it because 50 Hawthorne does; because at the same time that he recoils from the Puritan view of sin he honors its capacity to be a view at all. Sin for him, for Hester, and for the people who punish her is equally a solemn fact, a problem for which there is no solution in life. There was no other solution for his story, given Hester's strength, Dimmesdale's weakness, and Chillingworth's per- 55 version, than the one he found. Rather, as we read, it finds itself. And if the conclusion is not depressing, the reason is that nothing before it has been meaningless. This world has not been really bleak. It has been as beautiful as it was terrible; Hester's life has not been hollow, nor has her great nature been wasted. 60

QUESTIONS

1. Mark Van Doren's average sentence length is nearer to that of F. L. Lucas and Pierre Champion than to that of Thorstein Veblen and George Bernard Shaw. But as we know intuitively, the voice, the personality behind Van Doren's prose is different from that of any of the others. This difference in "assumed" personality combined with a different purpose and a different "assumed" ideal reader produces Van Doren's characteristic way of writing, his style. His style, in part, results from an effective interplay of sentence structure and diction. Note, for example, the balanced repetition of nearly identical phrases in the first clause of the first sentence: "brief *though it is*" coordinated with "barren of incident *though it seems*." Find other examples of this device. Is it frequent or infrequent? What two purposes does it serve? What is its effect upon the reader?

2. Related to this kind of structure is negative-positive restatement *. For example in line 16 we find ". . . this is not merely because of the scarlet letter . . ." The next sentence begins "It is because of herself . . ." Locate one or two similar examples.

3. Two of Van Doren's sentences are unusually long: the first beginning "Tall, with dark and abundant hair . . ." (11-18) is some 92 words long; the second beginning "She is a passionate woman . . ." (21-33) is some 148 words long. Are these sentences easy or difficult to comprehend? Do they have a clear shape? Why or why not? Would the writer's prose be improved if he had divided each long sentence into several shorter ones? Or would something impor-

tant (besides mere variety) have been lost? If most of a writer's sentences are short or moderately long, is a very long sentence likely to seem emphatic? Why or why not? Do Van Doren's long sentences seem to express strong feeling? Explain.

4. The voice behind this prose sounds clear, forceful, and authoritative. The author seems to have thought about his subject profoundly, and he expresses himself incisively. Point to phrases and sentences that convey this kind of tone *.

5. What is Mark Van Doren's attitude toward *The Scarlet Letter?* Toward Hester Prynne? What is his principal means of conveying these attitudes?

6. An effective style ought to make the reader approve of the man the writer seems to be. The style ought to persuade the reader or at least win his respect. Of the writers whom we have so far analyzed in this section, which do you think has the most persuasive style? Which one has the least? Why?

SUGGESTIONS FOR WRITING

1. Choosing a character from literature whom you admire, describe him in a sentence between 100 and 150 words long, using as a model Mark Van Doren's sentence beginning in line 26.

2. Write a short essay in which you describe as completely as possible the kind of man the writer of "Hester Prynne" seems to be. Use short quotations to support your points.

3. Write a short essay in which you describe the sort of person you seem to be in your best theme. Try to be as objective and as fair as you can. If appropriate, point out where and how you might have improved your style.

On The Scarlet Letter

D. H. Lawrence (1885-1930) wrote some of the most important fiction in twentieth-century British literature. While he was also a poet and essayist, Lawrence's reputation rests upon such novels as *Sons and Lovers* (1913), *Women in Love* (1920, 1921), and *Lady Chatterley's Lover* (final version, 1928). The last is among the first novels of stature in contemporary literature to treat sex explicitly and frankly. In 1922 Lawrence lived for about three years in Taos, New Mexico, becoming interested in nineteenth-century American writers such as Hawthorne, Franklin, Cooper, Poe, Dana, Melville, and Whitman—whose works, Lawrence believed, reflected the essential character of the United States. The result was *Studies in Classic American Literature* (1923), from which come the following comments about Hester Prynne, the heroine of Hawthorne's *The Scarlet Letter*. In style and tone, as you will see, Lawrence's prose is very different from Van Doren's.

1   *The Scarlet Letter* gives the show away.

2   You have your pure-pure young parson Dimmesdale.

3   You have the beautiful Puritan Hester at his feet.

4   And the first thing she does is to seduce him.

5   And the first thing he does is to be seduced.   5

6   And the second thing they do is to hug their sin in secret, and gloat over it, and try to understand.

7   Which is the myth of New England.

8   Deerslayer refused to be seduced by Judith Hutter. At least the Sodom apple of sin didn't fetch him.   10

9   But Dimmesdale was seduced gloatingly. Oh, luscious Sin!

10   He was such a pure young man.

11   That he had to make a fool of purity.

12   The American psyche.

13   Of course the best part of the game lay in keeping up pure appear-   15
ances.

14   The greatest triumph a woman can have, especially an American
woman, is the triumph of seducing a man: especially if he is pure.

15   And he gets the greatest thrill of all, in falling.—"Seduce me, Mrs.
Hercules."   20

16   And the pair of them share the subtlest delight in keeping up pure
appearances, when everybody knows all the while. But the power of pure
appearances is something to exult in. All America gives in to it. *Look
pure!*

17   To seduce a man. To have everybody know. To keep up appearances   25
of purity. Pure!

18   This is the great triumph of woman.

19   A. The Scarlet Letter. Adulteress! The great Alpha. Alpha! Adulteress! The new Adam and Adama! American!

20   A. Adulteress! Stitched with gold thread, glittering upon the bosom.   30
The proudest insignia.

21   Put her upon the scaffold and worship her there. Worship her
there. The Woman, the Magna Mater. A. Adulteress! Abel!

22   Abel! Abel! Abel! Admirable!

23   It becomes a farce.   35

24   The fiery heart. A. Mary of the Bleeding Heart. Mater Adolerata!
A. Capital A. Adulteress. Glittering with gold thread. Abel! Adultery. Admirable!

25   It is, perhaps, the most colossal satire ever penned. *The Scarlet
Letter*. And by a blue-eyed darling of a Nathaniel.   40

26   Not Bumppo, however.

27   The human spirit, fixed in a lie, adhering to a lie, giving itself perpetually the lie.

28   All begins with A.

29   Adulteress. Alpha. Abel, Adam. A. America.   45

30   *The Scarlet Letter.*

31   "Had there been a Papist among the crowd of Puritans, he might
have seen in this beautiful woman, so picturesque in her attire and mien,
and with the infant at her bosom, an object to remind him of the image of
Divine Maternity, which so many illustrious painters have vied with one   50

another to represent; something which should remind him, indeed, but only by contrast, of that sacred image of sinless Motherhood, whose infant was to redeem the world."

32   Whose infant was to redeem the world indeed! It will be a startling redemption the world will get from the American infant.

33   "Here was a taint of deepest sin in the most sacred quality of human life, working such effect that the world was only the darker for this woman's beauty, and more lost for the infant she had borne."

34   Just listen to the darling. Isn't he a master of apology?

35   Of symbols, too.

36   His pious blame is a chuckle of praise all the while.

37   Oh, Hester, you are a demon. A man *must* be pure, just that you can seduce him to a fall. Because the greatest thrill in life is to bring down the Sacred Saint with a flop into the mud. Then when you've brought him down, humbly wipe off the mud with your hair, another Magdalen. And then go home and dance a witch's jig of triumph, and stitch yourself a Scarlet Letter with gold thread, as duchesses used to stitch themselves coronets. And then stand meek on the scaffold and fool the world. Who will all be envying you your sin, and beating you because you've stolen an advantage over them.

38   Hester Prynne is the great nemesis of woman. She is the KNOWING Ligeia risen diabolic from the grave. Having her own back. UNDERSTANDING.

39   This time it is Mr. Dimmesdale who dies. She lives on and is Abel.

40   His spiritual love was a lie. And prostituting the woman to his spiritual love, as popular clergymen do, in his preachings and loftiness, was a tall white lie. Which came flop.

41   We are so pure in spirit. Hi-tiddly-i-ty!

42   Till she tickled him in the right place, and he fell.

43   Flop.

44   Flop goes spiritual love.

45   But keep up the game. Keep up appearances. Pure are the pure. To the pure all things, etc.

46   Look out, Mister, for the Female Devotee. Whatever you do, don't let her start tickling you. She knows your weak spot. Mind your Purity.

47   When Hester Prynne seduced Arthur Dimmesdale it was the beginning of the end. But from the beginning of the end to the end of the end is a hundred years or two.

QUESTIONS

1. One need hardly say that Lawrence's manner of writing in this selection is the most individualistic and most extreme expression of personality among all those represented in this textbook. Indeed, a more extreme manner would be difficult to find in all literature. Most immediately apparent are Lawrence's numerous devices to achieve emphasis. See if you can list and illustrate five or six ways Lawrence creates emphasis through sentence structure. Find at least three ways in which punctuation adds to his emphasis and tone *.

2. Lawrence's diction includes colloquialisms, highly connotative * words and phrases, many simple Anglo-Saxon words of one and two syllables, contractions, words chosen for their sounds, and rare or unusual words. Find examples of each kind.

3. Make a list of Lawrence's allusions *. Try to explain the significance of each one.

4. Lawrence also uses many formal, Latinate words. What is the proportion of these words to the simpler diction he employs? Is the total effect of his writing formal or informal? Can you justify his use of Latinate diction?

5. What virtues does Lawrence's prose have in this selection? What might be said to be its most serious, and perhaps fatal, defect? Lawrence had never used this style before and he never used it again in his novels or essays. Why not, do you think?

6. Although Lawrence admires *The Scarlet Letter* for its psychological insights and its essential truth, he calls it "the most colossal satire ever penned" (39) and in line 35 a "farce." In contrast, Mark Van Doren thinks of *The Scarlet Letter* as a tragedy. Is there any way to account for this difference in interpretation?

7. Which of the two writers seems to you the more objective and judicious? What is Lawrence's attitude toward himself? How does his prose reflect the way his mind works? How does he regard Hawthorne? Hester Prynne? Dimmesdale?

8. Most important of all, how does he regard the reader?

9. Which of the following judgments do you think comes closest to describing the voice and personality behind Lawrence's prose in this selection?

> (a) The writer assumes himself to be half infallible oracle, half secular preacher. Instead of treating his subject rationally or logically, he tries to persuade the reader almost entirely by emotion. He intones, he incants, he exaggerates, he sneers, he shouts; he intimidates and browbeats his reader. His interpretation of *The Scarlet Letter* is more concerned with his own personality and his own preoccupation with the battle of the sexes than with Hawthorne's novel.

(b) Lawrence is a courageous rebel who alone has seen through the humbug that permeates much of nineteenth-century American literature. His style is extreme because it expresses his contempt for tradition and propriety, both of which involve hypocrisy.

SUGGESTIONS FOR WRITING

1. Lawrence's prose is an extreme example of the segregating style. His sentences—exclusive of the quotations from Hawthorne—average only five or six words. Revise this selection using an aggregating style and conventional paragraph development. Make the tone emphatic but less so than the original.

2. Write a parody of Lawrence's style, using, say, *Hamlet, Macbeth,* or some novel you know well.

3. Both Lawrence and Shaw are writers who tend to preach. They often regard their reader as groping about in outer darkness and needing to be saved. Yet their effects upon their readers are very different. Contrast and evaluate Lawrence's and Shaw's methods of persuading their readers.

From In Our Time

Ernest Hemingway (1898-1961) wrote short stories and novels whose style has influenced hundreds of writers. Much of his finest work was done in the twenties—novels such as *The Sun Also Rises* (1926), *A Farewell to Arms* (1929), and collections of short stories like *Men Without Women* (1927). The following selection is taken from another collection of stories, *In Our Time* (1925), most of which have to do with a young man's encounters with the suffering, evil, and emptiness of life shortly before and after World War I. Between each pair of stories is a brief, untitled narrative vignette or "snapshot" unrelated to the stories themselves, except in so far as each depicts a scene of violence or horror typical of our time. The following piece is one of those vignettes. Keep in mind that it is a total composition, complete within itself.

They shot the six cabinet ministers at half-past six in the morning against the wall of a hospital. There were pools of water in the courtyard. There were wet dead leaves on the paving of the courtyard. It rained hard. All the shuttters of the hospital were nailed shut. One of the ministers was sick with typhoid. Two soldiers carried him down stairs and out into the rain. They tried to 5 hold him up against the wall but he sat down in a puddle of water. The other five stood very quietly against the wall. Finally the officer told the soldiers it was no good trying to make him stand up. When they fired the first volley he was sitting down in the water with his head on his knees.

QUESTIONS

1. This selection is about as simple as a style can be without appearing childish or child-like. At the same time this prose is highly sophisticated, and its impact upon the reader is powerful. What is its emotional effect?

2. Count the number of sentences and the number of words in each sentence. What is the number of words in the shortest sentence? In the longest? What is the average number of words in Hemingway's sentences? How does this average compare with the average length of sentences in Champion, Shaw, Veblen, Lucas, Van Doren, and Lawrence?

3. What is Hemingway's most common sentence opener? How many of these does he use? What variations does he employ and how often?

4. Sentences 1, 2, and 3 have about the same construction and the same rhythm. Demonstrate this fact by analyzing the structure of each sentence. What is the effect upon the reader of treating an execution and the description of a court-yard in exactly the same tone, or seeming lack of tone?

5. The fourth sentence—three words of one syllable—is a variation in sentence length and paragraph rhythm. Ordinarily such a variation underscores an important point. Here, it laconically describes the weather rather than the execution. Why?

6. Observe how many sentences end with a prepositional phrase or a series of prepositional phrases. How do these constructions affect the rhythm of the paragraph? Do they tend to make the sentences emphatic or unemphatic? Do they help to make the whole paragraph strongly rhythmic? Why or why not? Is a strong sentence rhythm an advantage or a disadvantage in this selection? Explain.

7. Hemingway's last sentence might have been written: "When he was sitting down in the water with his head on his knees they fired the first volley." Why does this revision detract from Hemingway's stylistic strategy and purpose?

8. Hemingway uses no punctuation within his sentences. Where might he have used semicolons, commas, or dashes? Why is this prose better without such internal punctuation?

9. Note the number of repetitions in this selection. For example, the second sentence ends "in the courtyard"; the third sentence ends "of the courtyard." Identify seven or eight similar repetitions or echoes. In this passage at least, they seem to be an important feature of Hemingway's style. What do you think is their purpose or their effect on the reader?

10. Hemingway uses very few adjectives in this prose. Most of these are merely denotative: there are *six* cabinet ministers; "*Two* soldiers carried him down stairs . . ." and so on. In each sentence Hemingway seems merely to be telling us tonelessly and precisely who did what, where, and when. The one exception is the reference to "wet dead leaves" in line 3. *Wet* and *dead* are, of course, concrete and denotative, but they have connotations too. Why doesn't Hemingway apply connotative adjectives to the ministers about to be executed?

11. Describe in detail the kind of man the writer of this prose seems to be. Does he succeed in making the reader like or respect him? Is his prose more or less persuasive than that of D. H. Lawrence?

SUGGESTIONS FOR WRITING

1. Revise Hemingway's sketch using an aggregating style. Supply details, sentence patterns, and diction that will more directly and obviously elicit the horror of the scene.

2. Imitating the principles of style employed by Hemingway, describe a combat operation, a painful event, a disaster or catastrophe that you have witnessed or taken part in.

Household Apples

William Gass, born in North Dakota, is a novelist and a teacher of philosophy. Among his most successful works are *Omensetter's Luck* (1966) and *Willie Master's Lonesome Wife* (1968). In the excellent collection of stories titled *In the Heart of the Heart of the Country* (1968), from which "Household Apples" is an excerpt, Gass's narrator—a teacher, philosopher, poet—has returned to the small town in Indiana where he spent his childhood. A part of his being merges with the daily life of the town, while another part observes, judges, interprets, and responds emotionally. The narrator's descriptions of the town, his friends and neighbors, the strangers on the street, his home, and the nearby countryside are colored by his feelings about his past, about an unhappy love affair, and about the deterioration of life in the geographical heart of America.

1   I knew nothing about apples. Why should I? My country came in my childhood, and I dreamed of sitting among the blooms like the bees. I failed to spray the pear tree too. I doubled up under them at first, admiring the sturdy low branches I should have pruned, and later I acclaimed the blossoms. Shortly after the fruit formed there were falls—not many—apples 5 the size of goodish stones which made me wobble on my ankles when I walked about the yard. Sometimes a piece crushed by a heel would cling on the shoe to track the house. I gathered a few and heaved them over the wires. A slingshot would have been splendid. Hard, an unattractive green, the worms had them. Before long I realized the worms had them all. Even 10 as the apples reddened, lit their tree, they were being swallowed. The birds preferred the pears, which were small—sugar pears I think they're called— with thick skins of graying green that ripen on toward violet. So the fruit fell, and once I made some applesauce by quartering and paring hundreds; but mostly I did nothing, left them, until suddenly, overnight it seemed, in 15

From *In the Heart of the Heart of the Country and Other Stories*. Copyright © 1967 by William H. Gass. Reprinted by permission of International Creative Management and Deborah Rogers Ltd.

that ugly late September heat we often have in Indiana, my problem was upon me.

2   My childhood came in the country. I remember, now, the flies on our snowy luncheon table. As we cleared away they would settle, fastidiously scrub themselves and stroll to the crumbs to feed where I would kill them in crowds with a swatter. It was quite a game to catch them taking off. I struck heavily since I didn't mind a few stains; they'd wash. The swatter was a square of screen bound down in red cloth. It drove no air ahead of it to give them warning. They might have thought they'd flown headlong into a summered window. The faint pink dot where they had died did not rub out as I'd supposed, and after years of use our luncheon linen would faintly, pinkly, speckle.

3   The country became my childhood. Flies braided themselves on the flypaper in my grandmother's house. I can smell the bakery and the grocery and the stables and the dairy in that small Dakota town I knew as a kid; knew as I dreamed I'd know your body, as I've known nothing, before or since; knew as the flies knew, in the honest, unchaste sense: the burned house, hose-wet, which drew a mist of insects like the blue smoke of its smolder, and gangs of boys, moist-lipped, destructive as its burning. Flies have always impressed me; they are so persistently alive. Now they were coating the ground beneath my trees. Some were ordinary flies; there were the large blue-green ones; there were swarms of fruit flies too, and the red-spotted scavenger beetle; there were a few wasps, several sorts of bees and butterflies—checkers, sulphurs, monarchs, commas, question marks— and delicate dragonflies . . . but principally houseflies and horseflies and bottleflies, flies and more flies in clusters around the rotting fruit. They loved the pears. Inside, they fed. If you picked up a pear, they flew, and the pear became skin and stem. They were everywhere the fruit was: in the tree still—apples like a hive for them—or where the fruit littered the ground, squashing itself as you stepped . . . there was no help for it. The flies droned, feasting on the sweet juice. No one could go near the trees; I could not climb; so I determined at last to labor like Hercules. There were fruit baskets in the barn. Collecting them and kneeling under the branches, I began to gather remains. Deep in the strong rich smell of the fruit, I began to hum myself. The fruit caved in at the touch. Glistening red apples, my lifting disclosed, had families of beetles, flies, and bugs, devouring their rotten undersides. There were streams of flies; there were lakes and cataracts and rivers of flies, seas and oceans. The hum was heavier, higher, than the hum of the bees when they came to the blooms in the spring, though the

bees were there, among the flies, ignoring me—ignoring everyone. As my ₅₅
work went on and juice covered my hands and arms, they would form a
sleeve, black and moving, like knotty wool. No caress could have been more
indifferently complete. Still I rose fearfully, ramming my head in the
branches, apples bumping against me before falling, bursting with bugs.
I'd snap my hand sharply but the flies would cling to the sweet. I could toss 6o
a whole cluster into a basket from several feet. As the pear or apple lit, they
would explosively rise, like monads for a moment, windowless, certainly,
with respect to one another, sugar their harmony. I had to admit, though,
despite my distaste, that my arm had never been more alive, oftener or
more gently kissed. Those hundreds of feet were light. In washing them off, 65
I pretended the hose was a pump. What have I missed? Childhood is a lie
of poetry.

QUESTIONS

1. "In the Heart of the Heart of the Country" consists of loosely connected
vignettes of small-town daily life and meditations thereon, with titles like
"Politics," "Place," "People," "My House, my Cat, my Company," and
"Weather." Recurring motifs and themes unify the several sections. From time
to time, for instance, the narrator addresses the woman he loves, even though
she is not present. Is he speaking to anyone in "Household Apples," or is it
more in the nature of a private meditation? What theme does he develop?
Observe that in each paragraph Gass rings changes upon the words *country*
and *childhood*. Identify these echoes and explain how each varies or develops
the key idea.
2. Does Gass combine a number of ideas in each sentence, or tend rather
to use a series of short sentences each containing a single idea? Underline each
short sentence (say, ten words or less) and bracket each sentence of twenty-five
words or more. Which is the writer's shortest sentence? Which his longest?
3. Sentences of description alternate with more abstract *, pithy sentences
which summarize or interpret. Find several examples of each type.
4. Explain why the revision that follows is less emotive and emphatic than
Gass's sentence:

> *Revision:* Some were ordinary flies; large blue-green ones were numer-
> ous also; there were swarms of fruit flies as well as many scavenger
> beetles; a few wasps could be seen, along with different kinds of bees
> and butterflies, but most of the insects were flies, which were swarming
> all over the rotting fruit.

Gass: "Some were ordinary flies; there were the large blue-green ones; there were swarms of fruit flies too, and the red-spotted scavenger beetle; there were a few wasps, several sorts of bees and butterflies—checkers, sulphurs, monarchs, commas, question marks—and delicate dragonflies . . . but principally houseflies and horseflies and bottleflies, flies and more flies in clusters around the rotting fruit." (36-41)

5. The following sentence illustrates the subtle interplay of style and sense which is a hallmark of good writing. Study it and then answer the questions listed after it:

"I can smell the bakery and the grocery and the stables and the dairy in that small Dakota town I knew as a kid; knew as I dreamed I'd known your body, as I've known nothing, before or since; knew as the flies knew, in the honest, unchaste sense: the burned house, hose-wet, which drew a mist of insects like the blue smoke of its smolder, and gangs of boys, moist-lipped, destructive as its burning." (29-34)

(a) Knowledge, this sentence suggests, comes from intense sensuous experience, especially that involving touch and smell. What word, repeated in various forms, emphasizes this theme? Show that the repetition of the key term is related to the parallelism * that gives the sentence its basic structure.

(b) How are the narrator and the woman he loves related to the flies and the burned, smoldering house? Note that in the phrase "the honest, unchaste sense," *honest* and *unchaste* are made synonymous. In what way do they mean the same thing?

(c) How are the boys like flies?

(d) *Hose-wet* and *moist-lipped* are nonce compounds invented by the author. Explain what each implies. How does Gass emphasize them within the sentence?

(e) Point to examples in the sentence of polysyndeton *, metaphor *, simile *, anaphora *.

6. In "Household Apples" the narrator feels a near-identity between the human and the natural, between himself and the trees, fruit, and insects. In several instances the narrator seems to merge with the insects, and, once, the behavior of the boys is identical to that of the flies. Explain how the sentence is constructed so as to suggest this identity.

7. At the same time the narrator is not being sentimental about insects by making them into persons. Where does he acknowledge their "otherness"?

8. In the sentence beginning "As the pear or apple . . ." (61-63), the narrator compares the flies to windowless monads, a phrase drawn from the German philosopher Leibnitz (1646-1716), for whom monads are the basic elements of

physical reality—indivisible, self-contained units, "windowless" because they are not subject to outside influence. What does the comparison reveal about the flies? Does it imply anything about the narrator?

9. As details about the flies accumulate, they become symbolic *. What do you think they represent?

10. The concreteness of Gass's diction creates an intensely sensuous reality, which is one source of our enjoyment. But at the same time Gass makes us feel deeply about his subject. One way in which he imbues his writing with emotion is to pay particular attention to the sounds of his words. For example, he uses alliteration *—not the Peter-Piper-picked-a-peck-of-pickled-peppers kind, but a more restrained, more elusive variety. Thus in the first paragraph he writes of "sitting among the blooms like the bees." Identify as many other instances of alliteration as you can.

11. One theme in "Household Apples" is nature's almost overwhelming super-abundance, richness, senuousness, and multiplicity. As a way of summarizing the qualities of Gass's prose, list all the stylistic techniques he uses to make this impression.

SUGGESTIONS FOR WRITING

1. Rewrite this piece, making your purpose to eliminate all subjective responses, all emotional coloring.

2. Imitate, generally but not slavishly, Gass's style and subject in any essay describing your close involvement with some part of the natural world.

3. Write an analysis of "Household Apples," stressing its similarity to poetry.

4. Read Robert Frost's poem "After Apple-Picking," and compare it with "Household Apples." Discuss particularly the different emotional impacts of the two works.

From Holiday Memory

Dylan Thomas (1914-53), one of the finest of modern British poets, also wrote stories, essays, and autobiographical sketches, which appeared in *Portrait of the Artist as a Young Dog* (1946) and *Quite Early One Morning* (1954), pieces collected by his publisher after Thomas's death. While some of these essays concern poets and writing poetry, others describe Thomas's childhood and adolescence in Swansea, Wales, where he was born and where he lived until 1934. The following excerpt from "Holiday Memory" reveals a poet's mastery of words and rhythm. It deserves to be read aloud more than once.

1   I remember the smell of sea and seaweed, wet flesh, wet hair, wet bathing-dresses, the warm smell as of a rabbity field after rain, the smell of pop and splashed sunshades and toffee, the stable-and-straw smell of hot, tossed, tumbled, dug and trodden sand, the swill-and-gaslamp smell of Saturday night, though the sun shone strong, from the bellying beer-tents, the   5
smell of the vinegar on shelled cockles, winkle-smell, shrimp-smell, the dripping-oily back-street winter-smell of chips in newspapers, the smell of ships from the sundazed docks around the corner of the sandhills, the smell of the known and paddled-in sea moving, full of the drowned and herrings, out and away and beyond and further still towards the antipodes that hung   10
their koala-bears and Maoris, kangaroos and boomerangs, upside down over the backs of the stars.

2   And the noise of pummelling Punch and Judy falling, and a clock tolling or telling no time in the tenantless town; now and again a bell from a lost tower or a train on the lines behind us clearing its throat, and always   15
the hopeless, ravenous swearing and pleading of the gulls, donkey-bray and hawker-cry, harmonicas and toy trumpets, shouting and laughing and singing, hooting of tugs and tramps, the clip of the chair-attendant's puncher, the

motor-boat coughing in the bay, and the same hymn and washing of
the sea that was heard in the Bible.   20

3   "If it could only just, if it could only just," your lips said again and
again as you scooped, in the hob-hot sand, dungeons, garages, torture-cham-
bers, train tunnels, arsenals (hangars for zeppelins, witches' kitchens, vam-
pires' parlours, smugglers' cellars, trolls' grog-shops, sewers, under the ponderous and cracking castle, "If it could only just be like this for ever and   25
ever amen." August Monday all over the earth, from Mumbles where the
aunties grew like ladies on a seaside tree to brown, bear-hugging Henty-land
and the turtled Ballantyne Islands.

4   "Could donkeys go on the ice?"
         "Only if they got snowshoes."   30
         We snowshoed a meek, complaining donkey and galloped him off in
the wake of the ten-foot-tall and Atlas-muscled Mounties, rifled and pem-
micanned, who always, in the white Gold Rush wastes, got their black-
oathed-and-bearded Man.
         "Are there donkeys on desert islands?"   35
         "Only sort-of-donkeys."
         "What d'you mean, sort of donkeys?"
         "Native donkeys. They hunt things on them!"
         "Sort-of walruses and seals and things?"
         "Donkeys can't swim!"   40
         "These donkeys can. They swim like whales, they swim like any-
             thing, they swim like—"
         "Liar."
         "Liar yourself."

5   And two small boys fought fiercely and silently in the sand, rolling   45
together in a ball of legs and bottoms. Then they went and saw the pier-
rots, or bought vanilla ices.

6   Lolling or larriking that unsoiled, boiling beauty of a common day,
great gods with their braces over their vests sang, spat pips, puffed smoke
at wasps, gulped and ogled, forgot the rent, embraced, posed for the dicky   50
bird, were coarse, had rainbow-coloured arm-pits, winked, belched, blamed
the radishes, looked at Ilfracombe, played hymns on paper and comb,
peeled bananas, scratched, found seaweed in their panamas, blew up paper-
bags and banged them, wished for nothing. But over all the beautiful
beach I remember most the children playing, boys and girls tumbling, mov- 55
ing jewels, who might never be happy again. And "happy as a sandboy" is
true as the heat of the sun.

QUESTIONS

1. This sample of Dylan Thomas's prose is taken from the essay "Holiday Memory," a composite, no doubt, of many August holidays by the seaside near the author's native town of Swansea, Wales. As often happens, a sophisticated adult is writing of childhood and sees it partly through the eyes of a child and partly from the more mature point of view * of an adult. This double vision gives to Thomas's essay a specific tone *. Point out passages which suggest the child's view; others that reveal the adult's.

2. The first paragraph is a single sentence of about 130 words. Should it have been divided into two or three shorter sentences? Explain why you think it is, or is not, overloaded.

3. In the first paragraph what is the ratio of verbs to adjectives? Which carries most of the description?

4. How many adjectives in the first paragraph are single words; how many are compounds; and how many are participles *, either past or present?

5. Thomas's compound adjectives are especially striking. What are some of their advantages? Can you easily find one-word equivalents for those Thomas uses in the first paragraph? Do they have any disadvantages?

6. If for emphasis a writer repeats a single word in several sentences or throughout an entire paragraph, he is using a rhetorical figure called *tautotes*. Identify the tautotes in paragraph 1.

7. Find two examples of polysyndeton * in the first sentence of this selection.

8. Why does Thomas include the details in line 11? What do they tell us about the child?

9. How are the diction and sentence structure of paragraph 2 like those of paragraph 1? How do the two paragraphs differ?

10. What is unusual about the structure of the first sentence of paragraph 3?

11. How does this revision alter the emphasis and movement of Thomas's sentence?

> *Revision:* I remember the noise as Punch pummelled Judy and both fell. A clock struck and told no time in the empty town; now and then a bell from a lost tower or a train on the lines cleared its throat. Hopeless, ravenous gulls pleaded and swore. Donkeys brayed and hawkers cried.
>
> *Thomas:* "And the noise of pummelling Punch and Judy falling, and a clock tolling or telling no time in the tenantless town; now and again a bell from a lost tower or a train on the lines behind us clearing its throat, and always the hopeless, ravenous swearing and pleading of the gulls, donkey-bray and hawker-cry. . . ." (13-17)

12. How many abstract * words can you find in this selection? How many rare words and technical terms? Are many of Thomas's words derived from Latin? Do many of his words, or only a few of them, refer to things intrinsically beautiful?

13. Dylan Thomas was a famous poet, and he has a poet's ear for language, exploiting such qualities of sound as onomatopoeia, alliteration *, assonance *, and consonance *. Point out examples of each of these.

14. Thomas is also fond of metaphor *, simile *, personification *, and puns, all of which are devices more common in poetry, though certainly found also in prose. Find instances of these.

15. Finally, he uses an occasional adjective in the post position * (that is, placed after the noun instead of before it) and employs grammatical shift now and then (the use of a word which is normally one part of speech to function as another, as a verb acting as a noun). Find some examples.

SUGGESTIONS FOR WRITING

1. Compare the prose styles of William Gass's "Household Apples" and the passage from "Holiday Memory," discussing both their similarities and their differences.

2. It has been claimed that "style is the man"; that is, that style is a manifestation of the writer's essential personality. Describe the personality of Dylan Thomas as it is reflected through his prose.

3. Write about some group activity that you have enjoyed. Try to be as concrete in your imagery as Thomas and to use a wide range of verbal effects (but don't fall into the bad habit of repeating any of these so much that it becomes a mannerism).

Glossary

This glossary offers brief definitions of those grammatical and rhetorical terms that are used in the questions. The first time such a term appears in any group of questions, it is marked with an asterisk, a signal that it appears in the Glossary.

ABSOLUTE CONSTRUCTION: A word or phrase grammatically unrelated to any one part of a sentence is absolute. "The candle stood on the counter, *its flame solemnly wagging in a draught;* and by that inconsiderable movement the whole room was filled with noiseless bustle and kept heaving like a sea: *the tall shadows nodding, the gross blots of darkness swelling and dwindling as with respiration, the faces of the portraits and the china gods changing and wavering like images in water.*" The italicized constructions are neither subjects, verbs, objects, nor modifiers of any one word in the main clauses. Independent of the grammatical structure of these clauses, each loosely modifies the whole statement.

The most common kind of absolute is the one illustrated above: the NOMINATIVE ABSOLUTE. It is used to show cause and effect: "*The search having failed,* the men returned to camp" and also attendant circumstances: "She fled down the stairs, *her hair streaming behind her.*"

ABSTRACT, ABSTRACTION: A word or phrase that refers to ideas, relationships, generalities is abstract: e.g. *truth, justice, democracy, realism, interdependent.* Unlike concrete words, which name specific things, abstractions make little or no appeal to the senses; they are qualities, characteristics, or essences shared by a large class of things. Not all abstractions, however, are equally general in meaning. The word *man*, for example, is more specific than *organism*. But *man* seems quite abstract when set beside "a sturdy, corpulent old man, with a three-cornered hat, red waistcoat, leather breeches, and a stout oaken cudgel." The more general the meaning of any given word the more abstract it tends to be.

Abstractions must be used with caution. They tempt the writer to speak in hazy generalities, to forget that good writing is specific. The writer

637

cannot avoid abstract words, especially in exposition, but he should anchor his thoughts as firmly as possible in concrete reality. The number of abstract words in any composition of course will depend upon the writer's subject and purpose: the philosopher discussing the nature of being will use more abstract words than a traveler describing the ruins of Rome. Wherever possible abstract words should be avoided. When the key words in any essay are abstractions, they should be defined and illustrated at the beginning. See CONCRETE.

ADJECTIVES IN POST POSITION: Adjectives placed after their nouns instead of before: "The blue noonday sky, *cloudless*, has lost its old look of immensity." (Lewis Thomas) "The national states are not physical groups; they are social symbols, *profound* and *terrible*." (Susan K. Langer) Such adjectives draw our attention and hence are emphatic.

ALLITERATION: The repetition in successive words of the same letter or sound is alliteration. Most often the sound in the first syllable is repeated: "The majestic, the magnificent Mississippi." Alliteration should be used only when the writer makes a strong emotional response to his subject; it is usually out of place in matter-of-fact exposition. But even in emotive writing alliteration must be used rarely and with extreme caution. Excessive alliteration is offensive. The effect of successful alliteration is beauty of sound and emphasis.

ALLUSION: An allusion is a reference to a generally familiar person, place, or thing, whether real or legendary: Queen Elizabeth, Cleopatra, Apollo, Adam, Paul Bunyan, Tom Sawyer, San Francisco, The Garden of Eden, the Eiffel Tower, the Great Pyramid, the shield of Achilles. Most allusions are drawn from history, geography, the Bible, mythology, and literature. One value of allusions is their economy; they allow the writer to evoke in one or two words an atmosphere, a whole story, a whole period of history.

AMBIGUITY, AMBIGUOUS: When a word or passage can be understood in either of two ways, it is ambiguous. (More loosely, the term applies even when three or more interpretations are possible.) Unintentional ambiguity is usually a fault, as in: "*He forgot his book on the piano*" where it is not clear whether the book was about the piano or was left lying on top of a piano. Sometimes, however, ambiguity is a deliberate strategy, either as a kind of humor or irony or as a way of suggesting the complexities and uncertainties of experience.

ANAPHORA: The repetition of a word, or group of words, at the beginning of successive clauses, sentences, or lines of poetry. Like most forms of deliberate repetition it is emphatic; it has the secondary effect of aiding the writer's coherence or flow. In the following passage Loren Eiseley is scolding modern man for his resistance to fact in his political and social thinking: "*We are always more willing* to accept mechanical changes in an automobile than to revise, or even to examine our racial prejudices, to use one painful example. *We are more willing* to swallow a pill that we hope will relax our tensions than to make the sustained conscious effort necessary to alter our daily living habits." [Italics ours.–Eds.]

ANTITHESIS, ANTITHETICAL: A balancing of two opposite or contrasting words, phrases, clauses, paragraphs, or even larger units of writing. Antithesis refers most often, however, to the balancing of opposites in independent clauses within a sentence or in two adjacent sentences. Sir William Osler, for example, writes: "The quest for righteousness is Oriental, the quest for knowledge, Occidental." Frequently, as here, the second clause is elliptical, the verb being represented by a comma. Mark Twain makes dependent clauses antithetical: "Good breeding consists in concealing how much we think of ourselves and how little we think of the other person." Samuel Butler creates antithesis in two short sentences: "God is Love, I dare say. But what a mischievous devil Love is." Antitheses are emphatic, often witty, and usually memorable. If not overused, they are effective in development by contrast.

APPOSITIVE: A noun that stands after another noun and repeats the meaning of the first is an appositive: "Francis Bacon, the youngest *son* of Sir Nicholas, was born at York House, his father's *residence* in the Strand, on the twenty-second of January 1561." Here *son* repeats and further identifies *Francis Bacon* just as *residence* repeats and further identifies *York House*. In each instance the second noun is said to be in apposition with the first. The appositive is in effect an abbreviated clause in place of "who was the youngest son of Sir Nicholas" and "which was his father's residence in the Strand."

ASSONANCE: The repetition of internal vowel sounds in successive words is called assonance: "a *deep green stream*." The same warnings that apply to alliteration also apply to assonance. See ALLITERATION.

ASYNDETON: The use of commas to separate members of a compound construction, most often a series of words. Rather than A, B, and C asyndeton employs A, B, C, which gives equal emphasis to each member of the series instead of placing slightly more stress on the last member, as in A, B, and C. Asyndeton speeds up the sentence: "Drays, carts, men, boys, all go hurrying to a common center, the wharf." (Mark Twain)

BALANCE, BALANCED CONSTRUCTION, BALANCED SENTENCE: A balanced construction or sentence contains two distinct halves or parts, each of about the same length and importance. Similar constructions appear in the same place in each half and balance one another: "Our heritage of Greek literature and art is priceless; the example of Greek life possesses for us not the slightest value."

CHIASMUS: A repetition and arrangement of two key terms in a sentence, forming the pattern A B B A: "We should eat to live, not live to eat." Chiasmus appears in proverbs and aphorisms, being unusual, emphatic, and easily remembered. G. K. Chesterton uses chiasmus as a kind of summary and punch line: "If the Superman may possibly be a thief, you can bet your boots that the next thief will be a Superman."

CLAUSE: A clause is a group of words containing a subject and verb. It may be *independent*, in which case it is capable of standing alone as a sentence. Or it may be *dependent*, in which case it usually functions as part of a sentence. Dependent clauses, according to how they function, are described as *noun*, *adjective*, or *adverbial clauses*.

CLOSING BY RETURN: To end a long paragraph or one section of an essay or an entire composition, the writer sometimes returns to an image, an idea, or a statement that occurs in the beginning. This completed cycle, or closing by return, signals to the reader that the unit of writing is done.

COLLOCATION: Generally "collocation" means the arrangement of words in a sentence. In linguistics it is a technical term signifying the probability of a word appearing in the context of other specific words. Thus since "oink" is often found in the same context as "pig," we say that "oink" collocates with "pig"; but it does not collocate with, say, "elephant." A good writer acquires a feel for collocation and is careful about violating the probabilities of word occurrence. As a feature of style unusual collocations may be a fault or a virtue. They are faulty when they are the result of ignorance or carelessness and violate our expectancies to no purpose. Probably, for instance, it would be awkward to write "the duchess grinned" because a duchess "smiles"; she does not "grin." On the other hand, an unusual word may be very effective. "Apoplectic," for example collocates with "man" but not with "flower"; yet when the Scottish poet Hugh MacDiarmid writes of "apoplectic peonies," it is, while an unusual collocation, a singularly apt one, evoking a sharp visual image of the bright and bursting red of the flower.

COLLOQUIALISM, COLLOQUIAL: A colloquial expression (or colloquialism) is language appearing more often in speech than in writing. Speaking of George Bernard Shaw, Joseph Wood Krutch says, "No one ever urged us more insistently *to stop mooning about, to get busy and do something.*" [Italics ours.— Eds.] Colloquialisms give writing something of the flavor of talk, making it more informal and more entertaining.

COMPLEX SENTENCE: A sentence containing one independent clause and at least one dependent clause: "Fifty years ago, when all type was set by hand, the labor of several men was required to print, fold, and arrange in piles the signatures of a book." (Carl Becker)

COMPOUND SENTENCE: Two or more independent clauses joined paratactically or by one or more co-ordinate conjunctions: "General Custer could fight all right, but there was a great deal of question about his competence as a commander." (Ralph K. Andrist)

CONCRETE: Words or phrases that name specific things as opposed to generalities are concrete: e.g. *coarse sandpaper, a rotten orange, a blue silk gown with four flounces, dirty snow, the buzzing of yellow bees.* It is not quite accurate to say that concrete words make a direct appeal to one or more of the five senses and abstractions do not. Some words, like *chair,* are at once both concrete and abstract. The word *chair* is a general term that names a large class of objects; yet *chair* brings to mind a clearer mental image than *furniture,* and it is more specific. However, *chair* is not as concrete as "the battered old Windsor chair in my grandmother's attic," which identifies a single object that really exists. Words move toward the concrete as they re-create actual, specific things. For most purposes, we can define concrete words as those that make us touch, smell, taste, hear, and see. Since, like good writing, concrete words are definite and specific, they are usually preferable to abstractions. See ABSTRACT.

CONJUNCTIVE ADVERB: A conjunctive adverb, like any conjunction, links two ideas. Like other adverbs, it answers the questions in what manner, under what conditions. Most conjunctive adverbs signify logical relationships like addition, contrast or contradiction, cause and effect. English is particularly rich in conjunctive adverbs. Among the most common are *therefore, however, nevertheless, moreover, consequently.* Unlike ordinary conjunctions, the conjunctive adverbs are absolute. They loosely modify the whole sentence and cannot co-ordinate clauses.

CONNECTIVES: Any word or phrase that signifies a relationship between two words, phrases, clauses, sentences, or paragraphs can be called a connective. Thus, the term encompasses parts of speech like prepositions, pronouns, conjunctions, and conjunctive adverbs in addition to connective phrases like *of course, for example, in fine, to be sure.* Most beginning writers need to build their active vocabulary of connective words and phrases, for although it is possible to overuse them, the student writer seldom uses them enough. Connectives express, among others, such ideas as (1) addition (*and, moreover, furthermore, in addition*); (2) contrast or contradiction (*but, yet, in contrast, however*); (3) cause and effect (*so, therefore, for this reason*); (4) disjunction and division (*some . . . others, either . . . or*); (5) conclusion (*finally, at last, ultimately*). These are only a few of the great number of connectives and only a few of the logical notions they can express. Connectives deserve the student's closest attention.

CONNOTATION: The connotation of a word is not the thing or idea the word stands for, but the attitudes, feelings, and emotions aroused by the word. Connotations tend to be favorable or unfavorable. Thus *village* and *hick town* both refer to a small settlement. *Village* is favorable, or at least neutral, in its connotations, but *hick town* suggests the writer's scorn or contempt. The denotation of a word refers only to the thing the word represents, stripped of any emotional associations the word might carry. The denotation of both *village* and *hick town* is the same; both identify a small community.

CONSONANCE: In verse, consonance is a kind of rhyme in which the same consonant follows different vowel sounds: for example, the rhyme of *late* and *light*. In prose, the term generally refers to a harmonious repetition of internal consonant sounds as in the phrase "a pale gold cloud."

CO-ORDINATE CLAUSES: Two independent clauses of equal importance joined together are said to be co-ordinate. They are linked either by a semicolon or by one of the co-ordinate conjunctions—*and, but, or, nor, for*. See SUBORDINATE CLAUSES.

CUMULATIVE SENTENCE: A cumulative sentence is an extended variety of the LOOSE sentence. Often used in description, the cumulative sentence begins with a general statement which it then expands in a series of particulars, as in this description of a ward in a state mental hospital: "The geriatric section is always the most unattractive, poorly lighted, no brightness, no pictures, no laughter. Just long green corridors, lined by doors; white-gowned nurses moving silently, expressionless; large wards with beds filling the room, allowing no space for anything." (Sharon R. Curtin)

DEPENDENT CLAUSE: See CLAUSE.

ELLIPSIS: This is the omission of words necessary to the syntax of a sentence but not to its sense, as in "He is taller than I," where words "am tall" are understood but not expressed. Ellipses often contribute concision and emphasis to one's style.

ENTHYMEME: An enthymeme is an abbreviated syllogism in which one of the premises is less than fully stated or else only implied. Consider, for example, the following syllogism:

> All men are mortal.
> Socrates is a man.
> Therefore Socrates is mortal.

As an enthymeme this syllogism might appear in some such form as this: "Being human Socrates is mortal." Needless to say, one seldom encounters a full-blown syllogism in most argument. Yet enthymemes can be expanded into syllogisms in order to test their validity.

ETYMOLOGY: The derivation or origin of a word, whatever its source—a person, a place, a thing, a word from another language—is called its etymology: *tele-*

scope . . .[NL. *telescopium* fr. Gr. *tēleskopos*, viewing afar, farseeing, fr. *tēle*, far, far off + *skopos*, a watcher.] Some dictionaries list etymologies in brackets just before the definition. Etymologies often help the writer to understand the first or root meaning of a word, from which any further meanings have been derived. Knowing an etymology helps the writer to remember a word and to use it accurately.

FIGURE OF SPEECH, FIGURATIVE, FIGURATIVELY: Any use of language for stylistic effect other than the plain, normal, straightforward manner of writing or speaking is called figurative. Some of the common figures (see this glossary) are metaphor, simile, personification, alliteration, assonance, irony, metonymy.

FLOW: The continuity, or coherence, among the sentences of a paragraph. Flow is created (1) by repeating a key word or its synonym in successive sentences; (2) by using logical connectives; (3) by using a pronoun whose antecedent is in the preceding sentence; (4) by using identical or similar grammatical constructions at the beginning of successive sentences. The following illustrates all of these techniques: "One never forgets Masefield's face. It is not the face of a young man, for it is lined and grave. And yet it is not the face of an old man, for youth is still in the bright eyes. Its dominant quality is humility." (Beverley Nichols)

FRAGMENT: Conventionally defined, a sentence is a grammatically independent statement containing a subject and a finite verb. Any construction punctuated as a sentence but not conforming to this definition is a fragment: e.g. *Men who live in Chicago. Men living in Chicago. When we visited Chicago.* Generally fragments are a serious fault; wisely employed, they may prove more emphatic or realistic than grammatically complete sentences: e.g. "I have another Sicilian memory that will not soon fade. *The waiter.*" It is worth noting, however, that a fragment such as this is deliberate effect of style, not, as is so often the case in student themes, the accident of carelessness or ignorance. Even such successful fragments quickly become an awkward mannerism if used very often. The student is well advised to leave fragments alone, or if he wishes to use one now and again to ask his instructor's advice.

FRAMING WORDS: To separate clearly and to introduce the several divisions of a subject or thought, the writer often uses framing words: *First, Second, Third; First, Next, Last; The most significant effect, A less important effect,* and so on. These usually occur in a paragraph introduced by an organizing sentence. See ORGANIZING SENTENCE.

FREIGHT-TRAIN SENTENCE: A freight-train sentence consists of three or more independent clauses, usually relatively short and joined either by coordinating conjunctions (commonly *and*) or by semicolons without conjunctions: "It was a hot day and the sky was very bright and blue and the road was white and dusty." (Ernest Hemingway)

IMAGE, IMAGERY: At its simplest an image is a picture made with words. Images also may appeal to touch, smell, hearing, and taste. Description and narration make frequent use of images, but imagery appears in exposition as well. See CONCRETE.

INDEPENDENT CLAUSE: See CLAUSE.

INTERRUPTED MOVEMENT: The normal word order of the English sentence is subject, verb, object (or complement). Normally, short modifiers like adjectives, adverbs, or prepositional phrases may stand between subject and verb or between a verb and its object. Such normal word order may be called straightforward movement. But to introduce a clause or an absolute word or phrase between subject and verb or between a verb (or verbal) and its object creates interrupted movement: "The Renaissance, as we have seen, has not yet reached Northern Europe." Here the clause *as we have seen* interrupts the normal order. Interrupted movement is an important variation of normal sentence structure, but it is more at home in a relatively formal style than in very informal writing.

INVERSION, INVERTED WORD ORDER: Any variation of the normal order of subject, verb, object (complement) is inversion. In some sentences the object stands first: "That story I did not believe." Occasionally a verb appears before the subject: "In the far corner of the room sat a very old man." Such inversions are emphatic, but like all variations of the normal their emphasis depends upon their rarity.

IRONY, IRONIC, IRONICALLY: When the writer uses words to mean something different from what they seem to say on the surface, he is ironic. The simplest form of irony means the reverse of what it says. Thus a terrible stench may be called a perfume; a stupid man a genius. Yet irony may range from a complete reversal of meaning to a subtle qualification of the surface meaning. Irony surprises and makes its point with the greatest emphasis because it forces us to contemplate two incongruous things. Most often a device of satire and persuasion, irony appears in all kinds of prose except the driest kind of exposition.

LOOSE SENTENCE: See PERIODIC SENTENCE.

METAPHOR: A metaphor is an implied comparison between two things seemingly quite different: "All the world's a stage, / And all the men and women merely players." Or to take an example from prose: "Man's imagination is limited by the horizon of his experience." Since one term of the metaphor is usually commonplace and concrete, the metaphor not only makes writing more vivid, it may help the writer to make his point clearly. Metaphors make the abstract, concrete; the elusive, definite; the unfamiliar, familiar.

METONYMY: The figure of speech called metonymy substitutes something closely associated with a thing for the thing itself. We may speak of Shakespeare to mean his works; we speak of seeing three sails on the horizon to mean three ships, of the Crown to mean the British monarch.

NEGATIVE-POSITIVE RESTATEMENT: A type of emphasis in which a statement of what is not the case is followed by an assertion of what is: "They did not leave because they were tired; they left because they were frustrated and angry."

NOMINATIVE ABSOLUTE: See ABSOLUTE.

ORGANIZING SENTENCE: Standing at the beginning of a paragraph or a major section of an essay or at the beginning of the composition, an organizing sentence indicates the subject to be treated, how it is to be divided, and into how many parts the division falls: "There were four underlying causes of World War II."

PARALLEL, PARALLELISM, PARALLEL CONSTRUCTION: Constructions are parallel when two or more words, phrases, or clauses of the same grammatical·rank are related in the same way to the same word or words. Thus two or more subjects of the same verb are parallel; two or more verbs with the same subject are parallel; two or more adverbial clauses modifying the same verb are parallel; and so on. In the following sentence Rachel Carson is describing the face of the sea:

```
Crossed                        by    colors,
                                     lights,
                               and   moving shadows,
sparkling
mysterious                     in the sun,
                               in the twilight,
                               its aspects
                         and   its moods
                               vary hour by hour.
```

Here the writer uses three parallel adjectives (two are participles) to modify the same parallel subjects *aspects* and *moods*. Each adjective is modified by a prepositional phrase, the first with three parallel objects.

In the eighteenth century many writers often strove for a more involved parallelism combined with balance. In the following example, Samuel Johnson balances a series of parallel independent clauses in the first half of the sentence against parallel dependent clauses in the second half. This already complex pattern he further complicates by parallel constructions within the dependent clauses:

```
. . . much of my life      has been lost under the pressures of disease;
       much                has been trifled away;
and    much                has always been spent in provision for the day
                               that was passing over me;
                                                      useless
              but I shall not think my employment or ignoble,
```

```
       if by my assistance        foreign nations,
                         and    distant ages,
                   gain access to the propagators of knowledge,
              and    understand the teachers of truth;
       if my labours           afford light to the repositories of science,
                         and    add celebrity
                                         to Bacon,
                                         to Hooker,
                                         to Milton,
                                   and   to Boyle.
```

This elaborate architecture has all but disappeared from even the most formal writing. Yet parallelism of a much simpler kind appears often in both formal and informal writing. In skillful hands it is an interesting variation of the normal sentence pattern, allowing the writer to compress many ideas into a small space. Parallelism may be used to sustain a mood or to suggest rapid action, as it does in this description of a boxing match by A. J. Liebling:

```
Instead of    flicking,
              moving around,
   and so     piling up enough unhurting points to goad Johnson into
                  some possible late activity,
```

he was reconnoitering in close, looking the challenger over as if he had never seen him before.

PARTICIPLE, PARTICIPIAL: A participle is a form of the verb. There are several types, but the most frequently used are the present active participle (for example, *exciting*) and the past active (*excited*). Participles function in verb phrases: "The people *were excited* by the news"; and also as modifiers: "An *exciting* trip to Paris," "The *excited* crowd rushed to the scene," or "*Excited*, the crowd rushed to the scene."

Participial phrases are word groups built around participles; as modifiers they are an efficient way of working additional information into a sentence.

PERIODIC SENTENCE: A sentence which delays the expression of a complete thought until the end, or until near the end, is called periodic. The following is an example from an essay by Virginia Woolf: "If behind the erratic gunfire of the press the author felt that there was another kind of criticism, the opinion of people reading for the love of reading, slowly and unprofessionally, and judging with great sympathy and yet with great severity, might not this improve the quality of his work?" One must read this entire sentence before a complete thought emerges. In contrast, most sentences exhibit what is called *loose structure*, as does this sentence from the same essay by Virginia Woolf: "Thus the desire grows upon us to have done with half-statements and approximations; to cease from searching out the minute shades of human character, to enjoy the greater abstractness, the purer truth of fiction." This sentence can be terminated at several points before the end and still make complete sense. The periodic sentence, because it is rare and because it demands closer attention from the reader than does the loose sentence, is one means of achieving emphasis through sentence structure. Although it appears in all kinds of writing, the periodic sentence, especially when long, is more suited to the formal than to the informal level of usage. If overused, the periodic sentence becomes an irritating mannerism, but it is extremely useful for variation and emphasis.

PERSONIFICATION: In the figure of speech called personification, ideas, animals, or things are given human attributes. Justice, for example, is often personified as a blindfolded woman of heroic proportions holding a pair of scales.

POINTER: A word or phrase (more conventionally called a conjunctive, or transitional, adverb) which stands at or near the beginning of a sentence and prepares the reader for a turn of thought. Thus the word *however* points to an approaching contradiction; *for instance* to an oncoming illustration; *therefore* to a logical conclusion. It is possible to overuse pointers, but more often students tend to use too few of them. See CONJUNCTIVE ADVERB, CONNECTIVE.

POINT OF VIEW: In the study of prose, a writer's point of view *does not* mean the writer's attitudes or values, does not mean his way of looking at things in general, his viewpoint. Rather a writer's point of view is the grammatical person of his composition. He may use *I*, explaining what happened to him, what he thought, or what he saw happen to others. This is the point of view of autobiography, much narrative, and often of the familiar essay. The third-person point of view detaches the writer from any personal relationship with his material. In place of *I*, the writer uses a noun or third-person pronoun; not "I like to travel," but "Traveling is the best of educations."

POLYSYNDETON: The use of *and* to separate each member of a compound construction, especially the members of a series. Instead of A, B, and C, polysyndeton uses A and B and C. Mark Twain, describing a steamboat, writes: "And the boat *is* rather a handsome sight, too. She is long and sharp and trim and pretty." Polysyndeton stresses equally each member of the series, but is slower and more emphatic than asyndeton. See ASYNDETON.

POST POSITION: See ADJECTIVES IN POST POSITION.

QUALIFICATION: Usually a sweeping statement must be slightly altered or modified in the interest of truth. This modification or adjustment we call qualification. Thus George Orwell writing of Dickens might have said, "One cannot point to a single one of his central characters who is primarily interested in his job." But what he does say in order to be accurate is this: "With the doubtful exception of David Copperfield (merely Dickens himself), one cannot point to a single one of his central characters who is primarily interested in his job." Qualifications are often necessary, but they must not overshadow the statements they qualify.

RHETORICAL QUESTION: A question asked for dramatic effect is a rhetorical question. It may or may not demand an answer. When it does, the answer may be supplied or left for the reader to infer. In prose, rhetorical questions often serve an organizing purpose, setting up the point the writer wishes to develop.

SCAN, SCANSION: Scansion is a method of analyzing the rhythm of prose or poetry by marking the stressed and unstressed syllables. In poetry the line is divided into feet, indicating the units of the rhythmic pattern. Stresses are usually indicated by ($'$), unstressed syllables by ($\smile$), and the foot division by ($/$). Thus, a line from a poem by Marvell scans:

$$\overset{\smile}{\text{The}} \overset{'}{\text{grave's}} / \overset{\smile}{\text{a}} \overset{'}{\text{fine}} / \overset{\smile}{\text{and}} \overset{'}{\text{pri}} / \overset{\smile}{\text{vate}} \overset{'}{\text{place.}}$$

In prose a rhythm is always present, but usually it does not, and should not, have the regularity of poetic rhythm.

SENTENCE: See COMPLEX SENTENCE, COMPOUND SENTENCE, SIMPLE SENTENCE.

SIGNPOST: Any word, phrase, clause, or sentence that tells us what the writer plans to do next, is currently doing, has already done, or will not do at all. Examples of signposts are: "Next we must consider . . ."; "This is a point we shall treat more fully in the following chapter; here we must concentrate upon . . ."; "As was noted in the preceding section . . ."; "This is a matter, which, interesting though it is, cannot be discussed in this essay." Like pointers (q.v.), signposts can be overused as well as used too little.

SIMILE: Using *like* or *as*, a simile makes a brief comparison between things seemingly unlike. "When all is done," writes Sir William Temple, "human life is, at the greatest and best, but like a froward child that must be played with and humored a little to keep it quiet till it falls asleep, and then the care is done." The purpose of simile is the same as that of metaphor. See METAPHOR.

SIMPLE SENTENCE: A simple sentence contains one subject-verb nucleus: "The *boys rowed* across the lake." It is possible for a sentence to have multiple subjects and verbs, yet to remain simple so long as these form only one nucleus: "The *boys* and *girls rowed* across the lake and *had* a picnic on the other side."

STRAIGHTFORWARD MOVEMENT: See INTERRUPTED MOVEMENT.

STRATEGY: In composition strategy is the means by which you achieve your purpose. Strategy determines organization, paragraph structure, sentence style, and diction. Thus purpose is realized in strategy, and strategy is manifest in style.

SUBORDINATE CLAUSE: A clause functioning within a sentence as an adjective, adverb, or noun is said to be subordinate. Since it is grammatically less important than the main clause, a subordinate clause should express ideas of lesser importance.

SYMBOL: A symbol is a person, place, or thing that exists both in its own right as something real and tangible and also as something greater than itself—an attitude, a belief, a quality, a value. The word *symbol* is sometimes loosely applied to an object, the only function of which is to stand for something other than itself. Thus, the American flag can be called a symbol of America.

TONE: A writer's tone results from (1) his attitude toward his subject and (2) his attitude toward his reader. A writer may love his subject, despise it, revere it, laugh at it, or seem detached from it. He may wish to shock his reader, outrage him, charm him, play upon his prejudices, amuse him, or merely inform him in the briefest and most efficient way possible. A writer conveys his tone largely through his diction, through the connotations of the words he uses. But tone may be carried by sentence structure as well.

TRICOLON: A tricolon is a sentence consisting of three clearly defined parts of roughly equal length and weight. Usually the three parts are independent clauses: "Her showmanship was superb; her timing matchless; her dramatic instinct uncanny." (Carey McWilliams)

UNDERSTATEMENT: To understate is to play down or soften something that is startling, horrifying, shocking, painful, or otherwise deserving of more emotion and attention than the writer gives it. The striking contrast between what the subject calls for and the restrained treatment with which it is dealt, effectively calls attention to the subject. Understatement, or litotes, as it is sometimes called, is therefore a device of emphasis. It has the additional advantage of relieving the writer of any charge of exaggeration or emotionalism. One possible disadvantage of understatement is that an uneducated audience may not respond to it, but may instead regard the writer as callous. Readers of any experience or sophistication, however, often prefer understatement to exaggeration—a more obvious form of emphasis.

VOICE: Generally in composition courses voice means whether the action designated by the verb originates in the subject or is received by the subject. Here, however, voice means the illusion—common in good prose—of a unique personality speaking to the reader.